Encyclopedia of Knots
And Fancy Rope Work

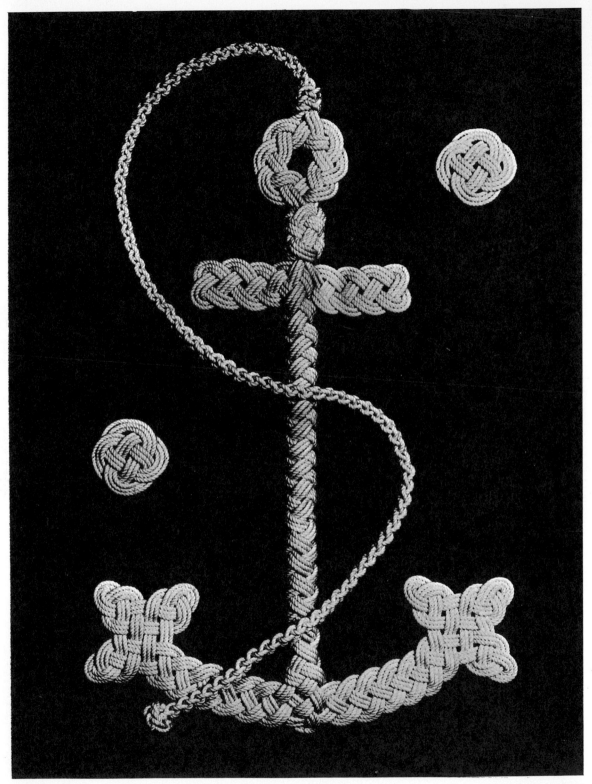

ROPE ANCHOR

Description on Page 438

ENCYCLOPEDIA OF
KNOTS
AND FANCY ROPE WORK

By
Raoul Graumont and John Hensel

FOURTH EDITION

Completely Revised and Enlarged
By Raoul Graumont

Cornell Maritime Press, Inc.

Cambridge *Maryland*

ISBN 0—87033—021-7

Cornell Maritime Press
Cambridge   Maryland

FIRST EDITION 1939

SECOND EDITION 1942

THIRD EDITION

1st Printing, 1943
2nd Printing, 1944
3rd Printing, 1944
4th Printing, 1945
5th Printing, 1946

FOURTH EDITION

1st Printing, 1952
2nd Printing, 1958
3rd Printing, 1964
4th Printing, 1970
5th Printing, 1972
6th Printing, 1977

Books by Raoul Graumont and Elmer Wenstrom
SQUARE KNOT HANDICRAFT GUIDE
FISHERMAN'S KNOTS AND NETS

By Raoul Graumont
HANDBOOK OF KNOTS

Printed and Bound in the United States of America

Acknowledgments

IN THE COMPILATION of this collection of knots and designs in fancy and ornamental rope work the authors wish to acknowledge the assistance of their many seafaring associates for their suggestions and for their contributions of many of the various knots and designs shown and described herein.

Acknowledgment is made also to the authors of countless books and magazine articles on the subject of knotting, which were consulted in the preparation of this work.

We thank the Whitlock Cordage Company for supplying the Manila rope used in constructing the examples of knots shown in the illustrations and for supplying the photographs and information relating to rope manufacturing.

To Capt. William Alford and Mr. William Christenson we extend our thanks for their assistance in making many of the useful knots and designs illustrated and described here for the first time.

Likewise, we wish to acknowledge the valuable aid and suggestions of Mr. Frank Parchen and Mr. I. Weinberg and we thank them for their contributions of knots and designs.

We make grateful acknowledgment to Cyrus Lawrence Day for the use of material from his book SAILORS' KNOTS. In the preparation of our "Notes on the History of Knots and Rope Making" we are especially indebted to his research in this field, and his presentation of it.

To P. C. Herwig Company we are indebted for the use of their material on the subject of Square Knotting.

For their co-operation and the use of their materials we acknowledge with thanks the assistance of J. McNamara & Son, Inc., in the preparation of the material having to do with canvas work.

We are indebted also to the Paulsen Cable Company for the use of their cable and equipment and desire to thank them for their assistance in this respect.

To the Seamen's Church Institute of New York we are indebted for their co-operation in enabling us to obtain photographs and descriptions of the two knotted picture frames illustrated here, which hang in the Conrad Library and the Museum of the Institute.

We also extend our thanks to Mr. William Stuart for his professional advice in making the engravings used as illustrations.

Likewise, we are indebted to Miss Louise Sampson and Mr. Newton Alfred for the art work and their able assistance in the preparation and arrangement of the illustrations of the various knots and designs.

To Mr. Harry Hartwick and Mr. William W. Baxter we extend our thanks for their aid in editing and arranging the manuscript of this book for publication.

In the second edition: We are indebted to Mr. Jack A. Garriott for numerous additional designs included herein, and we wish to express our thanks for his helpful co-operation.

To Mr. Elmer Wenstrom we wish to extend our thanks for his able assistance in making many of the additional designs included in the Appendix.

Raoul Graumont
John Hensel

Preface

THERE HAVE BEEN many useful books published on such subjects as Knots and Fancy Rope Work, but most of them relate to these arts—for they are arts—as they pertain to the sea and seamanship.

We are told by historians that rope making and knotting were generally well known by many civilized races, as well as by savage tribes, long before man took to the sea. There is little doubt, however, that the art of tying knots and that of making ornamental rope designs were further improved upon by the mariners of the earlier days.

Sailors, in the long sea voyages of the bygone days of sailing ships, and in their leisure hours, devoted much of their idle time to the tying of knots and to contriving many beautiful and ornamental rope designs.

Insofar as the authors of this work have any knowledge, there is no complete and comprehensive literature covering the entire subject of tying knots and the making of ornamental rope designs. Most of the knowledge on these subjects was never published, but was handed down from man to man, and from generation to generation, through actual contact with those who were familiar with the work.

Therefore, he who would today acquire knowledge in the art of Knotting and Fancy Rope Work must seek out some one of the ever-diminishing number of the older mariners who are still experienced in the intricacies of knot-tying.

The advent of steam in the place of sails and the extensive replacement of fiber with wire rope on the merchant ships of the present time have driven this fascinating art from the seas. Some designs of ornamental work in knots may be found in dictionaries of needlework, in books giving instructions in tatting and macramé lace, and in other publications, but in none of them is the art of knotting presented so completely and so comprehensively as it is in this work.

It is therefore the purpose of this book to include, insofar as it is possible, all of the known kinds, types, forms and designs of knots, macramé lace, tatting, braiding, and ornamental rope work, in order that the art may be preserved as an historical record for future generations.

The student of knot and rope work should understand that before he undertakes to make any of the many complicated and highly involved knots and other examples to be found in this work he must first master the details of simple knotting.

Too much emphasis cannot be placed upon this admonition, because of the fact that many of the knots and designs included here can be made only after a very thorough mastery of simple knotting, and even then the student will be compelled, in many instances, to exercise considerable ingenuity before he can hope to solve many of the intricate and ramified processes necessary to the completion of the knot or design.

It will be found in some cases that the work is so involved that no clear and complete explanation, which would be comprehensible to the layman, can be given as to how the work is done.

It is urged therefore that the student, in his own interest, make every effort to master the methods used in tying the basic knots. He should also learn thoroughly the many ways in which the various combinations of knots are used to form still other knots. This is the only way in which he can hope to understand the different ways of tying and combining knots.

The Ropewalk

In that building, long and low,
With its windows all a-row,
    Like the port-holes of a hulk,
Human spiders spin and spin,
Backwards down their threads so thin
    Dropping, each a hempen bulk.

At the end, an open door;
Squares of sunshine on the floor
    Light the long and dusky lane;
And the whirring of a wheel,
Dull and drowsy, makes me feel
    All its spokes are in my brain.

As the spinners to the end
Downward go and reascend,
    Gleam the long threads in the sun;
While within this brain of mine
Cobwebs brighter and more fine
    By the busy wheel are spun.

Two fair maidens in a swing,
Like white doves upon the wing,
    First before my vision pass;
Laughing, as their gentle hands
Closely clasp the twisted strands,
    At their shadow on the grass.

Then a booth of mountebanks,
With its smell of tan and planks,
    And a girl poised high in air
On a cord, in spangled dress,
With a faded loveliness,
    And a weary look of care.

Then a homestead among farms,
And a woman with bare arms
    Drawing water from a well;

As the bucket mounts apace,
With it mounts her own fair face,
    As at some magician's spell.

Then an old man in a tower,
Ringing loud the noontide hour,
    While the rope coils round and round
Like a serpent at his feet,
And again, in sweet retreat,
    Nearly lifts him from the ground.

Then within a prison-yard,
Faces fixed, and stern, and hard,
    Laughter and indecent mirth;
Ah! it is the gallows-tree!
Breath of Christian charity,
    Blow, and sweep it from the earth!

Then a schoolboy, with his kite
Gleaming in a sky of light,
    And an eager, upward look;
Steeds pursued through lane and field;
Flowers with their snares concealed;
    And an angler by a brook.

Ships rejoicing in the breeze,
Wrecks that float o'er unknown seas,
    Anchors dragged through faithless sand;
Sea-fog drifting overhead,
And, with lessening line and lead,
    Sailors feeling for the land.

All these scenes do I behold,
These, and many left untold,
    In that building long and low;
While the wheel goes round and round,
With a drowsy, dreamy sound,
    And the spinners backward go.

—LONGFELLOW

Contents

Rope Speaks!

I am the servant of man. I am the life line. My greatest joy is in sweet human functions. I am one with the old oaken bucket.

I am a friend to the children of the world; their happy feet jump tirelessly over me. I am the swing in which they dream their dreams. I ring the curfew which cuts off day's activity.

I scorn not holier uses. I am the clothes line: the wind and I flaunt banners of cleanly garments. I am the hammock rope. I poise securely the window weights.

I love my part in Sunday's services. I enable the bell to peal out over a quiescent and careless world its inviting call to worship. I thrill with the music of the chimes.

I have had no small part in some of history's tremendous moments. Through my pulsating length ran the force which rang the Liberty Bell. I sometimes thrill with pride and patriotism. I maintain aloft the starry flag, "living and dying momently in the breeze."

I am, next to the horse, the best beloved of the cowboy. I am the lasso. I hurtle unerringly to the mark. In skillful hands, I live, dance, and sing.

I am the trusted line upon which the tight-rope dancer pirouettes across the circus tent, or the chasm of Niagara. The daring feats of the trapeze performer are as much dependent upon me as on his own sure eye and firm hold.

I am an important factor in man's adventuring through open spaces. My staunch strength holds his tent in place. I stay his reluctant canoe.

I am the tried friend of man on dizzy mountain heights. I have borne many perilous strains. I am the safety of the pioneer and the explorer. I am no less reliable when winds wrack the tortured merchant vessel and its sails groan in protest.

I operate the derrick, hoist and pulley in mid air, as well as in the foundation pit. I have made the sky-scraper possible. Who shall say that I did not strain and bind and lift upon Egypt's sand to achieve the pyramids?

I cry aloud that I have often been put to shameful uses. All down the ages I have had to feel the stigma of those disgraceful words: "You shall be hanged by the neck till dead."

I was forced to bind Joan of Arc, Savanarola, and many another martyr of human liberty until cruel flames set their spirits free. Gladly I yielded my body to be burned with them.

I AM A ROPE.

—DAN F. MURPHY.

List of Illustrations

Notes on the History of Knots and Rope Making

DOWN THROUGH THE ages the tying of knots and the making of rope have played highly important roles in the life of Man. That there has always been a need for rope or cord of some kind can be readily appreciated. Since rope could have served but few useful purposes unless it could have been attached in some manner to the things it was desired to pull, lift, or secure, Man, at the time of his first conception of the use of rope, must have conceived of some means of tying knots.

History tells us that the first cords were made from the tendrils of vines, from the cord-like fibers of plants, and from strips cut from the skins of animals. When the vine tendrils and the cord-like fibers which were readily available failed to serve their immediate needs the primitive peoples of the world began to weave, twist, or braid these strands of fibers to make ropes of greater strength and added length.

Records are available to indicate that most of the ancient civilized nations of the world were accomplished rope makers, as were many of the savage tribes of the globe. Each of these races and tribes made use of the materials which were most easily accessible. These have been found to include the fibers of many different kinds of plants, the skins and sinews of animals, and the hair of both humans and animals.

Specimens of rope made by the early Egyptians of flax, papyrus, and rawhide have been found in tombs estimated to be not less than 3500 years old, while it is generally well known that rope was made in China at a very remote period.

Neolithic Man made rope and tied simple knots. The lake-dwellers during the Stone Age, and the Incas in Peru used the sheet-bend in making their nets. The Incas also had a decimal system of numbers based on knots tied in suspended cords, the type of the knot and its position in the cord each having a special significance.

Among some of the most interesting relics of these ancient Incas are these so-called *quipus*, or knot-records. It appears that this race of people never discovered the art of writing but that they developed a decimal system of numbers and with the aid of knots tied in cords were able to keep records of large sums and figures. It is supposed that they may have used their system of knots for difficult mathematical calculations, but this has not been determined definitely. Their method was substantially as follows: Several vertical cords were suspended from a horizontal cord and in each of the vertical cords knots were tied, the whole being called a *quipu*. It is assumed that a single overhand knot represented the figure one, a double overhand knot, two, and so on, up to nine. It has been found, too, that the figure-of-eight knot and the simple running knot were used and had particular significance. The knots representing the units were tied in the lower ends of the pendant cords, with the tens immediately above the units, the hundreds above the tens and the thousands above the hundreds. In this manner dates, astronomical records and other large numbers could be preserved. Since colored cords were used it is assumed that the various colors indicated the kind of thing being recorded. This system is said to be in use today by Peruvian shepherds for counting their sheep, and that similar devices were used in China before the invention of writing. Several of these Peruvian *quipus* are on exhibition in the American Museum of Natural History and the Museum of the American Indian, both in New York.

In Egypt and Persia knots were used in building bridges and in rigging ships. Rope played many important roles in ancient

3

world events. During his invasion of Greece (480 B. C.), Xerxes marched his army across the Hellespont over bridges of boats held together by huge rope cables stretched from shore to shore. The historian Herodotus relates that these cables were made of flax and papyrus, and that they measured twenty-eight inches in circumference.

In the historical records of the early Greeks and Romans are to be found many examples of the use of rope. An illustration of the triumphal arch at Orange (41 A. D.), shows in bas-relief a coil of rope, a pulley, and an anchor. As another example of early rope making a painting of a drinking cup in the British Museum shows an Attic sailing ship of about the sixth century fitted with sails and ropes.

The Indians of North America were also accomplished rope makers and used knots for recording dates, while from the sailor's point of view some very interesting specimens of aboriginal skill come from the Nootka and Clayoquot Indian tribes of Vancouver Island and the coastal regions of the state of Washington. These peoples made whaling lines out of small cedar limbs twisted into three-strand rope which was about four or five inches in circumference. One of these lines is known to have been 1200 feet in length. For the lanyards of their whale harpoons they employed the sinews of the whale, twisted into three-strand rope.

It is not definitely known whether the art of making rope was transmitted through the channels of trade and social intercourse, from one race of people to another, or whether it was independently evolved by the various peoples of the globe as they emerged from savagery. All that can be stated about this matter is that rope and cordage of some kind was one of Man's earliest and most useful tools, that its use was widespread, and that a high degree of skill in the making of rope was achieved long before the dawn of history.

In his work, "Sailors' Knots," Cyrus Law-

rence Day states in part that a photograph which I have seen of the door leading into the third shrine of Tutankhamen's tomb shows a piece of rope, used to tie the door shut, with a strange and rather ineffective-looking knot. Perhaps this particular door was sealed by an Egyptian landlubber—for I think it reasonable to suppose that among Egyptian sailors the art of knotting was pretty highly developed.

Oddly enough, in this connection, it is a significant fact in many of the drawings and other works of art of the early Egyptians, Greeks and Romans, no knots were shown where we today know they must have been used. In the strings or cords on loin cloths, in the fastenings of other clothing, and in the ropes with which animals were secured, there were no knots shown; the cords or ropes being merely looped or laid in place to indicate the form of a knot. This is attributed by historians to a superstitious or religious belief that the artist might draw or depict a knot that could not be untied, with dire results, either to himself or to the person or animal on whose person the knot was shown. In the illustration of the rope, pulley, and anchor, mentioned previously, it is clearly evident that there are no knots shown at the points where it is shown that the rope must have been attached to the pulley and the anchor.

Despite the fact that, in most instances, these artists of ancient times showed in intimate detail every minute part of their work, yet they failed to show a knot of any kind in its actual or true form. There is nothing to indicate that this was done purposely, but an examination of the specimens of the art of those early times clearly indicates that all knots were omitted.

In legendary history the rope knot ofttimes dictated the course of kingdoms. Consider for example one of the legends told about Alexander the Great. After the oracle of Zeus had counseled the Phrygians to choose as their sovereign the first person

In the preparation department of the cordage mills the bales of fiber are opened and the "hemp" is put through a series of operations, to straighten and parallel the fibers, until a small even ribbon of "sliver" is finally produced.

An intermediate step in the combing process. After their final working these "slivers" are transferred to the spinning department, where they are reduced in size by an additional combing and drawing operation, after which they are twisted into yarns.

to ride up to their temple in a cart, Gordius happened to be the first-comer, thereby becoming the Phrygian ruler. He gratefully dedicated his cart to Zeus, tying it by a rope of cornel bark to a pole in front of the temple. Soon, the oracle spoke again, proclaiming that whoever was able to undo the intricate knot would someday reign over all Asia. Many tried, but all failed— probably because they could not locate the knot-ends, which had been cleverly concealed. Then came Alexander the Great to give the famous Gordian knot a try. Puzzled over its complexity and becoming increasingly exasperated, the Great Alexander finally drew his sword and with one blow slashed the knot. Later Alexander ruled over a sizable portion of Asia. Since that time "to cut the Gordian knot" has been proverbial, yet no one seems to know just how this knot was tied or in what class of knots it would fall, as we know them today.

That the Reef knot was well known in ancient Greece and Rome may be seen in many existing works of the classical art. It was used in an ornamental manner in the handles of vessels, while it nearly always appeared on the staff of Mercury and in many instances in pieces of sculpture in the girdles of Roman vestals. These people called it the knot of Hercules (that is, *nodus Herculis* or *Herculaneus*), because they thought it had been originally tied by Hercules. One historian declares that it was the custom for Roman brides to wear a girdle tied with a Hercules knot, which their husbands untied on the marriage night, as an omen of fecundity. Pliny states in his *Natural History* that it was found that wounds healed much more rapidly when the bandages which bound them were tied with Hercules knots.

In some writings by Oribasius there are descriptions of some eighteen different kinds of knots used in surgery, but unfortunately the Greek names he employs do not serve to identify the knots at this time.

Probably one of the earliest knots familiar to the English people was the Carrick bend. This was used as an heraldic badge by Hereward Wake, the Saxon leader who refused to submit to William the Conqueror in 1066 A. D. This knot is now commonly called the Wake knot.

The names of the knots as we know them today afford no clues as to their origin. The familiar Reef knot was known to Man long before the origin of the English word reef. We are told that the word knot comes from the Old English *cnotta*, meaning to join together, while the sailors' "bend" comes from the Anglo-Saxon word *bygan*, which is to make a loop or fashion a "bight" in a rope. There are lovers' knots, matrimonial knots, the Gordian knot and others whose names are but figurative. The Stafford knot, the Bouchier knot, the Henage knot and others are in no sense knots, but badges of heraldry. Then, too, there is the Monkey knot, the Peruvian knot and the Wind knot, all of which are fancy knots.

Among the real and useful knots are the Weavers' knots, the Builders' knots, the Sailors' knots and the Fishermen's knots. Included in the classification with knots are bends, hitches, lashings, seizings, whippings, shortenings, stopperings, bowlines and splicing, which find many uses in everyday life.

The various methods by which any of these knots are tied are in large measure dependent upon three primary conditions; the material available, i.e., the rope or cord to be used; the purpose for which the knot is intended, and the ability to so manipulate the rope or cord into the form of knot desired.

The true lover's knot, while it has been mentioned repeatedly in early English literature, has never been identified with any particular knot known today. In one instance it is mentioned in an old English ballad, "Fair Margaret and Sweet Wil-

Spinning yarns—the units of twine and rope making. In various grades, sizes and degrees of twist or turn, yarns are either used singly, or are combined in twos, threes, or larger numbers, to make up practically all kinds of twines and the strands of rope.

Cordage up to about ½-inch diameter is often known as "thread rope" and is usually made on compound machines, which produce strands, each composed of two or more yarns, and, in a continuing operation, combine the multiple strands into the finished rope.

liam," which was written in the sixteenth century or earlier.

Margaret was buried in the lower chancel,
    Sweet William in the higher;
Out of her breast there sprung a rose;
    And out of his a brier.

They grew as high as the church top,
    Till they could grow no higher,
And then they grew in a true lover's knot,
    Which made all people admire.

In his famous *Sea Grammar*, published by Captain John Smith about 1627, he asserts that the three commonest knots used by sailors of that time were the "Boling" knot, the "Shepshanke" and the Wall knot, although he does not make mention of any of the bends, hitches and splices which surely must have been known at the time his Grammar was published.

There are countless stories told, purporting to relate the origin of many of our commonest knots. One of these is offered as the source of the name of the Thief knot. It has to do with a tale told about an old Cape Cod sea captain who suspected one member of his crew of stealing bread from the captain's bread-bag. One night, instead of tying the bag with a Reef knot, as had been the usual custom of the captain, he tied it with a Thief knot instead. Since the two knots are very similar the wiley captain anticipated that the thief would tie the bag again with a Reef knot, which he did. In this manner the thief was found out, and, so it is said, since that time the knot has been known by its present name. As a matter of fact, however, the Thief knot was known by many different peoples in many different lands long before there were any Cape Cod sea captains.

Among many of the primitive peoples of the world knots have often been associated with magical and supernatural powers. Wizards and witches, or persons who were regarded as such, have been known to contend that they had the power to tie

up the wind in knots. And mariners, who as a class are notoriously superstitious, bought these charmed cords of knots to be untied when they were becalmed at sea. There were supposedly three of these knots in the cord, which when untied in order had the property to release a wind of moderate force, then a half-gale and finally a blast of hurricane proportions. Such superstitious beliefs as these were prevalent in Lapland, Finland, Shetland, the Isle of Man, and other northern countries, particularly among sea-faring men. That the same superstitious beliefs were held by the early Greeks is evidenced in Homer's epic in which Ulysses was presented by Aeolus, king of the winds, with all of the winds tied up in a leather bag.

Other beliefs about the magic powers of knots which were generally widespread were that by a sort of sympathetic magic they bound up and restricted men and women in the performance of certain of their respective tasks. Among the Lapps, certain of the Germanic races, and the aborigines of Borneo, as well as among many other primitive races, it was taboo for pregnant women to wear any knots or knotted garments, lest their delivery be restricted. In other similar instances even the husbands of such women were prohibited from wearing knots, or rings, or from locking locks or sitting cross-legged.

In some sections of Scandinavia this belief was used as a form of birth-control. Thus the parents of large numbers of children, or those who desired to curtail the number of their offspring, gave to their last-born son the name of *Knut,* or in English *Canute,* which meant knot, thereby hoping to prevent the conception of another child.

That knots played an important part in magic and witchcraft in many countries and in many ages is also evidenced by the historians of early times. Plato, in his "Laws," states: "He who seems to be the sort of man who injures others by means

In making the larger sizes, the operations of forming strands with a suitable number of yarns and laying these strands into rope are carried out on separate machines. The reels on which the strands are wound (to the left) in the formers are then transferred to the "layers."

On these machines the strands are twisted or laid together to the right, in the final operation. All tensions and other adjustments are carefully regulated. Three right-laid ropes are twisted together to the left to make hawser-laid rope, or drilling cable.

of magic knots or enchantments or incantations or any of the like practices, if he be a prophet or divine, let him die." As related in the Koran the prophet Mohammed was once bewitched by a Jew, who tied some knots in a cord and threw the cord into a well. It was then only the intervention of the Angel Gabriel who revealed the hiding place of the knots and thus cured Mohammed of his illness. There are instances in Scotland and in France in which persons have been condemned to death for having bewitched others by the use of magic knots. One such event took place more than twenty years after the Salem witch trials.

At times we, today, are often caused to pause and wonder at the credulity of some of these early peoples and at some of the powers they attributed to magic and witchcraft. Among some European races there was once the belief that knots could either cause or cure illness. One such belief was that if a person had a fever he could rid himself of it by seeking out a willow tree and tying knots in the limbs of the tree—one for every day of the fever. Then by the incantation of certain magic words the tree would acquire the fever and the patient would be cured. In Germany, and even in some parts of this country, there was a belief that a person could rid himself of warts by tying knots in a string—one for each wart—after which the cord was to be buried or preferably hidden under a stone. When the cord had rotted the warts were supposed to have disappeared.

Even in Biblical times the value of strong rope and knots was recognized as is the case in the reference: "If they bind me fast with new ropes that never were occupied, then shall I be weak, and be as another man" (Judges XVI).

And so, throughout all history, and among the records of many civilized nations and savage tribes as well in all sections of the world there are many references to ropes and knots.

Chapter I

Elementary Rope Work

THIS CHAPTER BEGINS with elementary rope work in its simplest form. Starting with Clinches and Hitches, the types of knot work are developed gradually step by step, finally embracing the more intricate forms of knotting as the chapter advances. Bends, Bowlines and Sheep-Shanks are dealt with at length in all their various combinations with an adequate description of how they are tied, their different uses, and are exemplified by beautiful illustrations. Seizings and Whippings are also illustrated and explained in an easily understandable manner.

The beginner should master well all the details of construction and thoroughly understand the formation of the examples contained in this chapter before attempting the more intricate knot designs in subsequent chapters. This is imperative because practically all simple knots start from a clinch, hitch, loop or bight. The elementary simple knots are then combined and expanded to form the complex varieties and the ornamental knots which are described fully in the following chapters.

Plate 1—Clinches and Hitches

FIG. 1: The *Simple Clinch* is a Running Eye with a strong cross-seizing to make the moving part fast to the standing part. It is sometimes used to prevent a rope from running out through a block, and also to make the Running Clinches described below. This clinch has one seizing. A cross-seizing is shown in PLATE 19, FIG. 286.

FIG. 2: This *Simple Clinch* is made with two seizings and is more secure than FIG. 1, although its use is the same.

FIG. 3: The *Outside Clinch* is a Running Knot formed by reeving the standing part of the rope through the eye of a Simple Clinch (*see* FIG. 1 or 2).

FIG. 4: The *Inside Clinch* is similar to the preceding, except that it is somewhat more secure. When hauled taut around a spar or other object, it jams on itself. On the other hand, it is somewhat more difficult to release than the Outside Clinch. It is a good knot to use where a turn is to be taken about an object and after being drawn taut must be slipped quickly. These clinches, FIGS. 3 and 4, have a single cross-seizing.

FIG. 5: The *Double Clinch* may be used for a temporary eye when there is not sufficient end to tie a Bowline. Make a stout cross-seizing, then cross the moving part under the standing part, and make a second cross-seizing.

FIG. 6: This *Inside Clinch* is made with a double-seizing. It is more secure than FIG. 3 or 4, and is used for the same purpose.

FIG. 7. The *Overhand* or *Thumb Knot* is known to almost everyone, and has a wide utility. It has one chief function: to serve as a base or part of other knots. It is sometimes used as a Stopper Knot to prevent a rope from running out of a block or other hole, but should not be favored for this purpose, due to the fact that when it jams it is difficult to untie. Furthermore, it should not be used in preference to the accepted whipping or pointing to prevent unraveling or fraying in the end of a rope Overhand Knots often tie themselves spontaneously in loose pieces of cordage. And in this connection it is well to remember that a rope with an Overhand Knot in it possesses less than half the breaking-strength of an unknotted rope.

FIG. 8:   The *Figure-of-Eight Knot* has been called the perfect knot, because of its symmetry rather than its utility. It is used, as in the case of FIG. 7, as a Stopper Knot, and serves this purpose well, since it does not jam as hard as the Overhand Knot and by comparison opens quite easily. As a practical knot its uses are limited, but as an ornamental knot few can surpass it for beauty and simplicity of design.

FIG. 9:   The *Openhand Eye Knot* or *Binder's Loop* is a landsman's method of making a loop in the end of a line. It can be used in tying up packages, but should not be preferred to a Clinch or Splice, as it jams very hard and consequently proves difficult to untie.

FIG. 10:   The *Granny* or *Lubber's Knot* is often made when attempting to tie the Square Knot (FIG. 11), but should never be used, due to the fact that it either slips or jams. The beginner should learn the difference between the Granny and Square Knot before proceeding further in the art of knotting. When tension comes on only one of the standing parts of the Granny Knot, it upsets and jams. In this position it is unsafe and difficult to release.

FIG. 11:   The *Square* or *Reef Knot* is the most ancient and generally most useful method of joining two pieces of cordage. It is usually employed to tie up bundles or other objects, or to tie the reef points in a sail. However, it has two serious disadvantages: it does not hold if the ropes are of two different sizes or materials, and it jams very hard under great tension. Therefore, it should never be used to join two hawsers. To make the Square Knot, tie one Overhand Knot, as in FIG. 7, upon another (FIG. 11). Tie the second Overhand Knot in the opposite way from the first; in other

words, be sure that both the standing part and the end of each rope reeve together through the bight of the other rope. Otherwise, you will finish with a Granny Knot.

FIG. 12:   The *Single Half Hitch* is the basic element in the formation of many important knots. It is seldom used alone, except as in PLATE 2, FIG. 46, when the end is seized to the standing part.

FIG. 13:   *Two Half Hitches* is a widely used and excellent way to secure a rope to a ring spar or other object.

FIG. 14:   The *Round Turn and Two Half Hitches* is similar to FIG. 13, except that an additional turn is taken around the object. It is superior to FIG. 13, for when pulled taut it will grip the object much firmer and hold its position. Care should be taken that the Half Hitches are made the same way; otherwise a Sailor's Hitch will result, as in PLATE 2, FIG. 47. However, both forms are equally secure.

FIG. 15:   The *Lark's Head* or *Cow Hitch* is serviceable when tension is applied on both standing parts, but is valueless when a strain comes on one part only. It is familiar on baggage tags, or wherever a parcel is to be bound with the bight of a line.

FIG. 16:   The *Round Turn Lark's Head* is similar to FIG. 15, except that a round turn is taken with the bight around each standing part, thus jamming the knot and holding it more securely. It is used for the same purpose as the ordinary Lark's Head.

FIG. 17:   The *Clove Hitch* or *Ratline Hitch,* which has a number of uses, is frequently employed to secure a line to a stanchion or spar, or to fasten the ratlines to the shrouds; hence its name. This very useful knot is not only easily tied, but is quite secure when made on a spar.

FIG. 18:   The *Fisherman's Bend* or *Anchor Bend* is a remarkable knot because of its simplicity and great strength. It will not slip, chafe, or jam; much tension can be

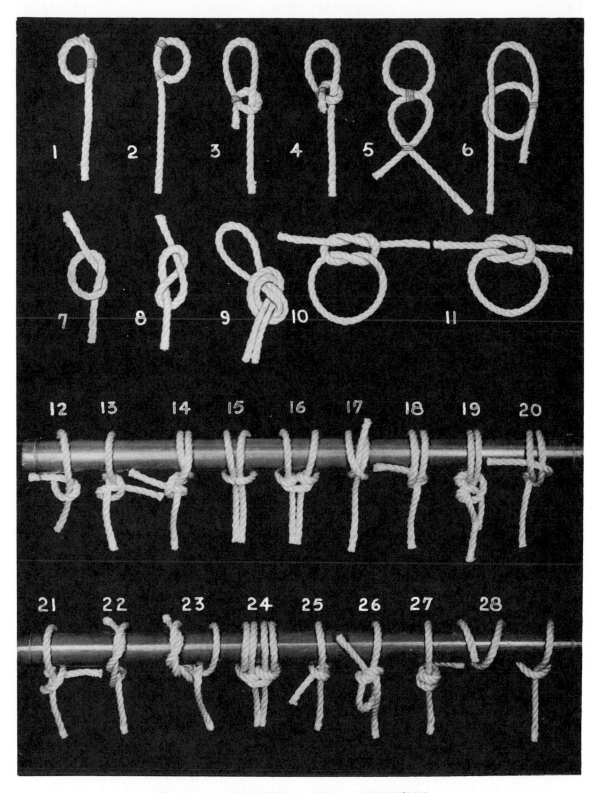

PLATE 1—CLINCHES AND HITCHES

applied to it, and when the strain is released, it is very easily untied.

FIG. 19: The *Fisherman's Bend and Half Hitch Seized*, First Method, is made in the same way as FIG. 18, except that a Half Hitch has been taken around the standing part and the end seized to it. If the tension is not continuous, it is best to do this, since the knot is liable to shake itself free if the end is not secured. Another method is shown in Chapter XI.

FIG. 20. The *Studding-Sail Boom Hitch* or *Stun-Sail Halyard Bend* is made the same as the Fisherman's Bend, but with the end brought back over the first turn, and under the second. This knot was used on the studding-sail booms of sailing vessels.

FIG. 21: The *Buntline Hitch* or *Studding-Sail Tack Bend* is made with an Inside Clove Hitch around the standing part. This hitch will jam and never slacken. It is used to make fast the tack of the studding-sail.

FIG. 22: The *Timber Hitch* is useful in securing a rope temporarily and quickly to a spar or piece of timber. It does not hold well unless it is kept taut. The twist should be in the same direction as the lay of the rope, which may be easily remembered by always thinking of it as "dogged" with the lay.

FIG. 23: The *Log Hitch* is similar to the Timber Hitch, except that it has a Half Hitch added to it. In actual use the Half Hitch is of course placed further away from the Timber Hitch than shown in the illustration. The addition of the Half Hitch tends to keep the log pointed in the right direction when being towed.

FIG. 24: The *Round Turn and a Cow Hitch* is made the same as FIG. 16, except that the standing parts are given a round turn on the spar before being inserted in the two loops in the bight.

FIG. 25: The *Halter Hitch* is formed by putting the end about the spar or object to which it is to be fastened, and then tying an Overhand Knot around the standing part. It is used to tie up horses.

FIG. 26: The *Slip Halter Hitch* is made in the same way as FIG. 25, but with the end tucked back through the body of the knot. This hitch can be easily untied by simply pulling the end.

FIG. 27: The *Inside Clinch Hitch* is tied by taking a turn around the spar and then putting a round turn around the standing part, so that the end is inside the knot. It is unsafe to use this knot unless the end is seized to the standing part. It has very little practical value.

FIG. 28: The *Stopper Hitch* is formed by making a Half Hitch with the end of the line around the spar, rope, chain, or whatever it is to be used on. Then the end is backed around the object in the opposite direction from which the strain is to be applied. In use, the part hanging down should lead to the right, almost parallel to the object upon which it is fastened, and be made fast to a stationary object. After the turns have been dogged around the rope or spar, the end is held in the hand. The authors have found that in actual practice these backing turns should always be taken with the lay of the rope (if it is put on a rope), as it tends to hold better due to the added cross-friction. The Stopper Hitch shown in PLATE 4, FIG. 92, is superior to this one, because the added turn gives it greater holding power, and if a heavy weight is to be suspended, it is much safer to use the stopper with more than one turn.

Plate 2—Hitches

FIG. 29: The *Inside Rolling Hitch* is tied as follows: with the end of a line, make a turn around the spar; then overlap the standing part and take another turn, overlapping the standing part again inside the first turn; continue around the spar again,

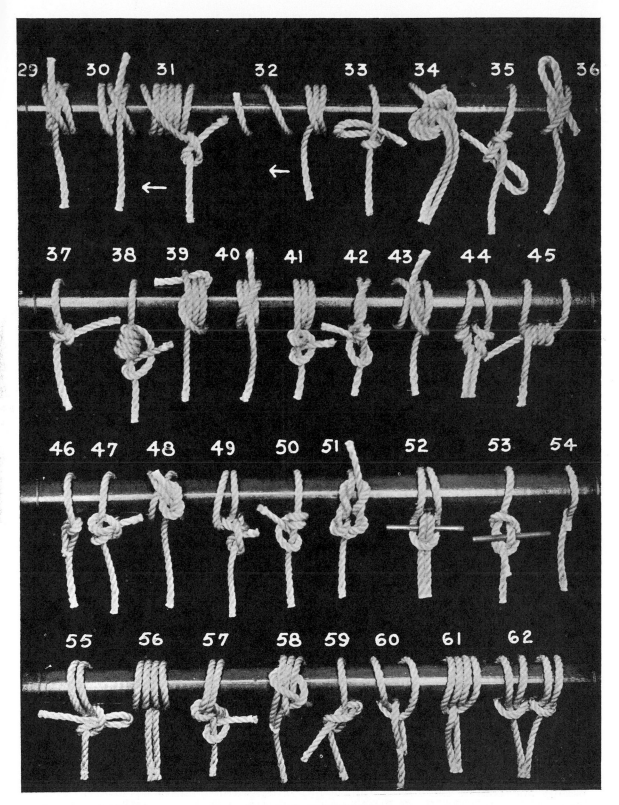

PLATE 2—HITCHES

and bring the end up under the second turn. This is a very valuable knot ashore or afloat, because it can be tied around a smooth surface without slipping. It can also be untied very easily. Another important feature about this knot is that it may be applied at a right angle to the spar or parallel with it.

FIG. 30: The *Outside Rolling Hitch* is made almost the same as FIG. 29, except that instead of overlapping the standing part with the first two turns, only one is overlapped, and a round turn is made the second and third times around, with the end brought up under two instead of one turn. It may be used for the same purpose as the Inside Rolling Hitch, but the latter is to be preferred.

FIG. 31: The *Lifting* or *Well Pipe Hitch* will also bear a strain parallel to the object to which it is fastened. It is used to secure the guy ropes of a circus tent to stakes driven into the ground; or, as the name indicates, to hold a well pipe being lowered into the earth. It is formed by first taking a number of round turns about the object, as many as desired (the more the better). Then when enough have been put on, the end is brought across the top of the turns, and two Half Hitches are made around the standing part. Tension is applied to the knot in the direction shown by the arrow.

FIG. 32: The *Round Turn Running Stopper Hitch,* although used for the same purpose, is inferior to the Stopper Hitch illustrated in PLATE 4, FIG. 92. One bad feature is that the "dogged" part reeves against the lay when made as on a hawser (*see* explanation, PLATE 1, FIG. 28). It is tied by overlapping the two round turns over the standing part, and then "dogging" the end. Tension is applied to the knot in the direction indicated by the arrow.

FIG. 33: The *Slip Hitch* is tied by first passing the end of the line a full turn around the spar. Then a full turn is taken around the standing part, and the bight of

the end is tucked under the turn on the spar. This knot may be used as a fastening where it is necessary to untie the end quickly; but it is not very safe.

FIG. 34: The *Lark's Head and Half Hitch* or *Check Knot* is a more secure method of tying the Lark's Head Knot (*see* PLATE 1, FIG. 15). The rope is weakened considerably by the addition of the Half Hitch, and is quite difficult to untie once a strain has been put on it.

FIG. 35: The *Halter and Manger Hitch* is formed as follows: a full turn is taken about the spar; then a twist is put in the moving part to form a loop and placed on top of the standing part; the end is next brought around the back of the standing part, and the bight is placed through the loop formed by the twist. This knot has little value, and is not very safe to use.

FIG. 36: The *Slip Clove Hitch* is a variation of the ordinary Clove Hitch (*see* PLATE 1, FIG. 17). It is made the same way except that on the last tuck the bight, rather than the end, is placed under the turn. This is a handy knot, as it can be slipped and untied quickly.

FIG. 37: The *Teamster's Hitch* is a very useful and secure knot, and is made in the same fashion as a Single Carrick Bend (*see* PLATE 6, FIG. 136).

FIG. 38: The *Snubbing Hitch* is made by first taking a full turn around the spar, and bringing the end down to the standing part. Next, make a bight, and hold it with your finger. Wind the end around the bight and the standing part, until four or five turns have been made. Then the end is put through the space between the spar and the knot. It is now brought down, and a Half Hitch taken around the standing part below the turns.

FIG. 39: The *Top Sail Halyard Bend,* First Method, is made exactly like the Studding-Sail Boom Hitch (*see* PLATE 1, FIG. 20), except that another turn is taken

[*Plate 2*] Elementary Rope Work 17

around the spar. The Yachtsman's method of tying this knot will be shown in Chapter XI.

FIG. 40: The *Magnus Hitch,* First Method, resembles the Inside Rolling Hitch, but differs in that it has one overlapping turn which goes from the left side completely across the knot to the right side. It is made by first making a round turn on the spar, then crossing over the two top turns and going completely around the spar again. The end is disposed of by putting it under the outside turn. Another commonly known method of tying this hitch will be shown in Chapter XI on Miscellaneous Knotting.

FIG. 41: The *Rolling Hitch and Two Half Hitches* is made by taking the end of the rope and passing it around the spar three full turns, then taking two Half Hitches around the standing part with the end. This is a very serviceable knot, and should be mastered by anyone working cordage. It is uniform, and when drawn taut will not slip or give, and if put on a varnished surface will not mar it as much as the two Half Hitches (PLATE 1, FIG. 13).

FIG. 42: The *Turning Hitch* is made by first taking a full turn around the spar. Then an Overhand Knot is made with the end and the standing part. To finish, the end is again passed around the spar, and two Half Hitches are made around the standing part with the end.

FIG. 43: The *Chain Knot Fastening* is tied as follows: the end is passed around the spar, then crossed over the standing part, and a Clove Hitch made on the left-hand side of the first Hitch. This knot can be used for the same purpose as a Rolling Hitch.

FIG. 44: This *Cat's Paw Hitch* has been made on a spar instead of a hook as illustrated in PLATE 256, FIG. 156. When a strain is to be put on one end only (although both ends may be used), a Cat's Paw can be made in the center of a line and put over the end of a spar. It will not slip, and in general is a useful knot.

FIG. 45: The *Bow Hitch* is begun by laying down a piece of line, with one end running to your left and one to your right. The end is taken, and an ordinary loop made, which is flattened down. Another loop is now formed with the standing part and is then wound around the center four or five times. There will then be a loop on each side of the center, and these are grasped and placed over the spar.

FIG. 46: The *Seized Half Hitch* is made more for temporary than permanent use, although it will stand up under considerable strain. It can be used for the same purpose as PLATE 1, FIG. 13.

FIG. 47: The *Inside Sailor's Hitch* is tied in the same manner as PLATE 1, FIG. 15, except that the Lark's Head Knot is made around the standing part instead of the spar. This knot is not used much, but is just as sturdy as the knot in PLATE 1, FIG. 13.

FIG. 48: The *Gunner's Combination Knot* is a Clove Hitch with an Overhand Knot made by using the end and the standing part. This knot has very little use, aside from being a more secure form of Clove Hitch.

FIG. 49: The *Backhand Hitch* is tied by putting a bight around the spar (just as in making a Lark's Head Knot, but without the ends rove through). The standing part is left hanging down; the moving part is put through the bight; and two Half Hitches are placed around the standing part. There is little use for this knot.

FIG. 50: The *Midshipman's Bend* is made somewhat the same as an Inside Clinch Hitch (*see* PLATE 1, FIG. 27), except that a Half Hitch is added below the knot on the standing part. It may be used in place of two Half Hitches, as it is very secure.

FIG. 51: The *Dogged Hitch* is begun by

taking a bight and laying it on the spar. The end is next brought around the back of the spar, put through the bight, and run around on one side against the lay for two turns. It is then taken across the front of the standing part, and "dogged" up around and with the lay.

Fig. 52: The *Lark's Head with Toggle* can be instantly released by withdrawing the toggle. It is unnecessary to have access to the ends of the rope in order to form this knot. It is effective, however, only when there is constant tension on both standing parts, and even then should be used only temporarily.

Fig. 53: The *Boat Knot* is an excellent temporary fastening for the end of a rope, and one that can be cast off in a moment. This knot is formed by making an Overhand Knot (*see* PLATE 1, FIG. 7) in the end of the rope, passing it over the spar (or ring), and bringing the bight of the standing part up through the center of the Overhand Knot and inserting the toggle. This knot has one disadvantage: it has a habit of jamming around the toggle at the wrong moment, making it difficult to release. Hence, the Lark's Head with Toggle (FIG. 52) is to be preferred.

Fig. 54: The *Seized Loop* is a temporary fastening, made by simply passing the end around the spar and seizing it to the standing part. It is not advisable to use this Loop if something heavy is to be placed on the standing part, as it is liable to carry away.

Fig. 55: The *Slip Fisherman's Bend* is made by precisely the same method as the ordinary Fisherman's Bend (*see* PLATE 1, FIG. 18), except that a Slip Hitch has been added. This knot is a bit more secure than the ordinary Fishermen's Bend, although used for the same purpose.

Fig. 56: The *Round Turn Lark's Head* is the same as PLATE 1, FIG. 15, with an additional turn taken around the spar with each standing part. When drawn tight, this Lark's Head will not slide or give.

Fig. 57: The *Thumb Knot Hitch* is made as follows: a round turn is taken on a spar; the end is passed around the standing part, tucked as in the Fisherman's Bend (*see* PLATE 1, FIG. 18), brought back across the turns, and put in toward the spar through the loop just formed by the end going around the standing part, forming a Thumb Knot; the end is then taken down and half-hitched to the standing part. This knot may well be called a variation of the Fisherman's Bend, but it will not shake loose.

Fig. 58: The *Lock Hitch* is a useful knot where there is a short standing part, for it is with this end that the Lock Hitch is tied. Hold a short end and take the standing part around the spar for three full turns. Next, bring it over across the turns and back under the three turns on the spar, then back over and through the loop on the far side. The end is then seized to the standing part.

Fig. 59: The *Sheet Hitch* is seldom used, and is too difficult to make to be of any practical value.

Fig. 60: The *Clove Hitch Seized* is made in the same fashion as PLATE 1, FIG. 17, except that the end is seized to the standing part. Although it can be used for the same purpose, it is more permanent than the ordinary Clove Hitch.

Fig. 61: The *Crossed Lark's Hitch* can be used only when there is equal tension on both standing parts. It is made by holding a bight in front of the spar, facing down. The standing parts are next given a round turn on the spar between the bight. Then one of the ends is run through the bight (the other runs straight down the outside), and both ends are seized.

Fig. 62: The *Treble Lark's Head* may be used for a Hitch, but is mainly employed to cover rings (Coxcombing). To make it, an ordinary Lark's Head is tied (*see* PLATE 1, FIG. 15). Then a Back Half Hitch is formed with each end.

[*Plate 3*] Elementary Rope Work 19

Plate 3—Hitches

FIG. 63: The *Double Lark's Head,* in this case, is made on the standing part, and can be used when a Hitch is to be made on the bight of a line.

FIG. 64: This *Seized Lark's Head* is made with the end of a line. The seizing is put on to give the knot added security. A Lark's Head of this type should always be seized; otherwise it is liable to slip.

FIG. 65: The *Backhanded Hitch* is made by putting a bight around the front of the spar, and bringing the two ends around the back. A turn is taken around the bight and the end, with the standing part. The end is then seized to the standing part to make the knot secure.

FIG. 66: The *Round Turn Seized* is made when there is not enough end left to make two Half Hitches. It is not very secure, and should not be used if there is to be great tension on the hauling part.

FIG. 67: The *Figure-of-Eight Clove Hitch* is made as follows: a Figure-of-Eight Knot is first tied with the end; the two loops are then taken and slipped over the end of the spar, drawn tight, and the end seized to the standing part.

FIG. 68: The *Midshipman's Hitch* is better known to yachtsmen and fishermen as a Topsail Sheet Bend, taking its name from the use to which it is put. It consists of a Half Hitch made with the end around the standing part, plus a Round Turn Inside Half Hitch just below it. It will not shake free when there is not a constant strain on it; hence, its use for securing the end of a topsail sheet to the clew cringle in the sail.

FIG. 69: The *Capstan Knot* is an application of the Figure-of-Eight Knot. It is unreliable, except for very light work or for a temporary fastening.

FIG. 70: The *Two Slip Half Hitches with a Bight* is made when it is desired to slip the knot quickly. To tie it, first take a bight, and form a Half Hitch around the standing part. Then take the bight again, and make a Slip Half Hitch around the standing part.

FIG. 71: The *Two Half Hitches and a Slip Knot* is tied by first taking the end around the spar, and making two Half Hitches around the standing part. Then a Slip Knot is tied just below the Half Hitches.

FIG. 72: The *Half Hitch and Thumb Knot* is made as follows: tie a Half Hitch, and then right under it make a Thumb Knot around the standing part. This knot is more secure than Two Half Hitches, but is very seldom used.

FIG. 73: The *Roband Hitch* was formerly used to bend the robands (rope bands) of a sail to a yard. The two ends are finished off with a Reef Knot to complete the Hitch.

FIG. 74: The *Strop Lifting Hitch* is made with a strop instead of the end of the rope. A block or other object may be hitched in the loop hanging down. This knot will bear great tension, and if put on a vertical spar will not slip down when a strain is placed on it.

FIG. 75: The *Weaver's Hitch* is really a Bowline, but it is made like a Weaver's Knot or a Sheet Bend. This is a very useful method of hitching a line to a spar or other object, because it will not give, and is easily untied.

FIG. 76: The *Lifting Hitch with a Bowline* serves the same purpose as the Lifting Hitch shown in PLATE 2, FIG. 31. The only difference is that this Lifting Hitch is made with a Bowline, whereas the other is made with two Half Hitches. Each serves its purpose equally well.

FIG. 77: The *Two Half Hitch Stopper Hitch* is used for the same purpose as the Stopper Hitch in PLATE 2, FIG. 32, although made slightly different. Every person who uses a Stopper Knot has his own pet method of applying it. Some prefer the Rolling Hitch or one of the other various types. Experimentation has shown that, if applied to a rope, two Half Hitches are the most satisfactory, because when a great amount of tension is applied to it, the knot can still be cast free easily. The Stopper Hitch shown in PLATE 4, FIG. 92, usually jams when a heavy weight is placed on it. Tension is applied to the knot in the direction indicated by the arrow.

FIG. 78: The *Killick Hitch* is an adaptation of the Log Hitch, and resembles PLATE 1, FIG. 23, except that the Half Hitch is passed in the opposite direction. It is a good way to secure a large stone or other object when a temporary mooring is needed. Tension is applied to the knot in the direction shown by the arrow.

FIG. 79: The *Reversed Check Knot* is an adaptation of the knot shown in PLATE 2, FIG. 34, except that the Half Hitch is made around the bight instead of around its own part.

FIG. 80: The *Lark's Head with Two Half Hitches* is a method of securing the end of the rope in a Lark's Head when only one end of the line is to be used.

FIG. 81: The *Clove Capstan Hitch* is made as follows: a Clove Hitch is first tied, and the end is taken from the right, brought to the left underneath the standing part, up between the Clove Hitch, and then from the right to the left, over under, and over.

FIG. 82: The *Round Turn and Half Hitch* is a good method of securing the end of a line permanently, and will bear quite a bit of tension. To make it, a round turn is first taken on the spar, and then the end is half-hitched around the standing part and seized.

FIG. 83: The *Inside Cow Hitch* is a variation of PLATE 1, FIG. 16, but the bight is on the inside instead of the outside of the knot.

FIG. 84: The *Lock Studding-Sail Boom Hitch* is made somewhat similar to the knot shown in PLATE 1, FIG. 20, but as can be seen, the end is brought around the standing part in the opposite direction from the ordinary Studding Sail Boom Hitch.

FIG. 85: The *Lock Clove Hitch* is made by beginning in the same way as the ordinary Clove Hitch. As the second part is being made, an additional turn is taken, and the end is then put under the second turn and finished in the same manner as the regular Clove Hitch.

FIG. 86: The *Clove Hitch and Half Hitch* is an adaptation of the Hitch in PLATE 2, FIG. 43, except that in this knot both ends are used instead of only one.

FIG. 87: The *Rolling Thumb Knot Hitch* has very little use, and when a strain is placed on it the Thumb Knot is liable to jam.

FIG. 88: The *Slide Knot* is a Slip Knot, and is made somewhat similar to the Figure-of-Eight Hitch. This knot has little use, and the Figure-of-Eight Hitch is to be preferred.

FIG. 89: The *Back Hitched Clove Hitch* is similar to the ordinary Clove Hitch. A Half Hitch is taken on one of the turns.

FIG. 90: The *Rolling Sailor's Hitch* is made by first taking a turn around the spar. Then a Half Hitch is placed around the standing part; the end is brought back as in the Lark's Head Hitch; and two full turns are taken. The end is then put through the bight on top of the turns to finish the knot.

FIG. 91: The *Riding Turn Hitch* is tied as follows: two full turns are taken around the spar to the left of the standing part; a third turn is taken, bringing the end across the front of the previous turns; the end is again taken and brought from the right to the left; then a Half Hitch is taken on the two left-hand turns, and brought down and seized to the standing part.

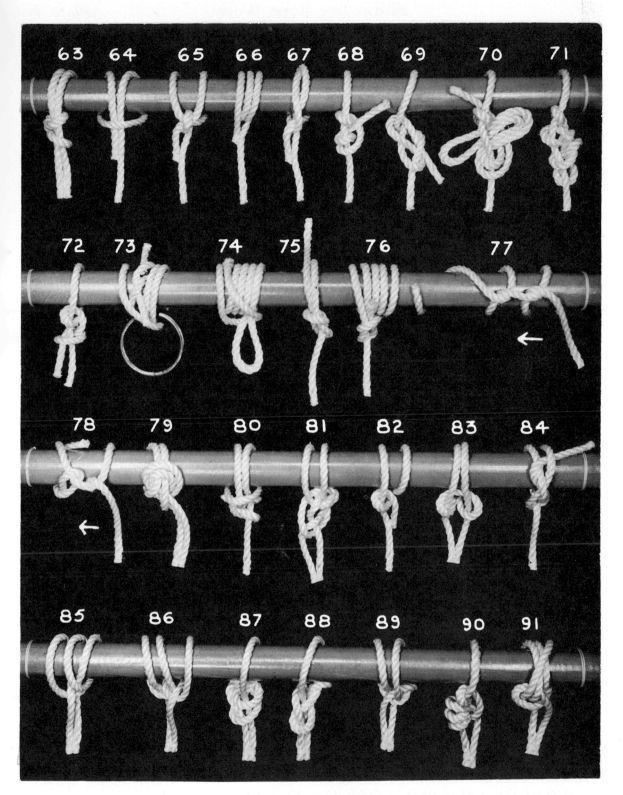

PLATE 3—HITCHES

Plate 4—Hitches

FIG. 92: The *Regular Stopper Hitch* is the most widely used of all Stoppers. This Hitch will hold even when the rope is wet or greasy, because the heavier the load the tighter the knot becomes. In this case, as in all Stoppers, the end made fast to the bitts or other object is marked *b,* and the end held in the hand is marked *a.* End *a* was left short in the illustration for obvious reasons, but in reality it is a little longer. First, take a turn around the rope, forming a Half Hitch. Next, take another turn around the rope and inside the original Half Hitch. The end should then be at point *c,* from where it is taken back and dogged with the lay. Notice the difference between this Hitch and the Hitch shown in PLATE 2, FIG. 32. Tension is applied to the knot in the direction shown by the arrow.

FIG. 93: The *Lark's Head with Interlocking Half Hitches* is another secure method of tying the Lark's Head Knot. However, it has one bad feature: when forced to carry a heavy load, it will jam very hard, and becomes difficult to untie.

FIG. 94: The *Round Turn Lark's Head Hitch* is a Lark's Head with a round turn made around the bight with each end.

FIG. 95: The *False Figure-of-Eight Hitch* has a knot on the bottom which appears to be a Figure-of-Eight. Close observation will show that it is not locked.

FIG. 96: The *Round Turn Clove Hitch* is an ordinary Clove Hitch, except that a round turn is taken with each end. This gives the knot added security.

FIG. 97: The *False Thumb Knot Hitch* apparently has a Thumb Knot in it. But when this Hitch is tied, it will be found to be an entirely different knot.

FIG. 98: The *Crossed Lifting Hitch* may be used for the same purpose as the Lifting Hitch in PLATE 3, FIG. 74, and also serves as a very good method to use in passing a strop around a stanchion to hook a block in. This Hitch can be put on a vertical spar or other object, and will not slip. Tension is applied to the knot in the direction shown by the arrow.

FIG. 99: The *Outside Magnus Hitch* is similar to the Hitch shown in PLATE 2, FIG. 40. However, the hauling part is on the outside, not in the center. Both of these Hitches will hold equally well.

FIG. 100: The *Log Clove Hitch* is made by first tying a Clove Hitch, and then with both ends, forming a Half Hitch around the spar on the left-hand side of the Clove Hitch.

FIG. 101: The *Blood Hitch* is made as follows: four complete turns are taken around the spar; the end is put under the turns to the right, around the standing part, back under the turns, then brought down and half-hitched to the standing part. and the end seized.

FIG. 102: The *Crossed Lark's Hitch,* First Method, is tied by first making a bight and putting it in front of the spar. One end is taken and a full turn is made around the spar. Both ends are taken, given another full turn on the spar, and brought through the bight under the turn on the right, back down over one turn, and under the two turns on the left-hand side.

FIG. 103: The *Interlocking Bight Lark's Hitch* is begun by taking a bight over the top and around the back of the spar. The two ends are then put through the bight and passed inside the Hitch, so that they will interlock as shown in the illustration.

FIG. 104: The *Backed Lark's Hitch* is tied as follows: first, an ordinary Lark's Head is made; then the end on the right-hand side is taken, and a Half Hitch made with it in the reverse direction, to form an opposite Lark's Head.

FIG. 105: The *Crossed Lark's Hitch,*

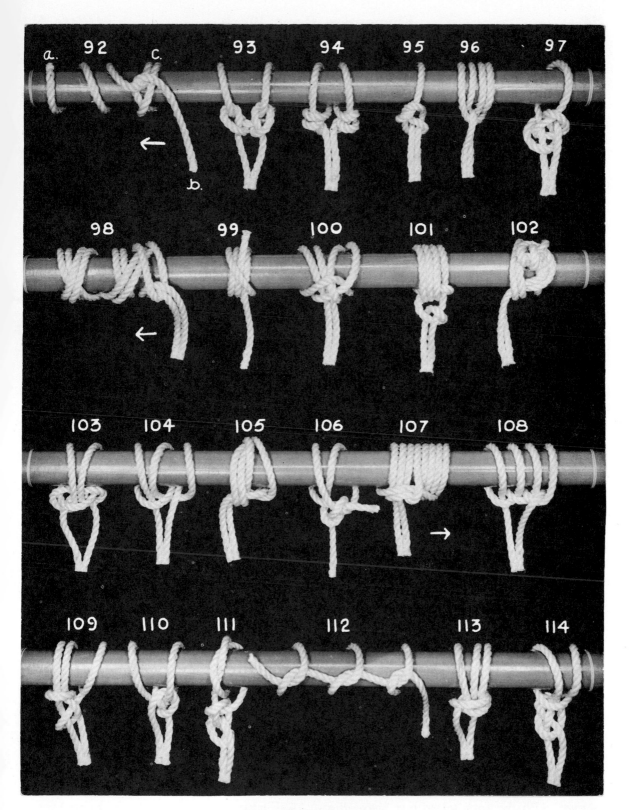

PLATE 4—HITCHES

Second Method, is made by first putting a bight on the front of the spar hanging down. The ends are next brought around, and up, and under the bight from left to right, then continued around, brought through the bight from right to left under the turn, and the knot drawn tight.

Fig. 106: The *Loop Hitch* is clearly shown in the illustration. It has no practical value.

Fig. 107: The *Killick Lifting Hitch* begins with a bight, taken and passed around the back three full turns. Then the ends are passed through the bight, and a Half Hitch is put on with the turn reversed as in the Killick Hitch, Plate 3, Fig. 78. This Hitch, when put on an object, will hold it more securely than the ordinary Killick Hitch. If put on a log for towing, this Half Hitch is slipped up about two or three feet, or as far as necessary away from the round turns in order to keep the log pointed in the proper direction. Tension is applied to this knot in the direction indicated by the arrow.

Fig. 108: This *Series of Half Hitches* is merely a group of Half Hitches made on the spar. The end is seized to the standing part. This Hitch can be made when it is necessary to have a Hitch that will not slip either to the left or right when used on a horizontal spar or other object.

Fig. 109: The *Rolling Hitch with Reverse Hitches* is made as follows: three full turns are taken around the spar; next, an Outside Half Hitch is taken with the end, and brought up and in back of the standing part, then placed as shown in the illustration.

Fig. 110: The *Round Turn Lock Hitch* begins with two complete turns taken on the spar. The end is placed through the center turn from the front to the back, brought back to the front again, taken around the standing part, and again hitched through the center turn—although in the opposite direction from which it was previously put through. Then the end is taken down and seized to the standing part.

Fig. 111: The *Twist Hitch with Two Half Hitches* is made by first bringing the end once around the spar. It is next twisted around the standing part twice, and brought around again. A Half Hitch is then taken with the end to the standing part. When this has been made, the remaining end is hitched as shown in the illustration.

Fig. 112: The *Marline* or *Hammock Hitch* consists of a number of Overhand or Thumb Knots (as many as necessary), made consecutively around an object, such as a yard, boom, stanchion. It has many uses, such as "marling down" the nettles or foxes when pointing a rope. Sails, bundles, or packages may be kept in a neat roll by marling them down with light rope. The Marline is also a very useful Hitch to apply when setting up wind dodgers to the jackstays.

Fig. 113: The *Round Turn with Lark's Head Hitch* is tied as follows: three full turns are taken on the spar to the left; the end is taken from left to right under all the turns; a bight is placed in front of the knot, and the end is led back under the turns to the left, then put through the bight to complete the knot.

Fig. 114: The *Crabber's Eye Lark's Head Hitch* is made by first tying a Lark's Head Knot on the spar. Then a Crabber's Eye Knot (Plate 26, Fig. 64) is formed on the standing part with the end or moving part.

Plate 5—Bends

Fig. 115: The *Loop* or *Bight Bend* is shown, with the rope seized just below the eye of each bight.

Fig. 116: The *Jam Bend* is of no practical value. It is tied by forming two Interlocking Round Turns.

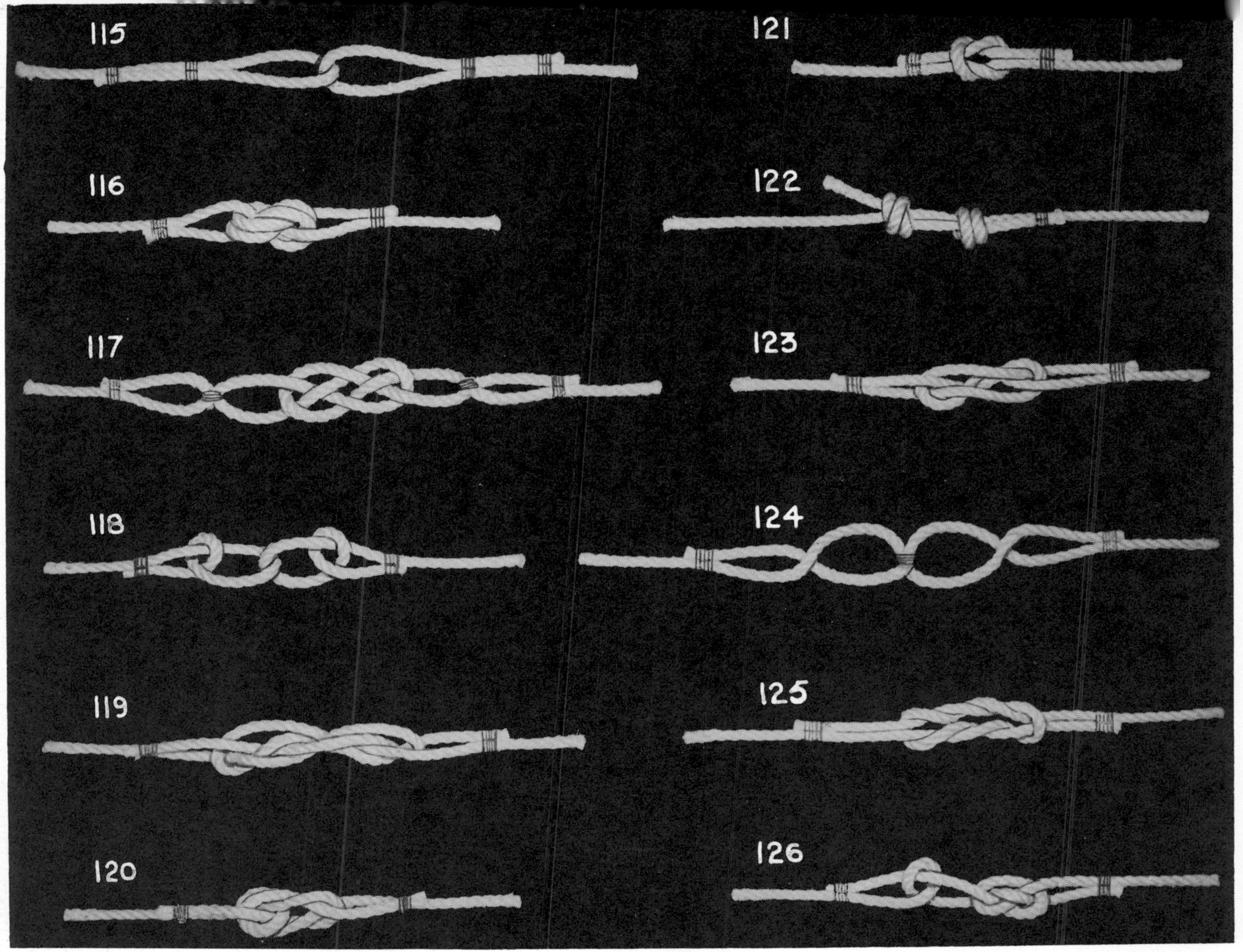

115 116 117 118 119 120 121 122 123 124 125 126

PLATE 5—BENDS

FIG. 117: The *Spanish Hawser Bend,* First Method, is used for joining the ends of two hawsers together. This is one of the many different combinations of Carrick Bends.

FIG. 118: The *Hawser Bend,* First Method, is probably the simplest way of joining the ends of two hawsers which are not going to be taken around a capstan or winch, and is nothing but two Half Hitches formed around each other's bights.

FIG. 119: The *Carrick Diamond Bend* is an ornamental way of forming a Bend.

FIG. 120: The *Open End Carrick Bend* is tied by forming a double round turn in the cross on one side, and leaving the cross in the other side open. It is seldom used.

FIG. 121: The *Square Knot* or *Reef Bend* is tied by merely forming a Square Knot with the ends of each rope.

FIG. 122: The *Blood Knot* or *Sliding Monkey Fist Bend* is tied by forming two Blood Knots as illustrated in PLATE 22, FIG. 16A and B. It is rarely used.

FIG. 123: The *French Carrick Bend* is another ornamental way of forming a Bend that is seldom seen. It is made by tying an Overhand Twist in the center and passing the ends out as illustrated.

FIG. 124: The *Temporary Bend* is tied by forming temporarily seized bights or eyes, which can be taken out very easily. It is used only when the strain is of short duration or a quick seizing of this type is needed.

FIG. 125: The *Surgeon's Knot Bend* is tied by forming a Surgeon's Knot in the form of a Bend.

FIG. 126: The *Crabber's Eye Bend and Hitch* is another novel way of forming a Bend that is rarely encountered. It is tied by making a Crabber's Eye Knot (PLATE 26, FIG. 64) and Half Hitch.

Plate 6—Bends

FIG. 127: The *Double Carrick Bend,* First Method, has a variety of forms, which are shown. Some of them, however, are more practical than others. The type shown here does not jam as hard as a Reef Knot or Sheet Bend, and can be pulled apart very easily after having tension exerted upon it, thus making it more practical for use in bending large hawsers together. This knot also is used for ornamental work in fancy gangway cloths, and fancy designs in Square Knot belts and ladies' hand-bags.

FIG. 128: The *Double Bowline on a Bight Bend* is tied by forming two Bowlines on a Bight together.

FIG. 129: The *Sennit Bend* is an attractive method of forming a Bend in two ropes. It is taken from a Four-strand Round Sennit, and slightly varied by merely passing the ends alternately through the bight of each cross, as illustrated.

FIG. 130: The *Hawser Bend,* Second Method, is another way of forming a Hawser Bend, with two Half Hitches in the bights instead of one.

FIG. 131: The *Hawser Bend,* Third Method, is shown with the Hitches taken on the other rope, rather than forming two bights and hitching the ends on their own part as in FIG. 130.

FIG. 132: The *Bowline Bend* is probably the strongest of all knotted Hawser Bends, and is formed by two Bowlines crossing the loops or bights of each other.

FIG. 133: The *Half Single and Half Double Carrick Bend* is another of the many variations of this Bend.

FIG. 134: The *Interlocking Bowline Bend* is a Bowline Bend tied or joined together as one part, instead of two as in the preceding Bowline Bend (FIG. 128).

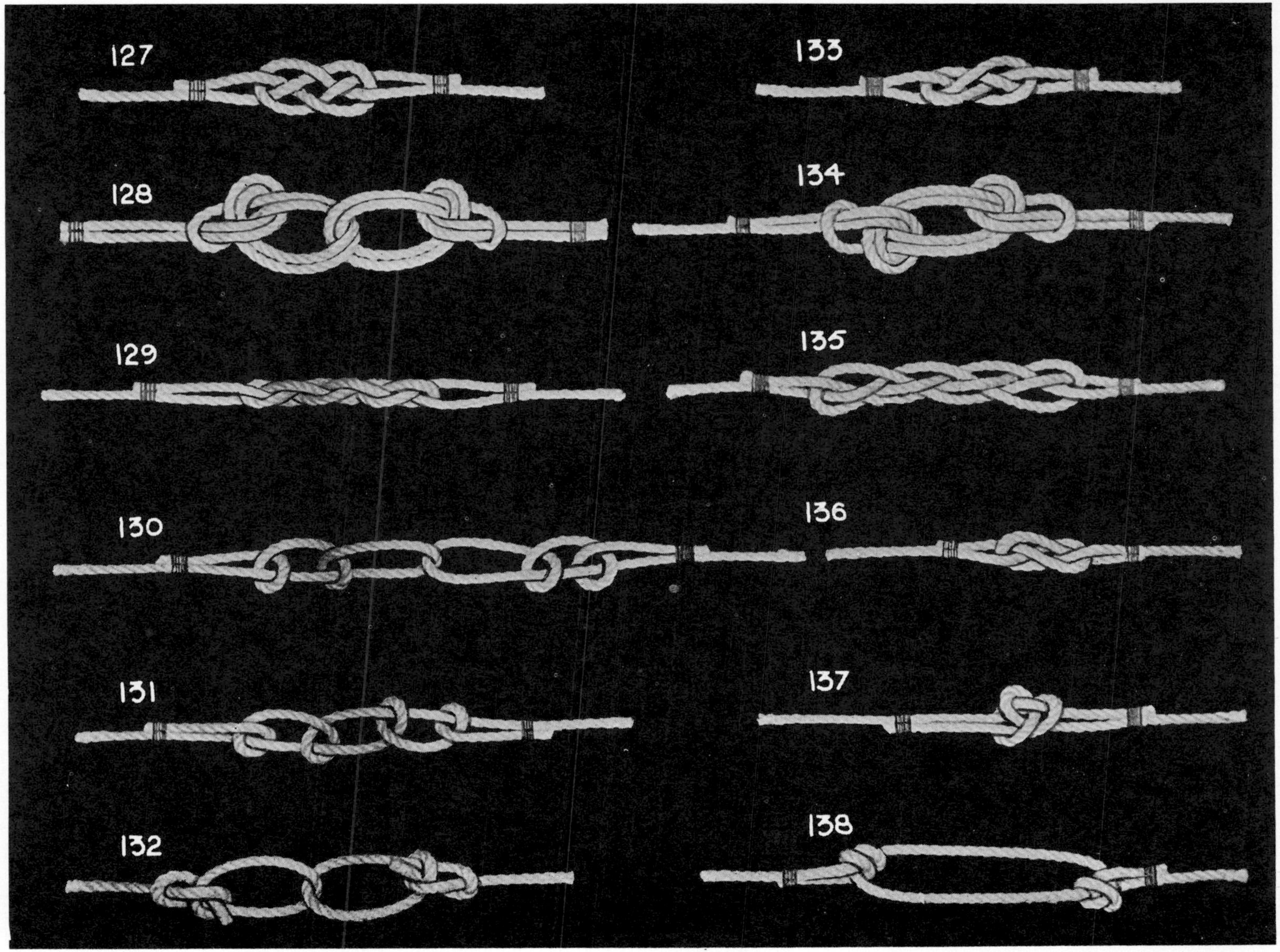

127 128 129 130 131 132

133 134 135 136 137 138

PLATE 6—BENDS

FIG. 135: The *Navy Carrick Diamond Bend* is quite often seen in the Navy, where it is used more or less as a decorative knot.

FIG. 136: The *Single* or *Open Carrick Bend* is another type of the various combinations. It is seldom used.

FIG. 137: The *Round Turn Open Car-* *rick Bend* is formed by leaving one end open, like a Sheet Bend, and making a round turn or Half Hitch around the cross of the other end.

FIG. 138: The *Rolling Hitch Bend* is formed with Rolling Hitches, taken with the ends of each rope on the standing parts of the other rope.

Plate 7—Bends

FIG. 139: The *Double Carrick Bend,* Second Method, is another type of Carrick Bend, and formed similar to some of the others. It is made by taking two turns around the cross on one side, and closing the other side as illustrated.

FIG. 140: The *Figure-of-Eight Bend* is made by tying a Figure-of-Eight in the body of the Bend.

FIG. 141: The *Bowline Splicing Bend* is made by forming a gooseneck in each standing part. Then passing each end or moving part as shown in the illustration, to form a Bowline. This bend is similar to that in FIG. 144.

FIG. 142: The *True Lover's, Englishman's* or *Halibut Bend* is made by tying two Overhand Knots back-to-back, with their ends pointing in opposite directions.

FIG. 143: The *Reeving Line* or *Single Marriage Bend,* First Method, is not safe unless both ends are well seized to standing parts.

FIG. 144: The *Bowline Splicing Bend,* Second Method, shown here, is practically the same as FIG. 141 except that the ends are tied somewhat differently, thus forming the Bowline in the opposite way.

FIG. 145: The *Gut Leader Bend* is made by tying a Twisted Hitch around the standing parts of both lines. Rarely used.

FIG. 146: The *Granny Bend,* like all forms of Granny Knots, is unreliable.

FIG. 147: The *Double Sheet Bend* is formed in the same way as the Sheet Bend, but with an additional turn around the bight and under its own part. This is a very good knot to use when bending together lines of two different sizes. Always use the larger line for the bight or loop.

FIG. 148: The *Sheet Bend on a Bight* is also formed the same way as the Sheet Bend, but with two ends of line through the loop instead of one. This knot is used when an occasion arises for the employment of two tackles.

FIG. 149: The *Sheet* or *Becket Bend* or *Swab Hitch* is also known as a Single Bend, Common Bend, and Simple Bend. It was once in very common use as a means of bending a sheet to the clew of a sail. When used for joining ropes of different sizes, it holds much better than the Reef Knot. It is made by forming a bight in one rope and a Half Hitch with the other rope. Weavers use this knot when a thread in a loom breaks; and it has also been used for centuries in the making of nets.

FIG. 150: The *Bending Loop* is another and more complicated method of bending a rope to a loop. It can be tied as shown by the illustration. When hauled taut, it holds securely. However, it takes longer to make a Bend of this type.

FIG. 151: The *Overhand* or *Gut* or *Leader Bend* is formed by tying an Over-

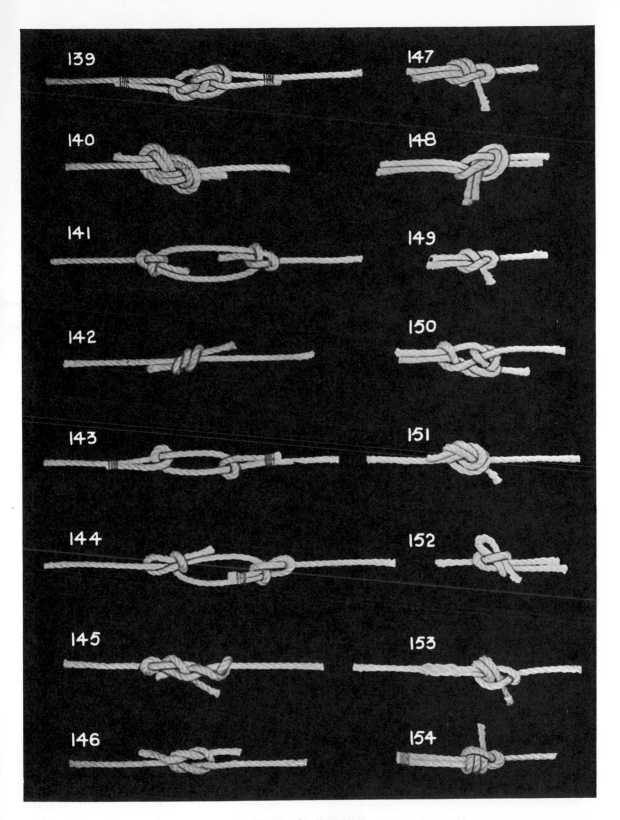

PLATE 7—BENDS

hand Knot in one rope, then following the knot around with the other rope. This is used by fishermen to splice gut leaders. To soften it, the gut should always be moistened before tying.

FIG. 152: The *Slip Sheet Bend* is seldom used. It can be untied instantly by pulling on the end of the Slippery Hitch.

FIG. 153: The *Double Sheet* or *Becket Bend with Spliced Eye* is the same as the ordinary Double Sheet Bend, but tied in a spliced eye instead of a bight.

FIG. 154: The *Triple Sheet* or *Becket Bend* is formed in the same way as the Double Sheet Bend, but with an additional turn, as shown in the illustration.

Plate 8—Bends

FIG. 155: The *Turning Bend* is another method that is rarely seen. It can be tied by forming a running loop on one standing part, and tucking the other end, as illustrated.

FIG. 156: The *Variated Reeving Line Bend,* First Method, is another way to make a Reeving Line Bend, and can be tied by closely observing the weave.

FIG. 157: The *Interlocking Reverse Reef Knot Bend* is an ornamental method of forming a Bend. It is made by first tying a Reef Knot. Then the ends of both sides are reversed back over the body of the knot, and out through the side of their own parts.

FIG. 158: The *Half Carrick Bend* is tied by forming a cross in one end, and leaving the other end open.

FIG. 159: The *Double Carrick Bend,* Third Method, is another of the numerous Carrick combinations.

FIG. 160: The *Half Granny Bend* is of no practical value.

FIG. 161: The *Double Carrick Bend,* Fourth Method.

FIG. 162: The *Spanish Hawser Bend,* Second Method, is another way of joining two hawsers together, similar to PLATE 5, FIG. 117.

FIG. 163: The *Double Carrick Bend,* Fifth Method, requires no explanation, as the illustration is very plain.

FIG. 164: The *Variated Reeving Line Bend,* Second Method, is similar to the other methods, and can be easily tied by following the illustration.

FIG. 165: The *Silk Gut Bend* is used by fishermen as a method of uniting silk lines.

FIG. 166: The *Sheet Bend with Toggle* is tied by placing the toggle between the lines, as shown. This method prevents the knot from jamming.

Plate 9—Bends

FIG. 167: The *Variated Reeving Line Bend,* Third Method, is quite easy to tie, and makes a neat way of joining ropes together.

FIG. 168: The *Half Hitch and Seizing Bend* is a very quick and useful way of uniting two lines.

FIG. 169: The *Double Marriage Bend* or *Splice* is made by forming an inside round turn around each other's standing

part. It is safe if both ends are well secured to standing parts, but jams under strain.

FIG. 170: The *Reeving Line Bend,* Second Method.

FIG. 171: The *Hitched Seizing Bend* is a novel method of bending two ropes together.

FIG. 172: The *Tucked Sheet* or *Double Bend,* First Method, is sometimes used when it is necessary to reeve a knotted

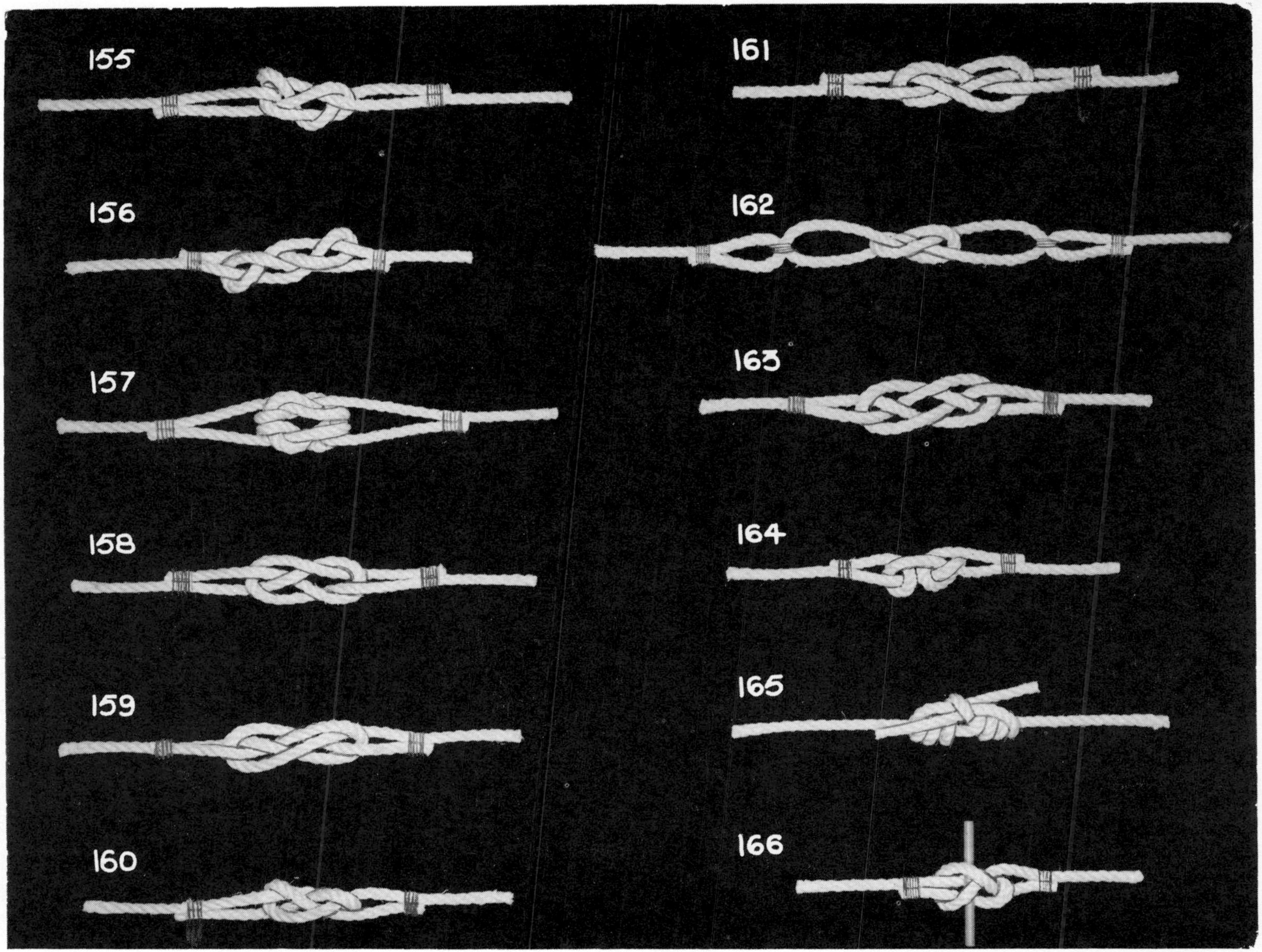

PLATE 8—BENDS

rope or piece of line through a small hole or opening.

Fig. 173: The *Half Hitch Open End Bend* has an open end on one side and a Half Hitch tied through the end of the other side.

Fig. 174: The *Tucked Hitch Bend* is made by forming a Thumb Knot with one end, then taking an additional turn and tucking the end out through the first bight.

Fig. 175: The *Tucked Sheet* or *Double Bend,* Second Method, is similar to the First Method and used for the same purpose.

Fig. 176: The *Interlocked Carrick Bend* is an unusual way of forming another type of Carrick Bend. It can be duplicated by studying the illustration closely.

Fig. 177: The *Left-Handed Sheet* or *Becket Bend* is practically the same as the ordinary Sheet Bend, the only difference being that the ends come out on opposite sides.

Fig. 178: The *Twin Hitch Bend* has one Hitch tied overhand and the other underhand, forming an attractive and novel way of joining two ropes, but not practical to use.

Plate 10—Bowlines

Fig. 179A: The *Bowline* is sometimes called the king of knots, and is the most useful way to form a loop in the end of a rope. Though simple in construction, it never slips or jams; and after severe tension has been applied to it, a simple push of the finger will loosen it enough to untie. The Bowline is really a Sheet Bend with a loop, but is made somewhat differently. To make it, the standing part is taken in the left hand. The end, in the right hand, is laid on top of the standing part and grasped with the thumb and the index finger, the thumb being underneath. Next it is twisted up and away from you until Fig. 179A is reached. Then the end is put around the standing part and down again through the loop, as the line shows.

B: This represents the finished Bowline.

Fig. 180A: The *Ring* or *Stopper Bowline* is made when you have a coil of rope and only want to use some of the end. In order to make the rope fast to something, the Ring Bowline is utilized, being formed as follows: first, the end is rove through a ring as much as desired; next, the end of the right side of the ring is taken in the right hand and made into a bight; the end on the left-hand side is taken in the left hand, and a Half Hitch is put over the

bight in the right hand, as in Fig. 180A; then the free end on the top is rove through the bight, as the line shows.

B: This shows the finished Ring Bowline. It can also be used on the cover, draw lines under the belly of a life boat.

Fig. 181A: The *French Bowline,* or the *Double Chaise de Calfat,* (Double Caulker's Chair) is superior to the ordinary Bowline as a sling, because a man can sit in the two loops more comfortably than in one. The formation of the French Bowline is illustrated in its first stage in Fig. 181A.

B: This shows the finished French Bowline in use. A man sits in one of the loops, passing the other one about his chest and back under the armpits. The weight from sitting in one of the loops draws the loop under the arm taut.

Fig. 182A: The *Portuguese Bowline* at first glance appears to be the same as the French Bowline, but is in reality slightly different, in that the second turn, instead of going through the gooseneck, goes over the top of it.

B: This represents the Portuguese Bowline in its finished form. It can be used for the same purpose as the French Bowline, but the latter is to be preferred.

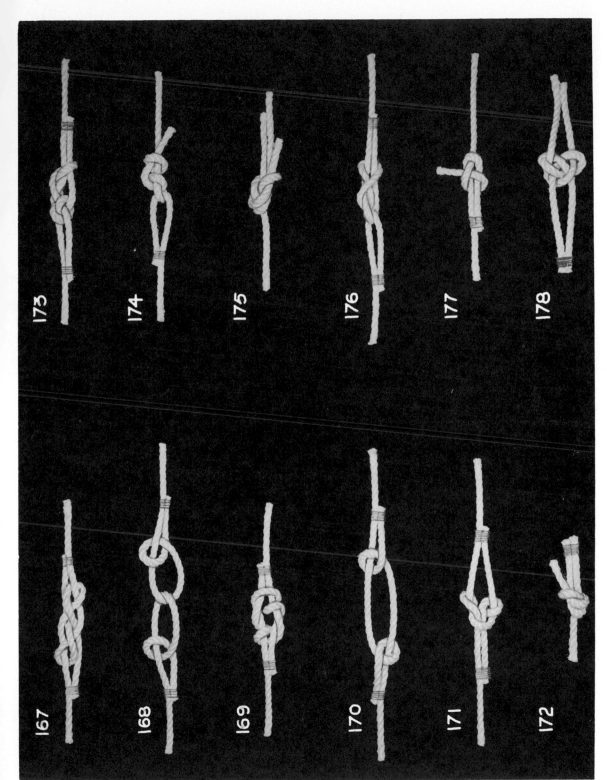

PLATE 9—BENDS

FIG. 183: The *French Bowline on the Bight* is made in the same fashion as FIG. 181A and B, and the end is put around in the same way as the ordinary Bowline on the Bight. It is made when there is not access to the ends and the knot made must consequently be tied in the middle of the rope.

FIG. 184: The *Slip Bowline* is similar to the ordinary Bowline, PLATE 10, FIG. 179, but with the end made into a bight and tucked through the gooseneck. This knot may be made in preference to the ordinary Bowline, as it is more easily released.

FIG. 185: The *Painter's Bowline* is made the same as the Bowline in FIG. 179A and B, except that a bight is run through the gooseneck instead of a single end. It can be used for the same purpose as the French, FIG. 181A and B. If a man is to be lowered into a smoke-filled place where he is liable to lose consciousness, it is much better to use the French Bowline, as it will jam about his body and prevent him from falling out.

FIG. 186: The *True Bowline* is made by forming a Figure-of-Eight Knot, then taking the end and passing it down through the loop in the Figure-of-Eight Knot. This knot has very little utility, and it is not recommended for any use other than instances where there will not be very much strain placed on it.

FIG. 187: The *Double Bowline* is made as follows: first, tie an ordinary Bowline and pull a little more end through than would ordinarily be used; then proceed to make another one (or just follow the original end through). This Bowline can be used where two separate loops are required.

FIG. 188: The *Running Bowline* is simply an ordinary Bowline made around the standing part of the line. It can be used to slip over the end of a spar or other object in place of the Timber Hitch.

FIG. 189: The *Fool's Bowline* is used by some as a chair instead of the French Bowline. This knot is unsafe, as the second loop is liable to slip and come free. It is made the same as the Double Bowline, except that the end is brought around the opposite way and merely put through the gooseneck.

FIG. 190: The *Jam Bowline* is so called because when it is made in small line it jams and is very difficult to untie. But when made in large rope, this is not true. It is formed by first making one gooseneck, then making another one on top of it, and proceeding as in an ordinary Bowline.

FIG. 191: The *Fisherman's Bowline* is used by the fishermen on the Grand Banks to snell their hooks. It is made by tying an Overhand Knot on the bight, then taking the end and putting it back down through the loop of the Overhand Knot.

FIG. 192: The *Eye Bowline* is tied by first forming a Bowline, then passing the end of the standing part back through the loop and following its own part around and under both standing parts. This knot has little utility.

FIG. 193: The *Lock Bowline* is made by taking a bight in the left hand, leading the end up to form a loop and back down through the bight, around to the right, and back to the body of the knot, with the bight put under the standing part. This knot is used but little, although it is quite safe.

Plate 11—Bowlines

FIG. 194: The *Carrick Bowline* is tied by first making a bight. The end is next carried down to make the loop, then up again and through the bight, around the standing part and back through the bight once more in the same direction as before, following the method used in an Open Carrick Bend.

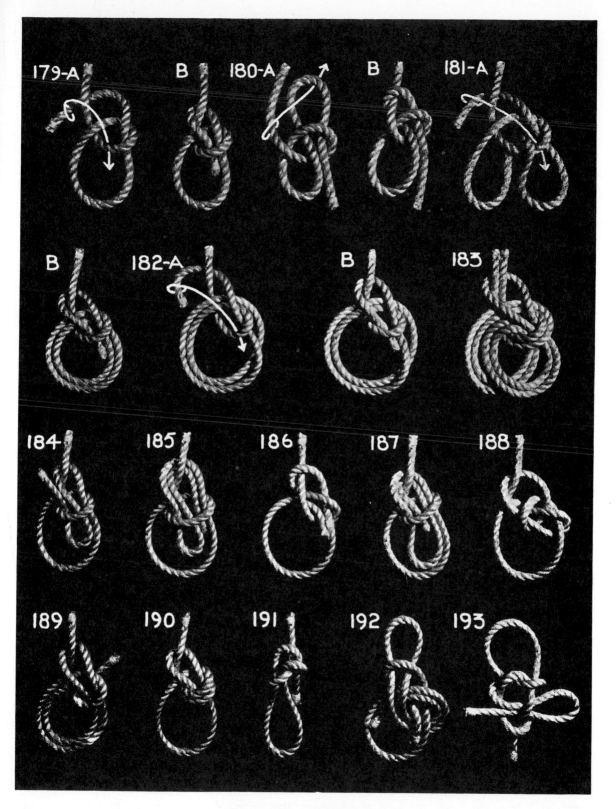

PLATE 10—BOWLINES

FIG. 195: The *Round Turn Bowline* is made in the same way as the ordinary Bowline, except that the end is passed completely around the standing part before it is put through the gooseneck again.

FIG. 196: The *Left-Hand Bowline* is identical to the ordinary Bowline, except that it is tied with the left hand; that is to say, the end is held in the left hand when tying the knot.

FIG. 197: The *Twist Bowline* is made as follows: the standing part is taken in the right hand; a bight is taken with the left hand, and given a twist; the end is then passed up through the gooseneck, around the standing part, and down through the gooseneck again. This completes the knot.

FIG. 198: The *Slip Noose Bowline* is begun by first tying a Slip Noose. Then a Half Hitch is made around the two ends of the Slip Noose, as shown in the illustration; and the standing part is put through the loop.

FIG. 199: The *Lineman's Bowline* is made by first taking a bight in the hand, with both ends hanging down. A Half Hitch is made on the bight with the end on the left-hand side. The other end is taken and passed through the bight above the Half Hitch, then around the other end, and back through the bight to finish the knot.

FIG. 200: The *Reverse Carrick Bowline* is somewhat similar to the Bowline shown in FIG. 194. A loop is formed in the standing part. The end is taken and put through the loop to the left, around the standing part, and then back through the loop to the left again, as in the illustration.

FIG. 201: The *Clinch Bowline* is begun by first making a loop in the standing part in the form of a Running Clinch. Then the end is taken, put through the loop to the right around the back of the standing part, and brought back through the loop again to the right, to complete the knot.

FIG. 202: The *Slip Noose French Bowline* is tied as follows: first, a Slip Noose is made in the standing part, leaving sufficient end; the end is taken and passed around, making a bight, and put through the center of the Slip Noose; another complete turn is taken, following the first turn, and then brought up and finished off, as shown in the illustration.

FIG. 203: The *Inverted Bowline* resembles the ordinary Bowline (PLATE 10, FIG. 179B), but differs in the fact that after the end is put through the gooseneck, the bight appears on the outside of the standing part, instead of the inside.

FIG. 204: The *Thumb Bowline* is fully explained by the illustration. It has little use, and is not recommended where a heavy weight is to be supported.

FIG. 205: The *Back Bowline* is tied by first making a gooseneck in the standing part of the rope. Next, the end is put through the gooseneck in the opposite direction from that in which the ordinary Bowline is put. It is then brought back up through the loop, around the standing part, and down again through the gooseneck.

FIG. 206A: The *Spanish Bowline* may be tied in many different ways. But this method is the simplest to illustrate. It is made with the bight of a rope, and laid out as shown. The two bights on each side on top are then put through the loops on the bottom, as indicated by the drawn line.

B: This shows the Spanish Bowline after the bights have been passed through the loops, and the knot drawn up tight. The knot pictured here can be used as a form of chair to sit in, although the French Bowline is to be preferred for this purpose.

FIG. 207: The *False Spanish Bowline* is made as follows: two bights are laid out in the center of the rope; one end is taken and half-hitched around the opposite bight; then the other end is hitched around the other bight. In other words, the end of the

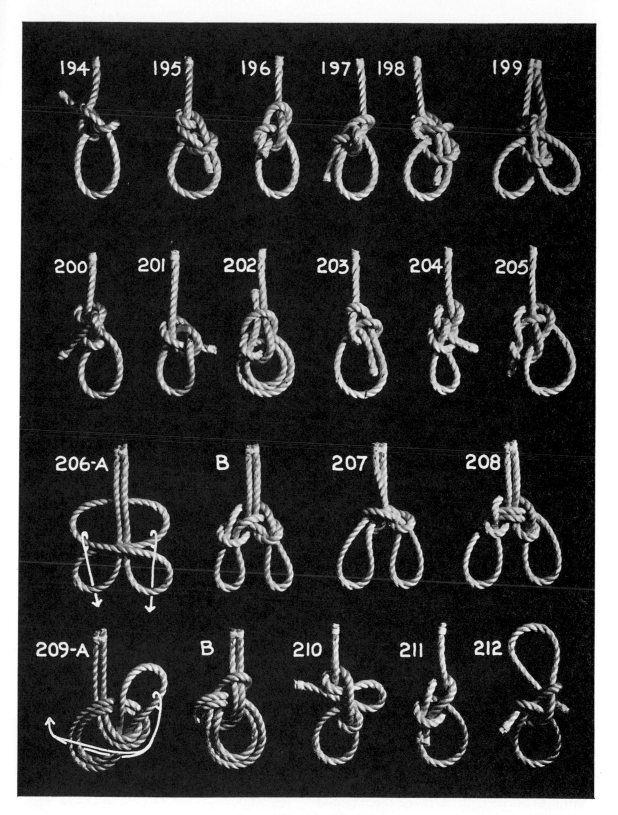

PLATE 11—BOWLINES

bight on the right-hand side is hitched on the bight of the left-hand side, and vice versa.

FIG. 208: The *Lark's Head Spanish Bowline* may be made in preference to the ordinary Spanish Bowline shown in FIG. 206B.

FIG. 209A: The *Bowline on the Bight* is formed on the bight of a line when the ends are inaccessible. To tie this knot, the bight of a rope is laid out to correspond with the illustration. It will be noted that the first step conforms to the beginning of the ordinary Bowline. The drawn line indicates how the bight is passed around the bottom of the knot, then up again around the standing part. To the novice, this knot may seem quite mysterious and difficult, although it is really very simple to master. Many years ago, mischievous boys would tie this knot in the reins of a horse while

the driver was engaged elsewhere. When he returned, he generally found it necessary to unhitch the reins entirely from the horse's head in order to straighten them out and untie the knot.

B: This shows the finished Bowline.

FIG. 210: The *Slip False Bowline* starts from a gooseneck, made with the end rove through it. The end is then brought around the standing part. But instead of passing it down through the gooseneck again, a bight is tucked under its own part, after being put around the standing part.

FIG. 211: The *Inside Bowline Seized* is made in the usual manner, but in this case, with the left hand. When completed, the end is seized to the loop.

FIG. 212: The *Bow Bowline* is an ordinary Bowline with the standing part tucked down through the body of the Bowline.

Plate 12—Bowlines

FIG. 213: The *Single Bowline on the Bight*, First Method, may often be utilized in place of the ordinary Bowline on the Bight. The latter has two loops, when made as in PLATE 11, FIG. 209. But at times this is undesirable. For instance, when the loops are to be put in a shackle which is large enough to accommodate only one loop, the Single Bowline on the Bight is employed. To make this Bowline, take the standing part of the rope in the left hand, and the end in the right hand. Take a complete turn around the left hand with the end, bring it up, and cross over the turn just taken, to the left. Bring it completely around the hand again, up and between the two original turns. Release the end, and with the right hand, put it under the first turn, and over the second turn, going from right to left. Then grasp the last turn with the thumb and index finger, and pull it through to the right, between the first and second turns. The slack is drawn out, and the knot is now finished.

FIG. 214: The *Single Bowline on the Bight*, Second Method, is similar to FIG. 213, and may be used for the same purpose. To make it, a bight is first taken and held with the thumb and index finger of the left hand, leaving the ends hanging down. With the right hand, take the end on the right-hand side and put two complete turns around the bight. Put the right hand through the bight, and grasp the lower of the two turns which have been placed around the bight. Then pull it up and through to finish the knot.

FIG. 215: The *Left-Hand Running Bowline* is the same as PLATE 10, FIG. 188, except that it is tied with the left hand instead of the right. Its purpose is the same as the one in PLATE 10, FIG. 188.

FIG. 216: The *Round Turn Hitch Bowline* is particularly useful because it will not slip when hitched around a spar. First, take two complete turns around the object. Put an Overhand Knot in the last turn;

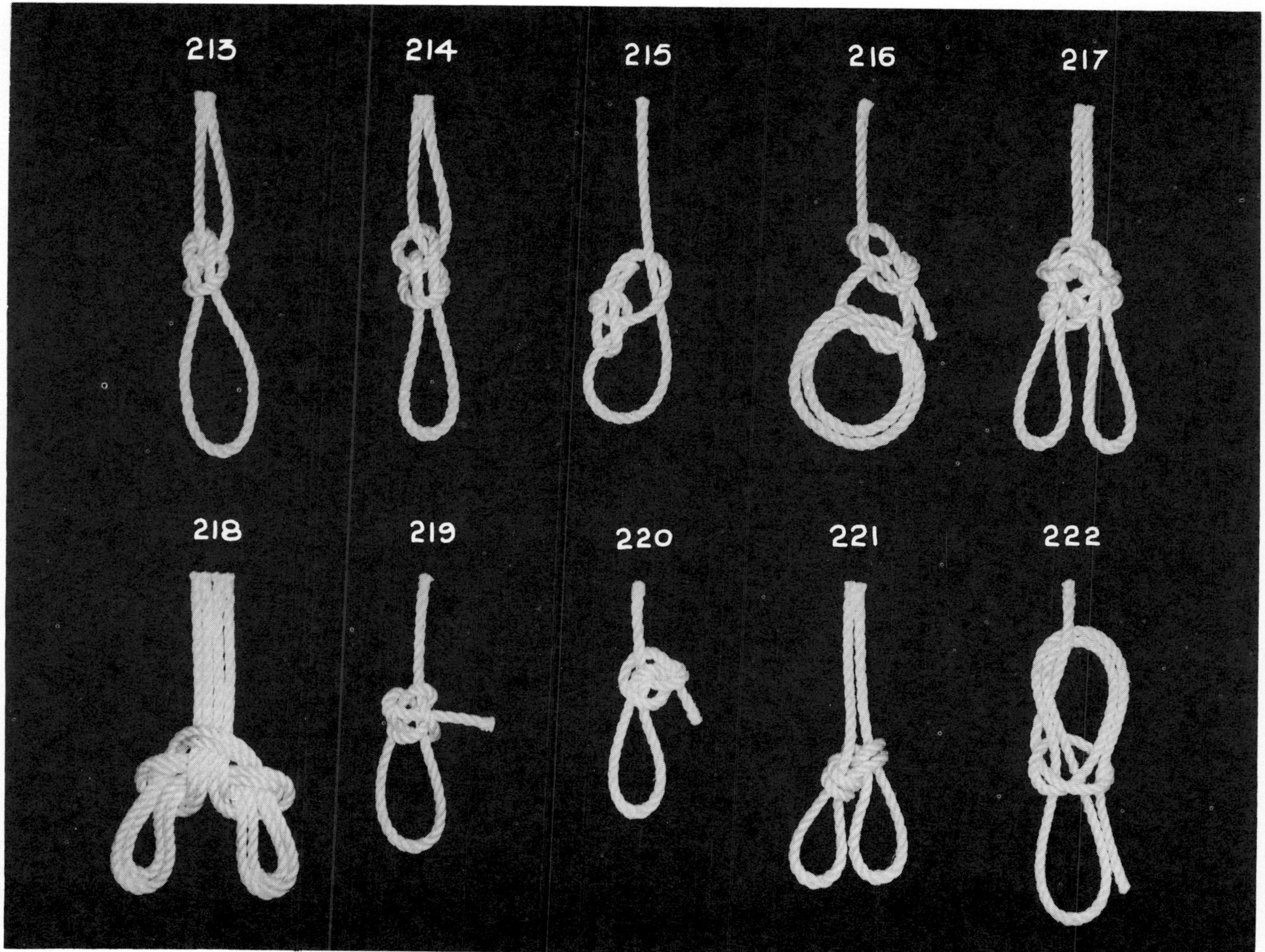

PLATE 12—BOWLINES

take the end and put it under the other turn; then bring it up and make an ordinary Bowline in the standing part to finish the knot.

FIG. 217: The *Double Knotted Spanish Bowline* is similar to the ordinary Spanish Bowline, except that it has two of the same type of knots back-to-back. First, make the ordinary Spanish Bowline (PLATE 11, FIG. 206B). Next, the bight going around the standing part is pulled up a bit. Then both ends are hitched into this bight, as shown in the illustration.

FIG. 218: The *Double Spanish Bowline* can be utilized whenever it is desired to form a Spanish Bowline with the bights of two lines. The two bights are first arranged as in PLATE 11, FIG. 206A. Then they are placed through the two loops in the same manner as FIG. 206B to finish the knot. These two knots are the same, except that one is made with a single bight, and the other with a double.

FIG. 219: The *Reverse Bowline* is made as follows: first, tie a Bowline (PLATE 10, FIG. 179A); twist the bight that goes through the gooseneck, until it becomes an Outside Bowline; finally, the end is brought from the left, over the first turn, and under the standing part, around the back of the body of the knot, then under both of the turns in front, as the illustration shows.

FIG. 220: The *Simple Bowline*, although it may appear to be insecure, is actually a knot that will bear quite a bit of strain. But its outstanding feature is that when a great amount of tension has been applied to it, a simple push of the finger will release it instantly.

FIG. 221: The *Interlocking Round Turn Bowline* is begun by first taking the center of the rope, then holding out two fingers, and placing a round turn on each one with the rope. The end on the right-hand side is put through the turns on the left-hand side. Then the end on the left is put through the turns on the right. The turns are drawn up snug to finish.

FIG. 222: The *Pulley Bowline* as illustrated by Commodore S. B. Luce, of the U. S. Navy, in his book *Seamanship,* is tied in the end of a rope, and a block or other object may be hooked into it. The top part is the standing part and the bottom part represents the bight where the hook is placed.

Plate 13—Sheepshanks

FIG. 223A and B: The *Ordinary Sheepshank* is used for shortening a rope. FIG. 223A is the beginning of the Sheepshank, with the rope laid out to form two bights. FIG. 223B shows the Sheepshank after it has been completed by forming a Half Hitch around the end of each bight with the ends of the rope.

FIG. 224: The *Sheepshank for a Free-Ended Rope* has the ends of the bights knotted.

FIG. 225: The *Sling Sheepshank* is an unusual method, seldom seen.

FIG. 226: The *Sheepshank with the Ends Seized.*

FIG. 227: The *Interlocking Overhand Knot Shortening Sheepshank* is tied by placing two Interlocking Overhand Knots in the center of the bights, and then half-hitching the ends to form a Sheepshank.

FIG. 228: The *Loop* or *End Shortening.*

FIG. 229: *Sheepshank with Outside Seizing.*

FIG. 230: The *Sheepshank Cinch.*

FIG. 231: The *Rolling Sheepshank Shortening.*

FIG. 232: The *Sheepshank with Ends Double-Hitched.*

FIG. 233: The *Variated Shamrock Knot Sheepshank* is a variation of the ordinary Shamrock Knot in the center of the Sheepshank.

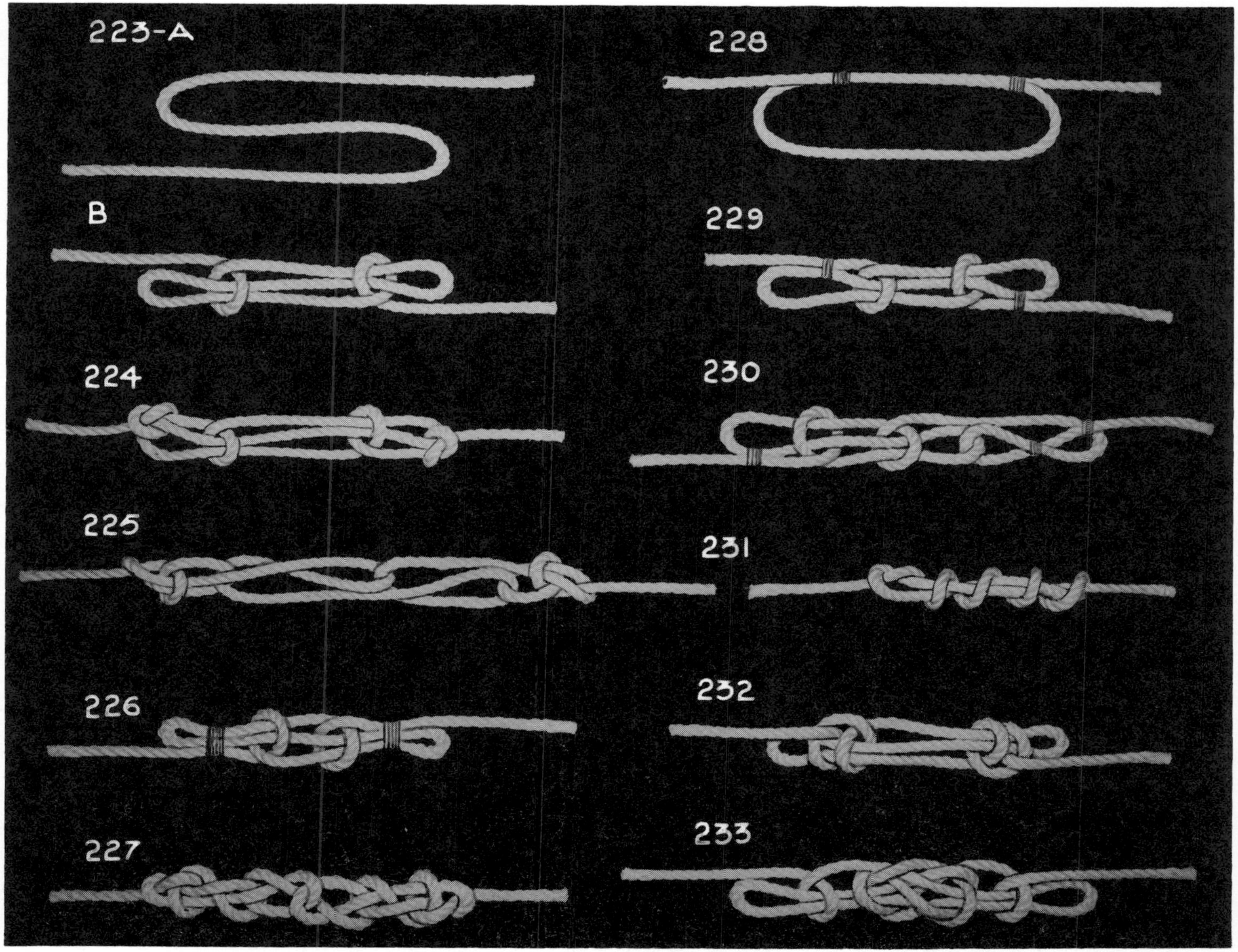

223-A

B

224

225

226

227

228

229

230

231

232

233

PLATE 13—SHEEPSHANKS

Plate 14—Sheepshanks

FIG. 234: The *Sheepshank with Bights Seized by Overhand Knots.*

FIG. 235: The *Knotted Sheepshank* is tied with the Overhand Knots passing out through the ends of the bights as well as their own parts.

FIG. 236: The *Marline Hitch Sheepshank*, First Method, has the Hitches reversed.

FIG. 237: The *Double Sheepshank* is made by forming double bights instead of the usual single ones.

FIG. 238: The *Overhand Shortening* is formed by tying an Overhand Knot in the middle of two bights, which have been made as though for a Sheepshank.

FIG. 239: The *Triple Knot Sheepshank* shown here as the body of the bights twisted around and rove through an Overhand Knot in the center. The ends are also knotted.

FIG. 240: The *Rolling Hitch Sheep-*shank is made with Rolling Hitches similar to PLATE 2, FIGS. 29 and 30, around the bights.

FIG. 241: The *Sheet Bend Sheepshank* represents another method of knotting the ends of a Sheepshank, with the ends passing around the bights, then through their own parts.

FIG. 242: The *Marline Hitch Sheepshank*, Second Method, has the Hitches coming out the same way at each end on their respective sides.

FIG. 243: The *Sheepshank with the Middle Crossed* is a novel method of tying the ordinary Sheepshank.

FIG. 244: The *Seized Sheepshank* is another way of forming a sling-shortening for a rope.

FIG. 245: The *Variated Surgeon's Knot Sheepshank* is tied by making a variation of the Surgeon's Knot in the middle.

Plate 15—Sheepshanks

FIG. 246: The *Overhand Sheepshank* is made by first tying an Overhand Knot (PLATE 1, FIG. 7). Then place the usual Hitches over the ends to complete the Sheepshank.

FIG. 247: The *Twin-Leaf Chinese Temple Sheepshank* is formed by tying a Temple Knot (PLATE 137, FIG. 5), then hitching the ends to make an ornamental Sheepshank.

FIG. 248: The *Square Knot Sheepshank with Spanish Knot Ends* is made by first tying a Square Knot (PLATE 1, FIG. 11). Then on each side tie a Spanish Knot, before placing a Half Hitch over the ends.

FIG. 249: The *Twin-Leaf Dragonfly Sheepshank* is formed by tying a two leaf Dragonfly Knot (PLATE 49, FIG. 363), then placing Hitches on the ends.

FIG. 250: The *Interlocking Overhand Sheepshank* represents another way of using the Overhand Knot in a Sheepshank.

FIG. 251: The *Square Knot Sheepshank* is made by tying the common Square Knot, then seizing the ends or bights with Half Hitches.

FIG. 252: The *Triple-Leaf Dragonfly Sheepshank* is another method of using an ornamental Dragonfly in a Sheepshank (PLATE 137, FIG. 1). Fancy rope shortenings like this one are merely novelties, and should not be employed for practical purposes.

FIG. 253: The *Triple-Leaf Chinese Temple Knot Sheepshank* is formed by making a Temple Knot with three loops (PLATE 137, FIG. 3).

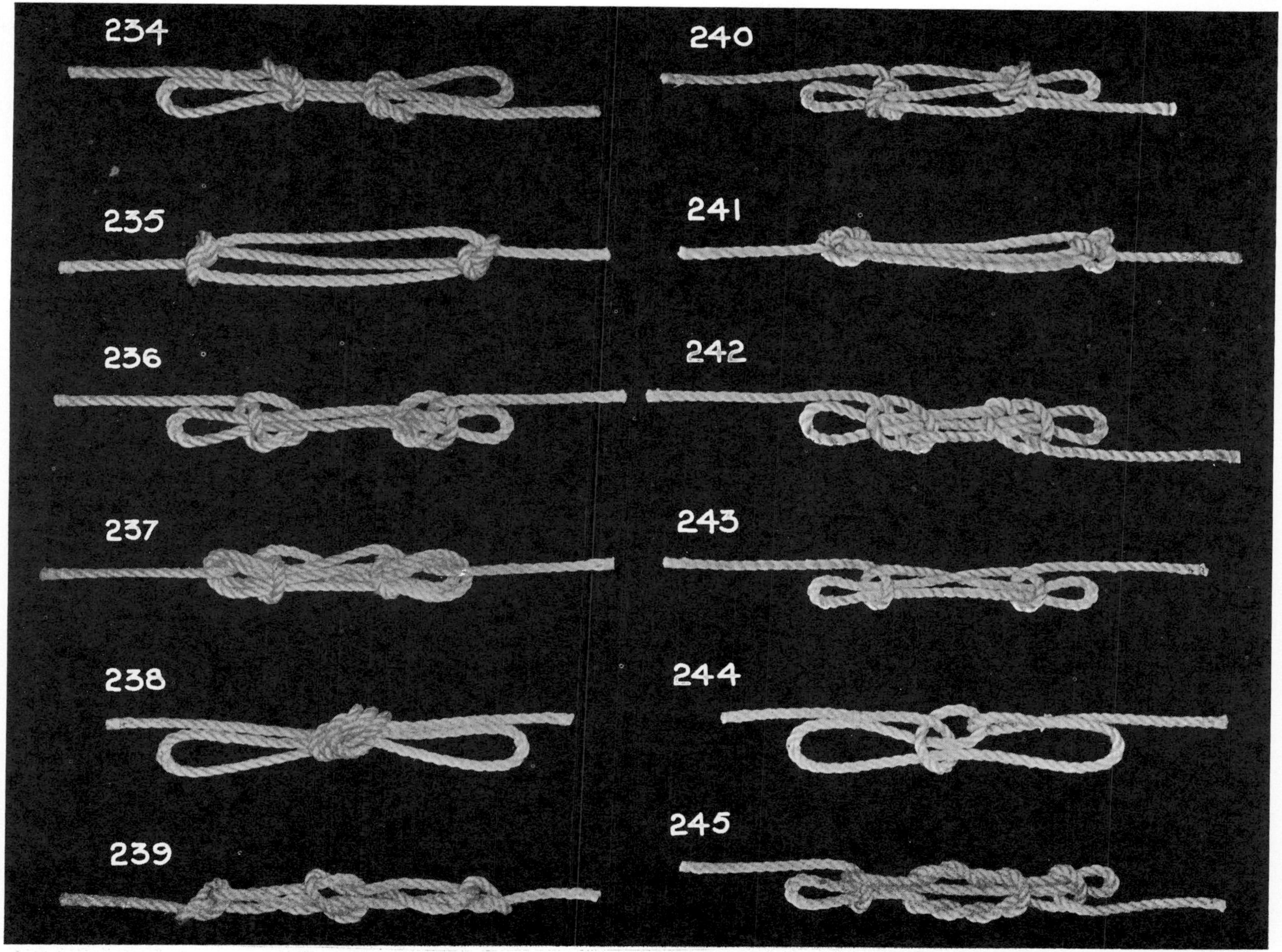

234   235   236   237   238   239

240   241   242   243   244   245

PLATE 14—SHEEPSHANKS

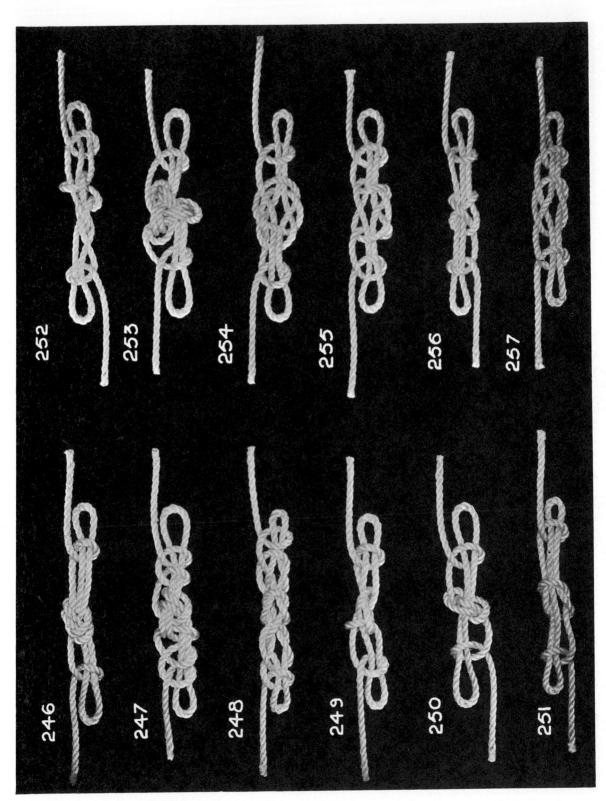

PLATE 15—SHEEPSHANKS

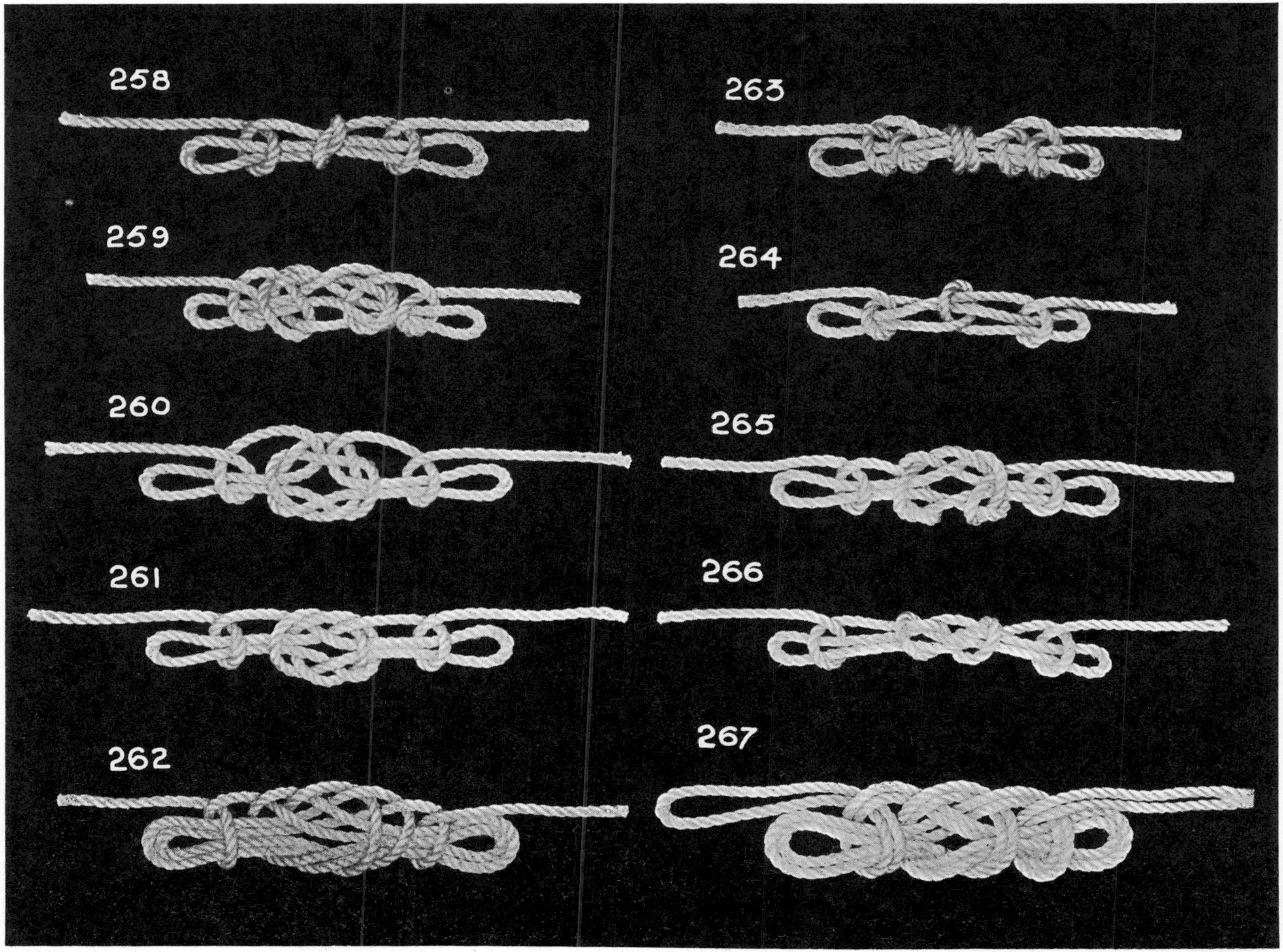

263

264

265

266

267

258

259

260

261

262

PLATE 16—SHEEPSHANKS

FIG. 254: The *Masthead Sheepshank* is made by tying a Masthead Knot in the middle, as in PLATE 24, FIG. 44.

FIG. 255: The *Shamrock Sheepshank* is constructed with a Shamrock Knot in the middle (PLATE 21, FIG. 11).

FIG. 256: The *Figure-of-Eight Sheepshank* is made with an ordinary Figure-of-Eight Knot (PLATE 1, FIG. 8).

FIG. 257: The *Man O' War Sheepshank* has a Spanish Knot tied in the middle of the bights (PLATE 23, FIG. 31).

Plate 16—Sheepshanks

FIG. 258: The *Overhand Sheepshank,* Second Method, is formed by tying an Overhand Knot in the center of the Sheepshank.

FIG. 259: The *Interwoven Hitch Sheepshank* has two Interwoven Hitches through the body of the Sheepshank.

FIG. 260: The *Variated Shamrock Knot Sheepshank,* Second Method, is tied the same as PLATE 25, FIG. 49.

FIG. 261: The *Double Jury Mast Sheepshank* has its center-knot illustrated in PLATE 24, FIG. 43.

FIG. 262: The *Cape Horn Sheepshank* is a rare, ornamental form of Sheepshank. See PLATE 293, FIG. 481 for the Cape Horn Knot.

FIG. 263: The *Blood Knot Sheepshank* is formed by tying a Blood Knot in the middle of the Sheepshank (PLATE 22, FIG. 16).

FIG. 264: The *Half Hitch Sheepshank* is made with a Half Hitch in the center. The Half Hitch is shown in PLATE 1, FIG. 12.

FIG. 265: The *Reverse Hitch Sheepshank* is tied with Reverse Hitches in the body of the Sheepshank.

FIG. 266: The *Twin Overhand Sheepshank* is made by forming two Overhand Knots in the order shown.

FIG. 267: The *Double Spanish Knot Sheepshank* is made in the same way as PLATE 23, FIG. 31.

Plate 17—Sheepshanks and Seizings

FIG. 268: The *Interlacing Sheepshank* is tied by placing two Interlacing Knots in the middle of a Sheepshank.

FIG. 269: The *Knotted Loop Sheepshank* is another of the many methods of forming knots in the loop or bights of a Sheepshank.

FIG. 270: The *Temporary Sheepshank* represents a temporary style of Sheepshank.

FIG. 271: The *Sailor's Breastplate Sheepshank* seems at first glance to be a Carrick Bend design in a Sheepshank. But it is merely similar. The Sailor's Breastplate is illustrated in PLATE 21, FIG. 10.

FIG. 272: The *Figure-of-Eight Knotted Sheepshank* contains a Figure-of-eight Knot in each end.

FIG. 273: The *Sheepshank with Toggle* is a method of tying the Sheepshank which makes the ends more secure when a steady tension is not maintained—especially if the ends are inaccessible.

FIGS. 274A and B: The *Flat Seizing,* First Method, is used only as a light seizing, where the strain is not too great, and when the tension on the two parts or ropes to be seized together is going to be equalized. First, take a sufficient length of marline or seizing twine and splice an eye in one end. Then place it around both of the ropes or shrouds and pass the unspliced end through its own eye, and heave it taut. Take the required number of turns, passing the end of the seizing line beneath the turns and between the two parts being seized together, then out through the eye of the seizing line, as shown in FIG. 274A. Next, take a round turn with the seizing line, passing it be-

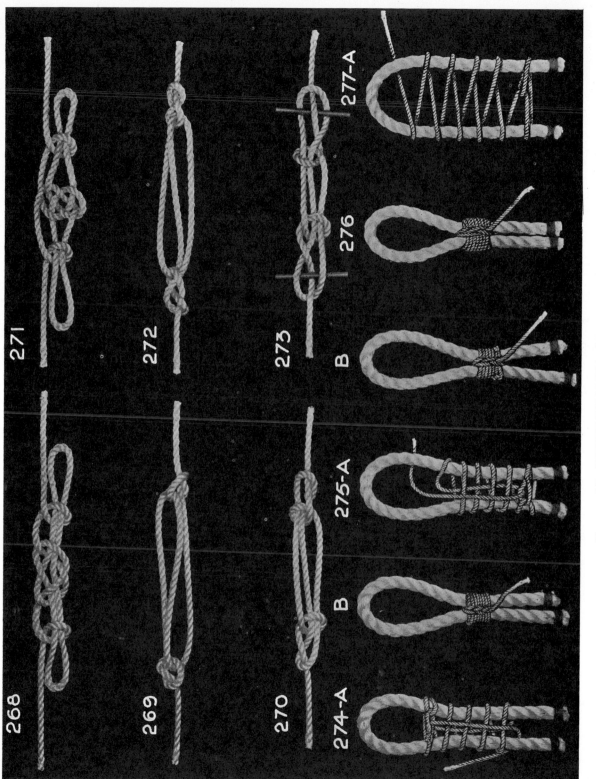

PLATE 17—SHEEPSHANKS AND SEIZINGS

tween the lines and over the turns already made, and heaving it taut. Then pass the seizing line around again, making two turns, before finishing off with a Braided Clove Hitch, as illustrated in FIG. 274B. These additional turns are called "Frapping Turns."

FIGS. 275A and B. The *Flat Seizing*, Second Method, resembles the first method, except that it is started in the opposite way, and finished off in the usual manner as shown in FIG. 275B.

FIG. 276. The *Round Seizing* is stronger than a Flat Seizing, and is to be preferred where the strain is very pronounced. Begin as in the flat version, but make an odd number of passes (say, seven or nine) before reeving the end of the seizing line beneath the turns and back through its own eye. Then heave taut. These turns make up the first layer, and are called the "lower turns." Next, the top or upper turns are made, with an even number of passes, or one less than the lower turns, which places the upper turns in the grooves formed between the lower ones. The end of the seizing line is then tucked under the last of the lower turns, and hove taut.

FIGS. 277A and B: The *Racking* or *Nippered Seizing* is the best method to use when an unequal strain is placed on two shrouds, as when turning in a dead eye. The seizing line should be well stretched before being used in a seizing of this type. Begin as in the Flat or Round Seizing, by forming a turn around the two parts to be seized, then reeving the end of the seizing line through its own eye. The turns are started in a sort of Figure-of-Eight fashion, as illustrated. After making about ten passes (if the strain is to be severe), start the second passes back in the direction of the beginning, fitting them between the grooves left by the first turns. Finish off by reeving the end of the seizing line through its own eye again. Then tie an Overhand Knot, and cut off short. A slightly different method of making this seizing can be used if desired. Before starting the second turns or passes, form a Half Hitch on the inside of the last Figure-of-Eight loop, and then follow back toward the beginning, as already described. The cross or frapping turns may also be applied to finish off. (FIG. 277B is illustrated on PLATE 18.)

Plate 18—Seizings

FIG. 278: The *Cuckold's Neck* or *Half Crown Seizing* is similar to a Round Seizing, except that it forms an eye at the point where both ropes cross each other. It was formerly used for the dolphin striker on sailing vessels. The illustration shows the ends brought together with a Flat Seizing.

FIGS. 279A and B: The *Overhand Seizing* is a rare and novel method of forming a seizing. Place a loop over the parts to be seized. Then take the required number of round turns over the loop and, at the same time, the parts being seized, reeving the end of the seizing line out through the eye of the loop on the opposite side. Heave taut and make an Overhand Knot across the front with both ends, passing the ends

through the seized parts and making an Overhand Knot on the opposite side. Repeat this once more by making another Overhand Knot next to the first one, and then finish off the opposite side by making an additional turn in the last Overhand Knot, for added security.

FIG. 280: The *Throat Seizing* is made in the same fashion as a Round Seizing, but without any cross turns. It was used for the same purpose as the Horseshoe Splice, to separate the legs of a pair of shrouds.

FIG. 281: The *Necklace Seizing* is begun in the same way as the Racked Seizing, by taking the required number of Figure-of-Eight turns, then tucking the end of the seizing line under the last turn and across

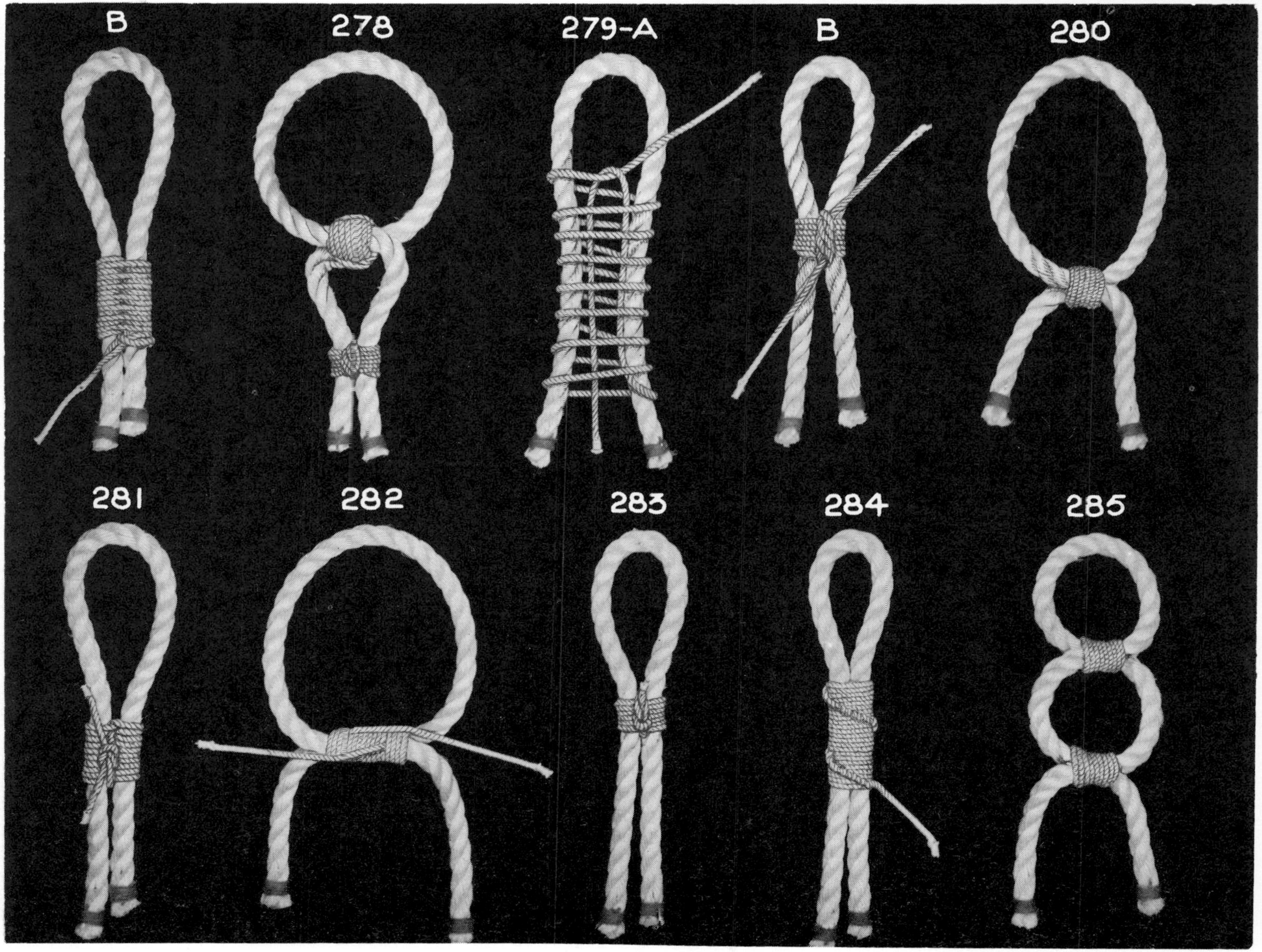

PLATE 18—SEIZINGS

the front, to form a Reef Knot with the line from the other side.

FIG. 282: The *Ring Throat, Half Crown,* or *Temporary Eye Seizing* is formed by first measuring the size of eye desired, and then making an ordinary seizing around the parts to be seized.

FIG. 283: The *Middle Seizing* closely resembles an Overhand Seizing, except that the bottom strand forming the loop is cut off short. Then the other end of the seizing line, after being rove through the eye of the loop on the opposite side, is passed around the seizing two times to form the cross or frapping turns. The seizing is finished off with a Reef Knot, as illustrated.

FIG. 284: The *French* or *Grapevine Seizing* is an ornamental type of seizing, made by half-hitching one strand around the body of the seized parts. It is started by overlapping one strand with the working part, and can be finished by either tying an Overhand Knot up close or tucking the end under.

FIG. 285: The *Temporary Clinch Seizing* is the same as FIG. 282, except that two eyes are formed instead of one.

Plate 19—Seizings and Whippings

FIG. 286: The *Single Crossed Seizing* is made as follows: splice a small eye in the end of the marline; reeve the end of the seizing line through the eye and around the parts to be seized; make eight or ten turns, and heave taut; then tuck the end down beneath the turns and between the seized parts, over the turns, and up between the seized parts, over the turns again, and finish off by tucking the end under its own two cross parts; heave taut in the opposite direction, which will bring the end between the two seized parts.

FIG. 287: The *Double Shroud Seizing* is a relic of the old clipper-ship sailing days, with their hemp shrouds, lanyards, and dead eyes. Splice a small eye in the marline, and reeve the end of the seizing line through and around the parts to be seized. Make about twelve turns, heaving each one taut. Use a marline spike to tuck the end back under the turns and out through its own eye. Then make eleven turns back in the same direction, or one less turn than the first group. To complete the seizing, use a marline spike to tuck the end back under both layers of turns; tie an Overhand Knot after heaving taut; and cut the end off short.

FIG. 288: The *Double Crossed Seizing* is begun by making an eye in the seizing line.

Reeve the end of the line through the eye, as in the Single Crossed Seizing. Take about ten turns around the parts to be seized, and heave taut. Make a second layer of riding turns back to the eye, and down through it, tucking the end beneath the riding turns between the seized parts, then take two frapping turns on the seizing turns. To finish off, tuck the end under the frapping turns and heave taut.

FIG. 289: The *Eye Seizing* is used in lines that cannot be spliced, such as hard lay braided line. It is usually necessary to put two or three cross seizings on lines of this type. Then the ends should be frayed, tapered, and served. This method of seizing is utilized for log lines, hand lines, and lead lines at sea.

FIG. 290: The *Nock Seizing* is an unusual method, but rather simple to make. Unlay the strands of the rope, and make a tuck as for an Eye Splice. Then form three Half Hitches by tucking each strand back under its own part, out through the eye of the Half Hitch formed by the next strand, and so on, until each strand has been passed under its own part and out through the eye of the next part. Finish off with an ordinary whipping.

FIG. 291: The *Clinch Seizing* shows the

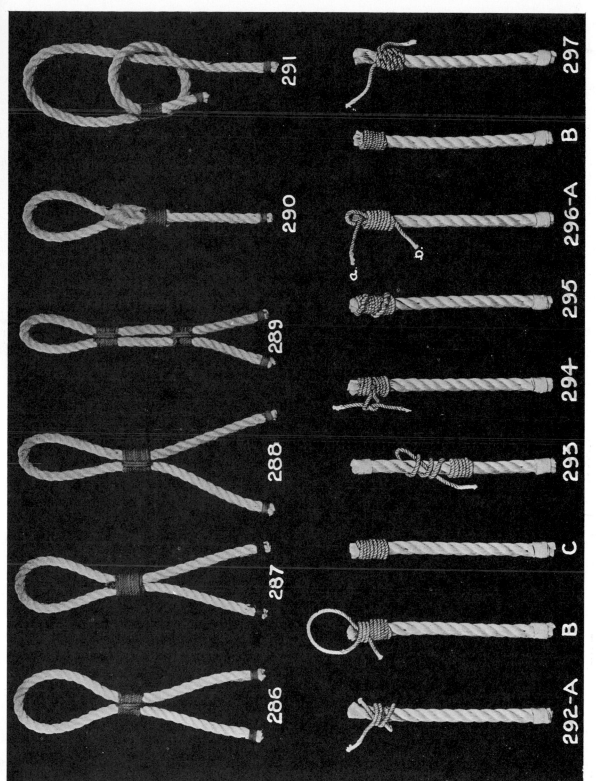

PLATE 19—SEIZINGS AND WHIPPINGS

method used in putting a Cross Seizing on a clinch. Either one or two seizings can be used, as desired, on either an inside or an outside clinch.

Fig. 292A: Is a *Plain Whipping*. (Whippings are always made with the twine wound against the lay of the rope. It is also customary to work the turns toward the end of the rope.) Fig. 292A shows the beginning of the whipping. One end is placed near the end of the rope, and then run back a short distance before the turns are begun.

B: After the desired number of turns have been wound around the rope, the end of the twine is laid in the direction shown in this illustration. Then three or four more turns are wound around the end of the rope with the bight of the twine.

C: After the finishing turns have been wound around, as just described, the last turn is drawn tight, and the ends are both cut off close to finish the whipping.

Fig. 293: The *Plain Whipping in the Middle of A Line* serves a special purpose. In most cases, a whipping is used to prevent the end of a rope from fraying out or becoming unlaid. But it sometimes becomes necessary to place a whipping in the center of a rope or other object. In order to do this, leave several turns slack, and pass the end of the whipping twine under them, as shown. Each turn is then hove taut, and the end pulled to take out the slack.

Fig. 294: The *American Whipping*, called by this name in England, is a variation of the Plain Whipping. Both ends of the twine are brought up in the middle of the turns, and joined with a Reef Knot. The Reef Knot should be made in the groove between two strands of the rope, so that it can be pushed down between them beneath the turns.

Fig. 295: The *French* or *Grapevine*

Whipping is a very secure and unique method of whipping the end of a rope. A suitable length of whipping twine is taken, and an Overhand Knot is tied a short distance back from the end of the rope. Next, a continuous group of Half Hitches should be put on against the lay of the rope, until the end is almost reached. Then two loose Hitches are taken, and the end of the twine is placed under them, the Hitches being drawn taut and the slack end pulled to complete the whipping.

Fig. 296A: The *Temporary Whipping* is made by first laying a bight on the rope a short distance from the end. A number of turns are taken about the rope and on top of the bight. End *a* of the whipping twine is put through the loop, and end *b*, which forms the bight, is drawn until the loop is under the turns. Both ends of the twine are then cut off close.

B: This figure shows the whipping after the ends have been cut off short to finish the whipping.

Fig. 297: The *West Country Whipping* is seldom used, although it is quite strong and secure. It is formed by first taking the middle of the whipping twine and tying an Overhand Knot around the rope at each half-turn, so that when finished there will be an Overhand Knot on each side of the rope. When a sufficient number of turns have been passed, finish off the ends with a Reef Knot.

Note: Very few people know, when asked, how long a whipping should be made. Some keep winding turns around the rope until it "looks right." But this is not a dependable method. The real thing to remember in making a whipping is that it should be made as long as the diameter of the rope upon which it is being placed.

Plate 20—Whippings

Fig. 298A: The *Palm and Needle Whipping* (three strands) is the neatest and most secure of all methods of finishing off the end of a rope. At first glance, it may seem diffi-

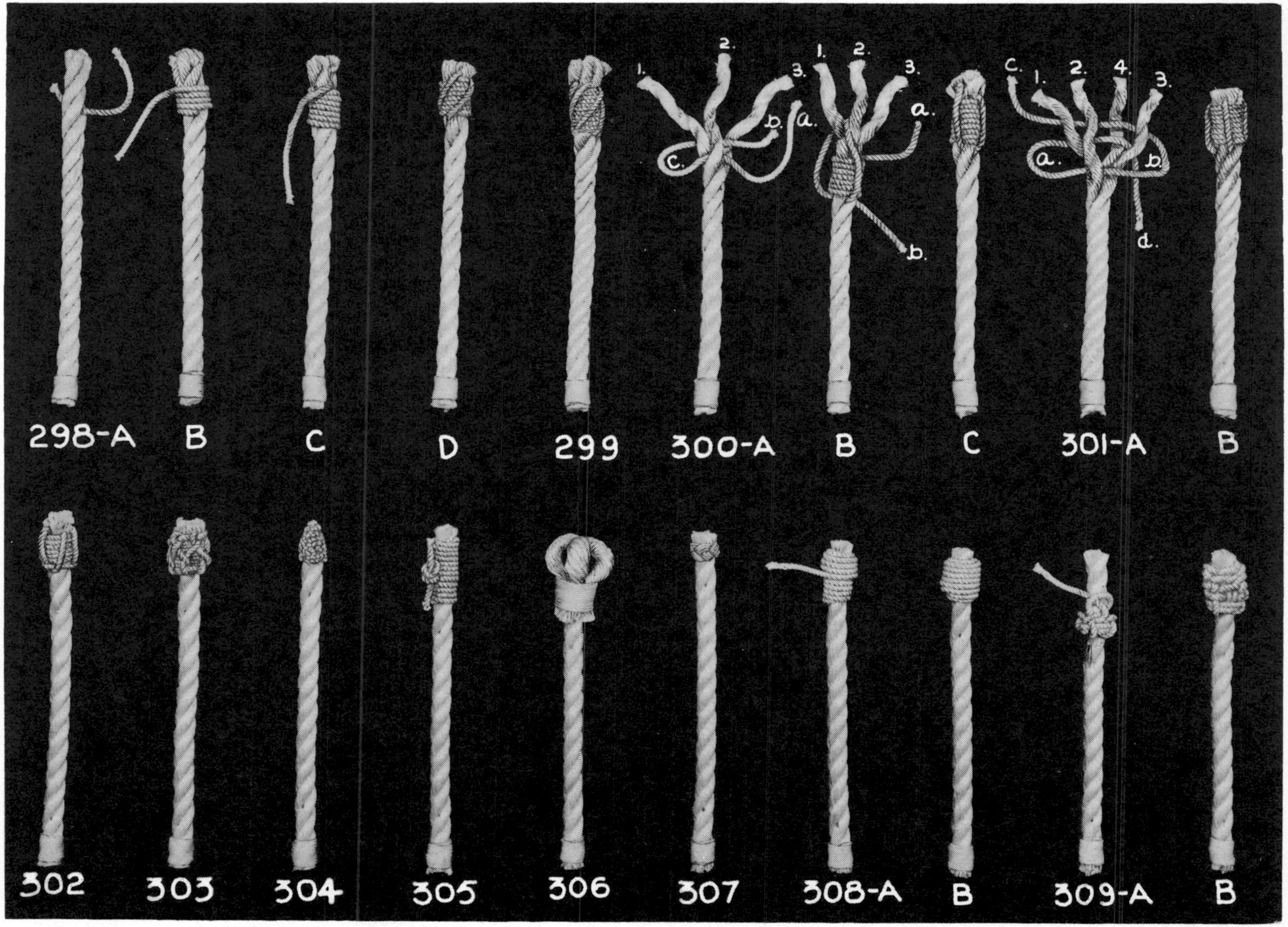

PLATE 20—WHIPPINGS

cult, but it is actually one of the simplest types of whipping. First, take a suitable length of twine. Wax it well, and stitch it through the rope under one strand, as shown here.

B: Next, take the proper number of turns around the rope and the short end of the twine, keeping each turn as taut as possible.

C: When enough turns have been taken, the twine is stitched through the rope again. Then bring the twine down on top of the turns, giving it its proper position along the lay of the rope. It is next stitched under another strand, and brought back up again over the top of the turns. This operation is repeated three times, until all the grooves between the rope strands have strands of the twine resting in them.

D: Finally, an additional stitch is taken through the rope with the twine, and cut off. The whipping, if properly made, will then appear as in this illustration.

FIG. 299: The *Palm and Needle Whipping* (four strands) is made in the same manner as the three-strand whipping, except that the operation described in FIG. 298c is repeated four times instead of three.

FIG. 300A: The *Sailmaker's Whipping* (three strands) is made as follows: the end of the rope is opened for a short distance; a bight of the twine is put around one strand, leading the ends between the other two strands, as shown in the illustration. End *a* in this case is the moving end, and end *b* is the standing end. The strands are next laid up again, and the proper number of turns taken around the rope. Then bight *c* is brought up and passed over the end of strand 1.

B: This illustration shows the whipping after bight *c* has been passed over strand 1. It is next heaved tight by the standing end of the twine, and the standing end is carried up alongside strand 3. Then the working and standing ends are knotted tightly

together between the strands, and trimmed off.

C: This shows the whipping after the ends have been trimmed, and the end of the rope cut off close to the whipping.

FIG. 301A: The *Sailmaker's Whipping* (four strands) is made by first unlaying the end of the rope and bringing the ends up, one on each side of strand 3, opposite strand 1. With the working end of twine *c*, make a bight around strand 3, and bring it out, passing strand 4 on the inside, as shown in the illustration. The strands are now laid up, and the proper number of turns are put around the rope with the working end of the twine. Bight *b* is passed over strand 3, and hauled tight by bight *a*. Bight *a* is passed over strand 1, and hauled tight by the standing end *d*. Carry the standing end up alongside strand 3. Then the standing end and the working end are tightly knotted between the strands, and trimmed off.

B: This shows the whipping after it is finished.

FIG. 302: *Snaking* is an old method of securing a whipping or seizing on a heavy rope or cable. When as many turns have been placed on the rope as desired, put the sail needle through the rope and haul the twine tight. The working end is then taken over and under the upper and lower turns of the whipping, as shown in the illustration.

FIG. 303: The *Herringbone Whipping* is somewhat similar to the whipping just described, except that when the twine is put through the upper and lower turns of the whipping, they are half-hitched rather than merely stitched through.

FIG. 304: The *Hitched End Whipping* is now seldom used, due to the labor involved. To make it, a temporary whipping is placed on the extreme end of the rope. With a sail needle, make the first round by hitching through one or more yarns in each strand of the rope. Then continue hitching as explained in PLATE 105, FIG. 16. After

[*Plate 20*]   Elementary Rope Work   **55**

two turns of hitching have been made, cut the temporary whipping and taper the end of the rope with a knife. When near the end, every other Hitch is skipped, in order to bring it to a pointed end.

Fig. 305: The *Seaman's Whipping* is made in exactly the same way as the American Whipping (PLATE 19, FIG. 294). But instead of cutting the ends of the whipping twine off close to the turns, they are reef-knotted together tightly on top of the turns. The ends are then cut off close to the Reef Knot.

Fig. 306: The *Royal Crown Whipping* is particularly effective with four-strand rope. An American Whipping is first placed a short distance from the end of the rope. After this has been done, the three or four strands (whichever the case may be) are opened up. Then they are brought down over the whipping, and stopped down to the standing part of the rope with a second whipping.

Fig. 307: The *Foot Rope Knot Whipping* is a unique method of finishing off the end of a rope, although it is seldom used, due to the time required to make it. PLATE 255, FIG. 149, shows how to tie the Foot Rope Knot.

Fig. 308A: The *Riding Turn Whipping* can be used on large ropes or cables where a stronger whipping is required. Begin as in the American Whipping, and put on the turns until they are almost to the end of the rope. Then begin to put another row of turns over the first row, as shown in this illustration.

B: When the twine has been brought back almost to the beginning, it is finished off in the same manner as the Whipping illustrated in PLATE 19, FIG. 293.

Fig. 309A: The *Straight Half Hitched Whipping* is made in almost the same way as the Whipping described in FIG. 304. But the end of the rope is not tapered down.

B: The hitching is continued until almost to the end of the rope. Then the twine is stitched through the rope several times, and cut off close.

NOTE: In the illustrations of **Whippings** the twine used is purposely much too large in proportion to the rope. This was done in order that the method of making the **Whippings** might be clearly shown in the photographs. The proper material to use for this purpose is ordinary sail twine.

Chapter II

Simple Knotting

THIS CHAPTER DEALS exclusively with all knots and ties which might be termed "Simple." Therefore, it embraces a great number of the many variations of this form of knotting in addition to all of the known orthodox methods. There are numbers of rare examples, such as the Indian Bridle or Hackamore Knot, the Star Hitch, and the Brahmin Knot, which is a sacred knot of India.

There is also the legendary Turkish Archers Knot which was said to have been a most effective method of attaching the string to the bow when shooting an arrow a great distance.

The more simplified forms of Heraldic and Oriental Knots are also included, with a great variety of Halter Ties and Novelty Knots, such as Handcuff Hitches. Jury Mast Knots, the Cape Horn Hitch, the Manifold, and Blockade Knots are among other interesting examples.

These knots and many others in this chapter should prove to be of special interest as they represent universal examples of the art of knotting.

Plate 21—Simple Knotting

FIG. 1A: The *Indian Bridle, Theodore* or *Hackamore Knot* was first a decoration on the horsehair bridle of the early Indians. Later it is said to have been used in the West as a temporary rope bridle and bit. There are several other names for this knot, such as Jug Sling; and in England it is known as a Bag, Bottle, or Beggarman's Knot. However, many of these names could also be applied to other knots; on the whole, the best choice seems to be Indian Bridle or Hackamore. The Indian Bridle is tied by making two loops, with the inside part on the right overlapping the inside part on the left, as illustrated in FIG. 1A. Next, pull the bottom bight up under the inside loop on the left, and between the overlapping center —going over, under, and over, as illustrated by arrow. Now invert the loops in front and back of the bight and the knot appears as in FIG. 1B. By inserting the center of the knot over the neck and pulling taut, this knot may be used to close the end of a bag or to make a handle or sling to carry a bottle or jar. Fishermen use it for fastening bladderfloats to their nets.

FIG. 2: The *Stevedore's Knot* is used to prevent a rope from unreeving. It is similar to a Figure-of-Eight Knot.

FIG. 3: The *Crossed Running Knot* is a Running Eye that gives extra friction. It is very seldom seen.

FIG. 4: The *Running Figure-of-Eight* or *Packer's Knot,* is the same as an ordinary Figure-of-Eight, the only difference being that one free end forms a loop by passing through the body of the knot.

FIG. 5: The *Surgeon's Knot,* First Method, is a Double Overhand Knot with a Reverse Overhand Knot on top, the ends coming out parallel with the standing part. This knot is used by surgeons in operations.

FIG. 6: The *Lineman's Knot* is tied by first making a bight, then with the free ends of the rope putting a Half Hitch around the bight, first from one side and then from the other with the Hitches interlacing.

FIG. 7: The *Running Overhand Knot* is tied the same as the ordinary Overhand

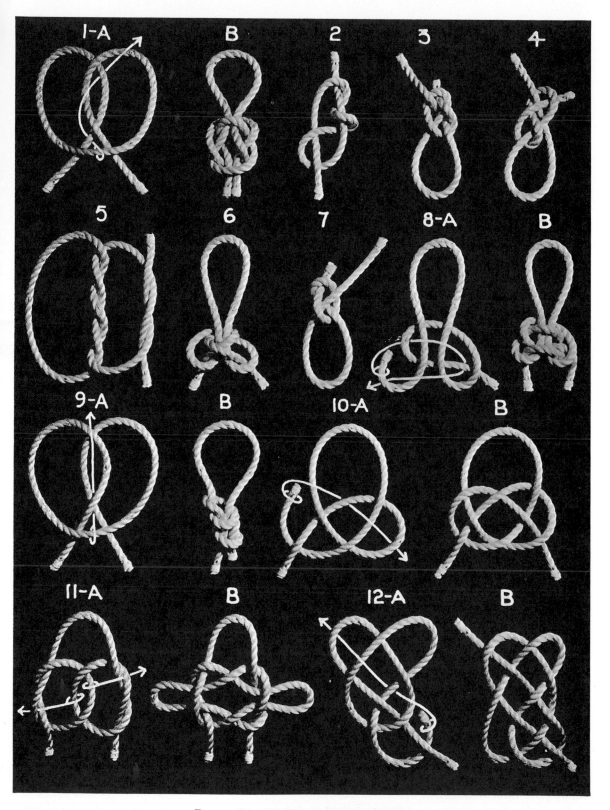

PLATE 21—SIMPLE KNOTTING

Knot, except that one free end forms a loop by passing through the body of the knot.

FIGS. 8A and B: The *Cask Knot* is tied by forming a bight and then placing an underhanded loop under the bight, as indicated in FIG. 8A. Close up the knot by passing the end on the left as shown by the arrow. The finished knot is shown in FIG. 8B. This knot has no practical value.

FIGS. 9A and B: The *Single Fisherman's, Englishman's True Lover's or Waterman's Knot* is generally used for gut, which is liable to slip when joined by a Reef Knot or Sheet Bend. It is tied by making two underhand loops, with the inside part on the left overlapping the inside part on the right. Then the bight is pulled through as illustrated by the arrow in FIG. 9A. FIG. 9B shows the knot complete.

FIGS. 10A and B: *"Sailor's Breastplate."* These figures represent a Double Carrick Bend tied in the end of a bight. It is made with an underhand loop crossed under, by reversing the strand pointing toward the right, and then passing underneath the body of the knot to the left side, closing it up with the strand from the left side, as indicated in FIG. 10A. FIG. 10B shows the knot as it looks when completed. This knot has no utility, and is used more as an ornamental version of the Double Carrick Bend.

FIGS. 11A and B: The *Japanese Masthead* or *Shamrock Knot* is another fascinating type of knot similar to the Masthead or Jury Mast Knot. It can be used as a decorative knot in the making of ornamental knot-board pictures, as will be explained in a later chapter. The knot is made by first forming two interlocking Overhand Knots, as shown in FIG. 11A. Then the inside bights are pulled through, as illustrated by the arrows. The finished knot is shown in FIG. 11B. It can also be used for a Jar Sling.

FIGS. 12A and B: The *French Carrick Knot* is another fancy way of tying a decorative knot. It is made by passing an underhand loop through an overhand loop, then closing it up with the end of the overhand loop, as shown in FIG. 12A. The finished knot appears in FIG. 12B.

Plate 22—Simple Knotting

FIGS. 13A and B: The *Triangle, Brahmin, or Sacred Knot* is said to be used for ceremonial purposes in India. It can be tied easily by observing the opened knot in FIG. 13A. FIG. 13B shows the knot as it looks when pulled up and turned over.

FIGS. 14A, B, and C: The *Japanese Crown or Success Knot* is very attractive and can be used in a number of ways for ornamental purposes. FIG. 14A shows how to start the knot. FIG. 14B shows the front of the knot as it looks when pulled up, and FIG. 14C shows the opposite side, or back, as it will appear when drawn tight. The square in FIG. B and the cross in FIG. C when combined form the word "Kanau," which means the wish realized.

FIG. 15: The *Surgeon's Knot,* Second Method, is slightly different from the First Method shown in PLATE 21, FIG. 5, as it shows the knot tied with two lines instead of one.

FIGS. 16A and B: The *Blood, Bullion, or Manifold Knot* is used when it is desired to shorten a small rope, or increase its diameter to prevent it from passing through the eye of a hole. The knot is formed by merely tying a series of turns through a loop, and then pulling taut. FIG. 16A shows the knot opened, and FIG. 16B shows it pulled up. This is a Two-Fold Blood Knot.

FIG. 17: The *Three-Fold Blood Knot* is the same as FIG. 16, except that it is tied with three turns instead of two.

FIG. 18: The *Four-Fold Blood Knot* is the same as the others, but with four turns.

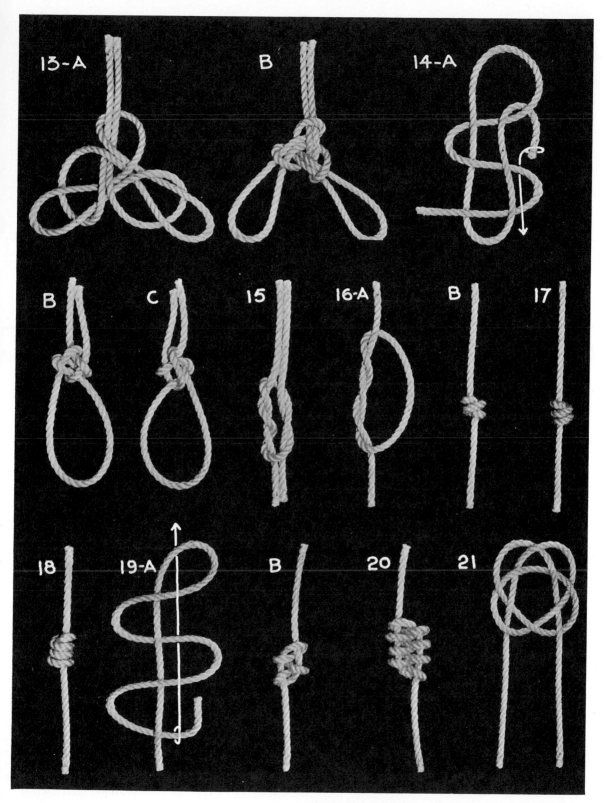

PLATE 22—SIMPLE KNOTTING

FIGS. 19A and B: The *Double Figure-of-Eight Knot* is shown open in FIG. 19A. FIG. 19B illustrates how it looks when pulled up.

FIG. 20: The *Four-Fold Figure-of-Eight Knot* is the same knot as FIG. 19A, tied with four turns instead of two.

FIG. 21: The *Napoleon Knot* is a very quick way of forming a simple ornamental knot, which will be found easy to duplicate. In reality, it is nothing but an open Three-strand Turk's Head flattened out. The method of tying is explained in PLATE 109, FIG. 1.

Plate 23—Simple Knotting

FIG. 22: The *Dalliance* or *Interlaced Overhand Knot* can be easily tied by following the illustration.

FIG. 23: The *Flemish Eye Knot* is tied without difficulty, but is seldom used.

FIGS. 24A and B: The *Japanese Good Luck Knot* is used as a ceremonial knot in Japan. It is shown in FIG. 24A opened up. FIG. 24B shows it with the loops *a* and *b* pulled out to close the knot. End *c* is tucked through bight *f* and the loop *a*, and end *d* is tucked through bight *e* and the loop *b*. Next tuck end *c* up under bight *e* and then tuck end *d* up under bight *f* and pull taut.

FIG. 25: The *Monkey Fist on a Bow* is tied by forming Blood Knots in opposite directions. It is of no practical value.

FIG. 26: The *Sliding Monkey Fist* is similar to a Blood Knot, except that it is tied with small line on a larger line. It has no value.

FIG. 27: The *Jig Knot* is formed by passing two round turns around a bight, then tucking the end out through the eye of the bight. It is occasionally used on the end of heaving lines.

FIG. 28: The *Overlapping Hitch* or *Water Loop Knot* is tied by forming a Two-Fold Blood Knot on the standing part, with the end of the rope.

FIG. 29: The *Blood Knot on A Bow* is the same as the usual Blood Knot, but tied on a bow.

FIG. 30: The *Leader Knot* is sometimes used for uniting silk line.

FIGS. 31A and B: The *Single Jury* or *Spanish Knot*. FIG. 31A illustrates how the knot is tied, and FIG. 31B shows how it looks when pulled up. It is used extensively in Sheepshanks.

FIGS. 32A and B: The *Japanese Knot* is a simple knot for ornamental decoration. FIG. 32A shows the method of construction, and FIG. 32B the finished knot.

Plate 24—Simple Knotting

FIG. 33: The *Topsail Sheet Bend* is similar to the Midshipman's Hitch. It is used as another method of securing a sheet to the clew cringle of a sail, and will not come unfastened, no matter how hard the sail may flap.

FIG. 34: The *Heaving Line Bend* is used for bending a heaving line to a hawser, or as a method of bending any small rope to a larger one.

FIG. 35: The *Water Bowline* is the same as the ordinary Bowline, except that it has an additional Half Hitch. This knot is used whenever a rope is liable to become soaked with water. The strain taken by the additional Half Hitch prevents the Bowline from drawing tight and becoming difficult to untie.

FIG. 36: The *Single Bowline on Bight*. Another Method, can be tied quickly, and forms a secure loop capable of being untied easily after having been drawn tight.

FIG. 37: The *Dutchman's Knot* is a relic

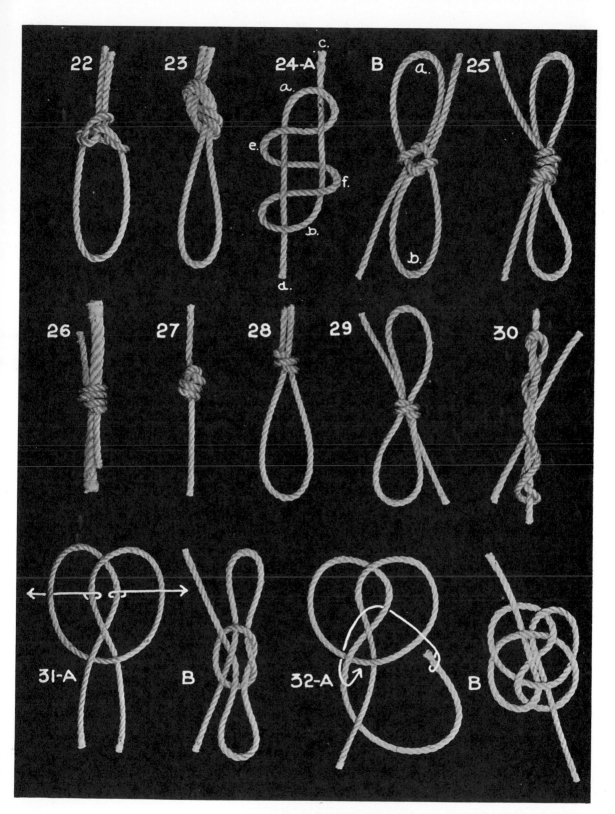

PLATE 23—SIMPLE KNOTTING

of bygone sailing ship days, and is now a curiosity.

FIG. 38: The *Clevis Knot* is another rare form of knot, which can be easily duplicated by closely studying the illustration.

FIG. 39: The *Interlocking Overhand Knots* is a simple method of uniting two Overhand Knots.

FIGS. 40A and B: The *Farmer's Loop* forms a secure loop, which can be tied without access to either end of the rope, and can be easily untied after being drawn tight. FIG. 40A illustrates the knot open and FIG. 40B shows how it looks when pulled up.

FIG. 41: The *Rurich Knot* is similar to a Running Figure-of-Eight, except that the running part is passed through in a slightly different way, as can be observed in the illustration.

FIG. 42: The *Tom Fool's Knot,* also known as a Conjurer's Knot, is said to have been used for rope handcuffs and as a Jar or Pitcher Sling.

FIGS. 43A and B: The *Double Jury Mast*

Knot is used for rigging a jury mast. Bights *a, b,* and *c* form a means of attaching supports to the mast. The center of the knot is slipped over the masthead, and stays are bent to the three bights by using Sheet Bends. The ends *d* and *e* are joined with a Bowline, with one of these ends serving as a fourth stay, in order to complete the staying of the jury mast. It is formed by three loops overlapping as shown. The loops are pulled through as the lines indicate, placing bight *a* on the left, and bight *b* on the right. Then bight *c* is pulled out on top.

FIGS. 44A and B: The *Jury Mast* or *Masthead Knot* is similar to the one above, and can be used for the same purpose. Both of these knots can also be used for Jar Slings, with the four bights serving as handles and the center of the knot placed over the neck of the jar or pitcher. Form three loops as shown in FIG. 44A. Then pull the bights through as the lines indicate, forming outside bights as in the Jury Mast Knot, and pulling the top part out at the same time to complete the knot as shown in FIG. 44B.

Plate 25—Simple Knotting

FIG. 45: The *Monkey Fist True-Lover's Eye* is similar to the Fisherman's Eye, as shown in PLATE 21, FIG. 9, except that it is tied with Blood Knots instead of Overhand Knots.

FIG. 46: The *Cohula Knot* is tied with interlacing Overhand Knots around the bight, as illustrated.

FIG. 47: The *Twin Overhand Bow* is tied by forming Overhand Knots in opposite directions around the center of the bights.

FIG. 48: The *Two-Strand Lanyard* or *Matthew Walker Knot* will be illustrated with three-strand rope in PLATE 60, FIG. 131. All other two-strand knots will likewise be shown in three-strand rope, as it is much easier to illustrate and describe the various keys with three strands instead of two. The

same key can be used for two-strand and three-strand knots.

FIG. 49: The *Variated Shamrock* or *Jury Mast Knot* is another method of forming one of the many versions of this type of knot.

FIG. 50: The *Twin Overhand Knots* have the parts interlocked as illustrated.

FIG. 51: The *Crossed Overhand Loop.*

FIG. 52: The *English Diamond Knot* is similar to the ordinary Diamond Knot, except that four ends are used instead of two, and there is a slight variation in the weave.

FIG. 53: The *Two-Strand Star Knot.* The key used in tying Star Knots is illustrated in PLATE 57, FIG. 78, which applies to any number of strands.

FIG. 54: The *Variated Jury Mast Knot*

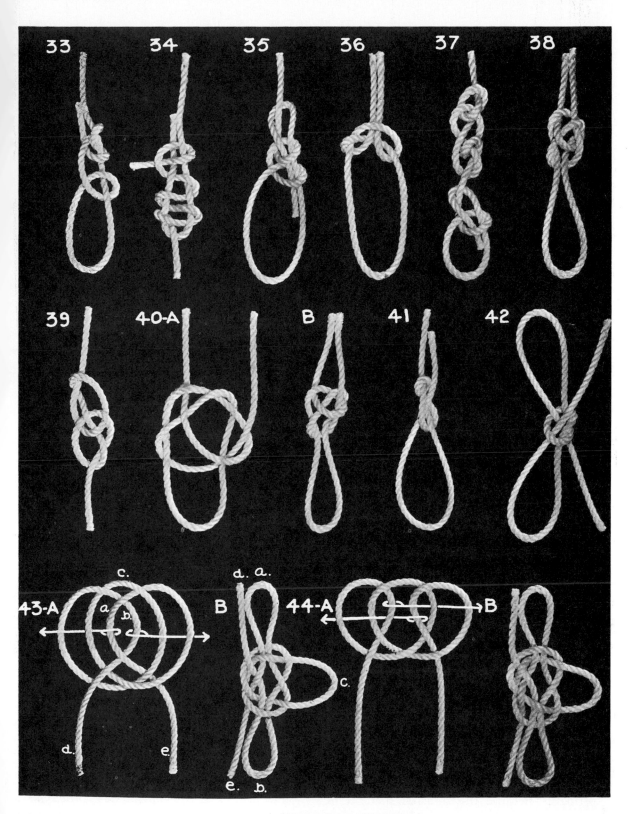

PLATE 24—SIMPLE KNOTTING

is another way of making the ordinary Jury Mast Knot.

FIG. 55: The *Stevedore's Loop Knot* is similar to the regular Stevedore's Knot, except that it is tied around a bight.

FIG. 56: The *Two-Strand Diamond Knot*. The key used for tying Diamond Knots is illustrated in PLATE 60, FIG. 140, which also applies to any number of strands.

FIG. 57: The *Two-Strand Sennit Knot*. The Key used for tying Sennit Knots of various numbers of strands is illustrated in PLATE 55, FIG. 33.

FIG. 58: The *Overlapping Overhand Knots* has the Overhand Knots formed around, or interlacing, each other.

FIG. 59: The *Interlocked Hitch Loop* is tied in the manner shown.

FIG. 60: The *Two-Strand Wall* or *Japanese Granny* is formed by walling the strands up through each other's parts, as illustrated in PLATE 53, FIG. 2. This is the Japanese method of tying a Granny Knot.

Plate 26—Simple Knotting

FIG. 61: The *Two-Strand Double Diamond*. The Key used for tying this knot is the same as PLATE 60, FIG. 140, except for the difference in the number of strands, which have two passes.

FIG. 62: The *Variated Lineman's Rider* is a slight variation on the ordinary Lineman's Rider.

FIG. 63: The *Double Running Knot* functions only when there is tension applied to both parts of the rope. It is formed by tying an Overhand Knot in the center of the rope, then reeving both ends of the rope through the Overhand Knot.

FIG. 64: The *Crabber's Eye Knot* is similar to the Crossed Running Knot, and is very seldom seen.

FIG. 65: The *Turkish Archer Knot* is said to have been used over one thousand years ago by the ancient Turkish archers, who were capable of shooting an arrow eight hundred yards with the attachment illustrated in FIG. 65. The part marked *a* represents the bight of the silk strings of the bow; the part marked *b* represents what was used as a leather thong for attachment to the bow. Incidentally, the remarkable distance the ancient Turks were capable of shooting an arrow has never been equaled, probably because the unusual method of using this knot apparently has been forgotten.

FIG. 66: The *Running Eye Knot* is used wherever a simple eye is needed.

FIG. 67: The *Lifeboat Draw* or *Slip Knot* is used in the draw lines under the belly of lifeboats to make the cover fast.

FIG. 68: The *Two-Strand Elongated Matthew Walker* is the same as the ordinary method of making this knot, except that it involves an additional pass with each strand. A Three-strand Elongated Matthew Walker Knot is shown in PLATE 54, FIG. 7.

FIG. 69: The *Slippery Reef, Draw Knot,* or *Half Bow* is slightly different from the Reef Knot. It is used in tying reef points on a sail. All that is necessary is to pull the end *a* when shaking out the reef.

FIG. 70: The *Staffordshire Knot* is of no particular use.

FIG. 71: The *Bell-Ringer's Knot Variation* is a rare form of a curious knot which is very seldom seen.

FIG. 72: The *Roven Overhand Knots* is made by tying Overhand Knots through each other's eye in the order shown.

FIG. 73: The *Overlapping Half Hitched Knot* is made by forming Half Hitches over each other's standing parts as illustrated.

FIG. 74: The *Crossed Carrick Knot* is an ornamental knot, which can be easily duplicated.

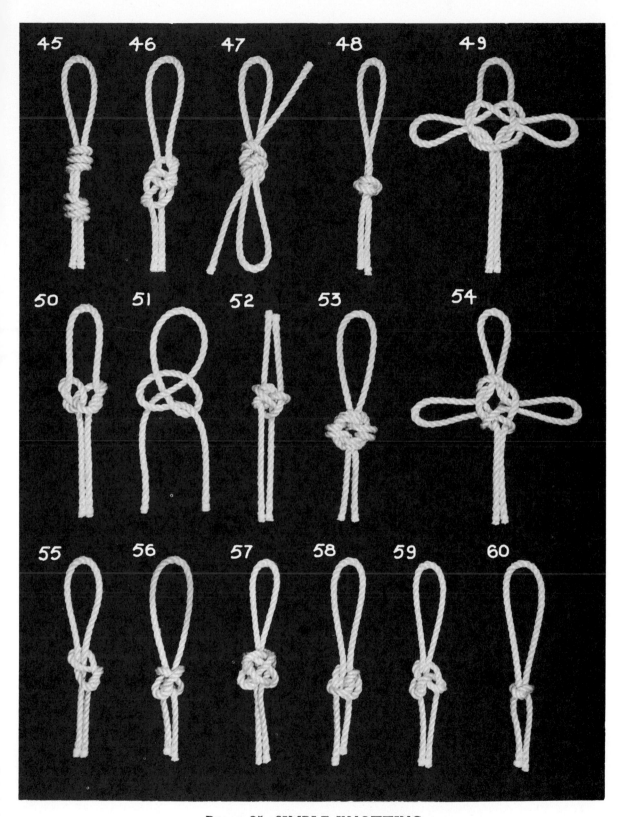

PLATE 25—SIMPLE KNOTTING

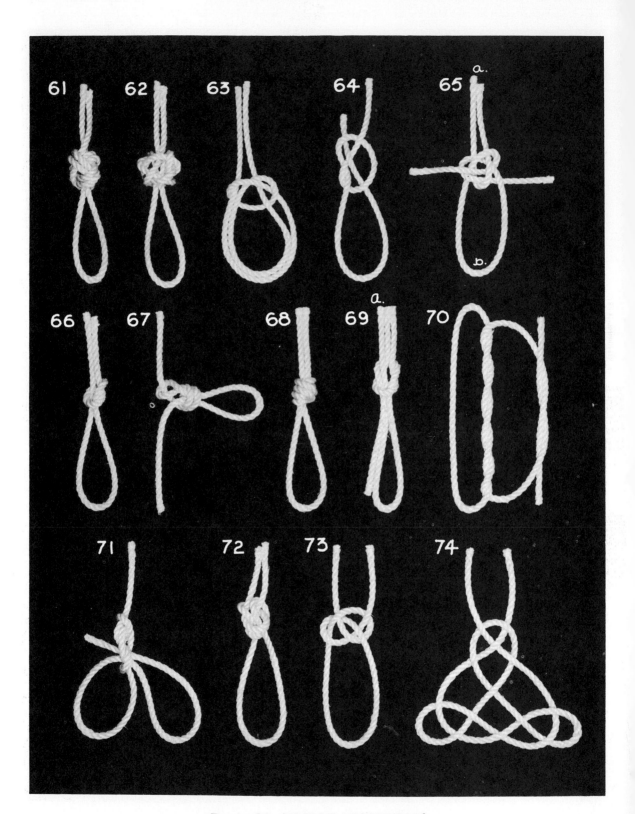

PLATE 26—SIMPLE KNOTTING

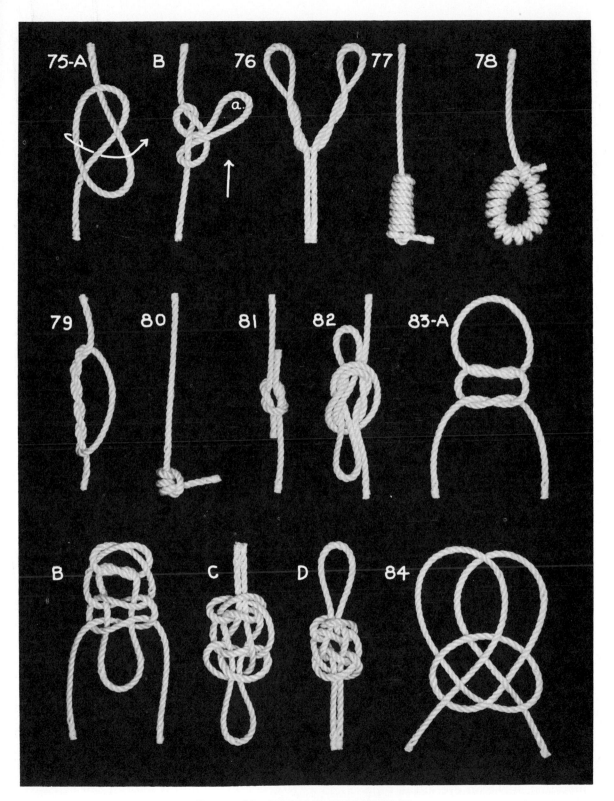

PLATE 27—SIMPLE KNOTTING

Plate 27—Simple Knotting

Fig. 75A: The *Man-Harness* or *Artillery Knot* is useful when several men have to haul a heavy object, such as a cannon or other piece of artillery, by means of a single line or rope. The rope is first placed in the position shown in this illustration; then the bight is pulled in the direction shown by the arrows.

B: After the bight has been pulled through as directed, the knot will appear as in Fig. 75B. Make as many knots as there are men. Each man puts his arm through the loop *a,* and places it over his shoulder. The strain is then exerted in the direction of the arrow, each man adding his share to the line.

Fig. 76: The *Cat's Paw* is a very useful knot to utilize when a hook is to be put in the middle of a line. When tension is applied to only one part of the rope, it will result in a crumpling and distortion of the knot, although it will still be quite secure. In making it, two bights are first laid out, and then each one is twisted inward as shown in the illustration. Both bights are placed on a hook and a strain is exerted on either end.

Fig. 77: The *Heaving Line Knot* is sometimes used in place of the Monkey's Fist (Plate 49, Fig. 362) to weight the end of a heaving line. This is more or less a landlubber's method, and is considered very unseamanlike aboard a vessel. First, make a bight on the end of a rope. Next, take the end of the line and begin winding it around and around toward the end of the bight, until the desired amount of turns have been placed on it. The end is then placed through the loop, and the standing part is pulled to draw the loop up taut.

Fig. 78: The *Terminal Knot* is another method of weighting the end of a heaving line. First, make an eye in the rope. Then take the end and begin winding it around the eye until the standing part is reached.

All the turns are now drawn taut, and the end is seized to the standing part.

Fig. 79: The *Multiple Overhand Knot* is, on the whole, quite a useless knot, although it served an interesting purpose among the ancient Incas of Peru (*see* Plate 243, Figs. 63 to 77). When used as a Stopper in place of the Stevedore's Knot (Plate 21, Fig. 2), it will not jam as hard as the ordinary Overhand Knot.

Fig. 80: The *Multiple Overhand Stopper Knot* represents Fig. 79 drawn up taut, and is used in this fashion as a Stopper Knot.

Fig. 81: The *Thief* or *Bread Bag Knot* resembles the ordinary Reef Knot. But it will be noticed that in this knot the ends come out on different sides, whereas in the regular Reef Knot the ends come out on the same side (Plate 1, Fig. 11). When tension is applied to the Reef Knot it will bear the strain without slipping. But the Thief Knot, when tension is applied, will keep on slipping until the ends are reached and the two lines separate. The reason for this is that when a strain is put on it, contiguous parts move in the same direction, and friction cannot be applied to make the knot secure. A captain once suspected a member of his crew was stealing bread, from the bread bag in the galley. This bag was usually tied with the common Reef Knot. One night he tied the bag with the knot illustrated here. The unsuspecting seaman of course retied the bag with the customary Reef Knot. And so unwittingly betrayed himself. The knot has since been known as the Thief Knot.

Fig. 82: The *Reef Knot in the Middle of a Line* is useful whenever it becomes necessary to shorten a rope after both ends have been made fast. Even though a severe tension is applied to this knot, it can be easily untied when the strain has been taken off the ends.

Fig. 83A: The *Brief Knot* is made as follows: a Reef Knot is first made, with a loop on top of the knot, as shown in this illustration.

B: The knot is next turned upside down, and a second Reef Knot is made, with the loop coming through the body of the knot.

C: The ends are then brought up and put through the body of the first Reef Knot.

D: After the step just explained has been completed, the knot is turned again with the loop facing up. When all the slack has been taken out of it, it will appear as in this illustration.

Fig. 84: *Handcuff Hitches* are said to have been used in place of iron shackles on prisoners in the old days of sailing ships; hence the name. When this knot is made, the two loops are placed over the wrists and drawn tight. The two ends are then reef-knotted together. If the reader will make this knot and place it over someone's wrists, it will leave no doubt in his mind as to its security.

Plate 28—Simple Knotting

Fig. 85: The *Japanese Square Knot.* This is the Japanese form of the ordinary Square Knot.

Fig. 86: The *Japanese Thief Knot.* This is the Japanese version of the Thief Knot.

Fig. 87: The *Japanese Crossed Running Knot* is another variety of Japanese knotting.

Fig. 88: The *Japanese Sheet Bend* is a left-hand Japanese-style Sheet Bend.

Figs. 89A and B: The *Square Knot Bow* is the ordinary Square Knot tied in a bow. Fig. 89A shows the knot opened, and Fig. 89B indicates how it looks when pulled up.

Fig. 90: The *Granny Knot Bow* is the ordinary Granny Knot tied in a bow, similar to the Square Knot method.

Fig. 91: The *Japanese Sheet Bend* shown here is a right-hand Japanese-style Sheet Bend.

Fig. 92: The *Granny Knot Sheepshank* represents a Granny Knot formed in the middle of a Sheepshank.

Fig. 93: The *Twin Loop Hitched Knot* has twin loops formed through opposite sides of the Hitch in the center.

Fig. 94: The *Japanese Single Carrick* (Right-hand Method) can be easily understood from the illustration.

Fig. 95: The *Japanese Single Carrick* (Left-hand Method) is the same as Fig. 94, except that it is tied in the opposite, or left-hand, way.

Fig. 96: The *Figure-of-Eight with Toggle* has the toggle to resist added tension.

Fig. 97: The *Stevedore's Knot with Toggle* is used for the same purpose as Fig. 96.

Fig. 98: The *Overhand Eye in Loop* is made by forming an Overhand Eye in the top of the loop as shown.

Plate 29—Simple Knotting

Fig. 99: The *Gunner's, Prolong,* or *Delay Knot* is simply the Carrick Bend with the upper loop put through two rings. Gunners themselves call this a Delay Knot.

Fig. 100: The *Chinese Loop* is another method of making a running eye in the end of a line, similar to the Crabber's Eye Knot.

Fig. 101: The *Marline Spike Hitch* is used when leverage is needed, as in heaving a seizing taut. It can be instantly formed and instantly released. Make a bight in the seizing twine or Marline, and bring it back over the standing part. Pass the spike over the bight on one side, under the standing part, and then over the bight again on the other side.

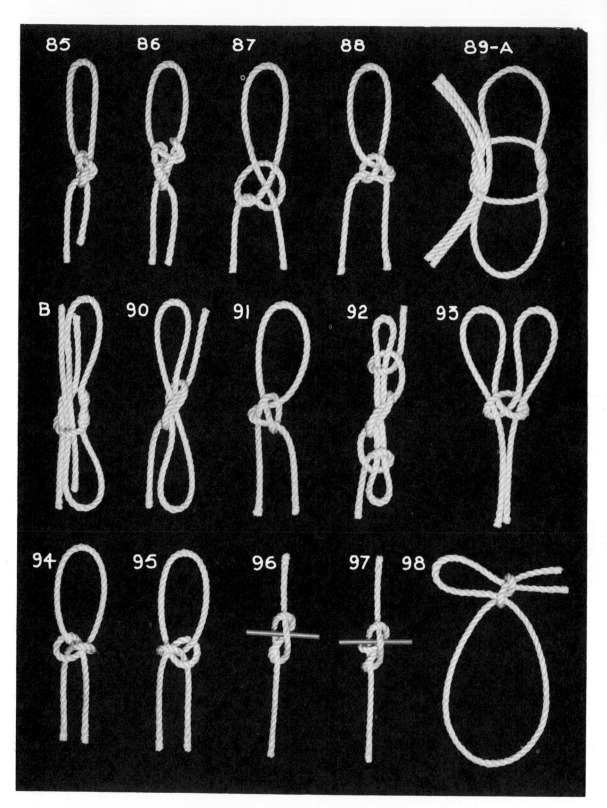

PLATE 28—SIMPLE KNOTTING

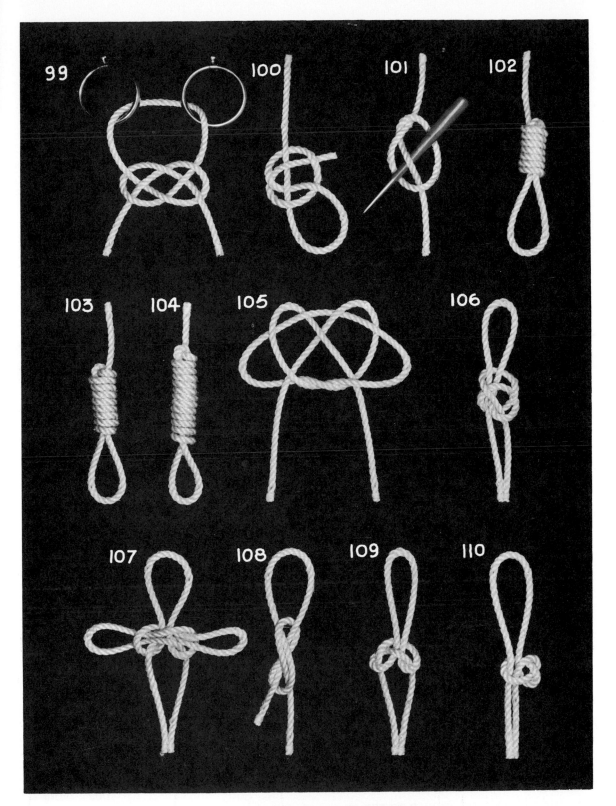

PLATE 29—SIMPLE KNOTTING

FIG. 102: The *Hangman's Noose with Seven Turns* is formed as follows: first, make a bight in the end of the rope; then take the end of the line and bring it back down toward the end of the bight. After this has been done, proceed to wind the end around the bight and the standing part away from the end of the bight until seven turns have been taken. The end is then placed through the small loop at the top of the turns, and this loop is pulled taut by grasping the bight and heaving it down.

FIG. 103: The *Hangman's Noose with Nine Turns* is made in precisely the same manner as the preceding one, except that nine turns are taken instead of seven. It was an old superstition that when white men were hung on the gallows they rated two extra turns. (*See* PLATE 327, FIG. 13.)

FIG. 104: The *Hangman's Noose with Thirteen Turns* is also made in the same way, except that thirteen turns are taken.

FIG. 105: The *Chinese Knot* is merely an ornamental knot, and has no practical value.

FIG. 106: The *Slip Running Eye Knot* is formed as follows: first, make a bight; take the end around and in front of the bight, making a loop; then make another bight with the end of the rope, and put it through the loop and up over the standing bight.

FIG. 107: The *Japanese Masthead Knot* is another novel method of forming the Masthead Knot shown in PLATE 24, FIG. 44.

FIG. 108: The *Running Eye Open Carrick Knot* is formed in much the same way as the Open Carrick Bend.

FIG. 109: The *Artillery-Man's Eye Knot* is formed in the same fashion as the Artillery or Man-Harness Knot shown in PLATE 27, FIG. 75. Instead of using it in a series along the length of a rope, it is made on the end of the line.

FIG. 110: The *Lock Slip Knot* can be formed by first making a slip noose. Next, take the end of the rope and put it up around the loop, then back down and under its own part.

Plate 30—Simple Knotting

FIG. 111: The *Two-Strand Outside Matthew Walker* has its key illustrated with three-strand rope in PLATE 54, FIG. 18.

FIG. 112: The *Blood Knot Noose* is the same as the ordinary Blood Knot, except that it is tied with an eye.

FIG. 113. The *Rolling Hitch Figure-of-Eight* is tied with a Combination Rolling Hitch Figure-of-Eight form.

FIG. 114: The *Round Turn Overhand Knots* design is tied with round turns in the usual Overhand Knots.

FIG. 115: The *Crossed Loop Hitched Knot* is tied with Hitches in a crossed loop as shown.

FIG. 116: The *Rolling Hitch Cinch* has a Rolling Hitch rove through an eye.

FIG. 117: The *Braided Figure-of-Eight* has an extra cross to form the additional weave.

FIG. 118: The *Ladder Hitched Knot* is similar to the Blood Knot. It is used in this style to make rope ladders, which is illustrated in PLATE 250, FIG. 130.

FIG. 119: The *Four-Fold Knot* is tied with four round turns, and brought out through the end as shown.

FIG. 120: The *Kettle-Drum Knot* has an ornamental weave on top of Interlocked Overhand Knots.

FIG. 121: The *Rolling Midshipman's Hitch* is an unusual variation on the ordinary Midshipman's Hitch.

FIG. 122: The *Twin Eye Sheet Bend* is a Sheet Bend made with twin eyes, in order to form a bight on each side of the knot.

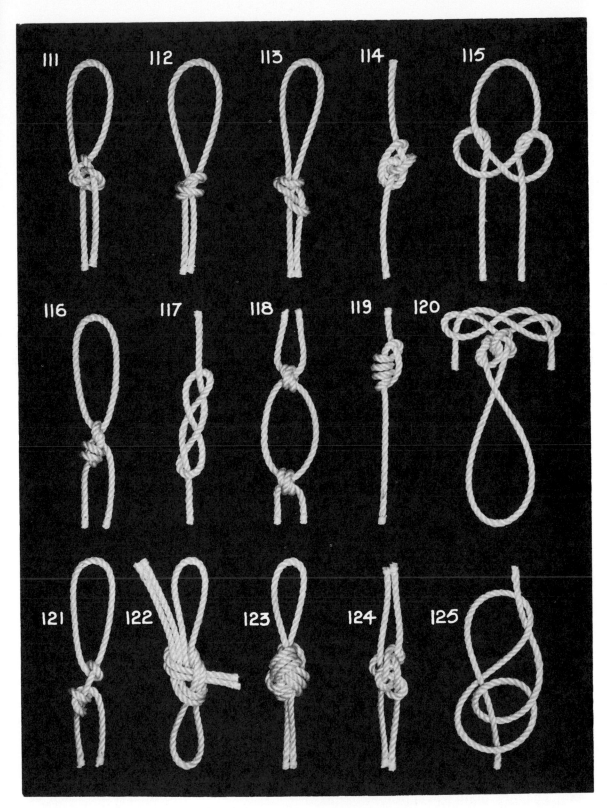

PLATE 30—SIMPLE KNOTTING

FIG. 123: The *Two-Strand Triple Diamond* is the same as the Double Diamond, PLATE 26, FIG. 61, but tied with three passes instead of two.

FIG. 124: The *Hitched Blockade* is a simple hitched method of joining two ropes.

FIG. 125: The *Cross Twin Figure-of-Eight* is a Figure-of-Eight with a Half Hitch taken on one standing part, as may be observed from the illustration.

Plate 31—Simple Knotting

FIG. 126: The *Hitched Overhand Eye* is a Half Hitch in a Slip Eye.

FIG. 127: The *Jug Knot* is similar to the Hackamore, but is almost unknown and rarely seen. This knot can also be used as a form of Jar or Jug Sling. It is tied by forming two Overlapping Overhand Knots in the end of a bight.

FIG. 128: The *Four-Strand Reef Blockade* is used for joining the bights of four different lines.

FIG. 129: The *Interlacing Bow* is a novel way of forming an Interlaced Knot into a bow.

FIG. 130: The *Double Running Eye Noose* is a method of tying a Double Running Noose in the form of an eye.

FIG. 131: The *Boat Knot*, First Method, is another knot for use in mooring a small boat. By withdrawing the toggle or any pin that is used, the knot instantly comes adrift.

FIG. 132: The *Rigged Jury Mast Knot* is a Jury Mast Knot rigged for staying a jury mast. The method of making this knot is illustrated in PLATE 24, FIG. 43.

FIG. 133. The *Interlocking Overhand Knot and Hitch* is a method of joining an Overhand Knot and a Half Hitch.

FIG. 134: The *Two-Strand Six-Fold Elongated Matthew Walker* is illustrated with each strand triple-passed. This knot is also illustrated with Three Strands in PLATE 54, FIG. 7.

FIG. 135: The *Four-Strand Spider Blockade* is used for blockading the bights of four ropes together.

FIG. 136: The *Loop Bend* is another method of bending a rope to a loop.

FIG. 137: The *Twisted Overhand Bight* is a bight that has the ends twisted around the standing part of the loop.

FIG. 138: The *Interlocking Figure-of-Eight Hitched Knot* consists of two Figure-of-Eights interlocked or hitched together.

Plate 32—Simple Knotting

FIG. 139: The *Toggle Bend* is a very useful knot to use when the eyes of two ropes are to be bent together. It is easily formed, and in an emergency can be cast off instantly. Slip the eye of one line over the eye of the other. Then take both parts of one bight, draw them up through the loop and insert the toggle.

FIG. 140A: The *False Round Braid* is illustrated in its first position.

B: The false braid will appear as in this illustration after it has been released. It assumes the twist automatically.

FIG. 141: The *Becket Loop* has no practical value.

FIG. 142A: The *Weaver's Knot* is in reality a common Sheet Bend. The four illustrations show how this knot is made by weavers when a thread in a loom breaks. When there is a "smash," as the weavers say (when all the threads in the warp break), they are knotted together in the following manner: two threads are taken between the thumb and the index finger of the left hand, and placed in the position

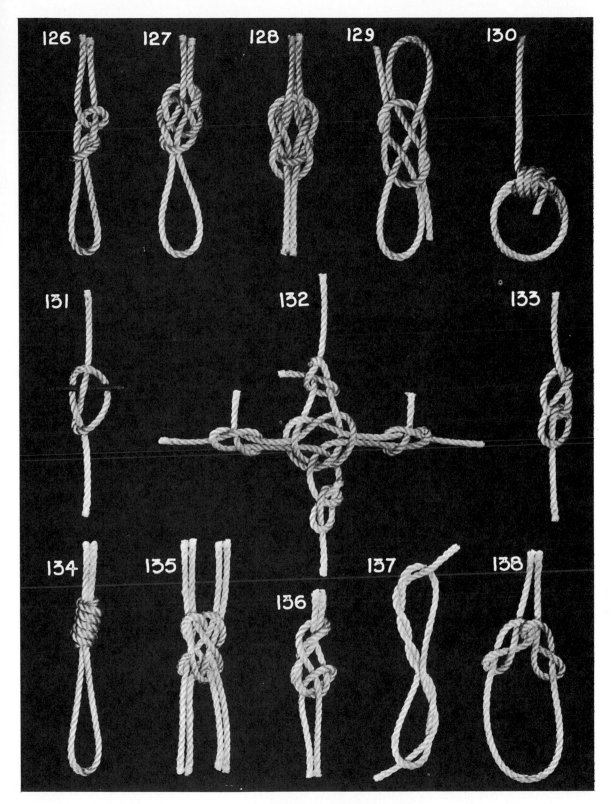

PLATE 31—SIMPLE KNOTTING

shown in this illustration. The drawn line shows the next step.

B: After the end has been brought around as shown in the preceding illustration, the other end is then brought down and through the bight as shown by the drawn line.

C: After this tuck has been made, the knot is now finished, and all that remains is to draw out the slack.

D: This shows the finished knot. The Weaver's Knot is sometimes called the smallest of all knots.

FIG. 143A: The *Thumb Bowline on the Bight* is first laid out in the position shown in this illustration.

B: After the rope has been placed in the position shown in the preceding picture, the bight is then grasped and pulled until it slips through the Thumb Knot into the position shown. This knot, when made in the middle of a rope, is very secure, but has a decided disadvantage in practical use as it will jam hard and become difficult to untie.

FIG. 144: The *Six-Fold Eye Knot* is a novel method of forming a loop in the end of a line. Take a line in the hand, then form a bight and pass three turns around the finger. After the third turn has been taken, the line is put around the standing part, and then down through the first turn.

FIG. 145: The *Double Round Turn Hitched Knot* is tied by first making a running loop in the middle of the line. Next, take one end and pass it through the loop twice, thus making a round turn. The other end is then given an additional turn, or in other words, doubled. The knot is now complete.

FIG. 146: The *Crow's Feet Hitched Knot* may be used for a sling-shortener. The illustration plainly shows how it is made.

FIG. 147: The *Butterfly Bow Knot* is formed as follows: a double loop is first made in the middle of a rope. A turn is next taken with each end around the middle of the bow. The ends are then crossed, and brought up and through the bights in opposite directions.

Plate 33—Simple Knotting

FIG. 148: The *Becket Loop* is made by forming a Becket Bend in the end of a rope, as shown in the illustration.

FIG. 149: The *Halter Tie,* First Method, is used to tie horses in their mangers. The illustration shows how it is made.

FIG. 150: The *Half-Open Carrick Loop* is in the form of a Carrick Bend. As the illustration shows, half of the Bend is open, with the other half made as in the Closed Carrick Bend.

FIG. 151: The *Half Hitch Loop,* First Method, is a very neat, secure method of forming a loop in the end of a rope.

FIG. 152: The *Double Becket Tie,* when formed with the ends of two lines and drawn taut, will assume the appearance of two Becket Bends.

FIG. 153: The *Lark's Head in Eye* is useful whenever it becomes necessary to hitch the end of one rope into the eye of another. This is an excellent knot to use for this purpose because any amount of tension may be applied and yet it can be easily untied.

FIG. 154: The *Clove Hitch in Eye* is another knot which may be utilized for the same purpose as the knot in FIG. 153.

FIG. 155: The *Half Hitch Loop,* Second Method, is another method of making a Half Hitch loop in the end of a line.

FIG. 156: The *Half Hitch Carrick Bend* is an ornamental method of forming the Carrick Bend.

FIG. 157: The *Lubber's Dragonfly Knot* resembles the common Dragonfly Knot.

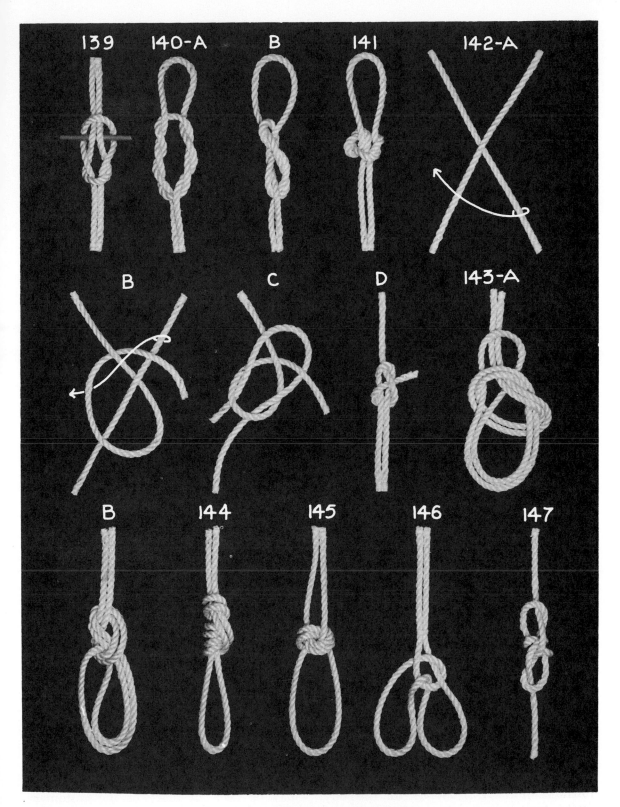

PLATE 32—SIMPLE KNOTTING

Yet it can be instantly seen that there is a great difference. A bight is first made a short distance from the end of the rope. Next, a loop is formed, and the end is brought down and around the bight. Another bight is then put through the loop around the first bight, forming a slip noose. The knot is now complete.

FIG. 158: The *Half Hitch Lineman's Loop* has no practical value.

FIG. 159: The *Reverse Loop Carrick Bend* is somewhat similar to the ordinary Carrick Bend. Instead of the loop being on opposite sides of the ends, it is woven in between them.

FIG. 160: The *False Handcuff Hitches* resembles the Handcuff Hitches shown in PLATE 27, FIG. 84, and may be used for the same purpose, although it is not as secure.

FIG. 161: The *Japanese Blood Knot Loop* is made as follows: two bights are made, and joined together; several turns are taken around the standing parts in opposite directions; the ends are then passed through underneath the turns; the end on the right goes through to the left, and the end on the left goes through to the right.

Plate ·34—Simple Knotting

FIG. 162: The *Crossed Running Knot with Toggle* is a way of using a toggle in an eye. It is another form of Boat Knot, Second Method.

FIG. 163: The *Honda,* or *Hondo Knot in Lariat* is shown as it is used in cowboys' lariats. It is made by first forming an eye through an Overhand Knot. Another Overhand Knot is then tied to keep the eye from pulling out.

FIG. 164: *False Hitches Interlaced* appear to be Hitches, but in reality are open eyes interlaced together.

FIG. 165: The *Double Pitcher Knot* is the same as a Double Jury Knot, except that it has the bottom ends spliced together to form another eye. This is a very good knot to use as a sling.

FIG. 166: The *Interwoven Twin Figure-of-Eight Knots* is a method of weaving Figure-of-Eight style knots in a loop.

FIG. 167: The *Double Overhand Weave* represents Double Overhand Knots woven as illustrated.

FIG. 168: The *Japanese Loop* is a Japanese method of forming a knot in a loop.

FIG. 169: The *Interlocked Bights* design illustrates how to interlock the bights of two ropes.

FIG. 170: The *Braided Figure-of-Eight in Eye* consists of a prolonged Figure-of-Eight placed in an eye.

FIG. 171: The *Laced Overhand Knots in Loop* represents Overhand Knots laced together to form a loop.

FIG. 172: The *Round Turn Slippery Sheet Bend* is similar to the ordinary Slippery Sheet Bend, except that it has a round turn, which gives it added strength.

FIG. 173: The *Ring* or *Shoe Lace Bow* is a knot that everyone should know since it represents the commonest form of tying an ordinary shoe-lace.

FIG. 174: The *Seized Bight* design illustrates how to seize two bights together.

Plate 35—Simple Knotting

FIG. 175: The *Heart Handcuff Hitches Knot* resembles the Handcuff Hitches illustrated in PLATE 27, FIG. 84. But the body of this knot is in the shape of a heart, and is interlocking throughout.

FIG. 176: The *Reef Knot Handcuff Hitches* is another form of Hitches which may be used in place of the customary shackles. In this case, the loop which hangs down in the center of the knot is placed

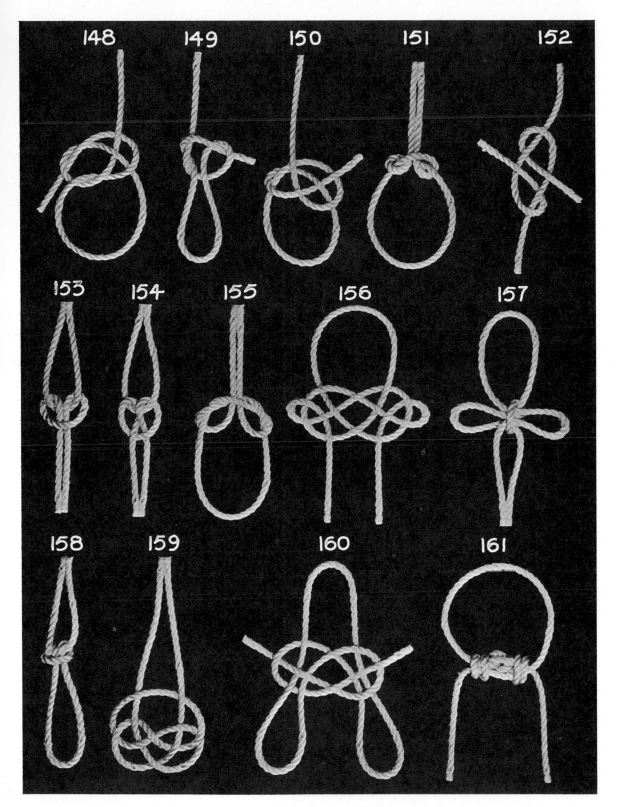

PLATE 33—SIMPLE KNOTTING

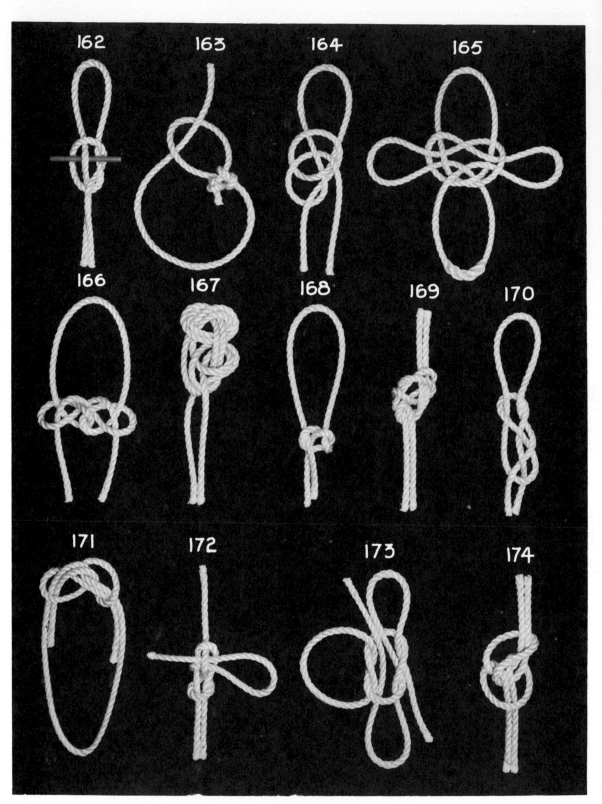

PLATE 34—SIMPLE KNOTTING

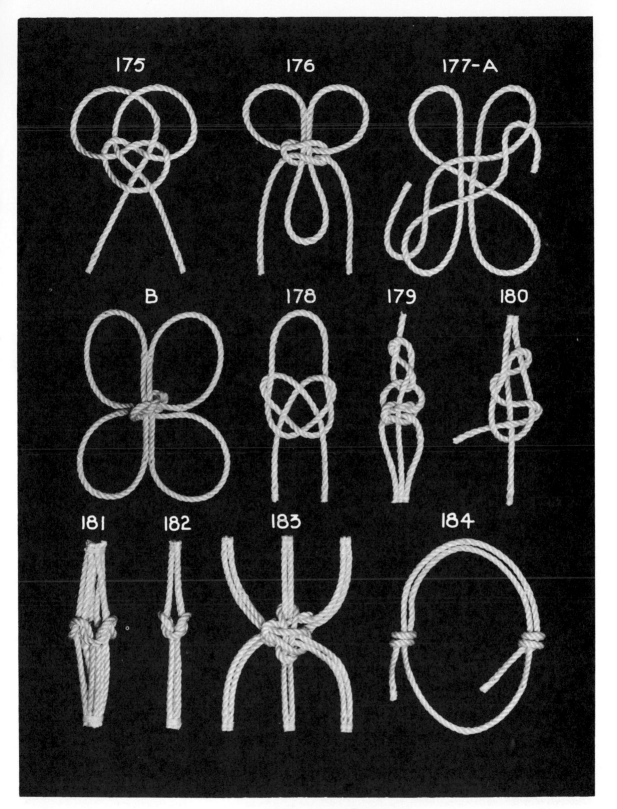

PLATE 35—SIMPLE KNOTTING

around the body, and the wrists inserted through the two loops. The slack is then taken out and all parts are drawn tight. The ends are made more secure by placing an additional Reef Knot in them.

FIG. 177A: The *Four-Loop Flower Tie* is illustrated in the first stage of the knot. Four loops are laid out, and the ends are put through the two loops in opposite corners.

B: The ends are now brought around to the back and reef-knotted together.

FIG. 178: The *Chinese Tassel Weave* can be used in making tassel designs in shade-pulls or lamp-cords.

FIG. 179: The *Two Ropes Bent Together in the Middle* is made by first forming a Figure-of-Eight Knot in the center of one rope, then reeving another rope through the body of this knot. The two ends of the rope which have been rove through the knot are next brought together, and a Square Knot is made, with the standing part of the first rope coming through the center of the Square Knot.

FIG. 180: The *Woven Hawser Bend* is made as follows: the end of one hawser is laid over the eye of the other, and then woven around the eye as shown in the illustration.

FIG. 181: The *Six-Strand Blockade Knot* can be used to join the bights of two or three lines to the bights of two or three other lines.

FIG. 182: The *Four-Strand Blockade Knot* is formed in the same manner as the preceding six-strand knot. The illustrations clearly show how these knots are made.

FIG. 183: The *Six-Strand Spider Blockade Knot* may also be used for the same purpose as the plain Blockade Knots. The only difference lies in the method of tying the knots, which are merely a series of Interlocking Reef Knots.

FIG. 184: The *Sliding Ring Knot* is formed as follows: a loop is first made in the middle of the rope; then a two-fold Blood Knot is made with each end, one on the right-hand side, and another on the left-hand side.

Plate 36—Simple Knotting

FIG. 185: The *Inside Double Round Turn Hitch* has two round turns on the inside, with Half Hitch seizing to complete the knot.

FIG. 186: The *Whip-Lash Knot* shows how to tie a lash to a whip.

FIGS. 187A and B: The *Japanese Loop* is shown opened in FIG. 187A. FIG. 187B shows the same knot closed or pulled up.

FIG. 188: The *Eight-Fold Jig Noose* is an Eight-fold Jig Knot in Noose.

FIG. 189: The *Japanese Bend* is a Japanese form of bending two ropes together.

FIGS. 190A and B: The *Two-Strand Carrick Diamond Knot* is made by first forming a Sailor's Breastplate, with one end coming out in the center of the loop, and

the other coming out on the outside, as shown in Fig. 190A. Now pass both strands underneath and out through the middle of the knot as illustrated by the arrows, and pull taut, working each strand up and in place as the knot is pulled up into its proper shape. Fig. 190B shows how it should look when pulled up properly. This is a very attractive and popular knot, and is still often used for decorative purposes.

FIG. 191: The *Two-Strand Carrick Diamond* (Double-passed) shows the same knot illustrated in FIG. 190 with two passes instead of one.

FIG. 192: The *Crossed Overhand Knots* design is a method of crossing two Overhand Knots through each other's parts.

Fig. 193: The *Overhand Loop Hitched*

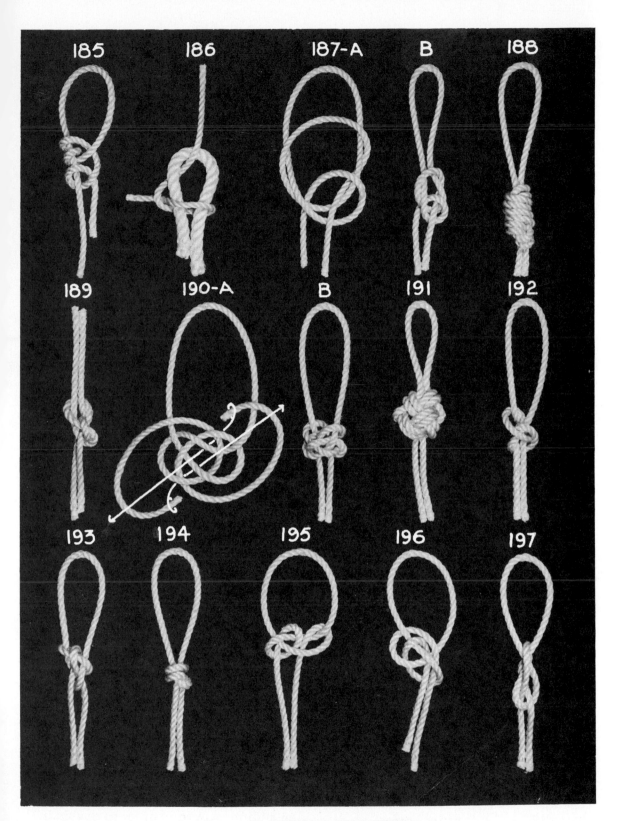

PLATE 36—SIMPLE KNOTTING

Knot is an unusual style of hitching, but can be easily followed from the illustration.

FIG. 194: The *Eye Jig Knot* represents an eye seized with a Jig Knot.

FIG. 195: The *Overland Half Hitch In-*terlocking Knot is a simple knot, easy to duplicate.

FIG. 196: The *Crossed Hitch Loop Knot* represents Crossed Hitches in a loop.

FIG. 197: The *Eye Braid Knot* consists of crossed passes in the form of a braid.

Plate 37—Simple Knotting

FIG. 198: A *Log Line Governor Hook Knot* is shown in this illustration. When a patent or taffrail log has been mounted in place, there is a fly-wheel or governor-wheel set just back of the clock. On this wheel is placed a hook, in which the log line is secured with this knot.

FIG. 199: The *False Hackamore Knot* somewhat resembles the ordinary Hackamore Knot, but there is really a decided difference between the two, as shown in the illustration.

FIG. 200: The *Bow Knot Bend* is formed by first making an Overhand Knot with the ends of two ropes, and then forming a Slippery Overhand Knot on top of it. The knot in general is tied in the same manner as the Square Knot. The difference is in the final tuck—the ends being tucked back through the center of the knot.

FIG. 201: The *False Two-Leaf Japanese Crown Knot* is formed as follows: first, make a bight in the center of the rope; reeve the ends through the bight, and make a Half Hitch around it; the ends are then brought over, and another Half Hitch is taken on the other part.

FIG. 202: The *Inside Clinch Loop* is begun by first making a bight on the end of a rope. Then the moving end is taken and brought around the standing part, and an Inside Clinch Hitch is made to finish the knot.

FIG. 203: The *Thief Knot Loop* is made somewhat similar to the Thief Knot, except that it is formed with a loop rather than with the ends of two ropes.

FIG. 204: **The *Single Bowline on the***

Bight Variation resembles the Single Bowline on the Bight, although it is actually quite different. The illustration clearly shows how it is made.

FIG. 205: The *Chinese Bow Knot* is the Chinese method of making the Bow Knot.

FIG. 206: The *Round Turn Loop* is a very secure, yet easily released, method of making a loop on the end of a rope.

FIG. 207: The *Rolling Hitch Loop* is formed by first making a bight on the end of the rope. The end is next brought back down and around the standing part with a round turn. Then the end is half hitched around the moving part of the bight.

FIG. 208: The *Whipping Loop with Two Half Hitches* has its turns made in the same manner as the turns on the knot described above, except that when the desired number of turns have been made, two cross turns are taken. Two Half Hitches are then taken on the standing part above the turns.

FIG. 209: The *Single Running Loop Hitch* is a novel method of hitching one rope to another. When a strain is placed upon it, the turns will not slip. First, make a running loop in the middle of a rope. Reeve the end of another rope through this loop. Then pass it around between the other two ends, and again through the loop.

FIG. 210: The *Double Running Loop Hitch* is made in the same manner as the preceding knot; but when making it, take an additional turn in order to double it.

FIG. 211: **The *Locked Running Noose***

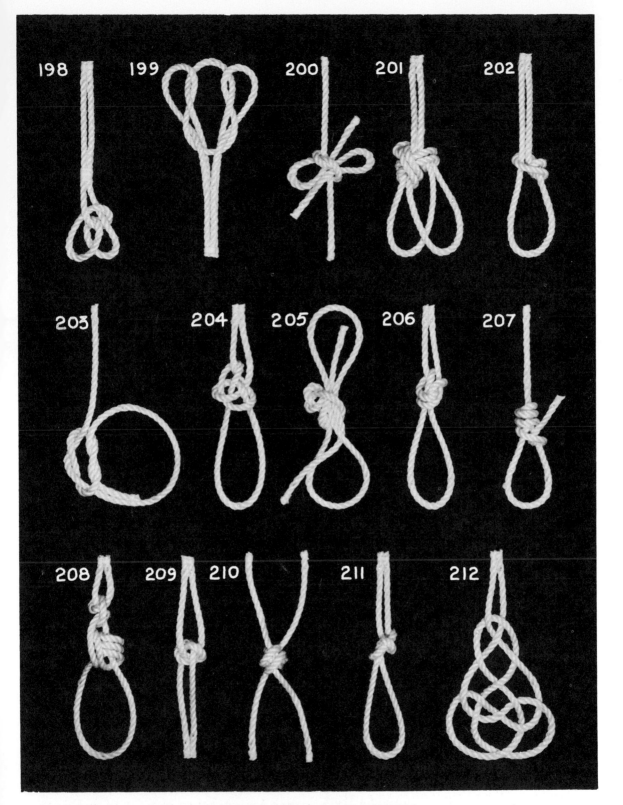

PLATE 37—SIMPLE KNOTTING

is formed as follows: first, make a Running Eye Knot or Slip Noose as in PLATE 26, FIG. 66. Then the moving end is brought up and down through the eye.

FIG. 212: The *Inverted Sailor's Breastplate with Interlocking Ends* is made by first tying the Sailor's Breastplate Knot shown in PLATE 21, FIG. 10B. A little slack is next taken in the loop at the top of the knot, and it is then turned over. The loop is then twisted as shown in the illustration, and the ends interlocked as indicated.

Plate 38—Simple Knotting

FIG. 213: The *Halter* or *Manger Tie* is the most common method used for tying horses to the mangers in their stalls.

FIG. 214: The *Hackamore Tie* can also be used for the same purpose as Fig. 213.

FIG. 215: The *Mooring Tie*, First Method, is a knot for mooring boats.

FIG. 216: The *Halter Tie*, Second Method, is another method of tying a halter.

FIG. 217: The *Halter Tie*, Third Method, is a particularly easy and convenient method.

FIG. 218: The *Weaver's Knot Hitch* is a Hitch in the form of a Weaver's Knot.

FIG. 219: The *Buntline Tie* is a variated method of the regular Buntline Hitch.

FIG. 220: The *Single Four-in-Hand Tie* is a common knot used for tying neckties.

FIG. 221: The *Double Four-in-Hand Tie* is another tie that all men should know, since, like the preceding knot, it has wide everyday use.

FIG. 222: The *Buntline Hitch* and *Oblique Granny Tie* consists of a Buntline Hitch and an Oblique Granny joined together.

FIG. 223: The *Grass* or *Strap Knot* is a good method to use for tying strops or straw together.

FIG. 224: The *Half Carrick Hitch* is a Hitch in the style of the Carrick Bend design.

FIG. 225: The *Mooring Tie*, Second Method, is another knot for mooring a boat. It is rather difficult to tie, but very secure.

FIG. 226: The *Packer's Noose* is a sort of Figure-of-Eight tied in the form of a noose. Similar to PLATE 50, FIG. 372.

FIG. 227: The *Variated Midshipman's Hitch* is slightly different from the ordinary form of this knot.

Plate 39—Simple Knotting

FIG. 228: The *Double Fisherman's* or *Waterman's Knot* is similar to the regular Fisherman's Knot, but is a trifle safer because it is doubled.

FIG. 229: The *Double Running Noose* is a double noose in the form of an eye.

FIG. 230: The *Twin Eye Sheet Bend* represents a double turn tied in the form of a Sheet Bend in order to make the eyes.

FIG. 231: The *Secured Eye Loop* is a simple way to secure an eye inside a loop.

FIG. 232: The *Sliding Blood Knot Noose* is made the same as the ordinary Blood Knot, except that it is tied in the form of a noose.

FIG. 233: The *Cross Turn Bend* is an unusual method of making a Bend with a cross turn in the middle.

FIG. 234: The *Surgeon's Bow* is the same as the ordinary Surgeon's Knot, but tied in the form of a bow.

FIG. 235: The *Hitched Figure-of-Eight Eye* is made by passing a Hitch through a Figure-of-Eight eye.

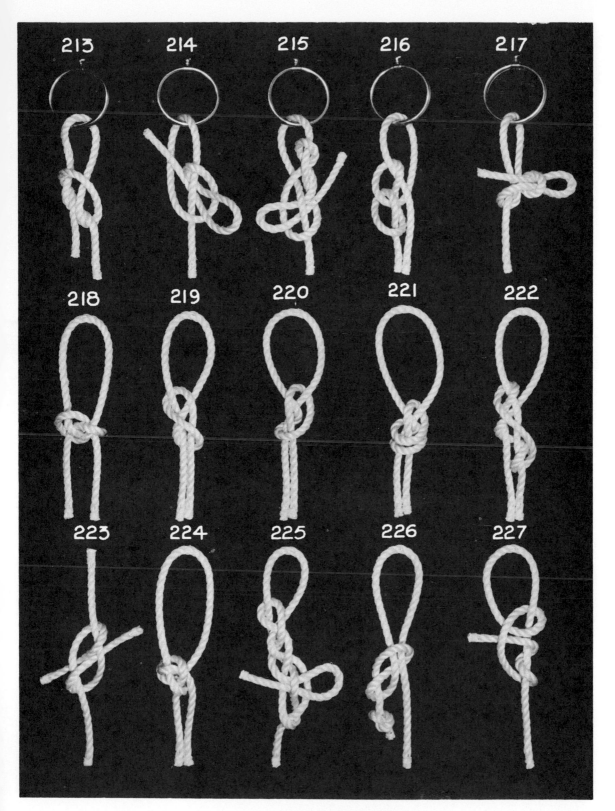

PLATE 38—SIMPLE KNOTTING

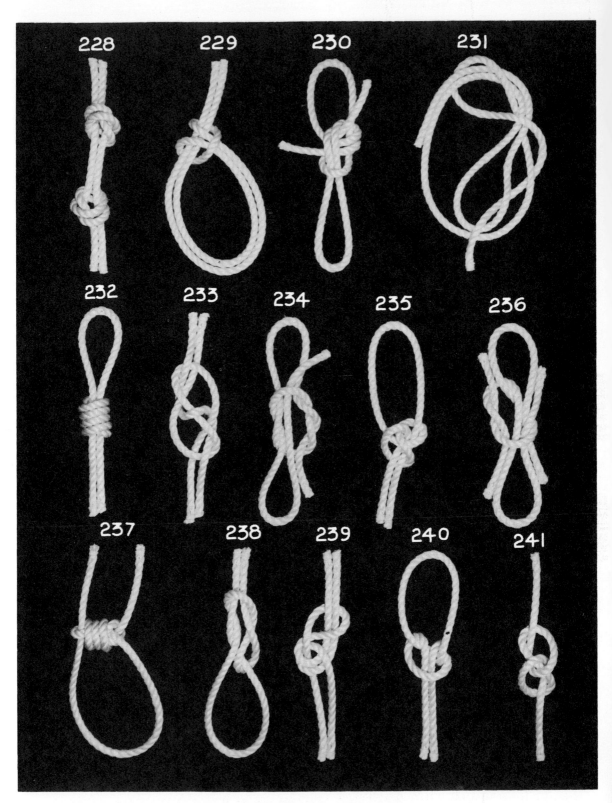

PLATE 39—SIMPLE KNOTTING

FIG. 236: The *Old-Fashioned* or *Double Bow* is the old-fashioned method of making a bow tie. It is tied with the bight of both ends.

FIG. 237: The *Sliding Monkey Fist in Loop* is another type of Monkey Fist, similar to the Blood Knot.

FIG. 238: The *Twisted Knot in Eye* is a method of tying a twisted knot in an eye loop.

FIG. 239: The *Half Double Figure-of-Eight Hitch* is a Figure-of-Eight in the form of a Hitch, half doubled.

FIG. 240: The *Round Turn Lark's Head Hitch* is somewhat like the ordinary Lark's Head, except that it is formed with a Running Eye and Half Hitch.

FIG. 241: The *Chained Overhands* consists of Overhand Knots tied in the form of an interlacing chain.

Plate 40—Simple Knotting

FIG. 242: The *Navy Neckerchief Tie* is used in the Navy to tie neckerchiefs. It consists of a Clove Hitch on the standing part.

FIG. 243: The *Single Bow Loop* is a loop and spliced eye joined together to form a single bow.

FIG. 244: The *Double Shoestring Bow* is the same as the ordinary Shoestring Bow, except that two turns are taken around the bow instead of one.

FIG. 245: The *Miller's Knot and Half Carrick* is a sort of combination Half Carrick and Miller's Knot.

FIG. 246: The *Interlocking Blood Knots* design consists of two ordinary Blood Knots tied through the body of each other.

FIG. 247: The *Halter Loop with Hondo* is a Hondo Knot in a Halter Loop.

FIG. 248: The *Double Halter Noose* is used as a halter for a cow. Part *a* is placed around the neck, and Part *b* is placed over the cow's muzzle.

FIG. 249: The *Hitched Bow* is made by tying two Hitches in the middle of a bow.

FIG. 250: The *Eye Toggle* is used for joining two eyes that may have to be cast loose instantly in an emergency.

FIG. 251: The *Twin Overhand Bights* has an Overhand Knot tied around each bight as shown.

FIG. 252: The *Square Knot Ring* is a Square Knot tied in a double ring.

FIG. 253: The *Inside Clove Hitch Loop* is an Inside Clove Hitch tied on the standing part to form a loop.

Plate 41—Simple Knotting

FIG. 254: The *Double Sheet Bend in Blood Knot Eye* is a Double Sheet Bend tied in an eye formed from a two-fold Blood Knot.

FIG. 255: The *Cape Horn Hitch* is an old-type Hitch, now seldom seen.

FIG. 256: The *Single Sheet Bend in Figure-of-Eight Eye* is a Single Sheet Bend tied in a sort of Figure-of-Eight Eye.

FIG. 257: The *Slip Hitch in Overhand Eye* is formed by first making an Overhand Eye with one strand, and then placing a

Slip Hitch underneath with the other strand.

FIG. 258: The *Jar Knot* is an unusual knot that has no practical use. It is tied by interlacing two open Overhand Knots.

FIG. 259: The *Inverted Hackamore* is tied by first making the usual Hackamore, then inverting or passing the strands back through the inside body of the knot and pulling taut.

FIG. 260: Another *Slip Hitch in Over-*

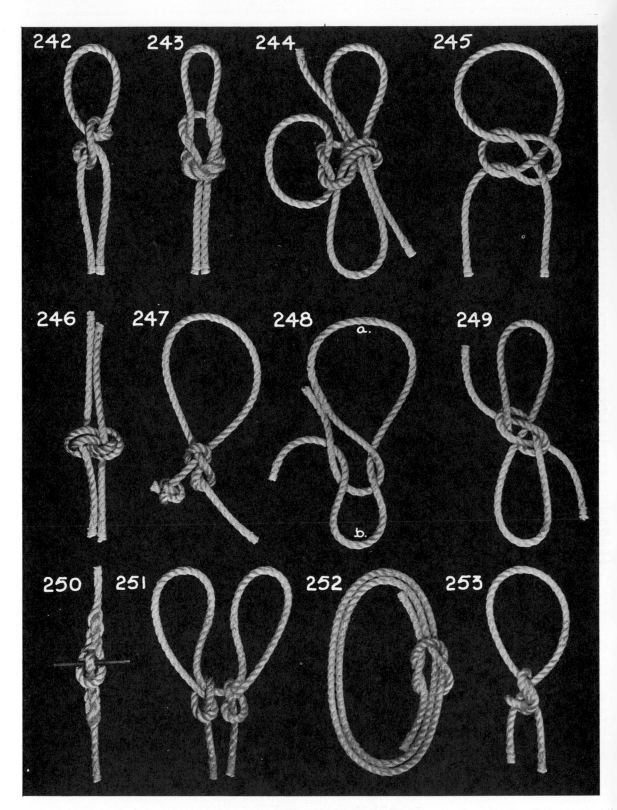

PLATE 40—SIMPLE KNOTTING

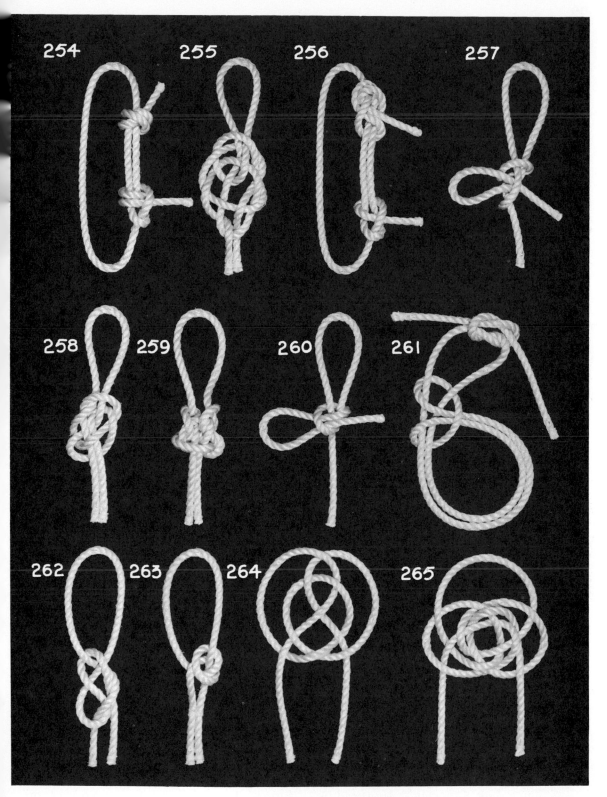

PLATE 41—SIMPLE KNOTTING

hand Eye is a Slip Overhand formed around an eye as shown.

FIG. 261: The *Square Knot Cinch in Double Noose* is a Double Noose capped with a Square Knot.

FIG. 262: The *Figure-of-Eight Halter Tie* is a sort of Figure-of-Eight made in the form of a Halter Tie.

FIG. 263: The *Seized Stopper Hitch* shows how to seize an Inside Stopper Hitch in a line.

FIG. 264: The *Four-Strand Open Turk's Head* is tied the same as the ordinary Four-strand Turk's Head, except that it is left opened and flattened out. Different methods of making Turk's Heads are illustrated in PLATE 109.

FIG. 265: The *Five-Strand Open Turk's Head* is a method of flattening the open Five-Strand Turk's Head, which is illustrated in PLATE 109, FIG. 3.

Plate 42—Simple Knotting

FIG. 266: The *Three-Strand Extra Cross Open Turk's Head* is a Three-Strand Turk's Head tied with an extra cross, left open, and flattened out.

FIG. 267: The *Spanish* or *Single Jury Knot with Carrick Diamond Ends* is made by first making the ordinary Spanish or Single Jury Knot, then tying a Carrick Diamond with the ends.

FIG. 268: The *Seized Eye* is made by forming an eye, and then placing a seizing around it.

FIG. 269: The *Four-part Masthead* is a Masthead Knot made from four parts instead of three.

FIG. 270: The *Three-Strand Blockade* is a method of joining the bights of three lines.

FIG. 271: The *Round Turn Inside Hitch* is a Round Turn Hitch tied in a loop.

FIG. 272: The *Two-Strand Variated Diamond* is slightly different from the ordinary Two-strand Diamond.

FIG. 273: The *Double Overhand Eye, Secured* shows how to secure an Overhand Eye.

FIG. 274: The *Crossed Hitch Weave* has Crossed Hitches placed in the ends as shown.

FIG. 275: The *Cross Lapped Overhands* has two Overhand Knots crossed through and lapped over each other.

FIG. 276: The *Interlocked Lark's Heads* has twin Lark's Heads interlocked together in the manner shown.

FIG. 277: The *Interlacing Hitch Weave* is an ornamental way of forming a simple weave. The Hitches overlap each other.

FIG. 278: The *Interlacing Knot* or *Dot Bend in Bow* consists of two bights interlaced to form a bow.

Plate 43—Simple Knotting

FIG. 279: The *Interlocking Overhand Knots* design has a central knot which appears to be an Overhand Knot. But in reality the two ends are merely laid over and under the bights respectively, and then interlocked by the two Overhand Knots on each side.

FIG. 280: The *Lineman's Masthead* is made as follows: a bight is first taken in the center of the rope; the end on the right-hand side is taken, put around the front of the bight, and pulled through its own loop to form a Slip Noose; then the other end is taken, and the process repeated, after which the knot is drawn up taut.

FIG. 281: The *Cat's-Paw in Eye* is formed by first reeving one end of the rope through the eye of the other rope, and

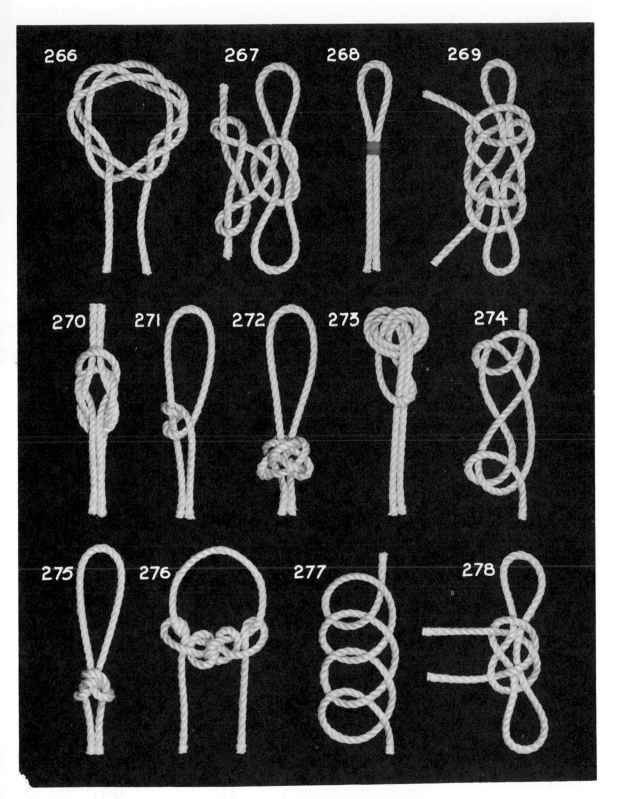

PLATE 42—SIMPLE KNOTTING

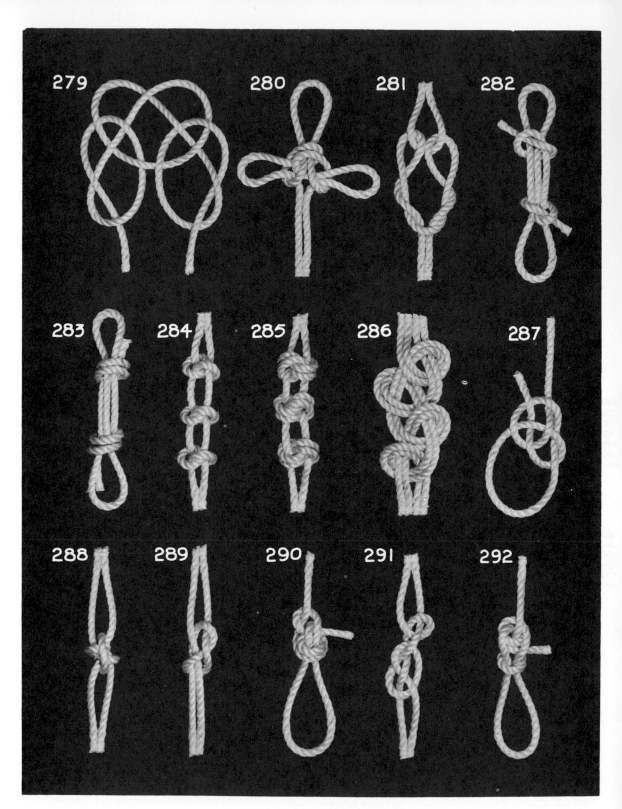

PLATE 43—SIMPLE KNOTTING

twisting it back around its own part one and a half turns. It is then brought back up and rove through the eye again in the opposite direction, and once more twisted around its own part until it appears as in the illustration.

FIG. 282: The *Double Sliding Loop with Overhand Knots* is made as follows: first, lay the rope out to form two bights; make an Overhand Knot around one of the bights; then take the other end and repeat this process on the other bight.

FIG. 283: The *Double Sliding Loop with Blood Knots* is made in precisely the same manner as the preceding knot, except that when the knots are made on the bights, a Blood Knot is used rather than an Overhand Knot.

FIG. 284: The *Single Running Loop Hitch in a Series* has its single knots made in the same manner as the knots shown on PLATE 37, FIG. 209. Instead of tying only one, several are made.

FIG. 285: The *Double Running Loop Hitch in a Series* has several single knots in its series instead of one. Otherwise, these knots are made in the same way as the double knots shown in PLATE 37, FIG. 210.

FIG. 286: The *Chain Hitch Shortening* is begun with two ropes laid out doubled, with the end of one half-hitched to the standing part of the other. The Hitches are then alternated, hitching one onto the other.

FIG. 287: The *Reef Loop* starts with a gooseneck made near the end of the rope. The end is brought around and passed un-der the gooseneck, then around the standing part, over both parts of the gooseneck, and under its own part.

FIG. 288: The *Interlocking Running Overhand Knots* is tied as follows: first, make an Overhand Knot in the middle of one rope; then make another Overhand Knot with the other end, so that they will interlock, as shown in the illustration.

FIG. 289: The *Draw Knot* is formed by first making a Figure-of-Eight Knot in the middle of one rope. Then reeve the other rope through the loop of the Figure-of-Eight Knot, as shown.

FIG. 290: The *Chinese Bowline* has no practical use, and when tension is applied it will jam very hard.

FIG. 291: The *Kay Knot* is a method of bending two ropes together. A Crabber's Eye Knot is first made with the ends of two ropes. Then a Half Hitch is made on the standing part of one rope with the end of the other rope. Both ends are now seized to the standing parts of the other ropes to finish the knot.

FIG. 292: The *Round Turn Single Bowline on the Bight* is made in the following way: first, take one turn around the left hand near the fingers, and take another turn back toward the wrist; two complete turns are next taken between these first two turns. Then with the right hand going to the left, put the thumb and the index finger under the first turn, over the next two turns, and finally grasping the fourth turn, pull it through to the right-hand side. All the slack is then drawn out, and the knot is complete.

Plate 44—Simple Knotting

FIG. 293: The *Halter Tie* is another of the many methods of tying halters. A Hitch is placed in a Slip Eye.

FIG. 294: The *Jam Hitch in Eye* is another method of placing a Jam Hitch in an eye.

FIG. 295: The *Slippery Square Knot* is tied in much the same way as the Square Knot, except that when finishing it, a bight of the left or right end is used instead of the straight end. By pulling the free end of the bight, the knot is easily untied. It

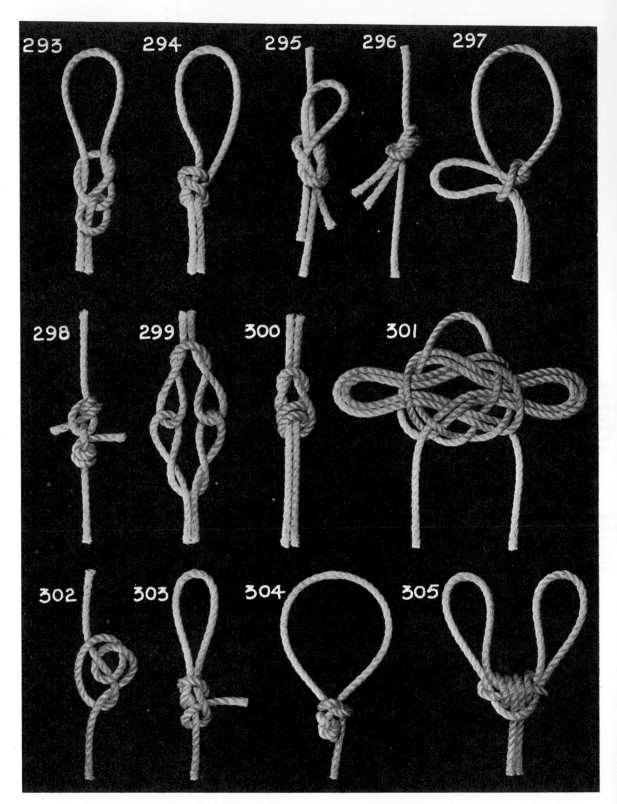

PLATE 44—SIMPLE KNOTTING

[*Plate 45*] Simple Knotting 97

is similar to the Slippery Reef Knot, and is particularly useful in tying reef points on sails, or for any other use where it must be quickly released.

Fig. 296: The *Binder Twine Bend* is made by first forming a bight in one rope or twine. Then bring the end of the other piece up through the bight, take a turn around the bight, and pass the end out through its own loop in the same direction as the end of the other part. Now pull the knot up taut. This knot is used for tying together the ends of balls of binder twine used on grain harvesters.

Fig. 297: The *Slip Eye in Loop* shows how to form a Slip Eye through its own part.

Fig. 298: The *Interlocked Round Turn Hitches* has two Round Turn Hitches interlocked in the manner indicated.

Fig. 299: The *Interlocking Cat's Paw Hitches* consists of two Cat's-Paw Hitches interlocked together.

Fig. 300: The *Rolling Hitch* or *Round Turn Sheet Bend* is slightly different from the ordinary Sheet Bend. Two round turns are taken. Then one end is passed through the eye of the bight from the outside, and the other from the inside.

Fig. 301: The *Cape Horn Masthead* differs somewhat from an ordinary Masthead Knot. This knot is partly doubled with a slight variation.

Fig. 302: The *Hitched Overhand Knot* consists of a Hitch in the body of an Overhand Knot.

Fig. 303: The *Slip Knot and Half-Hitch Knot* has a Half Hitch placed in the bottom of a Slip Knot, as shown. This knot may be used when an adjustable-size loop is required.

Fig. 304: The *Neck Loop for Hitching* is tied by first forming an Overhand Loop. Then slip the free end through the Overhand Knot, and place an Overhand Knot in the end of this also, drawing the knot up tight. This tie is used for securing horses and cattle. Its value lies in the ease with which the loop can be adjusted to any size desired.

Fig. 305: The *Round Turn Spanish Bowline* is made as follows: first, tie the regular Spanish Bowline; then take a round turn around the back of the knot with each end; then pass the ends out as in the usual method of tying this knot.

Plate 45—Simple Knotting

Fig. 306: The *Bowen Knot* is evidently of heraldic origin. It is one of the many forms of this type of knotting.

Fig. 307: The *Round Turn Half Hitch* design shows how round turns are placed in Half Hitches.

Fig. 308: The *Figure-of-Eight Throat* or *Emergency Tie* has a Figure-of-Eight tied through the bight. This knot is a handy tie to make when a quick fastening is required.

Fig. 309: The *Crossed Hitch Bow* consists of a Round Turn Hitch tied in the form of a bow.

Fig. 310: The *Sheet Bend Eye* is a Sheet Bend Tie placed in an Eye Loop.

Fig. 311: The *Combination Square Knot Hitch* has a Hitch tied through a Combination Square Knot.

Fig. 312: The *Victory Knot* is a nice knot for decorative purposes. In reality, it is a Triple Carrick Bend.

Fig. 313: The *Seized Loop* shows a loop with seizing.

Fig. 314: The *Surgeon's Reef Knot* is another heraldic form of knotting.

Fig. 315: The *Bowline Hitch* consists of

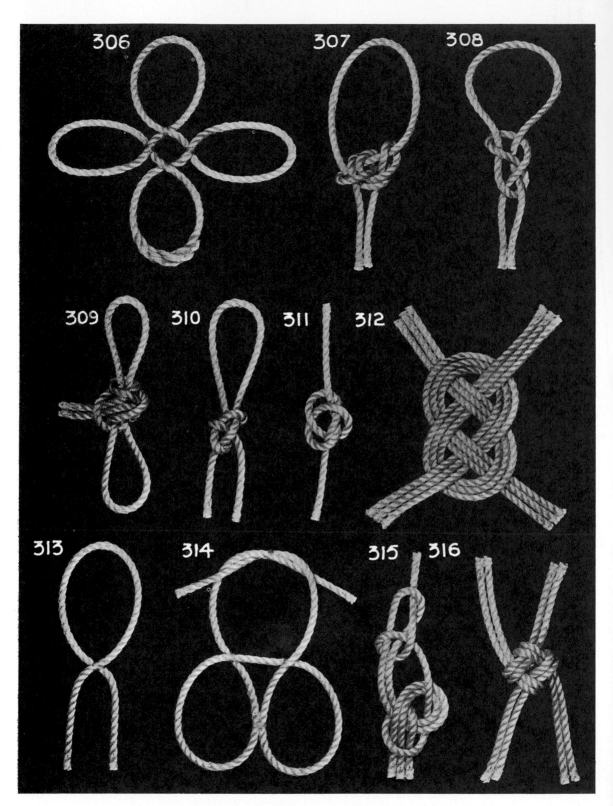

PLATE 45—SIMPLE KNOTTING

a Bowline Tie placed in the opposite end of a hitched bight.

FIG. 316: The *Double Japanese Crown* is the same as the Single Japanese Crown illustrated in PLATE 22, FIG. 14, except that it is double and tied with four ends instead of two. The method employed in making this crown is clearly shown in the illustration.

Plate 46—Simple Knotting

FIGS. 317A and B: The *Chinese Weave* is made by first placing one loop through the other one, as shown in FIG. 317A. Then the knot is closed by tucking the end through the body of the knot as indicated. FIG. 317B shows the knot as it appears when completed.

FIG. 318: The *Anne of Bohemia Knot* is of heraldic origin. More information is given on this style of knotting in PLATE 167.

FIG. 319: The *Figure-of-Eight Loop in Eye* consists of a Double Figure-of-Eight Weave with a Combination Eye.

FIG. 320: The *French Sheet Bend* is a novel way of forming a Sheet Bend. Take two round turns, and cross one part over from the back and the other part over from the front. Then reeve one end through the eye, with the other end passed between the eye and the end which has been rove through it.

FIG. 321: The *Hitched Overhand Locking Knots* design has two Hitched Overhand Knots locked through each other's eyes.

FIG. 322: The *Staffordshire Knot*, Heraldic Method, has two eyes formed in the manner shown.

FIG. 323: The *Bouchier Knot* is an Open Granny tied in the form of a Bend.

FIG. 324: The *Round Turn Loop* has a round turn placed in the middle of a loop.

FIG. 325: The *Wake Knot* is useful as a decorative knot. In reality, it is a Double Carrick Bend.

FIG. 326: The *Henage Knot* is another form of heraldic knotting.

Plate 47—Simple Knotting

FIG. 327: The *Variated Star Hitch*, First Method, is a slight variation of the Two-Strand Star Knot.

FIG. 328: The *Variated Star Hitch*, Second Method, is another variation of the Star Knot.

FIG. 329: The *Variated Diamond Knot* is a trifle longer weave than the ordinary Diamond, but is tied in somewhat the same way. After making the Diamond Knot, fill in with extra tucks over the next strands, then under the underneath strands.

FIG. 330: The *Triple-Pass Interlocking Round Turns* has two round turns laced together in the manner shown.

FIG. 331: The *Half Double Figure-of-Eight in Eye* is a Figure-of-Eight laced in the eye, which is partly doubled.

FIG. 332: The *Chain Hitches* design consists of Interlaced Chain Hitches.

FIG. 333: The *Double Chinese Weave* is the same knot as in PLATE 46, FIG. 317, except that it is doubled instead of single.

FIG. 334: The *Crossed Figure-of-Eight in Eye* is composed of two Figure-of-Eight Knots crossed around each other as shown.

FIG. 335: The *Knotted Shamrock* is a Shamrock Knot with Overhand Knots placed in the bottom ends.

FIG. 336: The *Triple-fold Figure-of-Eight Knot* represents a triple-fold made in Figure-of-Eight forms.

FIG. 337: The *Double Round Turn Sheet Bend in Eye* consists of two round turns tied in the form of a Sheet Bend on the eye loop.

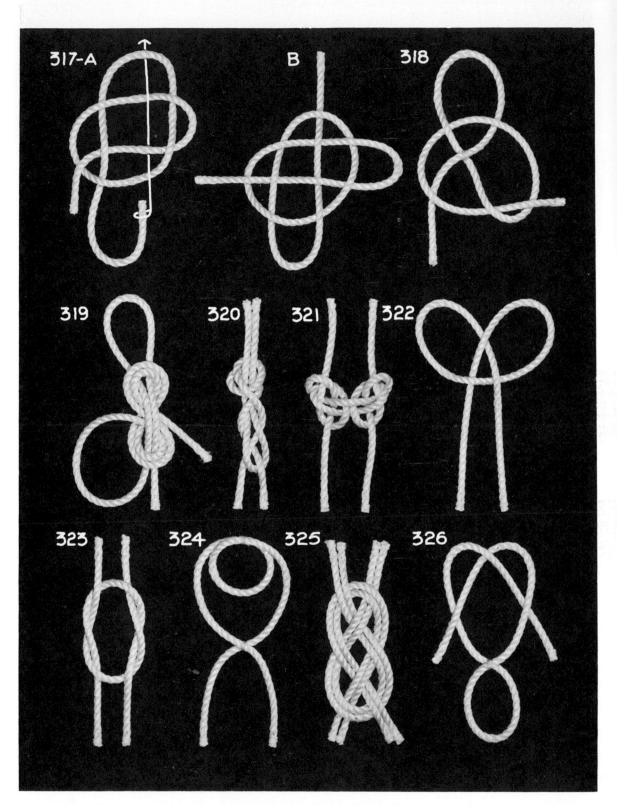

PLATE 46—SIMPLE KNOTTING

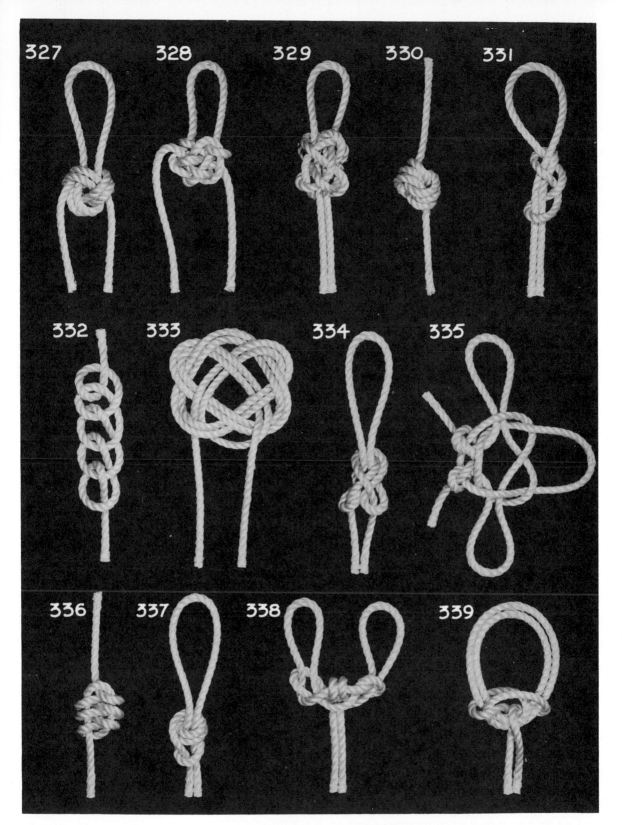

PLATE 47—SIMPLE KNOTTING

FIG. 338: The *Hitched Spanish Bowline* has two Hitches tied in the body of a Spanish Bowline as illustrated.

FIG. 339: The *Double Portuguese Bowline Hitch* is similar to the Portuguese Bowline; hence its name.

Plate 48—Simple Knotting

FIG. 340: The *Multiple* or *Five-fold Figure-of-Eight* is an extended variety of this form of knot with five passes.

FIG. 341: The *Draw* or *Single Bow* is similar to the Reef Knot, but easier to untie, as it is finished with one end on the bight.

FIG. 342: The *Single Pitcher Knot* can be used to take the place of a broken pitcher handle. The center knot is hauled taut, and the pitcher placed on it. Then the loops are brought up to form handles. To keep them in place, a lashing should be used, which is usually placed around the neck of the pitcher. This knot can also be utilized for slinging a shot, etc.

FIG. 343: The *Bundle Knot* is used for tying chaff, etc.

FIG. 344: The *Crossed Jam Knot* consists of a cross in a sort of Figure-of-Eight, which partly jams when pulled up taut.

FIG. 345: The *Lineman's Rider, "Star Method,"* is a Star Hitch form of this knot, similar to the ordinary Lineman's Rider.

FIG. 346: The *Lineman's Rider, "End Method,"* is another type that resembles the preceding knot.

FIG. 347: The *Wulah Hitch* is composed of a Slip Eye formed after taking two round turns.

FIG. 348: The *Overhand Sheet Bend* has an Overhand Knot formed in one part, with the other part passed through the body of the Overhand Knot, as indicated by the illustration.

FIG. 349: The *Running Noose* consists of, first, a simple Overhand Knot made on the end of the rope. Then the rope is knotted around the standing part as shown. It is one of the most common knots used in commerce.

FIG. 350: The *Surgeon's Knot Eye Loop* represents a Surgeon's Knot tied in the body of an eye.

FIG. 351: The *Double Sheet Bend Hitch* is tied by doubling a Sheet Bend in the form of a Hitch, as the picture indicates.

FIG. 352: The *Round Turn Star Hitch* is begun by making the first move of a regular Star Knot. Then a round turn is taken; in other words, it is partly doubled.

FIG. 353: The *Star Hitch* shown is a Star Knot which is finished by leaving the last parts single, instead of following around in order to make a completely doubled Star Knot.

FIG. 354: The *Variated Star Hitch, Third Method,* is another variation of the Star Knot.

Plate 49—Simple Knotting

FIG. 355: The *Strop Toggle* is used for placing a toggle in strops.

FIG. 356: The *Crossed Eye Tie* is a method for putting a crossed tie in an eye.

FIG. 357: The *Reversed Crown Blockade* is tied by first crowning four ropes together. Then the crown tie is reversed through to

the other side. This is an effective way of joining lines.

FIG. 358: The *One-Strand Monkey Fist* shown employs only one pass.

FIG. 359: The *Monkey Paw* consists of a Monkey Fist with a Hitch and seizing placed underneath.

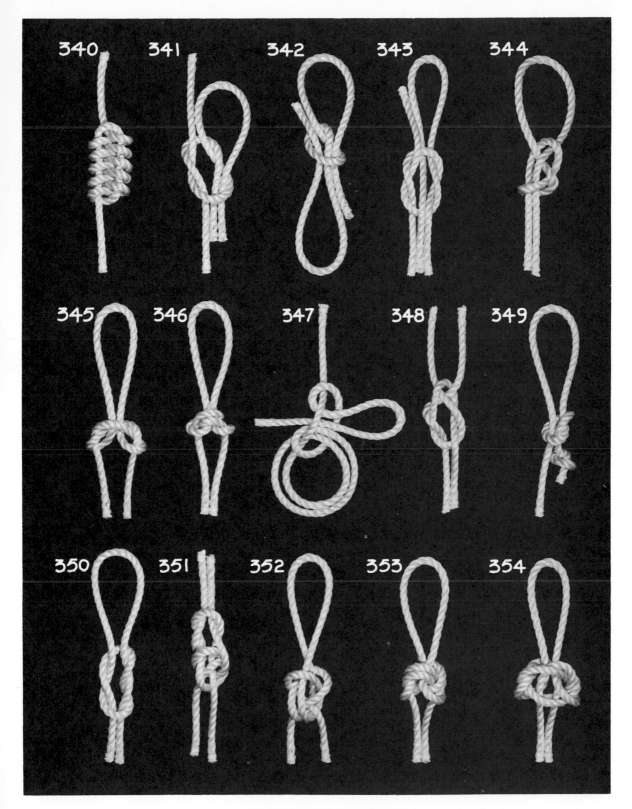

PLATE 48—SIMPLE KNOTTING

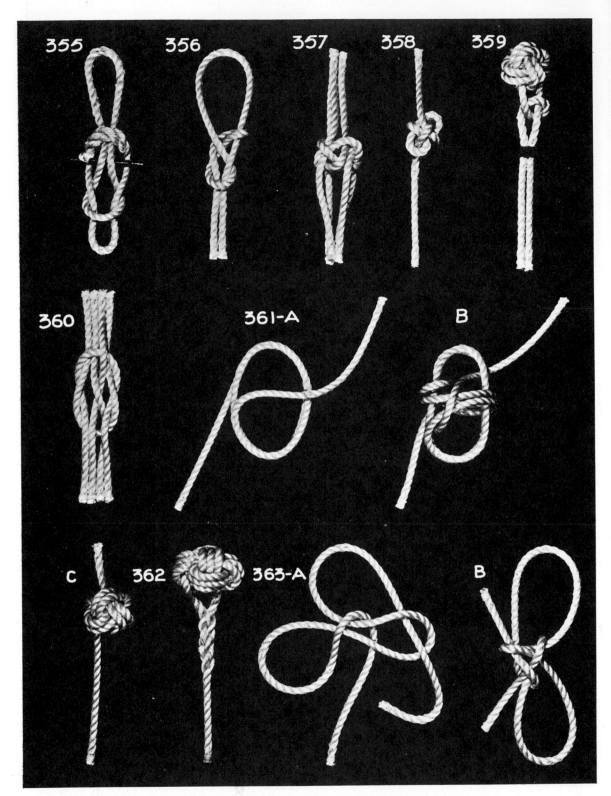

PLATE 49—SIMPLE KNOTTING

[*Plate 50*]   Simple Knotting   105

FIG. 360: The *Crossed Blockade* has two strands crossed under each other through the body of a Sheet Bend.

FIGS. 361A, B and C: The *Monkey Fist* is a type of knot used to put weight on the end of a heaving line. To make it, form two or three loops (usually three). Two are used here for the sake of clarity in the illustration. After forming the two loops as shown in FIG. 361A, pass the end around the first set of loops. Take two more turns, and pass the end through the first set of loops and around the second set of loops, as shown in FIG. 361B. Then take two more turns, the same as before, and pull up tight. Care should be taken in working

this knot up taut, in order to get the proper shape. FIG. 361C shows the knot as it looks when pulled up.

FIG. 362: The *Three-Strand Monkey Fist* is the regular form of Monkey Fist used for heaving lines. It is made by taking three turns instead of two, but is otherwise tied in the same way.

FIGS. 363A and B: The *Two Leaf Dragonfly* is formed in the manner shown in FIG. 363A. Then the end is passed over and around the two bottom parts, and back out by its own part. FIG. 363B shows the knot as it looks when pulled up. This is a decorative design.

Plate 50—Simple Knotting

FIG. 364: The *Double Loop Portuguese Bowline* can be used for the same purpose as the Spanish Bowline (PLATE 11, FIG. 206), and in practical use is quite secure.

FIG. 365: The *False French Bowline Seized* is tied as follows: first, make two complete loops with the end of the rope, and bring it around the standing part, forming a bight. This is next seized together to the two turns. Then the end is brought up and half-hitched to the standing part, and again brought up and seized to it.

FIG. 366: The *Japanese Twin Loop Bowline* has no practical value.

FIG. 367: The *Granny Loop* is begun by tying a Granny Knot a short distance from the end. It is then twisted, and the end rove through it, as shown.

FIG. 368: The *Clove Hitch Bend* has the end of one rope clove-hitched a short distance from the end of the other rope. Then the other end is clove-hitched a short distance from the Clove Hitch on the first rope. This is a very secure method of joining two ropes.

FIG. 369: The *Chinese Twin Loop Bowline* has little practical value.

FIG. 370: The *Reef Knot Spanish Bowline* is tied as follows: two bights are laid out in the middle of the rope, and an Overhand Knot is tied underneath the center part of the rope; the two ends are then brought up on each side of the center, and another Overhand Knot is formed to complete the Reef Knot.

FIG. 371: The *Variated Fool's Bowline* has a running end on one end of it.

FIG. 372: The *False Running Figure-of-Eight Knot* can be used to tie up packages.

FIG. 373: The *Locked Becket Bend* begins with a Becket Sheet Bend. Then the end is brought around and back through the body of the knot, as shown.

FIG. 374: The *Triple-Loop Bowline on the Bight* seems to be quite a tricky knot to tie, although it is really simple if the illustration is carefully followed. It will be noticed that there are three loops in this knot rather than the two found in the ordinary Bowline on the Bight.

FIG. 375: The *Chain Hitch Loop* has no practical value.

FIG. 376: The *False Hackamore Knot* appears similar to the Hackamore Knot, but close observation will reveal a distinct difference.

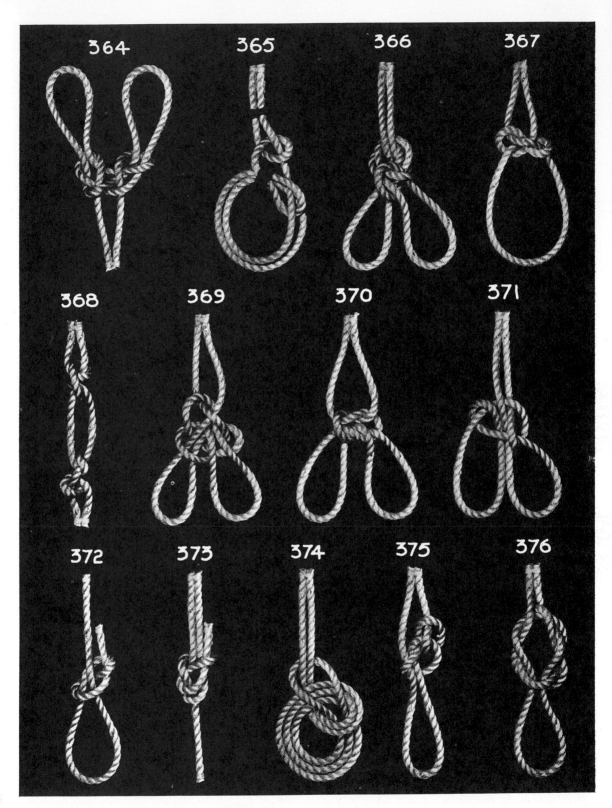

PLATE 50—BOWLINES

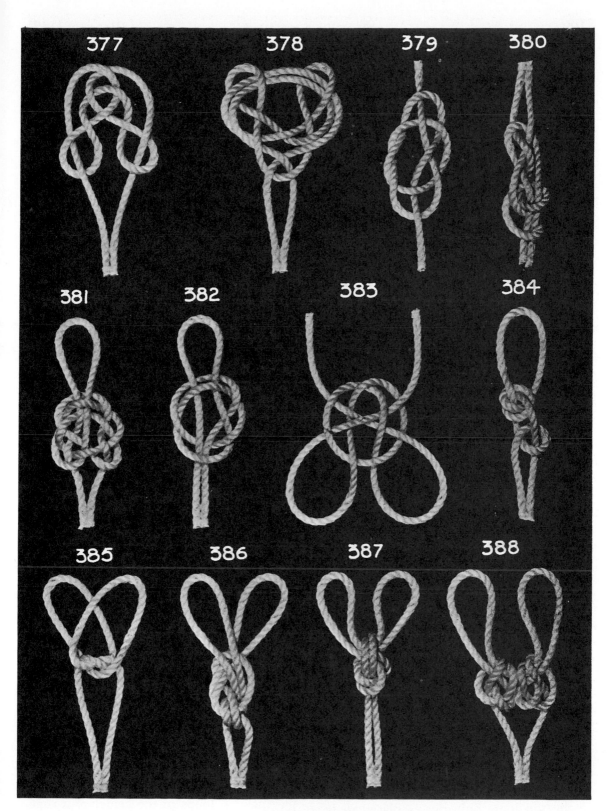

PLATE 51—SIMPLE KNOTTING

Plate 51—Simple Knotting

FIG. 377: The *Overhand Knot Weave* may appear complicated, yet it begins with a simple Overhand Knot.

FIG. 378: The *Simple Weave* is used only for decorative purposes.

FIG. 379: The *Ornamental Shortening* is an ornamental method of shortening a rope.

FIG. 380: The *Double Half Hitch Half Carrick Bend* has no real utility.

FIG. 381: The *Ornamental Loop* is an ornamental, and quite difficult, method of placing a loop in the end of a rope.

FIG. 382: The *Single Hackamore Loop* resembles the ordinary Hackamore Knot, except that it has fewer turns.

FIG. 383: The *Double Loop Interlocked Overhand Knot* can be used to tie two objects together, or may be utilized as Handcuff Hitches.

FIG. 384: The *Round Turn Overhand Knot and Half Hitch* is a very secure method of putting an eye in the end of a rope.

FIG. 385: The *Stevedore's Twin Loops Knot* is in reality a Sling Shortener in the reverse position. It is a very good method of forming two loops in the end of a rope.

FIG. 386: The *Dutchman's Bowline,* First Method, is a neat, secure method of forming two loops in the end of a rope.

FIG. 387: The *Dutchman's Bowline,* Second Method, seems similar to the knot in FIG. 386. Yet it is obvious that the cross turn comes between the loops in this knot, and between the two ends in the preceding one.

FIG. 388: The *Half-Hitched Twin Eyes* starts with two bights laid out in the center of the rope. Then two Half Hitches are taken on each bight with each end to complete the knot.

Plate 52—Simple Knotting

FIG. 389: The *Interlocking Round Turns* may be used to weight the end of a heaving line.

FIG. 390: The *Round Turns with Interwoven Half Hitches* has no practical value.

FIG. 391: The *Sailor's Breastplate Weave,* First Method, is tied as follows: first, make a Sailor's Breastplate (PLATE 21, FIG. 10). Both ends are then brought up from the outside, and the loop on top of the knot is given a twist and one end passed through. The same procedure is followed on the other side. On top, the loop is given another twist, and the ends are interlocked as shown.

FIG. 392: The *Sailor's Breastplate Weave,* Second Method, begins with a Sailor's Breastplate. Instead of putting three twists in the top loop, only one is placed in it; and the two bights on each side of the Car-

rick Bend are twisted to make the first two loops.

FIG. 393: The *Flemish Weave Loop* has no utility.

FIG. 394: The *Interlocked Round Turn Loop* is formed by first making two round turns a short distance from the end of the rope. Then make a bight, and with the end pass two more round turns through the two original turns. When the slack has been drawn up, the knot will appear as in this illustration.

FIG. 395: The *Four-fold Blood Knot Bow* starts with two bights laid out in the middle of the rope. Then a Blood Knot of four turns is made around all the parts.

FIG. 396: The *Granny Knot on a Bight* is another useful method of shortening or putting two loops in the center of a rope.

FIG. 397: The *Crossed Loop Shortening*

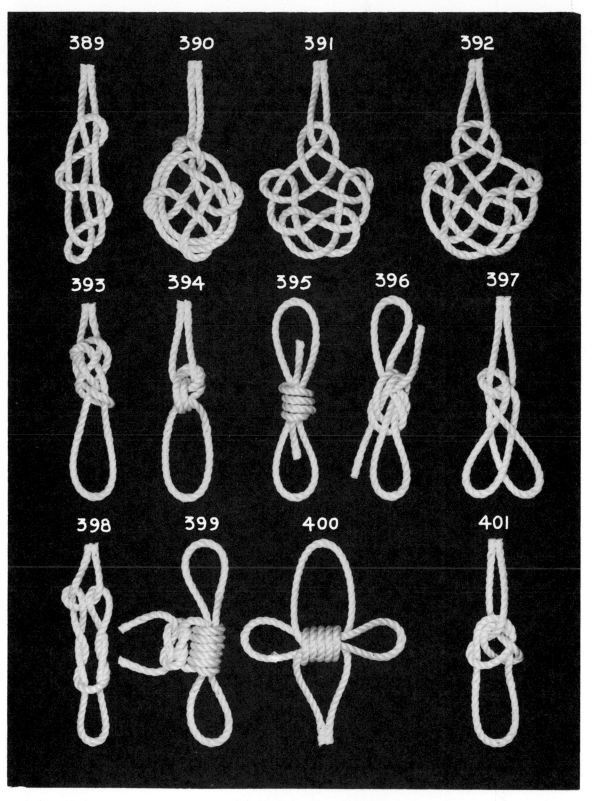

PLATE 52—SIMPLE KNOTTING

can be used as a Sling Shortener, or may be utilized in place of the Spanish Bowline.

FIG. 398: The *One-Strand Cat's-Paw* is made with one strand to form a loop.

FIG. 399: The *Blood Knot Handcuff Hitches,* when used as Handcuff Hitches or as a method of joining two objects, is very secure. The ends are made fast by the Reef Knot, as shown in the illustration.

FIG. 400: The *Blood Knot Masthead* has the loop on top made first. Next, the turns are passed around both ends and the loop. Then the ends are passed through the center of the turns to form two loops on each side.

FIG. 401: The *Single Portuguese Bowline Hitch* has two round turns made on the hand. Then both ends are passed around both turns to form an Overhand Knot of both parts. The Overhand Knot is then pulled apart, and the turn in the center of it is pulled through.

Chapter III

End Rope Knots

END ROPE KNOTS, or Knots tied with the unlaid strands of the end of a rope, have never before been presented in the complete and comprehensive manner shown herein. This particular phase of knotting probably has been neglected more than any other type.

Outside of a few ordinary examples, such as Wall or Crown Knots, which are still in everyday use, there has been very little development of the fascinating ties to which the old sailing ship men devoted so much of their leisure time. In fact, the fancy art of Rose Knotting and of tying intricate Shroud Knots has been almost forgotten and allowed to pass into oblivion. In this chapter are presented the most extensive variety known to exist. The authors have investigated almost every known variation of the different combination of keys which are used for the ordinary knots, such as the Manrope, Stopper, Diamond and Matthew-Walker Knots.

There are many different types of Rose Knots, besides a great variety of Star Knots and Shroud Knots, included among a host of many other useful and beautiful knots which can also be utilized for decorative as well as practical purposes.

Plate 53—Wall, Crown, and Matthew Walker Knots

FIGS. 1A and B: *The Three-Strand Crown Knot* is seldom used by itself, but usually as part of, or as a basis for, other knots, such as the Back Splice, and Rose Knot. Whip the rope near the end, according to the length of the strands desired. Unlay the strands, and lay the strand nearest to the right side over in front and on the inside of the center strand. Bring the center strand in the form of a bight down over the strand from the right, and bring the strand on the left over the center strand and through the bight of the strand on the right. The knot then will be opened up as in FIG. 1A. FIG. 1B shows the same knot pulled up.

FIGS. 2A and B: The *Wall Knot* is the opposite of a Crown Knot. In other words, you wall *up* and crown *down*. Each strand of a Wall Knot comes up through the bight of the strand next to it, as illustrated in FIG. 2A, whereas each strand of a Crown Knot goes down through the bight of the next strand. FIG. 2B shows the strands pulled up. This knot is used back-to-back for a Shroud Knot, in joining two ropes. There also are various other uses for it, such as finishing off seizings or forming a basis for other knots.

FIGS. 3A and B: The *Four-Strand Crown Knot* is tied the same as a Three-Strand Crown Knot, except that it is formed with four strands instead of three. FIG. 3A shows the knot opened, and FIG. 3B as it looks when pulled up.

FIGS. 4A and B: The *Four-Strand Wall Knot* is tied the same as a Three-Strand Wall Knot. It is shown open in FIG. 4A, and pulled up in FIG. 4B.

FIGS. 5A, B, and C: The *Matthew Walker Knot* at first looks rather difficult to tie, but is really simple when the illustrations are closely followed. Begin by taking the first strand lying nearest to the right, as shown in FIG. 5A. Pass it around the body

111

or standing part of the rope and up under its own part, forming an Overhand Knot. Then take the center strand and repeat the same move. The last strand on the left is also tucked in the same fashion. This gives the knot as it looks in FIG. 5B, with strands *a, b,* and *c* tucked under their own parts. Care should be used in pulling the strands of this knot taut, as each strand should lay around the knot in uniform appearance and in its proper place. When completed, the knot will look as it does in FIG. 5C.

with each strand leading up through its own bight or part, after interlacing the other two. This knot is used on the end of rigging lanyards. It will not slip.

FIG. 6: The *Wall and Crown Knot* is used mainly as a basis for the Double Wall and Crown, which then becomes a Manrope Knot. It is tied by first making a Wall Knot and then crowning the top of it. In years gone by it was used to form the cat-o'-nine-tails.

Plate 54—Miscellaneous End Rope Knots

FIG. 7A: The *Elongated Matthew Walker* (two passes) is tied in the same general manner as the ordinary Matthew Walker (PLATE 53, FIG. 5). The only difference is that instead of taking one turn around the body of the knot, there is an additional turn, making two turns in all, as shown. Strand *b* is next taken, and led down and around between the turns made by strand *a.*

B: This illustration shows strand *b* after it has been brought half-way around. It is given another full turn, as the drawn line indicates, before being passed up under the turns and through its own bight as in the regular Matthew Walker.

C: When the last strand *c* has been passed around in the proper way, the knot is drawn up taut and will then appear as in this illustration.

FIG. 8: The *Elongated Matthew Walker* (three passes).

FIG. 9: The *Elongated Matthew Walker* (four passes).

FIG. 10: The *Single Stopper Knot* (three strands) is made as follows: the rope is unlaid for a short distance; then a Crown Knot is made. After the Crown Knot has been drawn up taut, a Wall is made underneath it. In other words, instead of walling and then crowning, the Crown is made first, with the Wall following.

FIG. 11: The *Single Stopper Knot* (four strands).

FIG. 12: The *Single Stopper Knot* (six strands).

FIG. 13: The *Double Stopper Knot* (three strands) is begun by making the Single Stopper Knot, FIG. 10. The ends are next followed around to double the knot. Then all the slack is drawn out, and the ends cut off short.

FIG. 14: The *Double Stopper Knot* (four strands).

FIG. 15: The *Double Stopper Knot* (six strands).

FIG. 16: The *Tack Knot* (three strands) is used in tapering the "Tack Rope" where it passes through the clew of the sail. First, make a Wall, and then a Crown. The ends are next followed around, doubling the knot, and in reality forming a Manrope Knot. This leaves the ends on top of the knot; and they are passed downward through the body of the knot, bringing them out at the bottom. The strands are now opened up and scraped with a knife to taper them, then laid along the rope and marled down.

FIG. 17: The *Tack Knot* (four strands).

FIG. 18A: The *Outside Matthew Walker* (three strands) is a unique method of forming the Matthew Walker Knot, and so far as is known has never before appeared in any other work on knotting. It should be observed that in the ordinary Matthew

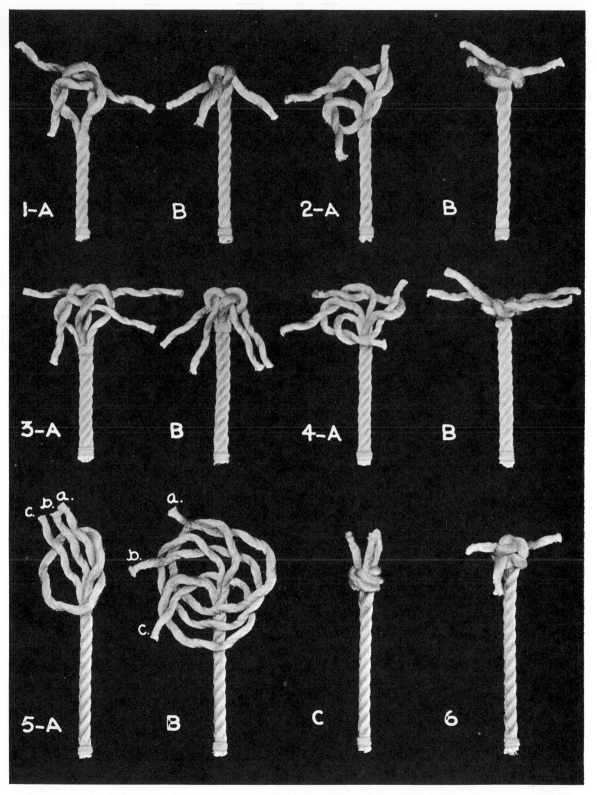

PLATE 53—WALL, CROWN, AND MATTHEW WALKER KNOTS

Walker Knot the end is passed *under* all
the other ends, when being passed around
the body of the knot. But in the Outside
Matthew Walker, the end is passed *over*
the other strands. Strand *a* is brought over
and passed through its own part, as shown
here. Strand *a* has already been tucked, and
strand *b* is next.

B: This shows how strand *b* is passed.
The next strand to be tucked is *c*.

C: Strand *c* is to be tucked as shown.
All the turns are pushed well down on the
body of the rope and carefully drawn up
into position.

D: After all the slack has been drawn
out of the knot, it will appear as in this
illustration.

FIG. 19: The *Outside Matthew Walker*
(four strands).

FIG. 20: The *Outside Matthew Walker*
(six strands) shows to the greatest advantage in six-strand rope, or in two three-
strand ropes joined to form six strands.

FIG. 21: The *English Rose Knot* (three
strands) is much too difficult to illustrate
in all its various stages of construction. To
make it, first tie the Wall Knot, followed
by a Crown. Then ends are half-hitched
through the bights formed by the Wall

Knot. They are brought back again over
the top of the knot, and another Crown
placed in them, but in the opposite direction from the first Crown. The ends are
then passed under the Half Hitches. When
this has been done, a fid is taken and
passed up through the center of the knot.
After the hole has been made and the fid
withdrawn, one strand is taken and passed
through this hole. This procedure is continued until all the strands have been
tucked in this manner. The ends are then
cut off short close to the top of the knot.

FIG. 22: The *English Rose Knot* (four
strands).

FIG. 23: The *English Rose Knot* (six
strands) shows this knot at its best.

FIG. 24: The *Royal Crown* (three
strands) is the simplest of the more ornamental methods of finishing off a rope end.
A whipping is first placed on the rope a
short distance from the end. The strands
are unlaid to the whipping, and brought
down alongside the rope to form loops.
Then the strands are half-hitched to each
other as shown in the illustration. After
this has been done, the ends are stopped
down to the standing part with a second
whipping.

Plate 55—Variations of Crown and Sennit Knots

FIG. 25: The *Royal Crown* (four strands).

FIG. 26: The *Royal Crown* (six strands).

FIG. 27: The *Royal Crown Spliced*
(three strands) is similar to the foregoing
knots. However, it has no whipping; and
the ends, rather than being stopped down
to the standing part of the rope, are spliced
in, as in the ordinary Back Splice (PLATE
79, FIG. 5).

FIG. 28: The *Royal Crown Spliced* (four
strands).

FIG. 29: The *Royal Crown Spliced* (six
strands).

FIG. 30A: The *Sennit Knot* (three

strands) is made as follows: begin by forming a Diamond Knot (PLATE 60, FIG. 140).
Then follow around only half-way, as
shown. Instead of continuing to follow
around, take each strand over the first crossing strand and under the next crossing
strand, as indicated by the drawn line. The
next strand to be tucked is strand *b*.

B: After each strand has been tucked in
this fashion, the entire knot is drawn up
taut, and the ends are then cut off short to
finish.

FIG. 31: The *Sennit Knot* (four strands).

FIG. 32: The *Sennit Knot* (six strands)
is particularly handsome.

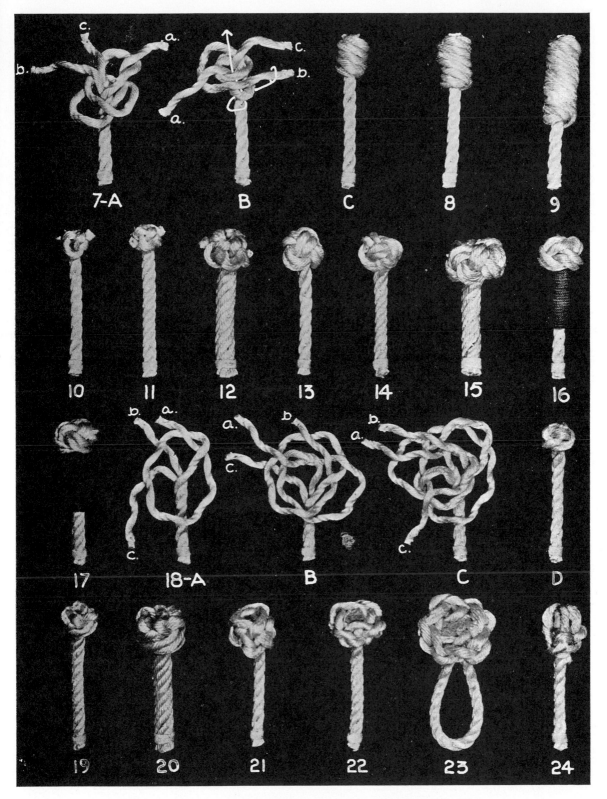

PLATE 54—MISCELLANEOUS END ROPE KNOTS

FIG. 33A: The *Sennit Rose Knot* (three strands) is one of the most uniform and attractive of the End Rope Knots, and can be quite easily mastered. To begin, two Crown Knots are made on the end of the rope, to give the knot a body. Then a Diamond Knot is made, and the ends are run down alongside the strand next to them, as though to double the knot. The ends now will be pointing downward. Strand *a* is tucked upward, over two and under two, as the line shows; *b* is tucked next.

B: This shows strand *a* already tucked and strand *b* tucked half-way. Strand *c* has not yet been tucked.

C: The knot now is drawn up taut. The knot will have a tendency to slip down the body of the core on to the standing part. Hence, it should be pushed well up until the Crown Knots which were made first are slightly below the top of the knot. It will be noticed that the weave around the side of the knot appears the same as the Five-Strand Running Sennit, which is over two and under two.

FIG. 34: The *Sennit Rose Knot* (four strands).

FIG. 35: The *Sennit Rose Knot* (six strands).

FIG. 36: The *Sennit Rose Knot Crowned and Spliced* (three strands) is the same as the preceding knot. After the last tuck has been made, the knot is crowned, and the ends are passed down through the knot and spliced into the standing part.

FIG. 37: The *Sennit Rose Knot Crowned and Spliced* (four strands).

FIG. 38: The *Sennit Rose Knot Crowned and Spliced* (six strands).

FIG. 39A: The *Single Reverse Diamond Knot* (three strands) is begun by unlaying the rope and crowning the end. Then work a Diamond Knot on the rope, but with the knot reversed, so that when the knot is tied the strands are lying down along the standing part of the rope, instead of being on top of the knot and clear of the rope, which is the ordinary way. This is a tricky piece of work, and will be found easier to tie if the knot is formed well down on the rope, and worked out to the end near the Crown after it is formed.

B: This shows the finished knot after it has been drawn taut.

FIG. 40: The *Single Reverse Diamond Knot* (four strands).

FIG. 41: The *Single Reverse Diamond Knot* (six strands).

FIG. 42: The *Double Reverse Diamond Knot* (three strands) is tied by first making the Reverse Diamond Knot just explained. Then proceed to double it. When drawn up taut, it will appear as in this illustration.

FIG. 43: The *Double Reverse Diamond Knot* (four strands).

FIG. 44: The *Double Reverse Diamond Knot* (six strands).

Plate 56—Sennit Rose and Lanyard Knots

FIG. 45: The *Sennit Rose with Spritsail Sheet* (four strands) is formed as follows: first, make the Sennit-Rose Knot illustrated in PLATE 55, FIG. 33; then make a Spritsail Sheet on top, which really amounts to a Crown Knot in four-strand rope. Next, the ends are taken over and put down through the body of the knot at the base of the **adjacent** strand, and then cut off close to **the** bottom of the knot.

FIG. 46: The *Sennit Rose with Spritsail Sheet* (six strands) is begun by taking a sufficient length of three-strand rope. Middle it, bring both ends together, and put a seizing on them, leaving a loop of any desired length. A Lanyard Knot (PLATE 60, FIG. 131) is then made, after which the Sennit Knot and Spritsail Sheet are tied as before.

FIG. 47: The *Sennit Rose with Spritsail*

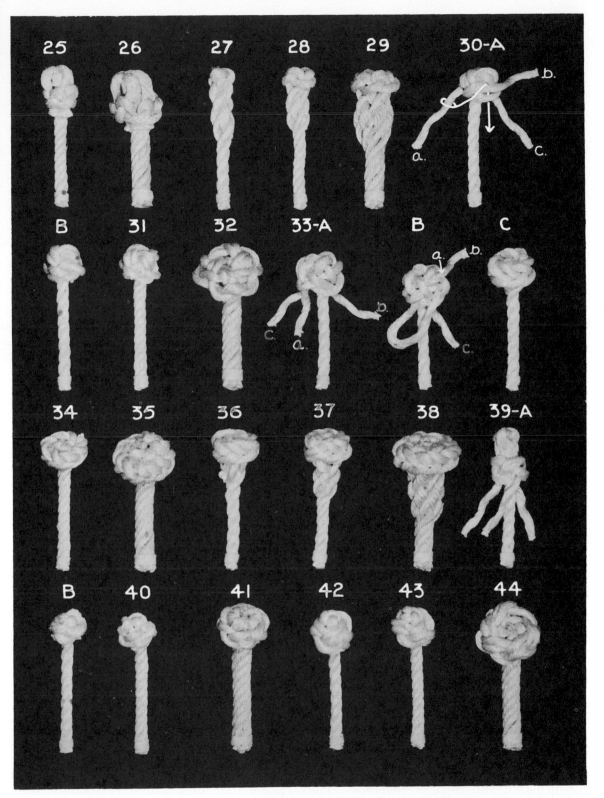

PLATE 55—VARIATIONS OF CROWN AND SENNIT KNOTS

Sheet (eight strands) is made in the same manner as the preceding knot.

FIG. 48: The *Sennit Rose with Spritsail Sheet* (twelve strands).

FIG. 49: The *Lanyard Knot with Spritsail Sheet* (four strands) is tied by first making the Lanyard Knot (PLATE 60, FIG. 131). Then bring the ends up and form a Spritsail Sheet Knot on top of it.

FIG. 50: The *Lanyard Knot with Spritsail Sheet* (six strands).

FIG. 51: The *Lanyard Knot with Spritsail Sheet* (eight strands) is formed by first joining a four-strand rope together to form a bight, and then proceeding as before.

FIG. 52: The *Crown and Wall Stopper Knot* (three strands).

FIG. 53: The *Crown and Wall Stopper Knot* (four strands).

FIG. 54: The *Crown and Wall Stopper Knot* (six strands).

FIG. 55: The *Crown with Lanyard Wall Underneath* (three strands).

FIG. 56: The *Crown with Lanyard Wall Underneath* (four strands).

FIG. 57: The *Crown with Lanyard Wall Underneath* (six strands).

FIG. 58: The *Lanyard Crown with Lanyard Wall* (three strands).

FIG. 59: The *Lanyard Crown with Lanyard Wall* (four strands).

FIG. 60: The *Lanyard Crown with Lanyard Wall* (six strands).

FIG. 61: The *Lanyard Wall with Plain Crown* (four strands).

FIG. 62: The *Lanyard Wall with Lanyard Crown* (three strands).

FIG. 63: The *Lanyard Wall with Lanyard Crown* (four strands).

FIG. 64: The *Lanyard Wall with Lanyard Crown* (six strands).

FIG. 65: The *Lanyard Wall with Lanyard Crown* (eight strands) begins with a plain Crown Knot, in order to give body to the knot. The Lanyard Wall is made underneath it. Then make the Lanyard Crown on top, draw the turns taut, and cut the ends off close to the knot.

FIG. 66: The *Three-Strand Crown and Six-Strand Lanyard Wall* is made as follows: first, seize together the ends of a three-strand rope, and unlay the ends; take up one strand and skip one; pick up the next one, then skip the next, and so on until three strands have been picked up. Make a Crown with these three, and then tie a Lanyard Wall Knot underneath with all six strands. Draw the knot up taut, and cut the ends off close.

FIG. 67: The *Four-Strand Crown and Eight-Strand Lanyard Wall* is made in the same way as FIG. 66, except that four strands are picked up instead of three.

FIG. 68: The *Six-Strand Crown and Twelve-Strand Lanyard Wall* has six strands picked up for the Crown.

Plate 57—Diamond, Star, and Pineapple Knots

FIGS. 69A and B: The *Long Diamond Knot* (three strands) is begun by unlaying the rope for a sufficient length and crowning the end. Then work a Diamond Knot on the rope, under the Crown, with the knot reversed, so that after the knot is tied the strands will be lying down along the standing part of the rope, instead of being on top of the knot and clear of the rope. The tying of the knot can be simplified by forming it well down on the standing part of the rope, and working it up to the end near the Crown. Another Diamond Knot is then worked on in the usual manner (with the strands pointing up) just below the first Diamond Knot. This will bring the strands out in the middle of the knot, as shown in the illustration. Next, the strands are followed around in the ordinary way until two passes have been made. The knot is then pulled up taut and the strands cut off short. The drawn line indicates where the first

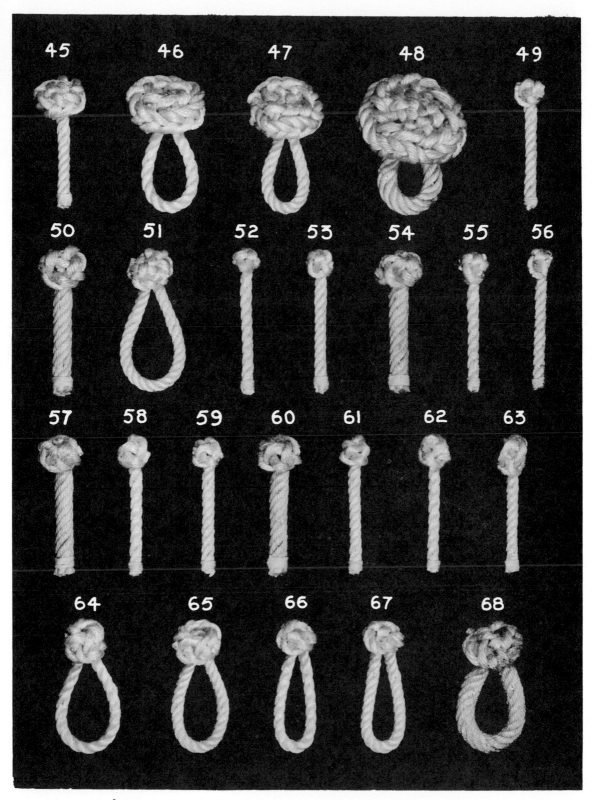

PLATE 56—SENNIT ROSE AND LANYARD KNOTS

strand is to be tucked. The Long Diamond Knot is shown complete in FIG. 69B.

FIG. 70: The *Long Diamond Knot* (four strands).

FIG. 71: The *Long Diamond Knot* (six strands).

FIG. 72A: The *Double Pineapple Knot* (four strands) is tied as follows: the rope is first whipped about two and one-half feet from the end; then the rope is unlaid to the whipping and a Crown made a short distance from the whipping, as shown in the illustration. The drawn line indicates where the next tuck is to be placed. Each strand in turn is then tucked through a bight in its proper place.

B: After two or more tucks have been put in each strand, they are brought from the left to the right under the nearest strand, and then followed up to double the knot.

C: When the knot has been doubled and the strands are again at the bottom of the knot, they are brought up through the center and trimmed off short, or left in a long tassel. This illustration shows the knot complete.

FIG. 73: The *Double Pineapple Knot* (three strands).

FIG. 74: The *Double Pineapple Knot* (six strands).

FIG. 75: The *Chair Rose Knot* (three strands) begins with a Diamond Knot. Follow around to double it. Then draw it up in such a way that it will be flat when pulled taut. Next, make another Diamond Knot. Follow around in the usual manner to double it, and then draw the knot taut in such a way that it will be round when finished.

FIG. 76: The *Chair Rose Knot* (four strands).

FIG. 77: The *Chair Rose Knot* (six strands).

FIG. 78A: The *Star Knot* (six strands) is made by first whipping the rope about two and one-half feet from the end, and unlaying it to the whipping. A Lanyard Wall should next be made as a base on which to form the knot, although this illustration omits the Lanyard Wall in order to make the knot appear less complicated. The strands are first placed in the position shown, with all the strands coming out on top (*see* strand *a*). The next step is to form a Crown, with all the ends coming out at the bottom of the knot. When forming the Crown, each strand is tucked through a loop, as is strand *b*. The line shows how to tuck strand *c*, which follows *b*. (Notice that each strand is tucked on the inside of the next strand when tucking through the loop.) Strand *a* is next tucked in the same fashion as strand *c*.

B: When all the strands have been tucked down, they are brought up again through the next loop, as is strand *a*. The arrow shows how strand *b* should be tucked in order to arrive at the position of *a*. When all the strands are again facing upward, they are tucked in the manner indicated by the arrow on strand *a*.

C: Strand *c* has been tucked like strand *a*, as explained in FIG. 78B. When all the strands have been tucked in this fashion, they are then brought around and tucked in the direction of the arrow. Strand *c* will now be in the position of strand *b*. Next, strand *a* is taken, first tucked like strand *c*, and then like strand *b*. The work is finally drawn up taut and the ends cut off short on top of the knot.

D: This shows the finished knot.

FIG. 79: The *Star Knot* (four strands).

FIG. 80: The *Star Knot* (three strands).

Plate 58—Star, Diamond, and Shroud Knots

FIG. 81: The *Star Knot* (five strands) begins with a length of three-strand rope, which is taken, middled, and seized. The

rope is next unlaid at both ends, forming six strands. A Lanyard Wall Knot is made with five strands, the sixth coming up

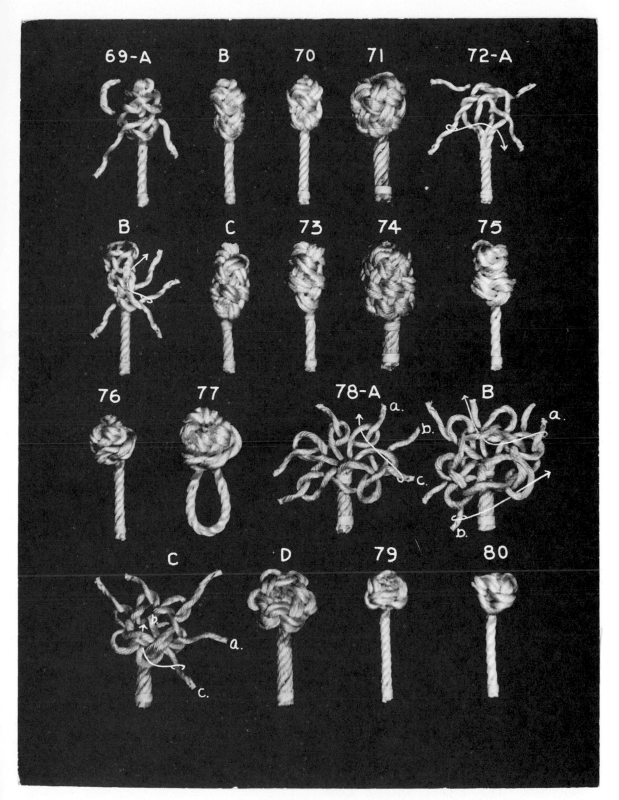

PLATE 57—DIAMOND, STAR, AND PINEAPPLE KNOTS

through the center of the Lanyard Knot and being cut off. Then proceed as in the regular Star Knot, PLATE 57, FIG. 78).

FIG. 82: The *True Star Knot* (three strands) is made in exactly the same manner as the regular Star Knot, except when the last tuck is being made before passing the strand under the two strands and up through the center of the knot. The strand is half hitched through the first loop, as shown, and is then put under the two strands and up through the center.

FIG. 83: The *True Star Knot* (four strands).

FIG. 84: The *True Star Knot* (five strands).

FIG. 85: The *True Star Knot* (six strands).

FIG. 86A: The *Variated Long Diamond Knot Doubled* (three strands) is made in the same way as the Pineapple Knot, PLATE 57, FIG. 72. However, instead of being made on top and clear of the rope it is made on the standing part of the rope. Begin by making a Crown. Then wind the strands down along the standing part of the rope in a direction contrary to the lay of the rope. After two complete turns have been taken, the strands are woven back through their own parts. This is begun by placing the strands in the position shown.

B: When the strands have been woven back to the top of the knot, as shown in this illustration, they are then brought back down and the weave doubled in the customary manner.

C: This shows the knot after it has been doubled and the ends cut off. It is now in its finished form.

FIG. 87: The *Variated Long Diamond Knot Doubled* (four strands).

FIG. 88: The *Variated Long Diamond Knot Doubled* (six strands).

FIG. 89A: The *Danish Shroud Knot Served* (three strands) is a type of knot that was used in the days before the introduc-

tion of wire-rigging to repair shrouds that had been shot away in action. Its particular advantage lies in the fact that it forms a neat, strong knot and requires very little rope. To make it, first unlay the ends of each rope for a sufficient length. Then marry them (PLATE 88, FIG. 78A shows how to "marry" two rope ends). With a piece of sail twine, take one or two turns about the ropes where they join, to hold both together until the knot is complete. (This procedure is not absolutely necessary, but simplifies the work a great deal.) Then form a Crown Knot on each side, as shown in this illustration. Take strands *a* and *b,* which have not yet been tucked, and tuck them under one strand of the opposite Crown, as indicated. The pair of strands, *c* and *d,* which have already been tucked are next tucked, followed by strands *e* and *f* which have not yet been tucked. After all the strands have been tucked in their proper places, the knot is drawn up taut simply by pulling each strand.

B: After the knot has been drawn taut, the strands are opened up, scraped to a taper, and marled down to the standing parts of each rope. The finished knot will then appear as in this illustration. The Shroud Knot is so pretty and ingenious that it is a pleasure to know it, even though there is practically no need for it in modern rope work.

FIG. 90: The *Danish Shroud Knot Spliced* (four strands) is begun by using the same method employed for the three-strand rope. Instead of marling the strands down, they are spliced into the standing parts of each rope.

FIG. 91: The *Danish Shroud Knot* (six strands) has the strands cut off close after the knot is made. Although this method has a neat appearance, it is not quite as secure as the other two methods of finishing off this knot.

FIG. 92: The *American Shroud Knot*

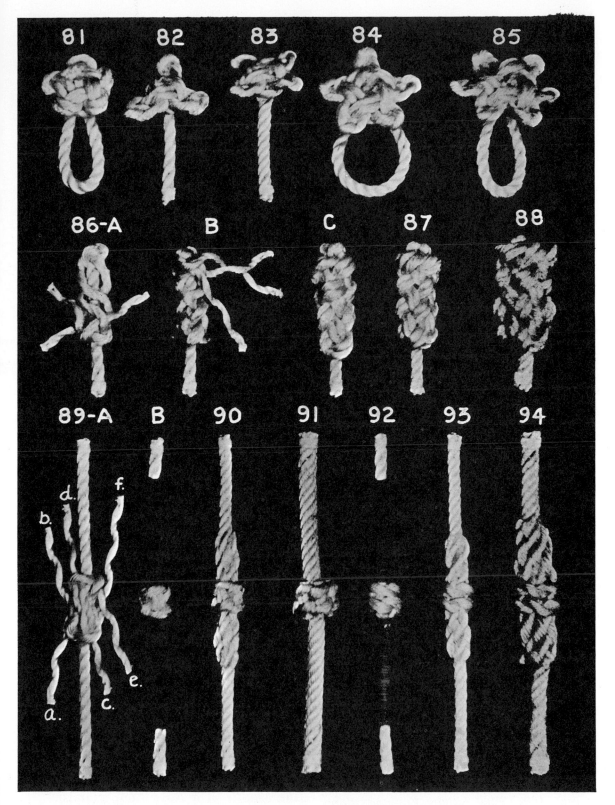

PLATE 58—STAR, DIAMOND, AND SHROUD KNOTS

Served (three strands) is made as follows: unlay the rope for a suitable length, and marry the ends; then form a Wall Knot on each side with each set of three strands, the strands going with the lay. The ends are then scraped, tapered, and marled down.

FIG. 93: The *American Shroud Knot Spliced* (four strands) is made in the same manner as the preceding knot. It has four strands, however; and the strands are spliced into the standing parts.

FIG. 94: The *American Shroud Knot Spliced* (six strands) is similar to FIG. 93.

NOTE: Some authors on the subject of knotting claim that in making this Shroud Knot the strands should be laid against the lay of the rope when forming the Wall Knot. Yet they give no basis for this claim. Commodore Luce, in his text-book for the United States Naval Academy at Annapolis, and Captain Felix Reisenberg, in his *Standard Seamanship,* form this knot in the way illustrated here, with the strands running with the lay of the rope. The authors of the present volume cannot see any special advantage or disadvantage in either of these methods.

Plate 59—Miscellaneous End Rope Knots

FIG. 95: The *Variated Star Knot* (three strands) somewhat resembles the Star Knot shown in PLATE 57, FIG. 80. To make it, begin in the same way as FIG. 78A. Instead of making only one loop, give the strand an additional turn, making two loops. Put the strands through both loops, but instead of putting them from the top down, put them from the bottom up. Take one strand and put it down through the center of the knot, around, and up through both loops once more, then down through the center of the knot again. This procedure is followed throughout with each strand. When all the strands have been properly tucked, the entire knot is drawn up taut and the strands cut off short.

FIG. 96: The *Variated Star Knot* (four strands).

FIG. 97: The *Variated Star Knot* (six strands).

FIG. 98: The *Single Variated Long Diamond Knot* (three strands) is formed in the same manner as the knot in PLATE 58, FIG. 86. Instead of doubling the knot, it is left with just one pass.

FIG. 99: The *Single Variated Long Diamond Knot* (four strands).

FIG. 100: The *Single Variated Long Diamond Knot* (six strands).

FIG. 101: The *Single Pineapple Knot* (three strands) is made in the same way as the Double Pineapple Knot shown in PLATE 57, FIG. 72, but with one pass rather than two. The strands are brought up through the center of the knot in an identical manner.

FIG. 102: The *Single Pineapple Knot* (four strands).

FIG. 103: The *Single Pineapple Knot* (six strands).

FIG. 104: The *Lanyard Wall Knot in the Middle of a Rope* (three strands) is made as follows: first, unlay the rope to the center (or a short distance from the end, whichever is desired), and form a Lanyard Wall Knot; then proceed to lay up the strands again, and place a whipping on the end.

FIG. 105: The *Lanyard Wall Knot in the Middle of a Rope* (four strands).

FIG. 106: The *Double Matthew Walker Knot in the Middle of a Rope* (three strands) follows the same method outlined in the two preceding knots; however, instead of tying a Lanyard Knot, a Matthew Walker is made (*see* PLATE 53, FIG. 5).

FIG. 107: The *Matthew Walker Knot in the Middle of a Rope* (four strands).

FIG. 108: The **Lanyard Wall Knot**

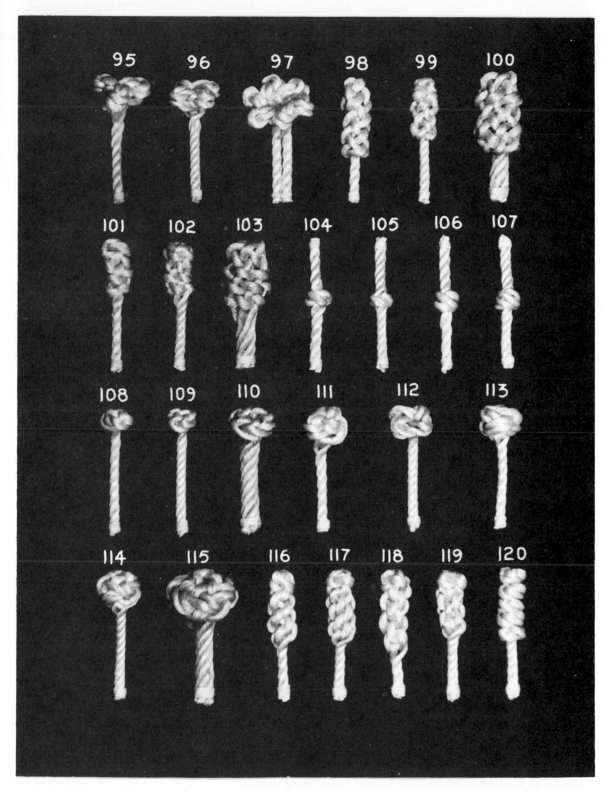

PLATE 59—MISCELLANEOUS END ROPE KNOTS

Crowned (three strands) is begun with a Lanyard Wall Knot. Before drawing it up taut, make a Crown on top of the Lanyard Knot, and bring the strands down through the body of the latter. Pull the Lanyard Knot taut first, then the Crown.

FIG. 109: The *Lanyard Wall Knot Crowned* (four strands).

FIG. 110: The *Lanyard Wall Knot Crowned* (six strands).

FIG. 111: The *Flat Diamond Knot* (three strands) is formed by first placing a whipping on the rope a sufficient distance from the end. Then tie a Diamond Knot, and draw it up so that it will lie flat on top when taut.

FIG. 112: The *Flat Diamond Knot* (four strands).

FIG. 113: The *Turk's Head Rose Knot* (three strands), in order to give it body, has three Crown Knots made one on top of the other, after the strands have been unlaid. Then form a Diamond Knot and double it. When drawing this knot up taut, the turns must be pushed out toward the end of the rope, as the knot has a tendency to slip back over the standing part of the rope below the Crowns. If this occurs, the knot will become flabby and lack the proper body.

FIG. 114: The *Turk's Head Rose Knot* (four strands).

FIG. 115: The *Turk's Head Rose Knot* (six strands).

FIG. 116: The *Spiral Crowning* (three strands) is made as follows: unlay the rope for a suitable length, and crown it; then continue crowning until the desired length of the knot is attained. Keep in mind that the Crowns are all made in the same direction, counter-clockwise.

FIG. 117: The *Spiral Crowning* (four strands).

FIG. 118: The *Alternate Crowning Knot* (three strands) is formed by first unlaying the rope and tying a Crown to the left, or counter-clockwise. Then form another Crown to the right, or clockwise. Continue this procedure, alternating the Crowns, one to the right and one to the left, until the desired length of the knot is reached.

FIG. 119: The *Alternate Crowning Knot* (four strands).

FIG. 120: The *Continuous Lanyard Walling* (four strands) begins with a Lanyard Knot, after the rope has been unlaid for a sufficient length. Draw the Lanyard Knot taut, and form another on top of the first one. This is continued until the desired number have been made.

Plate 60—Miscellaneous End Rope Knots

FIG. 121: The *Six-Strand Crown* is made exactly as the Three- or Four-Strand Crown, the only difference being in the number of strands used.

FIG. 122: The *Six-Strand Wall* is identical to the Three- or Four-Strand Wall, except that it uses six strands.

FIG. 123: The *Three-Strand Double Crown* is tied in the same way as the Single Crown, except that the strands are followed around and doubled.

FIG. 124: The *Three-Strand Double Wall* is the Single Wall, doubled.

FIG. 125: The *Four-Strand Double Crown*.

FIG. 126: The *Four-Strand Double Wall*.

FIG. 127: The *Six-Strand Double Crown*.

FIG. 128: The *Six-Strand Double Wall*.

FIG. 129: The *Six-Strand Matthew Walker* is tied in the same manner as the Three-Strand Matthew Walker.

FIG. 130: The *Four-Strand Matthew Walker*.

FIGS. 131A and B: The *Three-Strand Lanyard* or *Single Matthew Walker* is tied

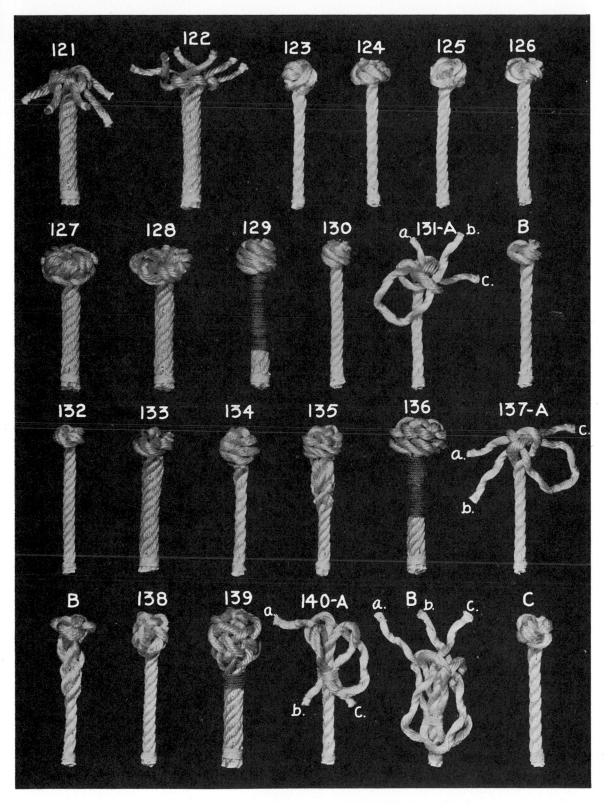

PLATE 60—MISCELLANEOUS END ROPE KNOTS

by first making a Wall Knot, then passing each strand up through the bight of the following strand and pulling taut. Strand *b* (FIG. 131A) is passed up through the bight of strand *a*. Strand *c* will go through the bight of strand *b*. And strand *a* will go through the bight of strand *c*. This is a very good knot to use as a base for other knots, as it pulls up neatly and holds fast. FIG. 131B shows how the knot looks when pulled up.

FIG. 132: The *Four-Strand Lanyard* is tied in the same manner as the Three-Strand Lanyard.

FIG. 133: The *Six-Strand Lanyard.*

FIG. 134: The *Three-Strand Rose Crown Lanyard* is tied as follows: first, make a Lanyard Knot; then a Rose Crown (illustrated in FIG. 137) is placed on top.

FIG. 135: The *Four-Strand Rose Crown Lanyard.*

FIG. 136: The *Six-Strand Rose Crown Lanyard.*

FIGS. 137A and B: The *Three-Strand Rose Crown* begins with an ordinary Crown. Then pass each strand over the next strand and out through its own bight. FIG. 137A shows strand *b* passed over strand *a* and out through its own bight as described above. FIG. 137B shows the knot as it looks when pulled up.

FIG. 138: The *Four-Strand Prolonged Crown* is tied in the same way as the Three-Strand Rose Crown, except that it has an additional tuck up in order to make the knot more secure.

FIG. 139: The *Six-Strand Prolonged Crown* resembles the other already described, except that the ends have been tucked up and passed out through the middle on top of the knot.

FIGS. 140A, B, and C: The *Three-Strand Single Diamond* should be begun by seizing the strands in the manner shown, as the knot will then be much easier to tie. Strand *a* is passed over the bight of *c* and through the bight of *b*, as shown in FIG. 140A. Strand *c* is next passed over the bight of *b* and through the bight of *a*. Then strand *b* is passed over the bight of *a* and through the bight of *c*. The knot will then appear as in FIG. 140B. FIG. 140C shows the knot as it looks when pulled up.

Plate 61—Combination End Rope Knots

FIGS. 141A and B: The *Three-Strand Double Diamond* starts with a Single Diamond Knot. Next, follow around and double the next strand leading down, as shown in FIG. 141A. Then follow and double the same strand leading up through the center of the knot. Continue this same method with the other strands until the knot is completely doubled. FIG. 141B shows the finished knot.

FIG. 142: The *Four-Strand Single Diamond.*

FIG. 143: The *Four-Strand Double Diamond.*

FIG. 144: The *Six-Strand Single Diamond* is made the same as the three-and four-strand methods. This also applies to all other six-strand knots that are reproductions of the same type of knot in a three- or four-strand rope.

FIG. 145: The *Six-Strand Double Diamond.*

FIG. 146: The *Single Diamond and Single Prolonged Crown* (three strands).

FIG. 147: The *Double Diamond and Double Prolonged Crown* (three strands).

FIG. 148: The *Single Diamond and Single Prolonged Crown* (four strands).

FIG. 149: The *Double Diamond and Double Prolonged Crown* (four strands).

FIG. 150: The *Single Diamond and Single Prolonged Crown* (six strands).

FIG. 151: The *Double Diamond and*

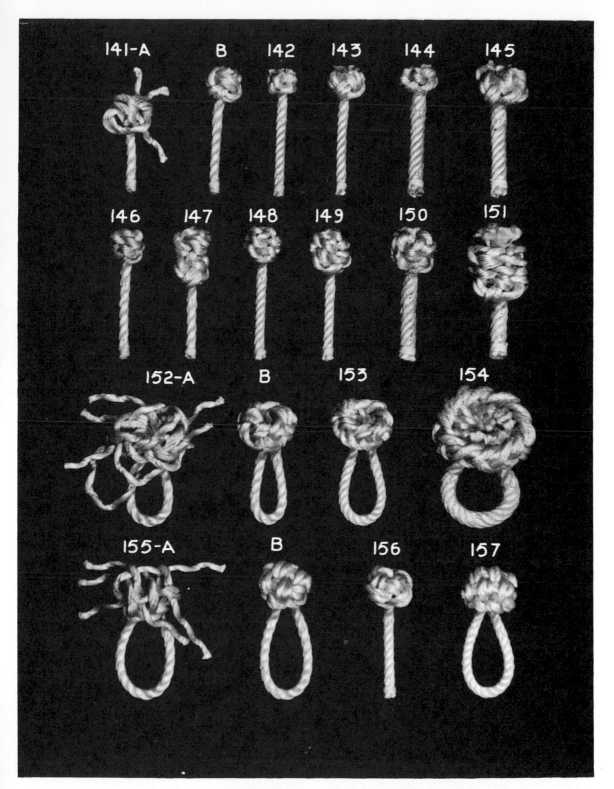

PLATE 61—COMBINATION END ROPE KNOTS

Double Prolonged Crown (six strands) is tied in the same way as the others, but with an additional tuck up to bring the ends out through the middle.

FIGS. 152A and B: *The Six-Strand Double Wall and Crown* is formed as follows: first, make a Wall Knot; then crown it and double around. FIG. 152A shows how the strands are followed around and doubled after tying the Crown Knot. FIG. 152B shows the knot as it looks when pulled up taut after being doubled.

FIG. 153: The *Eight-Strand Double Wall and Crown.*

FIG. 154: The *Twelve-Strand Double Wall and Crown.*

FIGS. 155A and B: The *Six-Strand Spritsail Sheet Knot* is made by first seizing the

strands together and tying a Wall Knot. When this has been done, take one strand from each side and lay in opposite directions over the body of the knot. Then close the knot up by alternately going over and under these two strands from each side with the remaining strands. FIG. 155A shows how the knot will then appear. Now follow around and double the Wall on the bottom, and continue by following and doubling the same strands through the top. Pull the knot up taut and it will appear as in FIG. 155B. In the old sailing-ship days, it was used in the clew of a sail as a Stopper Knot.

FIG. 156: The *Four-Strand Spritsail Sheet Knot.*

FIG. 157: The *Eight-Strand Spritsail Sheet Knot.*

Plate 62—Miscellaneous Wall and Crown Combinations

FIGS. 158A and B: The *Three-Strand Turk's Head Weave* is formed by passing each strand up under the second bight, after first making a Crown to begin the knot. FIG. 158A shows strand *a* passed under the second bight, or through its own part; and the other strands are tucked in the same fashion. FIG. 158B shows the knot as it appears when pulled up.

FIG. 159: *The Four-Strand Turk's Head Weave.*

FIG. 160: The *Six-Strand Turk's Head Weave.*

FIG. 161: The *Twelve-Strand Spritsail Sheet Knot.*

FIGS. 162A and B: The *Three-Strand Walled Crown* is made by passing each strand up under the first bight, after making a Crown. FIG. 162A shows strand *a* passed through the bight of *c*. Then pass strand *b* through the bight of *a*, and strand *c* through the bight of *b*. Pull the knot tight, and it will appear as in FIG. 162B.

FIG. 163: The *Four-Strand Walled Crown.*

FIG. 164: The *Six-Strand Walled Crown.*

FIG. 165: The *Three-Strand Lanyard with Prolonged Crown* is made the same as the regular Lanyard, with the Prolonged Crown added.

FIG. 166: The *Four-Strand Lanyard with Prolonged Crown.*

FIG. 167: The *Six-Strand Lanyard with Prolonged Crown.*

FIG. 168: The *Three-Strand Double Walled Crown* is a Single Walled Crown, doubled.

FIG. 169: The *Four-Strand Double Walled Crown.*

FIG. 170: The *Six-Strand Double Walled Crown.*

FIG. 171: The *Three-Strand Half-Doubled Walled Crown* is made by doubling only half of the knot, or the walled part.

FIG. 172: The *Four-Strand Half-Doubled Walled Crown.*

FIG. 173: The *Six-Strand Half-Doubled Walled Crown.*

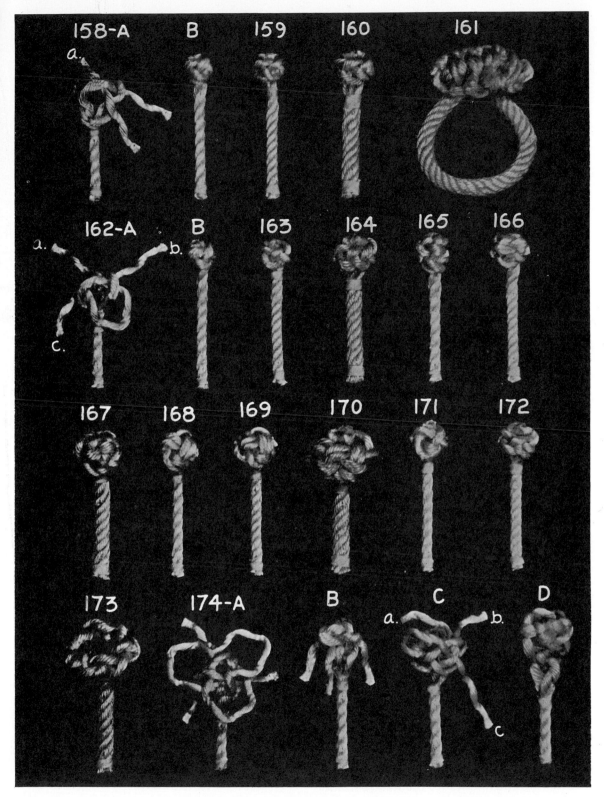

PLATE 62—MISCELLANEOUS WALL AND CROWN COMBINATIONS

FIGS. 174A, B, C, and D: The *Three-Strand Diamond Rose* is begun by making a base of two Crowns, one on top of the other. Then make a Rose Crown, which is shown opened up in FIG. 174A. Pull this up taut and it will appear as in FIG. 174B. Now make a Walled Crown (PLATE 62, FIG. 162A) around the body of the knot, with all three strands, and pull them up snug. Split the weave, as shown in FIG. 174C, by pulling each following strand out enough to make another tuck down with the working strand, which is represented here as strand *c*. It is passed under strand *b*. Then strand *b* is passed under strand *a*, after pulling it out enough to tuck underneath. Strand *a* in turn would be passed under strand *c* in the same manner. Now pull the knot up neat and taut, and it will appear as in FIG. 174D, after being spliced into the rope.

Plate 63—Rose Diamond and Shroud Knot Combinations

FIG. 175: The *Four-Strand Diamond Rose* follows the three-strand method.

FIG. 176: The *Six-Strand Diamond Rose*.

FIG. 177: The *Four-Strand Rose Crown* is made in the same way as the three-strand form of this knot, illustrated in PLATE 60, FIG. 137.

FIG. 178: The *Six-Strand Rose Crown*.

FIGS. 179A, B, C, and D: The *Three-Strand French Rose* has the same body as the Diamond Rose. Make a Wall around the body (FIG. 179A), and pull up snug. Pass each strand down through the bight of the following strand, as shown in FIG. 179B, with strand *c* passed down through the bight of strand *b*. Strand *a* is then passed down through the bight of strand *c*, and strand *b* is passed through the bight of strand *a*. After pulling the knot up, tuck each strand up under the following strand, which is pulled out through the weave in the same manner as for a Diamond Rose, except that you are tucking up instead of down. Continue to pass the working strand under the strand above it, which makes two strands it has been passed under. After completing this pass with all strands, pass the strands down again in the same way by pulling each following strand out and tucking under it, as in the Diamond Rose. The knot will now appear as it does in FIG. 179C. Draw up neat and tight and splice the ends into the rope, and it will appear as in FIG. 179D. This is one of the most beautiful of all the Rose Knots.

FIG. 180: The *Four-Strand French Rose* is made in the same way as the three-strand method.

FIG. 181: The *Three-Strand Star Shroud* is formed by marrying the strands together, and tying two Star Knots back-to-back.

FIG. 182: The *Four-Strand Star Shroud*.

FIG. 183: The *Six-Strand Star Shroud*.

FIG. 184: The *Three-Strand Single Lanyard Shroud* consists of two Lanyards shrouded back-to-back.

FIG. 185: The *Four-Strand Single Lanyard Shroud*.

FIG. 186: The *Six-Strand Single Lanyard Shroud*.

Plate 64—Wall, Crown, and Matthew Walker Knots

FIG. 187: The *Three-Strand Prolonged Rose Crown* is formed as follows: first, make a Rose Crown, as shown in PLATE 60, FIG. 137; then take an additional pass over the next strand and under the second strand, with each one in turn, until all tucks are made. Pull the knot up taut.

FIG. 188: The *Four-Strand Prolonged Rose Crown*.

FIG. 189: The *Six-Strand Prolonged Rose Crown*.

FIG. 190: The *Six-Strand Single Manrope* or *Single Wall and Crown Knot* begins

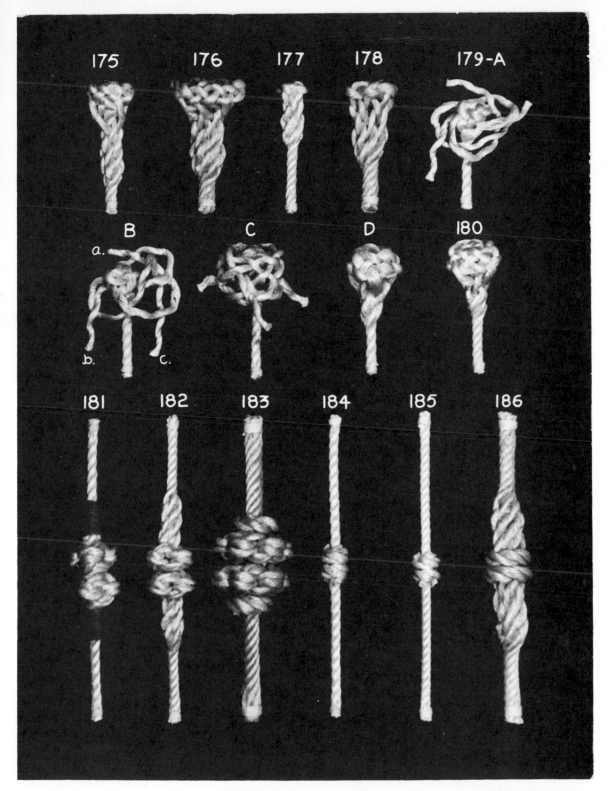

PLATE 63—ROSE, DIAMOND, AND SHROUD KNOT COMBINATIONS

with a Wall, which is crowned the same as for a Double Manrope Knot. It is then pulled up and spliced in, to make it hold taut.

FIG. 191: The *Three-Strand Diamond Crown* starts with a Crown Knot. Instead of passing each strand out under one, they are passed out under two strands, and then tucked up under the bottom strand, which is brought out from underneath by splitting the other strands, as for a Diamond Rose.

FIG. 192: The *Four-Strand Diamond Crown*.

FIG. 193: The *Six-Strand Diamond Crown*.

FIG. 194: The *Three-Strand Left-Hand* or *Back Wall Knot* is tied by walling to the right, or against the lay of the rope, instead of the usual method of walling to the left with the lay of the rope. A whipping should be used on the rope after unlaying the strands.

FIG. 195: The *Four-Strand Left-Hand* or *Back Wall Knot*.

FIG. 196: The *Six-Strand French Rose Knot* is tied the same way as the three- or four-strand method. Care should be taken in drawing the strands up even, as this knot is very difficult to draw up in the proper shape.

FIGS. 197A and B: The *Three-Strand Inverted Wall* is begun in the same way as a Three-Strand Star Knot, by forming an inside bight with each strand and then tucking the end of each strand through the following bight of the next strand, as shown in FIG. 197A. Pull taut, and the knot will appear as in FIG. 197B.

FIG. 198: The *Four-Strand Inverted Wall*.

FIG. 199: The *Three-Strand Button Knot* is tied as follows: first, make an Inverted Wall Knot; then make a Wall around the body of this knot and pass the ends up through the top of the knot and cut the ends off short to finish.

FIG. 200: The *Four-Strand Button Knot* is made by first tying an Inverted Wall. Then put a Wall around it, and crown the top. After crowning, pass the ends down through the Wall and up through the crown, and cut off short.

FIG. 201: The *Three-Strand Diamond Rose with Lanyard* begins with a Diamond Rose, made as shown in PLATE 62, FIG. 174. Then form a Lanyard Knot on top.

FIG. 202: The *Four-Strand Elongated Matthew Walker* (two passes) is tied the same as the three-strand method shown in PLATE 54, FIG. 7.

Plate 65—Round Turn and Chequer Knots

FIG. 203: The *Single Chequer Knot with Lanyard Knot* (eight strands) is a very pretty design, but its uses are limited to bell lanyards or manropes, etc. Although the knot appears difficult to make, it is in reality quite simple. The knot shown is made with eight strands, but it can also be made with any even number, from four upward. To begin, take a suitable length of four-strand rope, and form a bight in the middle. Put a seizing on a short distance from the end of the bight in order to form a small loop. Unlay the ends to the seizing, and form a Lanyard Wall Knot. A core or heart must

next be made. This can be done by making a ball out of spun-yarn, Marline, or by using some round object, such as a wooden ball. This heart is placed in the center of the Lanyard Knot, inside all of the strands. The strands are then brought up and a Spritsail Sheet Knot made on top of the ball. A Lanyard Wall Knot is used to finish off the ends.

FIG. 204: The *Double Chequer Knot with Round Turn Knot* is formed in the same fashion as the preceding knot, up to the point where the Lanyard Wall Knot is

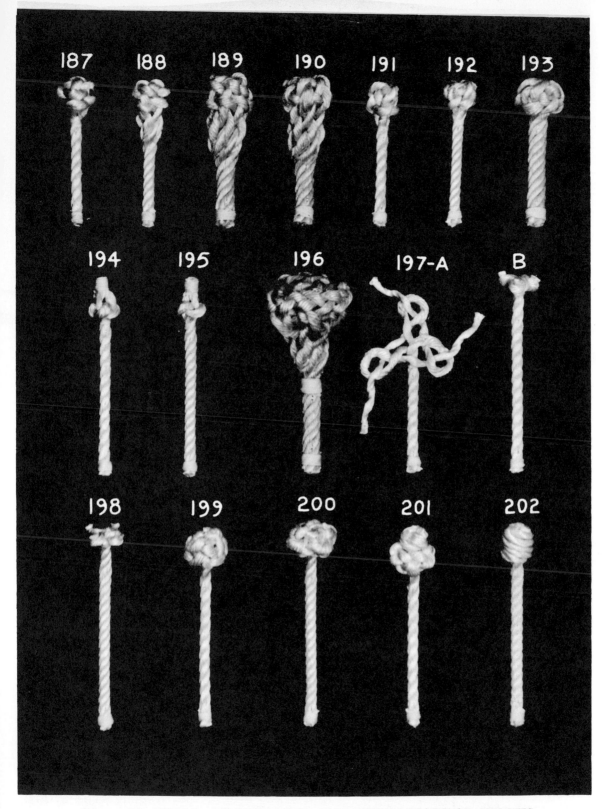

PLATE 64– WALL, CROWN, AND MATTHEW WALKER KNOTS

to be made. Then instead of making the Lanyard Wall, tie a plain Wall and follow the Spritsail Sheet Knot around to double it. When all the strands have been doubled and pulled up taut, the ends are cut off close to finish.

FIG. 205: The *Double Chequer Knot with Turk's Head* is similar to the knot in FIG. 204. But instead of cutting off the ends after doubling the Spritsail Sheet Knot, a Diamond Knot is formed and the ends followed around to double it. After drawing the knot taut, cut the ends off short.

FIG. 206: The *Double Chequer Knot with Star Knot* has the Spritsail Sheet Knot doubled, then a Star Knot formed with the ends as in PLATE 57, FIG. 78. Draw taut, and trim the ends to finish.

FIGS. 207A and B: The *Round Turn Knot* (four strands) is made as follows: put a whipping on the rope a suitable distance from the end, and unlay the strands; tie a Crown Knot, but do not draw it down taut. The Crown is formed to the left, or counter-clockwise. Then under it, or down toward the standing part of the rope, tie a Wall Knot, but in the opposite direction, or to the right. Next, bring the strands up to follow the Crown Knot, thereby doubling the Crown. The strand is then brought around to the left, under both crown strands, and up through the center of the knot, as indicated by the drawn line in FIG. 207A. FIG. 207B shows the finished knot, drawn up taut, with the ends cut off short.

FIG. 208: The *Round Turn Knot* (six strands) bears a remarkable resemblance to the Star Knot (PLATE 57, FIG. 78D).

FIG. 209: The *Eight-Strand Round Turn Knot with Lanyard Knot* is made in the same manner as the preceding knot; but instead of cutting off the ends at the top of the knot, a Lanyard Wall Knot is made, drawn taut, and the ends cut short.

FIG. 210: The *Three-Strand Crown Diamond Knot* is begun by unlaying the strands for a suitable length, and forming a Diamond Knot (PLATE 60, FIG. 140). Then before doubling it, instead of following the strand next to it, skip one strand and follow the next strand. Draw the knot taut, and cut the strands off close.

FIG. 211: The *Four-Strand Crown Diamond Knot* is made in the same way as the preceding knot; but the strands are brought up through the center of the knot, rather than being cut off as they come out from under the crossing strands.

FIG. 212: The *Six-Strand Crown Diamond Knot* is similar to the knot in FIG. 211. Instead of bringing the strands out in the center of the knot, they are cut off close as they come out from the crossing turns.

FIG. 213: The *Six-Strand Star Knot with Lanyard Knot* is made in the same manner as the Star Knot shown in PLATE 57, FIG. 78; however, instead of cutting off the strands on top of the knot, a Lanyard Wall Knot is first tied before the strands are trimmed.

Plate 66—Turk's Head Weave and Shroud Knots

FIG. 214: The *Three-Strand Turk's Head Weave Shroud Knot* is formed as follows: unlay the ends of each rope a short distance, and marry them; then tie the knot illustrated in PLATE 62, FIG. 158, with the three strands on one side; turn the work around and form another knot with the remaining three strands of the other rope; splice all six strands into the standing parts to finish.

FIG. 215: The *Four-Strand Turk's Head Weave Shroud Knot*.

FIG. 216: The *Six-Strand Turk's Head Weave Shroud Knot*.

FIG. 217: The *Three-Strand Interlocking Crown Shroud Knot* is made by first unlaying the strands and marrying them. Then form a Crown with each pair of

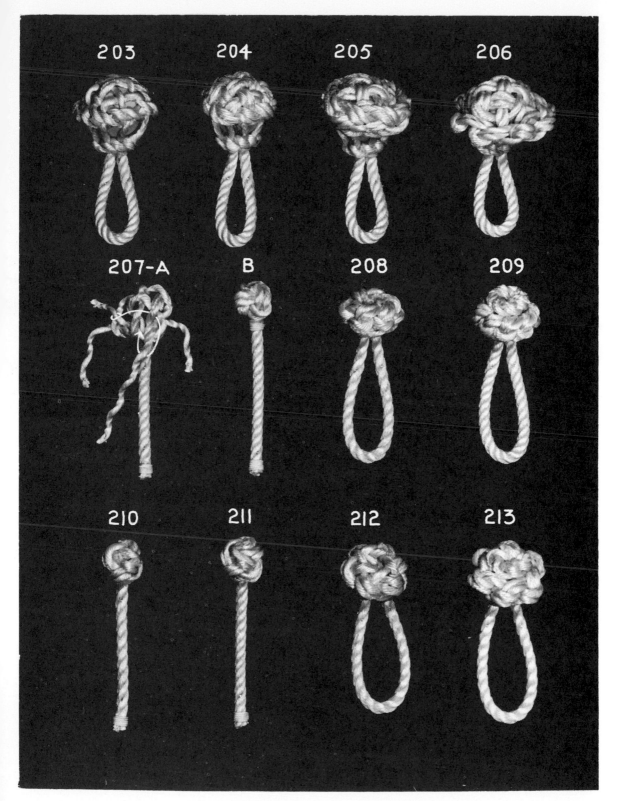

PLATE 65—ROUND TURN AND CHEQUER KNOTS

strands. Next, take the strands on the right side and follow the strands on the left side, until half of the knot is doubled. Then take the strands on the left side and follow the Crown on the right side, until the other half is doubled. The strands will now all be in the middle of the knot. To finish, the knot is drawn up taut, and the strands cut off close.

FIG. 218: The *Four-Strand Interlocking Crown Shroud Knot.*

FIG. 219: The *Six-Strand Interlocking Crown Shroud Knot.*

FIGS. 220A and B: The *Three-Strand Single Clipper-Ship Shroud Knot* may seem to have a complicated explanation; but if the illustration is carefully followed, it will be found to be really simple. The two ropes are married, and a temporary whipping is placed around the part where they join, to hold them in place until the knot is formed. The strands of one rope are laid back on their own part, thereby forming three bights. These strands are designated as *a, b,* and *c.* For the sake of convenience in illustrating, they have been seized to the standing part of one rope. Strand *d* of the other

rope is then taken over strand *b* and up to the right, through the bight formed by strand *c.* Strand *e* is next taken over strand *c,* and then up through the bight formed by strand *a.* The same process is repeated for the third strand. After all the strands have been properly tucked, the knot is pulled up taut and each pair of strands spliced into the standing parts of their respective ropes. FIG. 220B shows the finished knot.

FIG. 221: The *Four-Strand Single Clipper-Ship Shroud Knot.*

FIG. 222: The *Three-Strand French Shroud Knot* is begun by marrying both ropes and forming a Crown on each side. Next, bring the strands of the Crown on the right over the Crown on the left, and splice them into the standing part. Then take the strands of the Crown on the left over the Crown on the right, and splice them into the standing part.

FIG. 223: The *Four-Strand French Shroud Knot.*

FIG. 224: The *Six-Strand French Shroud Knot.*

Plate 67—Miscellaneous Shroud Knots

FIG. 225: The *Three-Strand Double Matthew Walker Shroud* is made by first marrying the ropes. Then a Matthew Walker Knot (PLATE 53, FIG. 5) is tied on each side. The knots are both drawn taut and the strands spliced into the standing parts.

FIG. 226: The *Four-Strand Double Matthew Walker.*

FIG. 227: The *Six-Strand Double Matthew Walker* is made in the same manner as the two preceding knots. Additional care must be taken in drawing the Matthew Walker taut when six or more strands are used.

FIG. 228: The *Three-Strand Sennit Shroud Knot* is made by first marrying the

strands, then forming the Sennit Knot shown in PLATE 55, FIG. 33.

FIG. 229: The *Four-Strand Sennit Shroud Knot.*

FIG. 230: The *Six-Strand Sennit Shroud Knot.*

FIG. 231: The *Three-Strand Double Manrope Shroud Knot* is formed in the same way as the Manrope Knot. First, make a Wall, then a Crown, and follow the ends around until the knot has been doubled.

FIG. 232: The *Four-Strand Double Manrope Shroud Knot.*

FIG. 233: The *Six-Strand Double Manrope Shroud Knot.*

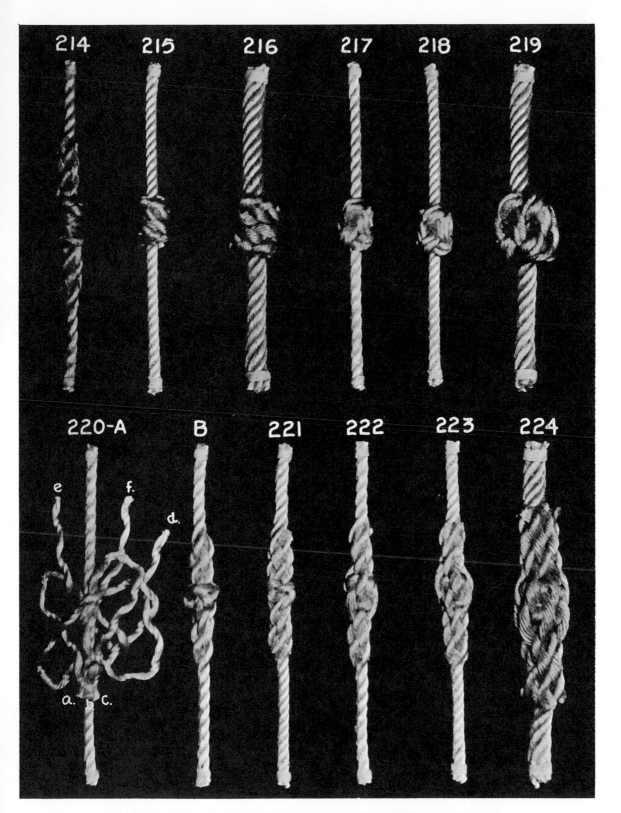

PLATE 66—TURK'S HEAD WEAVE AND SHROUD KNOTS

FIG. 234: The *Three-Strand Interlocking Pineapple Shroud Knot* is made as follows: after marrying the strands, form a Crown in each side, but do not draw them down taut; then bring each strand over one and under the next one, as in the knot shown in PLATE 57, FIG. 72, but instead of making several tucks, make only one. The strands of the knot on the right are brought over to follow the strands of the knot on the left, until the knot is half-doubled. The same process is repeated on the other side, until both sides are doubled. The knot is then drawn taut, and the strands cut off close.

FIG. 235: The *Four-Strand Interlocking Pineapple Shroud Knot.*

FIG. 236: The *Six-Strand Interlocking Pineapple Shroud Knot.*

Plate 68—Miscellaneous Shroud Knots

FIG. 237: The *Six-Strand Single Clipper-Ship Shroud* is made in the same way as the knot illustrated in PLATE 66, FIG. 220.

FIG. 238: The *Three-Strand Outside Matthew Walker Shroud Knot* is similar to PLATE 54, FIG. 18.

FIG. 239: The *Four-Strand Outside Matthew Walker Shroud Knot.*

FIG. 240: The *Six-Strand Outside Matthew Walker Shroud Knot.*

FIGS. 241A and B: The *Pineapple Mouse Knot* can be used either as a decorative covering for a short splice, or as a handle on the shrouds or stays of a small boat. If a splice is not made, build up a mouse with pieces of rag. After the mouse has been constructed to the desired thickness, cover it completely by marling it down. Then take two long pieces of Marline, and put one of them through the center of the rope near the end. Pull it through until there is the same amount of Marline on each side. Put the other piece through the center of the rope, but at right angles to the first piece, and pull this through until the middle of it is reached. There are now four ends of Marline, each protruding from a different point of the rope. The Marline is next brought up to the end of the mouse, and a temporary seizing placed on the rope and the four ends of Marline. A Crown is then made with them, and they are brought down to the lower end of the mouse spirally, as shown in the illustration. When the bottom of the mouse is reached, the cords are again crowned and woven alternately over and under against the spiral. This will lock the strands. When the top of the mouse has been reached, the temporary seizing is cut off and the ends are followed around three or four times (more, if desired). FIG. 241B shows how the knot will look when finished.

FIG. 242: The *Three-Strand Royal Crown Shroud Knot* shown is made in the same way as the Royal Crown Knot in PLATE 54, FIG. 24. The ends are then spliced into the standing parts.

FIG. 243: The *Four-Strand Royal Crown Shroud Knot.*

FIG. 244: The *Three-Strand Triple Clipper-Ship Shroud Knot* resembles the Single Clipper-ship Shroud in PLATE 66, FIG. 220, but three passes are made instead of only one.

FIG. 245: The *Four-Strand Triple Clipper-Ship Shroud Knot.*

FIG. 246: The *Three-Strand Reverse Hitched Shroud Knot* is made by first marrying the strands. Next, tie an Overhand Knot in each pair of strands, draw them up taut, and pull each standing part. The Overhand Knots will then topple and fall into position, after which the strands are spliced into the standing parts.

FIG. 247: The *Four-Strand Reverse Hitched Shroud Knot.*

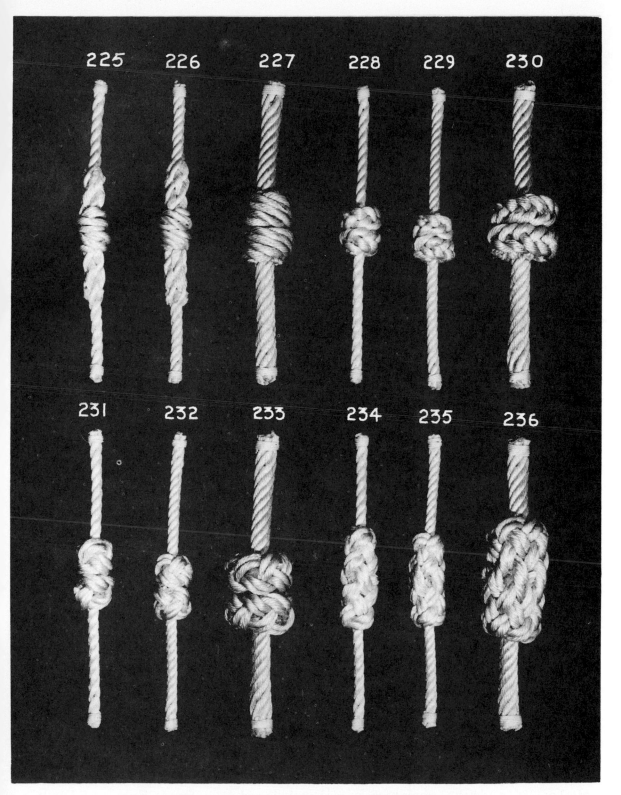

PLATE 67—MISCELLANEOUS SHROUD KNOTS

Plate 69—Miscellaneous Shroud Knots

FIG. 248: The *Three-Strand Double Stopper Shroud* is made by marrying the strands together and tying two Double Stopper Knots back-to-back. This knot is also shown in PLATE 54, FIG. 13.

FIG. 249: The *Four-Strand Double Stopper Shroud.*

FIG. 250: The *Six-Strand Double Stopper Shroud.*

FIG. 251: The *Three-Strand Double Lanyard Shroud* is made as shown in PLATE 60, FIG. 131.

FIG. 252: The *Four-Strand Double Lanyard Shroud.*

FIG. 253: The *Six-Strand Double Lanyard Shroud.*

FIG. 254: The *Three-Strand Quadruple Wall Shroud* consists of two Walls on each side back-to-back. Pull taut and splice the ends.

FIG. 255: The *Four-Strand Quadruple Wall Shroud.*

FIG. 256: The *Six-Strand Quadruple Wall Shroud.*

FIG. 257: The *Three-Strand Single Diamond Shroud* has two Diamond Knots (PLATE 60, FIG. 140) tied back-to-back, after marrying the ropes together.

FIG. 258: The *Four-Strand Single Diamond Shroud.*

FIG. 259: The *Six-Strand Single Diamond Shroud.*

Plate 70—Miscellaneous Shroud Knots

FIG. 260: The *Three-Strand Double Diamond Shroud* is made as follows: unlay the strands the required distance; then marry them in the usual manner. Put a temporary seizing on to hold them together, which is necessary in making nearly all types of Shrouds until the first knot is formed. Then tie two Stopper Knots back-to-back, and pull taut.

FIG. 261: The *Four-Strand Double Diamond Shroud.*

FIG. 262: The *Six-Strand Double Diamond Shroud.*

FIG. 263: The *Three-Strand Walled Crown Shroud* has two knots tied back-to-back to form the Shroud. These knots are the same as shown in PLATE 62, FIG. 162.

FIG. 264: The *Four-Strand Walled Crown Shroud.*

FIG. 265: The *Six-Strand Walled Crown Shroud.*

FIG. 266: The *Three-Strand Diamond Rose Shroud* has its Rose Knots formed back-to-back as shown in PLATE 62, FIG. 174.

FIG. 267: The *Four-Strand Diamond Rose Shroud.*

FIG. 268: The *Six-Strand Diamond Rose Shroud.*

FIG. 269: The *Three-Strand Double Clipper-Ship Shroud* consists of knots made the same as for the regular Clipper-Ship Shroud, except that they are doubled.

FIG. 270: The *Four-Strand Double Clipper-Ship Shroud.*

FIG. 271: The *Six-Strand Double Clipper-Ship Shroud.*

Plate 71—Miscellaneous End Rope Knots

FIG. 272: The *Combination Knot,* First Method, is made by combining several knots to form one large one. The first knot from the top down is a Six-Strand Wall fol-

lowed around. The next is a Star Knot, followed by a Sennit Knot, and finally a Diamond Knot. As each separate knot is tied, it is pulled taut before beginning the

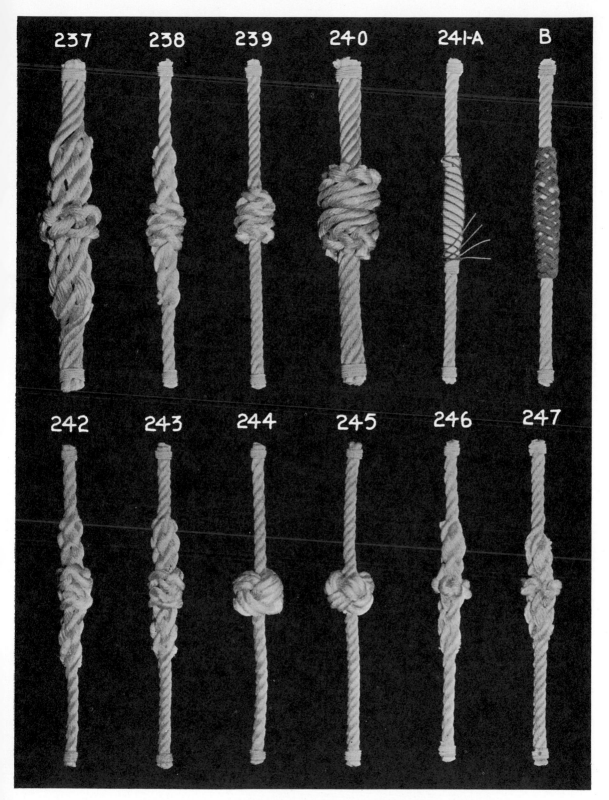

PLATE 68—MISCELLANEOUS SHROUD KNOTS

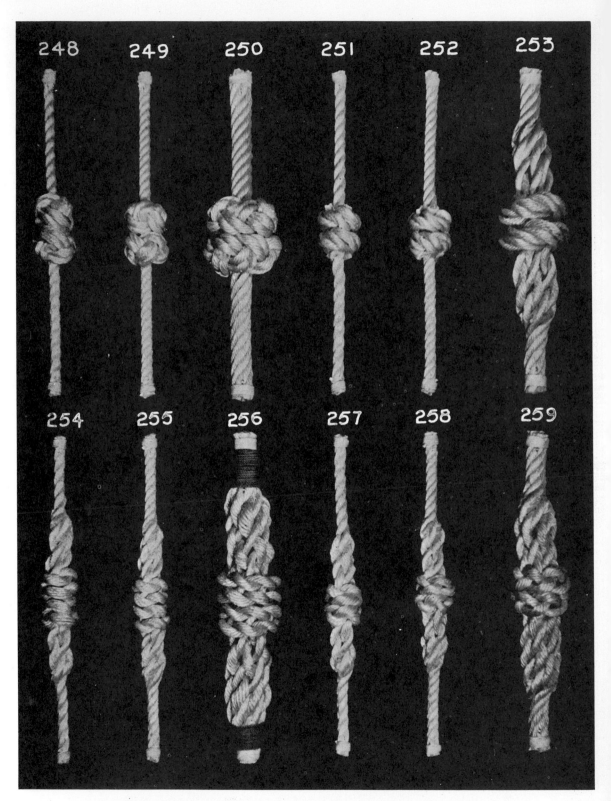

PLATE 69—MISCELLANEOUS SHROUD KNOTS

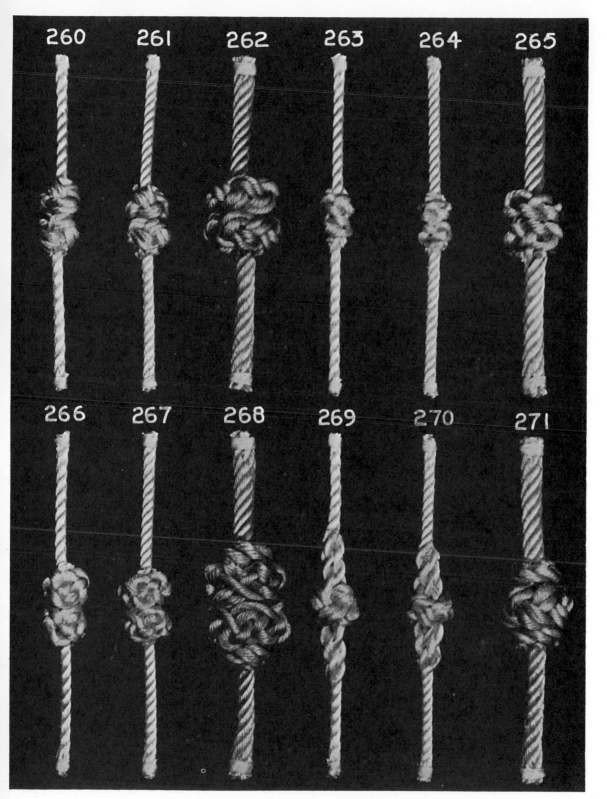

PLATE 70—MISCELLANEOUS SHROUD KNOTS

next one. After the Diamond Knot has been made and drawn up, the strands are opened, frayed out, and cut off about three or four inches from the Diamond Knot.

FIG. 273: The *Whale Eye Knot* makes a very attractive End Rope Knot of an ornamental character.

FIG. 274: The *Star Pineapple Knot* begins with a Star Knot. Then one series of crowns are made on top of another, gradually tapering the strands.

FIG. 275: The *Star Knot and Variated Cape Horn Rose Knot Combination.*

FIG. 276: The *Combination Knot,* Second Method, is tied as follows: first, make a Lanyard Wall and follow it around, thus doubling it; next, make a Star Knot. Then tie four Spiral Crown Knots, and finish the strands off by tying a Prolonged Crown Knot. They are then cut off a short distance from the end of the knot and frayed out.

FIG. 277: The *Monkey Fist End Rope Knot.*

FIG. 278: The *Spiral Crown Diamond Knot.*

FIG. 279: The *Variated Star Knot* begins with a Lanyard Crown Knot, which is left very loose. Pass each strand around the Lanyard Knot two times, as shown in the illustration. Bring each strand across the center of the knot. Then crown them and tuck them down through the center.

FIG. 280: Is a *Lamp-Stand Combination Design.*

FIG. 281: The *Variated Crowned Star Knot* closely resembles FIG. 279. Before making the final tuck, form a Crown Knot with the strands.

FIG. 282: The *Spritsail Sheet Star Knot* has the Star Knot and Spritsail Sheet Knot made simultaneously.

FIG. 283: The *Round Turn Interlocking Shroud Knot* should have the strands married very loosely. Then take a round turn with each strand around the nearest strand of the opposite rope, etc.

FIG. 284: The *Lanyard Star Pineapple Knot* is made by first tying a Lanyard Wall Knot and following it around. Then form a Star Knot, a Turk's Head Weave, and finally a Spritsail Sheet Knot.

FIG. 285: The *Sunflower Knot* is made with eight strands, and tied somewhat similar to the Star Knot.

FIG. 286: The *Toadstool Knot* is an ornamental design, embracing a Combination Reverse Crown base and Star Knot top.

FIG. 287: The *Spanish Rose Knot* is an ornamental knot. The method of forming it is too difficult to illustrate or explain, and any such attempt would only be confusing.

Plate 72—End Rope Knot Combinations

FIG. 288: The *Four-Strand Half Hitched Rose Knot* is formed by making a series of turns and Half Hitches.

FIG. 289: The *Lanyard Weave Knot* begins with a Lanyard Wall Knot. The strands are interwoven, finally coming out at the bottom. They are then put up through the knot, coming out at the top, and are cut off short to finish.

FIG. 290: The *Comb-Hanger Design* can be used in lieu of the knots of the Comb-Hangers illustrated in PLATE 230, FIGS. 7 to 9.

FIG. 291: The *Diamond Knot with Spiral Hitching* starts out with a Diamond Knot formed on the end of the rope. Then continuous crowning is put on the standing part of the rope below the knot, after it has been turned over. The ends are finished off by splicing them into the rope.

FIG. 292: The *Sennit Manrope Knot with Spritsail Sheet Crown* is tied as fol-

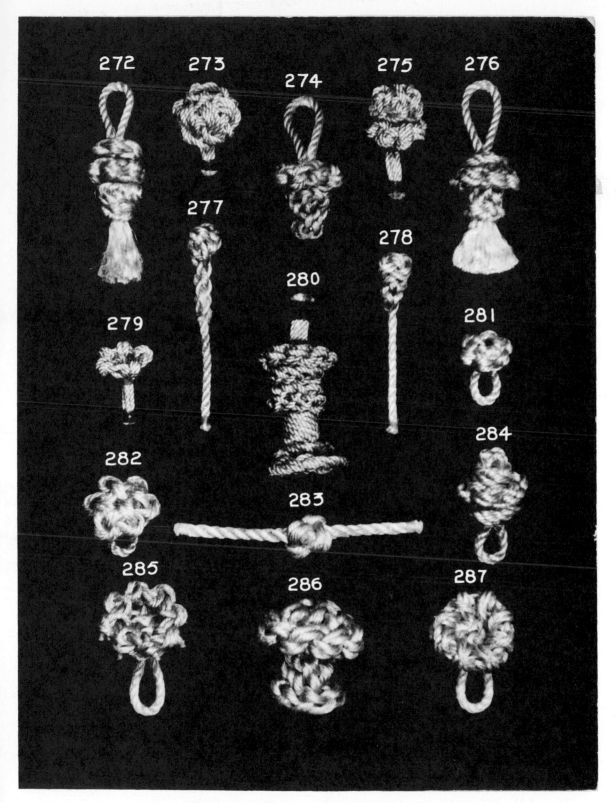

PLATE 71—MISCELLANEOUS END ROPE KNOTS

lows: first, make a Crown on the end of the rope; form the Manrope Knot and double it; the ends will now come out in the middle of the knot. They are next put under all the turns until they come out at the top. The Crown Knot made first on the end of the knot is then doubled, and the strands are again put down under the turns and spliced into the rope. The Manrope Knot made here is formed after the rope has been turned over, and is made on the standing part of the rope.

FIG. 293: The *Sennit Rose Knot with Inside and Outside Crowns* begins with a Crown. Then make the Sennit Rose Knot (PLATE 55, FIG. 33). Tie another Crown, tuck the strands through to the bottom of the knot, and cut them off short.

FIG. 294: The *Double Crowned and Single Walled Manrope Knot* has its strands spliced into the standing part of the rope.

FIG. 295: The *Star Knot and Cape Horn Rose Knot Combination*.

FIG. 296: The *Combination Cape Horn Rose and Sennit Rose Knot*.

FIG. 297: The *Spritsail Sheet with Lanyard Crown Doubled*.

FIG. 298: The *Variated Cape Horn Rose Knot*.

FIG. 299: The *Variated English Rose Knot* can be used for a drawer-handle by tying two knots on each side of the rope.

FIG. 300: The *Variated Manrope Knot*.

FIG. 301: Another *Variated English Rose Knot*, which does not follow the Half Hitches with the last tuck of the English Rose. Instead, another Half Hitch is formed, and the ends cut off short.

FIG. 302: The *Three Point Rose Knot* is made as follows: a Crown is first formed: the strands are brought through the knot from the right to the left, skipping one strand. They are then brought around the crown stand, and up to form another Crown on top. Finally, the knot is drawn taut and the strands cut off short.

FIG. 303: The *Spanish Manrope Knot* is similar to the ordinary Manrope Knot.

FIG. 304: The *Interlocking Hitched Knot* is made by taking a round turn with each strand on each adjacent strand and splicing the strands into the standing part.

FIG. 305: The *Variated Cape Horn Rose Knot* (four strands).

FIG. 306: The *Double Wall and Double Crown Rosette* (six strands).

FIG. 307: The *Interlocking Half-Hitched Manrope Knot* (three strands).

FIG. 308: The *Alternate Crown Hitched Knot* is begun by placing several Crowns on the end of the rope to build up body for the knot. Next, form a Crown Knot around the body to the left. Take each strand, bring it back to the right, and half-hitch it through the bight of the Crown. Then bring the strands back again to the left, and up and under the Crown. Draw the knot taut, and trim the ends.

Plate 73—End Rope Knot Combinations

FIG. 309: The *French Diamond Rosette* is similar to the French Diamond Rose.

FIG. 310: The *French Manrope* resembles the regular Manrope Knot (PLATE 238, FIG. 20).

FIG. 311: The *Turk's Head Rosette Spliced*.

FIG. 312: The *Star and Diamond Combination*.

FIG. 313: The *Danish Rose Knot*.

FIG. 314: The *Sennit Rosette*, First Method, is similar to the Sennit Rose Knot.

FIG. 315: The *Sennit Rose*, Second Method, is made by tying the Sennit Rose

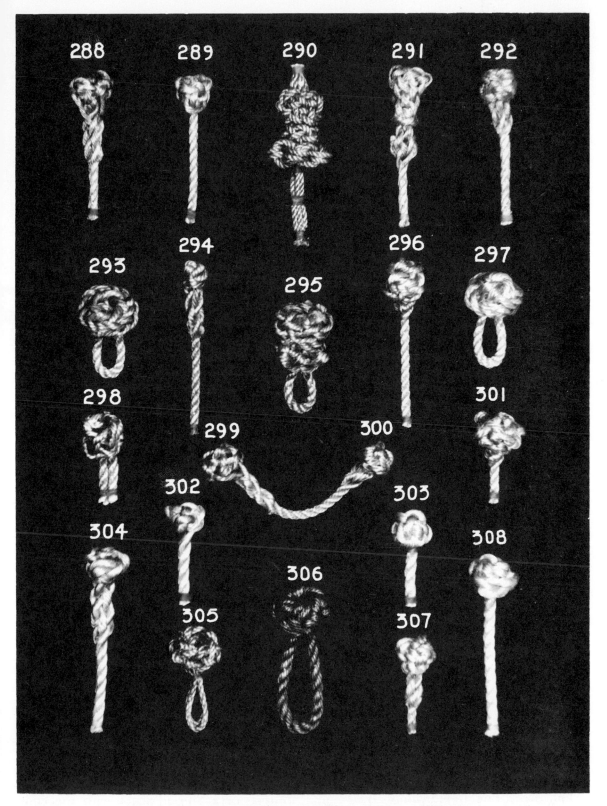

PLATE 72—END ROPE KNOT COMBINATIONS

Knot (PLATE 55, FIG. 33) and then drawing it taut, so that when finished it will lie flat.

FIG. 316: The *Turk's Head Rosette.*

FIG. 317: The *Lanyard Wall Doubled and Spritsail Sheet Knot.*

FIG. 318: The *Basket Knot* is a combination of the French, Diamond, and the Sennit Rose.

FIG. 319: The *Crown Weave Spliced.*

FIG. 320: The *Rose Crown Spliced.*

FIG. 321: The *Continuous Lanyard Crown Running Eye Knot.*

FIG. 322: The *Interlocking Japanese Rosette.*

FIG. 323: The *Three-Strand Variated Star Knot.*

FIG. 324: The *Raised Crown Sennit Rose Knot.*

FIG. 325: The *Cape Horn Rosette.*

FIG. 326: The *Diamond Head Monkey Fist.*

FIG. 327: The *Diamond Knot with Ends Combed Out.*

FIG. 328: The *Diamond Rosette.*

Plate 74—Miscellaneous End Rope Combinations

FIG. 329: The *Whaling Day Rose Knot* is similar to the French Rose (PLATE 63, FIG. 179), with the exception of an additional tuck over the next strand and under the second strand at the finish.

FIG. 330: The *Variated Tack Knot* is a slight variation of the Tack Knot.

FIG. 331: The *Interlocking Hitch Knot* is made as a Combination Lanyard, reverse hitch method.

FIG. 332: The *Combination English Rose* shows an English Rose made by joining two separate ropes.

FIG. 333: The *Combination Overhand Matthew Walker Crown Knot* is formed by combining a Crown with an Overhand Matthew Walker.

FIG. 334: The *Diamond Sennit Rose* represents a combination of a Diamond and a Sennit Rose Weave.

FIG. 335: The *French Rossette Knot* is a French Rose tied in the form of a Rosette.

FIG. 336: The *Basket Weave* is a Diamond Rose tied in the form of a Basket.

FIG. 337: The *Sennit Knot with Crown Weave* begins with a Sennit Knot. Then fill in the top with a series of Crowns.

FIG. 338: The *Combination Wall and Crown Weave* has the tucks interlacing.

FIG. 339: The *Combination Basket Weave* shows two separate ropes joined in the form of a Basket Weave.

FIG. 340: The *Variated Diamond Rose* is slightly different from the regular Diamond Rose, with the weave changed to form a Turk's Head type of design.

FIG. 341: The *Variated French Rose* differs slightly from the weave of the French Rose. In order to get a different type of knot, after becoming familiar with the basic formations of the more simple weaves, readers can easily form their own types of designs by using a combination of the various weaves.

FIG. 342: The *French Rose Crowned* has an additional Crown placed on top of the French Rose Weave and then tucked down and spliced in.

FIG. 343: The *Diamond Rose with Hollow Top* has the Diamond Rose Weave brought up over the body of the knot to form a hollow top.

FIG. 344: The *Variated Star Knot with Crown* shows a variation of a Star Knot, which is crowned and the ends passed down through the body of the knot.

FIG. 345: The *Hitched Shroud Knot* consists of a Shroud Knot with the ends hitched together.

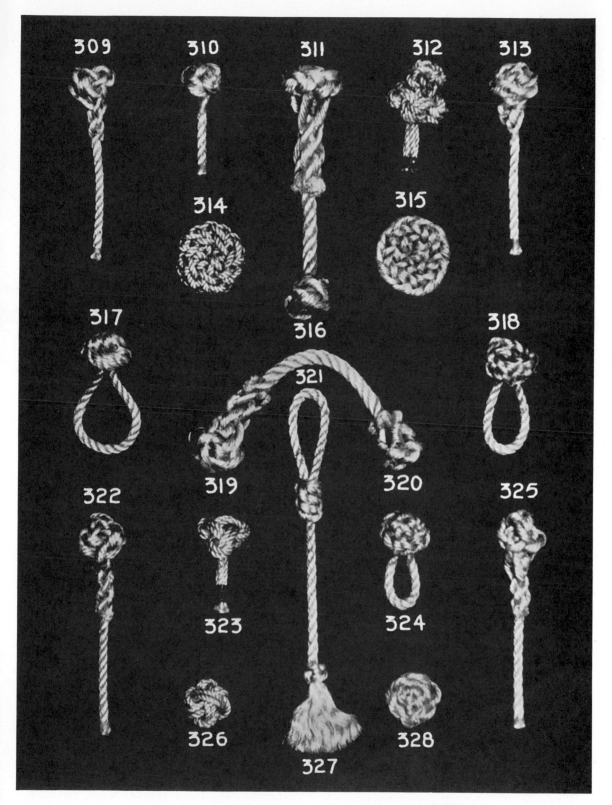

309 310 311 312 313
314 315
316
317 321 318
319 320
322 325
323 324
326 327 328

PLATE 73—END ROPE KNOT COMBINATIONS

FIG. 346: The *Lamp-Stand Design* is a combination of five different knots.

FIG. 347: The *Overhand Shroud Knot* consists of a Shroud Knot joined in the form of Overhand Knots.

FIG. 348: The *Open Basket Weave* is formed by using a Combination Lanyard and Diamond Rose Weave.

FIG. 349: The *Reverse Hitch Knot* is made up of a series of Hitches worked around in reverse form after first building a body of Crowns.

FIG. 350: The *Combination Sennit Knot* is a slight variation of the Sennit Knot, with the ends crowned over the top.

FIG. 351: The *Crowned Rose Knot* has a series of Crowns built first. Then a Wall Weave is passed around the body, crowned down through the body of the knot, and spliced in.

FIG. 352: The *Topsail Halyard Toggle* is a Manrope Knot formed in the opposite end of a spliced eye.

FIG. 353: The *Stopper Knot with Extra Crown* is a Stopper Knot with an additional Crown placed on top.

FIG. 354: The *Long Diamond Rose Bud* has a Long Diamond Weave shaped to form a hollow center.

FIG. 355: The *Diamond Rosette* shows a Diamond Rose tied in the form of a Rosette.

FIG. 356: The *Lock Tuck Crown Knot* has an additional Wall pass, which is then tucked down to lock the knot.

FIG. 357: The *Diamond Weave with Walled Crown Top* is tied by first joining the rope together leaving a small bight with a Lanyard Knot for a base. A Double Diamond Knot is formed. Then a Walled Crown is placed on top and finished off by tucking down through the body of the knot.

FIG. 358: The *Long Sennit Knot* is tied by forming a Sennit Knot with an additional Wall around the bottom.

FIG. 359: The *Lanyard Rose* is a Double Lanyard Knot tied in the form of a rose.

FIG. 360: The *Swivel Knot* is a Single Stopper placed on the opposite end of a series of Crowns.

Plate 75—Combination End Rope Knots

FIG. 361: The *Combination Eye* consists of a series of Crowns, then a Diamond, a Sennit, and a Lanyard Knot on top of each other, with a Spritsail Sheet Weave to finish off.

FIG. 362: The *Combination Walled Crown Knot* shows a Walled Crown Weave around the bottom of a Crown base.

FIG. 363: The *Weeping Willow Rose Knot* first has a base made the same as for any type of Rose Knot. Then the ends of the strands are opened up and frayed out, and a French Rose Weave is tied around the body of the knot.

FIG. 364: The *Stopper Knot Rosette* is a Stopper Knot tied in the form of a Rosette.

FIG. 365: The *Open Crown and Wall Weave in Eye.*

FIG. 366: The *Combination Star Knot* is tied with two separate ropes joined together.

FIG. 367: The *Hitched Rose Knot* is tied with a Diamond Rose Weave, and with each strand hitched through its own part.

FIG. 368: The *Combination Design with Frayed Ends* shows a Single Lanyard, Double Lanyard, and a Star Knot with the ends frayed.

FIG. 369: The *Matthew Walker Crown Knot* is a Matthew Walker Knot, crowned.

FIG. 370: The *Combination French and*

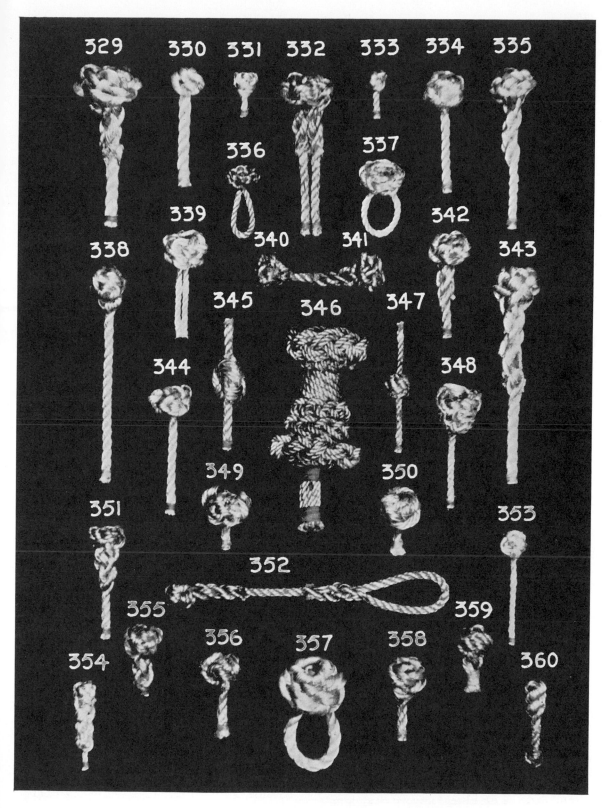

PLATE 74—MISCELLANEOUS END ROPE COMBINATIONS

Diamond Rose uses different weaves to achieve an unusual effect.

Fig. 371: The *Combination Rose Knot* is made with an additional Crown on top and by combining a Diamond and French Rose Weave.

Fig. 372: The *English Rose in Eye* is an English Rose Knot formed in an eye with frayed ends.

Fig. 373: The *Diamond Weave with Hollow Center* consists of a Diamond Weave tied on top of a Lanyard base to form a hollow center.

Fig. 374: The *Flower Knot* is tied as follows: five small ropes are seized together; each strand is opened up and the yarns separated. Then tie a Lanyard Knot for a base by using sets of three yarns each as an individual strand, which will make five working sets of three-yarn strands in all. Continue by tying a Wall around the body of the knot. Then pass each part down through the following part, and up under its own part, forming a Hitch with each set of yarns. The strands are cut off and frayed out to finish the knot.

Fig. 375: The *Portuguese Rose Knot* is a combination of a Lanyard, Matthew Walker, Diamond, and Long Diamond.

Fig. 376: The *Pineapple Knot with Frayed Ends* is a Pineapple Knot formed on a Lanyard base, with the strands frayed to finish off.

Fig. 377: The *Double Lanyard Crowned with Frayed Rope Ending*.

Plate 76—Combination End Rope Knots

Fig. 378: The *Crowned Star Knot* is a Star Knot crowned on top.

Fig. 379: The *Combination Crowned Lanyard Knot* consists of a Double Lanyard crowned on top, passed down, and spliced in.

Fig. 380: The *Cape Horn Rose Knot* is begun by making a body of Crowns. A Sennit Weave is formed around the body, and finished off with a Rose Crown on top. The strands are then tucked underneath the Sennit Weave and spliced in.

Fig. 381: The *Double Lanyard with a Double Rose Crown*.

Fig. 382: The *Double Walled Crown in Eye* is tied on a Lanyard base.

Fig. 383: The *Five-Fold Knot* is made up of a Lanyard, Triple Lanyard, Diamond, another Lanyard, and a Spritsail Sheet top.

Fig. 384: The *Baton Knot* consists of a Lanyard, Matthew Walker, Single Diamond, and a Double Lanyard and Single Diamond, with a Spritsail Sheet top.

Fig. 385: The *Two-Fold Knot* is a Lanyard and Diamond Rose Weave joined together.

Fig. 386: The *Heaving Mallet or Turk's Head Button*. A three-strand Turk's Head is first made. Next, leaving out a bight, take the other end, follow the first end around twice, making three passes in all. Draw the knot taut and cut the ends off short to finish.

Fig. 387: The *Combination Locked Hitch Knot* employs a Combination Rose Weave on top of a Lanyard base. Then the strands are locked under their own parts with a tucked hitch.

Fig. 388: The *Brush Knot* begins with ten small ropes seized together. Then a Lanyard Knot is formed, which is followed by a Diamond and a Walled Crown Weave. On top of this tie a loose Crown and tuck each strand down under the next part, then over the second part and in through the center, as in the Pineapple Knot. Fray all strands, and cut off.

Fig. 389: The *Star Knot with Sennit*

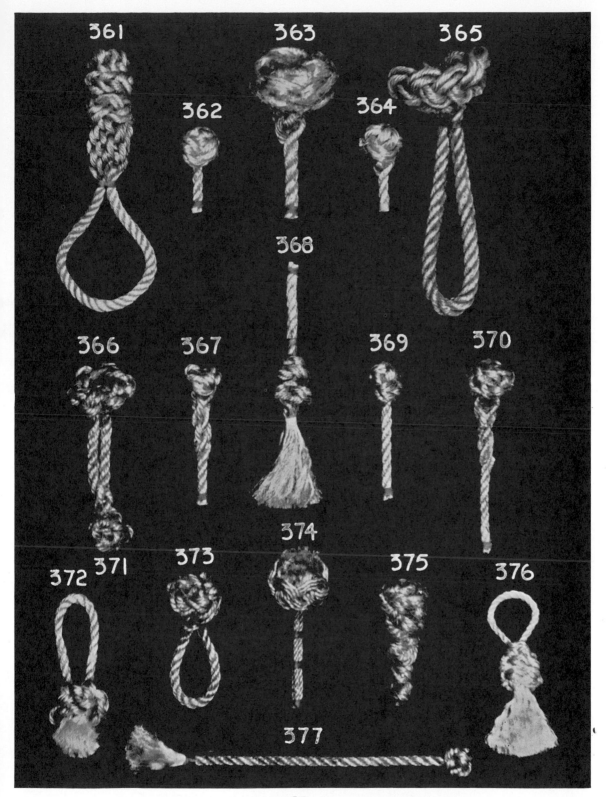

PLATE 75—COMBINATION END ROPE KNOTS

Top represents a Sennit Knot placed on top of an ordinary Star Knot.

Fig. 390: The *Triple-Passed Walled Crown.*

Fig. 391: The *Four-Fold Knot* shows a quadruple combination of a Walled Crown, Matthew Walker, another Walled Crown, and a Lanyard.

Fig. 392: The *Combination Double Crown and Wall Knot.*

Fig. 393: The *Combination Spritsail Sheet Knot* has a Lanyard base.

Plate 77—Combination End Rope Knots and Weaves

Fig. 394: The *Artichoke Knot* is a combination weave drawn up in the form of an artichoke.

Fig. 395: The *Variated Diamond Weave* is a variation of the ordinary Diamond Knot.

Fig. 396: The *Star Knot with Lanyard Top.*

Fig. 397: The *Combination Rosette* consists of a Double Wall and Crown Weave.

Fig. 398: The *Open Walled Crown with Lanyard.*

Fig. 399: The *Rose Weave with Spritsail Sheet Top* has six strands with two yarns comprising each strand.

Fig. 400: The *Combination Shroud Knot* has the strands doubled and the crowns formed with each group of strands interlocking.

Fig. 401: The *Rose Bud Knot* begins with three strands seized together and opened up into sets of three yarns each. Then a base knot is formed, after which the strands are crowned around and hitched up through their own parts.

Fig. 402: The *Variated Spritsail Sheet Knot* contains a variation of the single-passed weave.

Fig. 403: The *Hitched Fender Weave* has a hitched weave in eye.

Fig. 404: The *Variated Rose Knot* illustrates a slightly different weave in the form of a Rose Knot.

Fig. 405: The *Portuguese Man o' War Knot* is begun by first building up a body with a series of Crowns. Then a Diamond Knot and a Rose Knot Weave are tied, with a Triple-passed Crown on top.

Fig. 406: The *Combination Star with Spritsail Sheet Top.*

Fig. 407: The *Double Wall and Crown with Frayed Lanyard Top.*

Fig. 408: The *Double Combination Weave with Spritsail Sheet Finish.*

Fig. 409: The *Combination Lanyard Diamond Weave with Ends Frayed.*

Plate 78—Combination End Rope Knots and Weaves

Fig. 410: The *Crowned Turk's Head Weave* has a Rose Crown placed on a Double Turk's Head Weave, with the ends passed over the knot and spliced into the standing part.

Fig. 411: The *Variated Diamond Knot Weave.*

Fig. 412: The *Combination Star Knot Tassel* is tied with five strands joined together.

Fig. 413: The *Combination Crowned Lanyard Knot.*

Fig. 414: The *Sennit Knot with Rose Crown.*

Fig. 415: The *Double Stopper Knot with Rose Crown.*

Fig. 416: The *Interlocking Knot* consists of an Interlocking Crown and **Double Lanyard Weave.**

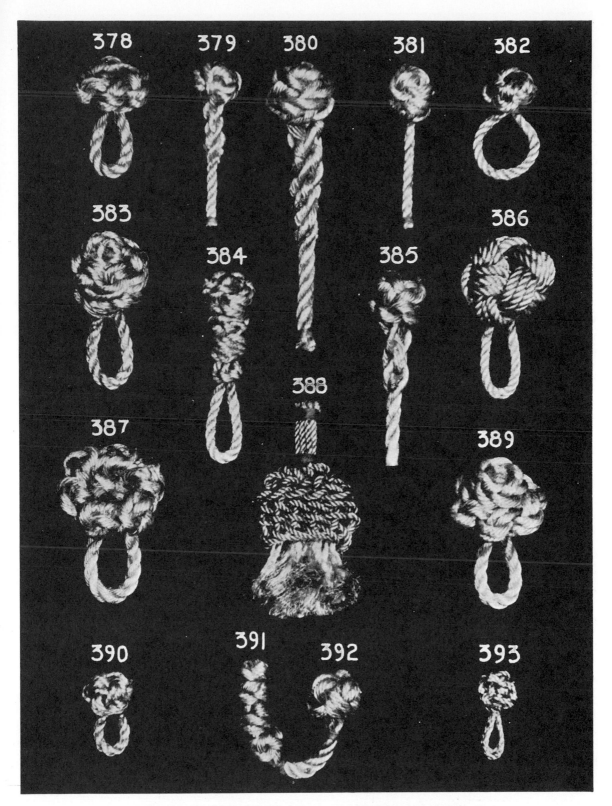

PLATE 76—COMBINATION END ROPE KNOTS

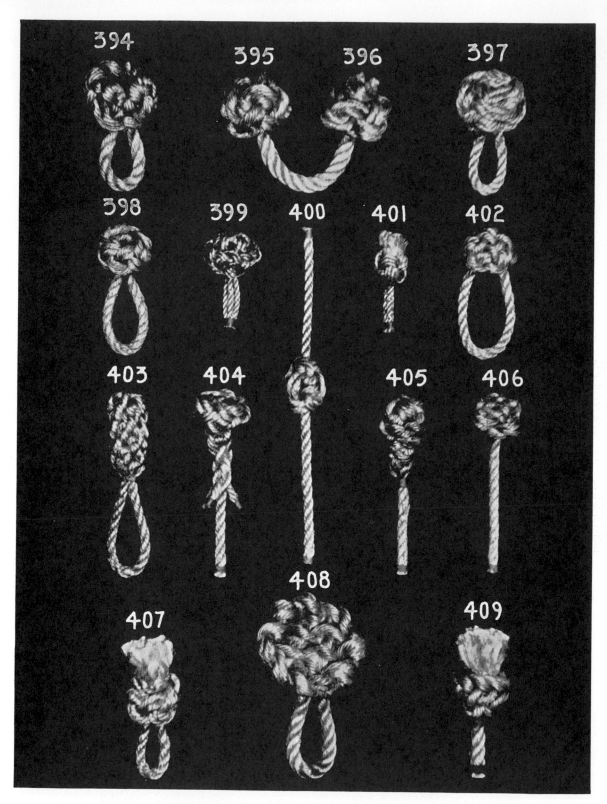

PLATE 77—COMBINATION END ROPE KNOTS AND WEAVES

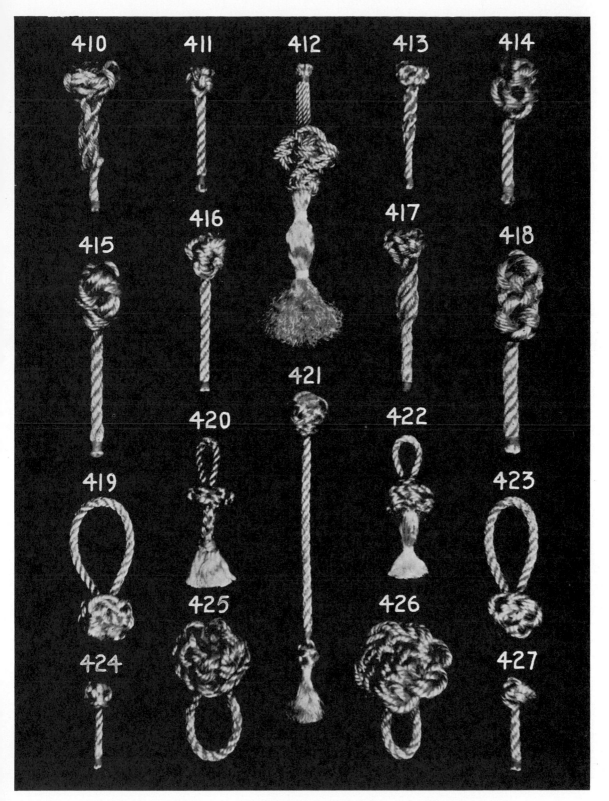

PLATE 78—COMBINATION END ROPE KNOTS AND WEAVES

FIG. 417: The *Variated Diamond Rose Weave with Spritsail Sheet Top*.

FIG. 418: The *Diamond Knot with a Series of Crowns*.

FIG. 419: The *Combination English and Sennit Rose Weave*.

FIG. 420: The *Star Knot with Ends Braided Out* is finished off with a Lanyard Knot, and frayed.

FIG. 421: The *Tulip Knot* is tied as follows: first, the body is built up with Crowns and covered with a Double Lanyard and Diamond; then the ends are opened up into separate yarns, and a Spritsail Sheet top is formed. The bottom design represents a frayed Diamond Knot.

FIG. 422: The *Double Lanyard with a Rose Weave and a Star Knot Heart and Frayed Ends*.

FIG. 423: The *Diamond Knot with Top Crowned Through*.

FIG. 424: The *Left-Handed Combination Walled Crown*.

FIG. 425: The *Combination Knot with Star Knot Heart*.

FIG. 426: The *Variated Star Knot Rosette*.

FIG. 427: The *Combination Lanyard Crown*.

Chapter IV

Rope Splicing

SPLICING HAS BEEN DEALT with heretofore in many different ways, but it has never been covered thoroughly until now. Like most of the other types of rope work it seems to have reached a certain stage and then never to have been developed or expanded any further.

Besides all the practical methods which are in common use there are presented in this chapter many universal examples, such as the Eight-Strand Braided Eye or Signal Halyard Splice, the Grecian Splice and various types of Halter Splices. Many examples of splicing have been carried out or extended from three to four and then six strands for the purpose of giving additional knowledge in the art of being able to splice all kinds of rope regardless of its type or the number of its strands.

Eye Splicing, Short Splicing and Long Splicing by both the regular and sailmaker's methods are explained and illustrated fully, as are the many other different examples of both practical and unusual types.

Plate 79—Three- and Four-Strand Eye and Back Splices

FIG. 1: The *Three-Strand Inverted Wall Eye Splice* is begun by making the first tuck of a Three-Strand Eye Splice. Then an Inverted Wall Knot (PLATE 64, FIG. 197) is tied around the standing part of the rope. The ends are spliced into the rope to finish off.

FIG. 2: The *Four-Strand Inverted Wall Eye Splice.*

FIG. 3: The *Three-Strand Double Manrope Eye Splice* begins with an Eye Splice tuck; then follows the regular Manrope Knot. This knot will lead out toward the eye on the last tuck; therefore the ends are cut off short, instead of being spliced in.

FIG. 4: The *Four-Strand Double Manrope Eye Splice.*

FIGS. 5A, B, and C: The *Three-Strand Back Splice* starts with a Three-Strand Crown. Then tuck each strand over the next strand and under the second strand, and pull taut. FIG. 5A shows the first tuck started, with strand *c* going over the first strand and under the second. FIG. 5B illustrates the second tuck, with strand *b* tucked in the same manner as strand *c*. Strand *a*

follows the same procedure. Make several tucks, and taper the splice down by splitting each strand in half for each remaining tuck. Then pull taut and trim all strands. FIG. 5C shows the splice as it will appear when finished.

FIGS. 6A and B: The *Four-Strand Back Splice* is made in the same way as the three-strand splice. FIG. 6A shows the Four-Strand Back Splice with the first set of tucks finished. FIG. 6B represents the completed splice.

FIGS. 7A, B, and C: The *Three-Strand Sailmaker's Back Splice* begins with a Crown, as in the regular splice. But instead of going over one and under one, each tuck is made over, around, and then under the next or following strand, which brings them out with the lay of the rope. FIG. 7A shows strand *b* tucked in this fashion. Strands *c* and *a* are tucked in the same way, until they take on the appearance of FIG. 7B. FIG. 7C shows the splice as it looks when pulled taut, tapered, and finished. This neat form of splicing is used by sailmakers for awnings.

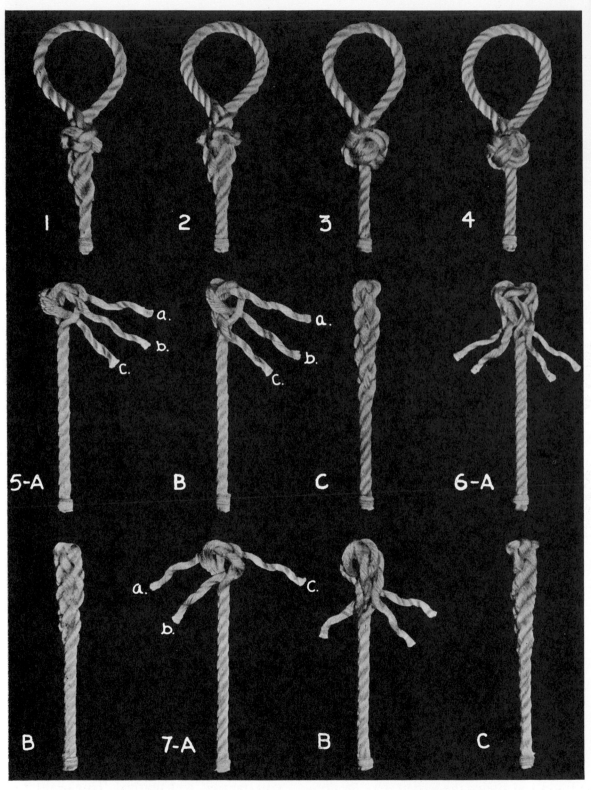

PLATE 79—THREE- AND FOUR-STRAND EYE AND BACK SPLICES

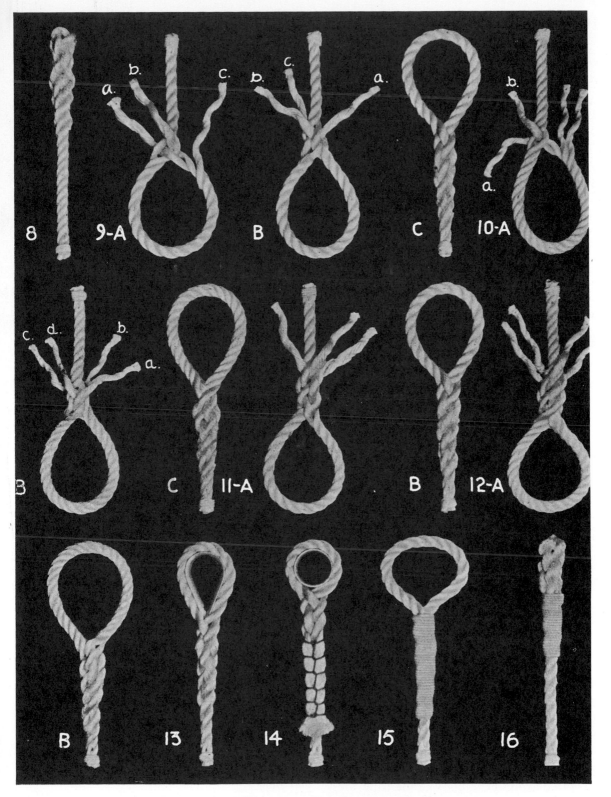

PLATE 80—MISCELLANEOUS EYE SPLICES

Plate 80—Miscellaneous Eye Splices

FIG. 8: The *Four-Strand Sailmaker's Back Splice.*

FIGS. 9A, B, and C: The *Three-Strand Eye Splice* is made as follows: unlay the rope a sufficient distance, and make an eye of the required size; tuck the bottom strand under one strand against the lay, and place the middle strand under the next strand in the same manner. Turn the splice over, and tuck the remaining strand as already described. Strands *a* and *b* are shown tucked in FIG. 9A. FIG. 9B shows the splice turned over, with strand *c* tucked. Tuck each strand a second time against the lay, over one and under one, and repeat as many more times as desired. After tapering down to finish off, the splice will appear as in FIG. 8C. This splice and all other splices can be rolled under the foot or hammered down to insure a neat, close-fitting job.

FIGS. 10A, B, and C: The *Four-Strand Eye Splice* is a repetition of the three-strand method, except at the beginning. The bottom strand is tucked under two strands, and the other strands are tucked under one each. Strand *a* in FIG. 10A is shown tucked under two strands as described, and strand *b* under one strand. Turn the splice over and tuck strands *c* and *d* accordingly. The splice will then appear as in FIG. 10B. Continue by tucking over one and under one against the lay, until the required number

of tucks have been made. FIG. 10C shows the splice as it looks when finished.

FIGS. 11A and B: The *Three-Strand Sailmaker's Eye Splice,* First Method, is begun by unlaying the rope and making the first tucks as though for the regular Eye Splice. Then continue by making the sailmaker's tucks as shown in FIG. 11A. When the required number have been made, taper down and cut the strands off short. FIG. 11B shows the splice as it appears when completed.

FIGS. 12A and B: The *Four-Strand Sailmaker's Eye Splice,* First Method, is made in the same way as the three-strand knot. FIG. 12A shows the splice with the first set of sailmaker's tucks completed. The finished knot is illustrated in FIG. 12B.

FIG. 13: The *Thimble Eye Splice* consists of a thimble spliced into an eye. It is used to prevent a hook from chafing the rope.

FIG. 14: The *Round Thimble Eye Splice with Ends Frayed* is a round thimble, spliced into an eye with the ends frayed out, and hitched along the body of the rope with Marline.

FIG. 15: The *Eye Splice Served* has the eye spliced in, tapered down, and served.

FIG. 16: The *Back Splice Served* represents a regular Back Splice tapered down and served in the usual manner.

Plate 81—Miscellaneous Eye Splices

FIG. 17: The *Three-Strand Wall Eye Splice* consists of a Wall Knot tied around the body of the rope, after splicing in the first round of tucks. The ends are spliced back into the rope, and cut off short.

FIG. 18: The *Four-Strand Wall Eye Splice.*

FIG. 19: The *Three-Strand Lanyard Eye Splice* has a Lanyard Knot (PLATE 60, FIG. 131) tied around the body of the rope, after the first tucks have been spliced in. The

knot is finished off by splicing and trimming the ends, as in FIG. 17.

FIG. 20: The *Four-Strand Lanyard Eye Splice.*

FIG. 21: The *Three-Strand Turk's Head Weave Eye Splice* is based on the Turk's Head Weave illustrated in PLATE 62, FIG. 158.

FIG. 22: The *Four-Strand Turk's Head Weave Eye Splice.*

FIG. 23: The *Three-Strand Walled*

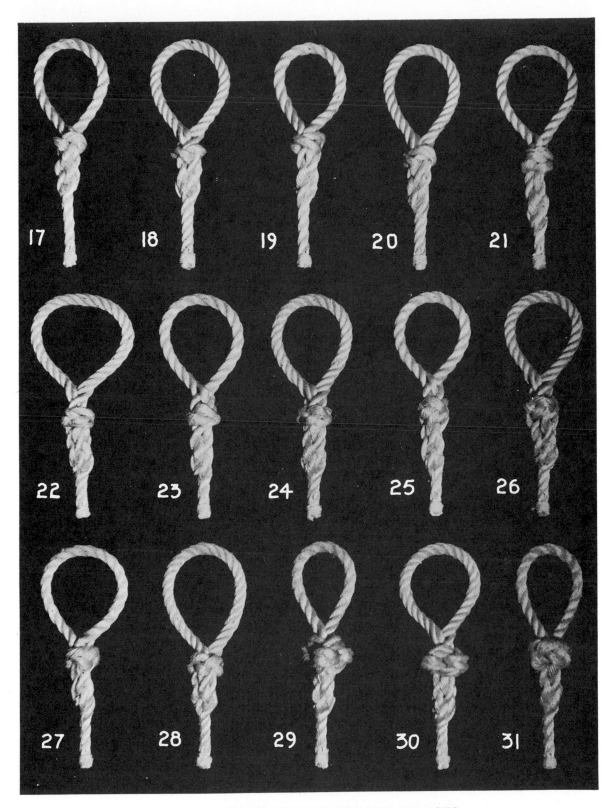

PLATE 81—MISCELLANEOUS EYE SPLICES

Crown Eye Splice utilizes the Walled Crown Knot shown in PLATE 62, FIG. 162.

FIG. 24:　The *Four-Strand Walled Crown Eye Splice.*

FIG. 25:　The *Three-Strand Single Stopper Eye Splice* is made by tying a Single Crown and Wall, and splicing in the strands.

FIG. 26:　The *Four-Strand Single Stopper Eye Splice.*

FIG. 27:　The *Three-Strand Single Diamond Eye Splice* begins with the eye spliced into the rope in the usual manner. Then form a Diamond Knot (PLATE 60, FIG. 140),

and finish off as in the preceding knots.

FIG. 28:　The *Four-Strand Single Diamond Eye Splice.*

FIG. 29:　The *Three-Strand Star Eye Splice* is formed with a Star Knot (PLATE 57, FIG. 78), and finished off as usual.

FIG. 30:　The *Four-Strand Star Eye Splice.*

FIG. 31:　The *Three-Strand Sennit Eye Splice* is begun by splicing the eye into the rope, just as in all knotted eye splices. Follow this with a Sennit Knot (PLATE 55, FIG. 33), and finish off by splicing and trimming the strands in the regular way.

Plate 82—Three- and Four-Strand Eye Splice Combinations

FIG. 32:　The *Four-Strand Sennit Eye Splice.*

FIG. 33:　The *Three-Strand Matthew Walker Eye Splice* is begun by splicing the first set of eye tucks. Then a Matthew Walker Knot is tied as shown in PLATE 53, FIG. 5. The ends are spliced into the rope and cut off short to finish.

FIG. 34:　The *Four-Strand Matthew Walker Eye Splice.*

FIG. 35:　The *Three-Strand Outside Matthew Walker Eye Splice* is tied with the Outside Matthew Walker illustrated in PLATE 54, FIG. 18.

FIG. 36:　The *Four-Strand Outside Matthew Walker Eye Splice.*

FIG. 37:　The *Three-Strand Single Manrope Eye Splice* follows the Eye Splice with first a Wall, and then a Crown, which is pulled up and spliced back into the rope.

FIG. 38:　The *Four-Strand Single Manrope Eye Splice.*

FIG. 39:　The *Three-Strand Double Lanyard Eye Splice* uses the Lanyard Knot shown in PLATE 60, FIG. 131 doubled, which is tied around the standing part of the rope in the usual way.

FIG. 40:　The *Four-Strand Double Lanyard Eye Splice.*

FIG. 41:　The *Three-Strand Double Diamond Eye Splice* is based on a Double Diamond Knot (PLATE 26, FIG. 61).

FIG. 42:　The *Four-Strand Double Diamond Eye Splice.*

FIG. 43:　The *Three-Strand Double Walled Crown Eye Splice* utilizes a Walled Crown Knot (PLATE 62, FIG. 162), doubled.

FIG. 44:　The *Four-Strand Double Walled Crown Eye Splice.*

FIG. 45:　The *Three-Strand Double Stopper Eye Splice* has a Crown and Wall doubled in the usual manner to form a Stopper Knot in the Eye Splice.

FIG. 46:　The *Four-Strand Double Stopper Eye Splice.*

Plate 83—Six-Strand Eye and Back Splices

FIG. 47:　The *Six-Strand Back Splice* is made by first removing the heart, then forming the splice as in the three- and four-strand methods.

FIG. 48:　The *Six-Strand Sailmaker's Back Splice* is tied in the same way as the three and four-strand versions.

FIGS. 49A, B, and C:　The *Six-Strand Eye*

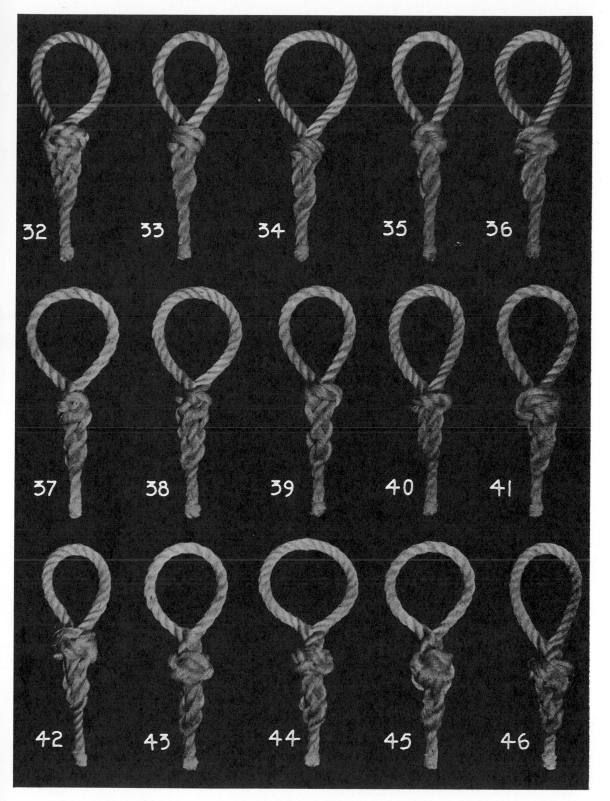

PLATE 82—THREE- AND FOUR-STRAND EYE SPLICE COMBINATIONS

Splice is begun by unlaying the strands the required amount and placing a whipping on to keep them from unlaying further. Next, remove the heart, and bend the rope in from right to left toward the standing part. Start with the underneath strand nearest the standing part of the rope, and tuck it through the middle, or under three strands, as shown with strand *a* in FIG. 49A. Then take the following strand on the right of the first tuck and tuck it through two strands, after first starting it through in the same place as the first tuck. But be careful to keep it slightly ahead, in order to bring it out in its proper place one strand above the first tuck, as shown with strand *b* in FIG. 49A. The next strand is tucked under one (*See* strand *c* in FIG. 49A), after which the Splice is turned over, and strands *d, e,* and *f* are then tucked under one strand each against the lay. It will then appear as in FIG. 49B. Make two or three tucks

over one and under one, then taper down and cut off. FIG. 49C shows the Splice as it will look when finished.

FIG. 50: The *Six-Strand Sailmaker's Eye Splice,* First Method, is made in the same manner as the three and four-strand methods, after first removing the heart, and starting the first tucks in the same manner as illustrated in FIG. 49.

FIG. 51: The *Six-Strand Double Manrope Eye Splice* is tied by first unlaying the strands the proper distance. Make the first set of tucks, then tie a Manrope Knot around the standing part of the rope. Pull taut, and cut off the strands to complete the knot. At times, the end of a rope that runs close to a block requires an eye; and as an ordinary Splice would have a tendency to jam, a knot of this sort is preferred. Any one of the various other Eye Splice Knots that are quick and easy to form might also be used.

Plate 84—Miscellaneous Six-Strand Eye Splices

FIG. 52: The *Six-Strand Wall Eye Splice* is begun, as usual, by unlaying the rope a sufficient distance. Next, seize it, remove the heart, and splice an eye into the rope as shown in PLATE 83, FIG. 49. Then make the first set of tucks, and tie the knot in the same manner as the three and four-strand methods. Splice the ends into the rope in the ordinary fashion to finish off.

FIG. 53: The *Six-Strand Lanyard Eye Splice.*

FIG. 54: The *Six-Strand Double Lanyard Eye Splice.*

FIG. 55: The *Six-Strand Single Diamond Eye Splice.*

FIG. 56: The *Six-Strand Double Diamond Eye Splice* follows the single-strand method, except that it is doubled.

FIG. 57: The *Six-Strand Single Stopper Eye Splice.*

FIG. 58: The *Six-Strand Double Stopper Eye Splice* is made in the same way as the single-strand knot, then doubled.

FIG. 59: The *Six-Strand Turk's Head Weave Eye Splice.*

Plate 85—Miscellaneous Six-Strand Eye Splices

FIG. 60: The *Six-Strand Star Eye Splice.*

FIG. 61: The *Six-Strand Sennit Eye Splice.*

FIG. 62: The *Six-Strand Matthew Walker Eye Splice.*

FIG. 63: The *Six-Strand Overhand Matthew Walker Eye Splice.*

FIG. 64: The *Six-Strand Single Walled*

Crown Eye Splice.

FIG. 65: The *Six-Strand Double Walled Crown Eye Splice.*

FIG. 66: The *Six-Strand Inverted Wall Eye Splice.*

FIG. 67: The *Six-Strand Single Manrope Eye Splice* contains a Wall and Crown tied and spliced in the usual manner.

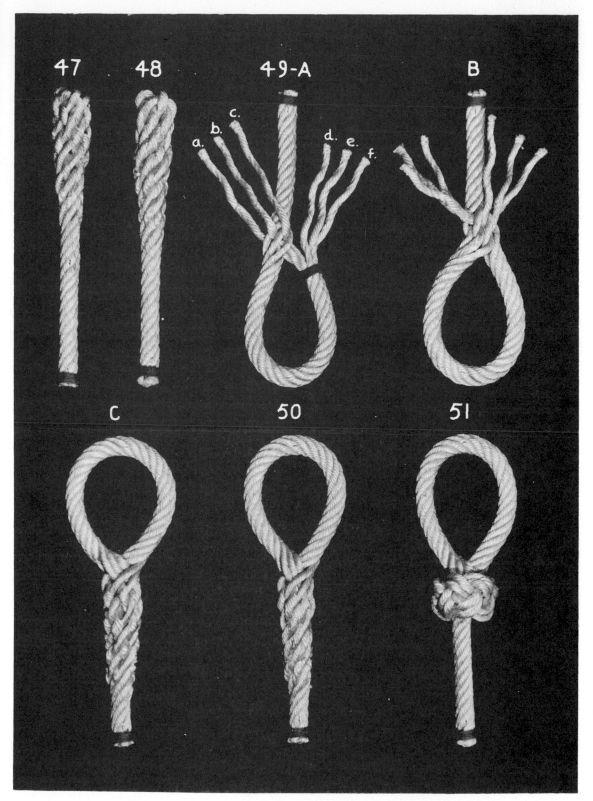

PLATE 83—SIX-STRAND EYE AND BACK SPLICES

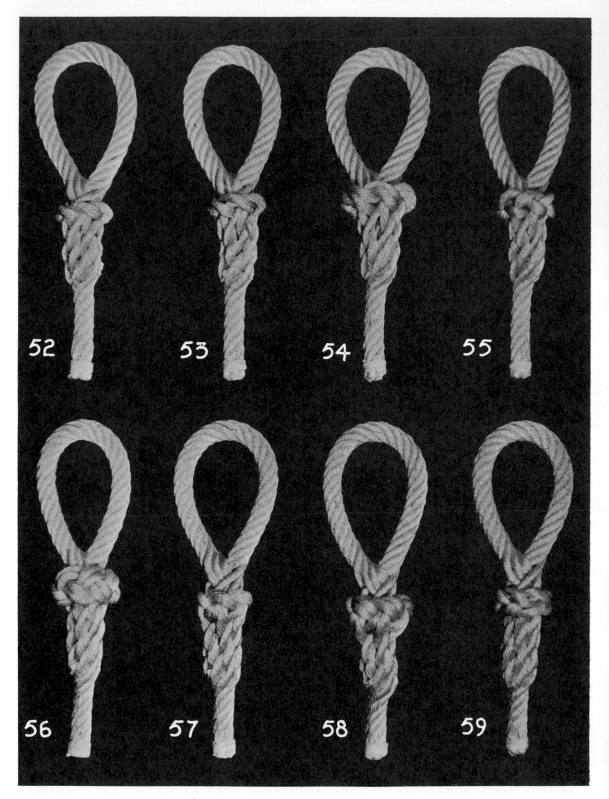

PLATE 84—MISCELLANEOUS SIX-STRAND EYE SPLICES

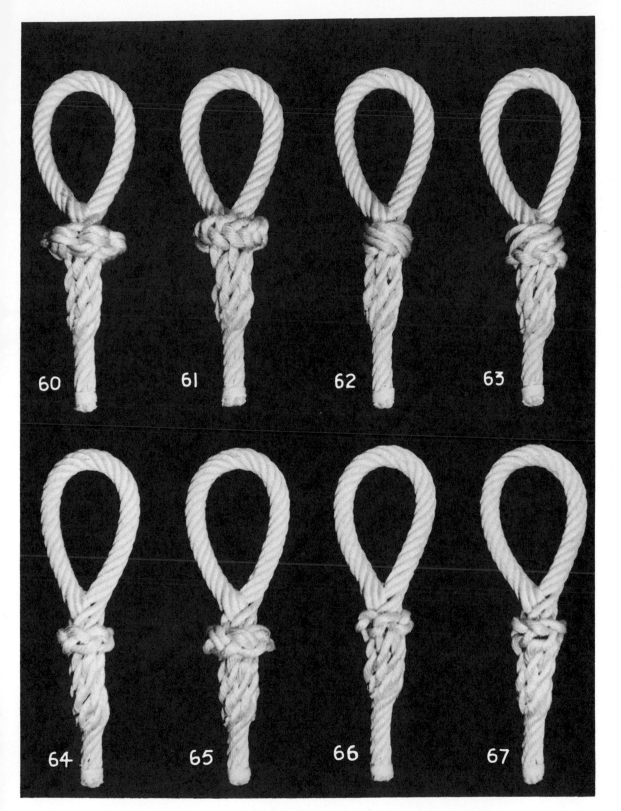

PLATE 85—MISCELLANEOUS SIX-STRAND EYE SPLICES

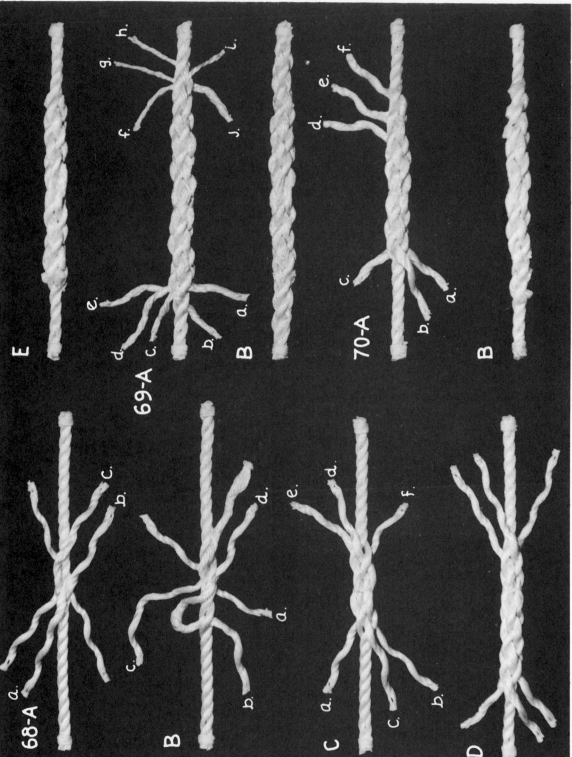

PLATE 86. THREE STRAND AND SHORT SPLICES

[*Plate 86*]   Rope Splicing   **173**

Plate 86—Three-Strand Short Splices

Fig. 68A: The *Three-Strand Short Splice* is the strongest and most secure method of uniting two ropes. It is stronger than the Long Splice, but increases the diameter of the rope, so that the spliced portion of the rope may be unable to pass over the sheave of a block. To begin this Splice, unlay the ends of each rope, and marry the strands as shown in the illustration. In marrying a rope, one strand of one rope comes between two strands of the other, as shown by strand *a,* which comes between the two strands *b* and *c.*

B: The work will be found much simpler to execute if a temporary seizing is placed at the point where both ropes have been married. This will serve to hold the ropes in position until the first tucks are made. The strands on the right-hand side are, for the moment, let alone. Begin with any strand on the left. Tuck it over one and under one against the lay. Strand *b,* as shown in the illustration, is tucked over strand *d* and under the next strand. Either strand *a* or *c* may be tucked next.

C: After strands *a, b,* and *c* have been tucked, strands *d, e,* and *f* are tucked once each. The Splice is begun on both sides, there now being one round of tucks. Two more tucks are put in with each strand, making three rounds of tucks in all, which is the proper amount for a secure Splice.

D: This shows the Short Splice after three rounds of tucks have been made. The Splice is now rolled under the foot and pounded with a fid or mallet, to make it round and work the strands into place. The strands are then cut off, but not too close, or they may work out when tension is applied.

E: This illustration shows the finished Splice. It is good practice for the beginner to put a whipping on the end of each strand to prevent unlaying. The ends can be sewn to the body of the rope with sail twine to make them more secure.

Fig. 69A: The *Short Splice Tapered,* First Method, is an especially neat form of Short Splice, because of its tapered strands. The tapering, however, should not be begun until three rounds of tucks have been made. Each strand is then split in half, as shown by strands *d* and *e.* In this case, *d* is tucked and *e* is cut off. Strand *b* has already been tucked, and its remaining half, *c,* is cut off. The full strand *a* has not yet been split. Two complete rounds of tucks are then made with each half-strand. They are halved again, making quarters, as shown by *f* and *g.* In this case, *f* is tucked and *g* is cut off. Strand *h* has already been tucked, and its other half *i* is to be cut off. The half-strand *j* has not yet been quartered. One round of tucks is made with the quartered strands.

B: After the Splice has been rolled and pounded, all the remaining strands are cut off, and the finished Splice will then appear as in the illustration. The Splice, it should be noted, will be found just as secure if only two rounds of full tucks are made before tapering.

Fig. 70A: The *Short Splice Tapered,* Second Method, is another and much more rapid method of tapering the Short Splice. First, marry the ropes and splice two rounds of tucks. Instead of tucking strand *a,* tuck both strands *b* and *c* once. Strands *a* and *b* are left as they are, and the remaining strand *c* is tucked again. When this has been done, the strands will appear in the position shown by strands *d, e,* and *f,* only pointing downward rather than up.

B: The Splice is then rolled and pounded and the strands cut off. The finished Splice is pictured in this illustration.

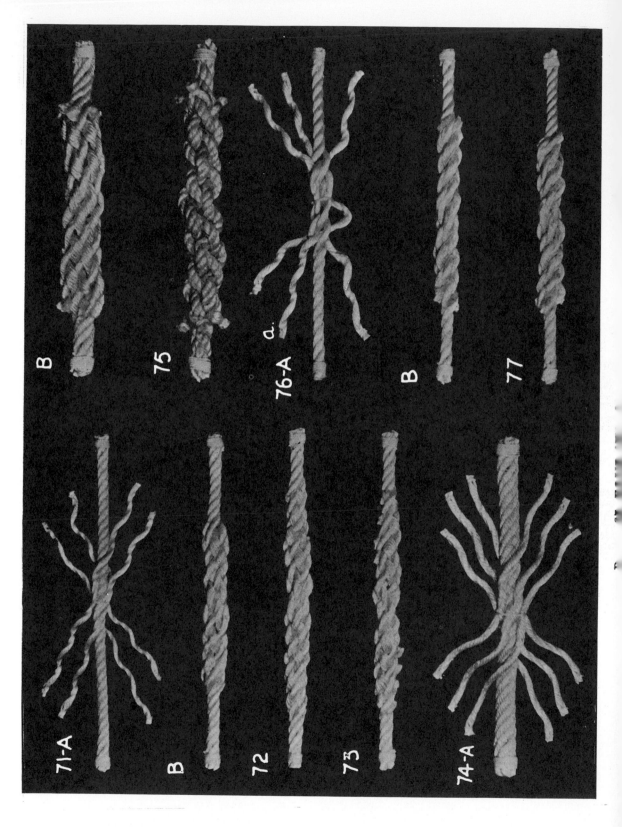

Plate 87—Four-Strand Short Splices

FIGS. 71A and B: The *Four-Strand Short Splice* has the strands married and spliced by means of the same method used for three-strand rope. FIG. 71B shows how the completed Splice will look after the required three rounds of tucks have been made and the strands cut off.

FIG. 72: The *Four-Strand Splice Tapered*, First Method, follows the procedure used for the Tapered Splice shown in PLATE 86, FIG. 69.

FIG. 73: The *Four-Strand Splice Tapered*, Second Method, is tied in the same way as the Tapered Splice in PLATE 86, FIG. 70.

FIGS. 74A and B: The *Six-Strand Short Splice* is begun by first placing a temporary whipping on each rope before unlaying the strands. Next, unlay the strands to the whipping, and remove the heart. Marry the strands in the same manner as the three and four-strand rope. And place a temporary whipping at the point where they join, to hold the ropes in place until the tucks have been made. After making one round of tucks, the temporary whippings on each rope are cut off. Then after two more rounds of tucks have been made, the whipping put on after marrying the strands is removed. The Splice is pounded and rolled under the foot, and the strands cut off short to finish. FIG. 74B shows the Splice completed.

FIG. 75: The *Short Splice (Cable-Laid Rope)* is made by first unlaying the three strands of each rope. Marry and splice them in the same manner as the three-strand rope. After three rounds of tucks have been made, the three strands that make up each strand of the rope itself are unlaid. Take a strand from one side and two from the other, making three. Then seize them together as shown in the illustration. They are now cut off close to the seizing.

FIG. 76A and B: The *Three-Strand Sailmaker's Short Splice* is begun by marrying the strands of each rope. Choose any two strands lying next to each other, in order to have one adjacent strand from each rope. Then instead of going over one and under one, as in the common Splice, tuck them around one another. As there is a right and wrong way of tucking these strands in the Sailmaker's Splices, the following method should be followed to eliminate the possibility of making any errors: when the strands have been married, select the proper strand with which the first tuck is to be made; look closely at the strand it is to be tucked under, and observe the direction the yarns of that strand follow; then tuck the strand in the same direction as the yarns, or in the direction of strand *a*. FIG. 76B illustrates the finished Splice, after three rounds of tucks have been made and the temporary whipping and strands cut off.

FIG. 77: The *Four-Strand Sailmaker's Short Splice*.

Plate 88—Three-Strand Long Splice

FIG. 78A: The *Three-Strand Long Splice* (over and under style), though weaker than the Short Splice and requiring more rope, does not appreciably increase the diameter of the rope, and can therefore be run over a sheave or pulley without jamming in the block. To begin, unlay the strands of both ropes four to five times farther than in a Short Splice. (In reality, the strands are unlaid much farther than the specimen in the illustration, since it was necessary to make the Splice shorter in order to get the work into the photograph.) Then marry the strands as shown here, and group them off into pairs. The next step is to take strand *a* and unlay it a short distance. Then take its mate, strand *b*, and lay it into the groove that was made when strand *a* was removed.

When strand *b* has been laid up to strand *a*, and they meet, tie an Overhand Knot with both strands to hold them temporarily. Next, go back to the center, and knot strands *c* and *d* together, as they will remain where they are. Take strand *f*' and unlay it to the left the same distance that strand *a* was unlaid to the right. Then lay strand *e* into the groove left when strand *f* was taken out.

B: This shows how the Splice will look after the preceding steps have been made. (The Overhand Knots have not been tied in the strands in this illustration.) Strands *a* and *b* are together on the right; and *c* and *d* are together in the center. Strand *f* has been unlaid, and strand *e* is being laid into the groove until it reaches strand *f*.

FIG. 79: *Finishing Off the Strands of a Long Splice.* The next and final step in long splicing shows the disposal of the strands. This can be accomplished in several ways. The method illustrated shows the whole strand Overhand Knotted. (Note the manner in which the strands are knotted together, with the strands coming out on the right on top, and coming out on the left on the bottom. When tied in this fashion, the strands lie flat and do not form a lump.) After they have been knotted together, splice them over and under against the lay, as in the ordinary Short Splice. This is done to each pair of three strands.

FIG. 80A: *Split Strand Method,* First Method, illustrates another method perhaps not as strong as the one described in FIG. 79, but forming a neater joint. It is made by first splitting the strands in half, then tying an Overhand Knot with the halved strands,

as indicated. In this case, the splicing strands, *a* and *b*, are the ones with which the Overhand Knots were formed. Strands *c* and *d* are left as they are until the Splice is completed. Then after the Splice has been rolled under the foot, they are cut off, leaving about an inch of each strand, so that when the Splice is stretched under tension the tucks will not pull out. Either an Over and Under or Sailmaker's Splice may be made in finishing off the strands.

B: This shows the Splice before the strands have been pulled up taut. Strands *a* and *b* are the strands with which the Overhand Knots are tied, and *c* and *d* are the dead strands to be cut off.

FIG. 81A: *Split Strand Method,* Second Method, shows another method in which the strands are first split and knotted together as in FIG. 80. Then take one strand and tuck it under the next one to it. In other words, the strand that comes out on the right is tucked under the next strand to its right, and the strand on the left is tucked under the next strand to its left. This illustration shows working-strand *a* already tucked, and *b* tucked halfway. The dead strands *c* and *d* are left until the Splice is finished, and then cut off.

B: The strands will now emerge from the other side of the rope, to be spliced in as a Sailmaker's Splice.

C: This shows the Splice after two tucks have been made. In a Splice of this type, it is good practice to put in at least four tucks with each strand.

D: The Splice in this illustration is shown as it looks when completed.

Plate 89—Six-Strand Long Transmission and Cable-Laid Splices

FIG. 82: The *Four-Strand Long Splice.* All strands were disposed of in this Splice by employing the method illustrated in PLATE 88, FIG. 81.

FIG. 83: The *Six-Strand Long Splice* is begun by seizing the rope the proper distance from the end, or about twice as far as in three-strand rope. Unlay the strands

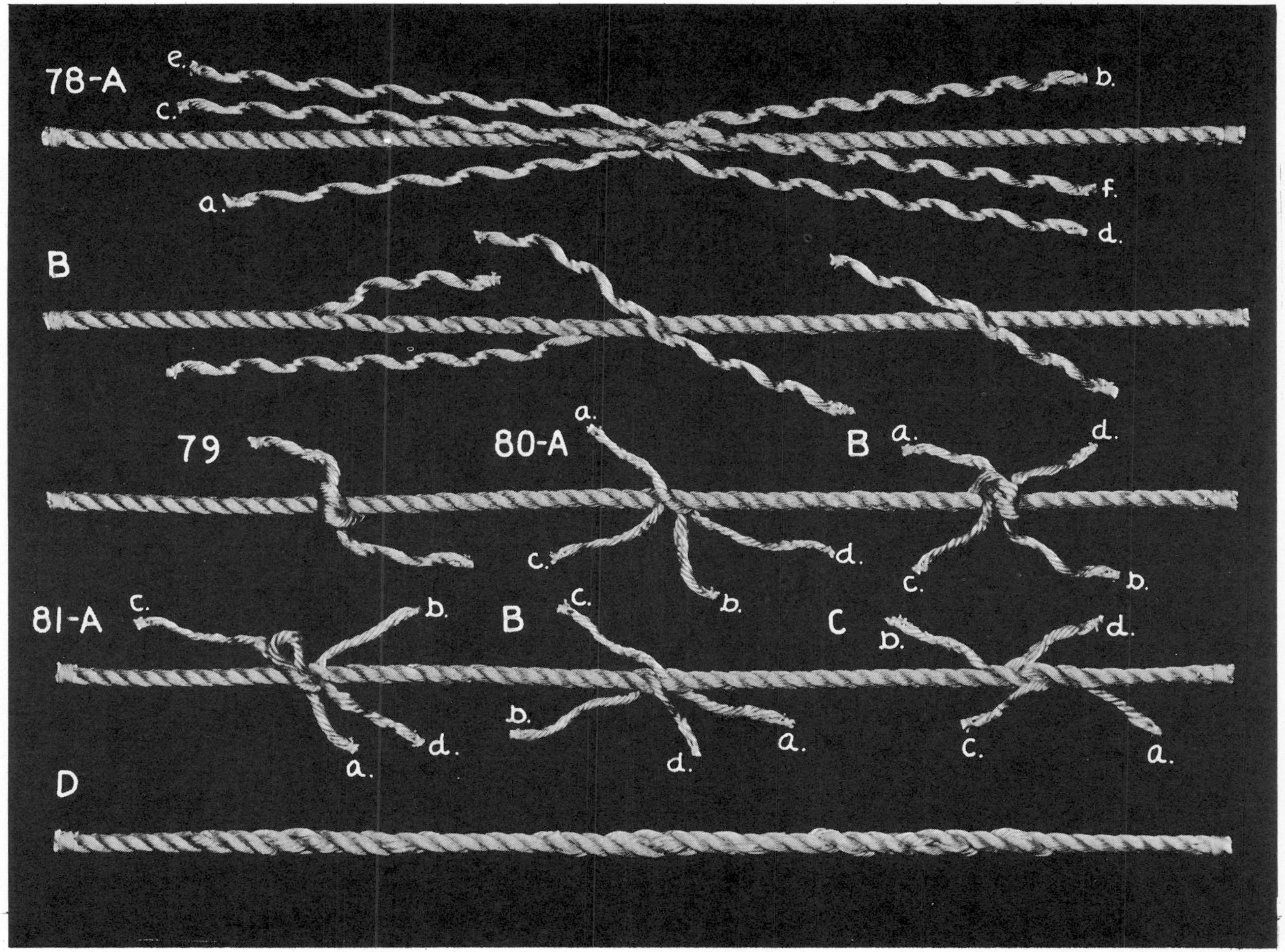

PLATE 88—THREE-STRAND LONG SPLICE

of both ropes to the seizing, cut out the hearts, and marry the strands. Select alternate strands on one rope, leaving three strands. Put a temporary seizing on these strands, to hold them secure to the standing part of the rope. Then cut off the seizing on the rope from which the three strands were selected, and taking the strands in pairs, proceed as in making a Three-Strand Long Splice. After this has been done, the seizing is cut off the other rope, and the same procedure is followed.

Fig. 84A: The *Transmission Splice* is similar to the Long Splice, but the manner of finishing off the strands is quite different. Whereas the common Long Splice will stand up when used on hand tackle, the strands would work loose if it were used as a Transmission Splice. (A Transmission Splice is tied in factories on ropes used to transmit power from motors to machinery, and is therefore subjected to high speeds.) This Splice, as a rule, is made in four-strand rope; but it can also be tied in three or six-strand rope. The first step is the same as in the common Long Splice. The difference lies in the method of tucking and finishing off the strands. After the strands have been laid up in their proper positions, take one strand—the one on the left-hand side—and unlay it three more full turns. Split the strand and name one half a, the other half a^1. Next, take the half-strand a and lay it up three full turns, until it reaches its original position. Take its partner, and unlay this strand to the right three full turns. Split the strand in half and lay it up to its original position, naming one half b and the other half b^1. In this illustration, strand b has been laid up to its original position, but strand a has not. (Note: as space was limited in the photograph, it was not possible to unlay the strands three full turns as required. But although they were unlaid only one turn, the principle is the same.)

B: When halves a and b meet, they are joined with an Overhand Knot in the usual manner. Tuck the half-strand b to the left, around half-strand a as in a Sailmaker's Splice, until b reaches a^1. The half-strand a is then tucked to the right around half-strand b, until b^1 is reached. This illustration shows b tucked until it has reached a^1. The half-strand a has not yet been tucked to reach b^1.

C: When the preceding step has been completed, take strand a^1 and open the strand in the center, close to the rope itself. Then insert strand b through this hole. After this has been done, it is tucked through the center of the rope, emerging from the opposite side. Strands b^1 and a show how this is handled.

D: The strands are now all drawn taut and cut off, leaving about an inch of each strand; for when the rope is stretched a small amount of slack will be taken up. After the rope has been run in for several days, the small remaining pieces of yarn from each strand may then be cut off.

Fig. 85: The *Three-Strand Transmission Splice*. All strands are disposed of in three-strand rope by using the same method as used in four-strand rope.

Fig. 86: The *Long Splice (Cable-Laid Rope)* or *Mariner's Splice* is tied by first unlaying the rope about two and one-half times the length that would be required for an ordinary Long Splice in a rope of the same size. Marry the strands and proceed as in the common Long Splice. When they have been spaced apart the proper distance, unlay the strands of one pair, marry them, and put in the common Long Splice. Then repeat the same procedure with the other two pair. Patience, perseverance, and a substantial amount of elbow-grease will be found necessary to turn in a Splice of this type neatly and securely.

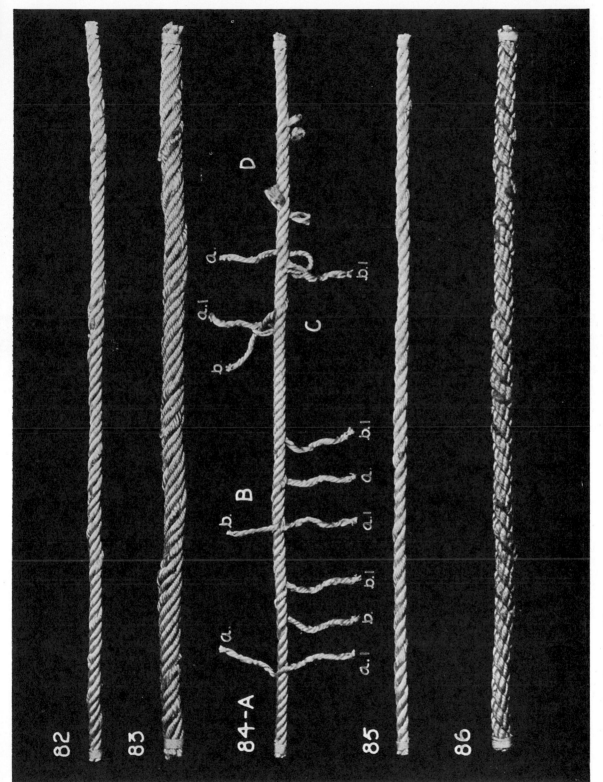

PLATE 89—SIX-STRAND LONG TRANSMISSION AND CABLE-LAID SPLICES

Plate 90—Rope Lengthening Splices

FIG. 87A: The *Splice for Lengthening a Rope with a Single Strand* is useful whenever it is desired to give a sail more spread by inserting a cloth. The head and foot rope can be lengthened in the following manner: cut a strand at the point marked *a;* unlay the cut strand to point *b,* and cut another strand; then unlay both cut strands to point *c,* and cut the last strand. By following this method, the wrong strand cannot possibly be cut.

B: Next, measure the distance from *x* to *z.* This will be the distance that the rope is to be lengthened. (Be certain to leave enough end on strand *2* for splicing.) Lay strand *2* up to the point *z.* Measure off the same distance on the other rope, and lay strand *b* up on strand *a.* Mate strand *a* with strand *2,* and lay strand *3* up until it mates with strand *b.* Select a strand from another rope of the same size, and measure it off to be at least eight inches longer than the distance from strand *c* to strand *1.* Take this strand and begin laying it in from strand *c* until it reaches strand *1.* The single strand is lettered *d.*

C: This shows how the Splice will appear after the steps just outlined have been completed. All that remains now is to splice the strands in the usual manner.

FIG. 88A: The *Splice for Lengthening a Four-Strand Rope* is accomplished in almost the same fashion as the Three-Strand Splice. Join strands *a* and *2,* and strands *b* and *3.* Strand *4* is then laid up on the left-hand rope until it mates with *c.* One long single strand is then taken from a four-strand rope of the same size, and laid in from strand *d* to strand *1.* This long strand is lettered *e.*

B: When the additional strand has been added, the Splice appears as in this illustration. Then splice the strands in the usual way.

Plate 91—Miscellaneous Splices

FIG. 89A and B: The *Grecian Splice* must have the rope unlaid twice the distance required for the common Short Splice. Then from each strand on both ropes take four yarns with which to form nettles for the cross-pointing. Lay up enough of each strand again so that a Short Splice with three rounds of tucks can be made. Marry the ropes, and make a Short Splice. After this has been done, bring each strand up between each group of nettles, and seize them temporarily to the standing part of the rope. Next, take each nettle, or yarn, and separate it from the next one in its group, until there are three sets of four yarns. Twist these down around the Splice in the same direction as the lay of the rope. When they meet the group of nettles from the other rope, lead them between the groups and seize them temporarily, just behind the second group. Unlay the second group in the same manner as the first. Then in groups of four, tuck them over four yarns and under four of the first group, just as in splicing, and against the lay. When the end of the Splice is reached, scrape-taper all the strands and marl them down well. FIG. 89B shows the finished Splice.

FIG. 90A and B: The *Eye Splice Wormed and Collared* is a very smart method of turning in an Eye Splice, and may be used on a rope that does not come close to a block. Unlay the rope about twice as far as in the common Splice. When the first tuck has been made, take four yarns from each strand, and with the remaining yarns make a Sailmaker's Eye Splice, tapering by leaving out several yarns at intervals. Next, take two yarns from each pair of four nearest the eye, and twist them up into two yarn nettles. These are then wormed into

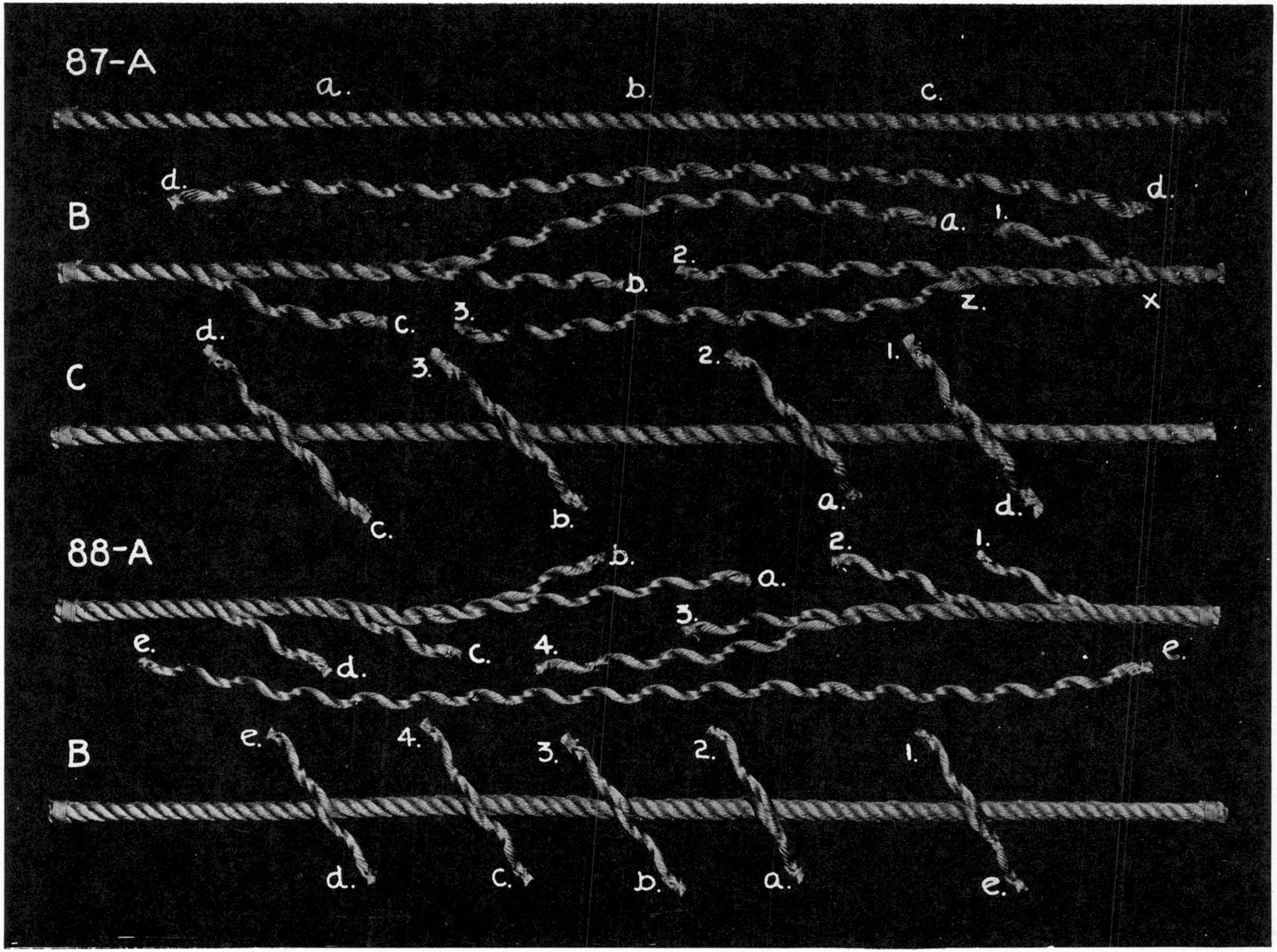

PLATE 90—ROPE LENGTHENING SPLICES

the lay until they reach the end of the Splice, where they are tucked under one strand. The remaining yarns, named group *a*, are twisted into three two-yarn nettles, and a Footrope Knot (PLATE 255, FIG. 149) is formed. Three passes are then made, the knot is drawn taut, and the ends are cut off short. Select two yarns, *b*, from each of the remaining strands of the Splice (not the worming nettles), and cut off all the other yarns. Roll each group of two yarns into nettles and form the second Three-Pass Footrope Knot. Draw it up taut, and cut the nettles off short. FIG. 90B shows the knot complete.

FIG. 91: The *Running Eye Splice on the Bight* is begun by twisting the rope in the middle, against the lay. The strands will then untwist spontaneously and begin twisting up on themselves. When they have one complete twist in them, they are spread apart, and the end rove through the eye of each strand.

FIG. 92: The *Ropemaker's Eye* is a type of eye that is formed only by people who manufacture rope. Instead of beginning to twist a cable-laid rope from the end, a long piece of rope is taken (in cable-laid rope, this would form two of the three strands of the rope), and the bight of this is taken. The third strand is bent to the size of eye desired. There is now one single end with an eye and one bight, which forms three strands. These three are twisted to make the rope. After a suitable length has been made, strands *a*, *b*, and *c* are wormed into the lay, instead of being spliced, and the eye and worming are then marled and served with good rope.

FIG. 93: The *Admiral Elliott's Eye* is similar to the Ropemaker's Eye, but no loop is formed by the bight of two of the strands. Instead, the loop is formed by taking two strands from the end of the rope and long-splicing them together. The third strand is bent around, and an eye of the proper size is spliced in. Then instead of cutting off the strands remaining from the Eye Splice, they are wormed into the lay of the rope, and the whole eye and worming are marled and served with good rope.

Plate 92—Cringles and Miscellaneous Eye Splices

FIG. 94A: The *Cringle*, like the Grommet, is made with a single strand of rope. Instead of being made by itself, it is worked into another rope, such as the leech rope of a sail. Take one strand of a three-strand rope, and stick one end through the rope and under two strands. Be sure that end *a* is toward you and end *b* leading away from you. In other words, stick the single strand against the lay of the rope. Also make certain that there are an odd number of kinks in the part of the strand that is to form the Cringle. The one shown in this illustration has three: *c*, *d* and *e*.

B: Selecting end *a*, proceed to lay it up on its own bight until it reaches the opposite strand.

C: Now take end *b*, and lay this strand up to form a three-strand rope.

D: The ends are now disposed of as in a common Splice. This illustration shows the completed Cringle.

FIG. 95: The *Cringle with a Thimble* is begun in the same manner as the Cringle described in FIG. 94, but using the strand from a four-strand rope. Lay the strands up as in the Three-Strand Cringle. When they are laid up until they meet the rope, they are rove through the rope again in the same direction they were first put through. They are then laid up again until they meet at

NOTE: Some authorities prefer to form the Cringle first and then hammer the thimble into position. This is a very good method, although considerable experience is necessary in order to avoid making the Cringle too small or too large.

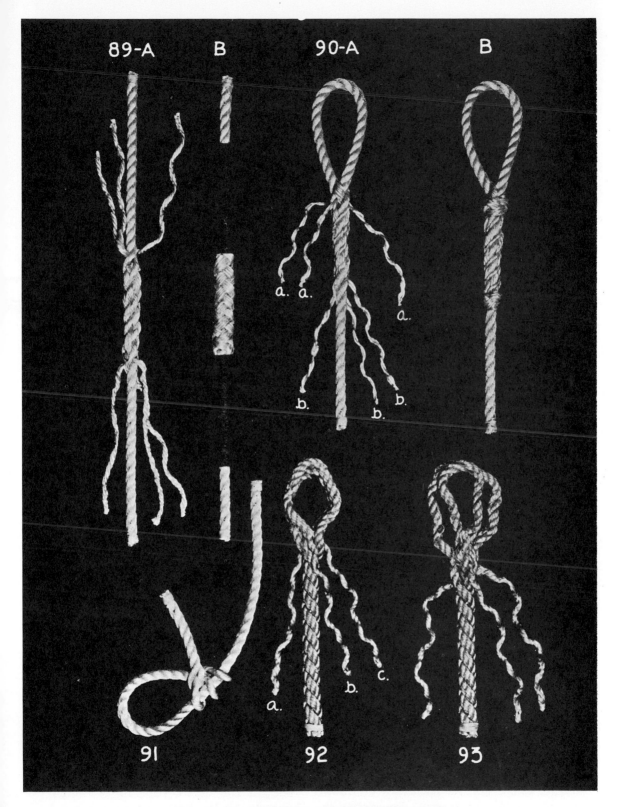

PLATE 91—MISCELLANEOUS SPLICES

the top of the thimble. The strands are next hove taut with the aid of a marlinspike, and the ends cut off short.

FIG. 96A: The *Flemish Eye Splice*, which is a little different from the common Eye Splice, can be used when there is a tendency to spread the eye apart. First, unlay the rope a sufficient length for turning in a common Eye Splice. Select one of the three strands and unlay it until the remaining two strands form an eye of the desired size. Bend these two strands down until they meet the single strand *a* again. Instead of laying it up on the standing part, lay it in the other direction, beginning a short distance from the end of the opening strands.

B: When strand *a* has been laid up again, proceed to dispose of the ends as in the common Splice.

FIG. 97: The *Flemish Eye Splice* (four strands) starts as usual with one strand. When this has been completed, select another strand, but not one adjacent to the first one used. Then splice in the strands as before.

FIG. 98A and B: The *Eye Splice on the Bight* is begun by untwisting the rope where it is desired to make the eye. Continue doing this, and the strands will untwist on themselves as shown. When these ends are long enough, form an eye and proceed to splice them into the rope, following the method used for a Three-Strand Splice. FIG. 98B shows the finished Splice.

FIG. 99: The *Eye Splice on the Bight* (four strands).

FIG. 100: The *Combined Horseshoe and Eye Splice* has the strands unlaid about four times more than in an ordinary Splice. Then splice an eye in the end of the rope. After three tucks have been made, lay the strands up again to form the horseshoe. Splice the remaining strands into the standing part of the rope.

Plate 93—Miscellaneous Splices

FIG. 101: The *Shoemaker's Splice* can be used in either old rope or rope with a loose lay. Marry the rope in the usual manner, and make one round of tucks against the lay of the rope. The next round of tucks is made with the lay, or sailmaker fashion, and the last round is again made against the lay. That is, one against, one sailmaker style, and the last against. Roll the Splice, and cut the strands off short.

FIG. 102: The *Four-Strand Shoemaker's Splice*.

FIG. 103: The *Drawing Splice* is a good way to short-splice a hawser or large rope, and enables one easily to pass the spliced portion of the line through a hawse-hole or chock. By using this method, the Splice may also be taken apart again without damage. Put a stop on each hawser, about two fathoms from the end, depending on the size of the rope. Each rope is unlaid to the stop, and another stop placed on each strand about four feet from the end. The strands are then scrape-tapered and laid up again. Each strand of both ropes is next worked into a long taper. Marry the hawsers, and short-splice them in the usual manner. When the end of the Splice has been reached, clap a stout seizing on each side. The tapered ends are now wormed around the cable. When half of the strand has been wormed, clap on another seizing. Then continue worming until the ends of the strands are reached. At this point, clap on another strong seizing. The finished Splice is shown in the illustration.

FIG. 104A and B: The *Splice for Adding a New Strand to a Rope* is often necessary when a strand has become frayed. Pick up the frayed strand and cut it in two. (Do not cut the entire rope in two—only one strand.) Unlay both cut ends a good distance on each side of the frayed portion.

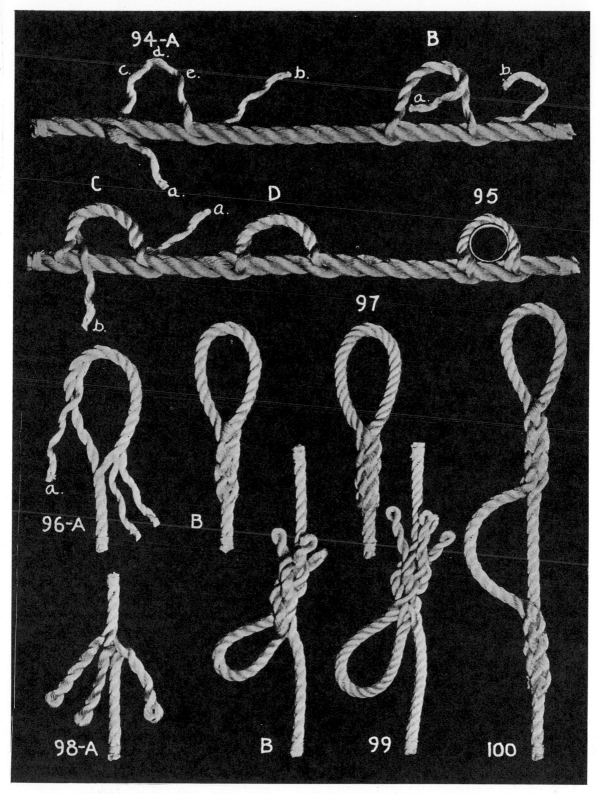

PLATE 92—CRINGLES AND MISCELLANEOUS EYE SPLICES

Then take a single strand from another rope of equal size, and lay it into the groove from which the cut strand was unlaid, leaving enough end with which to splice. Then dispose of the ends as in the common Long Splice. FIG. 104B shows the Splice completed.

FIG. 105: *Splicing Three-Strand and Four-Strand Rope Together* is as follows: unlay the strands of both ropes a sufficient distance, and marry them: unlay one strand of the three-strand rope, and fill the space with a strand of the four-strand. Next, unlay a strand from the four-strand, and fill the space with a strand from the three. There now remain two strands from the four, and one strand from the three. Divide the single strand from the three, by taking out one third. Knot this third to one of the remaining pair of the four. Then unlay the remaining strand of the four, and fill the space with the two thirds left from the three-strand rope. Finish off the strands as in the common Long Splice. This shows how the Splice appears before the ends are tucked. Another method is to work three strands as usual, and splice in the remaining fourth strand where it lies. The first method is the better.

FIG. 106: The *Splice for Shortening a Rope* is begun by cutting the rope in the same fashion as though you were preparing to lengthen it. Then marry the ends which were cut, and splice the strands in the usual way.

FIG. 107: The *Spectacle Splice* has the strands laid up in the same fashion as the Grommet (PLATE 103, FIG. 161). It should be done in such a way that when finished,

two strands of one will run under two strands of the other. This Splice is made of four strands. Finish off the ends as in a Long Splice.

FIG. 108: The *Twin Eye Splice* is made in the same manner as the preceding knot, but with three strands.

FIG. 109: The *Eye Splice in Eight-Strand Braided Hemp* or *Signal Halyard Splice* is made in the following way: unbraid a sufficient amount of the end, and separate the strands into two groups of four strands each; bend the end around until an eye of the desired size has been formed. Then take a pricker and tuck the four strands on the right-hand side, so that each one follows a strand in the standing part. The same is done with the strands on the left, in the opposite direction. Follow these same strands in the standing part until the desired amount of tucks have been made. Four tucks should be made if this Splice is to carry considerable weight.

FIG. 110: The *Grecian Eye Splice* requires about three times the amount of rope necessary for a common Splice. After making the first tuck, take eight yarns from each strand and seize them to the eye, to keep them out of the way temporarily. Continue with the common Splice, tapering the strands. Next, remove the temporary seizing and divide the strands so that there will be six sets of four strands each. Begin to cross-point, alternately taking three sets to the right and three to the left. When the entire Splice has been covered, put a stout seizing over all six sets of yarns, in this way securing them to the standing part of the rope.

Plate 94—Miscellaneous Splices

FIG. 111A and B: The *Horsehoe Splice* is begun by unlaying a short piece of rope as shown in FIG. 111A, and splicing it into the standing parts of another piece of rope which has been bent in horseshoe fashion.

The completed Splice will then appear as in FIG. 111B. This Splice was formerly used to separate the legs of a pair of shrouds.

FIG. 112: The *Sailmaker's Short Splice in Three-Strand Grommet* first has the

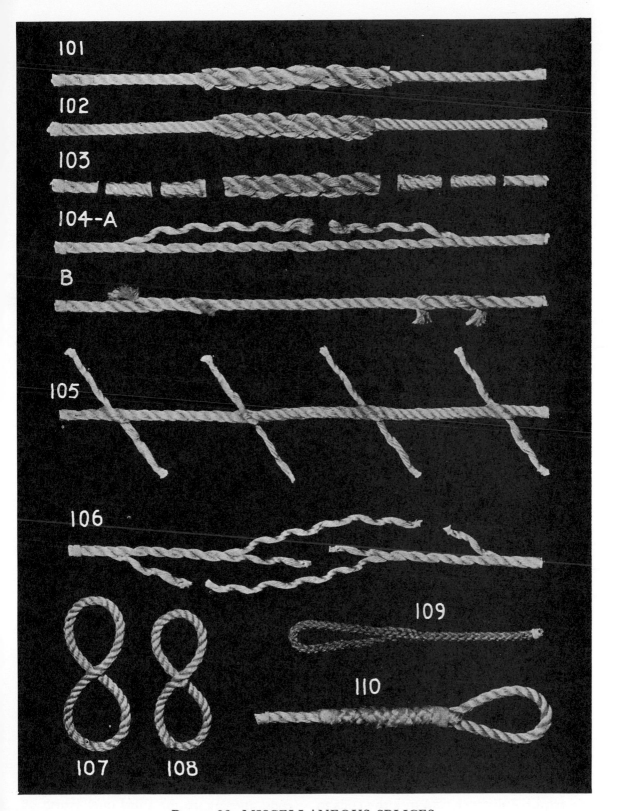

PLATE 93—MISCELLANEOUS SPLICES

strands married together. Then an Over-hand Knot is tied with each set of strands, which will bring the strands out in the form of a sailmaker's tuck. Continue with sailmaker's tucks and taper off. This Splice is seldom used.

Fig. 113: The *Sailmaker's Short Splice in Four-Strand Grommet.*

Fig. 114: The *Combination Three-Strand Splice,* First Method, is begun by first marrying the ropes. Then with each set of strands make a sailmaker's tuck in the form of an Overhand Knot. Make the next set of tucks as in a regular Splice (against the lay). Finally, taper down, and cut the strands off short.

Fig. 115: The *Combination Four-Strand Splice,* First Method.

Plate 95—Braided Eye, Horseshoe, and Cargo Strap Splices

Fig. 116: The *Three-Strand Braided Eye Splice* is made by taking the first set of tucks, as in a Three-Strand Eye Splice, and then separating the strands into braids of three strands each.

Fig. 117: The *Stirrup Splice with Eyes* is made by splicing one line into the stand-ing part of another line, with spliced eyes in both ends. By splicing hooks in the eyes, they can be used as a Barrel Sling or a Double Sling.

Fig. 118: The *Four-Strand Braided Eye Splice* is formed by first making a set of tucks, as in a Four-Strand Eye Splice, then separating the strands and making four-strand round braids out of each set.

Fig. 119: The *Horseshoe and Crossed Loop Splice* shows a Loop Splice crossed over and seized into the standing part of a Horseshoe Splice.

Fig. 120: The *Cargo Strap* can be made in various sizes, according to requirements. For an extra load, two straps can be used by splicing the loop of one over the loop of the other. Then pull the first strap through the loop. Do not taper these Splices, and use several additional tucks on each end. To shorten a strap, tie an Over-hand Knot with the two loops under the standing parts.

Plate 96—Cut Splice and Eye Splice with French Seizing

Fig. 121: The *Eye and Loop Splice with Horseshoe Splice in the Standing Part.*

Figs. 122A and B: The *Cut Splice* is made by measuring off the required dis-tance, then splicing each end into the standing part of the other rope. Fig. 122A pictures the rope in position for starting; and Fig. 122B shows the completed splice. The Splice is used to form an eye or collar in the bight of a rope.

Fig. 123: The *Three-Strand Eye Splice with French Seizing* consists of an eye spliced in, with the ends frayed out and seized to the standing part of the rope. This is a neat way of finishing off an Eye Splice in a hawser. It will also prevent the spliced portion of the rope from jamming in a hawse hole.

Fig. 124: The *Loop Splice* is a loop spliced into the standing part of a rope.

Plate 97—Miscellaneous Splices

Fig. 125: The *Eye Sling or Strap Splice* is made as follows: unlay the end of a line the required distance, and tuck the ends to the size of eye desired; then make about three full tucks, and lay up the strands. First, lay up two of the strands, seize the ends, and lay up the third one. Finish off by making a Short Splice with both ends.

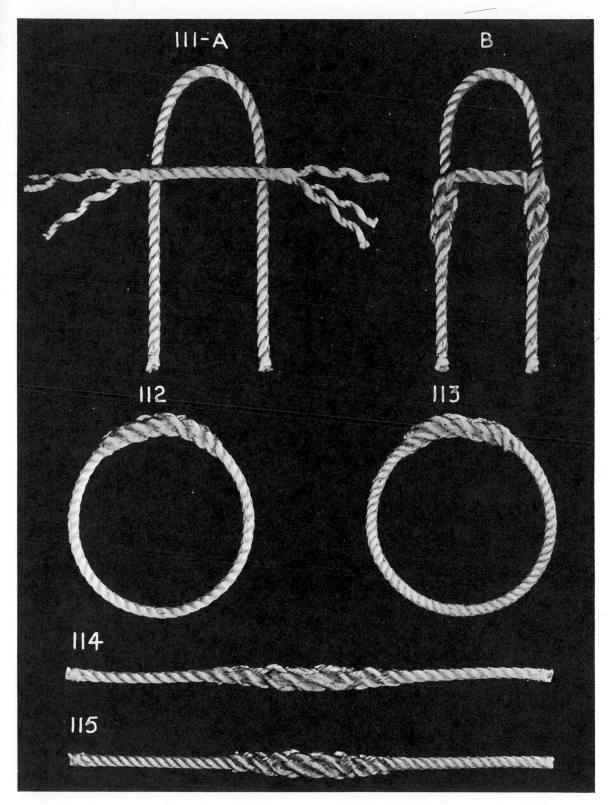

PLATE 94—MISCELLANEOUS SPLICES

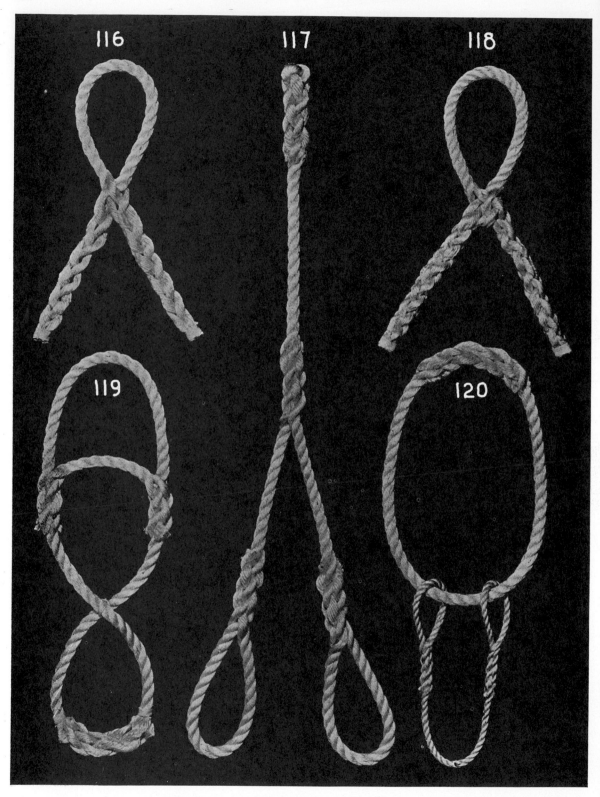

PLATE 95—BRAIDED EYE, HORSESHOE AND CARGO STRAP SPLICES

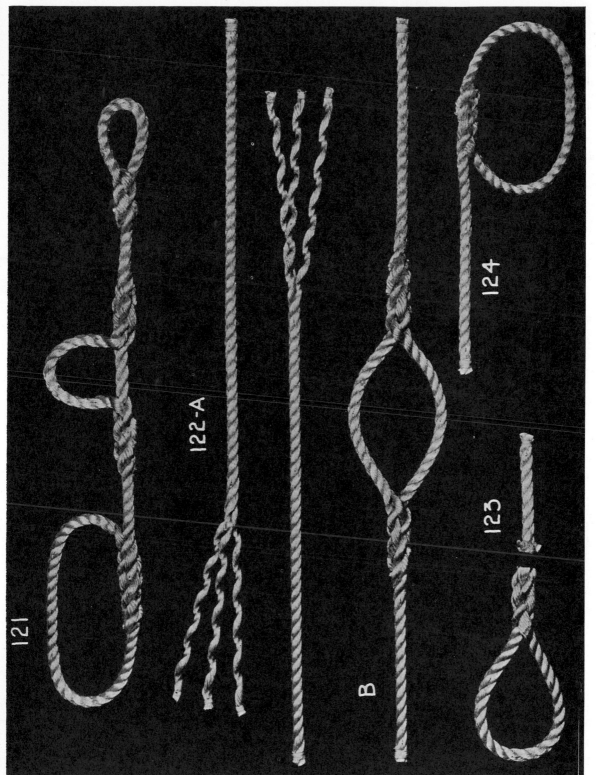

PLATE 96—CUT SPLICE AND EYE SPLICE WITH FRENCH SEIZING

FIG. 126: The *Loop and Eye Splice Halter* represents a halter formed with Loop and Eye Splices.

FIG. 127: The *Eye and Loop Splice* is an eye and loop spliced into the standing part of a rope.

FIG. 128: The *Short Splice Served* consists of an ordinary Short Splice tapered and served.

FIG. 129: The *Six-Strand Sailmaker's Short Splice*.

Plate 98—Rope Halter and Miscellaneous Splices

FIG. 130: The *Three-Strand Single Stopper Shroud* is made up of two Single Crown and Wall Knots tied back-to-back in the usual manner.

FIG. 131: The *Emergency Rope Halter* is made as follows: at the required distance from the end of the rope, form a Man-Harness Knot (PLATE 27, FIG. 75); then place the long end of the rope around the knee, with the short end on top, and join the short end to the long end with an Englishman's Tie (two Overhand Knots arranged in the manner shown). Pull this coupling up tight, and pass the long end through the eye of the Man-Harness Knot.

FIG. 132: The *Four-Strand Single Stopper Shroud*.

FIG. 133: The *Three-Strand Single Manrope Shroud* consists of two Single Wall and Crown Knots tied back-to-back in the usual fashion.

FIG. 134: The *Combination Eye and Back Splice in Slip Loop* shows a small Flemish Eye in the form of a Slip Loop. A Back Splice is tucked in with a regular Eye Splice, and each set of strands laid up and seized.

FIG. 135: The *Four-Strand Single Manrope Shroud*.

Plate 99—Sailmaker's Eye and Combination Splices

FIGS. 136A and B: The *Three-Strand Sailmaker's Eye Splice,* Second Method, has the eye bent in from left to right with the lay, instead of from right to left against the lay as in the First Method (PLATE 80, FIG. 11). Make the first tuck with the strand nearest the standing part, tucking it under one strand with the lay. Follow up with the other strands in rotation, making each tuck under one, and then continuing with the regular sailmaker's tucks. The eye will appear as in FIG. 136A when the first set of tucks has been completed. FIG. 136B shows the Splice when finished. This type of Sailmaker's Eye Splice lays in better and looks neater than the regular method, which has the first tucks made against the lay.

FIGS. 137A and B: The *Four-Strand Sailmaker's Eye Splice,* Second Method, follows the three-strand method, except that the first tuck is under two instead of one. FIG.

137A shows the first set of tucks completed. FIG. 137B shows the Splice as it looks when finished.

FIGS. 138A and B: The *Six-Strand Sailmaker's Eye Splice,* Second Method, is begun by unlaying the strands a sufficient length. Then seize them and remove the heart. Bend the eye in toward the standing part from the left, or with the lay, as in the three- and four-strand methods. Tuck the strand nearest the standing part under three with the lay; tuck the next or following strand under two; and continue by tucking each of the remaining strands under one. In other words, the tucks are the same as in the Liverpool Eye Splice in wire. The remaining tucks are over and under with the lay, as in the regular Sailmaker's Eye Splice. FIG. 138A has the first tuck completed, and FIG. 138B shows the Splice when finished.

FIG. 139: The *Three-Strand Lock Seiz-*

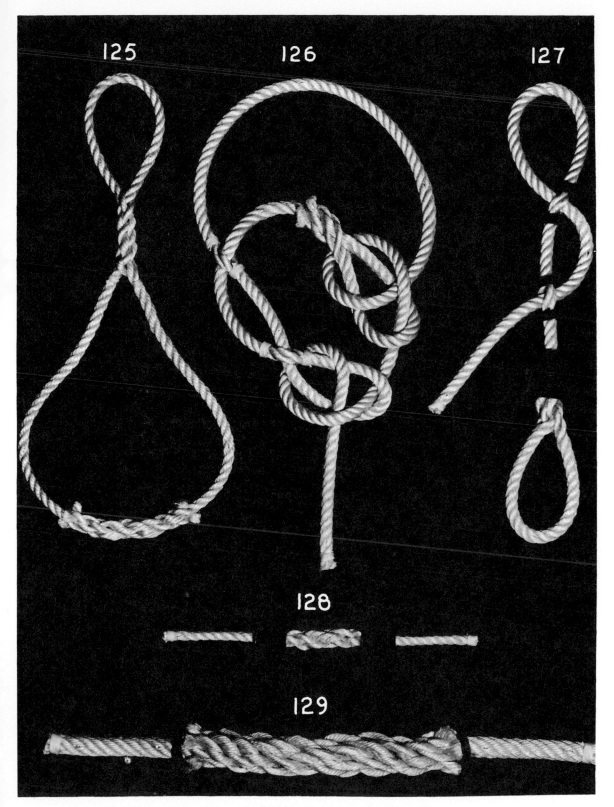

Plate 97—MISCELLANEOUS SPLICES

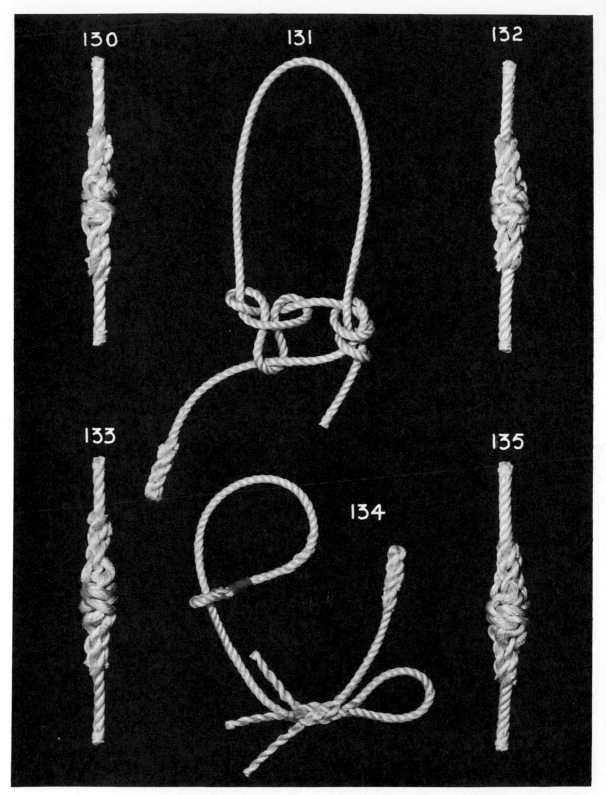

PLATE 98—ROPE HALTER AND MISCELLANEOUS SPLICES

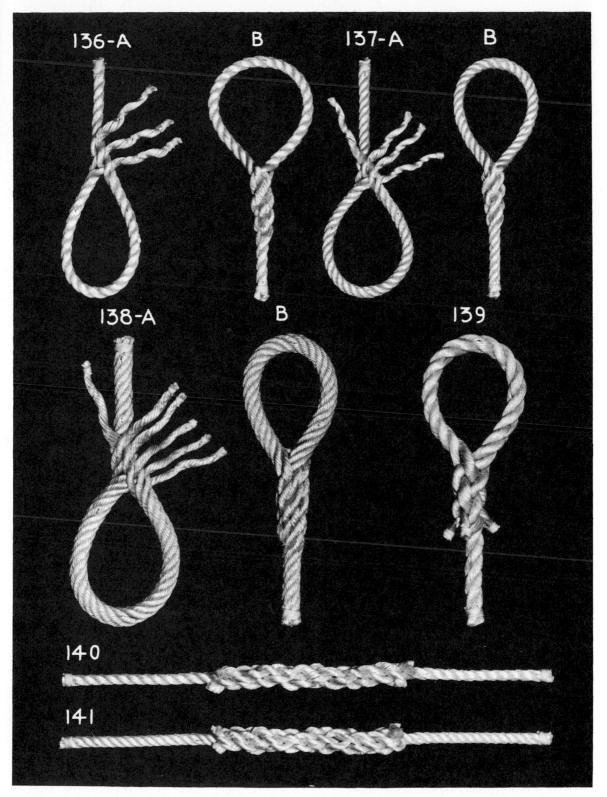

PLATE 99—SAILMAKER'S EYE AND COMBINATION SPLICES

ing in Hawser is begun by splicing the eye in with the required number of tucks. Then finish off by splitting the strands and seizing them together in pairs. This is done to prevent the strands from working out, as will happen when working with large rope.

FIG. 140: The *Three-Strand Combina-*

tion Splice, Second Method, starts with three tucks made against the lay after joining the ropes together. Then the next three tucks are made with the lay to complete the Splice.

FIG. 141: The *Four-Strand Combination Splice,* Second Method.

Plate 100—Halters and Bull Earing Splices

FIG. 142: The *Bull Earing Splice* can be easily and simply tied by following a method common in the days of the sailing-ships. An old and well-worn piece of manila was spliced into the standing part, forming a long bight in order to hitch around the yard outside the cleat. Then it was rove through the reef cringle and back to the yard, where it remained, instead of being left in the cringle.

FIGS. 143A and B: The *Loose Guard Loop Halter* is tied as follows: form the eye by making the first tuck with the long end of the rope, under two strands and toward the left as indicated; then tuck the short end of the rope under two strands of the long end, also toward the left, skipping about two strands before making the tuck. Bring the long end around to form the nose-piece, and tuck it through two strands of the short end, which is brought over from the eye on the right to form the head-piece. Tuck the short end through two strands of the long end, toward the right, passing it through the eye before making it secure by tying an Overhand Knot around the long end and through its own part. Long end and short end are represented as *a* and *b*.

FIG. 144: The *Bull Earing Splice with Twin Bights* is a type that was sometimes

made to give more parts in the first turn, by splicing an additional length into the first bight. The bights, however, had a tendency to twist up in wet weather, so the simpler form was usually preferred.

FIG. 145: The *Served Grommet* is a regular Grommet, served with Marline.

FIG. 146: The *Adjustable Halter* is begun by measuring off the proper length of rope according to the table below. Form an eye with the part of rope used for the long bight or nose-piece. Tuck it under one strand of the other part of rope representing the head-piece. Tuck the head-piece under two strands of the nose-piece, toward the right, to complete the eye. Bring the nose-piece around to form the proper length of bight, and splice it into the head-piece. Adjust the halter to the animal, and secure the lead to the loop if it is desired.

TABLE FOR ADJUSTABLE HALTER

	Diameter of rope	*Total length of rope*	*Length left for lead*
Large cattle....	½ inch	12 feet	6 feet
Medium cattle.	⅜ inch	11½ feet	6 feet
Small cattle....	⅜ inch	11 feet	6 feet
Calves and sheep	¼ inch	7½ feet	4 feet

FIG. 147: The *French Served Grommet* is a regular Grommet, served with French or Grapevine Hitching (PLATE 106, FIG. 22).

Plate 101—Miscellaneous Eye and Shroud Splices

FIG. 148: The *Four-Strand Eye Splice with French Seizing* is made by splicing the eye in, and then fraying the ends, which are finally laid around the standing part and seized.

FIG. 149: The *Regular Short Splice in Grommet.*

FIG. 150: The *Four-Strand Eye Splice with Lock Seizing* is tied by first splicing in the ends to form the eye. After the re-

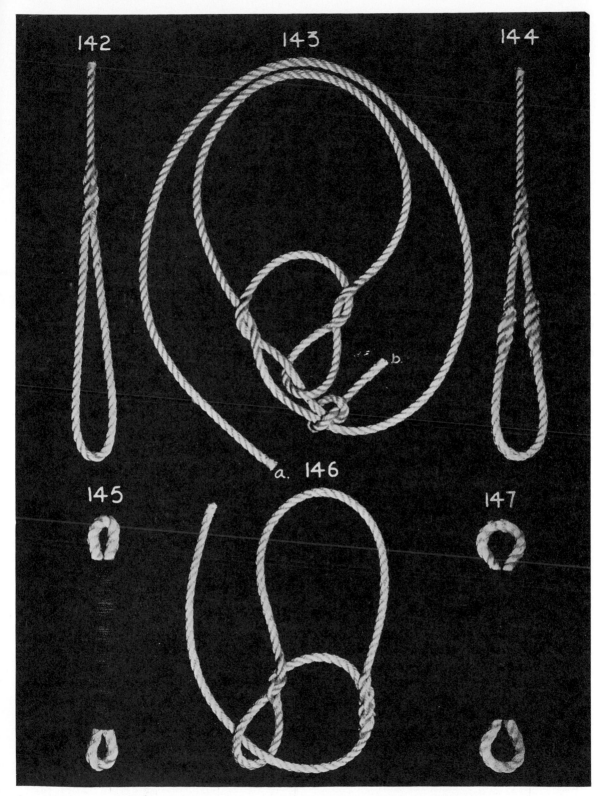

142   143   144

b.

a. 146

145   147

PLATE 100—HALTERS AND BULL EARING SPLICES

quired number of tucks have been made, each strand is split in half and seized to the opposite half of the next strand. This brings them all together in sets of two halves each.

Fig. 151: The *Three-Strand Inverted Wall Shroud* is composed of two Inverted Wall Knots (Plate 64, Fig. 197), tied back-to-back in the usual manner, and spliced into the standing part of the rope.

Fig. 152: The *Four-Strand Inverted Wall Shroud*.

Fig. 153: The *Eye Splice and Thimble*

Served has an Eye Splice made around a thimble, then tapered and served.

Fig. 154: The *Three-Strand Double Walled Crown Shroud* is made up of two Walled Crown Knots (Plate 62, Fig. 162), doubled and tied back-to-back in the usual way, then spliced into the standing part of the rope.

Fig. 155: The *Four-Strand Double Walled Crown Shroud*.

Fig. 156: The *Double Sheet Bend in Spliced Eye*.

Plate 102—Adjustable Halter and Chain Splices

Fig. 157: The *Non-Adjustable Halter* is formed by tucking the head-piece under one strand of the nose-piece, toward the left. Then skip two strands, and bring it back under one strand of the nose-piece, toward the right, to form the eye. After measuring the required length of bight for the nose-piece, splice the head-piece into the nose-piece at the proper distance. Splice one strand up toward the top of the bight and one strand down toward the bottom, with the other strand being spliced back into the head-piece.

Fig. 158: The *Standard Guard Loop Halter* is similar to the Loose Guard type, except that the short end is seized to the long end instead of being tied.

Figs. 159a and b: The *Chain Splice* is tied as follows: unlay the rope a considerable distance, and reeve strands *b* and *c* through the end link of the chain; then unlay strand *a* quite some distance down the rope; tuck strand *b* under strand *c*, and lay up strand *c* in the groove vacated by strand *a*. Join them together with an Overhand Knot, disposing of the strands by tucking against the lay, as in a regular Long Splice, with strand *b* also tucked over and under against the lay to finish. Fig. 159a illustrates the open Splice at the beginning; and Fig. 159b shows how it looks when complete.

Fig. 160: The *Sliding Chain Splice in Loop*.

Plate 103—Grommet, Eye and Back Splices

Fig. 161a: The *Three-Strand Grommet* represents a type of knot that can be utilized for making many different articles, such as strops, chest handles, or quoits. It is made from a single strand of rope, as follows: first, take a piece of rope of the desired thickness; determine the circumference of the Grommet you wish to make; then measure off three and one-half times this circumference. (In other words, if the circumference is one foot, three and one-half feet is the proper measurement.) Next, cut the rope and unlay one strand. Tie an

Overhand Knot in this strand, and begin laying up one strand as shown in the illustration.

b: When the ends meet, there will be a Grommet of two strands. Continue the strand around again, making three strands as illustrated here. (The strands have purposely been left short, in order to fit them into the photograph.)

c: When the strands meet again, halve them and tie an Overhand Knot. Then proceed to dispose of the ends as in the common Long Splice.

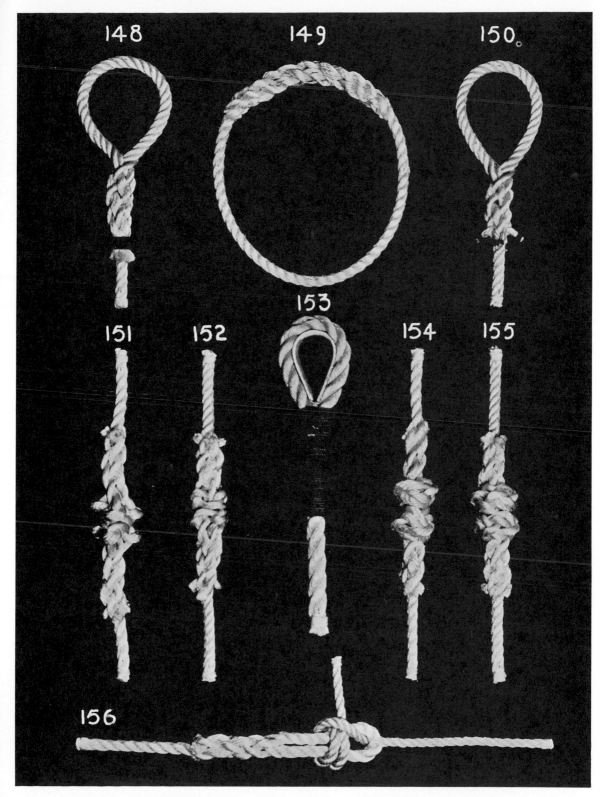

PLATE 101—MISCELLANEOUS EYE AND SHROUD SPLICES

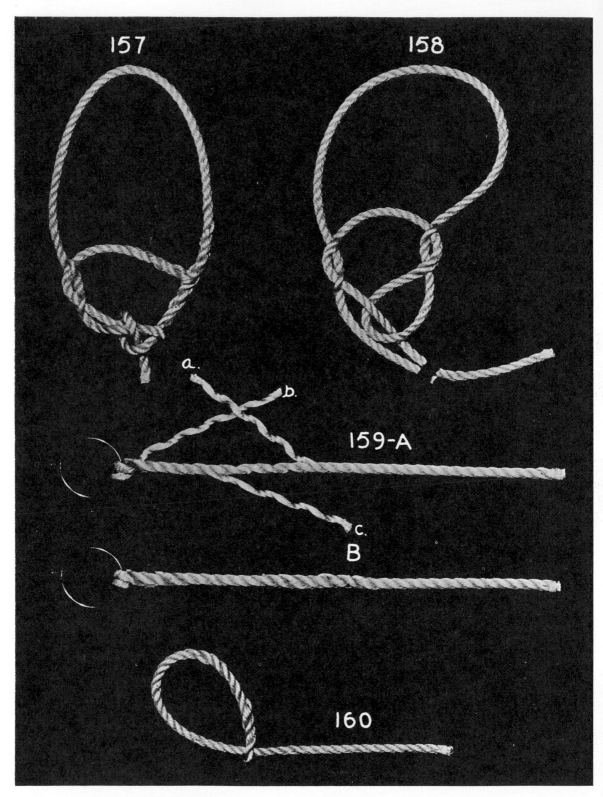

157

158

a.

b.

159-A

c.

B

160

PLATE 102—ADJUSTABLE HALTERS AND CHAIN SPLICES

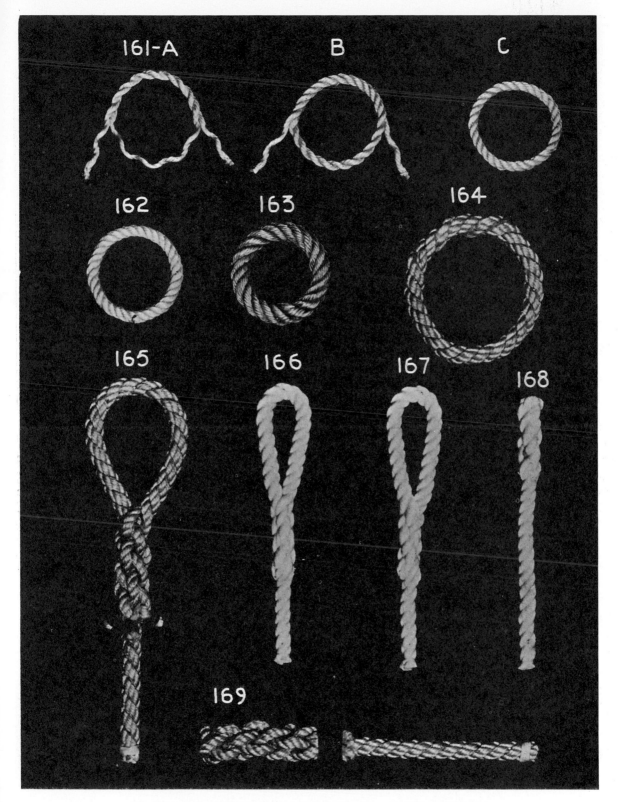

PLATE 103—GROMMET, EYE AND BACK SPLICES

FIG. 162: The *Four-Strand Grommet* is formed in precisely the same manner as the Three-strand Grommet. But the strand used must be *four and one-half* times the circumference of the desired Grommet. The strand must of course be unlaid from a four-strand rope.

FIG. 163: The *Six-Strand Grommet* is tied by first making a heart slightly larger than the inside of the finished Grommet itself. This heart is also a Grommet, but of three strands. Next, take a strand of six-strand wheel rope, *eight* times the circumference of the completed Grommet, and proceed as before.

FIG. 164: The *Cable-Laid* or *Mariner's Grommet* resembles the common Three-Strand Grommet. When the strands meet for the last time, the three strands which comprise one strand of the cable-laid rope are unlaid in each strand, and married. They are then long-spliced together, and the strands disposed of in the usual manner.

FIG. 165: The *Cable-Laid* or *Mariner's Eye Splice* is begun by unlaying the three strands and proceeding to splice in the ordinary way. Four tucks are usually made. When finished tucking, split the strands and take one-half of one strand and one-half of another and seize them together as indicated.

FIG. 166: The *Sailmaker's Eye Splice in Cotton Line* is made in the same fashion as the Sailmaker's Eye shown in PLATE 80, FIG. 11. The strands in cotton line are a little more difficult to keep in place, and so should be tucked very carefully.

FIG. 167: The *Eye Splice in Cotton Line* follows the same method as the common Eye Splice.

FIG. 168: The *Back Splice in Cotton Line* is tied in the same way as the common Back Splice.

FIG. 169: The *Cable-Laid* or *Mariner's Back Splice* is formed in the same manner as the common Back Splice. When three tucks have been made, the strands are unlaid and seized to the standing part as shown. They also may be finished off as in the Eye Splice (FIG. 165).

NOTE: The strands in cable-laid rope should always be finished off in the manner shown; otherwise the strands may work free when towing with the Splice under water.

Chapter V

Coxcombing

THIS CHAPTER IS DEVOTED to various types of Coxcombing, Coach Whipping and Cackling which are used extensively in the navies of many countries, serving as excellent decorative designs.

The work contained here may be summarized as follows: Coxcombing in various styles from one to six strands; Cackling in every known type of design; various methods of Fender Hitching and Spanish Hitching; Coach Whipping; and other different examples of work are dealt with extensively.

Ample explanations of how to tie each new example, and the various things for which they are used, are also covered. It will be found that as the student of rope work continues to master the different designs in this and the following chapters he will acquire the added ability of being able to execute the most beautiful and intricate designs in any kind of decorative examples that requires skill in fancy rope work.

Coxcombing is an ornamental method of covering hand-rails, rings, Flemish Eyes, or any round objects subject to wear and hard usage. In reality, Coxcombing and Half Hitching are the same. Hence, when it is desired to form a different type of Coxcomb, it is merely necessary to change the method of Half Hitching.

Plate 104—Channel and Running Coxcombing

Figs. 1a and b: The *Two-Strand Channel Coxcombing* is made as follows: two strands of line are seized to the rope or hand-rail, and a Half Hitch is taken to the right, on the right-hand side, as shown by strand *b*. Another Half Hitch is then taken with strand *a*, to the left, but below *b*. Next, make another Half Hitch to the right, with *b* again, but below *a*. This is continued until the desired length of Coxcomb is attained. Be sure to haul out all the slack and draw each Half Hitch up taut immediately after it is made. Fig. 1b shows the completed Coxcomb.

Figs. 2a and b: The *Coxcomb* illustrated is made in exactly the same way as the preceding Coxcomb, except that the crosses are put on the opposite sides. Fig. 2b shows the Coxcomb finished.

Figs. 3a and b: The *Two-Strand Cackling* is used for the same purpose as Coxcombing, but is given a different name. In reality, it is alternate crowning with two strands, and its formation is clearly shown in this illustration. Be certain, however, that where the strands hitch together these crosses are on opposite sides. Fig. 3b shows the finished Cackling.

Figs. 4a and b: The *Two-Strand Running Coxcomb* is made by seizing two strands to the rail and forming two Right-hand Hitches, followed by two Left-hand Hitches. Both Hitches are kept close to each other, so that they will appear together on top of the rail. The finished Coxcomb is shown in Fig. 4b.

Figs. 5a and b: The *Two-Strand Round Turn Running Coxcomb* is made in somewhat the same manner as the preceding Coxcomb, but the Half Hitch is supplemented by another full turn. Fig. 5b shows the completed Coxcomb.

Figs. 6a and b: The *Common Three-*

203

Strand Coxcomb is tied as follows: seize three strands to the rail; next, take one strand and form a Left-hand Half Hitch. With another strand, form a Right-hand Half Hitch. Then tie a Left-hand Half Hitch. In the illustration, *a* has been half-hitched to the left, *b* to the right, and *c* to the left. The next step is to begin with *a* again, hitching it to the right this time. The complete Coxcomb is shown in FIG. 6B.

FIGS. 7A and B: The *Three-Strand Running Coxcomb* is the same as the Coxcomb in FIG. 4, but with three strands. In the illustration, all the strands have been hitched to the left. Then they are all hitched to the right, beginning with *a*. FIG. 7B shows the finished Coxcomb.

FIGS. 8A and B: The *Doubled Two-Strand Running Coxcomb* is made with four strands. Two are worked into a Coxcomb resembling FIG. 5, on one side; and the other two are worked into the same type of Coxcomb on the opposite side. In the illustration, *a* and *b* have been hitched left-handed. Next, hitch *c* and *d* also left-handed. Begin over again with *a* and *b* in the same manner, but this time hitch them right-handed. Make sure that one set of Coxcombing is kept exactly opposite the other. FIG. 8B shows the Coxcombing complete.

Plate 105—Cackling and Spanish Hitching

FIGS. 9A and B: The *Three-Strand Cackling* resembles the Cackling described in PLATE 104, FIG. 3A, but is made with three strands instead of two. FIG. 9B shows the finished work.

FIGS. 10A and B: The *Two-Strand Coxcomb* is made in the following way: first stop down two lengths of small line to the rope or hand-rail; take one of these and make a Right-hand Half Hitch; bring the end back over to the left; take the other strand and again form a Half Hitch to the right, bringing the end back to the left after it has been drawn taut. This illustration shows strand *a* taken over to the left after the Half Hitch has been made. Strand *b* has been half-hitched to the right, and the end must now be brought over to the left. The complete Coxcomb is illustrated in FIG. 10B.

FIGS. 11A and B: The *Four-Strand Running Coxcomb* is begun by stopping four strands of line to the rope, then half-hitching each one in turn to the right, until all four have been hitched. Next, hitch each one to the left, beginning with the uppermost strand. The illustration shows all four hitched to the right. Begin again by hitching strand *a* to the left, then *b* to the left, and so on. The finished Coxcomb is shown in FIG. 11B.

FIGS. 12A and B: The *Four-Strand Cackling* follows the three-strand method. FIG. 12B shows the work complete.

FIGS. 13A and B: The *Three-Strand Coxcomb on Each Side with Six Strands* gives a distinct Three-Strand Coxcomb on each side of the work. It is made by working the strands in the same manner as in the common Three-Strand Coxcomb (PLATE 104, FIG. 6), but only one strand from each side is worked at a time. First, stop six strands of line to the hand-rail, placing three on each side. Hitch one strand of the right-hand group. Then hitch one strand of the left-hand group in the proper direction. Continue this, first taking one strand from one group, then one strand from the other, and hitching them as in a Three-Strand Coxcomb. The finished work is shown in FIG. 13B.

FIG. 14: The *Inside Spanish Hitching* is a very good way to make a fender for a small boat. Although it may appear difficult, this method of Coxcombing is in reality very simple. A suitable number of strands are first stopped to a piece of rope. Next, take a very long piece of line—

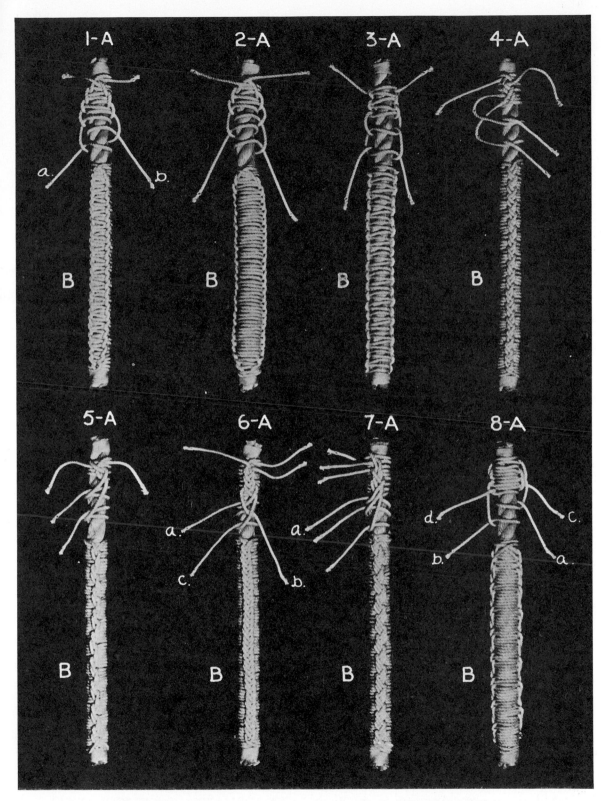

PLATE 104—CHANNEL AND RUNNING COXCOMBING

twenty-five to thirty times the length of the warp strands (*b*) used. This long strand will be called the filling strand (*a*). All the warp strands are then half-hitched on the filling strand, until the hitching has reached the desired length.

Fig. 15: The *Outside Spanish Hitching* is made in the same way as the preceding knot, but the warp strands are hitched so that the ends emerged on the outside of the filling strand. This type of knot is used for the same purpose as Fig. 14, but it has a much smoother surface. In this knot, *a* is the filling strand, and *b* the warp strands.

Fig. 16: The *Open Fender Hitching* is the method of hitching used to cover large fenders, such as those on the bow of a tug-boat, a familiar sight to everyone. This type of hitching is done with one strand. To begin, take two complete turns around the work with the end of the strand. Take the other end and begin half-hitching on these two turns until you have gone completely around the fender or rope. The next Half Hitch is taken on the bight, between two of the first group of Half Hitches that have been made. This is continued until the desired length is reached. It will be found necessary, when covering a large fender, to add a length of line from time to time; and this can be accomplished by long-splicing the two ends together. When working on an irregular surface a Half Hitch is left out or one can be added at intervals, whichever may be necessary.

Plate 106—Miscellaneous Coxcombing and Hitching Weaves

Figs. 17A and B: The *One-Strand Shade-Pull Coxcomb* is often used on the rings of shade-pull cords. It is formed by first placing a bight on top of the object to be covered. Next, bring one end of the bight around the object and pass it through the first bight from the opposite side, forming a small eye on top. Pass the line around underneath the object again, and form another bight alongside the first one. Bring the end back in the same way as before, to the opposite side, and form another small eye through both the bight and the eye made previously. Continue this method until the Coxcomb is as long as desired, taking care to keep the eyes on top and pulled up neatly. Fig. 17A shows the beginning, and Fig. 17B the completed Coxcomb.

Figs. 18A and B: The *Three-Strand Inside Hitch Weave* is made as follows: seize three strands around a core, and proceed by hitching each strand in turn to the next or following strand; pass the ends underneath their own part to form an Inside Hitch, pulling each Hitch up as snugly as possible to produce a neat-looking job. Fig. 18A shows the Hitches opened up, and Fig. 18B as they look when finished.

Fig. 19: The *Spiral Crown Hitching* is begun by seizing around a core as many strands of cotton line or Marline as desired. Then crown each complete set, pull up taut, and repeat the same method on top of the last set of Crowns until the required number have been completed. This method of crowning in the same direction produces a spiral effect.

Figs. 20A and B: The *One-Strand Chained Eye Coxcomb* is made by first seizing one strand to the object to be covered. Next, make a round turn and pass an eye under the turn, holding it in place on top while making the next pass, which is a complete round turn. Form another eye through the eye made previously. And make another complete round turn, which will bring the eye up through the previous eye, from the opposite side each time. This method is similar to Fig. 17, except that it has no bight under the eyes and lays flat instead of at an angle.

Fig. 21: The *Spiral Wall Hitching* is tied in the following way: seize around a

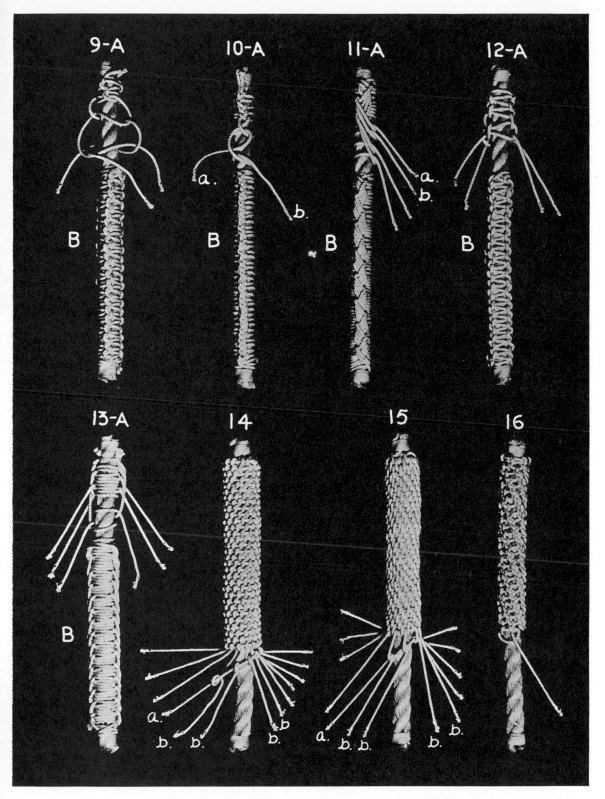

PLATE 105—CACKLING AND SPANISH HITCHING

core as many strands as desired; Wall each complete set, pull taut, and repeat as many times as necessary. The ends can be neatly finished off with Three-Strand Turk's Heads, as shown in the illustration.

FIG. 22: The *One-Strand French* or *Grapevine Hitching* is made by seizing one strand, and then hitching each turn around in rotation, pulling taut after each pass. This produces a spiral effect, as in the French Served Grommet.

FIG. 23: The *One-Strand Inverted Lark's Head Hitches* design is similar to the Lark's Head type of Cackling, except that the bights are passed underneath instead of on top, or just the reverse of the orthodox method.

FIG. 24: The *One-Strand Running Hitch Coxcomb* has each Hitch formed the same way, by passing the strand around from the same side each time, and forming the

Hitch or tucking underneath from the opposite side.

FIG. 25: The *One-Strand Running Coxcomb* is made by hitching the strand around to the left, then hitching it the opposite way, to the right, alternating each Hitch in turn.

FIG. 26: The *One-Strand Double Zig-Zag Coxcomb* is tied by making two Hitches to the left, then forming the next two Hitches the opposite way, to the right, reversing after each set of two Hitches.

FIG. 27: The *One-Strand French Coxcomb* is formed by hitching the line to the right, then making a complete round turn and hitching the opposite way. Make a round turn after each Hitch, and always hitch in alternate directions.

FIG. 28: The *One-Strand Triple Zig-Zag Coxcomb* is tied by making three Hitches in the same direction, then forming three more the opposite way, reversing after each set of three Hitches.

Plate 107—Miscellaneous Coxcombing and Hitching Weaves

FIGS. 29A and B: The *Four-Strand Coxcomb* is tied as follows: seize four strands to a core; hitch one of the strands one way, and then take a strand from the other side and hitch the opposite way; continue by taking from each side the strand nearest the top, and making alternate or opposite Hitches each time. FIG. 29A shows how to start, and FIG. 29B illustrates the finished appearance.

FIGS. 30A and B: The *Five-Strand Coxcomb* is made in the same way as the four-strand method, except that five strands are used instead. FIG. 30A shows how to begin the weave, which is complete in FIG. 30B.

FIGS. 31A and B: The *Six-Strand Coxcomb* follows the four- and five-strand methods. The Coxcomb is shown open in FIG. 31A and finished in FIG. 31B.

FIGS. 32A and B: The *Three-Strand Double Coxcomb* is similar to the ordinary

three-strand method, but with double strands instead of single. FIG. 32A shows the start, and FIG. 32B the completed weave.

FIGS. 33A and B: The *One-Strand Danish Coxcomb* is begun by seizing one strand to a core or any other desirable object. Then form a bight around the end seized, and pass the other end around the core and over its own part, tucking it under the previous pass. Next, bring it back toward the side it started from, and around the core again, then over its own part and under the previous pass as before. This creates a sort of hitched eye effect that resembles a Three-Strand Coxcomb. The Coxcomb is shown open in FIG. 33A, and finished in FIG. 33B.

FIGS. 34A and B: The *Four-Strand Coach-Whipping* or *Cross-Pointing* is tied by the same method as a Round Sennit Braid. In addition to its use as a braided line, it

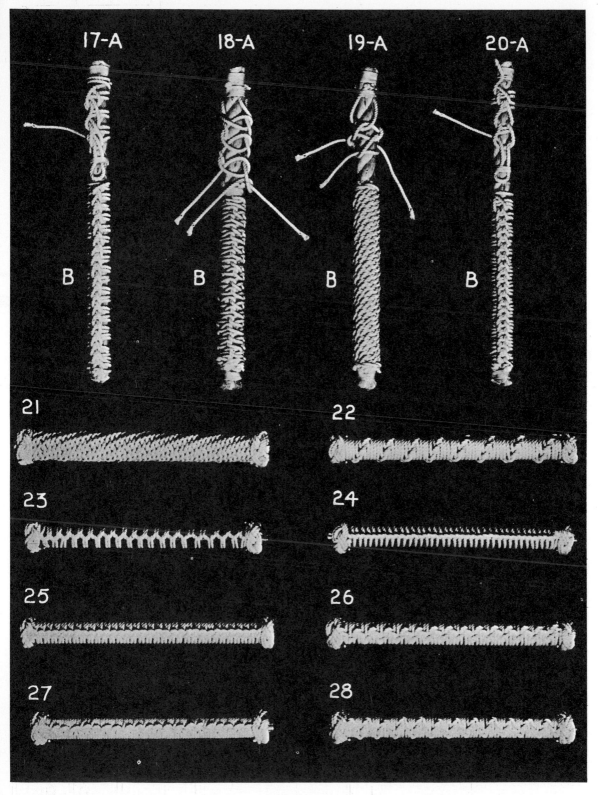

PLATE 106—MISCELLANEOUS COXCOMBING AND HITCHING WEAVES

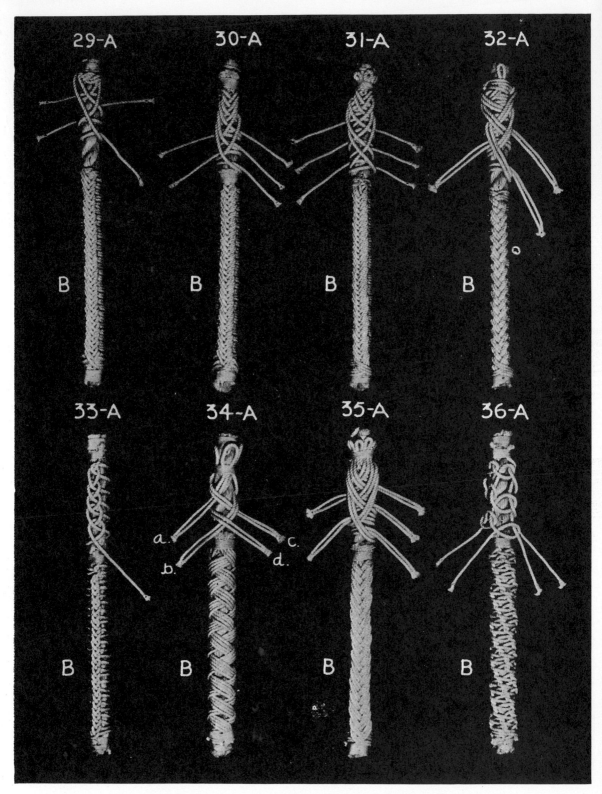

PLATE 107—MISCELLANEOUS COXCOMBING AND HITCH WEAVING

[*Plate 108*] Coxcombing 211

can also be formed around a core, as a covering for a stanchion, a telescope, a rope point, etc. It can be made with any even number of strands, which are often doubled, trebled, or quadrupled. To begin, take strand *c* and lay it across strand *a*. Strand *b* is brought around over *c* and under *d*, toward the opposite side. Follow up by bringing strand *a* around under *c* and over *d* to its own side. Then bring strand *c* around under *b* and over *a* to its own side —and so on, until the desired number of passes have been made. FIG. 34A shows how the seizings are made to start, and FIG. 34B shows the Coach-Whipping complete.

FIGS. 35A and B: The *Five-Strand Double Coxcomb* uses the regular five-strand method, except that the strands are double instead of single. FIG. 35A shows the open Coxcomb, and FIG. 35B illustrates how it looks when finished.

FIGS. 36A and B: The *Four-Strand Inside Hitch Weave* uses four strands, but follows the three-strand method. FIG. 36A pictures the Weave open, and FIG. 36B shows it when completed.

Plate 108—Hitching, Pointing, and Coach Whipping

FIGS. 37A and B: The *Diamond Hitching* is used for covering ropes, etc. It is made by stopping the desired amount of line around the rope to be covered, and then forming one set of Diamond Knots after another, until the required number have been completed. In FIG. 37A the Diamond Knots are shown open; in FIG. 37B, pulled up and closed.

FIGS. 38A and B: The *Three-Strand Hitching* represents another method of hitching a rope with three strands. It will be observed that each line is hitched under its own part and then through the eye of the following strand. On the third or last Hitch in each series, it is necessary to pull the line out to obtain enough slack for tying the Hitch. FIG. 38A shows the Hitches opened up, and FIG. 32B pictures them closed.

FIG. 39: The *Six-Strand Cackling.*

FIG. 40: The *Odd and Even Coach-Whipping* is begun by seizing one double strand, passing around the rope for the required number of turns, and then stopping down to the rope again. A single line is next passed over one double strand and under one double strand, following the groove of the rope. Bring it down and then up, and down again, alternating the over and under passes. In other words, make these passes back and forth, filling each groove of the rope.

FIG. 41: The *Spiral Pointing* is made as follows: a sufficient number of strands of small line (enough to cover the work closely) are seized to the core (be sure always to use an *odd* number of strands). Next, take a long piece of twine slightly smaller than the warp (cords leading up and down), and thread it through a sail-needle. This is called the filler. Then begin weaving around the work, over two and under two. After going around one complete turn, the filler cord will come up and go down between two strands of the warp, whereas the filling cord on the previous round went over or under these two. Although this may seem an error, it is quite correct, and when continued, the work will take on a spiral effect of its own accord. This type of Hitching can be used to cover fenders, like the Hitching shown in PLATE 105, FIGS. 14 and 15.

FIG. 42: The *Five-Strand Running Coxcomb* is made in the same manner as the Two-Strand Running Coxcomb, first hitching all strands to the right, then all to the left, etc.

FIG. 43: The *Running Pointing* is somewhat similar to the Pointing in FIG. 41; but it is not of the spiral variety. The warp

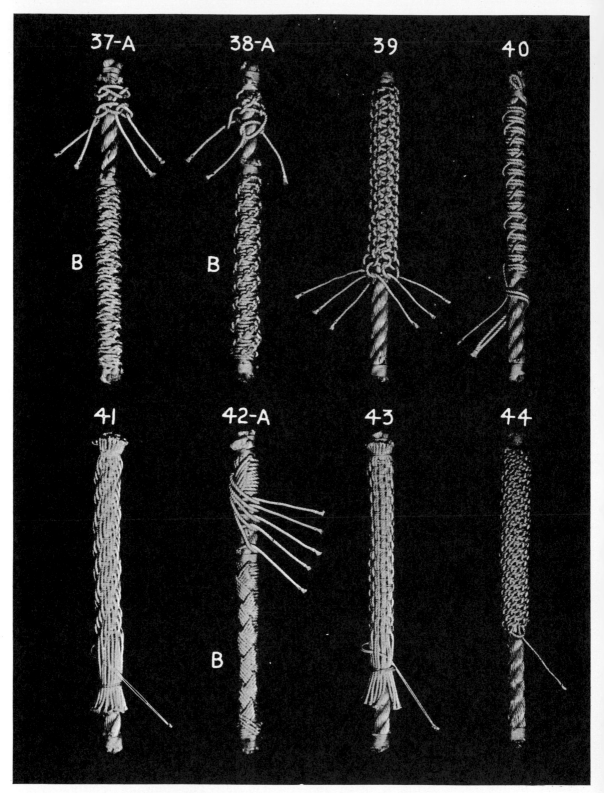

PLATE 108—HITCHING, POINTING AND COACH WHIPPING

here is merely a series of overs and unders. A sufficient number of strands are stopped to the core to cover it completely. (An *even* number of strands must always be used in this type.) Then a long piece of twine, smaller than the warp in diameter, is doubled and woven under two and over two, until the desired length is obtained.

Fig. 44: The *Closed Fender Hitching* is made in the same way as the Hitching in Plate 105, Fig. 16. But the Hitches are taken much closer together, so that the core upon which the work is being done can barely be seen through the Hitching, and the Hitching is inverted or the opposite from preceding method.

Chapter VI

Turk's Heads

THIS CHAPTER EMBRACES every style or method of tying a Turk's Head. It is one of the best known of all knots still in use today. There are many different types of Turk's Heads that are almost unknown and the majority of the examples presented here have an added interest for that reason.

There are several very rare designs such as the Five-Strand Endless Sennit Turk's Head which is made from one strand, the Bugler's Braid, and the Antique Braid Turk's Heads. Long Turk's Heads and various other designs will also be found novel and interesting.

The keys for extending the orthodox Turk's Heads to twenty-four and twenty-five strands, respectively, in both the even and odd types, were worked out while the authors served on sailing ships almost thirty years ago, and the other ideas and examples were acquired from almost every part of the world over a period of many years.

The Turk's Head is an ornamental knot, which may be used for decorating a stanchion or handrail, placed on a hammer handle in order to secure a firmer grip, or made into a beautiful napkin ring with the application of a little varnish. To follow the illustrations from step to step in tying this knot on a spar, turn your work with the top coming toward you as soon as you finish 1A, until stage B is reached. The first Turk's Head illustrated is one of three strands.

Plate 109—Detailed Illustrations of Turk's Heads

FIG. 1A: *Turk's Head,* First Stage, is represented in 1A. Now turn your work to B.

B: This shows the second stage of the work, with the free end taken from the right, up and between the two turns.

C: The turn *a* is to be pulled under the turn *b,* as shown by the drawn line.

D: The knot will now look as in D. The turn on the right-hand side was pushed to the left and under the left-hand turn. The moving end is now passed as shown by the arrow.

E: This shows how the Turk's Head should look after the tuck has been placed as previously described in D. The moving part is now taken from the right to the left, under and up through the center as the drawn line indicates.

F: The work is again turned to position F. At this position, *a* indicates the movement just executed in E. The working end was on the right-hand side, and has been passed through the right to the left. The Turk's Head is now complete, and all that is necessary is to follow the standing end with the moving end. However, be sure to watch that the passes taken to double the Turk's Head do not cross each other. After following around three times, the Turk's Head appears as in G.

G: This shows the Turk's Head as it looks when finished, if the directions have been carefully followed.

FIG. 2A: *Turk's Head Four-Strand.*

B: Notice that at *a* the moving part goes under both turns, instead of over and under.

C: The working end is then brought completely around the spar on the left-hand side, to the left of all the turns which have already been taken, and brought over

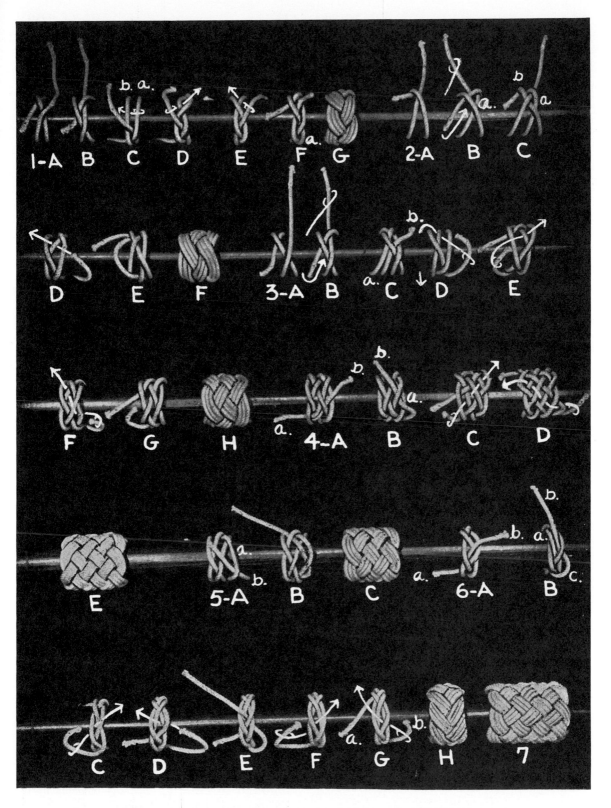

PLATE 109—DETAILED ILLUSTRATIONS OF TURK'S HEADS

b and under *a*, which will lock these strands.

D: The work is again turned until position D is reached. (Some of the turns may slip out of place as the knot is being worked on, and should be adjusted until they resemble the illustration). At this point the working end is put over, under, and over as the drawn line indicates. This is the final tuck to be made in the Turk's Head, and the work when turned appears as in E.

E: The moving end here follows the beginning as in the Three-Strand Turk's Head, until three passes are made. The ends are then put underneath the Turk's Head before it is drawn up; after it has been worked tight around the spar, the ends are cut off close.

F: The Four-Strand Turk's Head, when finished, appears as illustrated.

FIG. 3A: *Beginning a Five-Strand Turk's Head.* The first two movements (A and B) are in this case the same as the Three-Strand Turk's Head.

C: The end is brought completely around the spar on the left-hand side of the knot, to the left of all the turns, as in C of the Four-Strand Turk's Head just described. In this illustration, *a* is the standing part, and *b* is the moving part. The moving part is brought over and under, following strand *a*, to the right-hand side.

D: The work at this stage is turned to correspond with the illustration D, the drawn line indicating where the strand is to be put over, under, and over.

E: The work is now turned over, to correspond with E. At this point the two parallel strands are split and the moving strand is passed, as the drawn line shows.

F: The work is again turned until this position is reached. The moving part is then passed between the parallel strands under, over, under, and over for the last tuck to complete the Turk's Head as shown in G.

G: The moving end at this point fol-

lows the original beginning until three passes have been made.

H: The Turk's Head is now complete, and appears as in H. The ends are placed underneath, and the work drawn taut.

FIG. 4A: *To make a Turk's Head of any number of strands over four and five,* a "key" must be used. By using the "key" illustrated in 4A, any Turk's Head of an odd number of strands may be made, such as seven, nine, eleven, thirteen, etc. The first step in making this knot is to tie a Five-Strand Turk's Head, as in 3G. Then the moving part is passed up from left to right, as though in doubling it. The standing part is *a*, and *b* is the moving part.

B: The work is now turned. At this point the moving part *b* is crossed over the standing part *a*, and comes to the inside. It is then run from the right to the left, paralleling strand *a*.

C: The work is turned, and the moving part *b* is put over, under, over, under, and over as the drawn line shows, between the parallel turns.

D: The work is again turned over, and the moving part is passed between the parallel turns as indicated by the drawn line. This is the final tuck.

E: This illustration shows the Seven-Strand Turk's Head as it looks when it has been followed around three times.

FIG. 5A: *To make a Turk's Head of an even number strands over four-strands,* a "key" must be used, as in the Five-Strand Turk's Head; but it is made in a slightly different way. First, a Four-Strand Turk's Head is made. Then the end is followed up, just as in 4A. At this point compare 4B and 5A, because here is where the difference in the two knots lies. As is to be noticed in 4B, strand *b* is crossed *over* strand *a*, where as in 5A strand *b* crosses *under* strand *a*. After this, the same procedure is followed to close up the open parts as in 4C and 4D, by going in between the strands which have just been paralleled.

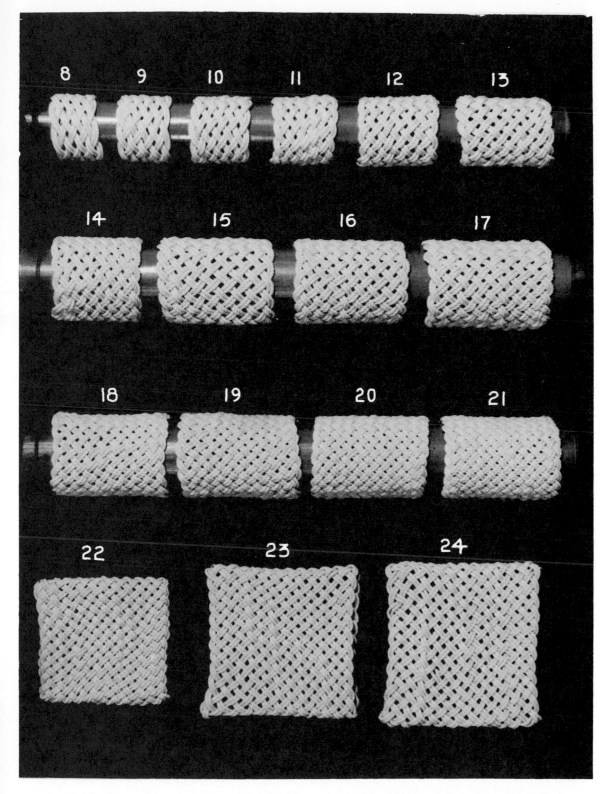

PLATE 110—NINE- TO TWENTY-FIVE-STRAND FINISHED TURK'S HEADS

B: This shows the Turk's Head after strand *b* has been pulled through.

C: The finished *Six-Strand Turk's Head* is represented in C.

FIG. 6A: *Five-Strand Unorthodox Endless Sennit Turk's Head.* This Turk's Head differs from the ordinary one, in that its strands go over two and under two. The first step is to make an ordinary Three-Strand Turk's Head, as in 1F. Then comes the most important move in the construction of this knot. The moving end *b* is brought up as if to double it, and placed just as in 6A. Note, however, that it must come in front of strand *a*.

B: This shows the second step. The moving end *b* is crossed over strand *a* and brought back down in front of it, from the right to the left. The step just completed in A is indicated by *c*.

C: The drawn line in this figure illustrates where the moving end must next be placed.

D: This step is traced by the drawn line.

Be certain that the strand goes under the first two and over the next two.

E: In this figure we see how the strand looks after it has been tucked through as explained in D.

F: The drawn line shows how the next tuck is placed, going from left to right.

G: The drawn line indicates how the final tuck should be made, again passed under two and over two.

H: Once the tuck in G has been made, the standing end *a* in G is followed by the moving end *b*, to double the strands. After it has been followed around three times, the finished Turk's Head appears as in H. The proper name for this knot is an *Endless Sennit Turk's Head.*

FIG. 7: *An Eight-Strand Turk's Head.* To tie it, a Four-Strand Turk's Head is first made. Then the "key" explained in 5A to 5C that is used to convert the Four- to a Six-Strand Turk's Head is also employed to transform the Six- into an Eight-Strand Turk's Head.

Plate 110—Nine- to Twenty-Five-Strand Finished Turk's Heads

FIG. 8: The *Nine-Strand Turk's Head* uses the "key" for Turk's Heads with an odd number of strands (PLATE 109, FIG. 4). Begin with a Five-Strand Turk's Head; then by use of the "key," form next the seven, and finally the nine.

FIG. 9: The *Ten-Strand Turk's Head* is formed by first making the Four-Strand Turk's Head, then using the "key" (PLATE 109, FIG. 5) to convert the four successively to a six, an eight, and a ten.

FIG. 10: The *Eleven-Strand Turk's Head.*

FIG. 11: The *Twelve-Strand Turk's Head.*

FIG. 12: The *Thirteen-Strand Turk's Head.*

FIG. 13: The *Fourteen-Strand Turk's Head.*

FIG. 14: The *Fifteen-Strand Turk's Head.*

FIG. 15: The *Sixteen-Strand Turk's Head.*

FIG. 16: The *Seventeen-Strand Turk's Head.*

FIG. 17: The *Eighteen-Strand Turk's Head.*

FIG. 18: The *Nineteen-Strand Turk's Head* and the following knots are made with smaller line than the preceding ones.

FIG. 19: The *Twenty-Strand Turk's Head.*

FIG. 20: The *Twenty-One-Strand Turk's Head.*

FIG. 21: The *Twenty-Two-Strand Turk's Head.*

FIG. 22: The *Twenty-Three-Strand*

[*Plate 111*]   Turk's Heads   219

Turk's Head and the next two Turk's Heads have been mounted flat, since they were much too large to mount on a spar.

Fig. 23: The *Twenty - Four - Strand Turk's Head.*

Fig. 24: The *Twenty-Five-Strand Turk's Head* required five and one-half hours to finish the first turn of five hundred and seventy-six tucks, and an additional four hours to complete the second pass, making a total of one thousand, one hundred and fifty-two tucks. One piece of line (60-thread seine twine), eighty-five feet in length, was used in making it.

Plate 111—Detailed Illustrations of Irregular Turk's Heads

Fig. 25: The *Three-Strand Irregular Turk's Head* is begun by tying an ordinary Three-Strand Turk's Head, and pulling it out rather loose. Make two extra tucks back and forth, as illustrated in Plate 109, Fig. 1c, which will bring it out in uniform order, so that it can be followed around in the usual manner.

Fig. 26: The *Four-Strand Irregular Turk's Head* (five crosses) is made by first tying an Overhand Knot around the hand or any suitable object, then working the crosses back and forth, over and under in the usual fashion, until it comes out correctly.

Fig. 27: The *Four-Strand Irregular Turk's Head* (seven crosses) is the same as Fig. 26, but with two additional crosses.

Fig. 28: The *Four-Strand Irregular Turk's Head* (nine crosses) begins with two Overhand Knots, tied as in the preceding knots. Then work the Turk's Head out in the usual way.

Figs. 29A and B: The *Five-Strand Irregular Turk's Head* is tied by first making an ordinary Three-Strand Turk's Head. Then cross over to the outside of the strand that is usually followed, in order to double the Three-Strand Turk's Head just completed. Follow this same strand around until it is necessary to split the strands after finishing the first passes, and pull the second strand from the outside, under the outside strand on each side, to make the tucks come out properly. Fig. 29A shows how to start the first pass, and Fig. 29B illustrates the completed knot.

Figs. 30A and B: The *Six-Strand Irregular Turk's Head* is extended from the Four-Strand Turk's Head with five crosses. After this knot has been made, tuck the line under the first cross in the center, doubling the underneath crossing-strand. Follow this strand around with a complete pass, until it is necessary to split the strands at the intersection, in order to work the tucks out correctly. Continue by tucking over and under in the usual manner. Fig. 30A shows how to begin the first pass, and the completed knot is pictured in Fig. 30B.

Fig. 31: The *Six-Strand Irregular Turk's Head* is an extension of the Four-Strand Turk's Head with seven crosses. After completing the four-strand knot, use the method of extending it explained in Fig. 30.

Fig. 32: The *Seven-Strand Irregular Turk's Head* is extended from the Five-Strand Irregular Turk's Head, by means of the same method used for extending the Five from a Three-Strand Irregular Turk's Head (*see* Fig. 29).

Fig. 33: The *Eight-Strand Irregular Turk's Head* is an extension of the Six-Strand Turk's Head with five crosses. It follows the method used in extending the Six from the Four-Strand Turk's Head with five crosses.

Fig. 34: The *Royal Carrick Bend Turk's Head* begins with a Royal Carrick Bend, tied as shown in Plate 138, Fig. 11, and then converted into Turk's Head form by passing a spar through the center of the knot.

Fig. 35: The *Japanese Turk's Head* is

made by tying a Japanese Knot as shown in PLATE 23, FIG. 32, and then converting it into the Turk's Head form.

FIG. 36: The *Five-Strand Endless Sennit in Four-Strand Turk's Head* necessitates doing two things at the same time. The Five-Strand Endless Sennit (PLATE 109, FIG. 6) has to be woven, and at the same time the Four-Strand Turk's Head must be tied. The whole operation is performed with only one strand, which should test the skill of the more advanced students in fancy rope work.

FIG. 37: The *Five-Strand Turk's Head Made with a One-Strand Bugler's Braid* begins with a Bugler's Braid as shown in PLATE 120, FIG. 131. Allow enough length to form into a Five-Strand Turk's Head, and then close it up in the same manner as the Bugler's Braid Turk's Head in PLATE 111, FIG. 50.

FIG. 38: The *One-Strand Chain Hitch Turk's Head* is made by first tying a Chain Hitch Braid as shown in PLATE 120, FIG. 134. Then close up and double.

FIG. 39: The *Four-Strand Turk's Head with One Carrick Bend* begins with a Four-Strand Turk's Head with five crosses, after which both ends are brought out in the center, with only one strand separating them. Tie a Carrick Bend with these ends, and make the required number of passes in the Turk's Head. By properly adjusting the weaving of the strands, it will be found that four complete passes will give two passes in the Carrick Bend.

FIG. 40: The *Four-Strand Turk's Head with Two Carrick Bends* is tied as follows: make a Four-Strand Turk's Head with five crosses, and form a Carrick Bend with both strands where the strands meet; double the same strand as usual, and work both ends around to the center on the opposite side. Tie another Carrick Bend in the same manner as before, and proceed by doubling in the usual strands after the Carrick Bends

are tied. This method gives the same number of passes in both the Carrick Bend and the Turk's Head.

FIG. 41: The *Five-Strand Turk's Head with One Carrick Bend* starts out with a Five-Strand Turk's Head tied in the usual way. Then form the Carrick Bend as previously explained.

FIG. 42: The *Five-Strand Turk's Head with Two Carrick Bends* is tied in the same way as FIG. 41, with an extra Carrick Bend.

FIG. 43: The *Two-Strand Turk's Head* is made by crossing one strand around the other, first over and then under.

FIG. 44: The *Three-Strand Simple Turk's Head* is formed by first tying a Clove Hitch. Then cross over the strands on the left side, with the working part coming out parallel to the standing part of the strand, in order to double it.

FIG. 45: The *Interlocking Hitch Turk's Head* shows a series of Interlocking Hitches tied in the form of a Turk's Head.

FIG. 46: The *Carrick Bend Turk's Head* pictures a series of Carrick Bends in the form of a Turk's Head.

FIG. 47: The *Napoleon Bend Turk's Head* consists of a Napoleon Bend converted into Turk's Head form.

FIG. 48: The *Seven-Strand French Sennit Turk's Head* represents a Seven-Strand French Sennit converted into Turk's Head form. The passes are over two and under one, instead of the usual Turk's Head method of over one and under one. An easy way to learn to tie this type of Turk's Head is to make the braid first, and then close it up, with all strands coming out correctly with their counterparts on the opposite end of the braid. Leave it open and trace through with one single strand. Pull the other strands out, and you have a Seven-Strand Turk's Head ready to double.

FIG. 49: The *Nine-Strand French Sennit Turk's Head* follows the "key" of over

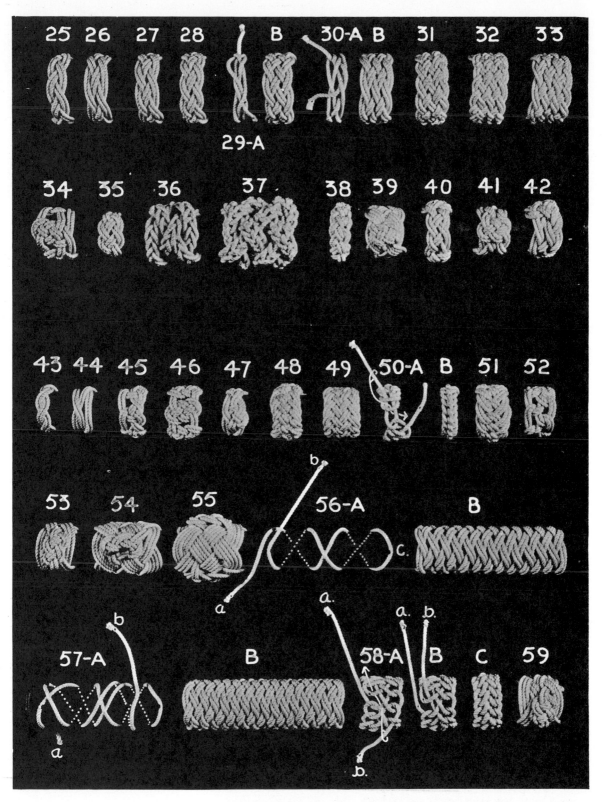

PLATE 111—DETAILED ILLUSTRATIONS OF IRREGULAR TURK'S HEADS

two and under two. It can be formed in the same manner as Fig. 48, and makes a very attractive Turk's Head.

Figs. 50a and b: The *Single Bugler's Braid Turk's Head* begins with an ordinary Bugler's Braid (PLATE 120, Fig. 131), which is next closed up as shown in Fig. 50a. It can be closed very easily by merely following the weave in the strands on both ends, and then making the closing tucks correspond accordingly. Fig. 50b shows how the knot appears when pulled up and closed.

Fig. 51: The *Double Bugler's Braid Turk's Head* is made in the same fashion as the single method, but doubled.

Fig. 52: The *Interlocking Figure-of-Eight Turk's Head* shows a series of Figure-of-Eights converted into Turk's Head form.

Fig. 53: The *Four-Strand Turk's Head with Vertical Carrick Bend* is made by first tying the Turk's Head. Then form a Vertical Carrick Bend with both ends of the line in the center. Follow the usual method in completing the additional passes.

Fig. 54: The *Five-Strand Turk's Head with One Carrick Bend* is tied as follows: first, form a Five-Strand Turk's Head; follow it around again to double it. Before going completely around, select the place where the Carrick Bend is to be formed, and then pull some slack through and twist the strand into the position of one loop of the Carrick Bend. Next, pass the moving part around the loop to double it. It will be found that if the loop is untwisted, one strand will cross the other at this point. Pass the strand through the Turk's Head again, but this time do not follow around the loop. The next pass, making the fourth, the moving part will be found to be on the inside of the three previous turns when it comes opposite the loop formed with the first two turns. The moving part is then passed around the loop on the right-hand side, and continued on until the standing

end is reached. There will now be a Turk's Head of four passes, with a Carrick Bend doubled on the right-hand side and a single on the left-hand side. All that remains is to follow around once more. This will double the last part of the Carrick Bend. When the moving and standing ends meet again, they are both tucked under the whole Turk's Head, and cut off short.

Fig. 55: The *Five-Strand Turk's Head with One Carrick Bend on Each Side* is formed in the same manner as the preceding Turk's Head, but instead of working with only one loop, two are worked, one on each side of the Turk's Head. Remember to form the loops on the right and not on the left-hand side.

Figs. 56a and b: The *Two-Turn "Even" Long Turk's Head* has a special purpose. When Turk's Heads are formed as shown in PLATES 109 and 110, they can be made to cover a larger surface by merely adding an additional strand. The larger they are, the larger the object must be that they cover. Therefore, if it is desired to cover the full length of an object, such as a hammer-handle or hand-rail, a Twenty-five-Strand Turk's Head probably would be long enough. However, its diameter would be much too great. In order to overcome this, use is made of another type of Turk's Head, which can be formed as long as necessary without increasing its diameter. In this type of Turk's Head, the number of "strands" can be counted by noting how many times the strand has reached the end of the knot and turned back. When forming this type of Turk's Head, it is advisable to place small studs or tacks in the object being worked on, in order to keep the line in place while tying the knot.

To begin, take a suitable length of line and place two complete turns around the spar, until it reaches stud *c*. (The word "turns" refers to the number of times the line has been passed entirely around the object being covered before reaching the

[*Plate 111*]   Turk's Heads   223

end and turning back.) If it is desired to make a longer Turk's Head, the studs may be placed farther apart; and instead of two turns being taken, three, four, five, or any number of turns can be made. The line must always be hooked on the stud directly opposite the stud where the work is begun. Then start going back to the beginning of the knot. The strand is given two complete turns around the spar, until it reaches the opposite stud. It is then brought back, but instead of going over and under on the return, it is taken over on each side, both front and back. When the beginning is reached, the strand is hooked to the next stud away from you, and brought back to the right again, paralleling the first strand, continuing to go over all the strands both front and back. When the end has been reached, hook the strand on the next stud and begin going back, under the first strand and over the second. Continue this until the end is reached. Proceed to weave over and under until the four studs have been taken up. The strand will have to be put under one and over two in order to pass in the reverse way at times. End *a* in this case is the standing end, and *b* the moving end. Fig. 56B illustrates the completed Turk's Head.

Figs. 57A and B: The *Two-Turn "Odd" Long Turk's Head* is similar to the "Even" Long Turk's Head. Five studs are used in this case, instead of four. Make a succession of overs and unders, going under in back and over in front. The line is then hooked on the next stud away from you, and led back, closely following the first strand, going over where the first strand goes under, and under where the first strand goes over. At times, the strand will have to be put over two and under two or over one and under two, in order to pass in the reverse way to the preceding strand. This apparent mistake will correct itself when the next turn is made. Follow this procedure until all of the five studs have been used. The work is now doubled, or three passes may be taken if desired. The finished Turk's Head is shown in Fig. 57B. End *a* is the standing end, and *b* the moving end.

Fig. 58A: The *Antique Braid Turk's Head* is formed by first tying the Antique Braid (Plate 136, Fig. 412). Make it long enough to go almost completely around the object being covered. Be certain that when both ends of the Braid meet part *a* is on the right-hand side, and part *b* on the left. Then proceed as in this illustration, working with end *b*.

B: After carrying the work this far, tuck end *a* in the manner shown. To complete the job, tuck end *b* back through the same opening from which end *a* emerges. The work is then drawn up taut, and the ends cut off short.

C: This shows the finished Turk's Head.

Fig. 59: The *Five-Strand Turk's Head with Vertical Carrick Bend* is similar to the Turk's Head explained in Fig. 53.

Chapter VII

Sennit Braiding

SENNIT BRAIDING OR PLAITING has been practiced in many countries at one time or another down through the ages. Mexican cowboys do quite a bit of this attractive work in leather and horsehair braiding, particularly their whips and sombrero chin straps. The cowboys of western America have also used it to some extent in the braiding of saddle ornaments and lariats. In France during the last century this beautiful art reached the peak of its development among French leather workers, who used an extensive variety of the different types of braiding in the making of harness, whips, belts, and many other useful articles. Fancy braiding also has been used more or less as a hobby by sailors on long sea voyages and in the making of decorative work as a cover for picture-frames and knot-boards.

After long years of laborious search and study in many different lands, the authors have acquired by far the most comprehensive knowledge of this subject ever compiled. Having originated a great many of the different braids, they have therefore had the added task of finding suitable names for them.

For the beginner, it probably would be better to first secure the strands to a board or ring, and letter them as they are lettered in the illustrations. Always keep right and left-hand groups of strands divided and in their proper places.

Plate 112—Sennit Braiding

FIG. 1: The *Three-Strand Sennit* is started with one strand, *a*, on the left, and *b* and *c* in the right group. Start with *c*, bring it down over and across *b* to the left side; then bring *a* down over and across *c* to the right side, and so on—repeating this method until you have the length of braid desired.

FIG. 2: The *Four-Strand Round Sennit* is made by bringing strand *a* down and in back, then under *d* and over *c*, toward the left side. Next, bring strand *d* down and in back, then under *b* and over *a*, toward the right side. Bring strand *b* down and in back, and between *c* and *d*, passing it over *d* toward the left side. Then bring *c* down and in back, between *a* and *b*, passing it over *b* toward the right side, and so on. This braid can be started from either side, which applies to all the other braids as well.

FIG. 3: The *Five-Strand Crabber's Eye Sennit* has its strands separated 3-2. Start with strand *e*; bring it down under from right to left; then pass it between *b* and *c* and over *c* toward the right, or its own side. Next, bring *a* down under from left to right and between *d* and *e* and over *e* toward the left, or its own side. Bring *d* down under from right to left, then under two and over one toward the right side, or in other words, between *c* and *a* and over *a*. Proceed by bringing *b* down from left to right and between *e* and *d* and over *d*. Continue by bringing *e* down under from right to left and between *a* and *b* and over *b* toward the right. The key to this braid is down under from left to right, then right to left, going under one and over one from one side, then under two and over one from the other side.

FIG. 4: The *Five-Strand Running Sen-*

224

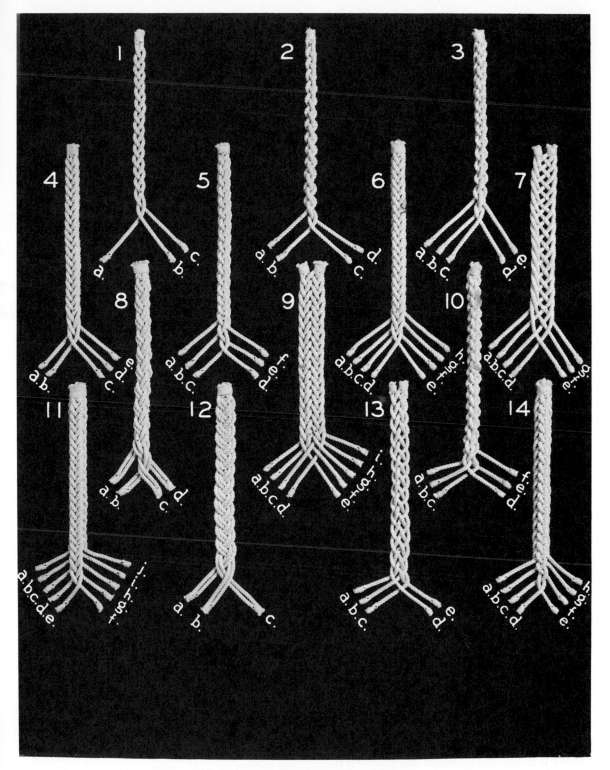

PLATE 112—SENNIT BRAIDING

nit is made the same as FIG. 1, the only difference being that the outside strand is brought down across the front, and over two instead of one as in the Three-Strand Sennit. Repeat from the opposite side, bringing strand *e* down across and over *d* and *c*. Then bring *a* down across and over *b* and *e*, repeating this as many times as necessary for the desired length of braid.

FIG. 5: The *Six-Strand Half Round Sennit* has its strands divided 3-3. Begin with *a* down and under from left to right and up between *d* and *e*, over *d*, then across to the left side or group. Bring strand *f* down and under from right to left and up between *c* and *a* and over *a* to the right side; then *b* down and over left to right and up between *f* and *d*, and over *f* to the left side, and so on. The rule is down and under from first one side and then the other, then under two and over one and back to its own side.

FIG. 6: The *Eight-Strand Square Sennit* divides its strands 4-4. Start with strand *h* down under and around from right to left, then up between *b* and *c* and over *c* and *d*, which will place it on the inside of *e*. Bring *a* down under and around from left to right and up between *e* and *f*, then over *h* and *e* to the inside of *d*. Next, repeat the same process with strand *g*, and so on. *Rule: each strand goes under and around, then under two and over two, and back to its own side.*

FIG. 7: The *Seven-Strand French Sennit* has the strands divided 4-3. Start with *a* across the front and over *b* and *c*, then under *d*. Bring *g* over *f* and *e*, then under *a* from the opposite side, and so on. *Rule: across the front from first one side and then the other, and over two and under one toward the opposite side.*

FIG. 8: The *Four-Strand Double Round Sennit* is made the same as the Four-Strand Single Round Sennit, with double instead of single strands (*see* FIG. 2).

FIG. 9: The *Nine-Strand French Sennit* divides its strands 5-4. Start with strand

i across the front and over *h* and *g*, then under *f* and *e* toward the opposite side. Now proceed with *a* over *b* and *c*, then under *d* and *i*. *Rule: use the odd strand on either side, then across the front, over two and under two toward the opposite side.*

FIG. 10: The *Six-Strand Round Sennit* has its strands separated 3-3. Start with strand *a* down and around in back from left to right, then over *f*, under *e*, and over *d* to the inside of *c*. Now bring strand *f* down and around in back from right to left, then over *b*, under *c*, and over *a* to the inside of *d*. *Rule: down and around in back, then over one, under one, and over one, toward its own side. Be very careful that the strands are held in place for this braid; otherwise you will lose the key and have to start over again.*

FIG. 11: The *Ten-Strand Comb Sennit* is tied as follows: divide the strands 5-5, and start with strand *j*, bringing it down under from right to left, then up between *c* and *d*, and over *d* and *e*, toward its own side. Proceed with strand *a*, bringing it down and around from left to right, then up between *g* and *f* and over *f* and *j*. *The rule to remember is down and around in back from the left side and then the right side, or vice versa, going under three and then over two toward its own side before repeating from the opposite side.*

FIG. 12: The *Three-Strand Double Sennit* is formed the same as the Three-Strand Single Sennit in FIG. 1, with double instead of single strands.

FIG. 13: The *Five-Strand Single Flat* or *English Sennit* has its strands divided 3-2. Then start with strand *a* and bring it across the front and over *b*, then under *c* toward the opposite side. Now take strand *e* across the front, then over *d* and under *a* toward the opposite side, and so on. *The rule to follow is over one, then under one, across the front toward the opposite side, and vice versa.* When braiding Flat Sennits, always remember that in the beginning you start

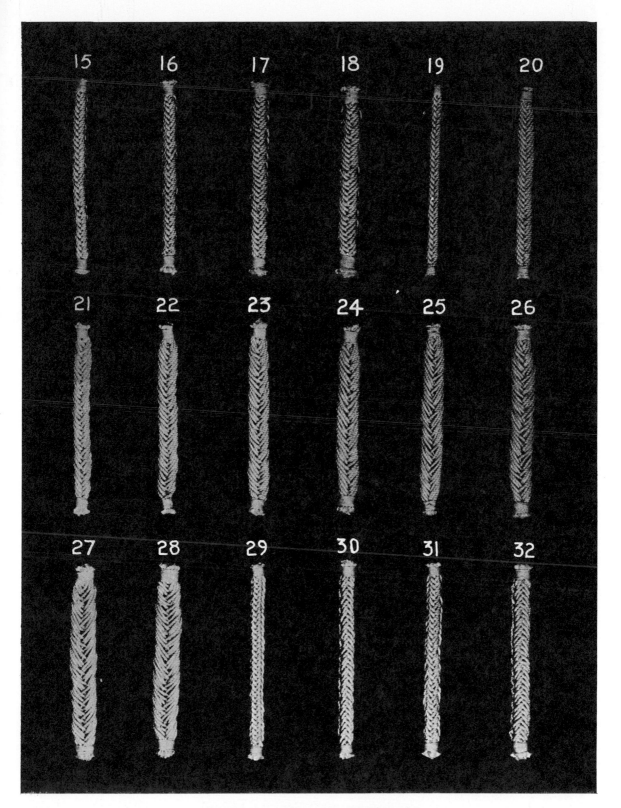

PLATE 113—SENNIT BRAIDING

over and then under from both sides on all odd number of strands; whereas on all even number strands you start over and under from one side, and then under and over from the other side.

Fig. 14: The *Eight-Strand Half Hexagonal Sennit* has its strands separated 4-4. Start with strand *h* down and under right to left, then up between *c* and *d* and over

d "left to right," and inside *e*. Bring strand *a* down and under left to right, then up between *e* and *h* and over *h* "right to left," then inside *d*. Proceed by next taking strand *g*, and so on. *Rule: take each strand down under and around, then under three and over one toward its own side.* This Sennit is flat on one side and three-sided on the other.

Plate 113—Sennit Braiding

Fig. 15: The *Twelve-Strand Square Sennit* is tied in the same way as the Eight-Strand Square Sennit in PLATE 112, FIG. 6. The key, however, is around in back from left to right, then right to left (or vice versa), and under three, then over three, toward its own side.

Fig. 16: The *Sixteen-Strand Square Sennit* duplicates the preceding methods. The key is under four and over four, from first one side and then the other, until the desired length of braid is attained.

Fig. 17: The *Twenty-Strand Square Sennit* follows the methods already described. The key is under five and over five.

Fig. 18: The *Twenty-Four-Strand Square Sennit* uses a key that goes under six and over six.

Fig. 19: The *Seven-Strand Running Sennit* is identical with the five-strand version in PLATE 112, FIG. 4, but the outside strand is brought down across the front, and over three, from first one side and then the other.

Fig. 20: The *Nine-Strand Running Sennit* is made in the same fashion as the preceding knots. The key, however, is over four, across the front, from first one side and then the other.

Fig. 21: The *Eleven-Strand Running Sennit* uses a key that goes over five, across the front, from both sides.

Fig. 22: The *Thirteen-Strand Running Sennit* is tied over six, across the front, in the usual way.

Fig. 23: The *Fifteen-Strand Running Sennit* is over seven, across the front.

Fig. 24: The *Seventeen-Strand Running Sennit* is over eight, across the front.

Fig. 25: The *Nineteen-Strand Running Sennit* is over nine, across the front.

Fig. 26: The *Twenty-One-Strand Running Sennit* is over ten, across the front.

Fig. 27: The *Twenty-Three-Strand Running Sennit* is over eleven, across the front.

Fig. 28: The *Twenty-Five-Strand Running Sennit* is over twelve, across the front.

Fig. 29: The *Twelve-Strand Comb Sennit* follows the ten-strand method in PLATE 112, FIG. 11, except that the key is under four and over two, from first one side and then the other.

Fig. 30: The *Fourteen-Strand Comb Sennit* duplicates the previous methods, but the key is under four and over three.

Fig. 31: The *Sixteen-Strand Comb Sennit* goes under five and over three, in the usual manner.

Fig. 32: The *Eighteen-Strand Comb Sennit* goes under five and over four, from first one side and then the other.

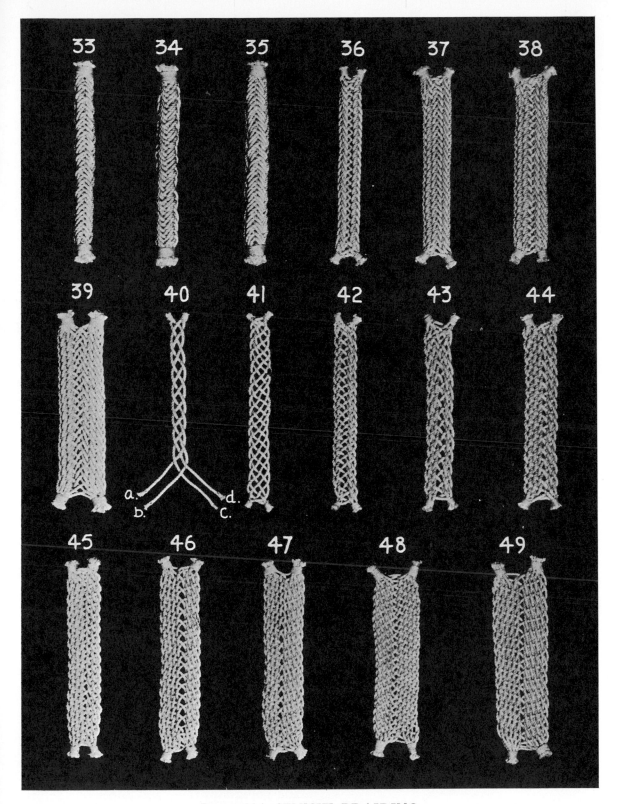

PLATE 114—SENNIT BRAIDING

Plate 114—Sennit Braiding

FIG. 33: The *Twenty-Strand Comb Sennit* is under six and over four, and so on.

FIG. 34: The *Twenty-Two-Strand Comb Sennit* is under six and over five.

FIG. 35: The *Twenty-Four-Strand Comb Sennit* is under seven and over five.

FIG. 36: The *Thirteen-Strand French Sennit* is made in the same manner as the nine-strand method in PLATE 112, FIG. 9. When increasing the strands in this type of Sennit, multiply the over and under tucks accordingly. Keep the key of over two and under two the same.

FIG. 37: The *Seventeen-Strand French Sennit.*

FIG. 38: The *Twenty-One-Strand French Sennit.*

FIG. 39: The *Twenty-Five-Strand French Sennit* shows how this type of Sennit changes in appearance as the number of strands are increased.

FIG. 40: The *Four-Strand Single Flat* or *English Sennit* is tied as follows: starting with strand *b*, bring it under strand *d* and over strand *c* to the center. Next, bring strand *a* over strand *b* to the center. Then pass strand *d* under strand *c*, and over strand *a*, and so on. Remember, when braiding

with an even number of strands in a flat braid, that the outside strand on one side has to be started under, and the one on the other side started over. With an odd number of strands, the outside strands on both sides are started over the next strand, then under, etc.

FIG. 41: The *Six-Strand Single Flat* or *English Sennit* is formed in the same way as the four-strand method, but with six strands.

FIG. 42: The *Eight-Strand Single Flat* or *English Sennit.*

FIG. 43: The *Ten-Strand Single Flat* or *English Sennit.*

FIG. 44: The *Twelve-Strand Single Flat* or *English Sennit.*

FIG. 45: The *Fourteen-Strand Single Flat* or *English Sennit.*

FIG. 46: The *Sixteen-Strand Single Flat* or *English Sennit.*

FIG. 47: The *Eighteen-Strand Single Flat* or *English Sennit.*

FIG. 48: The *Twenty-Strand Single Flat* or *English Sennit.*

FIG. 49: The *Twenty-Two-Strand Single Flat* or *English Sennit.*

Plate 115—Sennit Braiding

FIG. 50: The *Twenty-Four-Strand Single Flat* or *English Sennit.*

FIG. 51: The *Five-Strand Double Running Sennit* (ten strands) is identical with the five-strand single method shown in PLATE 112, FIG. 4, but the strands are doubled.

FIG. 52: The *Seven-Strand Double Running Sennit* (fourteen strands) is the same as the seven-strand single method.

FIG. 53: The *Six-Strand Even Irregular Sennit* (First Set) is braided across the front,

first from one side and then the other. The key is over one and under one from one side, and over two and under one from the other side. Strand *c* is brought down over strand *f* and under strand *e*. Then strand *d* is brought down over strands *a* and *b*, under *c*, and so on.

FIG. 54: The *Eight-Strand Even Irregular Sennit* is made by starting with the outside strands, as in the preceding methods, and going over three and under one across the front from one side, then over two and under one from the other.

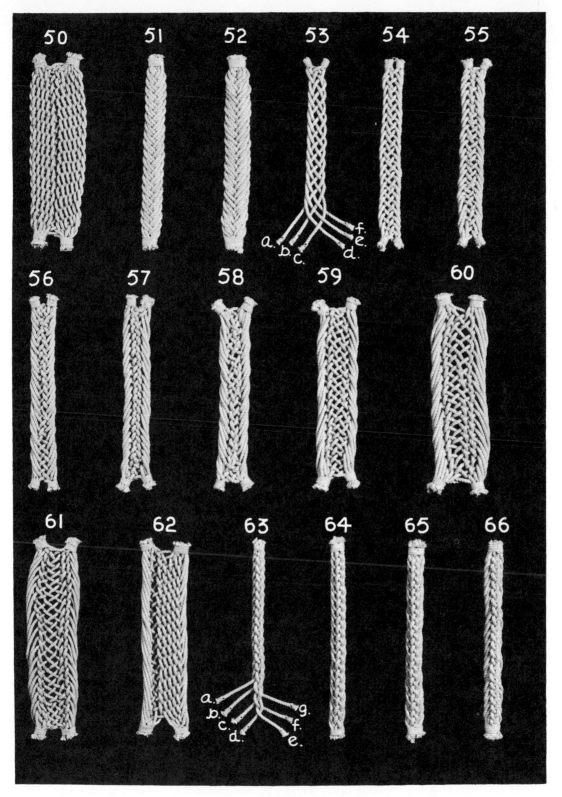

PLATE 115—SENNIT BRAIDING

FIG. 55: The *Ten-Strand Even Irregular Sennit* goes over four and under one from one side, then over three and under one from the other.

FIG. 56: The *Twelve-Strand Even Irregular Sennit* goes over five and under one, then over four and under one, and so on.

FIG. 57: The *Fourteen-Strand Even Irregular Sennit* goes over five, under one, and over one from one side; then over four, under one, and over one from the other side.

FIG. 58: The *Sixteen-Strand Even Irregular Sennit* goes over six, under one, and over one from one side; then over five, under one, and over one from the opposite side.

FIG. 59: The *Eighteen-Strand Even Irregular Sennit* goes over six, under one, over one, and under one from one side; then over five, under one, over one, and under one from the other side.

FIG. 60: The *Twenty-Strand Even Irregular Sennit* goes over six, under one, over one, under one, and over one from one side. Then on the other side, go over five, and repeat the procedure used on the opposite side—going under and over four times, in order to reach the center of the braid.

FIG. 61: The *Twenty-Two-Strand Even Irregular Sennit* first goes over six from one

side, and five from the other, repeating the under and over process five times after the first pass is made from either side.

FIG. 62: The *Twenty-Four-Strand Even Irregular Sennit* uses the same key as the preceding braid, except that six passes are necessary to reach the center, instead of five.

FIG. 63: The *Seven-Strand Odd Variated Sennit* (First Set) has its strands passed around in back from first one side and then the other. The key is under three and over one and back toward its own part from one side, then under two and over one and back toward its own part from the other side. Strand *e* is brought down in back from right to left, then under strand *c* and over strand *d*. Strand *a* is next brought down in back from left to right, then under strand *f* and over strand *e*.

FIG. 64: The *Nine-Strand Odd Variated Sennit* goes under four and over one from one side, then under three and over one from the other.

FIG. 65: The *Eleven-Strand Odd Variated Sennit* goes under five and over one from one side, then under four and over one from the other side.

FIG. 66: The *Thirteen-Strand Odd Variated Sennit* goes under six and over one from one side, then under five and over one from the other.

Plate 116—Sennit Braiding

FIG. 67: The *Fifteen-Strand Odd Variated Sennit* goes under seven and over one from one side, then under six and over one from the other.

FIG. 68: The *Seventeen-Strand Odd Variated Sennit* goes under seven and over two, then under six and over two.

FIG. 69: The *Nineteen-Strand Odd Variated Sennit* goes under seven and over three, then under six and over three from the other side.

FIG. 70: The *Twenty-One-Strand Odd Variated Sennit* goes under seven and over four, then under six and over four.

FIG. 71: The *Twenty-Three-Strand Odd Variated Sennit* goes under eight and over four from one side, then under seven and over four from the other.

FIG. 72: The *Twenty-Five-Strand Odd Variated Sennit* goes under eight and over five, then under seven and over five from opposite side.

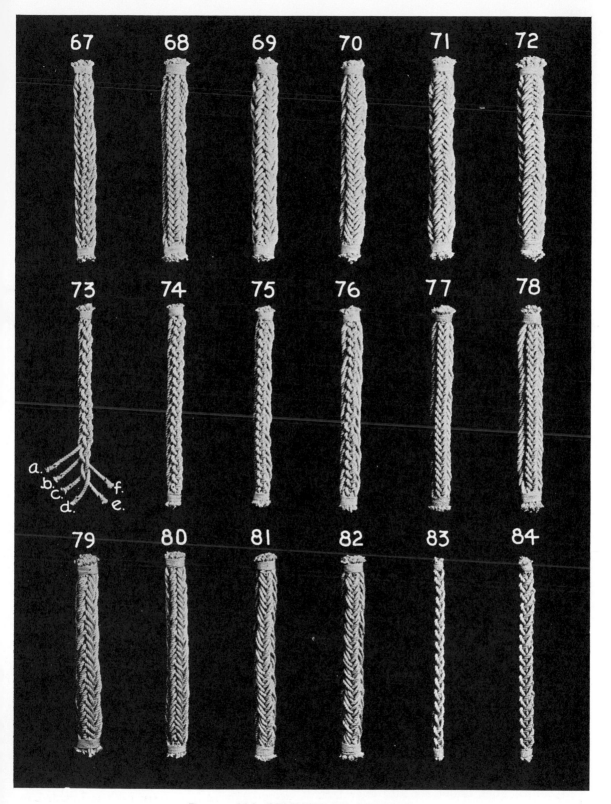

PLATE 116—SENNIT BRAIDING

FIG. 73: The *Six-Strand Even Variated Sennit* (First Set) follows the same principle that applies to the odd-numbered variated braids. Both are started with the outside strand on either side. Then alternate from one side to the other, always bringing each strand, in turn, down and around in back, under whatever number of strands the key stipulates, and over the given number of strands toward its own side to complete the pass, etc. Strand *d* in FIG. 73 is brought down around and under strand *f*, then over strand *e*. Strand *f* is next brought down around and under strand *c*, then over strand *d*, and so on. The key is under one and over one from one side, then under three and over one from the other.

FIG. 74: The *Eight-Strand Even Variated Sennit* goes under four and over one, then under two and over one from the other side.

FIG. 75: The *Ten-Strand Even Variated Sennit* goes under four and over one, then repeats from opposite side, using the same key.

FIG. 76: The *Twelve-Strand Even Variated Sennit* goes under five and over one, from first one side and then the other.

FIG. 77: The *Fourteen-Strand Even Variated Sennit* goes under five and over two from both sides.

FIG. 78: The *Sixteen-Strand Even Variated Sennit* goes under six and over two from both sides.

FIG. 79: The *Eighteen-Strand Even Variated Sennit* goes under six and over three from both sides.

FIG. 80: The *Twenty-Strand Even Variated Sennit* goes under seven and over three in the usual manner, from both sides.

FIG. 81: The *Twenty-Two-Strand Even Variated Sennit* goes under seven and over four from both sides.

FIG. 82: The *Twenty-Four-Strand Even Variated Sennit* goes under eight and over four.

FIG. 83: The *Six-Strand Even Variated Sennit* (Second Set) goes under two and over one from one side, then under one and over two from the other.

FIG. 84: The *Eight-Strand Even Variated Sennit* goes under three and over one from one side, then under one and over three from the other.

Plate 117—Sennit Braiding

FIG. 85: The *Ten-Strand Even Variated Sennit* goes under four and over one, then under one and over four from the opposite side.

FIG. 86: The *Twelve-Strand Even Variated Sennit* goes under four and over two, then under two and over four in the usual manner from each side.

FIG. 87: The *Fourteen-Strand Even Variated Sennit* goes under five and over two, then under two and over five.

FIG. 88: The *Sixteen-Strand Even Variated Sennit* goes under six and over two, then under two and over six.

FIG. 89: The *Eighteen-Strand Even Variated Sennit* goes under six and over three, then under three and over six.

FIG. 90: The *Twenty-Strand Even Variated Sennit* goes under seven and over three, then under three and over seven.

FIG. 91: The *Twenty-Two-Strand Even Variated Sennit* goes under seven and over four, then under four and over seven.

FIG. 92: The *Twenty-Four-Strand Even Variated Sennit* goes under eight and over four, then under four and over eight.

FIG. 93: The *Five-Strand Double Flat* or *English Sennit* (ten strands) is braided in the same manner as the single flat, but twice as many strands are used, and kept in

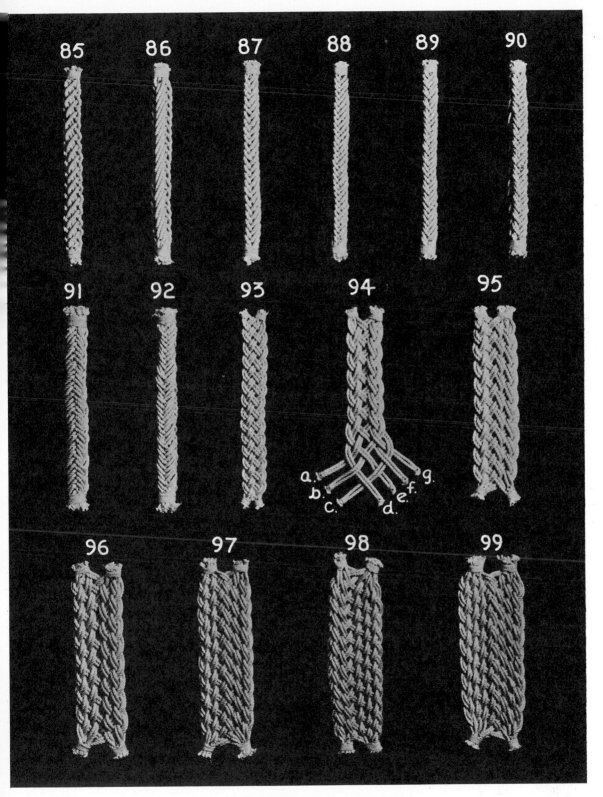

PLATE 117—SENNIT BRAIDING

pairs of two while braiding. PLATE 112, FIG. 13, shows the key for this type of braid.

FIG. 94: The *Seven-Strand Double Flat* or *English Sennit* (fourteen strands) is made by first bringing strand *c* down over strand *g*, under strand *f*, and over strand *e*. Strand *d* is then brought down over strand *a*, under strand *b*, and over strand *c*, etc.

FIG. 95: The *Nine-Strand Double Flat* or *English Sennit* (eighteen strands) is made in the same fashion as the seven-strand method. All Sennits of the odd-numbered type have the same key in flat braiding—over one and under one toward the middle, from both sides.

FIG. 96: The *Eleven-Strand Double Flat* or *English Sennit* (twenty-two strands).

FIG. 97: The *Thirteen-Strand Double Flat* or *English Sennit* (twenty-six strands).

FIG. 98: The *Fifteen-Strand Double Flat* or *English Sennit* (thirty strands).

FIG. 99: The *Seventeen-Strand Double Flat* or *English Sennit* (thirty-four strands).

Plate 118—Sennit Braiding

FIG. 100: The *Nineteen-Strand Double Flat* or *English Sennit* (thirty-eight strands).

FIG. 101: The *Twenty-One-Strand Double Flat* or *English Sennit* (forty-two strands).

FIG. 102: The *Twenty-Three-Strand Double Flat* or *English Sennit* (forty-six strands).

FIG. 103: The *Twenty-Five-Strand Double Flat* or *English Sennit* (fifty strands).

FIG. 104: The *Four-Strand Flat* or *English Sennit* (eight strands) illustrates how the even-numbered flat Sennits are started in a slightly different way from the odd. The first pass with the outside strands goes over from one side, then under from the opposite side; whereas the odd-numbered type starts over from both sides. Strand *c* in FIG. 104 is brought down under strand *a*.

Then strand *b* is brought down over strand *d*, under strand *c*, etc.

FIG. 105: The *Six-Strand Double Flat* or *English Sennit* (twelve strands).

FIG. 106: The *Eight-Strand Double Flat* or *English Sennit* (sixteen strands).

FIG. 107: The *Ten-Strand Double Flat* or *English Sennit* (twenty strands).

FIG. 108: The *Twelve-Strand Double Flat* or *English Sennit* (twenty-four strands).

FIG. 109: The *Fourteen-Strand Double Flat* or *English Sennit* (twenty-eight strands).

FIG. 110: The *Sixteen-Strand Double Flat* or *English Sennit* (thirty-two strands).

FIG. 111: The *Eighteen-Strand Double Flat* or *English Sennit* (thirty-six strands).

FIG. 112: The *Twenty-Strand Double Flat* or *English Sennit* (forty strands).

Plate 119—Sennit Braiding

FIG. 113: The *Twenty-Two-Strand Double Flat* or *English Sennit* (forty-four strands).

FIG. 114: The *Twenty-Four-Strand Double Flat* or *English Sennit* (forty-eight strands).

FIG. 115: The *Seven-Strand Odd Irregular Sennit* (First Set) is made in the same way as other irregular types, which are all braided across the front, alternately from each side. The key for this braid is over one strand and under two strands from one side, then over two strands and under one strand from the opposite side. In other words, the key for this and all the following braids in this set will be reversed from one side to

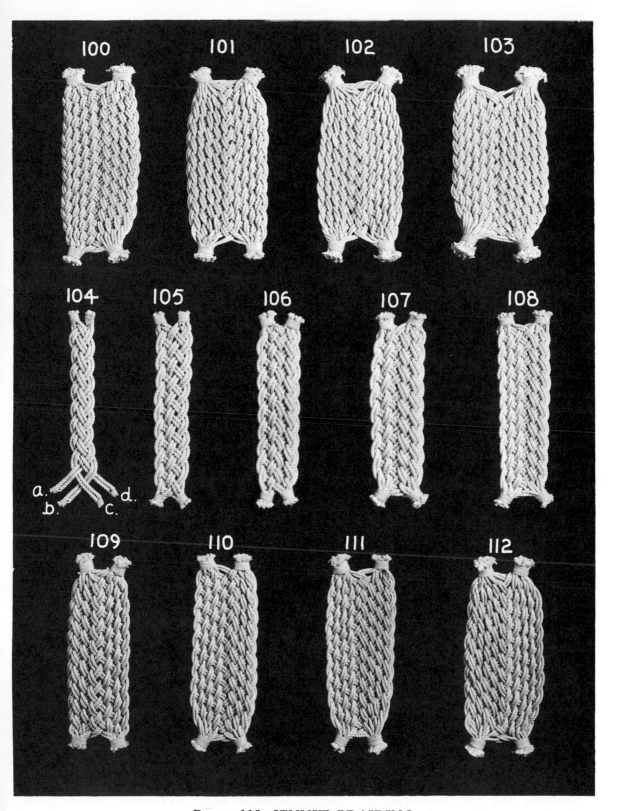

PLATE 118—SENNIT BRAIDING

the other. Strand *c* is brought down over strand *g*, then under strands *f* and *e*. Strand *d* is next brought down over strands *a* and *b*, then under strand *c*, etc.

Fig. 116: The *Nine-Strand Odd Irregular Sennit* goes over one and under. three, then over three and under one.

Fig. 117: The *Eleven-Strand Odd Irregular Sennit* goes over one and under four, then over four and under one.

Fig. 118: The *Thirteen-Strand Odd Irregular Sennit* goes over two and under four, then over four and under two.

Fig. 119: The *Fifteen-Strand Odd Irregular Sennit* goes over three and under four, then over four and under three.

Fig. 120: The *Seventeen-Strand Odd Irregular Sennit* goes over three and under five, then over five and under three.

Fig. 121: The *Nineteen-Strand Odd Irregular Sennit* goes over three and under six, then over six and under three.

Fig. 122: The *Twenty-One-Strand Odd Irregular Sennit* goes over four and under six, then over six and under four.

Fig. 123: The *Twenty - Three - Strand Odd Irregular Sennit* goes over five and under six, then over six and under five.

Fig. 124: The *Twenty-Five-Strand Odd Irregular Sennit* goes over five and under seven, then over seven and under five.

Fig. 125: The *Four-Strand Single Nelson Sennit* is a braid made by placing Reverse Crowns one on top of the other. First, crown to the right. Then pull up taut, and crown to the left on top of the previous right-hand Crown.

Fig. 126: The *Four-Strand Double Nelson Sennit* (eight strands) is woven in the same manner as the preceding braid, but with double strands.

Fig. 127: The *Four-Strand Triple Flat* or *English Sennit* (twelve strands) is identical with PLATE 118, FIG. 104, except that the strands are triple instead of double.

Fig. 128: The *Double Chain Sennit* is a duplication of PLATE 120, FIG. 134, except that the strands are double instead of single.

Fig. 129: The *Portuguese Square Sennit* is made with three strands. With the middle strand serving as a core, use the two outside strands for forming a chain of Square Knots, one after another. A quick and easy method of making a complete Square Knot at one time is illustrated in Chapter IX.

Fig. 130: The *Portuguese Spiral Sennit* uses the same number of strands as the Square Sennit. Let the middle strand serve as a core, and form a series of Hitches with the two outside strands. The Hitches are all tied in the same direction, which gives the braid a spiral effect. This method of Spiral-Hitching is illustrated in Chapter IX.

Plate 120—Sennit Braiding

Figs. 131A, B and C: The *Bugler's Sennit* is begun as shown in FIG. 131A. Two round turns are made to start with, one laid on top of the other. It is better to fold these round turns or coils to the left, as the picture illustrates. Then pass a bight under both round turns (to form another round turn of its own), pull the eye of the bight up uniformly, and pass each additional bight over the first round turn and under the next two, adjusting the size and shape with

the running part of the line as the braid is continued. FIG. 131B pictures the braid after the fourth tuck has been made, and FIG. 131C shows how it looks when completed.

Figs. 132A, B and C: The *Two-Fold Bugler's Sennit* follows the preceding method, except that three round turns are taken to begin with, and the eye of the bight is then passed over the first turn and under the next three. FIG. 132A shows the

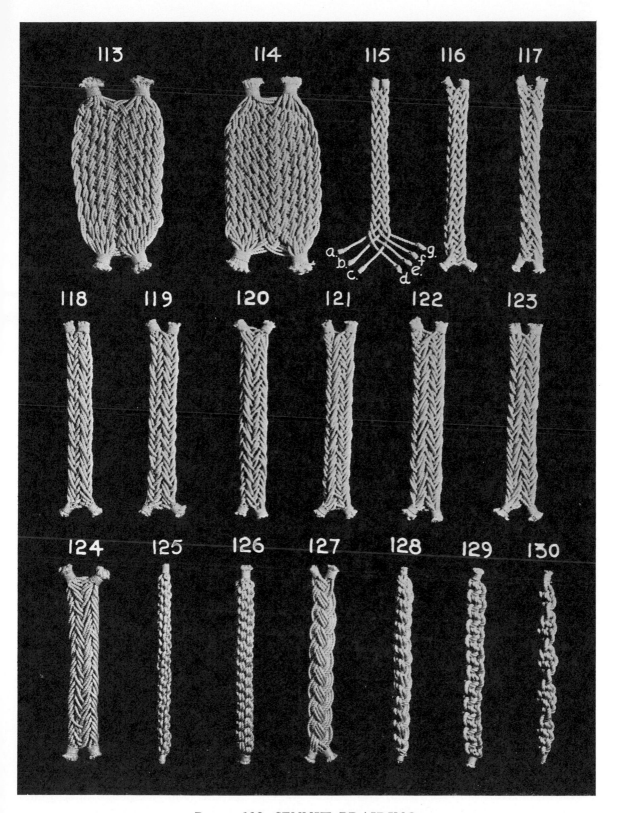

PLATE 119—SENNIT BRAIDING

braid started, with two tucks already tied, and FIG. 132B pictures the fourth tuck of the braid completed. FIG. 132C illustrates the finished design.

FIGS. 133A, B and C: The *Single Higginbotham Sennit* is formed as follows: tie a slip bight in an Overhand Knot to begin; then place another bight through the first one, from the opposite side, as shown in FIG. 133A. Pull the eye of the first bight up snug, and form another bight through the second one. Continue this procedure, pulling up the eye of each bight as the braid progresses. FIG. 133B shows the third stage of the braid, and FIG. 133C illustrates how it appears when finished.

FIGS. 134A, B, and C: The *Single Chain Sennit* is begun by forming a slip bight in an Overhand Knot. Then continue the braid by passing each additional bight through the eye of the last bight, etc. FIG. 134A shows the second tuck completed, and FIG. 134B the fourth tuck. FIG. 134C pictures it as it looks when finished and turned over.

FIG. 135: The *Four-Strand Double Running Sennit* (eight strands) is made in the same manner as the single running type in PLATE 122, FIG. 171, except that the strands are doubled.

FIG. 136: The *Six-Strand Double Running Sennit* (twelve strands).

FIG. 137: The *Three-Strand Crown Sennit* begins with a series of Crowns, one on top of the other, in the form of a braid with three strands.

FIG. 138: The *Four - Strand Triple Round Sennit* follows the double type in PLATE 112, FIG. 8, except that the strands are tripled.

FIG. 139: The *Three-Strand Wall Sennit* is made with a series of Wall Knots, one on top of the other, in the form of a braid.

FIG. 140: The *Seven-Strand Odd Variated Sennit* (Second Set) utilizes the same principle of braiding as the first set of this type. The key for this braid is under one and over three from one side, then under one and over two from the opposite side.

FIG. 141: The *Nine-Strand Odd Variated Sennit* goes under one and over three, then under two and over three.

FIG. 142: The *Eleven-Strand Odd Variated Sennit* goes under two and over three, then under two and over four.

FIG. 143: The *Thirteen-Strand Odd Variated Sennit* goes under three and over four, then under two and over four.

FIG. 144: The *Fifteen-Strand Odd Variated Sennit* goes under three and over four, then under three and over five.

Plate 121—Sennit Braiding

FIG. 145: The *Seventeen-Strand Odd Variated Sennit* goes under three and over five, then under four and over five.

FIG. 146: The *Nineteen-Strand Odd Variated Sennit* goes under four and over five, then under four and over six.

FIG. 147: The *Twenty-One-Strand Odd Variated Sennit* goes under four and over six, then under five and over six.

FIG. 148: The *Twenty-Three-Strand Odd Variated Sennit* goes under five and over six, then under five and over seven.

FIG. 149: The *Twenty - Five - Strand Odd Variated Sennit* goes under five and over seven, then under five and over eight from the opposite side.

FIG. 150: The *Seven-Strand Odd Irregular Sennit* (Second Set) is braided across the front, from first one side and then the other, starting with the outside strand on either side, in the same manner as the even-numbered types. The key to this braid is over three across the front from one side, then over one, under one, and over one, across the front, from the other side.

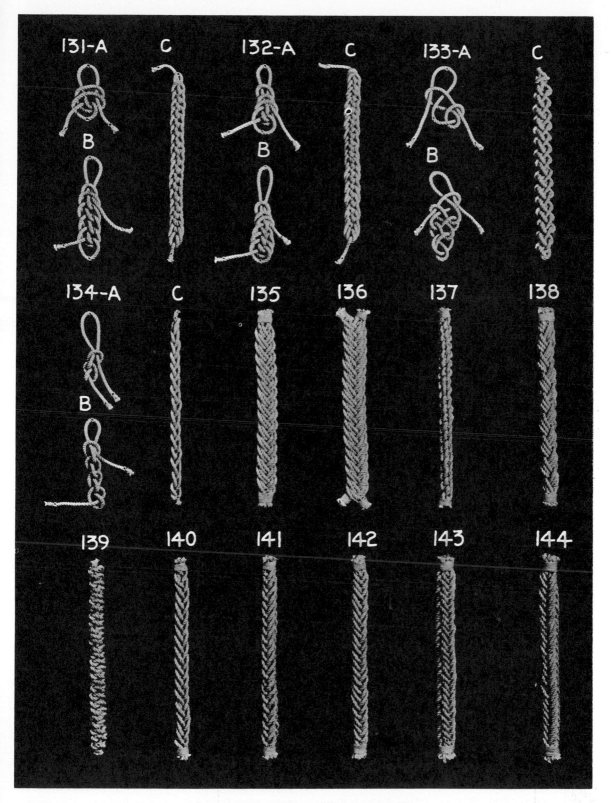

131-A

C

132-A

C

133-A

C

B

B

B

134-A

C

135

136

137

138

B

139

140

141

142

143

144

PLATE 120—SENNIT BRAIDING

FIG. 151: The *Nine-Strand Odd Irregular Sennit* goes over two and under one from both sides. Then keep on braiding over one and under one, until the center of the braid is reached alternately from both sides.

FIG. 152: The *Eleven-Strand Odd Irregular Sennit* goes over two and under one from both sides, as in the preceding method.

FIG. 153: The *Thirteen-Strand Odd Irregular Sennit* goes over two and under one from both sides.

FIG. 154: The *Fifteen-Strand Odd Irregular Sennit* goes over two and under one from both sides.

FIG. 155: The *Seventeen-Strand Odd Irregular Sennit* goes over three and under one from both sides.

FIG. 156: The *Nineteen-Strand Odd Irregular Sennit* goes over three and under two from both sides.

FIG. 157: The *Twenty-One-Strand Odd Irregular Sennit* goes over four and under two from both sides.

FIG. 158: The *Twenty - Three - Strand Odd Irregular Sennit* goes over five and under two from both sides.

FIG. 159: The *Twenty-Five-Strand Odd Irregular Sennit* goes over six and under two from both sides.

Plate 122—Sennit Braiding

FIG. 160: The *Five-Strand Odd Variated Sennit* (Third Set) is made in the same fashion as the previous types of this braid. The key is under one and over two from one side, then under one and over one from the opposite side. Strand *b* is passed down under strand *e*, and over strands *d* and *c*. Strand *e* is then passed down under strand *a*, over strand *b*, and so on.

FIG. 161: The *Seven-Strand Odd Variated Sennit* goes under two and over two from one side, then under two and over one from the other.

FIG. 162: The *Nine-Strand Odd Variated Sennit* goes under three and over two from one side, then under two and over two from the other.

FIG. 163: The *Eleven-Strand Odd Variated Sennit* goes under three and over three from one side, then under three and over two from the other.

FIG. 164: The *Thirteen - Strand Odd Variated Sennit* goes under four and over three from one side, then under three and over three from the other.

FIG. 165: The *Fifteen-Strand Odd Variated Sennit* goes under four and over four from one side, then under four and over three from the other.

FIG. 166: The *Seventeen - Strand Odd Variated Sennit* goes under five and over four from one side, then under four and over four from the other.

FIG. 167: The *Nineteen - Strand Odd Variated Sennit* goes under five and over five from one side, then under five and over four from the other.

FIG. 168: The *Twenty-One-Strand Odd Variated Sennit* goes under six and over five from one side, then under five and over five from the other.

FIG. 169: The *Twenty - Three - Strand Odd Variated Sennit* goes under six and over six from one side, then under six and over five from the other.

FIG. 170: The *Twenty-Five-Strand Odd Variated Sennit* goes under seven and over six from one side, then under six and over six from the other.

FIG. 171: The *Four-Strand Running Sennit* goes across the front, as in the odd-numbered type of this same braid. In the even-numbered type it is necessary to cross one more strand from one side than from

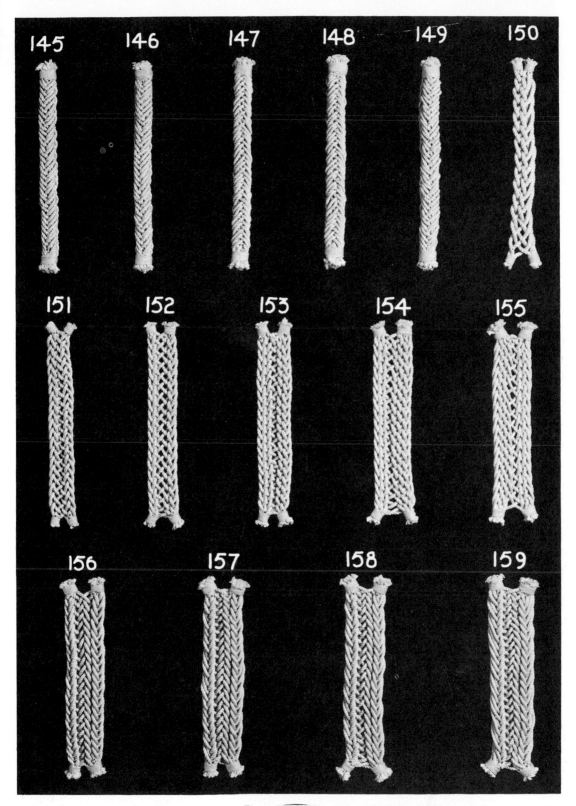

PLATE 121—SENNIT BRAIDING

the other. Strand *b* is brought down across the front and over strands *d* and *c;* then strand *a* is brought down over strand *b,* etc.

FIG. 172: The *Six - Strand Running Sennit.*

FIG. 173: The *Eight-Strand Running Sennit.*

FIG. 174: The *Ten - Strand Running Sennit.*

FIG. 175: The *Twelve-Strand Running Sennit.*

FIG. 176: The *Fourteen-Strand Running Sennit.*

FIG. 177: The *Sixteen-Strand Running Sennit.*

Plate 123—Sennit Braiding

FIG. 178: The *Eighteen-Strand Running Sennit.*

FIG. 179: The *Twenty-Strand Running Sennit.*

FIG. 180: The *Twenty-Two-Strand Running Sennit.*

FIG. 181: The *Twenty-Four-Strand Running Sennit.*

FIG. 182: The *Seven-Strand Odd Variated Sennit* (Fourth Set) is made in the same way as the previous types of this braid. The key is under one and over one from one side, then under three and over two from the other.

FIG. 183: The *Nine-Strand Odd Variated Sennit* goes under two and over one, then under four and over two.

FIG. 184: The *Eleven-Strand Odd Variated Sennit* goes under two and over two, then under four and over three.

FIG. 185: The *Thirteen-Strand Odd Variated Sennit* goes under three and over two, then under five and over three.

FIG. 186: The *Fifteen-Strand Odd Variated Sennit* goes under three and over three, then under six and over three.

FIG. 187: The *Seventeen - Strand Odd Variated Sennit* goes under four and over three, then under six and over four.

FIG. 188: The *Nineteen - Strand Odd Variated Sennit* goes under four and over four, then under seven and over four.

FIG. 189: The *Twenty-One-Strand Odd Variated Sennit* goes under five and over five, then under six and over five.

FIG. 190: The *Twenty - Three - Strand Odd Variated Sennit* goes under five and over five, then under nine and over four.

FIG. 191: The *Twenty-Five-Strand Odd Variated Sennit* goes under five and over five, then under ten and over five.

FIG. 192: The *Eight - Strand Single Round Sennit* follows the same procedure used in the six-strand method in **PLATE** 112, **FIG.** 10.

FIG. 193: The *Ten-Strand Single Round Sennit.*

FIG. 194: The *Twelve - Strand Single Round Sennit.*

FIG. 195: The *Fourteen-Strand Single Round Sennit.*

Plate 124—Sennit Braiding

FIG. 196: The *Sixteen - Strand Single Round Sennit.*

FIG. 197: The *Eighteen-Strand Single Round Sennit.*

FIG. 198: The *Twenty - Strand Single Round Sennit.*

FIG. 199: The *Twenty - Two - Strand Single Round Sennit.*

FIG. 200: The *Twenty - Four Strand Single Round Sennit.*

FIG. 201: The *Seven - Strand Double French Sennit* (fourteen strands) is made **in**

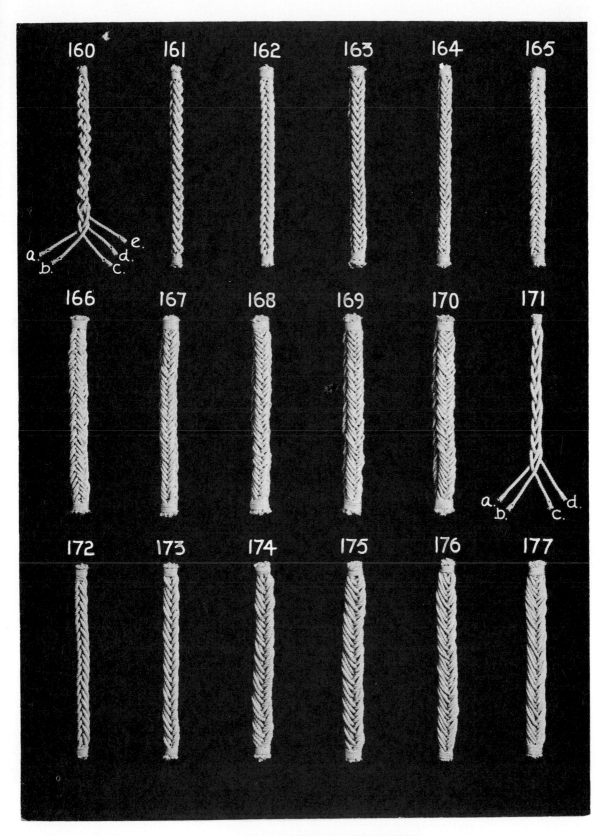

PLATE 122—SENNIT BRAIDING

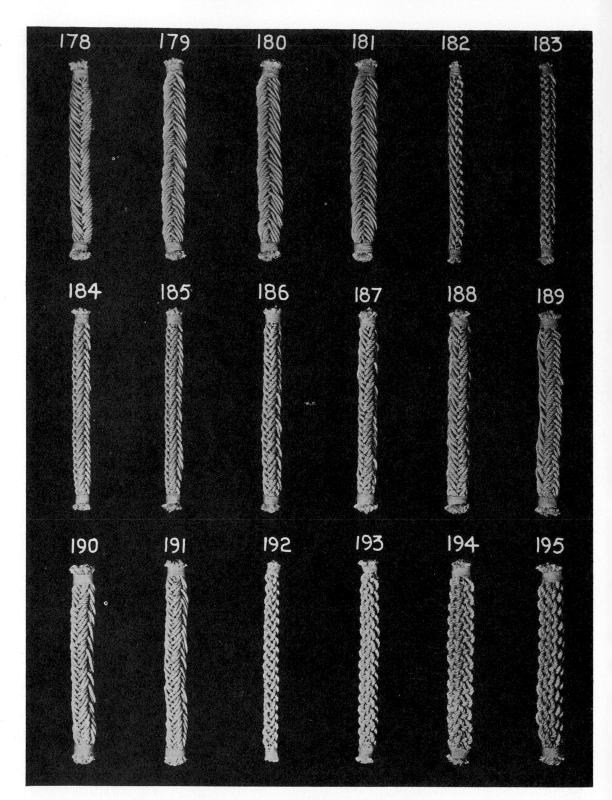

PLATE 123—SENNIT BRAIDING

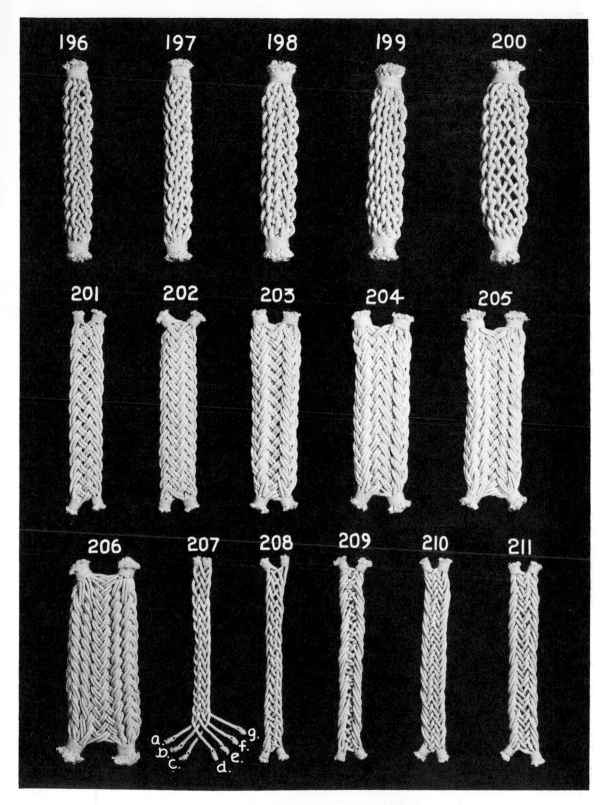

PLATE 124—SENNIT BRAIDING

the same manner as the single type, except that the strands are doubled and braided in pairs.

FIG. 202: The *Nine - Strand Double French Sennit* (eighteen strands).

FIG. 203: The *Thirteen-Strand Double French Sennit* (twenty-six strands).

FIG. 204: The *Seventeen-Strand Double French Sennit* (thirty-four strands).

FIG. 205: The *Twenty - One - Strand Double French Sennit* (forty-two strands).

FIG. 206: The *Twenty - Five - Strand Double French Sennit* (fifty strands).

FIG. 207: The *Seven-Strand Odd Irregular Sennit* (Third Set) is brought across the front, as in the previous methods of this type. The key is over one and under one from one side, then over two and under two from the other side. Strand *d* is brought down over strand *a* and under strand *b*. Then strand *c* is brought down over strands *g* and *f*, and under strands *e* and *d*, etc.

FIG. 208: The *Nine-Strand Odd Irregular Sennit* goes over three and under one from both sides.

FIG. 209: The *Eleven-Strand Odd Irregular Sennit* goes over four and under one from both sides.

FIG. 210: The *Thirteen-Strand Odd Irregular Sennit* goes over four and under two from both sides.

FIG. 211: The *Fifteen-Strand Odd Irregular Sennit* goes over four and under three from both sides.

Plate 125—Sennit Braiding

FIG. 212: The *Seventeen-Strand Odd Irregular Sennit* goes over five and under three from both sides.

FIG. 213: The *Nineteen-Strand Odd Irregular Sennit* goes over six and under three from both sides.

FIG. 214: The *Twenty-One-Strand Odd Irregular Sennit* goes over six and under four from both sides.

FIG. 215: The *Twenty - Three - Strand Odd Irregular Sennit* goes over six and under five from both sides.

FIG. 216: The *Twenty-Five-Strand Odd Irregular Sennit* goes over six, under three, and over three from both sides.

FIG. 217: The *Six-Strand Even Irregular Sennit* (Second Set) is similar to the other methods of this type of Sennit. The key is under two from one side, then over one and under two from the opposite side. Strand *d* is brought down under strands *a* and *b*. Then strand *c* is brought down over strand *f* and under strands *e* and *d*, etc.

FIG. 218: The *Eight-Strand Even Irregular Sennit* goes over one and under three from one side, then over two and under one from the other.

FIG. 219: The *Ten-Strand Even Irregular Sennit* goes over three and under three from one side, then over two and under one from the other.

FIG. 220: The *Twelve-Strand Even Irregular Sennit* goes over four and under two, then over three and under two.

FIG. 221: The *Fourteen-Strand Even Irregular Sennit* goes over four and under two, then over four and under three from the opposite side.

FIG. 222: The *Sixteen-Strand Even Irregular Sennit* goes over five and under three, then over four and under three.

FIG. 223: The *Eighteen-Strand Even Irregular Sennit* goes over five and under four, then over four and under four.

FIG. 224: The *Twenty-Strand Even Irregular Sennit* goes over six and under four, then over five and under four.

FIG. 225: The *Twenty-Two Strand Even*

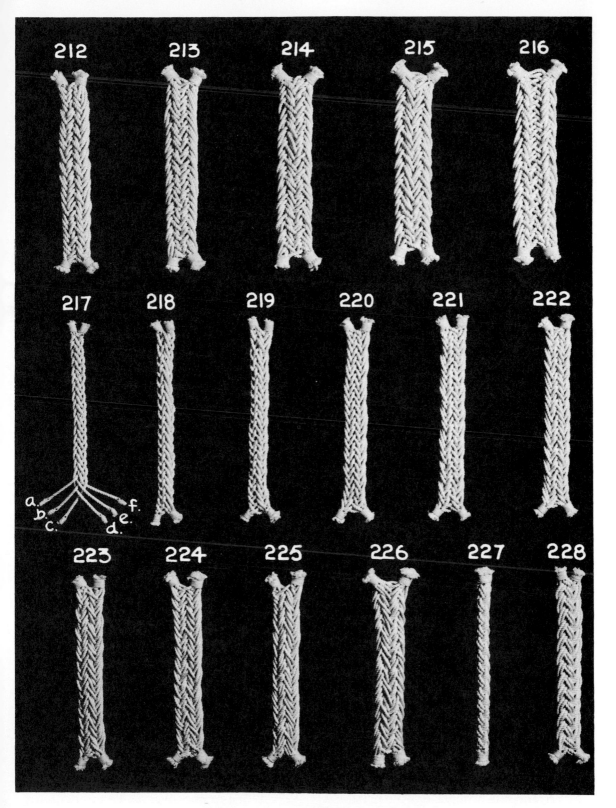

PLATE 125—SENNIT BRAIDING

Irregular Sennit goes over six and under five, then over five and under five.

FIG. 226: The *Twenty-Four-Strand Even Irregular Sennit* goes over seven and under five, then over six and under five.

FIG. 227: The *Six-Strand Double Half Round Sennit* is made in the same fashion as PLATE 112, FIG. 5, except that the strands are doubled.

FIG. 228: The *Six-Strand Double Irregular Sennit* (twelve strands) has two strands brought down over four strands on one side. Then two strands are brought down under four strands and over two strands from the opposite side, etc.

Plate 126—Sennit Braiding

FIG. 229: The *Six-Strand Even Variated Sennit* (Third Set) employs the same method as previous types. The key for this braid is under two and over two from one side, then under one and over one from the other. Strand *e* is brought down under strands *a* and *b,* and over strands *c* and *d.* Then strand *a* is brought down under strand *f* and over strand *e,* etc.

FIG. 230: The *Eight-Strand Even Variated Sennit* goes under three and over two, then under two and over one.

FIG. 231: The *Ten-Strand Even Variated Sennit* goes under three and over three, then under two and over two.

FIG. 232: The *Twelve-Strand Even Variated Sennit* goes under four and over three, then under three and over three.

FIG. 233: The *Fourteen-Strand Even Variated Sennit* goes under four and over four, then under three and over three.

FIG. 234: The *Sixteen-Strand Even Variated Sennit* goes under five and over four, then under four and over three.

FIG. 235: The *Eighteen-Strand Even Variated Sennit* goes under five and over five, then under four and over four.

FIG. 236: The *Twenty-Strand Even Variated Sennit* goes under six and over five, then under five and over four.

FIG. 237: The *Twenty-Two-Strand Even Variated Sennit* goes under six and over six, then under five and over five.

FIG. 238: The *Twenty-Four-Strand Even Variated Sennit* goes under seven and over six, then under six and over five.

FIG. 239: The *Six-Strand Even Variated Sennit* (Fourth Set) is braided in the same way as previous types. The key is under one and over three, then under one and over one.

FIG. 240: The *Eight-Strand Even Variated Sennit* goes under one and over four, then under two and over one.

FIG. 241: The *Ten-Strand Even Variated Sennit* goes under three and over two, then under two and over three.

FIG. 242: The *Twelve-Strand Even Variated Sennit* goes under four and over two, then under two and over four.

FIG. 243: The *Fourteen-Strand Even Variated Sennit* goes under four and over three, then under three and over four.

FIG. 244: The *Sixteen-Strand Even Variated Sennit* goes under five and over three, then under three and over five.

FIG. 245: The *Eighteen-Strand Even Variated Sennit* goes under five and over four, then under four and over five.

FIG. 246: The *Twenty-Strand Even Variated Sennit* goes under six and over four, then under four and over six.

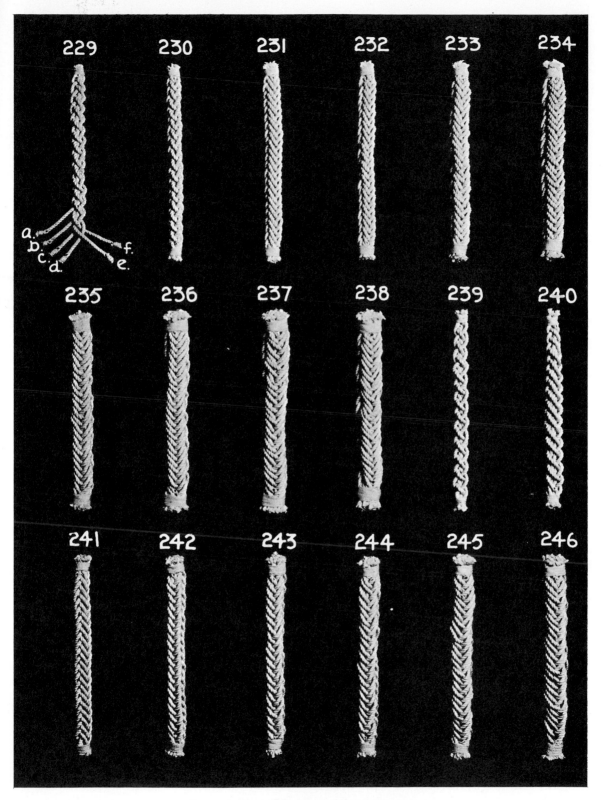

PLATE 126—SENNIT BRAIDING

Plate 127—Sennit Braiding

FIG. 247: The *Twenty-Two-Strand Even Variated Sennit* goes under six and over five, then under five and over six.

FIG. 248: The *Twenty-Four-Strand Even Variated Sennit* goes under seven and over five, then under five and over seven.

FIG. 249: The *Six-Strand Even Irregular Sennit* (Third Set) is made in the same manner as the other sets of this type. The key is under two from one side, then over two and under one from the other side. Strand *d* is brought down under strands *a* and *b;* then strand *c* is brought down over strands *f* and *e*, under strand *d*, and so on.

FIG. 250: The *Eight-Strand Even Irregular Sennit* goes over two and under one; then under two, over one, and under one from the opposite side.

FIG. 251: The *Ten-Strand Even Irregular Sennit* goes over three and under one; then under three, over one, and under one, etc.

FIG. 252: The *Twelve-Strand Even Irregular Sennit* goes over three and under two; then under three, over two, and under one from the opposite side.

FIG. 253: The *Fourteen-Strand Even Irregular Sennit* goes over four and under two, then under four, over two, and under one from the other side.

FIG. 254: The *Sixteen-Strand Even Irregular Sennit* goes over four and under two; then under four, over three, and under two, and so on.

FIG. 255: The *Eighteen-Strand Even Irregular Sennit* goes over four and under three from one side; then under four, over three, and under three from the opposite side.

FIG. 256: The *Twenty-Strand Even Irregular Sennit* goes over five and under three; then under five, over three, and under three from the other side.

FIG. 257: The *Twenty-Two-Strand Even Irregular Sennit* goes over five and under four from one side; then under five, over four, and under three from the opposite side.

FIG. 258: The *Twenty-Four-Strand Even Irregular Sennit* goes over five, under three, and over three; then under five, over three, under three, and over one from the other side.

FIG. 259: The *Six-Strand Even Irregular Sennit* (Fourth Set) is made in the same way as previous methods. The key for this braid is over one and under one from one side, then over one and under two from the opposite side. Strand *d* is brought down over strand *a*, then under strand *b*. Strand *c* is next brought down over strand *f*, then under strands *e* and *d*, and so on, repeating the key in the usual manner.

FIG. 260: The *Eight-Strand Even Irregular Sennit* goes over two and under two from one side, then over two and under one from the other.

FIG. 261: The *Ten-Strand Even Irregular Sennit* goes over three and under two from one side, then over two and under two from the other.

FIG. 262: The *Twelve-Strand Even Irregular Sennit* goes over three and under three, then over three and under two, etc.

FIG. 263: The *Fourteen-Strand Even Irregular Sennit* goes over four and under three, then over three and under three from the opposite side.

Plate 128—Sennit Braiding

FIG. 264: The *Sixteen-Strand Even Irregular Sennit* goes over four and under four, then over four and under three from the opposite side.

FIG. 265: The *Eighteen-Strand Even Irregular Sennit* goes over five and under three, then over five and under four.

FIG. 266: The *Twenty-Strand Even Ir-*

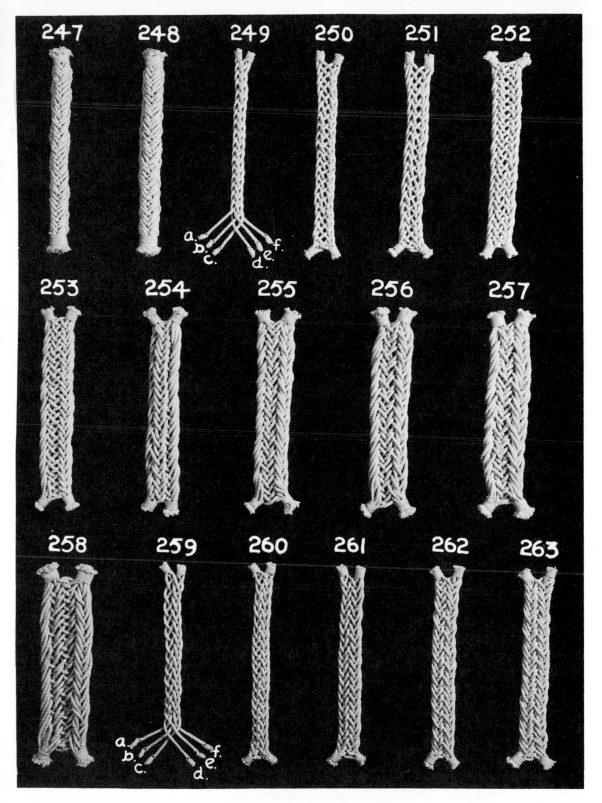

PLATE 127—SENNIT BRAIDING

regular Sennit goes over five and under five from one side, then over five and under four from the other.

FIG. 267: The *Twenty-Two-Strand Even Irregular Sennit* goes over six and under five, then over six and under four.

FIG. 268: The *Twenty-Four-Strand Even Irregular Sennit* goes over six and under six, then over six and under five.

FIG. 269: The *Seven-Strand Odd Irregular Sennit* (Fourth Set) is made in the same fashion as previous methods of this type. The key for this braid is over one, under one, and over one from one side; then under two and over one from the other. Strand *c* is brought down over strand *g*, under strand *f*, and over strand *e*. Next, bring strand *d* down under strands *a* and *b*, over strand *c*, and so on.

FIG. 270: The *Nine-Strand Odd Irregular Sennit* goes over two, under one, and over one from one side; then under two and over two from the opposite side.

FIG. 271: The *Eleven-Strand Odd Irregular Sennit* goes over two, under one, and over one from one side; then under three and over three from the other side.

FIG. 272: The *Thirteen-Strand Odd Irregular Sennit* goes over two, under two, and over one; then under four and over three from the opposite side.

FIG. 273: The *Fifteen-Strand Odd Irregular Sennit* goes over two, under two, and over two from one side; then under four and over four from the other side.

FIG. 274: The *Seventeen-Strand Odd Irregular Sennit* goes over four and under three from one side; then under three, over three, and under three from the opposite side.

FIG. 275: The *Nineteen-Strand Odd Irregular Sennit* goes over four and under four; then under four, over three, and under three from the other side.

FIG. 276: The *Twenty-One-Strand Odd Irregular Sennit* goes over four and under four; then under four, over four, and under four from the opposite side.

FIG. 277: The *Twenty-Three-Strand Odd Irregular Sennit* goes over five and under four; then under five, over four, and under four from the other side.

FIG. 278: The *Twenty-Five-Strand Odd Irregular Sennit* goes over five and under four; then under five, over five, and under five from the opposite side.

FIG. 279: The *Ten-Strand Mound Sennit* uses two strands instead of one. Begin with the two outside strands on either side, bringing them down across the front, then over one and under three. Repeat this same key from the opposite side. In other words, the key is two over one and under three, alternating from both sides.

FIG. 280: The *Fourteen-Strand Interlocking Sennit* is made in the same manner as the preceding mound type Sennit. The key for this is two over three, under one, and over two from one side; then repeat the same key from the other side, and so on.

Plate 129—Sennit Braiding

FIG. 281: The *Twelve-Strand Flat Sennit* is braided in the same way as other flat type Sennits, except that the strands are divided into sets of four and two. Start from the outside and bring two strands down over four from one side, and down under four from the other side. Then bring four strands down over two from one side, and

down under the two from the other side.

FIG. 282: The *Fourteen-Strand Flat Sennit* is a duplication of FIG. 281. But two additional strands are used, and it is started with four strands from the outside instead of two.

FIG. 283: The *Eight-Strand Double Half-Hexagonal Sennit* (sixteen strands) is

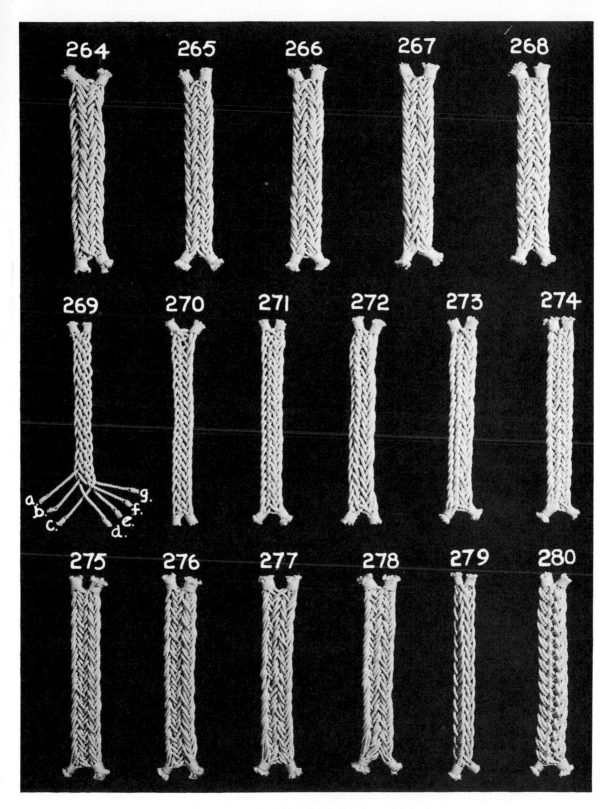

PLATE 128—SENNIT BRAIDING

made in the same fashion as the single type in PLATE 112, FIG. 14, except that the strands are doubled.

FIG. 284: The *Combination Odd Variated Sennit* is started with nine strands, then reduced to seven at the points marked *a* and *b*. A strand is dropped on both sides and the braid is then continued with seven strands for a short distance. At points *c* and *d*, two more strands are dropped, and a Crabber's Eye Sennit is used to finish off. The key for the nine-strand braid is down around in back from first one side then the other, and under three; then over one from one side, under four and over one from the opposite side, etc. The seven-strand braid is under two and over one from one side, then under three and over one from the other in the same manner. Turn to PLATE 112, FIG. 3, for the Crabber's Eye Braid key.

FIG. 285: The *Six-Strand Woven Sennit* follows the key of two over one, then under one, from each side. Two strands are joined together as strand *b,* and brought down over strand *d* and under strand *c.* The two strands joined together as strand *a* are next brought down through the middle of the two *b* strands, over the first and under the second. Strands *d* and *c* are then joined together and passed through the two *a* strands in the same manner.

FIG. 286: The *Eight-Strand Interwoven Sennit* starts with the two outside strands on either side. Bring them down over two and under one across the front, repeating the same key from the opposite side.

FIG. 287: The *Ten-Strand Interwoven Sennit* is braided in the same manner as the preceding method. The key is two over three, and under one from first one side and then the other.

FIG. 288: The *Twelve-Strand Interwoven Sennit* is two over four, and then under one, from both sides in the usual manner.

FIG. 289: The *Fourteen-Strand Interwoven Sennit* is two over five and under one from both sides in the same way as previous methods.

FIG. 290: The *Cape Horn Sennit* is one started with a Six-Strand Double Flat or English Sennit. It is then changed into a twelve-strand single braid of the same type, and tapered down, by dropping a strand on each side, into a ten, eight, six, and then four-strand braid of the same kind. A great variety of designs can be formed by utilizing different combinations of the various keys.

FIG. 291: The *Seven-Strand Angular Weave Sennit* uses the key of one over two, and then under two, across the front from both sides alternately.

FIG. 292: The *Seven-Strand Double Angular Weave Sennit* (fourteen strands) is made in the same way as the preceding braid. The key is two over four and under four from each side in turn.

FIG. 293: The *Seven-Strand Single Mound Sennit* uses the key of one over one, and then under two, from first one side and then the other.

FIG. 294: The *Seven-Strand Double Mound Sennit* (fourteen strands) follows the single strand method, except that the key is doubled, going two over two, and under four, from each side in turn.

FIG. 295: The *Nine-Strand Single Mound Sennit* is similar to the seven-strand type. The key for this braid is one over one, and under three, from first one side and then the other.

FIG. 296: The *Nine-Strand Double Mound Sennit* (eighteen strands) is the same as the single method, except that the key is doubled, going two over two and under six from each side.

FIG. 297: The *Eleven-Strand Single Algerian Sennit* uses the key of one over three, then under two, across the front from either side in turn.

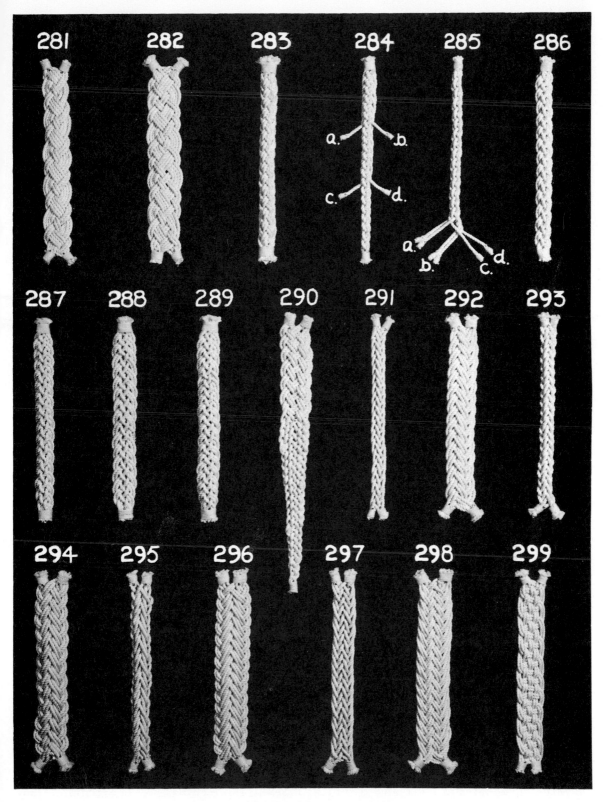

PLATE 129—SENNIT BRAIDING

FIG. 298: The *Eleven-Strand Double Algerian Sennit* (twenty-two strands) is a duplication of the single strand method, except that the key is doubled, going two over six and then under four from each side.

FIG. 299: The *Twelve-Strand Cross Sennit* can be followed from the illustration better than it can be described. The key is two over two, under two, then over two and under two again, from left to right. This will bring the working strands to the outside of the six core strands on the opposite side. Next, pass the two working strands on this side under the two working strands that were passed to begin with; then go over two, under two, and over two, from right to left. The first move is then repeated, and so on.

The two outside strands on both sides are the only working strands; the six middle strands merely serve as a core for the weave.

Plate 130—Sennit Braiding

FIG. 300: The *Combination Running Sennit* is started with seven strands, and then reduced to five and three strands in turn, by dropping two outside strands each time.

FIG. 301: The *Five-Strand Double Crabber's Eye Sennit* (twelve strands) is made in the same manner as PLATE 112, FIG. 3, except that the strands are doubled.

FIG. 302: The *Eight-Strand Double Square Sennit* (sixteen strands) duplicates PLATE 112, FIG. 6, but the strands are doubled.

FIG. 303: The *Combination Even Flat Sennit with Doubled Strands* represents a six-strand double flat braid (with twelve strands) tapered down to a four-strand double braid (with eight strands). The letters *a* and *b* show how the strands appear when dropped, cut short, and seized.

FIG. 304: The *Combination Odd Flat Sennit with Doubled Strands* is a seven-strand double flat braid (with fourteen strands) tapered down to a five-strand double braid of the same type. The letters *a* and *b* show how the strands are dropped in the usual manner.

FIG. 305: The *Combination Double Running Sennit* has ten strands braided double into a five-strand single type, then tapered down at strands *a* and *b* into a three-strand double braid of the same variety.

FIG. 306: The *Three-Strand Combination Sennit* is made by first braiding three separate single running braids of three strands each. Then braid the three completed Sennits together as one unit, to form another Sennit of the same type.

FIG. 307: The *Four-Strand Combination Round Sennit* is tied by first making four separate four-strand round braids. Then join them together in the same manner, to form one braid of the same type, as previously described.

FIG. 308: The *Combination Double Half-Round and Round Sennit* begins with a Six-strand Double Half-round Braid. Then this is tapered down into a four-strand double round braid in the usual manner. Letters *a* and *b* show where the double strands are dropped on both sides.

FIG. 309: The *Combination Tapered Sennit* starts out with a six-strand double round braid. Then this is tapered into a Ten-Strand Combination Sennit by dropping two strands in the usual way. Next, drop two more strands, and continue with an Eight-Strand Square Sennit. Follow this same method by tapering down first to a six-strand half-round, and then a four-strand round braid.

FIG. 310: The *Combination Clew Hitch Sennit* represents a series of Six-Strand Clew Hitches changed into a Three-Strand Double Running Sennit.

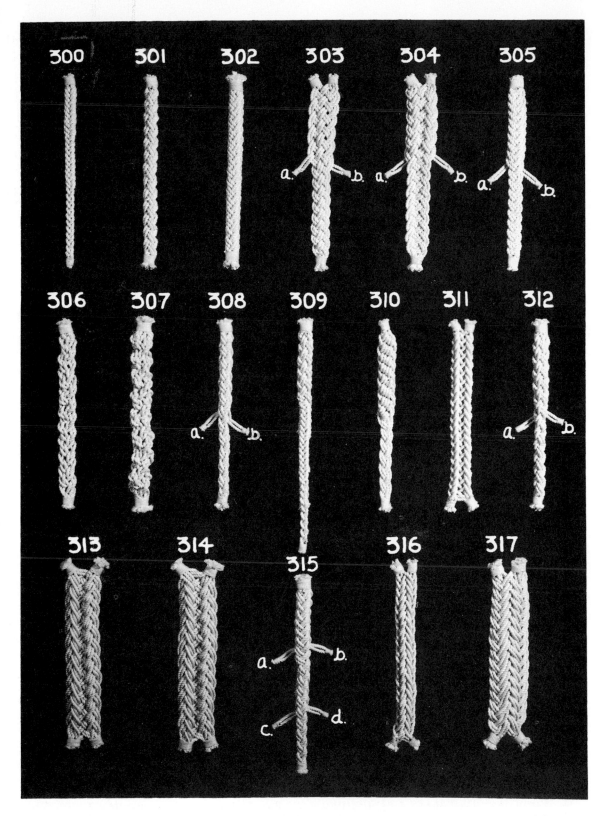

PLATE 130—SENNIT BRAIDING

FIG. 311: The *Eleven-Strand Channel Sennit* is made by braiding down across the front from first one side and then the other. The key for this braid is one over one, then under two, and over two from each side alternately.

FIG. 312: The *Combination Round Sennit* is made by combining a Six-Strand Double Round with a Four-Strand Double Round Sennit. Letters *a* and *b* show where the double strands are dropped in changing the braid.

FIG. 313: The *Eighteen-Strand Overlapping Sennit* is braided down across the front in the usual way. The key for this braid is two over three, under three, then over two from each side, alternating in turn.

FIG. 314: The *Twenty-Strand Overlapping Sennit* follows the preceding method.

The key is two over four, under three, then over two from each side alternately.

FIG. 315: The *Combination Triple Sennit* is started with an Eight-Strand Double Square Sennit, and then tapered into a Six-Strand Double Half-Round Sennit, where the double strands are dropped at *a* and *b*. It is then tapered into a four-strand double round braid where the double strands are lettered *c* and *d*.

FIG. 316: The *Eleven-Strand Single Mound Sennit* is made by braiding down across the front from both sides in the usual way. The key is one over two, then under three from each side, and so on.

FIG. 317: The *Eleven-Strand Double Mount Sennit* (twenty-two strands) is made in the same way as FIG. 316, except that the key is doubled, going two over four, then under six, from each side, etc.

Plate 131—Sennit Braiding

FIG. 318: The *Thirteen-Strand Mound Sennit* is braided in the same way as PLATE 130, FIG. 316. The key is one over three, then under one, and over two from each side in turn.

FIG. 319: The *Seventeen-Strand Mound Sennit* is one over three, under one, over two, and under two from each side.

FIG. 320: The *Twelve-Strand Mound Sennit* follows the preceding method, except that the key is two over three, under one, and over one from each side.

FIG. 321: The *Twelve-Strand Interlacing Sennit* is braided with two strands, which are passed under two and over two from one side. Then make the same pass from the opposite side, going under two, and over two. This will bring both sets of working strands to the middle where they are split and passed through each other, after each pass is completed from both sides. Next, repeat the original key and continue the braid in the same manner.

FIG. 322: The *Twelve-Strand Interlock-*

ing Sennit has two strands passed over two, under one, and over two. The same key is repeated from the other side.

FIG. 323: The *Twelve-Strand Cross Sennit*, Second Method, is braided in the same way as PLATE 129, FIG. 299, except that the six core-strands are divided into two sets of three strands each.

FIG. 324: The *Half Combination Running Sennit*, begun with a three-strand double running braid, and then tapered down into a three-strand single running braid. (*See* PLATE 112, FIG. 1, for detailed instructions.) Letters *a*, *b*, and *c* show where the three extra strands are dropped.

FIG. 325: The *Twelve-Strand Interlacing Sennit*, Second Method, is braided in the same way as FIG. 321, except that a slight variation of the previous key is used. Two strands are brought down over two and under three from each side in turn.

FIG. 326: The *Combination Comb Sennit* begins with a Twelve-Strand Square Sennit, going under three and over three

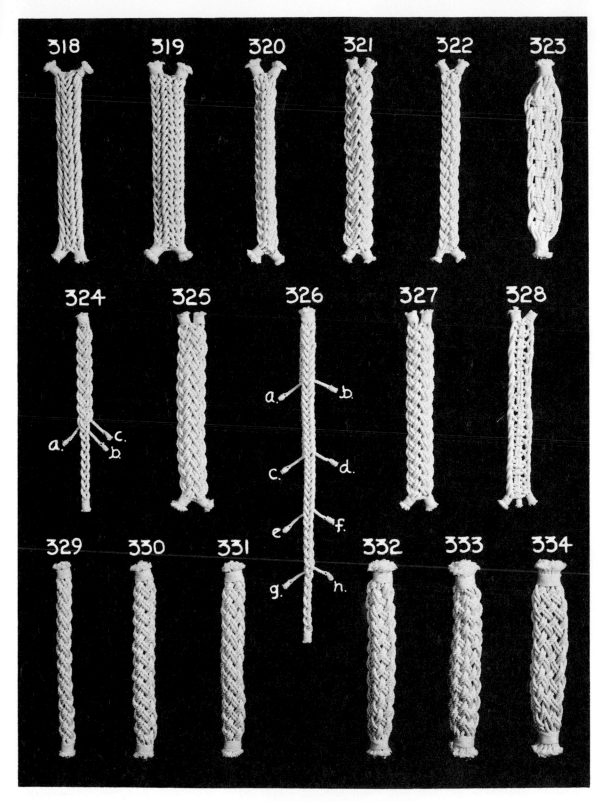

PLATE 131—SENNIT BRAIDING

around in back from each side. Next, where strands *a* and *b* are dropped, the braid is tapered into a Ten-Strand Comb Sennit, which goes under three and over two from each side. Then at strands *c* and *d*, the braid is again tapered into an Eight-Strand Square Sennit, going over two and under two from each side. Letters *e* and *f* show where two more strands are dropped. Then the braid is continued with a six-strand half-round key, which goes under two and over one from each side. Finish off with a four-strand round braid, going under one and over one, after dropping strands *g* and *h*.

FIG. 327: The *Twelve-Strand Cross Weave Sennit* is made by bringing two strands down across the front, over two, under two, then over one. Repeat the same key from the opposite side.

FIG. 328: The *Nine-Strand Core Sennit* uses two strands for a core, which leaves three strands on one side and four strands on the other. Begin on the side with four strands by bringing the outside strand down over two, then under one, and over the two core-strands. Next, bring the outside strand from the opposite side down under two, then over one, and under the two core-strands, etc.

FIG. 329: The *Six-Strand Double Round Sennit* (twelve strands) is braided in the same way as PLATE 112, FIG. 10, except that the strands are doubled.

FIG. 330: The *Eight-Strand Double Round Sennit* (sixteen strands).

FIG. 331: The *Ten-Strand Double Round Sennit* (twenty strands).

FIG. 332: The *Twelve-Strand Double Round Sennit* (twenty-four strands).

FIG. 333: The *Fourteen-Strand Double Round Sennit* (twenty-eight strands).

FIG. 334: The *Sixteen-Strand Double Round Sennit* (thirty-two strands).

Plate 132—Sennit Braiding

FIG. 335: The *Eighteen-Strand Double Round Sennit* (thirty-six strands).

FIG. 336: The *Twenty-Strand Double Round Sennit* (forty strands).

FIG. 337: The *Twenty-Two-Strand Double Round Sennit* (forty-four strands).

FIG. 338: The *Twenty-Four-Strand Double Round Sennit* (forty-eight strands).

FIG. 339: The *Sixteen-Strand Alternating Sennit* is made by bringing four strands down over three, then under three. Repeat the same key from the opposite side.

FIG. 340: The *Eight-Strand Interlacing Sennit* has two strands brought down over one, and under two, from first one side and then the other.

FIG. 341: The *Eight-Strand Interlacing Sennit*, Second Method, is begun by bringing three strands down over one from one side. Then from the opposite side, bring three strands down under one and over three. Repeat these two keys alternately from first one side and then the other.

FIG. 342: The *Ten-Strand Interlacing Sennit* has three strands brought down over two from one side, then three strands down under two and over three from the opposite side.

FIG. 343: The *Cable-Laid Sennit* is laid up in the same way as a cable-laid rope, which is composed of three right-handed hawser-laid three-strand ropes laid up together left-handed, consisting of nine strands in all. Two strands to each rope or a total of six strands, were used here.

FIG. 344: The *Square Knot and Half Hitch Sennit* consists of a series of ordinary Square Knots formed around a core, and then changed into a series of Hitches.

FIG. 345: The *Combination Alternate Hitch Sennit* is made of a series of Overhand Hitches formed from first one side

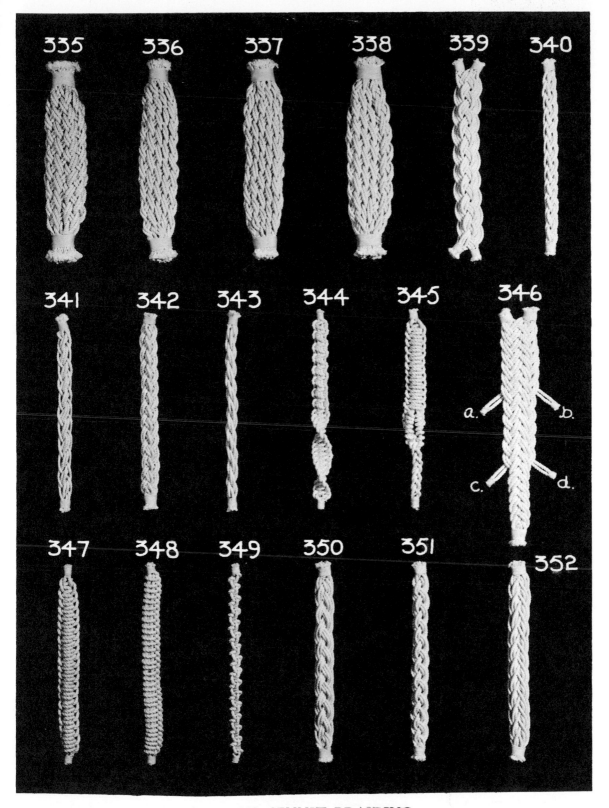

PLATE 132—SENNIT BRAIDING

and then the other around a core, then forked and changed into a running braid.

FIG. 346: The *Combination French Sennit* begins with a Double Nine-Strand French Sennit, which is then changed into a Double Seven-Strand French .Sennit where strands *a* and *b* are dropped. It is continued, after dropping strands *c* and *d,* with a Five-Strand Double Running Sennit. PLATE 112, FIGS. 9, 7, and 4, shows how these Sennits are made.

FIG. 347: The *Overhand Alternating Hitch Sennit* is formed by placing Overhand Half Hitches around a two-strand core, from first one side and then the other.

FIG. 348: The *Half Hitched Sennit* consists of a series of Hitches formed around the side of a three-strand core as illustrated.

FIG. 349: The *Interlocking Hitch Sennit* is made of two strands joined together in a series of Interlocking Underhand Hitches.

FIG. 350: The *Eleven-Strand Interlacing Chain Sennit,* First Method, is tied by bringing three strands down over one and under three across the front, then repeating from the opposite side.

FIG. 351: The *Eleven-Strand Interlacing Chain Sennit,* Second Method, is formed by bringing three strands down over two and under two, then repeating from the opposite side in the same manner as FIG. 350.

FIG. 352: The *Thirteen-Strand Interlacing Chain Sennit,* First Method, begins with three strands brought down over one and under four. Then repeat the same key from the other side.

Plate 133—Sennit Braiding

FIG. 353: The *Thirteen-Strand Interlacing Chain Sennit,* Second Method, is made by bringing three strands down over one, then under two and over two. Repeat from the opposite side.

FIG. 354: The *Fifteen-Strand Interlacing Chain Sennit,* First Method, brings three outside strands down in the usual way, over two and then under four. Repeat from the other side.

FIG. 355: The *Fifteen-Strand Interlacing Chain Sennit,* Second Method, has three strands brought over four, then under two from each side, as in the preceding methods.

FIG. 356: The *Seventeen-Strand Interlacing Chain Sennit,* First Method, brings three strands down over two, then under five across the front. Repeat from the opposite side.

FIG. 357: The *Seventeen-Strand Interlacing Chain Sennit,* Second Method, reverses the preceding method, going three over five and under two from each side.

FIG. 358: The *Nineteen-Strand Interlacing Chain Sennit,* First Method, has three strands brought down over two and under six across the front. Repeat from the opposite side.

FIG. 359: The *Nineteen-Strand Interlacing Chain Sennit,* Second Method, brings three strands down over two, then under three, and over three from each side in turn.

FIG. 360: The *Twenty-One-Strand Interlacing Chain Sennit,* First Method, has three strands brought down over two, then under three, and over four. Repeat from the other side.

FIG. 361: The *Twenty-One-Strand Interlacing Chain Sennit,* Second Method, brings three strands down over four, then under three, and over two. Repeat from the opposite side.

FIG. 362: The *Twenty-Three-Strand Interlacing Chain Sennit,* First Method, brings three strands down, in the usual way, over two, then under four, and over four. Repeat from the other side.

FIG. 363: The *Twenty-Three-Strand Interlacing Chain Sennit,* Second Method,

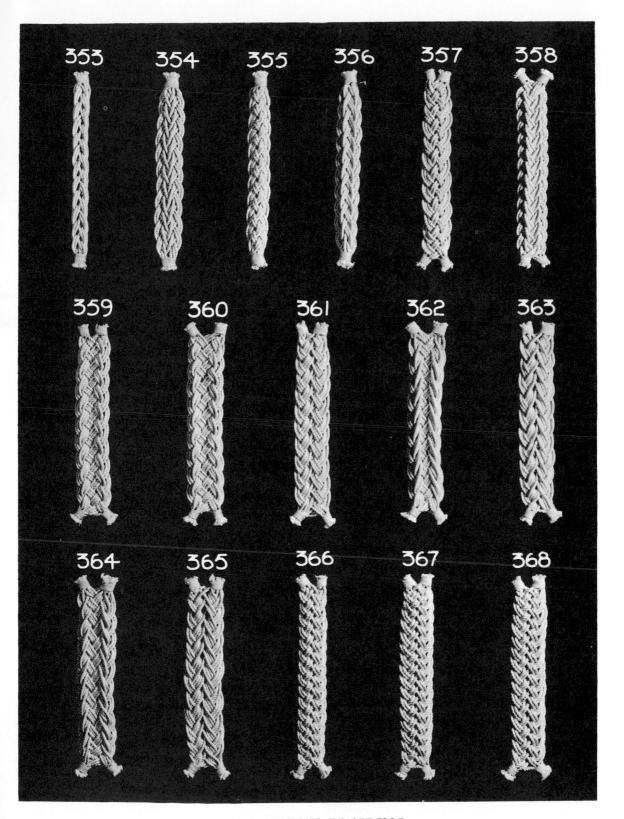

PLATE 133—SENNIT BRAIDING

brings three strands down over four, then under four, and over two from each side.

FIG. 364: The *Twenty-Five-Strand Interlacing Chain Sennit,* First Method, brings three over two, then under four, and over five, across the front from both sides in turn.

FIG. 365: The *Twenty-Five-Strand Interlacing Chain Sennit,* Second Method, is three over five, then under four, and over two. Repeat from the other side.

FIG. 366: The *Fourteen-Strand Cross Weave Sennit* brings two strands down across the front, over three, then under two, and over one from each side.

FIG. 367: The *Sixteen-Strand Cross Weave Sennit* brings two strands down over four, then under two, and over one, across the front. Repeat from the opposite side.

FIG. 368: The *Eighteen-Strand Cross Weave Sennit* is two over five, then under two, and over one from both sides in the usual way.

Plate 134—Sennit Braiding

FIG. 369: The *Twenty-Strand Cross Weave Sennit* brings two strands down over six, under two, and over one. Repeat from the other side.

FIG. 370: The *Twenty-Two-Strand Cross Weave Sennit* is two over six, under three, and over one from both sides.

FIG. 371: The *Twenty-Four-Strand Cross Weave Sennit* is two over six, under four, and over one from both sides.

FIG. 372: The *Twenty-Two-Strand Overlapping Sennit* brings two strands down over five, under three, and over two. Repeat from the opposite side.

FIG. 373: The *Twenty-Four-Strand Overlapping Sennit* is two over six, under three, and over two, from first one side and then the other.

FIG. 374: The *Sixteen-Strand Overlapping Sennit* has two strands brought down over two, under three, and over two, from first one side and then the other.

FIG. 375: The *Sixteen-Strand Interwoven Sennit* brings two strands down over six and under one. Repeat from the other side.

FIG. 376: The *Fifteen-Strand Interlocking Sennit* brings one strand down over four, under one, and over two, from each side in turn.

FIG. 377: The *Sixteen-Strand Interlocking Sennit* brings two strands down over four, under one, and over two, from first one side and then the other.

FIG. 378: The *Eighteen-Strand Interlocking Sennit* is two over five, under one, and over two from each side in the usual way.

FIG. 379: The *Twenty-Strand Interlocking Sennit* is two over six, under one, and over two. Repeat from the other side.

FIG. 380: The *Twenty-Two-Strand Interlocking Sennit* is two over six, under one, and over three, from first one side and then the other.

FIG. 381: The *Twenty-Four-Strand Interlocking Sennit* goes two over six, under one, and over four. Repeat from the opposite side.

FIG. 382: The *Thirteen-Strand Channel Sennit* brings one strand down over one, under three, and over two. Repeat from the other side.

FIG. 383: The *Fifteen-Strand Channel Sennit* goes one over one, under four, and over two from each side in turn.

FIG. 384: The *Seventeen-Strand Channel Sennit,* First Method, goes one over two, under four, and over two. Repeat from the other side.

FIG. 385: The *Seventeen-Strand Channel Sennit,* Second Method, goes one over four, under two, and over two. **Repeat from the opposite side.**

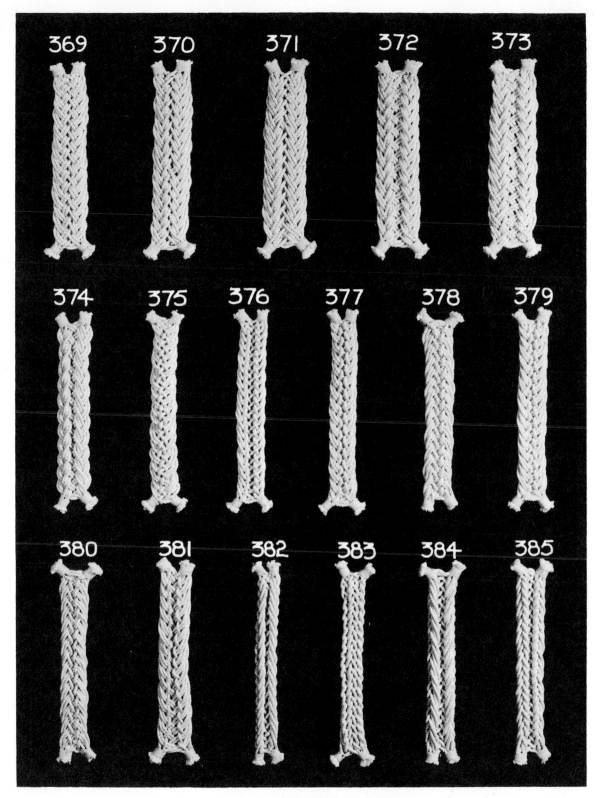

PLATE 134—SENNIT BRAIDING

Plate 135—Sennit Braiding

FIG. 386: The *Nine-Strand Interlocking Chain Sennit,* First Method, brings three strands down across the front, then over one, and under two. Repeat from the other side.

FIG. 387: The *Nine-Strand Interlocking Chain Sennit,* Second Method, uses the key of three over two and under one from each side.

FIG. 388: The *Nine-Strand Irregular French Sennit* brings one strand down over three and under one from each side.

FIG. 389: The *Half-Round Combination Sennit* starts with a Half-Hexagonal Sennit (PLATE 112, FIG. 14), where strands *a* and *b* are dropped; it is tapered into a Six-Strand Half-Round Sennit (PLATE 112, FIG. 5). Strands *c* and *d* are then dropped, and the braid is finished with a Four-Strand Round Sennit (PLATE 112, FIG. 2).

FIG. 390: The *Nine-Strand Double Irregular French Sennit* (eighteen strands) uses the same key as FIG. 388, except that the strands are doubled. This requires a double key, or two over six and under two from each side.

FIG. 391: The *Hitched Chain Sennit* begins with a Chain Sennit, as illustrated in PLATE 120, FIG. 134. Then hitch the end of the strand back through one side of the braid. After one side is completely hitched, begin at the other end of the braid and hitch the opposite end of the strand back through the other side in the same way.

FIG. 392: The *Double Chain Sennit* is the same as PLATE 120, FIG. 134, except that double strands are used.

FIGS. 393A, B, and C: The *Interwoven Bight Sennit* is made as follows: form a slip bight in an Overhand Knot; next, bring the working end of the line on the right side up through the center of the Overhand Knot and between its own parts. Then form another bight, and pass it under the first bight. Continue by passing the eye of each bight up through the center of the preceding bight, then over it, forming a new bight under the previous one. Pull the braid up neatly as each move is completed. FIGS. 393A and B show the two steps in the construction of this braid. And FIG. 393C illustrates how it looks when finished.

FIG. 394: The *Diamond Sennit* consists of a series of Four-Strand Diamond Knots, formed on top of one another until the braid is the desired size.

FIG. 395: The *Combination Eye Sennit* begins with an Eight-Strand Square Sennit (PLATE 112, FIG. 6). Put on a whipping for convenience, and divide the braid into two Four-Strand Round Sennits (PLATE 112, FIG. 2). After joining the two braids again to form the eye, continue with another Eight-Strand Square Sennit. Then taper down to a Six-Strand Half-Round Sennit (PLATE 112, FIG. 5), and finish off with a Four-Strand Round Sennit (PLATE 112, FIG. 2).

FIGS. 396A, B, and C: The *Crossed Bight Sennit* begins with a slip eye bight in an Overhand Knot. Form the eye of the next bight through the right side of the eye of the first one. Then pass it over and out under the eye of the first bight. FIGS. 396A and B show the two steps in beginning this braid; FIG. 396C illustrates its finished appearance.

FIGS. 397A, B, and C: The *Triangle Sennit* is begun by first attaching the line to a ring, or some other object to braid from. Next, tie a slip eye bight in an Overhand Knot with one end of the strand. Then with the other end, form a bight through the preceding one, as shown in FIG. 397A. Continue by bringing the bottom strand up over the braid each time, and passing the bight through the eye of the bight of the strand on top, which is then pulled up. FIG.

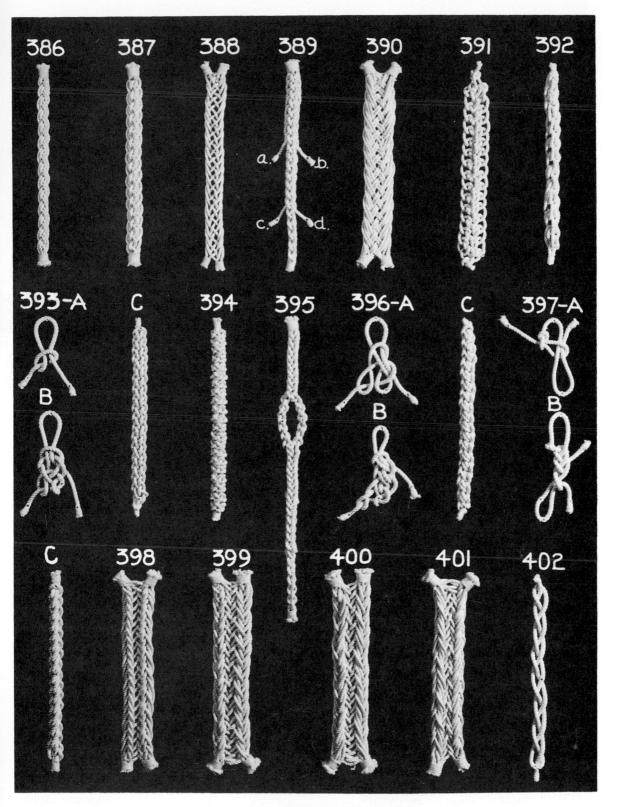

PLATE 135—SENNIT BRAIDING

397B illustrates the first three passes; Fig. 397c shows how the braid looks when finished with a three-sided or triangle effect.

Fig. 398: The *Nineteen-Strand Channel Sennit* brings one strand down across the front, over four, under two, and over three. Repeat from the other side.

Fig. 399: The *Twenty-One-Strand Channel Sennit* is one over four, under three, and over three from both sides.

Fig. 400: The *Twenty-Three-Strand Channel Sennit* is one over four, under four, and over three. Repeat from the opposite side.

Fig. 401: The *Twenty-Five-Strand Channel Sennit* goes one over four, under four and over four from both sides.

Fig. 402: The *Three-Strand Endless Sennit* is braided from one strand in the manner illustrated.

Plate 136—Sennit Braiding

Figs. 403A, B, and c: A *Combination Bight Sennit* is begun by forming two slip eye bights in two Overhand Knots, then lay the eye of one bight over the other one as shown in Fig. 403A. Next form two separate bights, one from each side, and pass them through the eyes of the bight that was previously made. After adjusting the eyes of the bights uniformly, as illustrated in Fig. 403B, form two more separate bights, one from each side, and pass them under their own parts or the individual bights that were made previously, then repeat the first move and continue with the same alternating moves. Fig. 403c shows the braid as it appears when finished.

Figs. 404A, B, and c: An *Intercrossing Bight Sennit* is begun by forming two slip eye bights, then pass the bight on the left side through the eye of the bight on the right side. Next, form another bight on the right side and pass it up under the side of its own previous bight, then over the top of same and out under the eye of the bight from the left side. Repeat same move from opposite side, etc. Figs. 404A and B show the two steps of formation and Fig. 404c as the finished braid appears.

Figs. 405A, B, and c: An *Overlapping Bight Sennit* is begun by forming two slip eyes in twin Overhand Knots. Then pass the bight of one eye through the other in an overlapping manner and form a separate eye from each side through the previous ones as shown in Fig. 405A. Continue by overlapping the eye of one bight with the other as shown in Fig. 405B. Pull the eyes of the bights up snug and repeat same move over again, etc. Fig. 405c shows how it appears when finished.

Figs. 406A, B, and c: A *Twin Chain Sennit* is begun with twin-slip eye bights in Overhand Knots in the usual way. Then pass the eyes of both bights through the eyes of the previous ones as shown in Fig. 406A. Adjust these bights so that their eyes are turned inward as shown in Fig. 406B. Then pass the two additional bights that are formed on each side of the weave (as illustrated) through the previous ones. Care should be taken in adjusting and pulling the eyes of the bights up in place as they are formed, before proceeding with the next stage of the work. Fig. 406c shows the completed Sennit.

Figs. 407A, B, and c: A *Diagonally Crossed Sennit* is started in the same way as Fig. 406. As illustrated, the line on the left side is passed from the front to the back through its own eye and the line on the right side is passed from the back to the front through its own eye. The eye of the bight on the right side is then passed in front of the weave and through the previous eye of the bight that was formed on the left side. Next pass the eye of the bight on the left side in back, or on the opposite side of the weave, and through the pre-

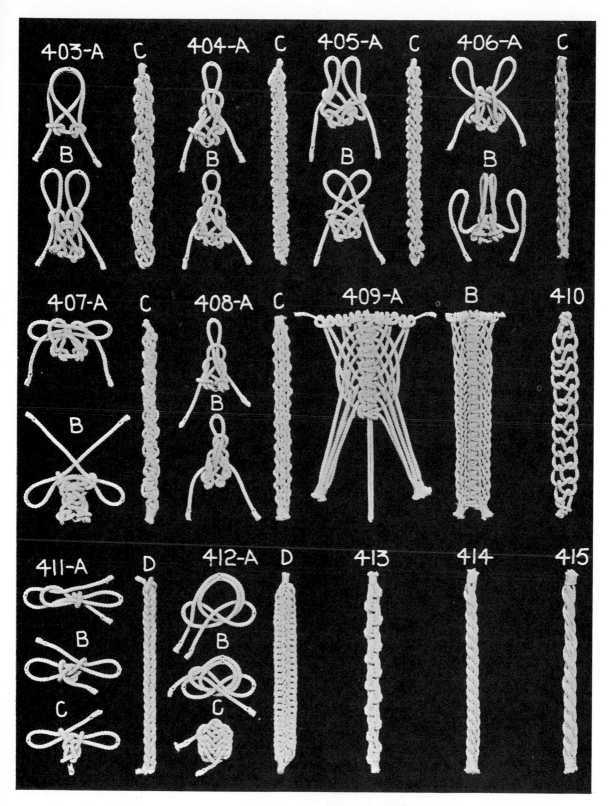

PLATE 136—SENNIT BRAIDING

vious eye of the bight that was formed on the right side. Note in FIG. 407A that after forming the first two bights, the end of the line on each side is then passed through the eyes to the opposite side before starting the weave. The first stage of the weave is now complete as it appears in FIG. 407A with the end of each line passed through the eye of the bight that was formed with the opposite end of the line. Proceed by bringing the line from the right side around in back of the weave and form an eye through the eye of the bight on the left side. Next, bring the line from the left side around in front of the weave, and repeat the previous procedure. The weave will then appear as in FIG. 407B, which shows the move as it has been described after several additional passes have been made. Pull the eyes of the bights up snug after each set of alternating passes have been made and continue the weave in the same manner until the desired length of Sennit has been reached. FIG. 407C shows the finished Sennit.

FIGS. 408A, B, and C: A *Twin Bight Intercrossed Sennit*. First, form two slip-eye bights in the usual manner, pass the bight on the left side through the eye of the bight on the right side as illustrated in FIG. 408A. Then form another bight with the line on the right side and pass it up through the inside of its own previous bight, then over the top of it and out through the eye of the previous bight that was formed from the left side. Repeat this same procedure from the left side and continue with the same alternating moves until the Sennit is finished. FIG. 408B shows the second stage of the work; FIG. 408C as it appears when finished.

FIGS. 409A, B, and C: A *Fourteen-Strand Combination Flat and Portuguese Square Sennit* is made by forming a Square Knot Weave around two core strands in the heart of the Sennit. The strands are then braided over and under to and from the Square Knot

heart as illustrated in FIG. 409A. After the strands on both sides are braided down to the core, they are formed into a Square Knot around the core and braided out again in turn. The finished weave is shown in FIG. 409B.

FIG. 410: A *Figure-of-Eight Chain Sennit*, formed with a Figure-of-Eight Weave in the manner shown.

FIGS. 411A, B, C, and D: A *Double Higginbotham* or *One Strand Square Sennit* is made by forming two bights in an Overhand or Thumb Knot; then with the working part of the line form another bight, through the eye of the bight on the left side as illustrated in FIG. 410A. Next, form another bight through the eye of the bight on the right side, which is illustrated in FIG. 410B. Pull the eyes of the bights up snug on each side of the braid as the work continues and follow this same alternating procedure throughout. FIG. 410C shows the third stage of the work; FIG. 410D as it appears when finished.

FIGS. 412A, B, C, and D: The *Antique Sennit* is made by taking two round turns, clockwise, from left to right and then with the working end of the line go around the two parts on the left side and out through the middle. Next, cross over and around the two parts on the right side and bring the line out through the middle again by crossing over the pass that was made previously. This completes the first move as shown in FIG. 412A. Next bring the line around the two bottom parts and cross through the middle over the previous pass toward the opposite side again. Continue in the same way by picking up the two bottom strands with each alternating pass and crossing over the previous pass through the middle of the weave. FIG. 412B shows the second stage of the work; FIG. 412C shows the third stage; FIG. 412D as it appears when finished.

FIG. 413: A *Double Interlocking Hitch Sennit* is tied in the same manner as PLATE

[*Plate 136*]   Sennit Braiding   273

132, Fig. 349, except strands are doubled.

Fig. 414: A *Six-Strand Angular Weave Sennit*. Two strands are brought down over one strand from one side and two strands are then brought down over three strands from the opposite side. Repeat the same key by alternating each time.

Fig. 415: An *Eight-Strand Angular Weave Sennit*. Three strands are brought down over one strand from one side and then three strands are brought down over four strands from the opposite side.

The same key is repeated after each alternating pass.

Chapter VIII

Ornamental Knotting

ORNAMENTAL KNOTTING has been used in Japan and to a certain extent in China for many centuries. It is probably the oldest form of recognized knot work, as it goes back almost to the dawn of history. It has been employed for ceremonial purposes in Japan since ancient times where it apparently was a subject of deep study. It was also prominent in Europe before and during the Middle Ages. It appeared in heraldic form and in many other different examples of designing of that time. It was later employed in the weaver's art where it was used for decorative purposes, but at the present time it has become almost a lost art, because there is very little information available dealing with the subject.

Other books on knot work have given a certain amount of information on ornamental knotting from time to time, but there has never been a complete treatise on this subject until now.

The authors have gone to considerable effort and have searched the entire world for the many different types of examples which are presented here in every known form of weave and combination. Some of them were copied from Oriental designs in the Far East many years ago, while others were gathered in San Francisco's Chinatown, the South Seas, Turkey, Asia, North Africa, France, England and many other countries, which also contributed their share of information from textbooks and individuals.

Plate 137—Chinese Double Braiding and Temple Knots

FIG. 1A: The *Three-Leaf Dragonfly Knot* has many uses in ornamental knotting, and should be thoroughly mastered. The work is first laid out as shown in this illustration, and a bight is pulled through the loop as the arrow indicates. If this knot is first tied on a table or some other flat surface until it is learned, it may then be tied in the hand much more rapidly.

B: Following FIG. 1A, the work appears as shown. The end is then put through the loop as indicated by the arrow.

C: Next, the end is again put through as the arrow shows.

D: After FIG. 1C has been completed, the work appears in the opposite manner to this figure, which is tied in the reverse way. The knot is now finished, and all that remains is to draw the slack out of it.

E: When all the slack has been drawn out, the completed knot appears as shown.

FIG. 2A: The *Chinese Double Braiding* is a very rare form of knotting or weaving, seldom seen in English-speaking countries except on Oriental lamp tassels. This type of work is distinctly different from any other type of weaving; for when it has been drawn taut, two separate weaves will be found on each side, and it will be hollow in the center. The work may appear difficult in the illustration, but in reality it is quite simple to duplicate, once the key has been mastered. It is almost impossible to do this work in the hand. A better plan is to lay it out on a board or other flat surface, and place inside each loop or bight a dowling pin, a peg, or small nail. By using this method, all the work will be kept in position, and there will be less danger of a mistake. To begin, take a piece of line of suitable length, middle it, and place the center around a nail. Name the end on the

274

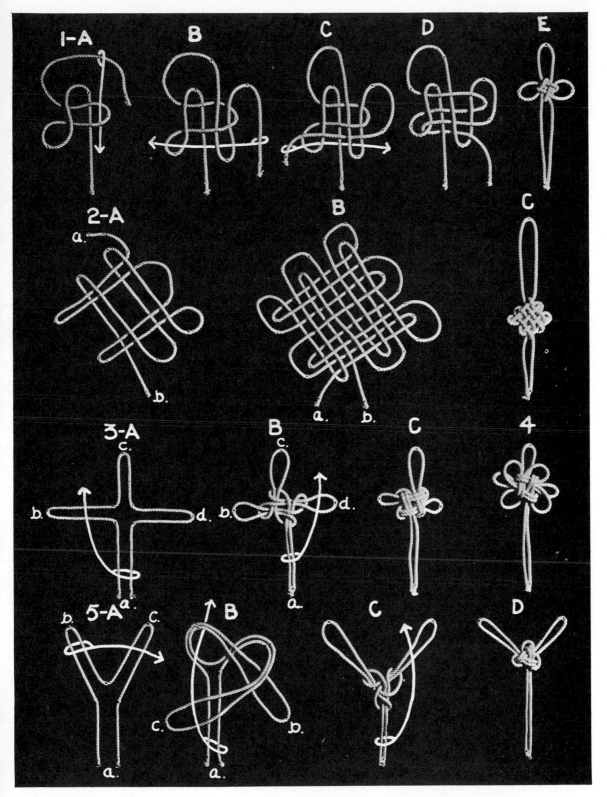

PLATE 137—CHINESE DOUBLE BRAIDING AND TEMPLE KNOTS

left *a,* and then end on the right *b.* Then take end *b* and work it into the position shown in this illustration.

B: End *a* is next woven through as shown. This completes the knot, which is then drawn up snug.

C: The knot is pictured after all the slack has been drawn out of it. It is now in its finished form.

FIG. 3A: The *Three-Leaf Chinese Temple Knot* is a very useful knot in ornamental work, and surprisingly simple to make. The cord is first laid out on a table, as shown in the illustration. Ends *a* are laid over bight *b,* bight *b* is laid over bight *c,* bight *c* is laid over bight *d,* and bight *d* is then put through the loops left by ends *a* when they were brought up. This final tuck is made in the same manner as in FIG. 5B.

B: After the operation just described, the work appears as in this figure. The next step is to repeat this procedure, and tie another Crown on top of the knot just made. This time crowning to the left rather than to the right. The drawn line indicates the next step.

C: After the Crown has been made, the finished knot appears as shown.

FIG. 4: *Three-Leaf Chinese Temple Knot,* Finished. When the small loops in each corner of the body of the knot are pulled out, the design takes on the appearance of a flower, as in this illustration.

FIG. 5A: The *Two-Leaf Chinese Temple Knot* is made in the same general way as the Three-Leaf Chinese Temple Knot, but with two bights instead of three. End *b* is crossed over end *c,* end *c* is crossed over end *a,* and then end *a* is brought up through the loop for the final tuck, as indicated by the arrow in FIG. 5B.

C: This shows the knot after the last tuck has been made and the slack taken out of it. The ends are then crowned as in FIG. 5D.

D: The complete knot is shown in D. The slack has been drawn out, and both the loops have been made the same size. Notice that the knot shown in FIG. 3C has four ends, while this one has three. FIG. 3C shows a back view and FIG. 5D a front view of both knots.

Plate 138—Ornamental Interlocking Carrick Bends

FIGS. 6A, B, and C: The *Interlocking Carrick Bend with Outside Overhand Knots.* This and the following knot can easily be tied by studying the illustrations.

FIGS. 7A and B: The *Interlocking Carrick Bend with Inside Overhand Knots.*

FIGS. 8A, B, and C: The *Interlocking Rosette Carrick Bend* is somewhat similar to FIG. 7, except that it has a Loop or Rosette in the design.

FIGS. 9A, B, and C: The *Interlocking Sennit Carrick Bend* has a Four-Strand Sennit between the Carrick Bends. To make the Sennit larger, merely take an additional turn with the two ends at the point lettered *a,* before bringing the ends up and starting to weave the second half of the Sennit, as in FIG. 9B. FIG. 9C is the finished design.

FIG. 10A: The *Arrow-Head* designs are woven out as shown. This key is used when forming the Snowflake design (PLATE 142, FIG. 77). But instead of tying the Three-Point Arrow-Head Weave on each end, plain pointed ends are woven. This figure shows the beginning of the knot. (Ends *a, b, c,* and *d* may be woven as long as desired.) The strands are then separated into groups of two each, and ends *c* and *d* are woven out as shown in FIG. 10B.

B: After this part of the weave has been made, strands *c* and *d* are given a final tuck, so that they appear as in FIG. 10C.

C: This shows the second part of the knot completed. Next, take strands *a* and *b* and repeat the procedure described for strands *c* and *d,* but weaving to the left

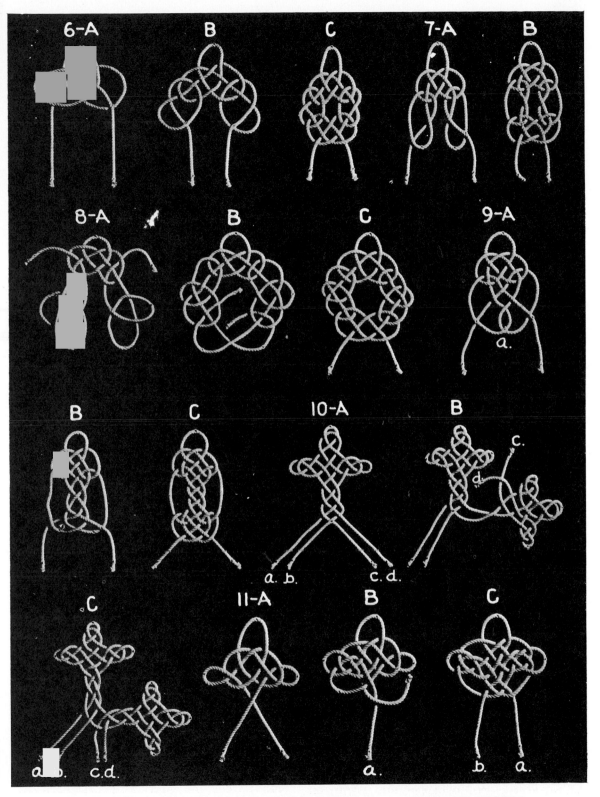

PLATE 138— ORNAMENTAL INTERLOCKING CARRICK BENDS

rather than to the right. When this has been done, three corners of the knot will be finished, and all of the strands again will be in the center. Finally, complete the fourth part, using all four strands to weave the last corner (*see* PLATE 144, FIG. 104).

FIG. 11A: The *Royal Carrick Bend* is first laid out in the position shown.

B: Strand *a* is then taken up and woven as illustrated.

C: Next, take strand *b* and weave it as shown, to complete the knot.

Plate 139—Sailor's Breastplate and Ornamental Designs

FIG. 12: The *Two Interlocked Carrick Bends* can be tied by following the illustration.

FIG. 13: The *French Carrick Knot* is a variation of the Carrick Bend.

FIG. 14: The *Variated Sailor's Breastplate* is similar to the knot shown in PLATE 21, FIG. 10B.

FIG. 15: The *Ornamental Sailor's Breastplate* is begun by first forming the Sailor's Breastplate (PLATE 21, FIGS. 10A and B). Next, an Overhand Knot is made with both ends. The knot is turned over, and the bights on each side are twisted, after which the ends are inserted in the loops, then woven through the remaining loop.

FIG. 16: *An Ornamental Knot*. This design is a combination of two single knots joined together.

FIG. 17: The *Carrick Bend Variation* shown in this figure begins with the tying of a Carrick Bend. Then two ends of both sides are brought down and braided into a Four-Strand Sennit.

FIGS. 18, 19, 20, 21: *Ornamental Knots*. These are simple forms of ornamental knotting which can easily be tied by tracing the knots in the illustration.

FIG. 22: The *Carrick Bend Variation* starts from the Carrick Bend at the top. Next, the knot itself is formed by tracing

the weave. When the weave has been completed, it is drawn up and an Elongated Diamond Knot (PLATE 165, FIG. 407) is then formed, drawn taut, and the ends cut off short.

FIGS. 23, 24, 25, 26, 27, 28 and 29: *Ornamental Knots*. Variations of the Sailor's Breastplate (PLATE 21, FIGS. 10A and B), and the Napoleon Bend (PLATE 242, FIG. 55). These variations can be tied by first mastering these two knots.

FIG. 30: The *Royal Carrick Bend Variation* shown is a modification of the knot pictured in PLATE 138, FIGS. 11A to C.

FIGS. 31, 32, and 33: *Ornamental Knots and Variated Handcuff Hitches.* (*Also see* PLATE 142, FIG. 82; PLATE 150, FIG. 178; PLATE 152, FIG. 236.) Knots which can be used in making knotted picture frames are described in Chapter X.

FIG. 34: The *Carrick Bend Variation* in this illustration can be easily made by tracing the weave. First, the upper Carrick Bend is formed. The ends are next brought down and twisted around each other twice, in a clockwise direction. After this has been done they are brought back up and passed through the ears of the Carrick Bend. The Four-Strand Sennit is then completed, and when the end is reached another Carrick Bend is tied. This knot is formed in almost the same manner as PLATE 138, FIG. 9.

Plate 140—Ornamental Weaving

FIG. 35: The *Nine-Strand Inverted Turk's Head* starts out with a Nine-Strand Turk's Head made on a spar, and given an additional pass to double the knot. Then remove it from the spar and flatten it out

until it assumes the shape of the Turk's Head in the illustration (*see* PLATE 109, FIG. 4).

FIG. 36: *An Ornamental Breastplate*. It is a variation of FIG. 48; close observation

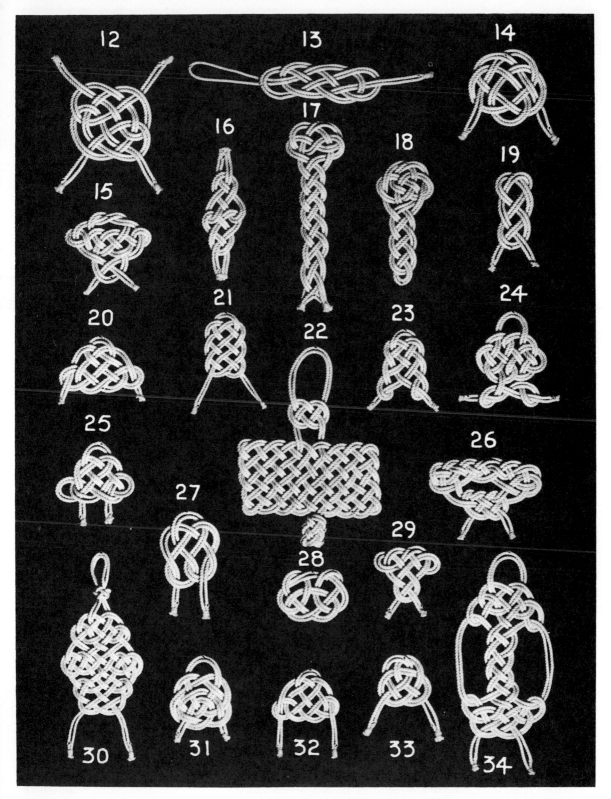

PLATE 139—SAILOR'S BREASTPLATE AND ORNAMENTAL DESIGNS

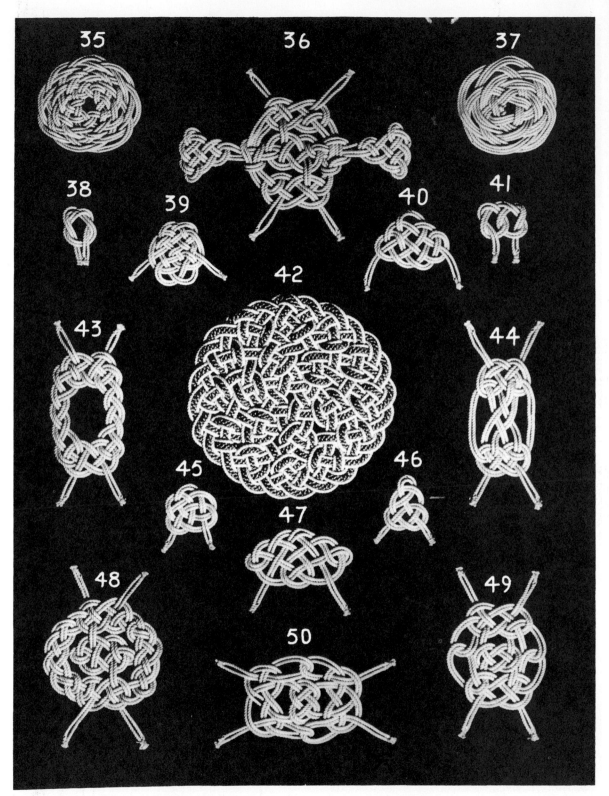

PLATE 140—ORNAMENTAL WEAVING

[*Plate 141*]   Ornamental Knotting   281

will show where the difference in the two knots lies.

Fig. 37: The *Six-Strand Inverted Turk's Head* is made in the same manner as the knot in Fig. 35, but with six strands rather than nine (*see* Plate 109, Fig. 5).

Figs. 38, 39, 40 and 41: *French Ornamental Knotting.* These examples of French Ornamental Knotting will be useful in picture framing as illustrated in Chapter X.

Fig. 42: The *Center-piece Design* can be tied more easily if it is made on a cushion or similar object, with pins placed through a cord as the weave is being formed. To add additional strands of different colors on each side of the main strand, take two pieces of line and tuck them completely around the entire weave following the main strand. When these lines meet, they are bound together, and cut off short on the reverse side of the Center-piece. This design is shown opened up in Plate 280, Fig. 373.

Figs. 43, 44, 48, 49 and 50: *Variated Ornamental Breastplates.* In tying these designs it will be found helpful to first study the knots illustrated in Plate 138, Figs. 6, 7, 8 and 9.

Figs. 45, 46 and 47: *Miscellaneous Ornamental Knots* can easily be duplicated by studying the illustrations.

Plate 141—Bugler's Braid and Other Ornamental Designs

Fig. 51: The *Five-Strand Inverted Turk's Head* is made by following the procedure outlined in Plate 140, Fig. 35.

Fig. 52: The *Bugler's Braid Design* shown is formed by first making two separate Bugler's Braids (Plate 120, Fig. 131a) and placing them in the position indicated. The Bugler's Braids are then closed, as shown in the chapter on Turk's Heads, to dispose of the ends (*see* Plate 111, Fig. 50).

Fig. 53: The *Three-Strand Inverted Turk's Head* is formed as usual but with an additional turn, and then flattened out (*see* Plate 109, Fig. 1).

Fig. 54: A Series of *Interlocking Carrick Bends* can be made as long as desired by simply continuing to form the Carrick Bends in the manner illustrated.

Fig. 55: *Variated Carrick Bends.* This knot is somewhat similar to the Square Mat illustrated in Plate 139, Fig. 21.

Fig. 56: The *Pendant* is formed in the same manner as the knot shown in Plate 138, Fig. 9. Instead of merely filling in the Sennit in the center, on the second time around a Half Hitch is taken on the outer strands when the working strands come out on each side before turning back. After completing the body of the knot, a Three-Strand Turk's Head is woven out with the two strands, and finished off with an Elongated Diamond Knot, illustrated in Plate 165, Fig. 407.

Figs. 57, 58 and 59: *Simple Ornamental Knots* which can easily be tied by closely observing the illustrations.

Fig. 60: The *Chinese Temple Shamrock Knot* begins with the Shamrock Knot shown in Plate 240, Fig. 45. Then crown the three bights and two ends, as in the Common Chinese Knot (Plate 137, Fig. 3).

Fig. 61: The *Five-Leaf Chinese Temple Knot* is formed in the same manner as the Three-Leaf Chinese Temple Knot, but with four bights instead of three as in Plate 137, Fig. 3.

Fig. 62: *A Carrick Bend Variation.* Another variation of the Square Mat, Plate 139, Fig. 21.

Fig. 63: The *Closed Sailor's Breastplate* is made by first tying the knot illustrated in Plate 21, Fig. 10. This is done with a single cord. Next, take one end and follow the other until the entire knot is doubled.

The ends are then seized together on the reverse side of the knot and cut off short.

Fig. 64: The *Three Strand Inverted Turk's Head* is formed by inverting the Turk's Head illustrated in PLATE 109, FIG. 1.

FIGS. 65, 66 and 67: *French Ornamental Knotting*. These knots can be tied by following the illustrations.

FIG. 68: The *Military Weave* is made from a single strand of cord. After beginning at the small loop on top of the knot and tracing out the design, it is given two additional passes, making three in all. This knot is often used on military uniforms.

FIGS. 69, 71 and 72: *Ornamental Designs* which can be used in making a knot board. When these knots are symmetrically mounted on plain varnished veneer boards there are few objects which can surpass them in beauty.

FIG. 70: The *Three-Strand Turk's Head Woven into another Three-Strand Turk's Head and Inverted* begins with a single Three-Strand Turk's Head, doubled. On the third turn, the two preceding passes are woven left and right, and the third strand is woven through these two to form a Three-Strand Turk's Head Weave. The entire knot is then doubled, with the ends secured on the reverse side and cut off short.

Plate 142—Snowflake Design and Other Ornamental Weaves

FIG. 73: The *Two-Leaf Chinese Temple Rosette* begins with the Two-Leaf Chinese Temple Knot (PLATE 137, FIG. 5). The two bights are then cut and a crown is formed around the edge of the knot, using the ends. To finish, the ends are taken in back of the knot, seized together and trimmed off short.

FIG. 74: *Ornamental Four-Strand Sennit Braid.*

FIG. 75: The *Three-Leaf Chinese Temple Rosette* is formed in the same manner as FIG. 73. The same procedure is followed in tying the Four-Leaf (FIG. 76) and Five-Leaf (FIG. 78) Chinese Temple Rosette.

FIG. 76: *Four-Leaf Chinese Temple Rosette.*

FIG. 77: The *Snowflake Design* is woven out with two separate cords. It can be made either by tracing the weave, or by first forming each one of the four sides separately and joining them together in the center. After two long pieces of line have been followed through, the separate pieces are removed, and the remaining ends from the single pieces are woven back to double the design (*See* PLATE 138, FIG. 10).

FIG. 78: *Five-Leaf Chinese Temple Rosette.*

FIG. 79: *Variated Arrow-Head Designs, First Method*, is used as a border knot in the Chinese Double Braiding illustrated in PLATE 160, FIG. 349.

FIG. 80: A *Spear Head* is frequently used as added ornamental weaving on double braiding.

FIGS. 81 and 82: *Carrick Braid and Variated Handcuff Hitches.* (*Also see* PLATE 139, FIG. 33; PLATE 150, FIG. 178; PLATE 152, FIG. 236.) These knots can be tied by closely observing the illustrations.

FIG. 83: *Variated Arrow-Head Knot, Second Method*, is made with two separate pieces of line, beginning with one point, and then weaving out the second. When the ends meet after the fourth point has been completed, they are woven around the design, following their original ends until three complete passes have been made. The ends are then seized together on the reverse side of the knot, and cut off short.

FIGS. 84 and 85: *Variations of the Overhand Knot* shown in PLATE 1, FIG. 7.

FIG. 86: *Variated Arrow-Head Knot, Third Method*, is formed in the same manner as the preceding knot, except for a slight variation in the weave.

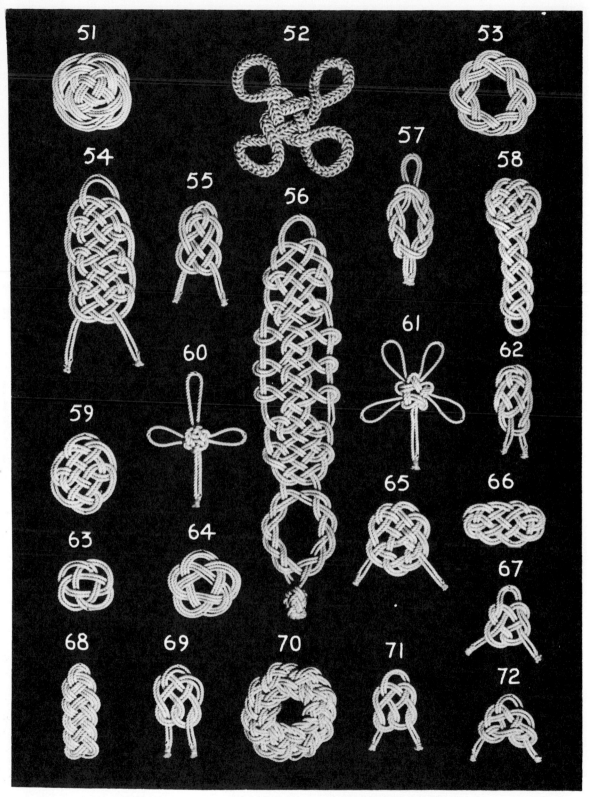

PLATE 141—BUGLER'S BRAID AND OTHER ORNAMENTAL DESIGNS

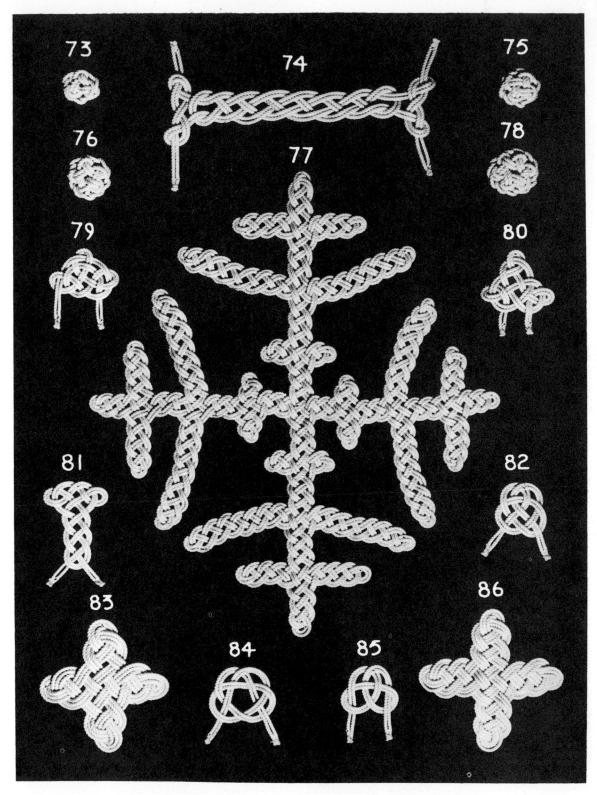

PLATE 142—SNOWFLAKE DESIGN AND OTHER ORNAMENTAL WEAVES

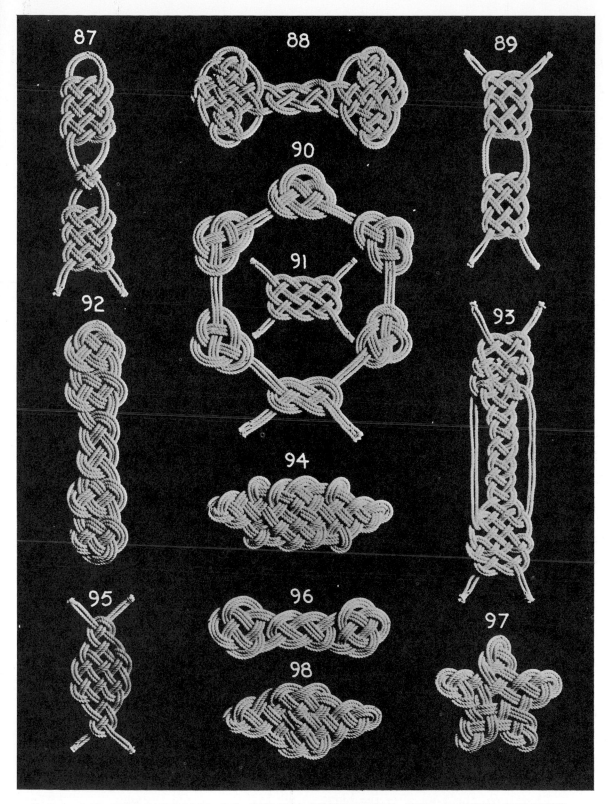

PLATE 143—VARIATIONS OF CELTIC KNOTTING AND OTHER WEAVES

Plate 143—Variations of Celtic Knotting and Other Weaves

FIGS. 87, 88 and 89: These *Variations of Celtic Knotting* can be easily duplicated by merely tracing the designs.

FIG. 90: The *Victory Wreath* is made by forming a series of Sailor's Breastplate Knots (PLATE 21, FIG. 10B), as shown.

FIG. 91: The *Open Carrick Bend* is made by carefully tracing the weave in the illustration.

FIG. 92: A *Sailor's Breastplate Design.* This figure is made with two separate cords. The weave is begun by forming a Carrick Bend in the middle of the knot, using the middle of both cords to tie it. Carrick Bends at both ends are then formed, and the entire knot is given two additional passes with the remaining ends at each side.

FIG. 93: *Combination Carrick Bend Four-Strand Sennit.* It can be made by first observing the knot illustrated in PLATE 138, FIG. 9.

FIGS. 94, 95 and 98: *Open Carrick Bend Variations.* Variations of the knot in FIG. 91. This knot is first made, then the center bight on the top and bottom are drawn out to form a large bight; the two upper ends are then woven into the top bight, and the lower ends into the bottom bight.

FIG. 96: *Variated Sailor's Breastplate Knot* (PLATE 21, FIG. 10). This particular knot is tied with two separate pieces of cord.

FIG. 97: *Five Point Star Weave* is tied in somewhat the same manner as the head of the Weave illustrated in PLATE 138, FIG. 10.

Plate 144—Combination Weaves in Ornamental Designs

FIGS. 99, 101, 102, 103, 106, 107, 108 and 109: These *Variations of Celtic Knotting* are woven with two or three separate pieces of cord. FIG. 106 requires three separate pieces.

FIG. 100: The *Girdle* is made as follows: four long pieces of line are first middled, then taken in two groups of two each. Next, tie the Royal Carrick Bend (PLATE 138, FIG. 11) in the center of these two groups. Then form four Japanese Crown Knots (PLATE 22, FIG. 14) on each side. Using the two center cords from each group, place a series of Lark's Head Knots on two brass rings as shown. (The original rings were one inch in diameter.) When the end of the

Four-Strand Sennit is reached, tie two Elongated Diamond Knots with the double strands (PLATE 165, FIG. 407). Finally, the strands are unlaid, combed out, and cut off to the desired length.

FIG. 104: The *Arrow-Head Cross* looks like this, after finishing the weave and doubling it as illustrated in PLATE 138, FIG. 10.

FIG. 105: The *Latin Cross* is tied by following the same key indicated in PLATE 138, FIG. 10. Plain pointed ends are woven instead of arrow-head ends, and the lower corner is woven out with an additional turn in order to make it longer.

Plate 145—Chinese and Oblong Mats

FIG. 110A: The *Chinese Square Mat* has the cord first laid out as shown in this illustration; then another bight *a* is passed through as indicated by the arrow.

B: This shows the knot after the bight has been tucked. These mats can be woven

to any size, simply by continuing to form bights and passing them over and under as many times as desired, each bight making the knot larger. To finish off, the end (not the bight) is passed through the weave, as shown by the arrow.

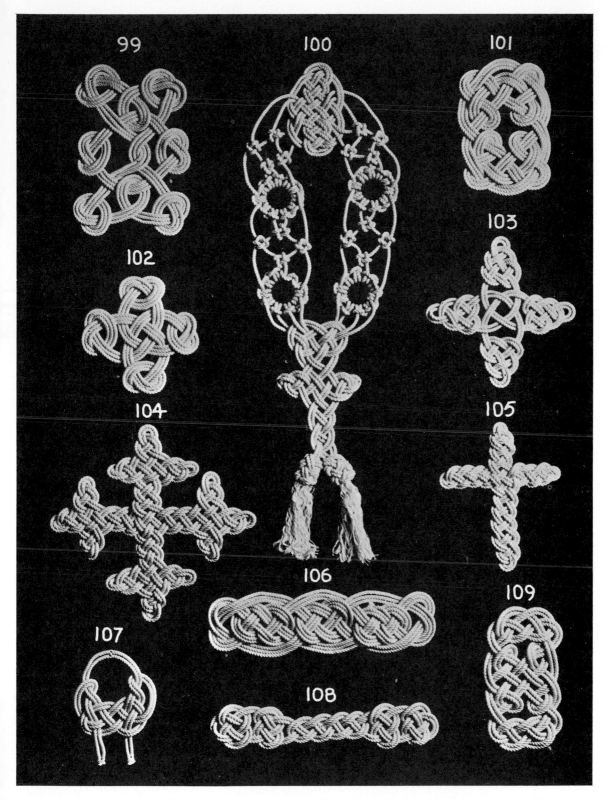

PLATE 144—COMBINATION WEAVES IN ORNAMENTAL DESIGNS

c: This shows the knot after the end has been tucked.

D: The knot is now drawn up until it is perfectly square. This mat is made of one bight.

FIG. 111: The *Chinese Square Mat with Two Bights* is composed of two bights, making it slightly larger than the preceding one.

FIG. 112: The *Chinese Square Mat with Three Bights* (*see* FIG. 110A).

FIG. 113: The *Chinese Square Mat with Four Bights* (*see* FIG. 110A).

FIG. 114A: The *Oblong Mat* begins with a Square Mat. Any one of the preceding designs is suitable. In this particular case, FIG. 111 was used. Then draw out all the bights on the bottom of the knot, leaving a generous amount of slack, as shown.

B: Next, bights *b* and *c* are crossed, as shown. Bights *a* and *d* are then woven over and under, until they appear as in FIG. 114C.

c: This shows *a* and *d* after they have been woven into place. Ends *e* and *f* are then woven diagonally, strand *e* going over and under between bight *a*, and strand *f* over and under between bight *d*.

D: This shows the completed Oblong Mat.

FIG. 115: The *Oblong Mat* in a larger size can be made by merely repeating the key described in FIG. 114. The knot illustrated was made by first forming the knot shown in FIG. 114D, and then repeating the key once.

FIG. 116: The *Oblong Mat* shown in this figure was made from the Square Mat of Three Bights (FIG. 112). It will be noticed that in this knot there are five bights at the bottom, instead of four as in FIG. 114. To overcome this, twist the center bight a half-turn; then take one bight on each side and begin weaving them in the same manner as FIG. 114.

Plate 146—Miscellaneous Ornamental Designs

FIG. 117: The *Interlocking Chinese Knot* is another form of Chinese Square Matting, in which all four ends are free. The knot may be made in a small size, as in the illustration, or it may be enlarged in the following way: first, tuck strand *a* through the body of the knot, parallel to itself, always tucking under the last strand. The drawn line pictures this initial step.

FIG. 118A: The *Interlacing Chinese Knot* is shown after the strand has been tucked as described in FIG. 117. The next step is to take strand *b* and tuck it as the arrow indicates.

B: This shows the completion of the step outlined in FIG. 117 and FIG. 118A. The knot is now in its finished form. This process for enlarging the knot can be repeated as often as desired, by using the key just described. The knot shown has the key carried out once.

FIG. 119: The *Interlacing Chinese Knot*

in this illustration has the key carried out twice.

FIG. 120: The *Interlacing Chinese Knot* in this instance has the key carried out three times.

FIG. 121: The *Rosette Carrick Bend with Tassels* has small round balls on it as tassels. These balls are in reality Three-Strand Turk's Heads drawn up taut.

FIG. 122: A *Chinese Ornamental Knot* can easily be duplicated by tracing the weave.

FIGS. 123 and 125: The *Ornamental Weaves* illustrated are designed for gold braid. They are made by taking two single pieces of cord and weaving out the design After it has been formed, the ends are followed around two times more, making three passes in all.

FIG. 124: The *Carrick Bend Design* pictured is somewhat similar to the knot illustrated on PLATE 138, FIG. 9A.

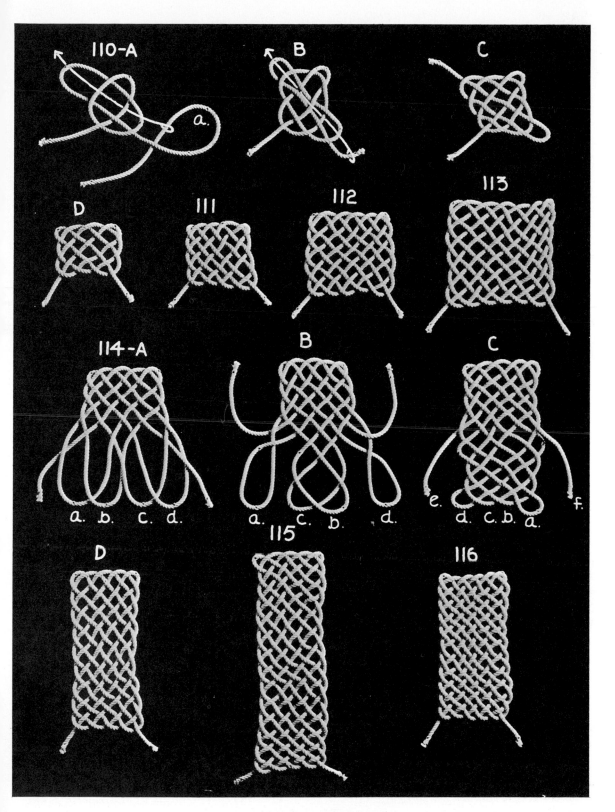

PLATE 145—CHINESE MATS

Fig. 126: A *Square Knot Design* is begun by forming the Macramé Square Knot or Flat Knot doubled at the top (PLATE 168, FIGS. 1A to F). Next, take a Half Hitch with each center cord on each outside cord. Form a Japanese Crown Knot in the center with the two center double strands (PLATE 22, FIG. 14), and take another Half Hitch on the outside strands. Then one more Flat Knot is made on the center strands. All four double strands are then braided into a Four-Strand Flat Sennit. The ends are seized when the Sennit has reached the desired length.

Fig. 127: The *True Dragonfly Knot* is tied as follows: a Diamond Knot (PLATE 36, FIG. 190) is first formed in the center of a piece of line and drawn taut, allowing the upper bight to be drawn into the center of the knot. A Shamrock Knot (PLATE 240, FIG. 45) is then made and drawn taut a short distance from the Diamond Knot. Another Shamrock Knot is formed just below the first one, and drawn taut. To finish off the tail, a Blood Knot (PLATE 22, FIG. 16) of six turns is made, drawn taut, and the ends cut off short.

Figs. 128 and 129: *Ornamental Sailor's Breastplate Designs*. These designs are also made from Sailor's Breastplate Knot (PLATE 21, FIG. 10).

Fig. 130: The *Flower Knot* begins with the Shamrock Knot (PLATE 240, FIG. 45). Then take the uppermost bight and pass it down through the body of the knot. This will provide an additional bight at the top of the knot, and also another one at the bottom.

Plate 147—Butterfly Knot and Other Insect Designs

Fig. 131A: The *Donkey Ear Knot* is first laid out as illustrated. Then bights *a* and *b* are pulled, and the knot worked taut.

B: This shows the completed knot.

Fig. 132: The *Mosquito Knot* has its body made in the same manner as the preceding knot, but both ends are passed through the body of the original knot to form two additional bights. Next, tie a series of three Two-Fold Blood Knots (PLATE 22, FIG. 16A).

Fig. 133: The *Patriarchal Cross* is formed by using the key illustrated in PLATE 138, FIG. 10, but instead of weaving the Arrowheads, the ends are woven to plain points.

Fig. 134: The *Double Mosquito Knot* is tied in the same way as FIG. 132. After passing the ends through the body of the knot once, pass them back through again, thus making six bights in all.

Fig. 135A: The *Rabbit's Ears Knot* has the cord laid out as shown, and the ends then tucked as the arrows indicate.

B: The knot is next drawn taut, until it appears as in this illustration.

Fig. 136: The *Royal French Carrick Bend* is made in somewhat the same fashion as the ordinary Royal Carrick Bend (PLATE 138, FIG. 11).

Fig. 137: The *Butterfly Knot*, First Method, is formed from the Chinese Temple Knot (PLATE 137, FIG. 5).

Fig. 138: The *Flower Knot*, First Method, is also made from the Three-Leaf Chinese Temple Knot, by drawing out all the bights.

Fig. 139: The *Butterfly Knot*, Second Method, is formed by first making the Bugler's Braid, and then closing it up as illustrated in PLATE 111, FIG. 50A. It is so designed that, when closed up, there will be five bights, which are then drawn out as shown.

Fig. 140: The *Flower Knot*, Second Method, is also made from the Bugler's Braid, as in the preceding knot. The bights are then pulled out, as indicated.

Fig. 141: *Variation of the Beetle Knot* shown in FIG. 144.

Fig. 142: *Caterpillar Knot*, which is a

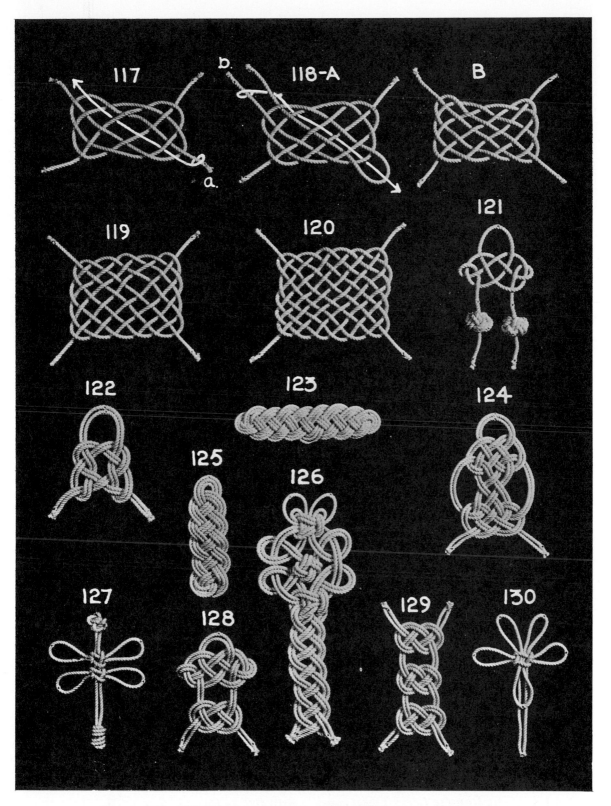

PLATE 146—MISCELLANEOUS ORNAMENTAL DESIGNS

Three-Strand Sennit made with a **single** cord. (*See* PLATE 135, FIG. 402.)

FIG. 143: The *Celtic Weave,* another form of Celtic Knotting, is made with two separate pieces of line.

FIG. 144: The *Beetle Knot* is composed of Macramé Square Knots, made in groups of two.

FIG. 145: The *Centipede Knot* has the Macramé Square Knots formed on their own bights. The Square Knots are made as illustrated in PLATE 168, FIG. 10.

Plate 148—Chinese Combination Designs

FIG. 146A: *Combining Dragonfly Knots,* First Stage; in some ornamental designs, a group of Dragonfly Knots (PLATE 137, FIGS. 1A to E) are used together. This illustration shows how to form a *Dragonfly* on either the right- or left-hand side of the original one. Strand *a* is first rove through bight *b,* and placed as shown.

B: The knot is then finished in the same manner as PLATE 137, FIG. 1B, C and D.

FIG. 147: *Combining Dragonfly Knots,* Second Stage. The next step is to form the Dragonfly Knot with two bights and two ends. This is done as follows: bight *b* is first rove through bight *a;* the bight of strand *c* is next rove through bight *b;* then *end d* is passed in the manner indicated by the arrow, to complete the knot.

FIG. 148: The *Chinese Book Mark* has the *a* portion of its design explained in FIGS. 146 and 147. For a detailed description of *b,* see PLATE 137, FIG. 2. (NOTE: The Carrick Bends are made from the bights of the Double Braid while it is being woven.) At *c,* four Macramé Square Knots are tied, after two strands have been added (*see* PLATE 35, FIG. 179).

FIG. 149: *The Pendant.* A combination of the knots illustrated in PLATE 143, FIG. 91; PLATE 138, FIGS. 6C and 7B.

FIG. 150: A group of *Dragonfly Knots* which has been formed by using the method illustrated in PLATE 137, FIGS. 1A to E.

FIG. 151: A *Simple Ornamental Weave* which can easily be duplicated by following the illustrations.

FIG. 152: The *Chinese Lamp Tassel* consists of *a,* a Bugler's Braid with six corners (PLATE 147, FIG. 139), which has been closed as indicated in PLATE 111, FIG. 50A. The knot at *b* is a Chinese Double Braid with three bights. Its construction is shown in detail in PLATE 137, FIG. 2.

FIG. 153: The *Bugler's Braid of Six Bights* is made as described in PLATE 147, FIG. 139.

FIGS. 154A, B, C and D: The *Four-Leaf Dragonfly* can be made with as many bights as desired by the following method: begin as in PLATE 137, FIG. 1A; pull a bight through, as shown by the arrow. Then instead of working with the end at this point, another bight is pulled through the bight just made. Finally, close up the knot as illustrated in FIGS. 1B, C and D.

FIG. 155: The *Five-Leaf Dragonfly* is made in the same manner as the preceding knot.

FIG. 156: The *Bugler's Braid* with **Seven** Bights and a Dragonfly contains a Diamond Knot at the bottom, which is shown in detail in PLATE 36, FIGS. 190A and B.

FIG. 157: The *Tombstone Knot* is tied as follows: after the Bugler's Braid has been made and closed up, the bights are drawn up snug, and a Dragonfly Knot is formed. Next, take another short length of line, place it between the original two and proceed to make a Four-Strand Round Braid. Finish off the design with an Elongated Diamond Knot (PLATE 165, FIG. 406A).

FIG. 158: The *Five-Leaf Chinese Temple Knot* is made in the same way as the Three-Leaf Chinese Temple Knot (PLATE 137, FIG. 3A). This knot, however, is formed with five bights and two ends, rather than three bights and two ends.

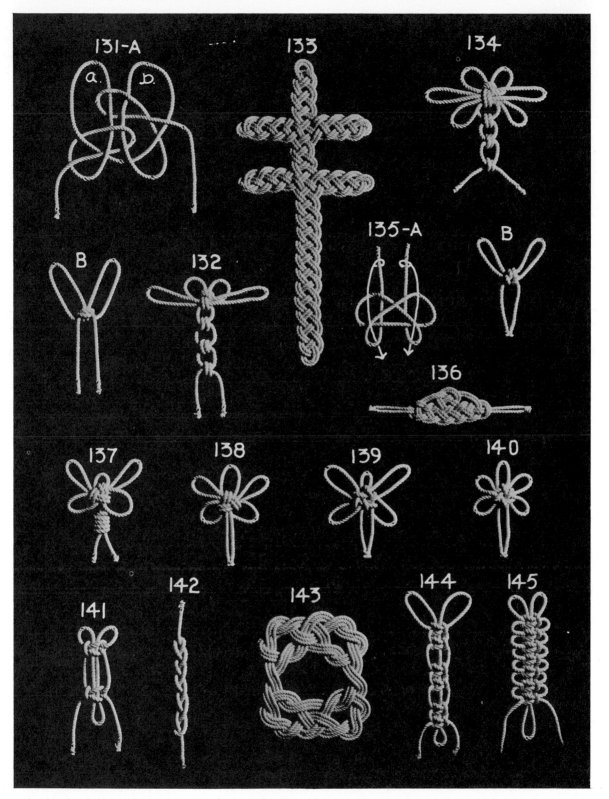

131-A 133 134
a. b.

B 132 135-A B

136

137 138 139 140

141 142 143 144 145

PLATE 147—THE BUTTERFLY KNOT AND OTHER INSECT DESIGNS

Plate 149—Dragonfly Combinations

FIG. 159A: The *Variated Dragonfly Knot* is tied in basically the same fashion as the Dragonfly. Its construction, however, will be simplified by using tacks to hold the work in place while tying it. The Dragonfly Knot is formed with single bights. Therefore, this knot, which is made with two bights, might properly be called a Double Two-Leaf Dragonfly Knot. The work is laid out as illustrated, and bights *a, b, c, d,* and *e* are pulled out to form the five bights of the design.

B: This shows the completed knot.

FIG. 160: The *Triple Dragonfly Knot* is formed in the same way as FIG. 159, but instead of laying out two bights, lay out three in each group.

FIG. 161: The *Double Three - Leaf Dragonfly Knot* is made by the same method as FIG. 159, but instead of laying out three groups of bights, lay out four but with only two bights in each group, keeping the procedure the same.

FIG. 162: The *Three - Leaf Triple Dragonfly Knot* is made in the same manner as FIG. 161, except that three bights are laid out in each group instead of two. (*See* PLATE 49, FIG. 363.)

FIG. 163: The *Two-Leaf Dragonfly Knot* is made in the same manner as PLATE 137, FIG. 1. Lay out the work as in FIG. 1A, but instead of pulling the bight through as indicated by the arrow, pass the end through, and then finish knot as in FIGS. 1B and 1C.

FIG. 164: The *Three - Leaf Chinese Temple Knot with Additional Bights* is made as follows: first, form the Chinese Temple Knot in PLATE 137, FIG. 3A; turn the knot over when it is finished, take one of the ends, and begin passing it in and out of the small bights on the corners of the

knot itself, until it emerges from the opposite side of the knot. Three bights should be added with this strand. The same procedure is followed with the other strand.

FIG. 165: The *Five-Leaf Dragonfly Knot* is in reality only a four bight knot, but upon close observation it can be seen that one end has been half-hitched into the next bight.

FIG. 166: The *Two-Leaf Chinese Temple Flower Knot* is tied by first forming the Two-Leaf Chinese Temple Knot (PLATE 137, FIG. 5). Next, draw out the bights in each corner, until there are five in all. Then tie a series of Overhand Knots with the ends.

FIG. 167: The *Chinese Double Braid Butterfly Design.* (For detail of this knot *see* PLATE 137, FIG. 2.)

FIG. 168: The *Chinese Double Braid with a Square Knot.* (*See* PLATE 137, FIG. 2A.)

FIG. 169: The *Seven-Leaf Bugler's Braid Flower Knot.* (*See* PLATE 147, FIG. 139.)

FIG. 170: The *Flower Knot* shown is made by first forming a Bugler's Braid which has been passed through three bights, not two (*see* PLATE 147, FIG. 139). Then close it up, and draw it into shape. This knot is one of eight points, or bights.

FIG. 171: *An Ornamental Design* which can easily be tied by closely following the illustration.

FIG. 172: The *Dandelion Knot* is also made from the Bugler's Braid of three bights (PLATE 120, FIG. 132).

FIGS. 173 and 174: *Dandelion Knot Variations* are made in the same manner as the previous knot, only with an additional number of bights.

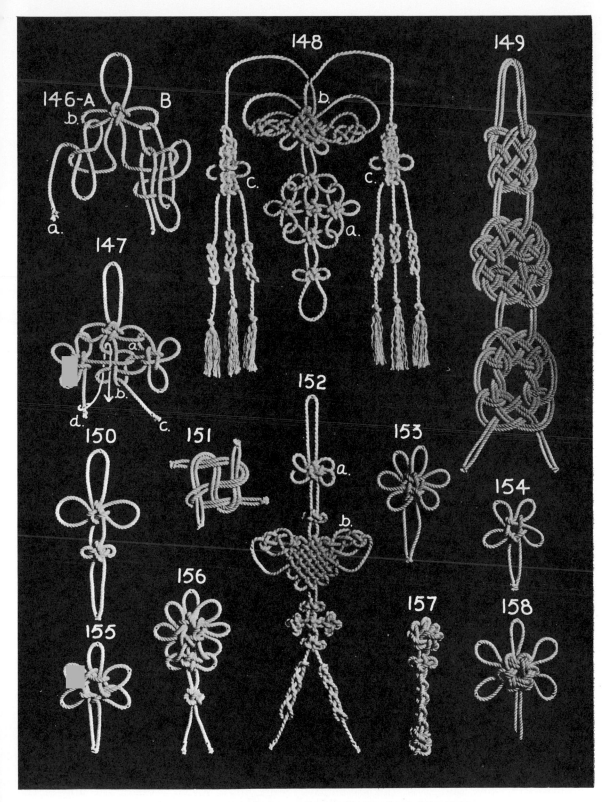

PLATE 148—CHINESE COMBINATION DESIGNS

Plate 150—Miscellaneous Ornamental Designs

FIGS. 175 and 176: These *Simple Ornamental Designs* can be tied by observing the illustrations.

FIG. 177: The *Four-Strand Nine-Cross Inverted Turk's Head* is illustrated in PLATE 111, FIG. 28.

FIGS. 178, 179, 180, and 181: *Variated Handcuff Hitches* and forms of *Japanese Knotting*. (*Also see* PLATE 139, FIG. 33; PLATE 142, FIG. 82; PLATE 152, FIG. 236.)

FIG. 182: The *Mariner's Wheel* is tied as follows: first, make the Bugler's Braid *(a)* with thirty-two bights, and close it; it will then have thirty-six bights. (Four bights are added while closing the ends.) This will allow six bights for each spoke. Next, tie a Chinese Temple Knot of six parts. Cut each bight, and place the knot in the center of the Bugler's Braid. From the Chinese Temple Knot, take two of the cut strands of one of the bights, and reeve them through the center of the Bugler's Braid, one strand on each side of one bight. Taking another pair of the severed strands, count six bights away on the Bugler's Braid from the point where the first set of strands were rove through, and reeve through the second pair. This procedure is repeated until all the strands have been passed through. Next, take a very long piece of cord, and make a Three-Leaf Dragonfly Knot in its middle.

Begin tracing this piece through the Bugler's Braid and into the Chinese Temple Knot (PLATE 137, FIGS. 3A to C). In the process of doing this, the original pieces of cord are of course removed. Each time the long piece goes through the Bugler's Braid, a Three-Leaf Dragonfly Knot is made, with its bight hitched through one of the previous Dragonfly Knots, so as to join them. When the knot is finished and drawn up evenly, both ends are bound together on the reverse side of the Chinese Temple Knot. In order to stiffen the entire knot, and make the Bugler's Braid round, bend a piece of stiff wire until it is perfectly round and slightly larger than the circumference of the Bugler's Braid itself. Then place this wire inside the braid, to keep it in its proper shape.

FIG. 183: The *Seven-Strand Inverted Turk's Head* is made by first tying the Turk's Head as in PLATE 109, FIG. 4A.

FIGS. 184, 185, 186, 187, 188 and 189: Examples of *Turkish Knotting*.

FIG. 190: *This Ornamental Design* is made with two separate pieces of cord, which are doubled by following the ends around; when they meet secure them on the reverse side of the design and cut off short.

FIGS. 191, 192, 193, 194 and 195: Examples of *Turkish Knotting*. They can be made by closely observing the illustrations.

Plate 151—Miscellaneous Ornamental Weaves

FIG. 196: *Combination Carrick and Napoleon Bends* can be duplicated by following the illustration.

FIG. 197: The *Tree Leaf* is another method of forming a leaf similar to the one shown in PLATE 155, FIG. 272.

FIG. 198: The *Inverted Antique Braid* is illustrated in PLATE 136, FIG. 412. PLATE 111, FIGS. 58A and B shows how to close it.

FIGS. 199, 200, and 201: *Ornamental Knots* which can be used for picture frame work, as shown in Chapter X.

FIG. 202: The *Teapot* has for its basic weave the Eleven-Strand Round Mat (PLATE 158, FIGS. 313A, B and C). The handle and legs are, of course, woven out during the forming of the knot.

FIGS. 203 to 211: *Ornamental Weaves*. These weaves are adaptable to picture frame work. The selection of these knots must, of course, be done with discretion. Only knots which are suitable and of the proper shape and size are to be used.

FIGS. 212 to 218: *Ornamental Weaves*.

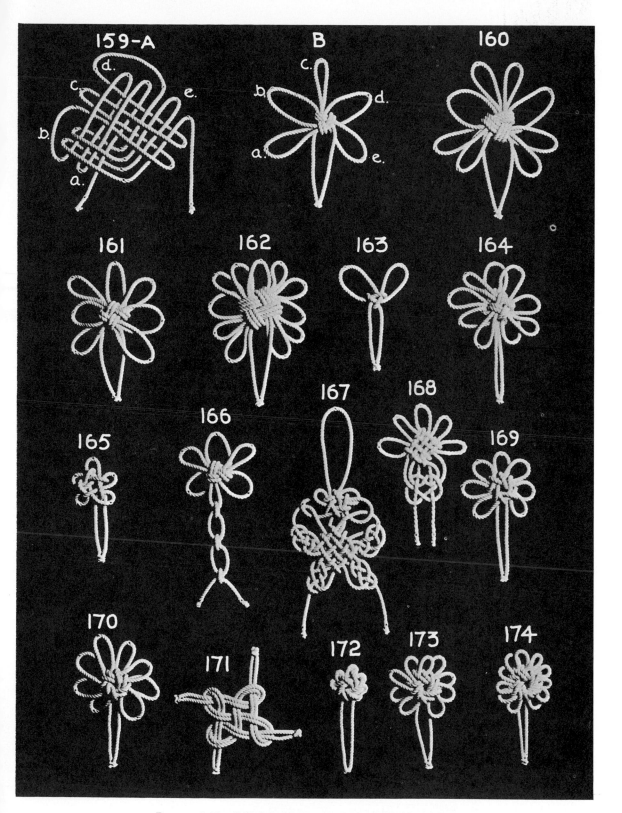

PLATE 149—DRAGONFLY COMBINATIONS

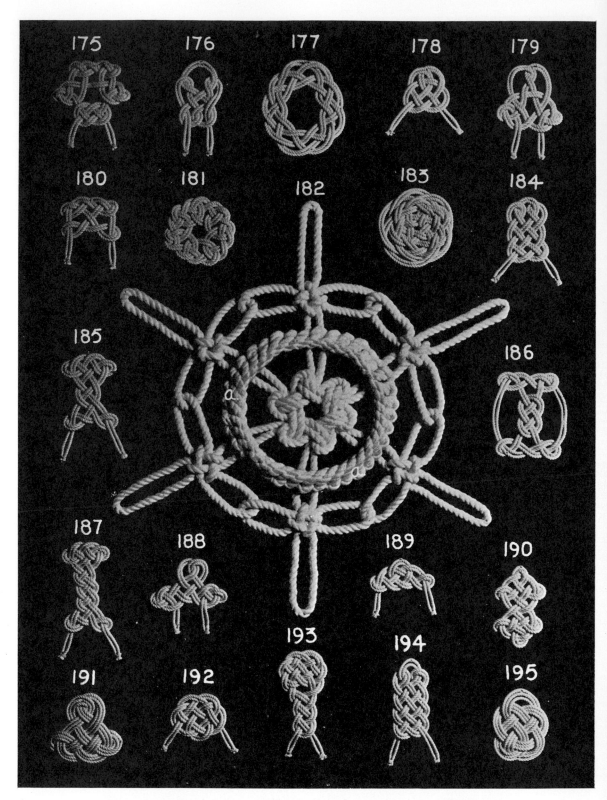

PLATE 150—MISCELLANEOUS ORNAMENTAL DESIGNS

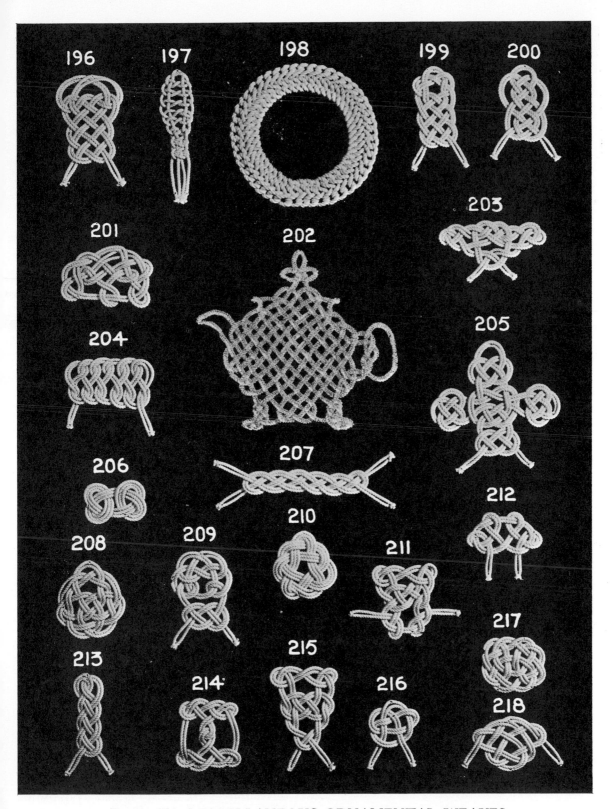

PLATE 151—MISCELLANEOUS ORNAMENTAL WEAVES

Plate 152—Combination Weaves in Decorative Designs

FIG. 219: The *Ten-Strand Inverted Turk's Head* is made by first tying the Turk's Head as illustrated in PLATE 109, FIG. 5, then inverting it.

FIGS. 220, 222, 223, 224, 225 and 226: *Turkish Ornamental and Japanese Knots* can be tied by observing the weave.

FIG. 221: The *Arrow-Head Weave* has its head woven from the knot illustrated in PLATE 158, FIG. 317. The shaft is a Three-Strand Sennit, and the feathers can easily be copied by examining the picture shown. The small round knot at the lower end is an Elongated Diamond Knot with two passes (PLATE 165, FIG. 407).

FIG. 227: *Open Carrick Bend Variation.* This design is made with two separate pieces of cord.

FIGS. 228, 229, 230 and 241: *Variations of the Napoleon Bend* (PLATE 242, FIG. 55).

FIGS. 231, 232, 233, 234, 235, 236, 237, 239 and 242: Examples of *French Knotting and Variated Handcuff Hitches.* (*Also see* PLATE 139, FIG. 33; PLATE 142, FIG. 82; PLATE 150, FIG. 178.) They can be duplicated by tracing the designs in the illustrations.

FIG. 238: The *Bugler's Braid of Three Bights.* (See PLATE 149, FIG. 172.)

FIG. 240: *A Turkish Ornamental Design.* This knot is begun by first weaving out the upper portion of the knot. Next tie a Double Carrick Bend but do not interlock the bights. Next form two non-interlocking Overhand Knots and finish off with a Double Carrick Bend as illustrated in the figure.

Plate 153—Closed Royal Carrick Bend and Other Designs

FIG. 243: The *Closed Royal Carrick Bend* begins with the Royal Carrick Bend illustrated in PLATE 138, FIG. 11. Then take one of the two ends, which have both been left long, and follow the other end around, so as to double the knot.

FIGS. 244, 246 and 247: *French Ornamental Knots* which can easily be duplicated by tracing the designs in the figures.

FIG. 245: The *Snowflake Design* is made as follows: take two long pieces of line, and weave the cross as illustrated in PLATE 138, FIG. 10. When the design has been completed, the ends are followed around to double the knot. Next, take two more pieces of line, and begin weaving the four points lettered *a*. When this has been woven, double as before. All the ends are seized on the knot's reverse side, and cut off short.

Plate 154—Miscellaneous Ornamental Designs

FIGS. 248, 249, 251, 252, 253, 254, 255 and 256: Examples of *French Knotting* which can be duplicated by observing the illustrations.

FIG. 250: *An Ornamental Design.* This design is formed with two separate pieces of cord, each one doubled. Beginning at the top proceed to trace the weave until the design has been completed. The knot is then drawn up, the ends seized and cut off.

FIG. 257: The *Royal Crown Carrick Bend* is woven from a single piece of line.

When the weave has been completed, the ends are secured on the reverse side of the knot, and cut off short.

FIGS. 258, 260, 261 and 262: *Miscellaneous Ornamental Knots* which will be found useful in making ornamental knot boards.

FIG. 259: The *Inverted Five-Strand Endless Sennit Turk's Head* is tied by doubling and inverting the Turk's Head illustrated in PLATE 109, FIG. 6.

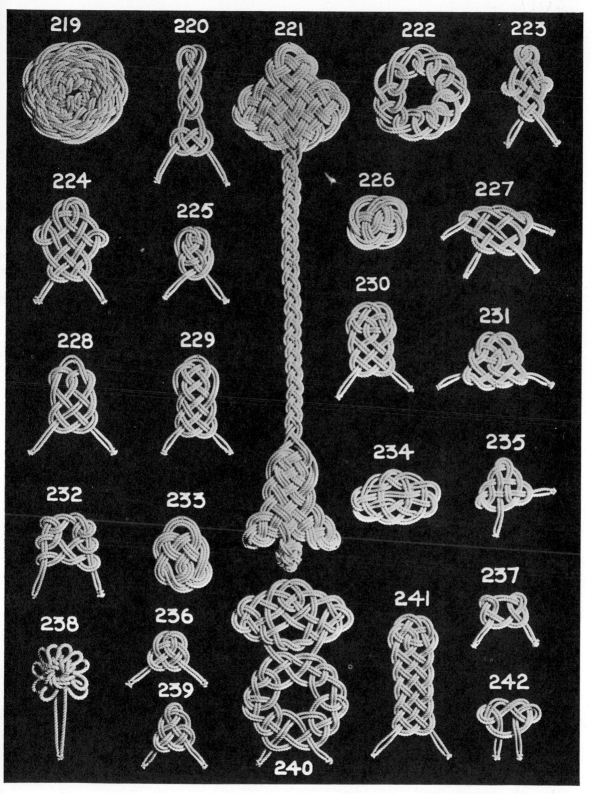

PLATE 152—COMBINATION WEAVES IN DECORATIVE DESIGNS

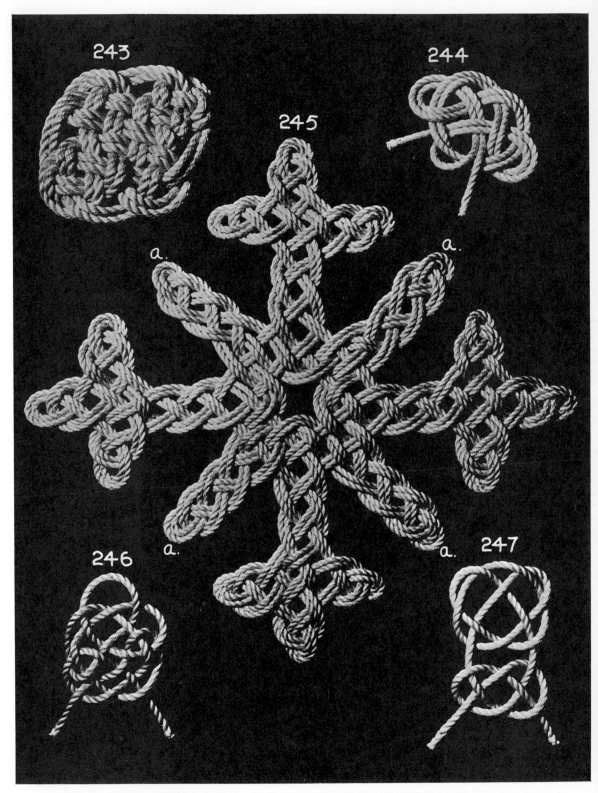

PLATE 153—CLOSED ROYAL CARRICK BEND AND OTHER DESIGNS

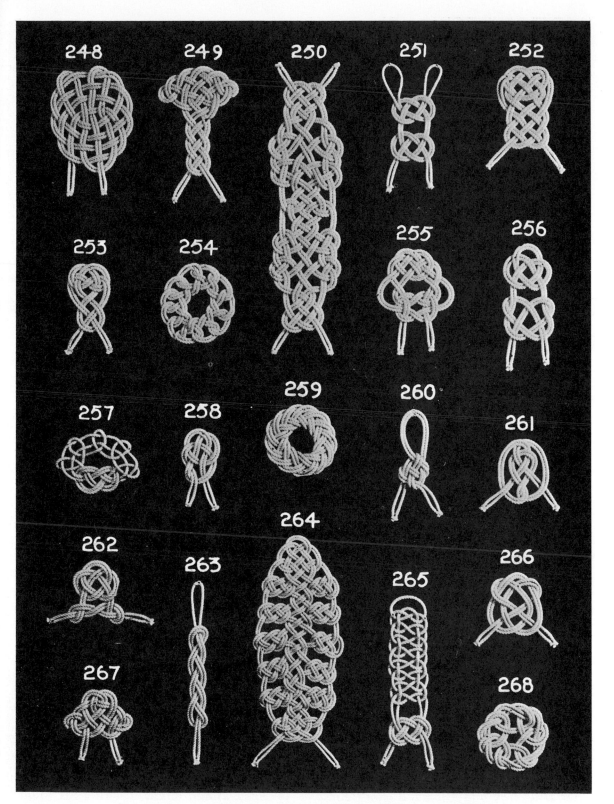

PLATE 154—MISCELLANEOUS ORNAMENTAL DESIGNS

Fig. 263: A *Three-Strand Sennit Braid* made out of one double strand.

Fig. 264: *Combination Sennit and Carrick Bend Design* shown is begun in the same manner as PLATE 138, FIG. 9A; but instead of twisting the two inside strands of each bight but once, they are twisted three times. In other words, one and one-half full turns. Next the Sennit is begun;

and each time that the two strands come out on either side of the Sennit Weave, a Carrick Bend is formed. This is accomplished by twisting the free outer strand, and then weaving the free end to make a Carrick Bend.

FIGS. 265, 266, 267 and 268: *Miscellaneous Ornamental Knots* which can be made by following the illustrations.

Plate 155—Miscellaneous Ornamental Designs

Fig. 269: The *Bugler's Braid Design*, First Method, pictured in this design is the Bugler's Braid illustrated in PLATE 120, FIG. 131. When sufficient length has been achieved, form the knot, and close the braid as shown in PLATE 111, FIG. 50.

Fig. 270: The *Butterfly Design* has for its body the Chinese Double Braid in PLATE 137, FIG. 2. The knot at the head is a Diamond Knot (PLATE 36, FIG. 190). The neck is a Blood Knot of five turns (PLATE 22, FIG. 16).

Fig. 271: The *Bugler's Braid Design*, Second Method, is tied as follows: two rings are made from the Bugler's Braid in PLATE 120, FIG. 131, each one with forty bights; a third Bugler's Braid is then tied, leaving thirty-eight bights; this is woven into the first two rings as illustrated. Next, close the braid. Four additional bights are formed in closing the braid, which brings the number of bights up to forty-two.

Fig. 272: The *Tree Leaf* can be made by observing the weave illustrated. After the weave has reached the desired length, all the strands are brought together and seized.

The small additional strands on each side are brought down until they reach the stem. Then they are square-knotted on it.

Fig. 273: A *Carrick Bend Design*.

Fig. 274: The *Chinese Tassel*, First Method, shown consists at *a* of a Six-Bight Chinese Double Braid. The part marked *b* is a Royal Carrick Bend, illustrated in PLATE 138, FIG. 11.

Fig. 275: The *Chinese Tassel*, Second Method, is another type of Butterfly Knot. The part marked *a* is the Brief Knot illustrated in PLATE 27, FIG. 83. That marked *b* is a Four-Bight Chinese Double Braid, pictured in PLATE 137, FIG. 2.

Fig. 276: The *Crowned Bugler's Braid* starts out with a Bugler's Braid of any desired size, which is closed with one of the ends. Next begin to take a series of Half Hitches in each bight of the Bugler's Braid, as shown by strand *a*.

Fig. 277: The *Cross Patonee* is made from a series of Dragonfly Knots, illustrated in PLATE 137, FIG. 1. PLATE 148, FIG. 146, shows how these knots are joined together in a series. Also *see* PLATE 148, FIG. 147.

Plate 156—Chinese Weaving

FIGS. 278, 282, 283, 286 and 289: *Dragonfly Knot Designs*. (*See* PLATE 137, FIG. 1, and PLATE 148, FIGS. 146 and 147.)

FIGS. 279, 281, 284 and 285: *Combination Dragonfly and Closed Bugler's Braid Designs*. (*See* PLATE 148, FIG. 153, and PLATE 137, FIG. 1).

FIG. 280: The *Chinese Book Mark* illustrated in this figure is begun with a Three-Leaf Dragonfly Knot. Next, tie a Six-Bight Chinese Double Braid (*see* PLATE 137, FIG. 2) and follow it with a Six-Bight Closed Bugler's Braid. At point *a*, make a Figure-of-Eight Knot, and after reeving an-

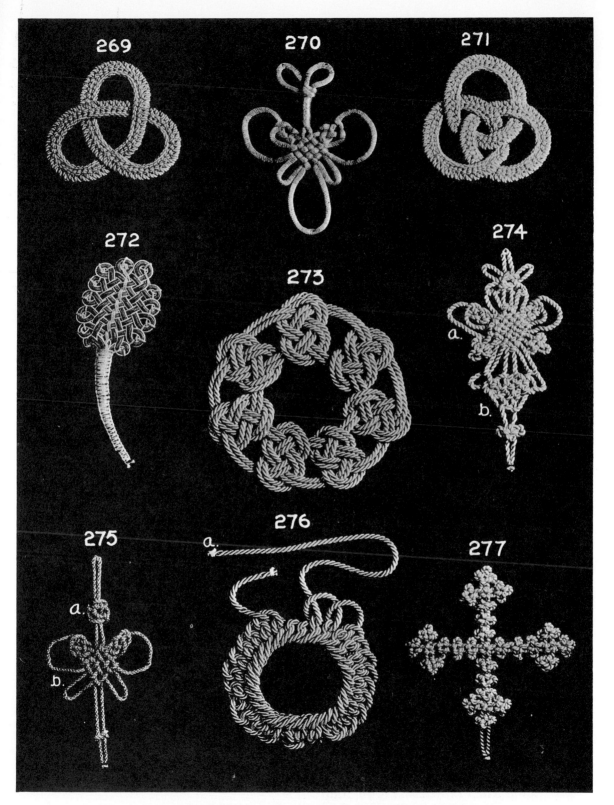

PLATE 155—MISCELLANEOUS ORNAMENTAL DESIGNS

other piece of line through the body of it, tie a Macramé Square Knot as in PLATE 35, FIG. 179. A Four-Bight Chinese Double Braid is next made, and the odd piece of line is passed through the body of it. Then tie another Macramé Square Knot, and finish off the design with a Brief Knot (PLATE 27, FIG. 83).

FIG. 287: The *Chinese Lamp Pull* takes its outside weave from the Single Higginbotham Braid (PLATE 120, FIG. 133). The round weave in the center is a Closed Bugler's Braid. A bight from this Bugler's Braid is hitched into a bight on the Higginbotham Braid at the points marked *a*. At point *b*, the two ends of the Higginbotham Braid are brought together. Then form a Dragonfly Knot, and hitch the bight on each side into the ends of each Higginbotham Braid.

FIG. 288: The *Four-Bight Chinese Double Braid with a Three-Leaf Dragonfly Knot in Each Corner*. (See PLATE 137, FIGS. 1 and 2.)

FIG. 290: The *Oblong Chinese Double Braid* has four bights horizontally and twelve vertically. A Dragonfly Knot is tied on every other bight. PLATE 167, FIG. 434, illustrates how this weave is made.

FIG. 291: The *Right Angle Chinese Braid*. (*See* PLATE 167, FIG. 434.)

FIGS. 292 and 293: *French Ornamental Knots.*

FIG. 294: The *Two-Leaf Chinese Temple Knot* shown has the end run back through the body of the knot and seized on the reverse side. (*See* PLATE 137, FIG. 5.)

FIG. 295: The *Three-Leaf Chinese Temple Knot* is made in the same manner as the previous knot but has four bights rather than three (*see* PLATE 137, FIG. 3).

FIG. 296: The *Four-Leaf Chinese Temple Knot* is made in the same manner as the preceding knots, but with five bights.

FIG. 297: The *Five-Leaf Chinese Temple Knot* is formed in the same manner as the preceding knots but with six bights.

Plate 157—Ornamental Mat Weaves

FIGS. 298A, B, and C: The *Pear Knot* is used as an ornamental decoration on women's dresses. It may be easily duplicated by noting the weave in the pictures shown. The weave may be continued to any length, making the knot larger and larger. To finish it off, reeve the moving end through the hole in the center of the knot, as illustrated in FIG. 298. Since this knot is not interlocking, it is necessary to sew the strands on the reverse side.

FIGS. 299A, B, and C: The *Turk's Cap* is fully illustrated. If this knot is used as a Turk's Head, and placed on a cone-shaped object, it will cover the object evenly, due to the fact that it has only four bights, which meet in the center of the knot.

FIG. 300: The *Inverted Turk's Cap Doubled* is made by first forming the knot in FIG. 299. Then take one end and follow

the other, thus doubling the completed knot. An Inverted Turk's Cap will result.

FIG. 301: The *Double Turk's Cap*. (See FIG. 299.)

FIGS. 302 and 303: *French Ornamental Knots.* FIG. 302 is same as PLATE 141, FIG. 59.

FIG. 304A: The *Five-Strand Turkish Round Mat* is first laid out as illustrated. Then ends *a* and *b* are passed as shown by the arrows.

B: The knot is drawn up evenly to finish.

FIG. 305: The *Triple-Pass Five-Strand Turkish Round Mat* is made in the same manner as the previous knot but with three strands.

FIG. 306: The *Closed Five-Strand Turkish Round Mat* begins with the knot shown

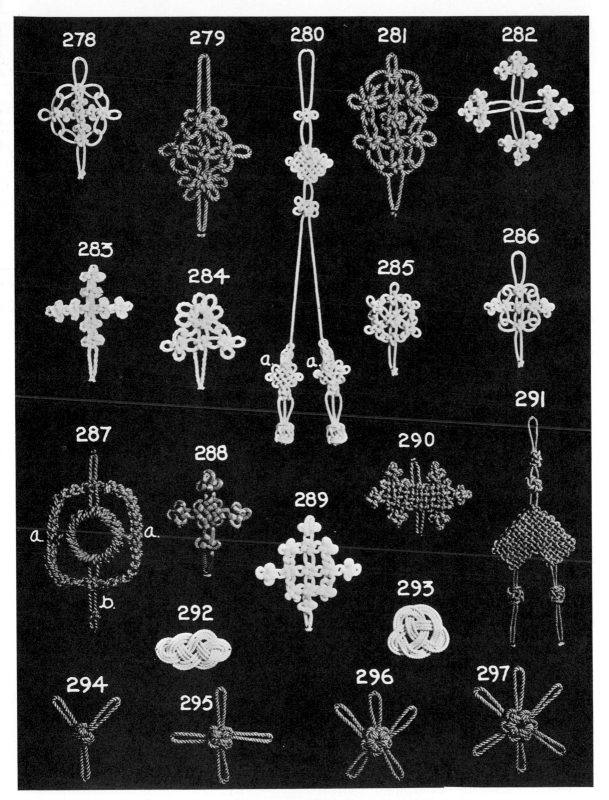

PLATE 156—CHINESE WEAVING

in Fig. 304. Next, follow one of the ends around and double the knot. Then secure the ends on the reverse side, and cut the strands off close.

Fig. 307A: The *Seven-Strand Turkish Round Mat* has the line first laid out as shown. Bights *a* and *b* are next given a half-twist to lock them. Then they are passed into the position shown in Fig. 307B.

B: When bights *a* and *b* have been placed in this position, both ends are passed

through the knot until they reach the position shown in Fig. 307C.

C: After the ends have been tucked and are in the position shown, they are tucked until they are in the position illustrated in Fig. 307D.

D: This shows the finished knot.

Fig. 308: The *Doubled Seven - Strand Turkish Round Mat.*

Fig. 309: The *Closed Seven - Strand Turkish Round Mat.*

Plate 158—Turkish Mat Weaves

Fig. 310A: The *Nine-Strand Turkish Round Mat* has the line first laid out until it is in the position shown in Fig. 307C. The ends are next passed down parallel to the outside strand on each side, until they reach the position shown. Finally, they are tucked over and under on the outside, and then over and under on the inside of the next strand, as indicated by the arrow.

B: This shows the completed knot.

Fig. 311: The *Doubled Nine-Strand Turkish Round Mat.*

Fig. 312: The *Closed Nine-Strand Turkish Round Mat* begins with the knot illustrated in Fig. 310B. Then follow one end around with the other, until the entire knot is doubled. The ends are seized on the reverse side, and cut off short.

Fig. 313A: The *Eleven-Strand Turkish Round Mat* is made by first completing the design shown in Fig. 310A. The ends are then run back parallel to their own parts, forming bights *a* and *b*.

B: After completing the knot up to the stage pictured in Fig. 313A, tuck the strands back down. Then pass them back up again between the bights, as shown by the drawn line.

C: The ends are now passed over and

under on the outside of the knot, as indicated in this illustration.

Fig. 314: The *Doubled Eleven-Strand Turkish Round Mat.*

Fig. 315: The *Closed Eleven - Strand Turkish Round Mat.*

Fig. 316A: The *Six-Strand Rosette Round Mat* is made in the same way as Figs. 307A and B. Notice, however, that strand *a* in this knot is brought up through the bight, and strand *b* is passed down through the other bight. They are then tucked as shown by the arrows.

B: This is the completed knot.

Fig. 317: The *Arrow-Head Knot* is tied as follows: first, make the knot illustrated in Fig. 316A and B; then take strand *a* and follow strand *b*. As strand *a* is being passed through, strand *b* is removed. This is continued until the center bight on the opposite side is reached. The knot is then turned around and it will then appear as in this figure.

Fig. 318: The *Closed Arrow-Head Knot* begins with the knot illustrated in Fig. 317. Next, follow end *b* with end *a* until the knot is doubled. It will then appear as shówn.

Plate 159—Combination Ornamental Weaves

Figs. 319 and 320: Examples of *Chinese Knotting.* They can be duplicated by tracing the weave in the illustration.

Fig. 321: The *Six-Bight Chinese Double Braid with Carrick Bends.* (*See* PLATE 137, Fig. 2.)

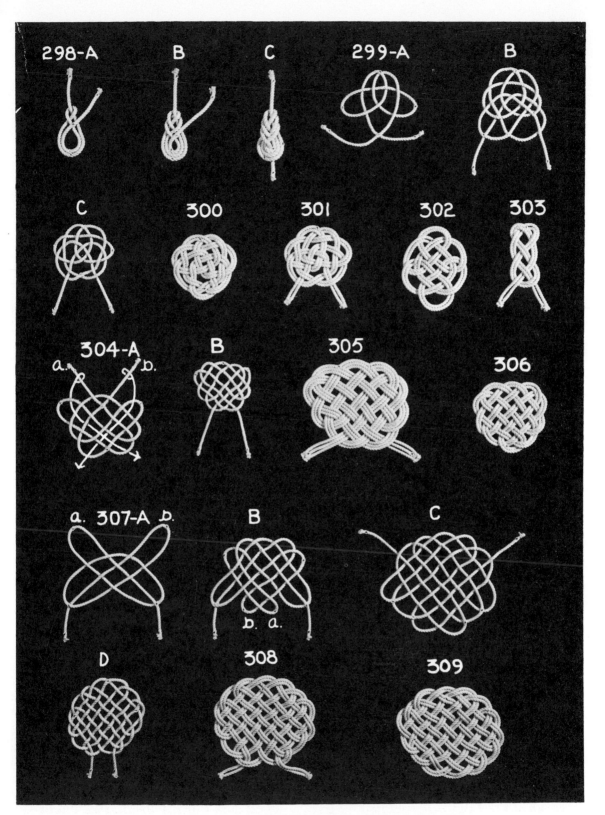

PLATE 157—ORNAMENTAL MAT WEAVES

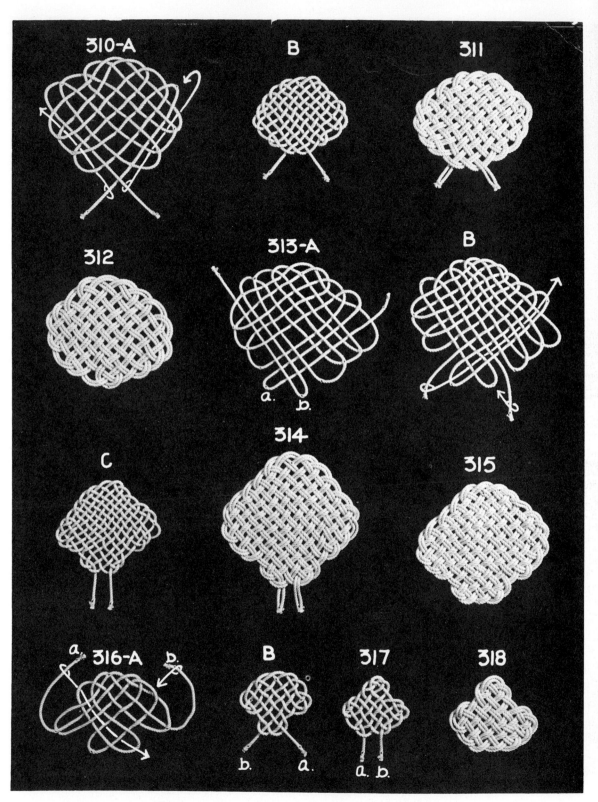

PLATE 158—TURKISH MAT WEAVES

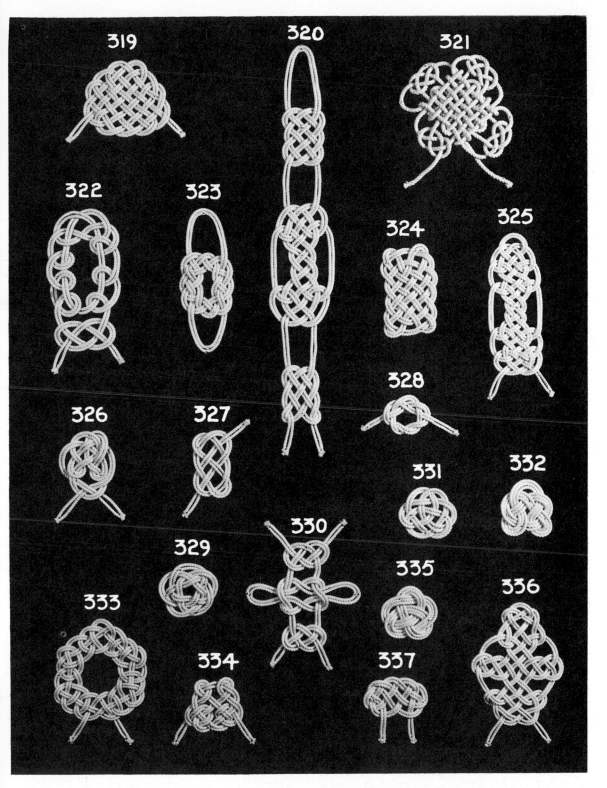

PLATE 159—COMBINATION ORNAMENTAL WEAVES

FIGS. 322, 323, 325, 326, 327 and 328: Examples of *Celtic Knotting*.

FIG. 324: The *Celtic Square Mat* is woven with two separate pieces of cord.

FIG. 329: The *Four-Strand Turk's Head with Five Crosses* is illustrated in PLATE 111, FIG. 26.

FIGS. 330, 331 and 332: *Miscellaneous*

Ornamental Knots which can be made by observing the design.

FIG. 333: The *Interlocking Sailor's Breastplates* are made from a series of Sailor's Breastplate Knots (*see* PLATE 21, FIG. 10).

FIGS. 334, 335, 336 and 337: Examples of *French Knotting*.

Plate 160—Antique Braid and Numerous Designs

FIG. 338: The *Chinese Double Braid Butterfly Knot* is constructed at *a* along the lines of the Single Higginbotham Braid illustrated in PLATE 120, FIG. 133.

FIG. 339: The *Napoleon Bend* is shown in detail in PLATE 241, FIG. 47.

FIG. 340: The *Chinese Double Braid Covering a Mirror* is made by the following method: first, tie a Chinese Double Braid Knot, a size larger than the mirror; draw it up taut, and lay the mirror on top of the knot. If the mirror is oblong, measure, then count, the number of bights on each side; make another Double Braid of the proper number of bights. Then the mirror is placed inside the knot, and the Double Braid is drawn taut.

FIG. 341: The *Long Turk's Head* shown is one of six strands. It is illustrated in PLATE 111, FIG. 56.

FIG. 342: The *Star Knot* is a Four-Leaf Chinese Temple Knot with the bights secured on the reverse side.

FIG. 343: The *Closed Triple Inverted Antique Braid* may be closed by making the braid with one color on one side and another color on the other. It is then a

simple matter to see just how to weave two ends together and close the braid. The braid itself is illustrated in PLATE 136, FIG. 412.

FIG. 344: *A Carrick Bend Mat.* This design is made from a series of Double Carrick Bends. Two separate pieces of cord are used to weave this knot.

FIG. 345: The *Chinese Tassel* consists at *a* of an Eight-Bight Chinese Double Braid. Each part marked *b* is a Four-Bight Chinese Double Braid (PLATE 137, FIG. 2). The smaller Double Braids at *b* are woven in while the larger design is being formed.

FIG. 346: The *Chinese Lamp Pull* is made at *a* of a Four-Bight Chinese Double Braid. The small knot over the Double Braid is a Brief Knot (PLATE 27, FIG. 83). Two small round wooden molds are then used to complete the design.

FIG. 347: The *Tree Leaf.* This knot is woven in exactly the same manner as the knot shown in PLATE 155, FIG. 272.

FIG. 348: The *Four-Bight Chinese Double Braid.* (See PLATE 137, FIG. 2.)

FIG. 349: The *Twelve-Bight Chinese Double Braid.* (See PLATE 137, FIG. 2.)

Plate 161—Mould Weaves in Various Designs

FIG. 350A: The *Six-Point Flat Mould Weave* uses a round flat object for its body, as do all such weaves. It is begun as shown in this illustration. The arrow indicates the next step.

B: In weaving this type of knot, the line is of course taken directly from a spool. The moving end has been cut off short in the picture. The line must always pass directly across the center of the mould, on the

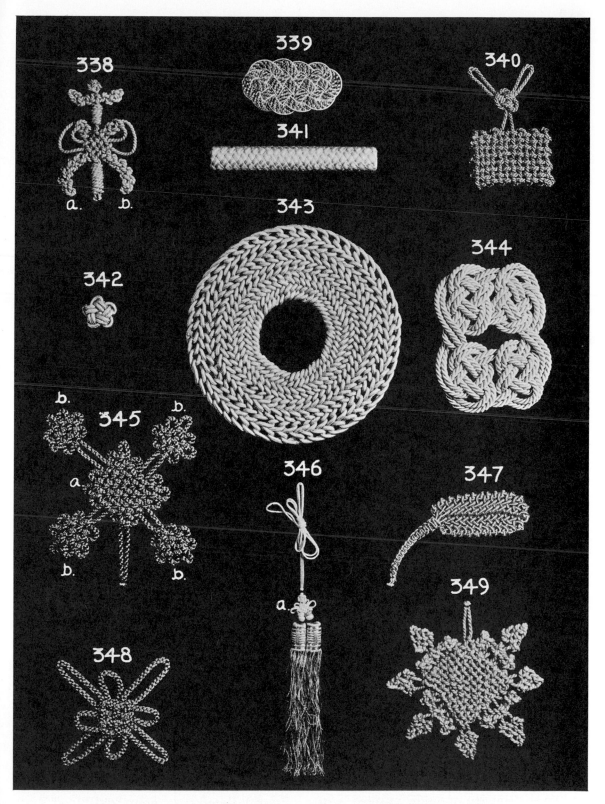

PLATE 160—ANTIQUE BRAID AND NUMEROUS DESIGNS

upper side, when weaving this knot. Continue to weave the line around the mould until it is completely covered.

c: This shows the finished knot.

FIG. 351: The *Flat Mould Weave* (FIG. 350) is shown turned over. A six-point star results.

FIG. 352A: The *Mould Weave* can be made with any number of points. This shows how to begin the weave with eight points.

B: The reverse side of the Eight-Point Mould Weave is illustrated.

FIG. 353: The *Five-Point Star Mould Weave,* like other Mould Weaves, can be woven in many colors, and the colors can be placed in any desired position.

FIG. 354: The *Mould Weave* in this illustration has the small crosses and background first woven out horizontally and vertically. Then the white cord and the green between the white running diagonally are woven until the design is completed.

FIG. 355: The *Mould Weave* shown is diamond-shaped. One color is woven horizontally and the other vertically.

FIG. 356A: The *Tassel Mould* is the body of the following two knots. These moulds can be purchased in a great variety of sizes and forms.

B: To cover the mould, four or five pieces of thread of the desired color are threaded into a needle. Then it is passed around and around the mould, going up through the center and down on the outside, until the mould is entirely covered. The weave around the body of the mould is a Three-Strand Turk's Head with additional crosses (*see* PLATE 109, FIG. 1).

FIG. 357: The *Mould Weave* covering this mould is Half Hitching, illustrated in PLATE 105, FIG. 16.

FIGS. 358 and 359: The *Celtic Knot* is woven from two separate pieces of line.

Plate 162—Six-Point Star Knot and Other Weaves

FIGS. 360, 361 and 362: Examples of *French Ornamental Knotting.*

FIG. 363: The *Six-Point Star Knot* is woven with four separate pieces of rope. When the ends meet, they are followed around three times, making three passes in the knot.

FIG. 364: The *Masthead Knot* shown is illustrated in PLATE 24, FIG. 44. The ends are passed through the bights on each side, and then interlocked through the lower

bight, as the illustration shows.

FIG. 365: The *Open Napoleon Bend Doubled* uses the key illustrated in PLATE 242, FIG. 55. Same as PLATE 139, FIG. 21.

FIG. 366: *The Six-Strand Rosette Round Mat Variated* is pictured in PLATE 158, FIG. 316.

FIGS. 367 and 368: Examples of *French Ornamental Knotting.* These designs can easily be made by observing the weaves in the illustrations.

Plate 163—Bugler's Epaulet and Other Designs

FIG. 369: The *Epaulet* is used in dress parade by buglers in the army. Detail *a* is a Three-Strand Flat Sennit made from one strand (*see* PLATE 135, FIG. 402). Detail *b* is a Seven-Strand Turkish Round Mat, illustrated in PLATE 157, FIG. 307. Slides *c* and *c* are small wooden moulds, covered with Fender Half Hitching (PLATE 108, FIG. 44).

FIGS. 370, 371 and 372: *Miscellaneous Ornamental Knots,* which can easily be duplicated by tracing the weave.

FIG. 373: The *Butterfly Design* consists, at *a,* of an Eight-Bight Bugler's Braid Closed. Detail *b* is illustrated in PLATE 142, FIG. 80. Detail *c* is a Four-Fold Blood Knot shown in PLATE 22, FIG. 18. The body of

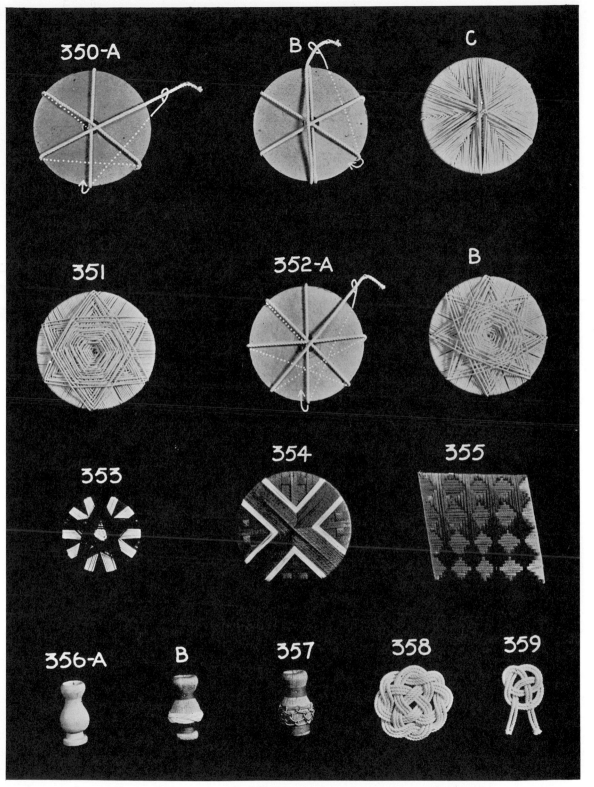

PLATE 161—MOULD WEAVES IN VARIOUS DESIGNS

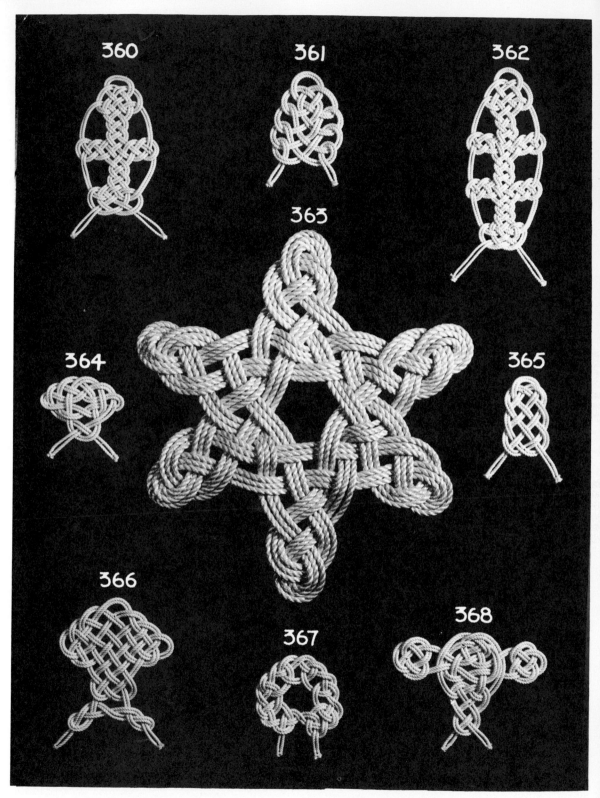

PLATE 162—SIX-POINT STAR KNOT AND OTHER ORNAMENTAL WEAVES

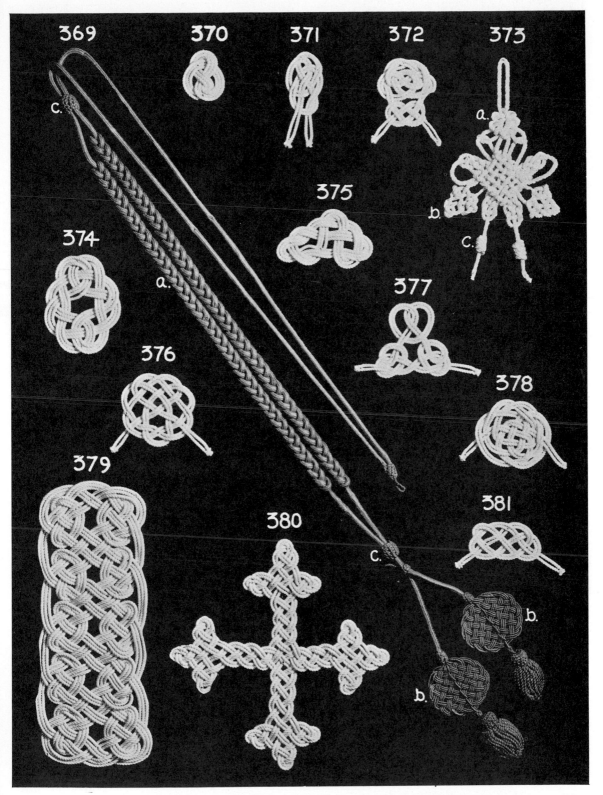

PLATE 163—BUGLER'S EPAULET AND OTHER DESIGNS

the design is a Six-Bight Chinese Double Braid (PLATE 137, FIG. 2).

FIGS. 374, 375, 376, 377 and 378: *Turkish Ornamental Knots.*

FIG. 379: The *Celtic Knot Design* pictured is made from three separate pieces of line. After the basic design of the knot has been worked out, the ends are followed around to give the design three full passes.

FIG. 380: The *Cross* in this illustration has its weave explained in detail in PLATE 138, FIG. 10. The ends are, of course, much longer than shown in FIG. 10. When the weave is completed, the ends are followed around once to double the knot. Then they are seized on the reverse side of the knot, and cut off short to finish.

FIG. 381· *False Napoleon Bend.* Although this knot appears somewhat similar to that in PLATE 241, FIG. 47, examination will prove it different (*see* FIG. 403).

Plate 164—Miscellaneous Ornamental Weaves

FIG. 382: *False Pyramid Knot.* Although this knot appears similar to the Knot illustrated in PLATE 165, FIG. 409, inspection will show, however, a slight difference.

FIG. 383: The *Flower Basket Design* shown was made from the Eleven-Strand Turkish Round Mat illustrated in PLATE 158, FIG. 313. The Three-Leaf Chinese Dragonfly Knots, on each side of the handle and the base of the basket, are tied while the Round Mat is being woven.

FIG. 384, 385, 386, 387, 388, 389, 390 and 391: Examples of *Persian Knotting.* These designs can be worked out by tracing the Weaves in the illustrations.

FIG. 392: The *Five-Cross Closed Sailor's True Lover Mat Weave* uses the key illustrated in PLATE 240, FIG. 42.

FIGS. 393, 394 and 395: *French Ornamental Knots.*

FIG. 396: The *Five-Strand Nine-Cross Inverted Turk's Head* is shown in PLATE 111, FIG. 29. After the knot is tied with one pass, it is flattened out. Next, follow the end around once, to double the knot. Then draw it up evenly, seize the ends on the reverse side, and cut off short to finish.

FIGS. 397, 398 and 399: *Ornamental Designs* worked out by using the Sailor's Breastplate Knot (PLATE 21, FIG. 10) as the fundamental knot.

FIG. 400: The *Four-Strand Inverted Turk's Head* is pictured in PLATE 109, FIG. 2. After the basic knot has been tied, it is flattened out, and another pass is made to double the entire knot. The ends are seized on the reverse side of the knot, and cut off short.

FIGS. 401, 402, 403 and 405: *Miscellaneous Ornamental Knots.* They can be duplicated by observing the weaves in the illustrations.

FIG. 404: The *Variated Sailor's Breastplate* shown is based on the Sailor's Breastplate Knot with a Half Hitch in each bight. It can easily be tied by following the weave in the illustration.

Plate 165—Diamond Knot and Other Combinations

FIG. 406A: The *Elongated Diamond Knot* is much longer than the knot shown in PLATE 36, FIG. 190, and has many more uses. The line is laid out as illustrated for the first stage in the formation of this knot. End *a* is then passed as indicated by the arrow.

B: End *a* is again passed as the arrow shows. When passing the end through the center of the knot, make sure that it is tucked through the proper space.

C: End *b* is next passed around one strand of the bight, and then through the center of the knot, in the same manner as

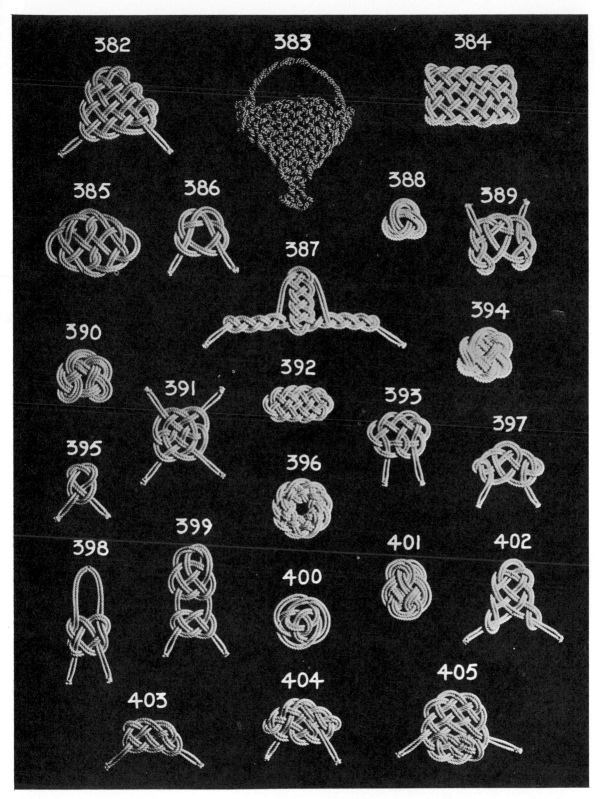

PLATE 164—MISCELLANEOUS ORNAMENTAL WEAVES

strand *a,* shown at the left in FIG. 406B.

D: The weaving of the knot is now complete, and all that remains is to draw it up evenly.

E: This shows the finished knot after it has been snugly drawn up.

FIG. 407: The *Elongated Diamond Knot Doubled* is formed in the same fashion as the preceding knot, but with two doubled strands rather than two single strands.

FIG. 408: The *Elongated Diamond Knot Tripled* is made in the same way as the knots in FIGS. 406 and 407, but with SIX strands.

FIG. 409A: The *Pyramid Knot,* when drawn up taut, assumes the shape of a triangle or pyramid; hence the name. The tying of this knot is a mechanical process, and it can be made as large as desired by merely adding more bights. The key remains the same throughout. First, lay the line out as shown here. Then pass a bight (not the end) as indicated by the arrow.

B: To enlarge the knot, pass another bight as shown by the arrow. It may be finished at any time by passing the end (not the bight) as the arrow indicates.

C: This shows the completed knot, made with two bights.

FIG. 410: The *Pyramid Knot of Four Bights Doubled* was made with four bights before tucking the end. This type of knot is more attractive when it is double-passed, as shown.

FIG. 411: The *Pear Pyramid Knot* was made from soft silk cord, which is indispensable in ornamental weaving. It was tied with six bights. Then the lower part was drawn up a little tighter, in order to give the knot a pear shape.

FIG. 412A: The *Royal Diamond Knot* is made on a round flat mould. The dotted line shows, in part, how the reverse side is woven. At this stage, the reverse looks the same as the front. Note that each cord crosses over and under as it goes from one side to the other. When the four sides have been completed, the ends will automatically meet. Now follow the standing end *b* with the moving end *a,* in order to double the entire design. When the beginning is again reached, strand *a* will be on the left-hand side of its own original part. Cross over this to come between the two doubled strands. Then where the two strands that run parallel go over, strand *a* is put under. And where the two go under, strand *a* is put over. This complete process is repeated once again. Then by following the original standing part *b,* the knot is given three full passes. Finally, the ends are cut off short to finish the knot.

B: This shows the completed Royal Diamond Knot.

FIG. 413A: The *Japanese Oblong Mat* has the line first laid out as illustrated. Then strand *a* is passed as shown by the arrow.

B: The bights are crossed and placed in the position shown. End *a* is then passed as indicated by the arrow.

C: The knot is now drawn up evenly to finish.

Plate 166—Japanese Girdle and Other Oriental Designs

FIG. 414: The *Japanese Girdle* is begun from the Interlocking Carrick Bend with Outside Overhand Knots (PLATE 138, FIG. 6C). Double Carrick Bends are then placed on each side, until the desired length is reached. Next, sew a hook to the cord with which both ends of the girdle are fastened. Take another piece of twine, and make a Diamond Knot (PLATE 36, FIG. 190) to form a button. Draw the knot up taut, leaving no bight on top of the knot. Pass both ends through the center hole of the Interlocking Carrick Bend, and then out again between the cross at the bottom of the knot. Tie another Diamond Knot. Then cover two small round moulds with Fender or Half Hitch-

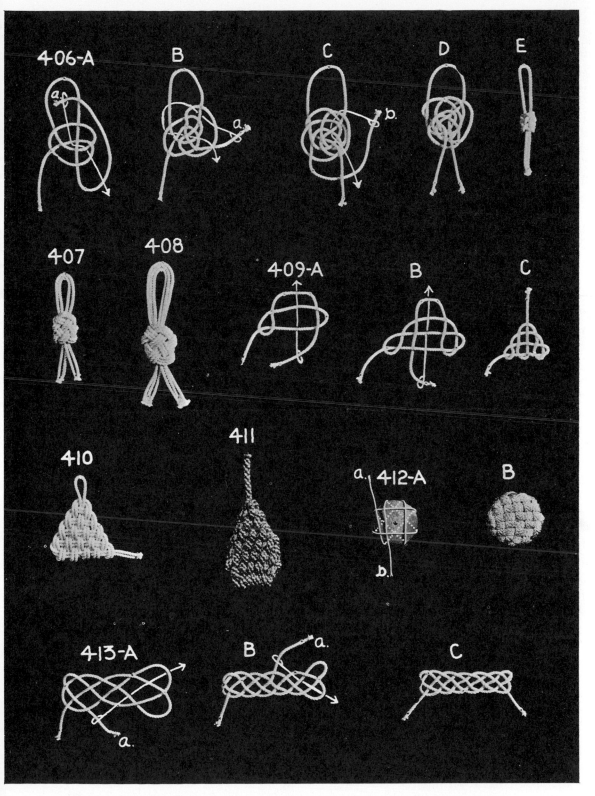

406-A B C D E

407 **408** **409-A** B C

410 **411** **412-A** B

413-A B C

PLATE 165—DIAMOND KNOT AND OTHER COMBINATIONS

ing (*see* PLATE 105, FIG. 16), and seize a tassel to the mould. Next, take the ends with the Diamond Knot in them, and put each one through one mould, tying an Overhand Knot under each tassel, in order to prevent the moulds slipping off the cords. To finish the design, form a Three-Strand Turk's Head on the cords, on top of each mould. This Turk's Head should be made of very small twine of a different color.

FIG. 415: The *Chinese Lamp Cord* shown is separated with a piece of round cut-glass. First, make the Butterfly Knot at *a*. Pass the ends through a hole in the round glass disk, and secure them to the standing part with an Overhand Knot. Then cover this Overhand Knot with a Three-Strand Turk's Head. The body of the Butterfly Knot in this illustration is a Four-Bight Chinese Double Braid, and can be made as large as desired. Next, hitch another piece of line into the lower end of the glass disk, and make another Four-Bight Chinese Double Braid, with each bight on the edges pulled out loosely. After this, a cone-shaped mould is covered. Then pass the ends of the cord through the body of the mould, and tie an Overhand Knot in them. One or two small Turk's Heads can be made on the line, just above the mould, to complete the design.

FIG. 416: The *Lamp Pull* shown is covered in the same way as a rope pointing. Enough threads are laid on the mould to cover it completely. Wind a very fine piece of wire around the mould horizontally for a short distance. All the threads are then laid down on the mould, and the wire wrapped around both mould and threads. By varying this procedure, designs can be worked into this covering.

FIG. 417: The *Lamp Pull,* Second Method, uses for its first knot, *a*, the Six-Bight Closed Bugler's Braid. The next knot, *b*, is a Four-Bight Chinese Double Braid, with the two uppermost bights hitched into the two lower bights of *a*. Two round

moulds are now covered as in FIG. 416. Then put two small round beads on each end of the twine, after the Double Braid has been drawn up taut. Next, pass each cord through the hole in the moulds. When they emerge from the lower side, they are brought together and joined with a Reef Knot. A small Turk's Head is made on the standing parts wherever a space occurs between the knots.

FIG. 418: The *Three-Leaf Chinese Temple Knot with Dragonfly Knots* is made as follows: first, tie three Dragonfly Knots a short distance from each other on one piece of line; then, using these knots to represent the three bights, tie the Chinese Temple Knot as illustrated in PLATE 137, FIG. 3. When the knot has been completed, and drawn up taut, another Three-Leaf Dragonfly Knot is made with the two ends. Then pass one end in back of the knot, following the other end, and seize them together. Cut the ends off short to finish.

FIG. 419: The *Triple-Tassel Shade Pull* has its body, *a*, illustrated in detail in PLATE 278, FIG. 361. Then form one Six-Bight Closed Bugler's Braid on top of the body, and another one below.

FIG. 420: The *True Star Knot Shade Pull* is made in the following way: first, take six pieces of line, and seize their middles to a small piece of wood; on one side of the seizing, form a True Star Knot (PLATE 58, FIG. 85). With the six ends on the other side of the seizing, form two Spiral Crowns. A Diamond Knot is next made, followed by two more Spiral Crowns. Then pass these six strands down through the center of the entire knot. Take a long piece of cord, middle it, and tie a Diamond Knot in it near the bight. Next, farther down the cords, form an Elongated Diamond Knot. Pass these two ends down through the center of the Star Knot, and make an Overhand Knot in them. Take six of the fourteen ends at the bottom of the knot, and tie a Diamond Knot around all the remaining strands.

PLATE 166—JAPANESE GIRDLE AND OTHER ORIENTAL DESIGNS

Then the Star Knot, Spiral Crowns, and Diamond Knots are all drawn up snug. Fray out the strands, and cut off evenly, to complete the design.

FIG. 421: The *Pendulum Knot,* at the point marked *a,* is the Racking Weave (PLATE 278, FIG. 361) closed up. It has twenty-four bights. On the inside, a Three-Leaf Dragonfly Knot is formed on every fourth bight. The top bight on each Dragonfly Knot is left longer than the two side bights. Then from these make a Six-Bight Closed Bugler's Braid. The detail at *b* is a series of Three-Leaf Dragonfly Knots, joined together as illustrated in PLATE 148, FIGS. 146 and 147.

FIG. 422: *Lamp Pull.* The tassel of this knot is made around a metal mould. The body of the mould is covered with Half Hitching and then the tassel is secured to the mould. A Shamrock Knot (PLATE 240, FIG. 45) is formed a short distance from the middle of a piece of cord. The ends of this cord are passed through the hole in the mould and secured by tying an Overhand Knot in them.

FIG. 423: The *Chinese Double Braid Tassel* is made from four strands (two sets of two each), rather than two single strands. A tassel is formed on each end, after the knot has been drawn taut.

Plate 167—Miscellaneous Ornamental Designs

FIG. 424: The *Five-Strand Inverted Endless Sennit Turk's Head* is illustrated in PLATE 109, FIG. 6. Instead of having three passes, this knot has only two. It also has one more cross than the Turk's Head shown in PLATE 109, FIG. 6. This, of course, is accomplished by making an additional cross in the Three-Strand Turk's Head before proceeding to weave the Endless Sennit Turk's Head.

FIG. 425: The *Hennepin Knot* is of heraldic origin.

FIG. 426: The *Five-Leaf Chinese Temple Knot with Interlocking Dragonfly Knots* is made as follows: first, form the Five-Leaf Chinese Temple Knot; in the center of another piece of line, tie a Three-Leaf Chinese Dragonfly Knot. Take the two ends, and with each one, trace through the Chinese Temple Knot, tracing one cord to the right and the other to the left. When the cords emerge on the outside of the Chinese Temple Knot (at the point where there is a bight), tie a Dragonfly Knot, so that one bight interlocks with one bight on a Dragonfly Knot previously made. The original cord forming the Chinese Temple Knot is of course withdrawn while the new piece is being traced in.

FIG. 427: The *Wake (Ormond) Knot* is of heraldic origin.

FIG. 428: *Variated Napoleon Bend.* This design has as its beginning the design illustrated in PLATE 240, FIG. 42. The remainder of the knot can easily be traced by observing the illustration.

FIG. 429: The *Knot of Savoy of the Annunciation* also is a heraldic knot.

FIG. 430: The *Six-Bight Chinese Double Braid with Dragonfly Knots* is made by first taking a sufficient length of line, then forming a Three-Leaf Dragonfly Knot in its middle. Next, weave out a Chinese Double Braid as illustrated in PLATE 137, FIG. 2. A Dragonfly Knot is tied in the bights at each corner, as the design is woven out.

FIG. 431: The *Bouchier Knot,* another method, is of heraldic origin.

FIG. 432: The *Elongated Open Napoleon Bend.*

FIG. 433: The *Elongated Closed Napoleon Bend* begins with the design shown in PLATE 240, FIG. 42, made with a single piece of line. When this has been completed, take one end and follow the other end, doubling the design. When the ends meet, they are

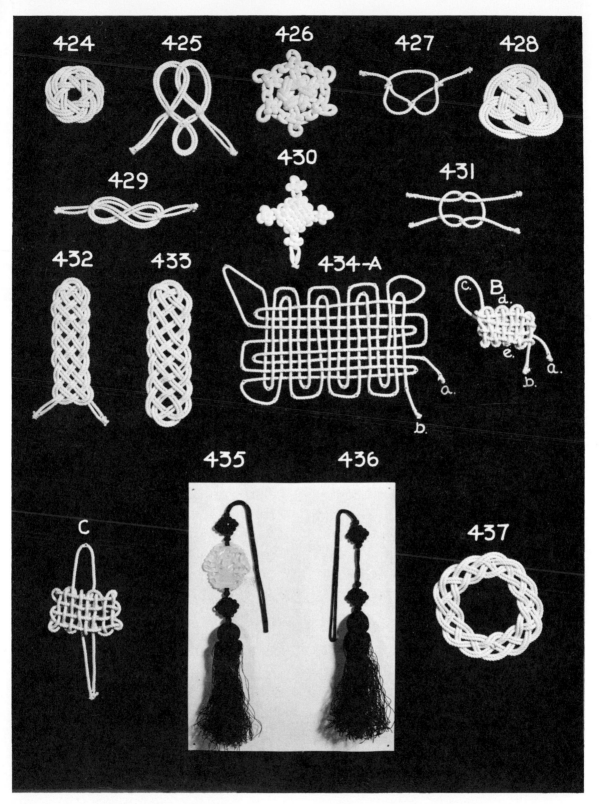

PLATE 167—MISCELLANEOUS ORNAMENTAL DESIGNS

seized together on the reverse side of the knot, and then cut off short to finish.

FIG. 434A: The *Oblong Chinese Double Braid* should be compared with the Square Chinese Double Braid illustrated in PLATE 137, FIG. 2B. It will be noticed that the latter has four bights in each direction, while the former has four bights vertically and eight horizontally. Although the shape and number of bights may differ in this type of knot, the principle of weaving never varies. Strand *a* is woven out first; then strand *b*.

B: When the knot has been pulled up snug, it will appear as in this illustration. Next, work the slack from bight *c* up to point *d*. Take strand *a* and trace it through the knot, following strand *b*. Strand *b* is, of course, withdrawn as strand *a* is filled into its place. This is continued until both strands come out at point *e*.

C: This shows the completed knot.

FIGS. 435 and 436: The *Chinese Lamp Pulls* shown have all their knots made from the Six-Bight Chinese Double Braid.

FIG. 437: The *Thirteen-Cross Four-Strand Inverted Turk's Head* will be found illustrated in the chapter on Turk's Heads.

Chapter IX

Macramé Tatting, Fringe, Needle-Work

THE WORD MACRAMÉ, of Arabic origin, is given to certain types of work produced by plaiting or knotting threads together. But the term "square knotting" is the one generally applied to this type of work in English-speaking countries. It was introduced into France during the fourteenth century, practiced for a time, and then allowed to die out. After many years, this work appeared again in France and in America as a novelty, and has since rapidly found its place in the field of knotting and fringe work. It has beyond a doubt been exploited more and is recognized more extensively in France than anywhere else, but it is steadily gaining favor in this country. As a useful diversion it is unexcelled; and for originality of design it has no equal. The durability of the work and the uniformity of its construction should bring it into favor wherever it is seen.

The method of its construction is difficult only in appearance; and after the rudiments of its formation have been mastered, even the most difficult-appearing designs may be executed by the novice with comparative ease. As a preliminary to the actual work, the various combinations of knots which go into the formation of the different designs are illustrated. After they have been learned, the same "keys" will be used throughout in duplication of the work.

Plate 168—Typical Macramé Knots

FIG. 1A: *The Square Knot* shown in this illustration explains the construction of the basic knot in this work. FIG. 1A indicates how to hitch the cords on a line.

B: The first step in making the Square Knot is to take the bight up over the two center cords. The thumb and index finger are next placed through the loop, and the two pieces of cord are grasped as the drawn line indicates. They are then pulled through until they are in the position shown in FIG. 1c.

C: This shows the cords after they have been pulled through the bight, as has just been explained in FIG. 1B. The strand *b* is then passed as shown by the arrow.

D: Strand *b* has been pulled through the bights held in the index finger and the thumb. Strand *a* in this illustration is then pulled until it appears as in FIG. 1E.

E: After end *a* has been pulled, FIG. D will look like this. The two bights are pulled until half of the knot is drawn up snug; and ends *a* and *b* are then pulled until the knot appears as in FIG. 1F.

F: This shows the completed Square Knot as it will look after having been drawn up snug. At first glance this method may seem difficult, but it is in reality very simple.

FIG. 2: *The Half Hitch* is another important knot used in this work. Most Macramé work is done with Half Hitches, as this gives a greater variety of design. Its construction is plainly pictured here.

FIG. 3: *Cords Half Hitched in a Series* are shown in this illustration.

FIG. 4: *When Making Two Rows of Hitches,* the last end *a* is brought down as shown.

FIG. 5: *To Begin a New Row of Hitches,* end *a* is brought across the front of the work and end *b* is then hitched on first; the ends *c, d, e,* and *f* follow one after the other in turn. Bear in mind that two Half Hitches are always put on with each cord.

FIG. 6: *A Continuous Row of Flat or Square Knots* may be formed as illustrated.

FIG. 7: *The Spiral or Waved Knot* is in reality only a half of a Square Knot. When tied one after the other they will twist or form a spiral by themselves. Notice the difference between the two by comparing FIG. 6 and FIG. 7. These knots are not made in the same way as the Square Knot, but are tied as shown in this figure, by making one half at a time and drawing each half up snug as it is made. In doing this work, remember to draw the work up snug (but not tight), and it will then be made more uniform. This will take a little time, but after a short period the knack will be acquired.

FIG. 8: *The Single Chain* is made by taking two cords and half hitching one on the other.

FIG. 9: *The Double Chain* is made in the same way as the Single Chain, except that it is made with two sets of cords of two each. Three cords are also used at times. Both of these chains are very common in Macramé work, as they are a means of passing from one color to another, or leading the threads from one place to another in order to carry out the color design.

FIG. 10: *Looped Square Knots* are made along a series of Square Knots, placed a little distance apart, so that the cord left between the knots forms a loop when they are pushed together.

FIG. 11: *To Make a Square Knot Design.* This shows which cords are taken to make a plain Square Knot design. First, hitch the middle of two cords to the line,

leaving four ends. A Single Knot is then made in these ends, two more cords are hitched on, and another Single Knot is tied in these.

FIG. 12: *The Small Shell Knot* is tied as follows: first, make a single Square Knot; then take the two center cords and tie an Overhand Knot in them. The two outside cords are then brought down and another Square Knot is tied in these ends.

FIG. 13: *The Knotted Loop Square Knot* is similar to FIG. 10, except that when the ends are taken down to tie the second knot, an Overhand Knot is made in the loops before the second Square Knot is formed.

FIG. 14A: *The Beaded Knot* is made by first making a series of three Square Knots as shown. Then ends *a* and *d* are crossed over in front of the two center cords *b* and *c*.

B: Ends *b* and *c* are taken up and through the space at the top of the series of knots, and then brought back down.

C: The series of Square Knots is rolled up to form a button. Then ends *a* and *d* are taken and made into another Square Knot.

D: The finished knot is shown here after the Square Knot has been drawn up snug.

FIG. 15: *When Two Rows of Half Hitches are made*—one slanting to the right, the other to the left—they are joined in the center by taking the two center cords *a* and *b*, and putting the Hitches on *a* with *b*.

FIG. 16: *Collecting Knot* is the name given to a knot which collects more than two cords together in the center of a Square Knot. It is used when it is necessary to collect more than two cords together in order to carry out a design.

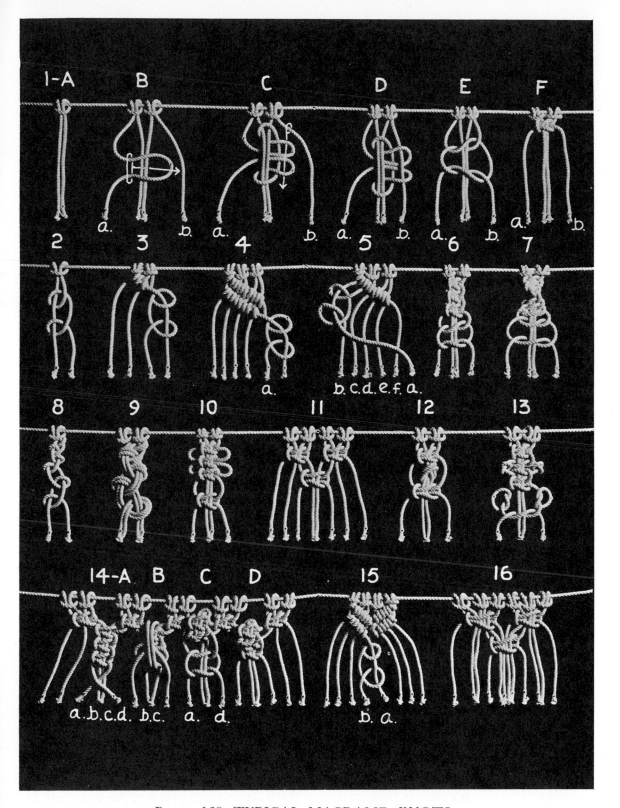

PLATE 168—TYPICAL MACRAME KNOTS

Plate 169—Square Knotting and Half Hitching

FIG. 17: *This Lark's Head Design* illustrates the use of Lark's Head Knots (PLATE 217, FIG. 177), in a single cord with small loops between them. Such patterns are used frequently in making fringes.

FIG. 18: *The Olive Design* is merely a series of Flat Knots made on a center of two cords as illustrated.

FIG. 19: *This is a Design of Split Bars of Half Hitching.* The bars are made diagonally to the left across the full width of the design, or in some cases only for a short distance. Then taking two cords make two Half Hitches on one with the others as illustrated.

FIG. 20: *A Figure-of-Eight Border Design* is made by putting the first and third cords on the hook (PLATE 218, FIG. 188), rather than the second and third. Then the knot is tied with the second and fourth cords and not the first and fourth, as is customary. This procedure applies to both the right and left sides of the design.

FIG. 21: *The Diamond Knot Design* is usually made in drawn thread and tassel work (*see* PLATE 231, FIG. 13). It is also commonly used in the more simple fringe designs. The design is made by taking half of one group of cords and half of another group and joining them, after which one cord is selected from each group and these are tied together with Half Hitches.

FIG. 22: *This Design is Composed of Spiral Half Hitched Bars.* The method employed in forming these groups of knots gives to them a spiral appearance (*see* PLATE 226, FIGS. 362 and 365).

FIG. 23: *Open Netting with Flat Knots* is made as shown here. Instead of drawing the knots up close together, as in FIG. 20, a small space is left in between each Flat Knot.

FIG. 24: *This Design is Formed with Horizontal Half Hitching.* This form of Half Hitching is quite different from that shown in Plate 168, Figs. 3 and 4. Instead of taking the outside cords and half hitching them diagonally a long piece of cord is used in this case and the Half Hitches are made on the vertical cords. The long single cord is called the filling and the vertical cords are called the warps. To variate the design the Half Hitches can be made with the warps on the filling cord (*see* PLATE 224, FIGS. 323 and 324).

Plate 170—Square Knotting

FIGS. 25A and B: *Square Knots* as they are used in making belts and other articles in which the Square Knot is used are shown in the accompanying illustration. Four strands of cord grouped together form the required number to make each Square Knot, the two center strands being the filler while the knot is actually formed with the two outside strands (*see* PLATE 168, FIG. 1).

Make the first row of Square Knots with each group of four strands as shown in FIG. 25A. The second row is then started with the third and fourth strand from the first group, and the first and second strands first group, and the first and second strands from the second group. This row is then continued in the same manner (*see* FIG. 25B).

The third row of Square Knots is made with the same strands as the first row, while the fourth row of Square Knots is made with the same strands as the second row, and so on.

FIG. 26: *Pointing,* or bringing to a point any such article as a belt in which Square Knots are the base of the design. Two strands are dropped on each side of each row of Square Knots until the four center strands are worked down to a point.

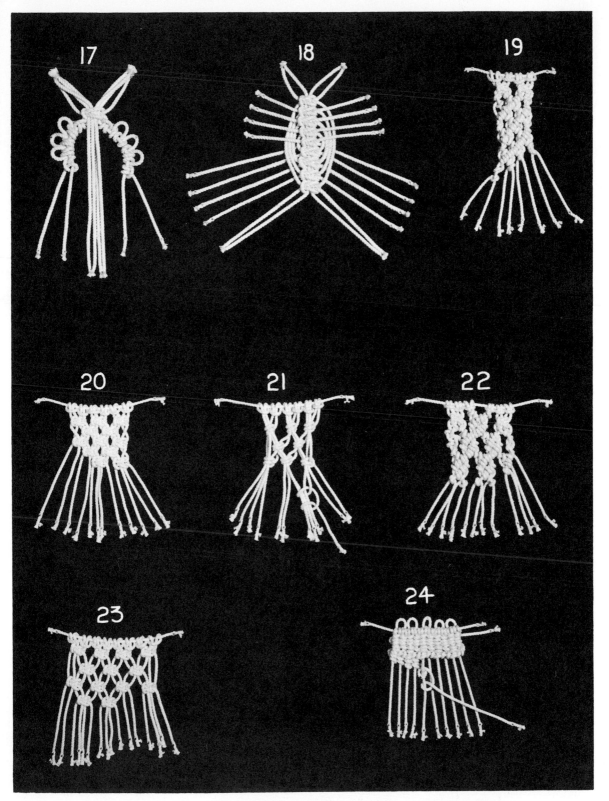

PLATE 169—SQUARE KNOTTING AND HALF HITCHING

If it is desired to form a point on one side of an article made with Square Knots two strands are dropped from the opposite side of each row of Square Knots.

FIG. 27: *Pointing,* as it is used to form points on each side of an article made with Square Knots. Two strands are dropped from the center on each side of each row of Square Knots.

FIG. 28: *Finishing a Belt with a Point* for the purpose of forming a belt-loop is shown in the accompanying illustration, as described in PLATE 171, FIG. 33.

FIGS. 29A and B: *Forming a Belt-Loop* as described in PLATE 171, FIG. 33.

FIGS. 30A and B: *A Smooth-Edged Belt* is shown in the accompanying illustration. Separate the strands into groups of four and after making a row of Square Knots across, take the second strand on each side and form a Half Hitch around the second strand with the outside strand. Now bring the second strand to the outside, which will make it the first strand. Continue by making a row of Square Knots with the remaining strands. Next begin on the left again and make another row of Square Knots. Continue the belt by alternately forming a Half Hitch around the second strand with the first strand on every alternate row of Square Knots.

Plate 171—Square Knotting in Making Belts

FIGS. 31A, B, and C: *To Start a Belt from the End* opposite to that to which the buckle is attached make certain that the width of the number of strands of cord to be used is the same as the width of the buckle. Cut the strands into lengths about seven times the desired length of the belt. Two strands are middled and hung over two small nails, as shown in FIG. 31A. Using the inside strands as a filler make a Square Knot with the two outside strands. Add a double strand on each side, below the Square Knot just tied. Then, using each double strand and the two adjoining strands, make a Square Knot on both sides as shown in FIG. 31B. After adding each set of double strands remove the strands from the nails and pull the knots up taut. Continue with the same method until the belt is of the required width, filling in with Square Knots across the belt each time a pair of double strands is added. FIG. 31C shows the point as it is worked part way down the belt.

FIGS. 32A and B: *To Start a Belt from the End* to which the buckle is attached select a number of strands whose combined width is equal to the width of the buckle. Cut the strands as before into lengths about

seven times that of the desired length of the belt. To begin the belt loop start in the middle of the strands by making a Square Knot on the left side with the first four strands, then continue with a row of Square Knots across and proceed with rows of Square Knots on each side from the middle. Next work one edge on each side to a point (*see* FIG. 32A). Make certain that the points on each side correspond with equivalent strands on both sides of the middle. For a belt of the average size about fourteen Square Knots are needed from point to point, counting down the outside, but in order to have an accurate measurement for any width of belt desired, allow a distance of about two and one-third times the desired width of the belt, between the points. Now bring the ends of the two points together in order to form the loop, then start the belt by selecting the second strand from each point and using these two strands as a filler, make a Square Knot with the first strand from each point (*see* FIG. 32B). Proceed by making rows of Square Knots, using two strands on each side for each successive row until all the strands from each side of the loop are joined. The

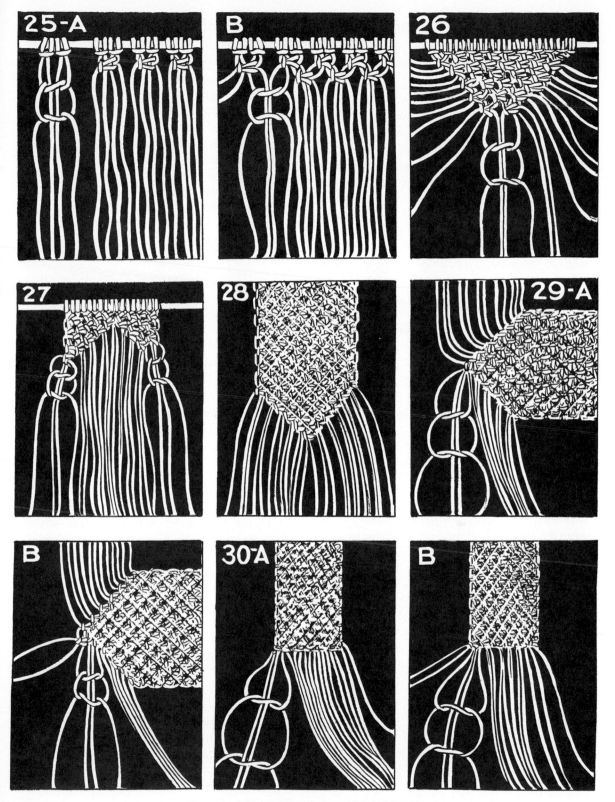

PLATE 170—SQUARE KNOTTING

belt is then continued desired of pattern.

FIGS. 33A and B: *After Starting a Belt from the End* and working to the required length the center is brought to a point (*see* PLATE 170, FIG. 28). Next select the four strands on one side of the point (*see* PLATE 170, FIG. 29A) and make a Square Knot. Continue by working at right angles from the belt (*see* FIG. 29B) and bring the Square Knots out to a point as shown in FIG. 33A, forming the loop. The point on the end of the loop must be on the same side of the strands as the point in the belt. Now bring the strands from the loop around to the strands on the end of the belt and with corresponding or equivalent strands from the loop and the end of the belt, tie Square Knots with each two strands. Draw each knot up taut and cut the strands off short. Be certain to turn the belt loop inside out before attaching the buckle to the belt. (*See* description of PLATE 312, FIG. 5.)

FIGS. 34A and B: *Another Method of Starting a Belt from the End* is shown in the accompanying illustration. Begin by using two doubled lengths of cord and then form Square Knots in the manner shown in FIG. 34A. Additional cords are then added in the same manner. A hole for the tongue of the buckle is worked in by dividing the cords into two equal groups and then knotting each separate group and bringing both groups together again after skipping one knot in the middle. Two Spiral designs are shown in FIG. 34B.

FIG. 35: *The Method of Forming Open Mesh Work* is shown in the accompanying illustration. Space the first half of the Square Knot the proper distance from the last row of Square Knots and then pull the second half of the Square Knot up taut on first half, to keep rows evenly spaced.

FIG. 36: *This Illustration Shows How the Strands are Attached to a Buckle* when the belt is started from the buckle.

Plate 172—Pointing Square Knot Work

FIG. 37A: *Pointing Square Knot Work with Half Hitches.* Lead the outside strand from one side to the center and make two Half Hitches around it with each strand, which also includes the strand lead to the center from the opposite side. When making several rows of Half Hitches, first lead the outside strand from one side to the center and then the outside strand from the opposite side to the center, at the same time making two Half Hitches around each strand, including the strand that was first led to the center from the opposite side. Repeat this same method again for each additional row (*see* FIGS. 37B and C).

FIG. 37D: To *Form a Row of Half Hitches from the Center to Each Side,* each side is first worked to a point. Next, begin with the two inside strands and make an Overhand Knot. Then pull the inside strand which was on the left at the start out taut and lead it to the left, after which form two Half Hitches around it with each strand until it becomes the outside strand on the left side. Repeat the same procedure with the inside strand on the right, which is led to the right and half-hitched with each strand until it becomes the outside strand on the right. Next, form another Overhand Knot with the two inside strands on each side and then proceed with another row of Half Hitches as before.

If an additional row of Half Hitches from the center to each side is desired, form two Half Hitches with each strand around the strand leading from the center. This also includes the strand from the last row of Half Hitches. In this way the strand from the center will become the outside strand on each side (*see* FIG. 37E).

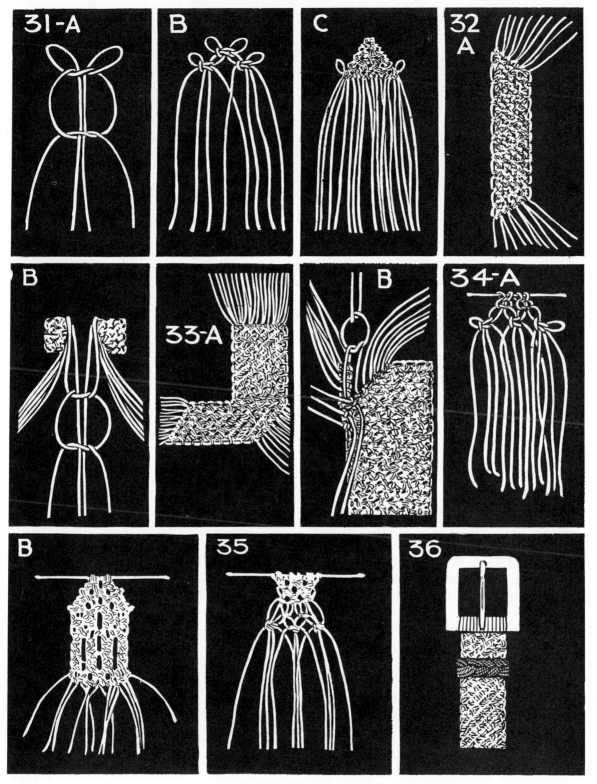

PLATE 171—SQUARE KNOTTING IN MAKING BELTS

If a diagonal row of Half Hitches all the way across is wanted one side is worked to a point, then the outside strand on the opposite side from the point is selected and two Half Hitches are made around it with each strand until it becomes the outside strand on the opposite side.

When a Half Hitch Diamond Design is wanted proceed by bringing each side of the work to a point and form a row of Half Hitches on each side by bringing the center strands to the outside, as already described. After completing the row of Half Hitches on each side begin in the center and form Square Knots down to the point on each side (*see* FIG. 37E). Work this Square Knot center down to a point as shown in PLATE 170, FIG. 26. Proceed with a row of Half Hitches to the center by bringing the outside strand on each side to the center (*see* FIGS. 37 F and G).

In forming a cross of Half Hitches work the center to a point from a row of Half Hitches to the center on each side (*see*

FIG. 37A). Continue by working each side to a point (*see* FIG. 37B). The rows of Half Hitches are continued with the strands in a line with the rows which were formed previously (*see* FIG. 37C).

In forming a pointed ridge, work the knots to a point, then work Square Knots down each side to the center at the same time keeping the work to a point, reversing every other row of Square Knots as the work proceeds towards the center. Begin by selecting the first, second, third and fourth strands on each side to form the Square Knot in the first row. Next, select the third, fourth, fifth, and sixth strands from each side to form the Square Knots in the second row, and then proceed by selecting the fifth, sixth, seventh, and eighth strands from each side to form the Square Knots in the next row. This method of knotting is followed down each side until the four center strands are formed into a square (*see* FIG. 38).

Plate 173—Belt Designs

FIG. 39: *An Attractive Belt* in a simple design. It is made entirely of white cord and the design is so simple that anyone, with a minimum amount of study, can follow the design.

FIG. 40: *An Attractive Belt* in another type of design in which colored cords are used.

FIG. 41: *This is a Braided Belt* made with brown cotton material. Belts of this kind can be made with any desired number of strands. A Flat or English Sennit Braid is used and the belts are started from

the end. The buckle is sewed on with an extra piece of material.

FIG. 42: *Another Braided Belt* similar to that shown in FIG. 41 is shown in the accompanying illustration. It is also made entirely of white material.

FIG. 43: *Another Belt Design* that is somewhat broader than the average. The design is worked out with two sets of four white cords in a manner easily followed.

FIG. 44: *A Rug Cord Belt Design* represents a novel method that is very easy to follow.

Plate 174—Belt Designs

FIG. 45: *One of the Many Varieties of Designs* that are offered here for the first time. These designs are presented in response to popular demand and to enlarge

upon the heretofore limited types of belt making. This is a combination of Half Hitches and Square Knots with the Half Hitches carried diagonally across with two

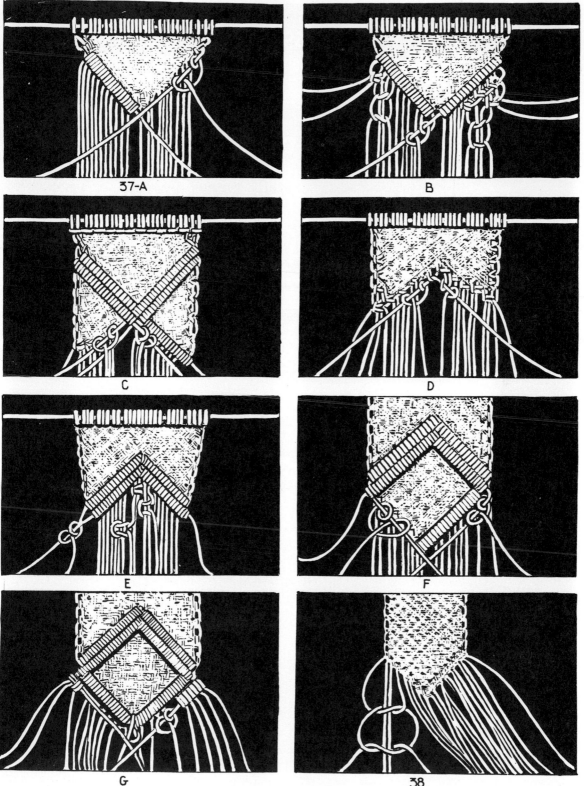

37-A

B

C

D

E

F

G

38

PLATE 172—POINTING SQUARE KNOT WORK

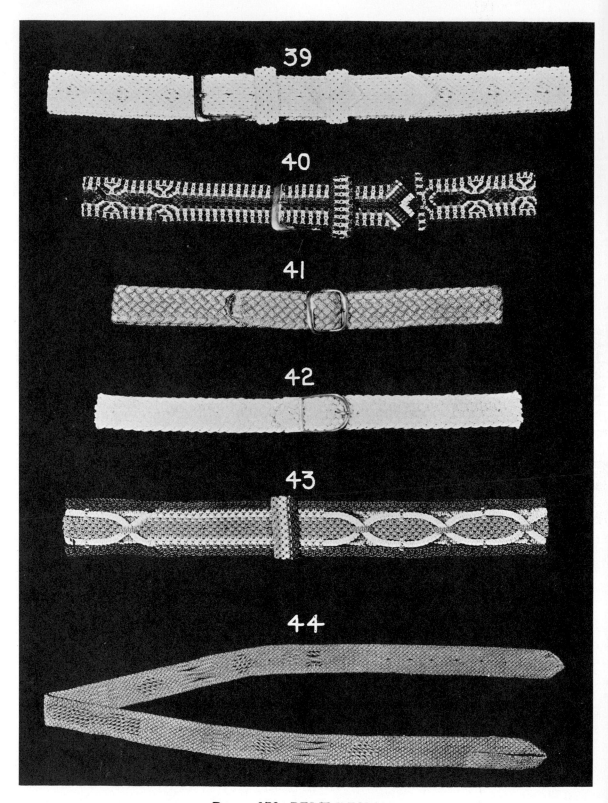

PLATE 173—BELT DESIGNS

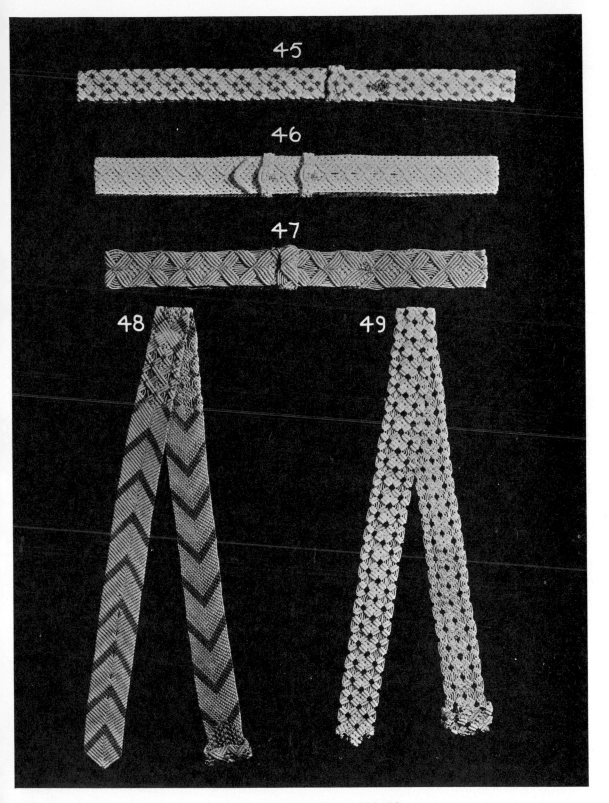

PLATE 174—BELT DESIGNS

rows of Half Hitches. The space in between is filled in with Square Knots. To obtain the color design shown, the order of tying the Half Hitches is changed with the dark cords becoming cover cords at different intervals.

FIG. 46: *A Chain of Half Hitched Diamonds* worked in the same colors as the Square Knot parts. Those who have studied the designs of belts illustrated previously will find this and the following types of belts and other Square Knot work very easy to duplicate, by simply following the methods shown in the illustrations.

FIG. 47: *An Attractive Belt Design* worked in one color with four rows of hitching to form the squares, which are alternately filled with a Square Knot center and then an open design.

FIG. 48: *A Somewhat Different Type of Belt* design with Hitching on the ends and squares worked in the center. The design should not be difficult to follow.

FIG. 49: *The Design of This Belt* is similar to that shown in FIG. 45, except that the method is worked with more strands, thus producing a broader color effect.

Plate 175—Color Combinations in Belt Designs

FIG. 50: *Another Belt* that represents an elaborate style of designing. This and the other belt designs shown on this plate should add a number of new and novel ideas to the knowledge of the student of Square Knots.

FIG. 51: *A Series of Double Row Hitches* worked into squares with open cord centers to make an attractive sports belt.

FIG. 52: *Rare Color Designing* to make

a beautiful belt is shown in this illustration.

FIG. 53: *A Multi-Colored Belt* such as that shown is an example of the possibilities of color varieties and different types of designing which can be utilized in making belts, once sufficient experience in the art of belt weaving has been acquired.

FIG. 54: *An Advanced Style in Belt Design* is shown in this illustration which should appeal to those experienced in the art of forming designs with Square Knots.

Plate 176—Attractive Belt Designs

FIG. 55: *An Artistic Belt Design* in which the belt is fastened with a pearl buckle. This and the other designs on this plate will supply the student of Square Knot work with many new ideas in color blending and forming designs. All of the illustrations are comprehensive and the various designs are easy to master with but a slight knowledge of Square Knot design.

FIG. 56: *A Belt Design Similar to Several Others* shown in other illustrations, but it has the darker colored cords worked into different formations.

FIG. 57: *A Combination Belt Design* of squares worked throughout the body. It

has a plain end with a fancy buckle to give added attraction.

FIG. 58: *An Unusual Suggestion* in a large, wide type of design. Belts such as this can be made with any desired number of strands.

FIG. 59: *A Twin-colored Combination Weave* that is worked throughout with Half Hitches.

FIG. 60: *A Buff Colored Belt with a Pearl Buckle.* It is worked with two rows of Hitches to form each square, while the space on each side is filled in alternately with Square Knots on one side and open

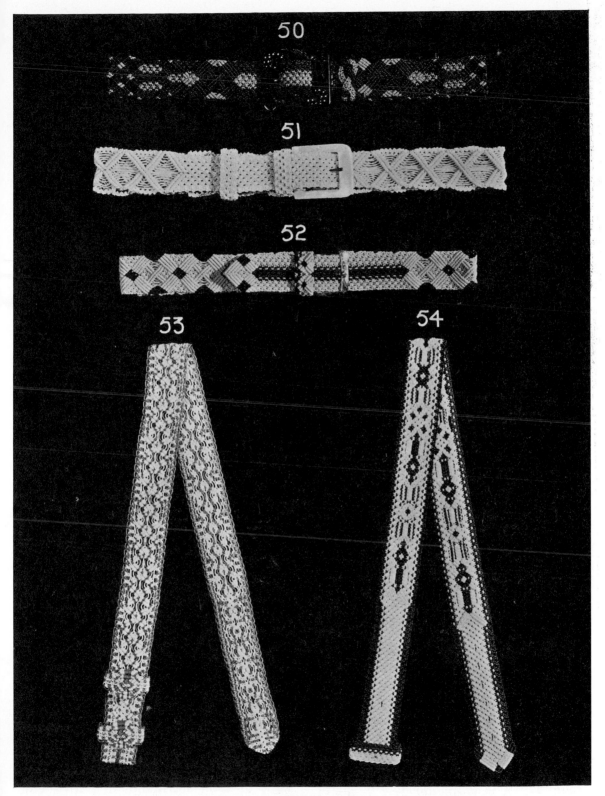

PLATE 175—COLOR COMBINATIONS IN BELT DESIGNS

work on the other. Square Knots are used to fill the center of each square.

FIG. 61: *A Large Black Belt* with white flower designs worked with Half Hitches throughout. French macramé belts of this type are apt to prove somewhat difficult to make unless the student has thoroughly mastered the art of macramé construction.

Plate 177—Suggested Designs for Belts

FIG. 62: *A Multi-colored Belt* with four rows of Diagonal Hitches worked on both sides of a Square Knot center at different intervals.

FIG. 63: *An Attractive Belt Design* that can be followed easily by observing the pattern.

FIG. 64: *A Belt Pattern That Is Easy to Follow* is shown in this illustration. Such a belt can consist of any desired number of strands.

FIG. 65: *Two Views of Another Type of Belt,* similar to that shown in PLATE 174, FIG. 49, are shown in this illustration.

FIG. 66: *A Striking Example of Color Weaving* is shown in this belt design. It may be observed that the colors alternate back and forth through the chain of squares in the center.

Plate 178—Color Combinations in Belts

FIG. 67: *A Belt of Japanese Style* worked with Carrick Bends. The Bends are made with four parts of silk cord in two pieces. Any kind of buckle may be added to suit the individual taste. This type of belt is suitable for wear on women's lounging garments.

FIG. 68: *An Unusual Belt Design* with the color combinations arranged in an attractive manner at different intervals in each four rows of Hitches.

FIG. 69: *A Wampum or Half Hitched Belt* with the colors interweaving to form a chain of squares.

FIG. 70: *An Outstanding Design in Colors* as shown in this illustration may be used to form an attractive belt in any color.

FIG. 71: *A Good Suggestion for a Sports Belt* is shown in this illustration. It is a simple open design that can be duplicated easily.

FIG. 72: *Another Outstanding Example of Unusual Color Weaving* is shown in this illustration. It is done with Half Hitches worked throughout.

Plate 179—Dog Leash and Belts

FIG. 73: *An Open Design or Sports Belt* with double rows of Half Hitches to form the squares throughout the body of the belt is shown in this illustration.

FIG. 74: *An Interesting Type of Belt* that is easy to make. The fancy designs represent the Full Diamond, the Braided Carrick, the Half Diamonds and a double row of Hitching in the shape of a square with a Spiral center. The end is finished off with four rows of Hitching.

FIG. 75: *Another Form of Color Blending in a Wampum Belt* with Half Hitching throughout is shown in this illustration.

FIG. 76A, B, and C: *This Illustration Represents a Dog Leash.* There are several ways in which this type of Square Knot work may be made. One of the simplest forms is shown at B and C. The leash is made by using six strands in a strip with the four outside strands on either side being formed alternately into Square Knots

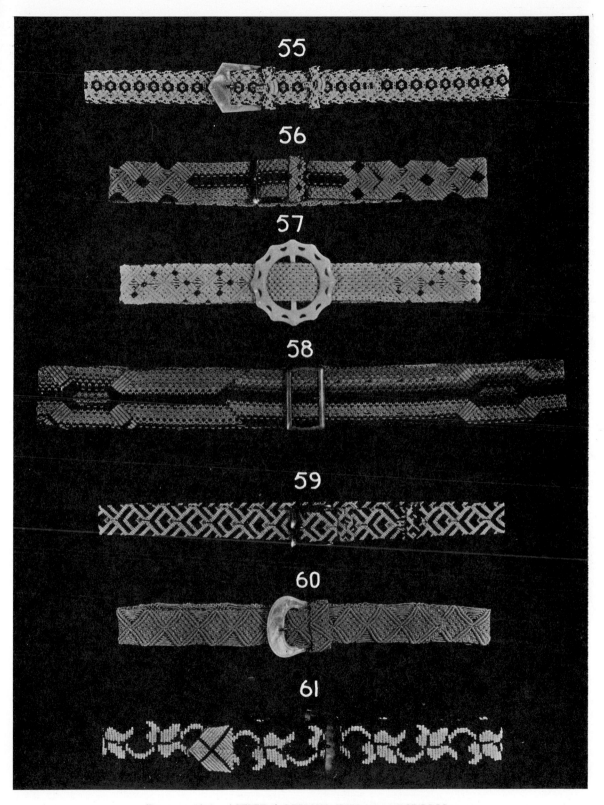

PLATE 176—ATTRACTIVE BELT DESIGNS

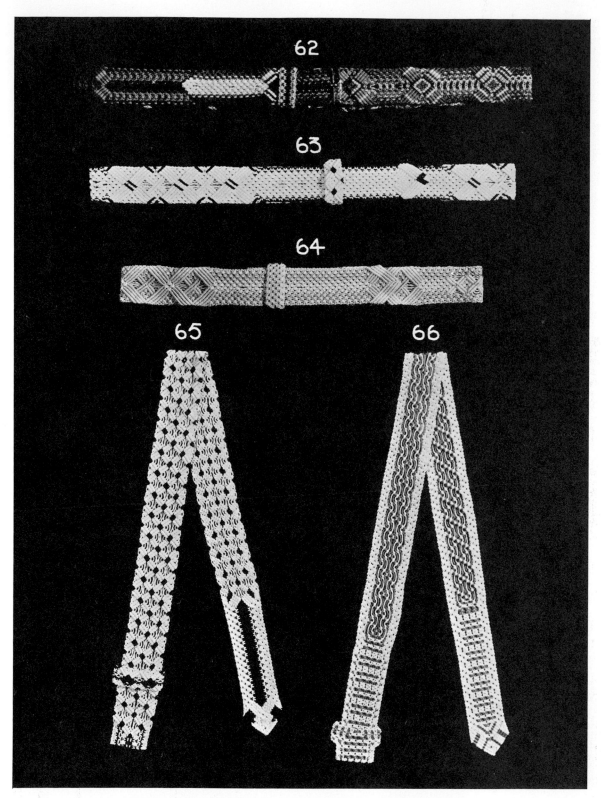

PLATE 177—SUGGESTED DESIGNS FOR BELTS

PLATE 178—COLOR COMBINATIONS IN BELTS

by using two strands as a filler and the two strands on either side of the filler to form the knot. It should be worked down to about five feet in length. The strip is ended with a loop by bending the end back on itself, then seizing the loose ends of the cord to the body of the strip with a Four or Five-Strand Turk's Head that should have about four or five passes. A loop can be formed on the other end to secure the leash to the snap. A narrower strip can also be made with four cords by using the center strands for the filler and the two outside strands for the knot. Heavy dreadnaught cord is the most suitable for this kind of work.

A Lanyard for a Whistle can also be made by using a narrow strip of four cords. Cut two filler cords about a foot longer than the strip, which should be between three and four feet, then select the tying cords in a contrasting color and about nine times as long and proceed with the knotting. At one end the loop is made around the body of the strip to provide a sliding loop to be used around the neck. A loop is then formed on the other end to secure the whistle.

An Attractive Watch Guard can be made by combining the narrow and wide styles of strips just described. Two lengths of cord sixty inches long and one cord forty inches long are needed. Double them and knot a sufficient distance of the wide strip to form a suitable belt loop, then tie these strands off securely and cut off the two shorter cords. The remaining four are then used for the narrow strip. These are worked down to a length of about six inches. Divide the four strands into pairs of two strands each and tie Square Knots with each pair without any filler cord until the ends are long enough to pass through the watch ring and back to the body of the strap where they are tied firmly or seized with a Turk's Head.

A Hat Cord can also be made with the wide strip of six strands. It is lapped over at the ends and seized with Sliding Turk's Heads and tassels are added on both ends of the strips to finish it.

Plate 180—Miscellaneous Belts and Other Work

FIG. 77: *A Unique Design in Belts* done in checkered coloring with hitched diamonds.

FIG. 78: *Another Belt Design* with open work on either side.

FIG. 79: *A Closely Woven Belt* made by hitching black and white cords to form the color design.

FIG. 80: *A Twelve-cord Square Knot Dog Leash.* It is made similar to the leash shown in FIG. 76, except that double the number of cords are required, which are looped to the ring attachment of the snap to start the leash. To form the split near the end divide the cords into two parts of six cords each. They are then brought back together and the end is finished off as for a belt.

FIG. 81: *A Fancy Design for a Shade Pull* which is made in a manner similar to PLATE 210, FIG. 158, except that the tassel is formed like a handbag tassel, as illustrated on PLATE 194, FIGS. 124F to I.

FIG. 82: *Additional Suggestions for Making Belt Loops* are shown in this illustration.

FIG. 83: *A Design for a Head Band* for keeping the hair in place is shown in the accompanying illustration. It is made from twelve cords with an elastic attachment and can be easily duplicated by studying the illustration.

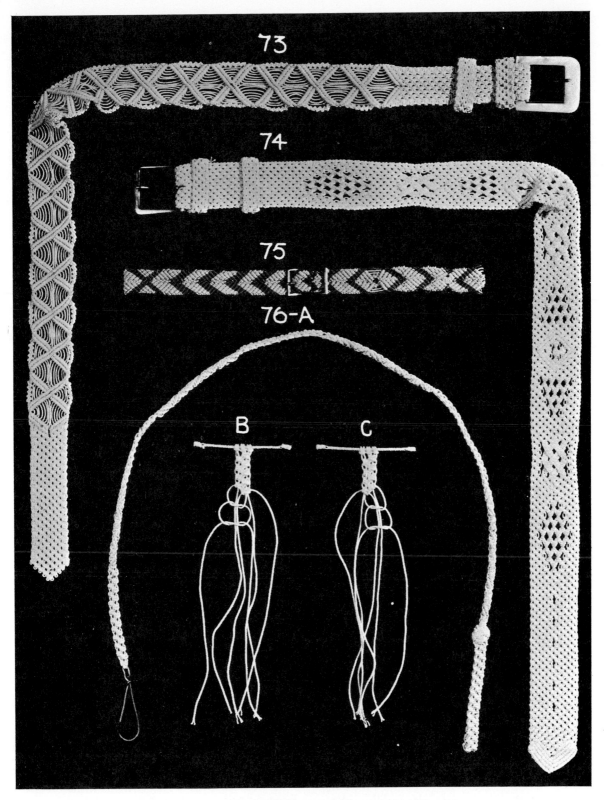

PLATE 179—LEASHES, CORDS, AND BELTS

Plate 181—Dog Harness and Half Hitch Work

FIG. 84: *Still Another Wampum Belt Design* consisting of Half Hitch weaving of colored cords.

FIG. 85: *An Interesting Belt Design of a Fancy Color Style* that can be easily worked in the end.

FIG. 86: *A Black and White Design* of French style macramé that can be utilized in making belts.

FIG. 87: *An Interesting Design in Colors* which can be blended is shown in this illustration. It has both edges in colors.

FIG. 88: *A Half Hitch Design* that is worked in criss-cross fashion makes an interesting design.

FIG. 89: *A Dog Leash and Harness* with a buckle and snap attached. This is but another example of the wide usage of Square Knotting, showing to the student who has mastered the art the many possibilities available in making many articles for practical use.

Plate 182—Belt Designs

FIG. 90: *A Belt Design in Black and White* with the white running through the center of the belt in an attractive manner.

FIG. 91: *Another Indian Wampum Belt Design* which illustrates a method of coxcombing around the buckle in which three cords of different colors are used.

FIG. 92: *An Interesting Belt Design* using black and red, Braided Flat Sennit fashion. Eight strands are used with three cords to each strand and these are braided together in the same manner as was used in making an Eight-Strand Flat Sennit.

FIG. 93: *A Belt Design* using a combination of Half Hitches in the center with a Square Knot edge through the body. A novel idea is presented in the manner of fastening the end on either side of the belt loop with buttons.

FIG. 94: *A Belt with Carrick Bends* designs formed over the body of the belt by working four black strands on each edge and then joining them across the top in the manner referred to. The other designs can be duplicated easily.

FIG. 95: *Another Suggestion in Colored Belt Work* is offered in this illustration.

FIG. 96: *Still Another Belt Design Suggestion,* slightly different from that previously described.

FIG. 97: *A Simple Belt Design* that can be duplicated easily.

Plate 183—A Bath Robe Cord Design

FIG. 98A to G: *A Spiral Knotted Cord Design for a Bath Robe* is shown here. Any contrasting colors of cords may be used. Cut four strands of one color, 30 feet long, and four strands of the same length from the cords of another color, with one cord of either color forty feet long to be used as a filler cord. Start knotting in the middle with part of each length tied up in a hank. Form a row of knots around the filler cord with all eight of the strands (*see* FIG. 98A). The ends of the row are then brought together as at FIG. 98B and the knotting is continued in Spiral fashion by hitching each strand around the filler cord as the work progresses. Each color will then form a Spiral design. After the knotting has been worked down to about 28 inches from the middle, turn the work around and continue with the same amount of work on the opposite side (*see* FIG. 98C).

When the Spiral Knotting is finished the work should be stretched out to a length of about six feet. Any kind of reasonably

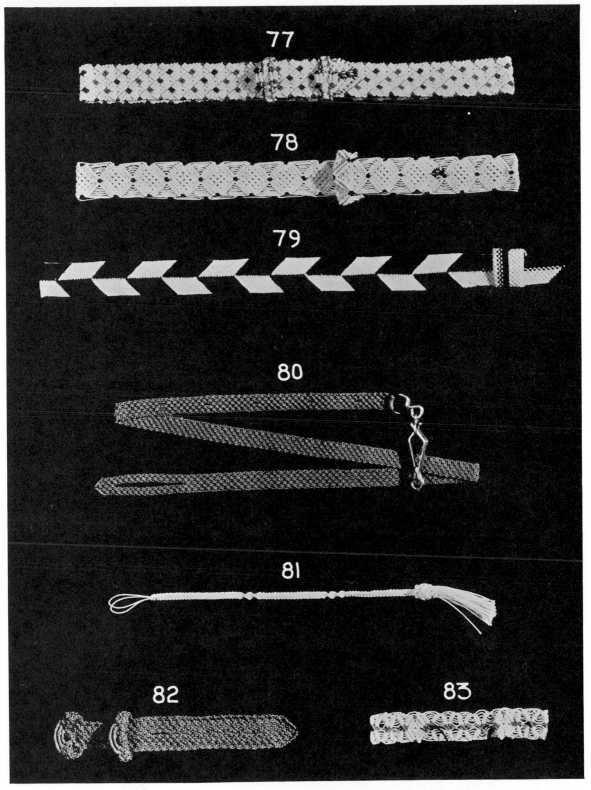

PLATE 180—MISCELLANEOUS BELTS AND OTHER WORK

PLATE 181—DOG HARNESS, AND HALF HITCH WORK

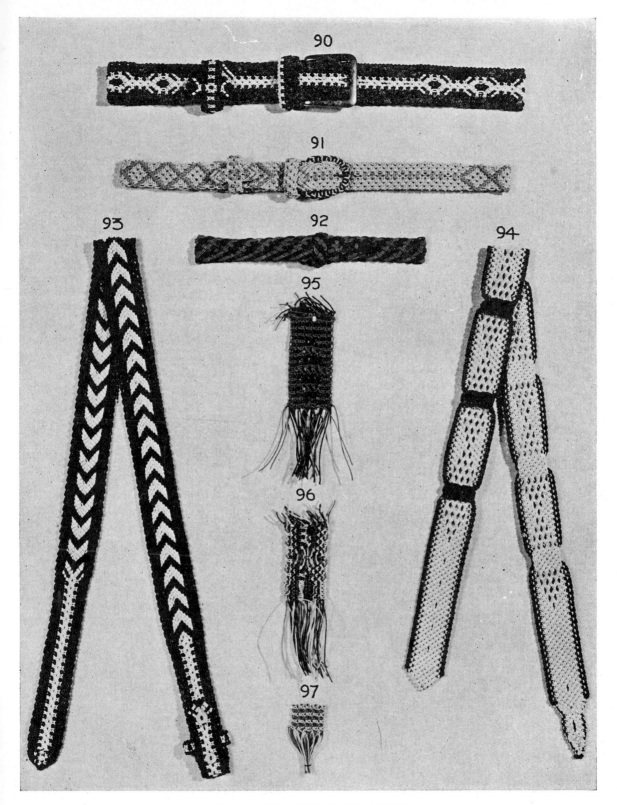

PLATE 182—BELT DESIGNS

rigid wire may be used to form the triangular or arrow-head-shaped pieces which form the ends of the cord. These pieces of wire are shaped by bending them around a triangular block having a length of about two inches on each side, after which the ends are soldered together. The ends of the Spiral Cord are then hitched to the triangular end pieces as shown in FIG. 98D. The arrow-head is then covered with a One-strand Coxcomb, which can be seen also in FIG. 98D. The center strip is then brought down inside the arrow-head by being hitched in the same manner as a Wampum belt (*see* FIG. 98E). FIG. 98F shows the finished arrow-head design and FIG. 98G the bath robe cord as it appears when completed.

FIG. 99A to E: *Blending Colors in Wampum Belt Making* are shown in these illustrations. The distinction between the lines of black and white is to show the possibilities of using contrasting colors in the designs.

To make one of these belts thirty-four inches long cut four strands of white cord twenty-five feet long and one strand of black cord forty-eight feet long. Double these strands and loop them over a buckle with the black cord in the center. Then, using the outside cord on the left as a filler, add two Half Hitches with the next four strands. This will bring the filler cord to the center (*see* FIG. 99A). Repeat the same operation by using the outside cord on the right for a filler and add two Half Hitches with the next four strands. The two filler cords are now knotted together by forming two Half Hitches over the cord coming from the right with the cord from the left (*see* FIG. 99B). FIGS. C, D and E show the next three stages in forming the design as the belt is worked down.

Plate 184—Wampum Belt Designs

FIG. 100: *Some of the Many Beautiful Designs* it is possible to incorporate in making belts are shown in these illustrations. The belt shown in this figure is a simple design in Wampum Weaving.

FIG. 101: *The Wampum Belt* shown here is made in a manner to that explained in the making of the belt shown in PLATE 183, FIG. 99.

FIG. 102: *Another Type of Wampum Belt* design in which the colors cross in similar fashion to that shown on PLATE 183, FIG. 99.

FIG. 103: *Belts* such as that shown here are not difficult to make, once one has mastered the art of Wampum Weaving. It is an interesting example of the possibilities of the manner in which different colors can be combined into attractive patterns.

FIG. 104: *This Belt Design* is slightly different to one that is described in PLATE 183, FIG. 99.

FIG. 105: *The Design in This Belt* is in the form of squares, with the colors crossing in the middle much as in the design shown on PLATE 183, FIG. 99.

FIG. 106: *This is an Attractive Design* for a sports belt with a zig-zag row of Square Knots running through the open part of the weave.

Plate 185—A Knotted Cord Cigarette Case

FIG. 107: *A Cigarette Case* made with Square Knotted cords. To start the weaving cut sixteen white cords and two dark blue cords eight feet long. Double the two blue cords and hang them over a lashing that is securely anchored. Form a Square Knot with these four colored strands and separate them into two strands of two cords each. Next add a double strand of white cord to each part just below the first knot.

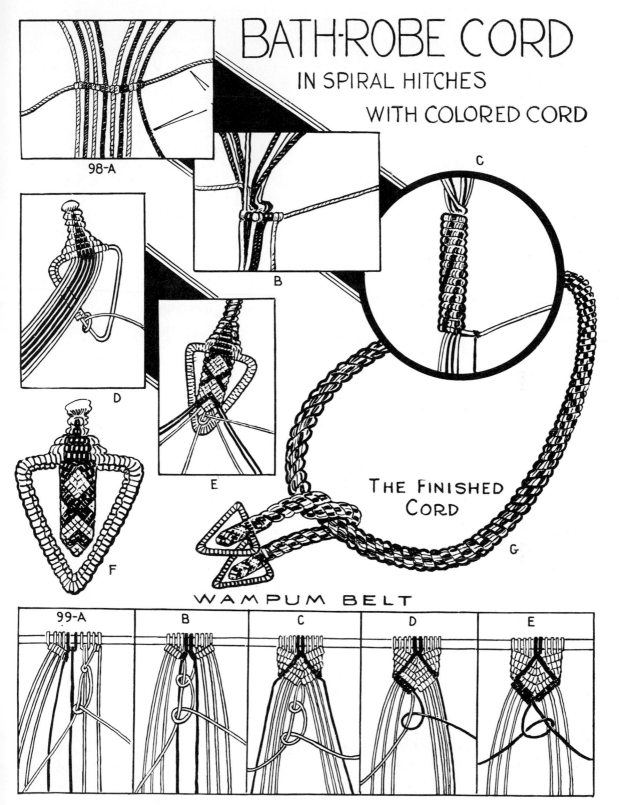

BATH·ROBE CORD
IN SPIRAL HITCHES
WITH COLORED CORD

98-A

B

C

D

E

F

THE FINISHED CORD

G

WAMPUM BELT

99-A   B   C   D   E

PLATE 183—A BATH ROBE CORD DESIGN

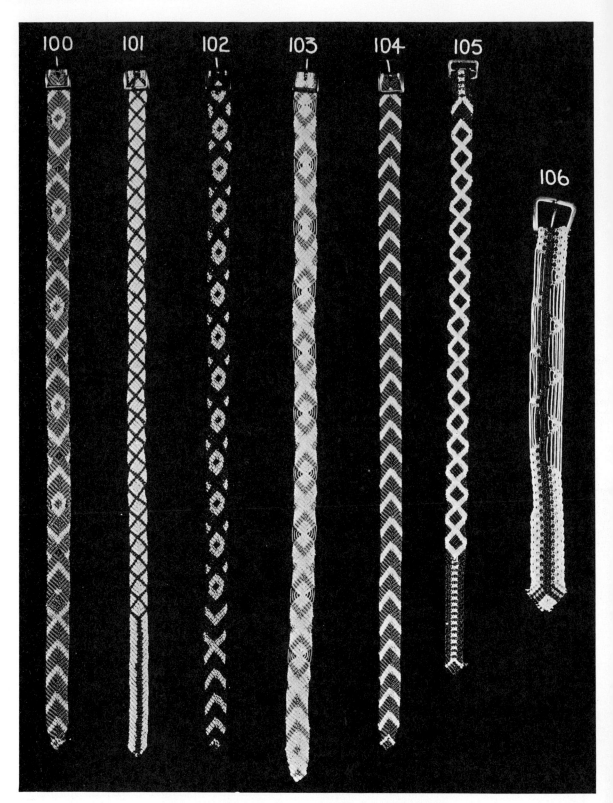

PLATE 184—WAMPUM BELT DESIGNS

CIGARETTE CASE
SQUARE KNOTTED WITH CORD

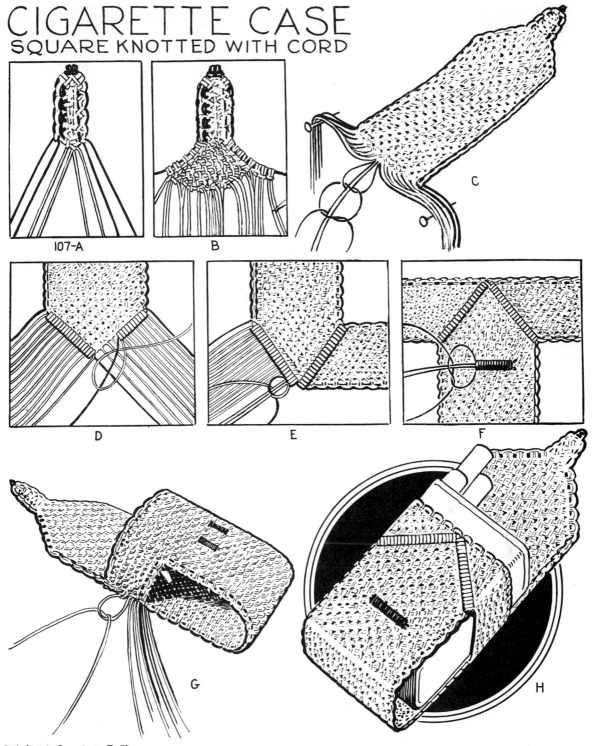

107-A

B

C

D

E

F

G

H

TYING CASE
TOGETHER WHEN REVERSED

READY FOR USE

PLATE 185—A KNOTTED CORD CIGARETTE CASE

Then with all eight strands make five rows of Square Knots. This will complete the tongue piece. (Shown at A.)

Next loop seven doubled white cords to each pair of blue cords. This will serve to widen the tongue into a flap. As each additional pair of white cords is added a row of Square Knots is made across the flap. (Shown at B.) This method of knotting is continued until the flap is worked down about nine and one-half inches from the tip of the tongue. It is then attached to the edge of a table with push pins as at C. The work is then brought to a point by dropping two strands in each row on each side.

Proceed by adding a single row of Half Hitches around a single blue strand from the outside on each side. (Shown at D.) Continue knotting with each half of the end at right angles to the body of the main piece. These knots are worked down to a distance of one and one-eighth inches on either side. (Shown at E.) Next place the hold-down for the tongue one and three-quarter inches from the point that was formed with the Half Hitches. Double two twenty-four inch cords and slip them through the diamond-shaped openings from the back so as to form a loop about a single Square Knot. A series of Square Knots is then made with the two inside strands serving as a filler. (Shown at F.) This piece should be about one inch long. Slip the ends through the diamond openings to the back and tie securely and cut short. Make certain that the piece which serves as a hold down for the flap is placed in the center.

The next step is to turn the case inside out and proceed to tie the cords from the right-angled pieces to the sides of the main piece. (Shown at G.) The exact point at which these cords are to be tied is to be determined by folding the case over a package of cigarettes. Draw the knots up taut while tying the loose cords and cut them off short. Turn the case right side out and the work is finished. (Shown at H.)

Plate 186—Miscellaneous Designs

FIG. 108: *A Bath Robe Cord* which is made in a similar manner to that shown on PLATE 183, FIGS. 98A to G.

FIG. 109: *A Necktie* made by tying Square Knots to form the design. It is started with thirty-six strands and then tapered down to twenty-four strands at the finish. The designs are worked out with nine rows of flats across the broad part, with three Square Knots to each flat, which are tapered down to six rows of flats across the narrow part with three Square Knots to each flat. The ends are changed into open work and then finished off in the same manner as a belt.

Any contrasting colors may be used and for the average tie the amount of material required is two balls of crochet silk, one of each color. To start a two-color tie cut twenty strands of one color, as red, and eight strands, as blue, about ten feet long.

Group the strands as follows: two strands of red and ten strands of blue; four strands of red and ten strands of blue; and then two more strands of red.

Attach the strands to any suitable support in the order given and then tie the first Square Knot. It should be placed fifty-two inches from the point at which the cords are supported. Starting at the left make these first Square Knots by using strands one, two, three, and four. Use strands five, six, seven, and eight for the second knot. Continue in this manner by using the succeeding four strands toward the right until the last four strands have been tied. This will form the seventh Square Knot in the first row. In tying this last Square Knot in the row the last half of the knot must be tied first and the first half last. In other words, the knot must be reversed to retain the balance of the colors.

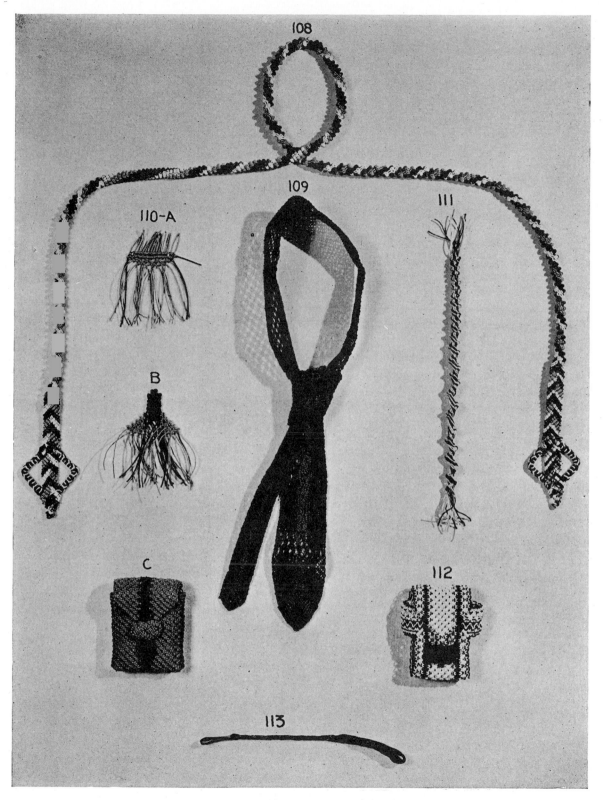

PLATE 186—MISCELLANEOUS DESIGNS

The second row of Square Knots is started from the left by using strands three, four, five, and six to make the first knot in the row. In this row it is necessary to reverse the fourth instead of the last knot. Repeat this procedure until thirty rows of Square Knots have been tied, taking care to pull each knot up snugly. After finishing the thirty rows of knots, continue as before but do not pull the knots up tight. Gradually increase the distance between rows until there is a space of about one-eighth of an inch between knots and follow this method until the tie is about twenty inches long. Finish the end by bringing the Square Knots to a point in the center and by tying three rows of Half Hitches. Turn the tie around and make solid Square Knots for a distance of about ten inches and then continue with about two inches of open work. Finish off by working the end down to a point as before.

Fig. 110: *A Cigarette Case* is shown at c, while A and B show the preliminary steps in the weaving. A similar case is illustrated on PLATE 185, FIGS. 107A to H.

Fig. 111: *Another Bath Robe Cord Design.*

Fig. 112: *Another Design for a Cigarette Case* similar to those illustrated previously is shown here.

Fig. 113: *A Braided Leather Watch Lanyard* is shown in this illustration.

Plate 187—Knotted Cord Bath Slippers

Fig. 114: *Making a Pair of Slippers with Square Knotting.* The knot work can be attached to either a pair of leather or sponge rubber soles. Obtain suitable material for the soles and trace the outline of the soles on the material by using a pair of shoes as a pattern. This will give the correct size of the soles, after which they may be cut out of the material. Then, with a length of Square Knot cord and a sail needle proceed to sew the edges around the soles as shown at A. Make the stitches a trifle wider on the top than they are on the bottom of the soles, by slanting the needle toward the inside as it is pushed through to the bottom.

Select about twenty or more strands (depending upon the size of the slippers) and cut the cords into lengths of about five feet. The cords may be of any color of cotton or other material but dreadnaught cord is probably the most suitable as it is strong and serves the purpose well. Double each one of the cords and attach them to the stitching around the edges of one sole as illustrated at B. Each group of four cords is used to form the Square Knots with the two center strands acting as fillers, as shown at c. Continue tying Square Knots in this manner until the covering for the end of the slipper is partly completed.

Next fit the slipper to the foot to insure the correct size and at the same time determine the spacing of the knots. In the process of weaving, the slippers should be slipped onto the feet occasionally to insure a correct fit. After the toe has been finished, as at D, the knotting should be worked back toward the heel. It is necessary to secure the work to each side with push pins to eliminate difficulties in tying the knots in the middle (*see* E).

After the knotting has been completed with all of the cords attach each row of knots to the soles by passing the side cords through the loops in the stitching (*see* F). Finish off with a row of Half Hitches. A loose cord from one side is brought over and across the width of the slipper. Next take each of the other loose cords and form Half Hitches around the single cord, making enough Hitches with each cord to fill the row in properly (*see* G). Pull these Half Hitches up very tight and then cut the cords off short. Rubber heels may be added. The finished slippers are shown at H.

BATH SLIPPERS
OF KNOTTED CORD
AND A SPONGE RUBBER or
FELT PAD

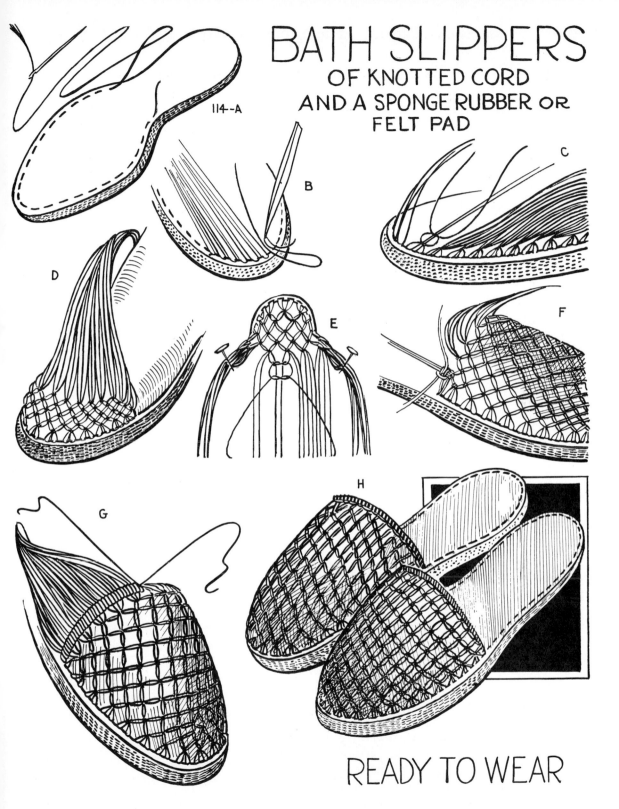

114-A

B

C

D

E

F

G

H

READY TO WEAR

PLATE 187—KNOTTED CORD BATH SLIPPERS

Plate 188—Forming Letters in Designs

FIG. 115: *The Weaving of Initials* as well as names into belts. The entire design including the checkerboard colors and the numbers as well as the name are all done with Half Hitch work. Such work as this requires a certain amount of initiative on the part of the weaver, depending of course upon the type of design and the letters or numbers included. However, once the student has mastered the principals of knot work and belt making such designs as this will be found relatively easy to make.

FIG. 115A: *A Suggestion for Another Type of Sandal* made with Square Knots. An industrious worker, with but a little patience and experience, can originate a great variety of designs and patterns in almost every type of Square Knot work, thereby making the work interesting and at the same time a constructive way to while away idle hours.

FIGS. 116A and B: *The Design for a Pair of Slippers* shown in this illustration includes the lining for the slippers.

Plates 189, 190 and 191—Steps in Making a Pillow Top Design

FIG. 117A: *The Start of a Pillow Top Design* as it would appear from the front side. In making pillow tops and other similar designs it is first necessary to construct a wooden frame to hold the work. It should be square or rectangular in shape and of the same size as that of the finished design. A row of small nails or brads is then added all around the entire frame, spacing all of the brads an equal distance apart.

Some such material as No. 3 Silkine Pearl Cotton is suitable for the base cords. It can be selected in a wide variety of colors, to suit individual tastes. To start the work place the cords selected for the bottom or body of the design on the frame, stretching them tight from nail to nail in both vertical and horizontal directions. The manner in which this cord is applied may be seen from reference to any of the three accompanying illustrations. It is to be understood that the number of cords applied in this manner is to be determined by the individual—the greater the number and the more varied the colors are the heavier and more attractive the design will be. There should be however, at least five or six strands in each of the vertical and horizontal rows.

After all of the different colored cords have been attached securely to the frame,

turn the work over. It will then appear as in the upper right side of PLATE 190, FIG. 117B. Clove Hitching is added next. This is indicated in the illustrations by means of the small black lines, drawn diagonally across the frame in both directions. The Clove Hitches are made at each intersection of the base or body cords, and in both directions. Such cord as No. 3 D.M.C. may be used for this purpose. When all of the intersecting body cords have been clove-hitched on one side of the frame, turn it over and proceed to make Clove Hitches at each intersection on the other side of the work. It is important to point out at this time that care should be exercised in forming the Clove Hitches for the reason that in the end they aid in supporting or holding together the entire design or pillow top.

Assuming that as many as six cords have been used for the base or body of the work, and working from the top or front of the frame, proceed to cut the colored cords in the following manner: starting in the extreme lower left-hand corner of the frame, with the first horizontal row, separate the four bottom cords and the Clove Hitch cord from the remaining strands and cut the top cords exactly in the center between

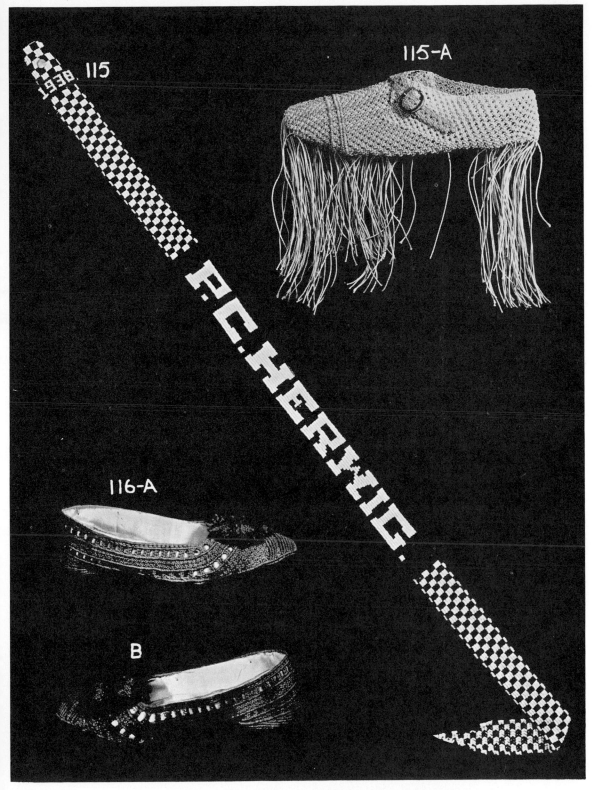

PLATE 188—FORMING LETTERS IN DESIGNS

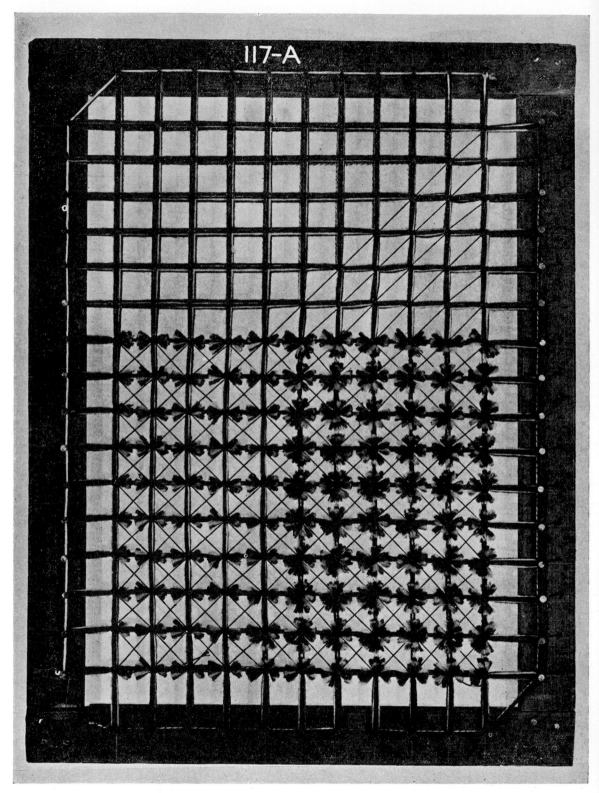

PLATE 189—THE INITIAL STEPS IN MAKING PILLOW TOPS

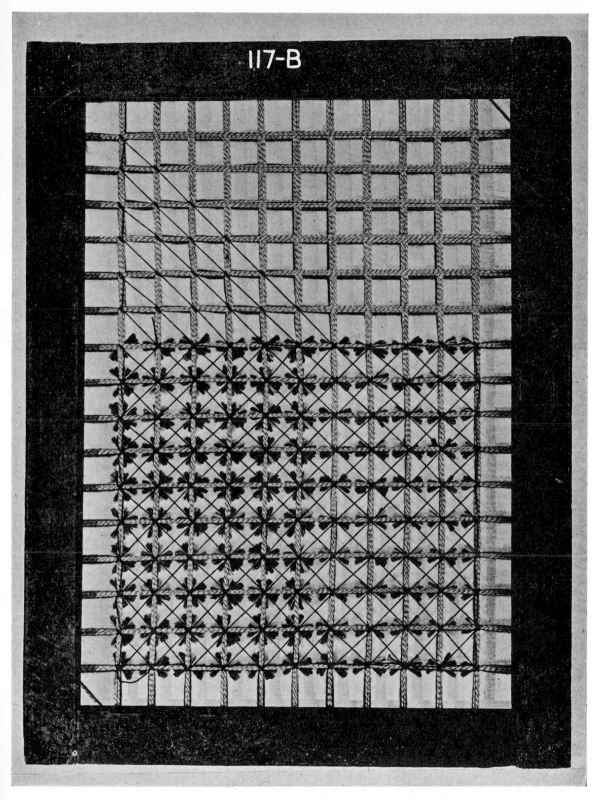

PLATE 190—THE SECOND STEP IN MAKING PILLOW TOPS

the intersection. Proceed to the next square to the right, and again separating four of the six cords, cut the top cords exactly in the center as between the first and second vertical rows. Follow this procedure for each succeeding square for all of the horizontal rows, after which turn the frame and continue to cut the cords in each square in all of the vertical cords. The appearance of the work and the manner in which it is done is shown clearly in the illustrations.

After all of the cords, in each of all of the vertical and the horizontal rows, have been cut in two as explained, proceed to fray the ends of the cords to form tufts at each of the Clove Hitches, or cord intersections. The work will then appear as in PLATE 191, FIG. 117C.

Plate 192—Tatting and a Watch Fob Design

FIGS. 118A, B, and C: *A Design in Tatting* is shown in its various stages in these three views. It is started by forming the line into a loop, and then, with the standing part on the inside, make a Lark's Head with the working part around the standing part, as illustrated at A. Next make a Lark's Head in the opposite way or from underneath instead of on top. Continue these alternating Lark's Heads until the loop is filled. FIG. 118B shows the second stage of the work and FIG. 118C illustrates the finished design. Tatting designs are used extensively in needlecraft and at the same time are useful in other forms of fancy work.

FIG. 119: *A Tatting Design Finished Off with Blood Knots*, then a Japanese Crown and finally a Dragonfly Knot. It is an example of the many possibilities of combining tatting and knot designs.

FIG. 120: *Another Tatting Design* is shown in this illustration. It is made with a Round Braid, then a Two-Strand Double Diamond Knot and is finished off with two Sliding Blood Knots.

FIGS. 121A and B: *A Four-Strand Round Sennit Braided in a Loop.* The illustration at A shows how the Braid is started and the completed loop is shown at B.

FIG. 122: *A Watch Fob Design* is shown in this illustration. To start the fob double a strand of cord and hang it on a nail or hook. Then take another cord and form about eight or ten Square Knots which are finished off with a Diamond Knot after which the ends are cut off.

Plate 193—A Handbag Handle Design

FIGS. 123A to H: *How a Handle for a Handbag Is Made* and at the same time how it is attached to the bag. The material required for the handle is sixteen strands of cord five feet long. Start the work by separating the strands into four groups of four strands each, middle each group and form Square Knots with each of the four groups, as shown at FIG. 123A. Next, form another Square Knot by joining the third and fourth cords in the first group of four strands to the first and second cords of the second group of four strands, as shown also at FIG. 123A. Follow this with another Square Knot made by joining the third and fourth cords in the second group of four strands to the first and second cords of the third group of strands. Continue to form Square Knots in this manner until all of the groups have been joined. This will shape the groups of cords into the form of a round handle.

The next step is to add twenty more rows of Square Knots, as shown at FIG. 123B. Continue by taking the outside strand on each side and forming a Spiral, as shown at FIG. 123C. After the Spiral has been made the cords are again paired off

PLATE 191—AN ATTRACTIVE PILLOW TOP DESIGN

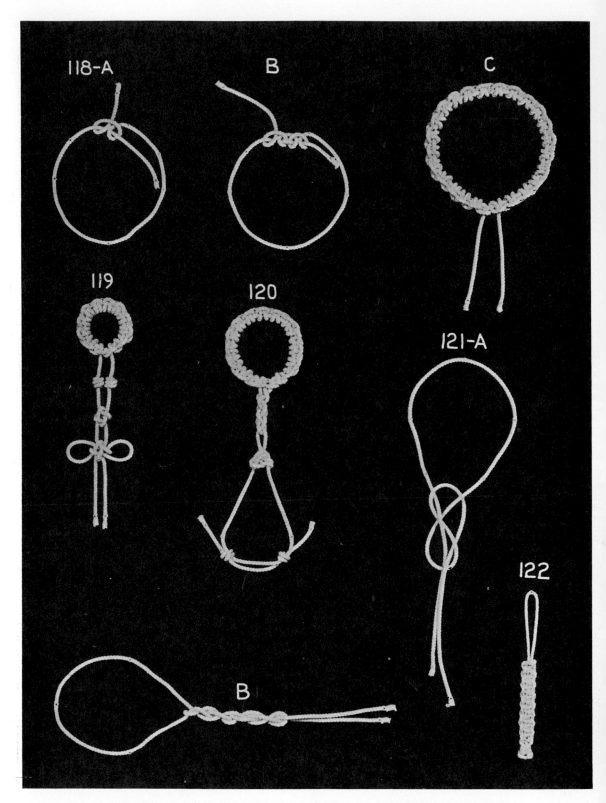

PLATE 192—TATTING, AND A WATCHFOB DESIGN

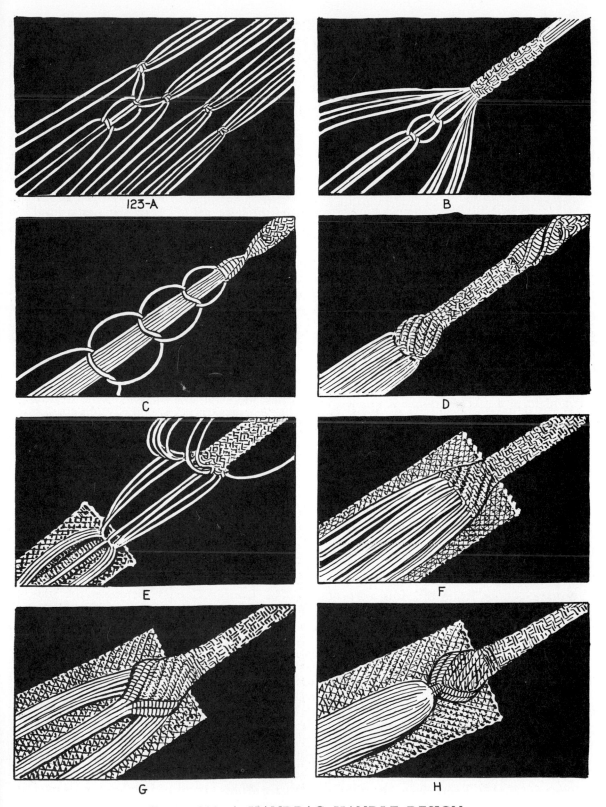

PLATE 193—A HANDBAG HANDLE DESIGN

into groups of four strands each and a Flat is formed about one inch long with each group of four strands. This is followed by again taking the two outside strands from each Flat and forming a Spiral one inch long with the two adjoining strands from the next Flat. When these Spirals have been completed add ten more rows of Square Knots and reverse every other row. In this manner a square is formed with the sixteen strands.

Continue by making four rows of flat Square Knots without connecting the strands on one side (*see* Fig. 123d). Beginning at the left take every other strand and insert it through the fourth row of Square Knots—counting down from the top of the bag—and bring the strand out again through the fifth row as shown in Fig. 123e. After all of the strands have been worked in this manner pull them down taut and form a row of Square Knots with all of the sixteen strands, beginning with the first four strands on the left (*see* Fig. 123f). Follow this step by adding three more rows of Square Knots, at the same time dropping two strands from each side of all three rows.

Proceed by selecting the outside strand on the left side and lead it down towards the right. Form Half Hitches around this strand with each of the seven following strands which will bring the outside strand from the left to the center. Repeat this operation with the next outside strand from the left, making Half Hitches around it with the next six strands. Next, bring the two outside strands on the right side to the center in the same way (*see* Fig. 123g). Make a Flat one-half inch long with the four strands in the center which lead out from the two rows of Half Hitches. Finish the work by inserting the remaining strands through and into the inside of the bag, tie or Half Hitch them and cut the ends off short. Twenty strands are cut eight inches long for the Tassel. The strands from the Flat on the handle of the bag are then tied around the center of the additional strands which are allowed to fall down over the Knot (*see* Fig. 123h).

Plate 194—Miscellaneous Macramé Work

Figs. 124a to c: *A Double Carrick Bend* which is used on the handbag illustrated on Plates 197 and 198, Figs. 126a and b. To start the work count down three rows of Square Knots from the top row of Spirals and then count over thirty-two strands from the left side and insert two double strands one foot long inside the bag. Proceed by forming a Flat between three and four inches long, then count down fifteen rows of Square Knots in the same manner as before and over fourteen strands from the left side and insert two more double strands one foot long, the same as before. Form another Flat with these strands the same length as that already made. Form a Double Carrick Bend with these two Flats. To finish off, tuck the loose strands from the Flats down through the bag one row of Square Knots below and eight strands over to the right of where the Flats were started. Tie them on the inside and cut off the ends.

The Double Carrick Bend on the bottom is formed in the same manner as the one at the top, except that two double strands are inserted four rows up from the row of Spirals at the bottom and then thirty-two strands over from the right side, to form the first Flat. The second Flat is then formed by inserting two double strands fourteen rows up from the bottom row of Spirals and fourteen rows over from the right side. Tuck the loose strands from the Flats through the bag, one row of Square Knots above and eight strands over to the left of where the strands were started. Tie them inside and cut off the ends.

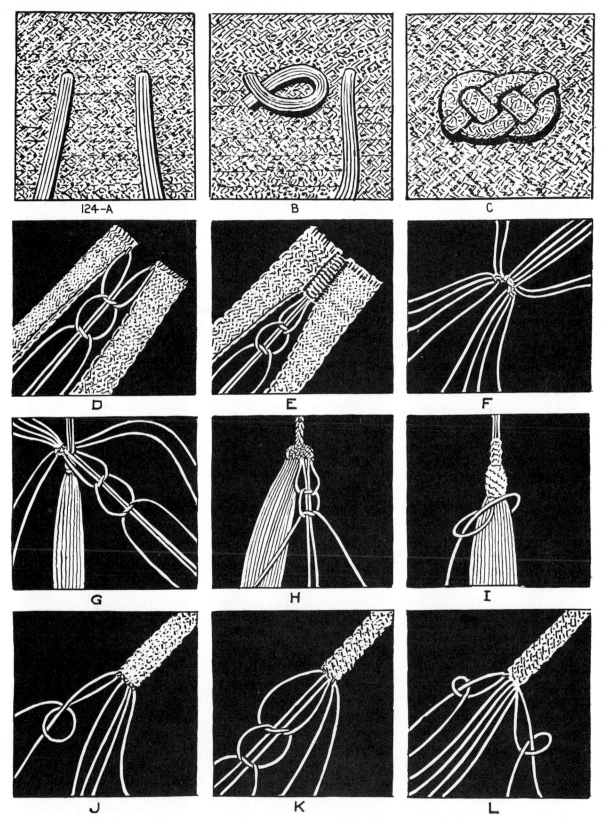

124-A   B   C

D   E   F

G   H   I

J   K   L

PLATE 194—MISCELLANEOUS MACRAMÉ WORK

FIGS. 124D and E: *To Join the Sides of a Handbag Together*. One double strand is inserted in each side of both upper corners of the bag by tucking the strands through the outside strands just below the second row of Flats near the top. Make certain that the outside or working strands are somewhat longer than the two filler strands and then proceed by working a row of Square Knots down the side, inserting the outside or working strands through the outside strand on each side of the bag after every two Square Knots are made (*see* FIG. 124E). Continue to form Square Knots down the side in this manner until the sides of the bag are completely joined.

FIGS. 124F to I: *To Start a Tassel for the Handle of a Handbag*. Cut eight strands about eighteen inches long. Begin in the middle of these strands and form a Square Knot with the four center strands (*see* FIG. 124F). Continue with two Square Knots in the second row by using the four outside strands on each side. All eight strands are then looped around the Flat of the Tassel, which will bring four strands on each side of the Flat (*see* FIG. 124G). Using the four center strands of the eight that were just brought around the Tassel, make a Square Knot; this will join all eight strands around the Flat. Allow the strands from each side to fall down over the Tas-

sel which will then double the number of working strands from eight to sixteen. Proceed by forming five rows of Square Knots around the Tassel (*see* FIG. 124H). One of the outside strands is now selected, with which four Half Hitches are formed around the remaining strands directly below the last row of Square Knots (*see* FIG. 124I). This strand is now brought to the center where a knot is tied with it and one of the center strands from the Tassel, at the same time allowing all of the strands to fall down over the knot. Repeat the same method for the other half of the handle.

FIGS. 124J to L: *Forming Independent Strips of Square Knot and Half Hitch Work* which may be used for the top of a handbag where rings are employed. Three double strands are looped to each ring. A Square Knot is then formed with the four strands on the left. The strip is continued by selecting the outside strand on the right and forming a Half Hitch around this strand with the second strand (*see* FIG. 124L), which is illustrated with eight strands. Begin now on the left and form a Half Hitch around the outside strand with the second strand (*see* FIG. 124J). Continue by forming a Square Knot with the next four strands on the right (*see* FIG. 124K). Repeat this method until the desired number of rows have been made on each ring.

Plates 195 and 196—Steps in Making a Moroccan Handbag

FIGS. 125A to E: *The Moroccan Handbag* represents the modern form of bag construction. The material required to make it is one hundred strands of dreadnaught cord eighty-four inches long. These cords are doubled by looping them in the' middle. The bag is started from the right and half hitched with the left-hand strand, using the same strand all the way across. Continue by hitching back and forth until four rows of Hitches have been formed, as shown at A. Then proceed as before, dropping the two outside strands

on either side, as shown at B. Make four rows of Square Knots all the way across, working them down into five points around which two rows of Half Hitches are formed, as shown at the left at B. FIG. 125C illustrates how the work appears after being continued with additional designing. By counting down and following the pattern from one design to another with each stage of the work, it will be found easy to duplicate this type of handbag. The opposite side is formed in the same manner with the same number of strands. Handbags are

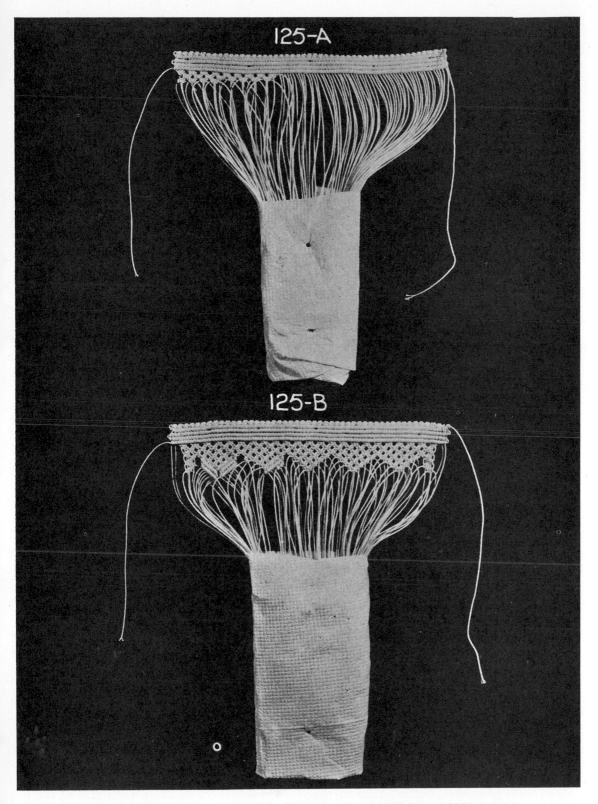

125-A

125-B

PLATE 195—THE INITIAL STEPS IN MAKING HANDBAGS

always made the same length and the same width on both sides so that they may be joined together accurately as illustrated on PLATE 194, FIGS. D and E.

A completed separate handle for a handbag is shown in FIG. 125D. See PLATE 193, FIGS. 123A to H for illustrations and descriptions for attaching the handles. The completed bag is shown in FIG. 125E.

Any similar or still other types of designs can be worked into handbags. They must all be figured out in advance, however, so that the space to allow and the number of strands to be used will fit into the design. After such bags as this are finished they may be lined with any suitable material and this can be attached with zippers for easy removal.

New bags made with dreadnaught cord should be washed and stretched over wooden blocks to dry in the sun. Never use lye or strong chemicals.

Plates 197 and 198—Tahitian and Snug Harbor Handbag Designs

FIG. 126A: *The Tahitian Handbag* is started from the flap. Six strands are cut ten feet long, then doubled and hung over a support. Using the two inside strands for a filler, make a Square Knot with the two outside strands (*see* PLATE 171, FIG. 31A). Next add a double strand on each side below the Square Knot just made (*see* PLATE 171, FIG. 31B). With the inside strand just added and the next or adjoining strands, make a Square Knot on each side. The second row of Square Knots is now completed. After the double strands are added on each side pull the second strand from the outside on either side down. Repeat the same operation after adding each additional double strand. Add double strands on each side in the same manner for the third row, then with these strands make ten additional rows of Square Knots, starting with the third, fourth, fifth and sixth strands for one row, then with the first, second, third and fourth strands for the next row. This forms the complete tongue of the flap.

Add a double strand to each side. They should be a little over nine feet in length. Continue to add double strands on the sides of each succeeding row of Square Knots until there are one hundred strands in all. After sixteen rows of Square Knots have been completed, form a Spiral of six knots with the four center strands, then continue with three rows of Square Knots on each side of the Spiral, at the same time adding a double strand to each side of each row of Square Knots.

Now select the eight center strands and form two Spirals of six knots each for the second row of Spirals and continue with three rows of Square Knots on each side of these Spirals. Proceed by adding another Spiral for every three rows of Square Knots. Two additional strands on each side are picked up for this purpose and then a Spiral is formed with each four strands. Repeat this same method until seven rows of Spirals have been formed. After the seventh row of Spirals has been made, there should be one hundred working strands. Two more rows of Square Knots are added after the Spirals. Proceed by selecting the outside strand on one side, then pass it to the opposite side and form two Half Hitches with each strand all the way across from one side to the other. After the first row of Half Hitches is completed, the second row of Half Hitches is added in the same manner, by selecting the outside strand on the opposite side. Two rows of Square Knots are now added.

Select the eight strands on each side and form three rows of Square Knots, then start with the next four strands and make a row of Spirals of six knots each, and follow this with another row of Square Knots. Spirals are now worked down each side of the bag by starting each time with the ninth, tenth, eleventh, and twelfth strands from each

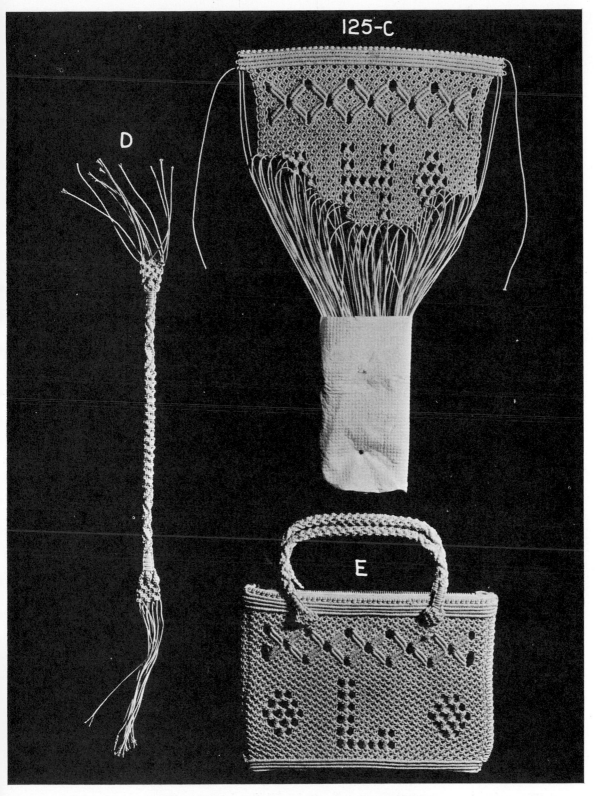

PLATE 196—A MOROCCAN HANDBAG

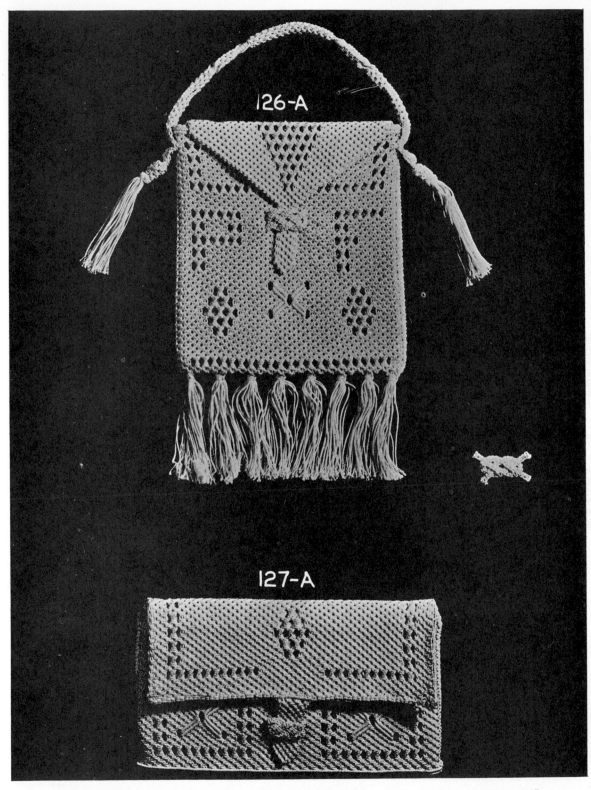

**PLATE 197—FRONT VIEW OF TAHITIAN AND SNUG HARBOR
HANDBAG DESIGNS**

PLATE 198—BACK VIEW OF TAHITIAN AND SNUG HARBOR
HANDBAG DESIGNS

side. Three rows of Square Knots are then worked on each side of these Spirals with a row of Square Knots also worked between each row of Spirals the whole length of the bag. Three rows of Square Knots are formed on each side of every Spiral of six knots all through the bag but this does not include the additional row of Square Knots between each row of Spirals.

After four rows of Square Knots have been formed, counting down from the row of Spirals at the top, count over from the right side and select the twenty-third, twenty-fourth, twenty-fifth, and twenty-sixth strand with which a six-knot Spiral is formed. Continue by forming two Spirals in the next row with two additional strands that are picked up on each side of the strands from the first Spiral, of which each Spiral is formed with six knots with each four strands. The Spiral in the third row is formed with the four middle strands of the eight strands from the two last Spirals. After forming three rows of Square Knots from the Spirals at the top select the four middle strands and form a six-knot Spiral, then continue by making two Spirals of six knots each in the next row. Pick up two additional strands on each side of the strands from the first Spiral for this purpose, after which the knots are formed with each four strands.

Now continue with four more rows of Spirals, one on each side, going two strands further on each side for each row of Spirals. A Flat of three Square Knots is now added between the Spirals of the third row. After the sixth row of Spirals has been completed, two additional Spirals are added on the outside of each Spiral. Continue with six more rows of Spirals, one Spiral on each side and directly underneath the outside Spiral just made. This will make a row of Square Knots between each row of Spirals. After the Spirals have been completed in the last row, two additional Spirals are added on each side towards the middle.

Proceed to make five more rows of Spirals, one on each side, and go two strands toward the middle on each side for each row of Spirals. After the twenty-third row of Square Knots, from the row of Spirals at the top, has been completed, select the four middle strands and form a Spiral of six knots. This is followed by a row of Square Knots and then another Spiral directly underneath the first one. Six additional strands are next picked up on each side of the strands from the last Spiral, and Spirals are formed with each four strands which makes four Spirals of six knots each in this row. Now select the four center strands again, and form another six-knot Spiral. Add another row of Square Knots and another Spiral which is also placed underneath the last Spiral. After fifty-one rows of Square Knots have been completed, counting from the top row of Spirals, select the twenty-third, twenty-fourth, twenty-fifth and twenty-sixth strands from the left and form a Spiral of six knots. Then form two Spirals in the next row by picking up two strands on each side of the strands from the first Spiral making the Spiral with each four strands.

Add another Spiral in the third row underneath the Spiral in the first row. After the last Spiral in the center at the bottom has been completed, form a row of Square Knots across the bag. Next form a row of Spirals across the bag starting with the ninth, tenth, eleventh, and twelfth strands from each side. Two more rows of Square Knots are formed across the bottom of the bag which completes the back side. For instructions as to how to add the Double Carrick Bends (*see* PLATE 194, FIG. 124).

The next step is to cut fifty strands, each seven feet long. These are doubled over a lashing to start the front part of the bag. The strands are paired off in groups of fours and knotting is begun in the usual way. The same design can be used as that described for the back part of the bag and if initials are desired, allowance must be

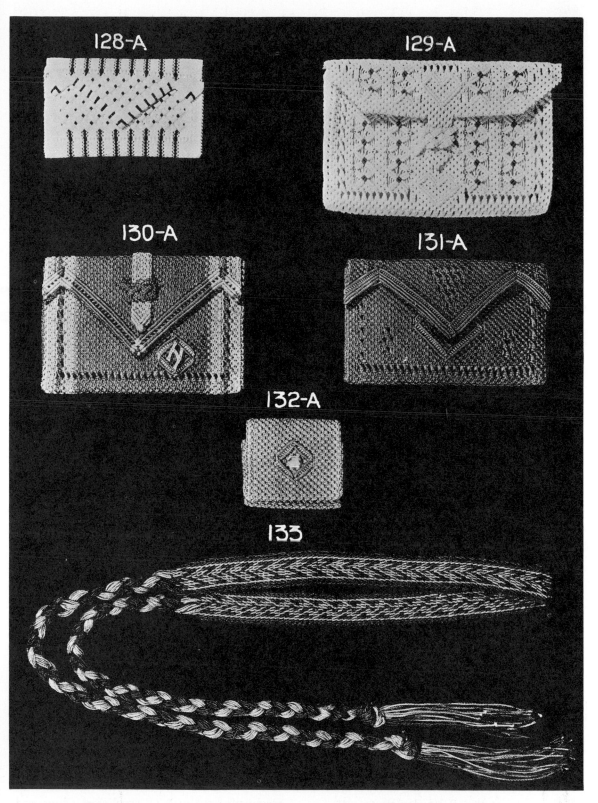

PLATE 199—HANDBAG DESIGNS AND CARD WEAVE BELT

made and figured out, according to the number, size and shape of the letters to be worked into the bag by the use of Spiral Hitching. *See* PLATE 193, FIGS. 123A to H, for instructions on how the handle is formed. *See* PLATE 194, FIGS. 124F to I, for instructions as to how to form the tassels.

To join both sides of the bag at the bottom, separate sixteen strands on each side from both sides of the bag, then start with the outside strand on one side and form five Half Hitches around the remaining strands, directly below the last row of Square Knots (*see* FIG. 124I). Following this proceed by bringing this strand to the center, then form a knot with it and one of the middle strands from the tassel, allow-ing the strands to all fall down over the knot. Separate the remaining strands into groups of twenty-four or twelve from each side of the bag and form five Half Hitches around each group in the manner just described. To complete the handbag cut the tassels and the fringe off to any length desired.

FIG. 127A: *The Snug Harbor Handbag* represents another type of pattern that is also started from the flap. The general method of construction can be followed easily by counting the designs from both the front and the back (*see* FIG. 127B). Lining can be included with this type of bag if desired.

Plate 199—Handbag Designs and Card Weave Belt

FIG. 128A: *A Beautiful Handbag Lined with Silk.* The design presents an interesting suggestion for the experienced Square Knotter.

FIG. 129A: *An Up-to-Date Handbag Design* that can be duplicated with but little effort on the part of an experienced knotter.

FIG. 130A: *A Design for a Novel Handbag* that involves the interweaving of an initial in the pattern.

FIG. 131A: *Another Handbag Design* similar to that in FIG. 130A.

FIG. 132A: *A Folding Cigarette Case* is shown in this illustration. Such a case may be made in a wide number of designs and patterns, depending upon the ingenuity of the knotter.

FIG. 133: *An Egyptian Card Weave Belt* which may be used for a bath robe cord. The ends are braided down as for an ordinary Round Sennit.

Plate 200—Miscellaneous Handbag Designs

FIG. 128B: *The Same Handbag* as that shown on PLATE 199, FIG. 128A, but with the flap open. This bag has the same design on both sides.

FIG. 129B: *The Back View of the Handbag* described and illustrated on PLATE 199, FIG. 129A.

FIG. 130B: *A Back View of the Hand-bag* illustrated and described on PLATE 199, FIG. 130A.

FIG. 131B: *The Back View of the Same Handbag* illustrated and described on PLATE 199, FIG. 131A.

FIG. 132B: *The Cigarette Case* shown open in this illustration is the same case illustrated on PLATE 199, FIG. 132A.

Plate 201—A Handbag and a Mat

FIG. 134: *The Handbag* shown in this illustration is made in one piece and has a blue satin lining. A close study of the pat-tern will show that the type of open work is simple and easy to duplicate. The other designs are made in much the same man-

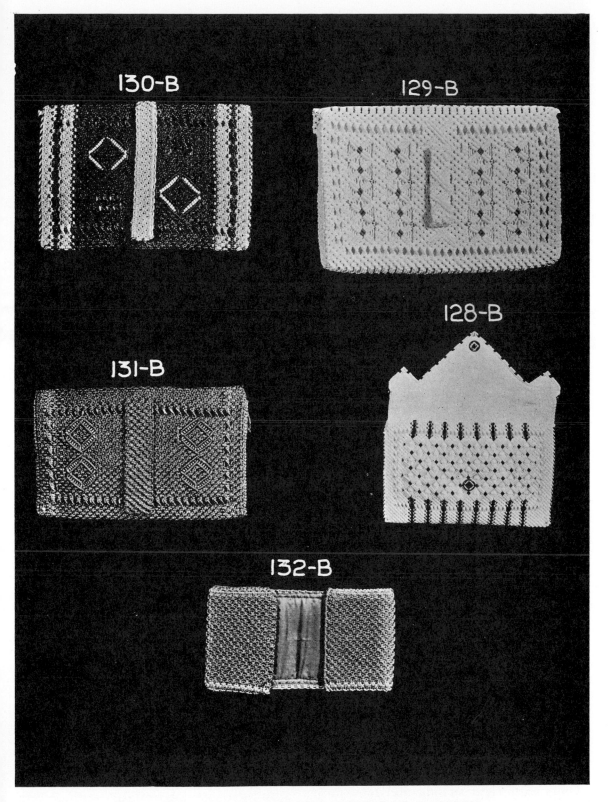

PLATE 200—MISCELLANEOUS HANDBAG DESIGNS

ner as employed in any handbag work.

FIG. 135: *A Square Knotted Mat.* These mats are made in the same manner as Square Knotted belts. Any number of strands may be used up to one hundred or more, depending upon the size of the mat. The ends are finished off with the usual forms of Macramé Half Hitches.

Plate 202—A Handbag and Half Hitch Work

FIG. 136: *The Tunisian Handbag* is made with one hundred and twelve strands. These are cut six and one-half feet long. Fourteen rings are used for each side of the bag loop, with four double strands on each ring. Make Square Knots with each group of four strands. After the first row of Square Knots has been completed, select the outside strand on each side and form a Half Hitch around the first strand with the second strand. Next, with the four center strands, make a Square Knot. Make the third row the same as the first row, and the fourth row the same as the second row. Using this same method make twelve rows of Square Knots on each ring. Both sides of the bag are now the same and the strands from each ring are ready to be joined.

Starting with the strands on the ring at the left select two strands on the right of this ring and form a Square Knot with these two strands and the two adjoining strands on the second ring. Continue this method all the way around the bag, using the next four strands each time, which will join the strands from each ring. Proceed by making another row of Square Knots the same as before. Next, form a row of Spirals of six knots each all the way around the bag, and select the eight center strands on each side of the bag and form two Spirals of six knots each. Using the next eight strands on each side of these Spirals, make three rows of Square Knots, then form two Spirals of six knots each. Continue around the bag by making three rows of Square Knots with eight strands, and then form two Spirals of six knots each with the next eight strands. Three complete rows of Square Knots are next made around the bag.

Proceed by again selecting the eight center strands on each side of the bag and with these eight strands form two six-knot Spirals of four strands each. Continue by forming three rows of Square Knots with the next eight strands on each side of these Spirals, then select the next eight strands on each side of the Square Knots and form two Spirals of six knots each. Repeat this same method all the way around the bag, by first making three rows of Square Knots with eight strands followed by two Spirals of six knots each with the next eight strands. Add two additional rows of Square Knots around the bag. Continue by forming three rows of Square Knots with the twenty center strands on each side of the bag, and proceed by adding ten Spirals of six knots each with the next thirty strands on each side of the Square Knots that were formed previously, after which continue by adding three rows of Square Knots with the remaining strands. Again form three more rows of Square Knots with the twenty center strands on each side of the bag and repeat with ten more Spirals of six knots each with the next thirty strands on each side of the Square Knots. Now add three more rows of Square Knots with the remaining strands the same as before.

Continue by forming a row of Square Knots with the sixty-four center strands on each side of the bag. Again form four Spirals of six knots each with the sixteen strands on each side of these Square Knots. Add three additional rows of Square Knots with the remaining strands. Continue with nine rows of Square Knots with the twelve center strands on each side of the bag, then

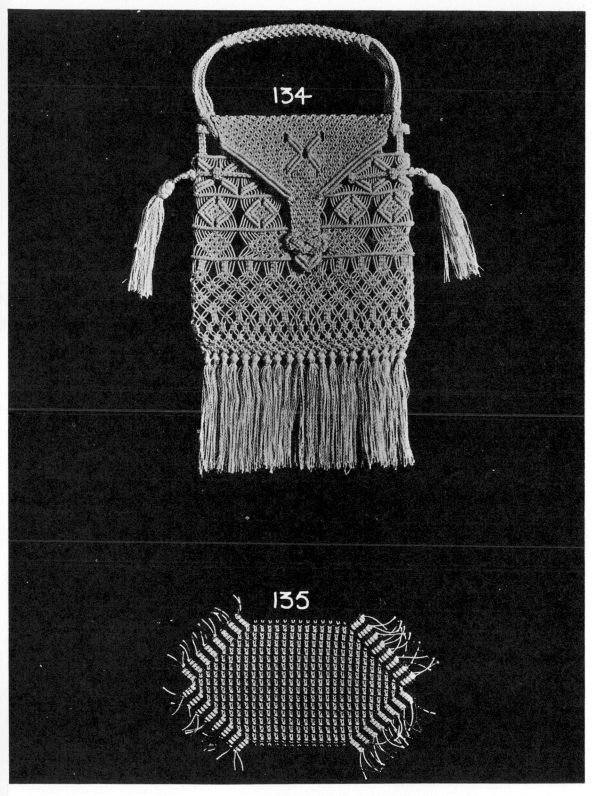

PLATE 201—A HANDBAG AND A MAT

form a Flat three inches long with the next four strands on each side of the Square Knots just referred to. Now form two rows of Square Knots with the next twenty-two strands on each side of the Flats that were just made.

Starting with the strands on the outside of each Flat, make one row of Square Knots with the remaining strands, then with the first twenty-two strands on each side of these Flats form three rows of Square Knots. Continue by forming four Spirals of six knots each with the next sixteen strands on each side of the Square Knots. Add three rows of Square Knots with the remaining strands. Begin once more with the strands on the outside of each of the Flats and form a row of Square Knots with the remaining strands. Again start the same as before with the strands on the outside of each Flat, by selecting the first twenty-two strands on each side and forming two rows of Square Knots. Proceed with four Spirals of six knots each with the next sixteen strands on each side of the Square Knots. Continue by forming a Double Carrick Bend with the two Flats on each side of the bag (*see* PLATE 194, FIGS. 124A, B, and C).

The strands from the Double Carrick Bend are worked into the bag again on the next or following row of Square Knots. Now continue by forming a row of Square Knots with the sixty-four center strands on each side of the bag which also includes the strands from the Double Carrick Bend. Add three additional rows of Square Knots with the twenty center strands on each side of the bag, then add ten Spirals of six knots each with the next thirty strands on each side of the Square Knots that were just made. Three rows of Square Knots are now added with the remaining strands. These are followed with a row of Square Knots all around the bag. Again add three more rows of Square Knots with the twenty strands on each side of the bag, then form ten Spirals of six knots each with the next

thirty strands on each side of the Square Knots that were just made. This is followed with another row of Square Knots all around the bag. Three additional rows of Square Knots are now formed with the twenty center strands on each side of the bag. A row of Spirals of six knots each is now added around the bag with the remaining strands. Continue by adding three more rows of Square Knots around the bag.

Form a Spiral of six knots with the four center strands on each side of the bag and form three rows of Square Knots with the next twenty-four strands on each side of the Spirals that were just made. Continue by forming a Spiral of six knots with the next four strands on each side of the Square Knots. Add two Spirals of six knots each with the eight center strands on each side of the bag and then form three rows of Square Knots with the next twenty strands on each side of the Spirals that were just made. These are followed by two Spirals of six knots each, with the next eight strands on each side of the Square Knots. Continue by adding three rows of Square Knots with the next twenty strands on each side of the Spirals, then form two Spirals of six knots each with the next eight strands on each side of the Square Knots. A Spiral of six knots is next added with the four center strands on each side of the bag and then two more Spirals are formed with the two strands from each of the two Spirals that were just made, and then the bag is continued with seven rows of Square Knots which are formed with the twelve strands on each side of the Spirals that were just made.

Two strands are dropped from each side of each succeeding row and the strands from the Spirals are picked up in the fourth row. Next turn the bag out with the strands passing out through the bottom. Form a Turk's Head around each set of strands under the last row of Square Knots at the bottom. After forming the tassels with the Turk's Heads, cut the

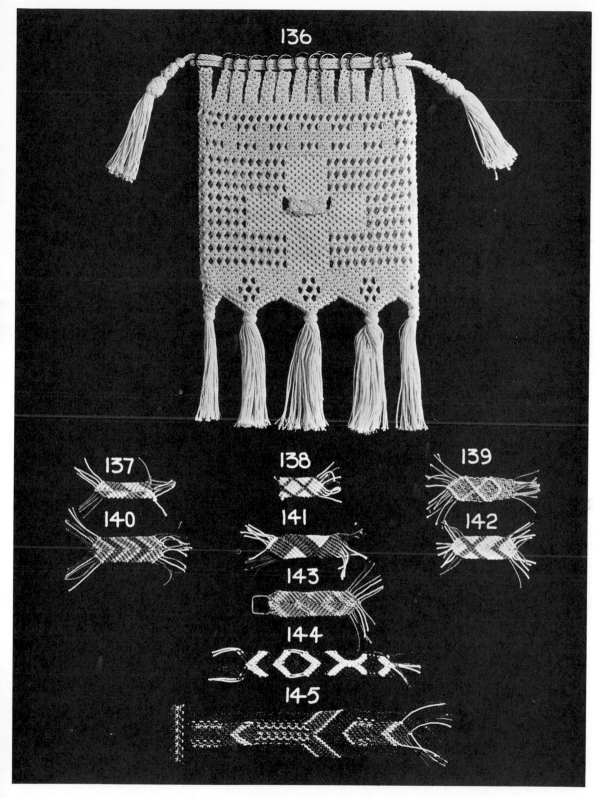

PLATE 202—A HANDBAG AND HALF HITCH WORK

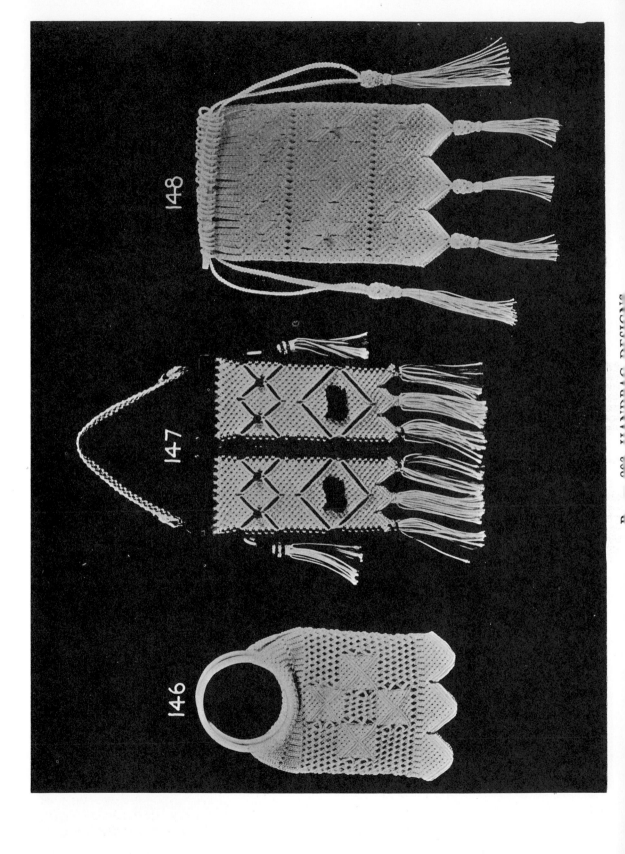

strands off to the desired length to complete the bag.

There are several ways in which to make the draw-cords but the Flat method is the simplest. Nine strands are cut three feet long for each draw-cord. Secure them to a lashing and proceed by forming a Nine-strand Flat or English Sennit with each set of nine strands which are both made the same length. After completing the draw-cords, pass one of them through all the rings, bringing it back to the same side from which it started. Repeat the same thing with the other draw-cord, by passing it through the rings from the opposite side. These draw-cords may be joined at each end with a Turk's Head or by Half Hitches which are formed with one of the strands (*see* PLATE 194, FIG. 1241). Square Knots can also be made around the body of the remaining strands with the two outside strands.

To make a Cable Laid Draw-Cord, cut nine strands twelve feet long and secure them to a support. Holding each set of three strands, twist them together toward the right until they are laid up together. Repeat this with the other two sets of three strands. Then twist the three sets together toward the left until the Sennit is completed. In other words, lay them up like a cable-laid rope, which consists of three right-handed, hawser laid three-strand ropes laid up together left-handed. The finished draw-cord is passed through the rings and the ends are joined in the same way as for the Flat method.

FIGS. 137 to 145: *Additional Patterns of Wampum Belts* are shown in different designs and color combinations.

Plate 203—Handbag Designs

FIG. 146: *Another Form of Handbag* in which the handles are made of celluloid rings. These various types and designs of handbags are presented for the purpose of broadening and adding to the knowledge of the advanced student of Square Knotting. They exemplify that with but a minimum of effort and a little initiative many kinds, types and varieties of bags may be made and that in them may be incorporated any number of interesting and beautiful designs.

FIG. 147: *The Bag Shown* in this illustration was made with No. 1 Cordonnet and is constructed on the typical handbag frame.

FIG. 148: *Another Handbag of Unusual Design.* It will further serve to illustrate that these bags can be made up in different sizes, designs and colors to suit the individual. In such bags as these about one hundred to one hundred and ten strands are required, about eight feet in length depending of course upon the size of the bag and the type of design. Cords of contrasting colors may be used if desired.

Plate 204—Handbag Designs

FIG. 149: *A Miniature Handbag* of unique design and striking appearance is shown in this illustration. It may be made with rug cord or any other suitable material of small size.

FIG. 150: *Another Form of Handbag* of somewhat picturesque design using a pair of rings as handles.

FIG. 151: *Another Suggestion in Handbag Making* in which the same type of weaving is employed as that used on PLATE 257, FIG. 164. This bag has a silk lining.

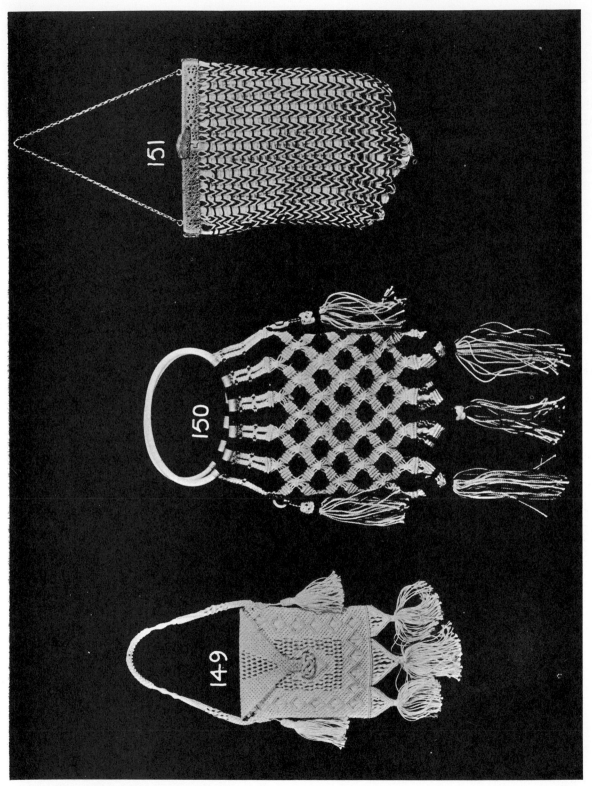

PLATE 204—HANDBAG DESIGNS

Plate 205—An Algerian Handbag Design

The Algerian Handbag requires 120 strands of No. 1 D.M.C. Cordonnet, nine feet long, and twelve pearl rings, one inch in diameter. To start the bag middle ten strands and loop them around each ring, which will then make twenty strands four-and-one-half feet long. Make two rows of Square Knots next to each ring. Tie six more Square Knots in a row followed by a row of Square Knots across. Next tie twenty-five Square Knots with each four outside strands and then with the twelve center strands tie five Square Knots. Continue by tying twenty-five Square Knots with each four ends of the eight center strands, then form the first Double Carrick Bend, which is secured with a Square Knot. Repeat the same method for the second row. Now divide the strands into groups of twenty strands each and tie Points. Next form three rows of Half Hitches, which are worked down to a point and then fill in between them with Square Knots.

The bag is now divided into four equal parts and worked down to a point with Granny Knot Spirals. Six knots are included in each Spiral. At the same time allowance is made for a diamond on the Square Knots which are in the center. Form another Carrick Bend in the diamond as before and then fill in between the point with Square Knots, allowing for a Double Carrick Bend in the upper part of the point. Next divide in equal parts of twenty strands to the point, then fill in with Square Knots. Now divide the strands into five equal parts and work each part down to a point with one row of Half Hitches to a point.

To make the bottom part of the bag, divide into five parts by counting nine Square Knots from the top of the Half Hitching to the bottom, and continue by working a row of Double Half Hitches on each side of the five parts. Turn the bag inside out and join it on the inside, leaving sixteen strands come through the center at the bottom for a tassel.

Plate 206—Pillow Top Handbag Designs

FIG. 152: *A Handbag* in which the pattern is formed in the same manner as is employed in making pillow tops. That is, the design is worked out by attaching the cords to a frame while the pattern is formed from the back of the frame. After the Clove Hitches have been made the squares are left intact instead of being cut to form clusters. The work is then folded over and sewed together on each side with the lining included. This may be any suitable material. A zipper is then attached along the top of the lining for opening and closing the bag while a tassel is put on the end of the two strands which are attached to and left hanging down from the upper left side.

Any combination of colors may be used of about the same quality as No. 3 Silkine Pearl Cotton.

FIG. 153: *Another Form of Handbag Design* which is constructed on a frame the same as a pillow top. The bottom is worked down to a point with the strands left hanging down to give a fluffy effect, after which they are cut off evenly. The bag is sewn together on the sides and along the bottom with the lining included. A drawstring made of two parts of heavy cord is attached around the top with tassels placed on the ends. The same kinds of materials as are used in pillow tops may be used for this type of work.

PLATE 205—AN ALGERIAN HANDBAG DESIGN

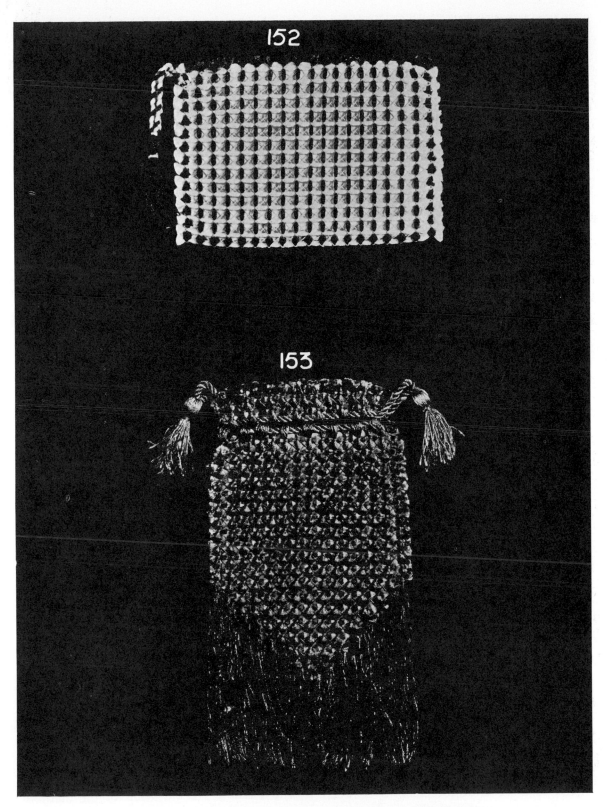

PLATE 206—PILLOW TOP HANDBAG DESIGNS

Plate 207—Miscellaneous Designs

FIG. 154: *A Mat That May be Made into a Cushion* is shown in the accompanying illustration. Like other work of this kind it too is made on a frame. Heavy woolen cord is used and the clusters are left in rounded ball-like shapes. Many different color combinations may be used with a variety of designs.

FIG. 155: *A Dog Collar with a Ring* is made with Square Knots. After having mastered the art of Square Knot work, the student can easily duplicate such designs.

FIG. 156: *A Napkin Ring* of interesting design is presented in this illustration. It is made of Square Knots with the letter H worked in the center with Half Hitches. It also affords an easy pattern for duplication.

Plates 208 and 209—Steps in Making a Center-Piece Design

FIG. 157A: *A Square Knot Center-Piece* such as that illustrated may be started with any number of strands from twenty to thirty-six. The first step is to measure and cut the strands about six times the estimated length of the center-piece, measuring from the center to the edge. Double each of the strands in the middle and loop them around the ring of cord which forms the center. This ring should be about one-half inch in diameter.

Separate the strands into groups of four and tie Square Knots all around the ring, as illustrated in FIG. A. These knots should be drawn up very snug before proceeding with the second row. The latter should be spaced about one-sixteenth of an inch from the first row. Continue tying Square Knots, spacing the third row about one-eighth inch from the previous row. The next row is spaced about one-quarter of an inch from the last row. Each of the succeeding rows should be spaced about three-eighths of an inch apart. Continue knotting until there are seven rows of Square Knots around the center. The eighth row, spaced three-eighths of an inch from the last row, is a row in which Flats are made of the seven Square Knots, using four strands all the way around. When this row is completed insert two double strands between each Flat and continue the Square Knot open work. The first row of knots should be spaced about three-eighths of an inch from the row of Flats. Continue this method and the same spacing until four additional rows of Square Knots have been made. The second row of Flats is then added, spacing the row of Flats about three-eighths of an inch away from the last row of knots.

Next insert two more double strands between each Flat, with which additional Flats are formed, after which follow the same method as described. Each row of Flats is then added until the center-piece reaches the desired width. After the last row of Flats has been made one row of Square Knots is tied around the center-piece and these should be spaced about three-eighths of an inch from the last row of knots. Tie the last row of Square Knots with eight strands instead of four. This is done by selecting four strands for the filler and, using the two strands on either side, form a Square Knot in the same manner as is used in tying a Single Knot. Cut the strands off to any desired length to complete the center-piece.

This is the orthodox method of making a center-piece. However, there are many styles, patterns and designs which can be worked out to suit the individual taste.

FIG. 157B: *Another Center-Piece Design* which is a slight variation of the method just described. It can be duplicated easily by a little study of the design.

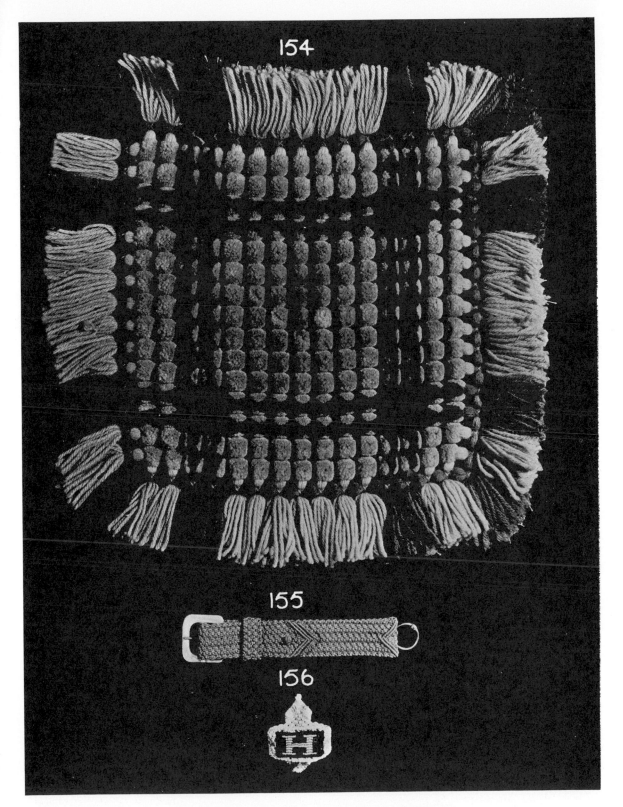

PLATE 207—MISCELLANEOUS DESIGNS

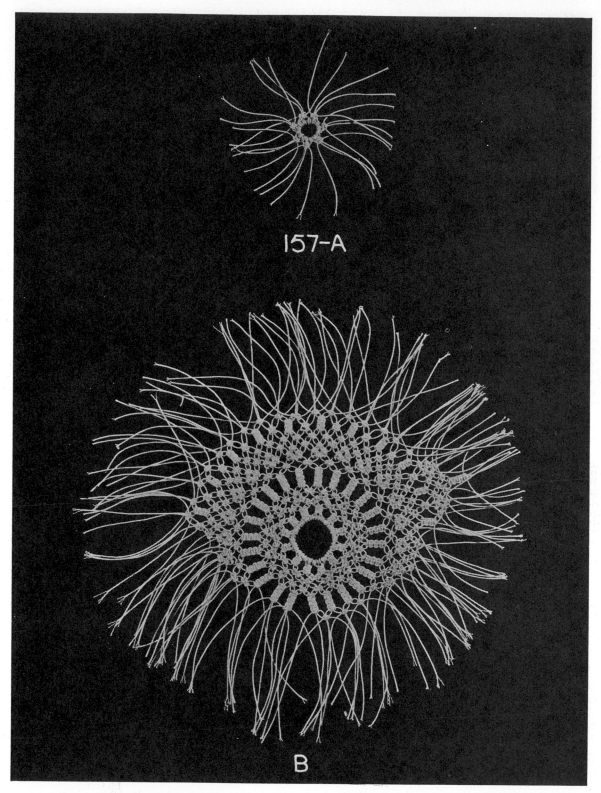

157-A

B

PLATE 208—THE INITIAL STEPS IN MAKING A CENTER-PIECE

157-C

PLATE 209—FINISHED CENTER-PIECE DESIGN

Fig. 157c: *A Finished Center-Piece* of still another style is shown in this illustration. It may be noticed that there are four rows of Flats and that three different rows of open work are used in this design.

The first rows of Flats have three complete Square Knots, the next row has four and the last row has three.

Plate 210—Shade Pull and Leather Work

Figs. 158a, b, c, and d: *A Shade Pull of Ornamental Design* made with Square Knots. It may be made in any length, size or color and with any pattern or design. One ball of dreadnaught cord will make ten shade pulls complete with tassels. The design is made up entirely of Square Knots and Spirals or Granny Knots, all of which have been explained previously.

A hook is required to hold the core or filler cords such as is used in making belts. For the filler cords use two lengths about two yards in length. Double these cords and hang them on the hook, making them fast to the hook. Next take a cord about three yards long and tie the center of it around the filler cord at a point about ten inches from the hook, as shown at A. Continue with a series of about ten Square Knots and then follow with about thirty Spiral or Granny Knots, as shown at B. Add ten more square knots and finish off by tying all of the cords into an Overhand Knot, which is pulled up into a ball-like shape to be used in forming the tassel (shown at c).

To form the tassel cut about thirty pieces of cord into lengths of six or seven inches and group them around the last knot. Place these cords so that about two-thirds of their length is above the base knot with one-third below. Tie another cord around the tassel cords just above the base knot, and then pull the tassel cords down over the base knot, taking care to arrange them symmetrically. Proceed by tying the tassel cords all together just below the base knot, using still another cord in the form of a Whipping. Trim the ends of the tassel evenly to finish.

Fig. 159: *A French Whip* made with tapered leather braids somewhat similar to Plate 211, Fig. 165, is shown in this illustration. This style of whip is an outstanding example of the French leather worker's art of a bygone day. Whips such as this were very popular among the sheiks and other horsemen of the French North-African colonies.

Fig. 160: *A Five-Strand Braided Leather Belt.* The leather is stripped and then braided into a Five-Strand Flat Sennit, with the end sewed to the buckle with an additional piece of material.

Fig. 161: *Another Example of a Braided Leather Belt.* It is made with Four-Strand Round Sennit.

Plate 211—Leather Belt and False Braids

Figs. 162a, b, and c: *An Example of Leather Belt Making* using a method which might be called False Braiding. To make such a belt take a piece of leather and cut holes in it at intervals as shown at A. Wet the leather to make it soft and pliable and then pull each part of the strap in alternate order through the slots as illustrated at B. The finished braid is shown at c.

Fig. 163: *Another Illustration of False Braiding* in which three parts of leather are joined in the manner indicated.

Fig. 164: *A Type of False Braiding of Four Parts* is shown in this illustration. The holes are cut as each stage of the work progresses.

Fig. 165: *Another Method of Braiding Leather* is shown in the accompanying

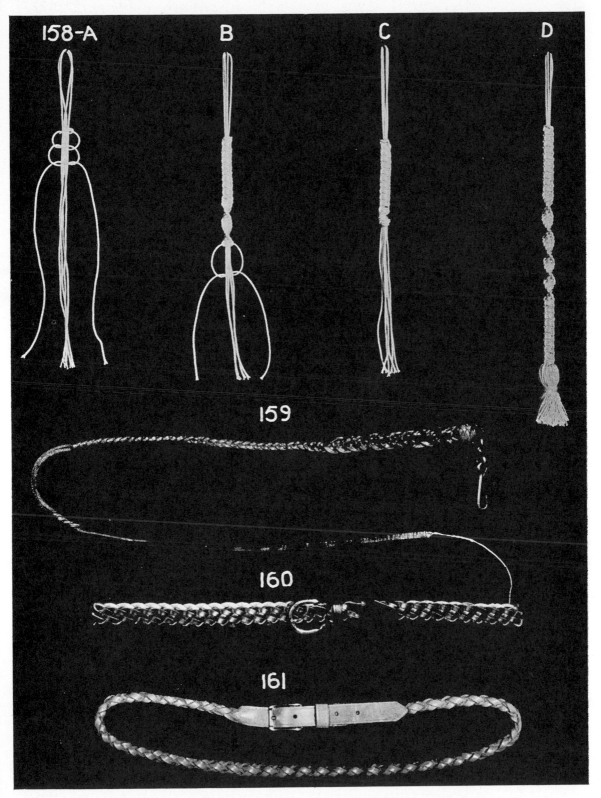

PLATE 210—SHADE PULL AND LEATHER WORK

illustration. This is a tapered leather braid which is reduced from four parts to three and then to two by the simple expe-dient of dropping a strand at intervals.

This form of braiding may be used in making quirts.

Plate 212—A Braided Leather Camera Case

FIGS. 166A to H: *A Leather Plaited Camera Case for a No. 1 Kodak* is shown in the various steps of construction in these views. The materials required include one piece of four-ounce strap leather and one piece of light-weight suède, about five inches wide by twenty-four inches long. These will make up the outside and the lining as well. Two pieces of six-ounce strap leather with two pieces of suède, 2½ by 8 inches make up the sides. Light leather thongs four feet long are used for the lacing. The shoulder strap is made from two pieces of strap leather, ½ inch wide and 30 inches long. One nickel-plated buckle, ½ inch wide, is also required for the shoulder strap. In addition, for the purpose of attaching the shoulder strap to the sides of the case, two ⅝-inch D's are needed. The list of materials is completed with a nickel-plated snap fastener, and a tube of house-hold or leather cement.

To start the case measure and mark off the width of the piece of leather for the outside. This should be done on a line one inch from the end of the leather. Draw the lines into 26 parts of equal size, then cut the piece of leather into 26 narrow thongs or strips, which are held together by the one-inch piece left on the end. Separate the thongs into pairs and braid each pair under one and over one, in the same manner as making a Thirteen-Strand Double Flat or English Sennit (*see* FIG. 166A). Be sure to space each pair of thongs an equal distance apart while braiding them.

A border line can be tooled on the uncut one-inch end after it has been softened by moistening with water. Or, monograms and initials may be used if desired. This work is done with a small pointed tool as shown in FIG. 166B. Continue by cement-ing a piece of the suède lining to the uncut end of the braided leather, as at FIG. 166C.

The side pieces are made with their corners rounded and trimmed to the correct size. Lacing holes are punched in the side pieces, one inch apart, and the D's are attached with short straps and are affixed to the sides of the case with small rivets. The placement of the D's and the manner of attaching them is shown in FIG. 166F.

The suède lining is then cemented in place with one end of the lacing thong cemented under the lining, between the lining and the side piece. The braided sections are then laced to the sides, by passing the lacing thong around the inside thong of the outside pair of braided straps nearest to each hole (*see* FIG. 166D). When the last hole is being laced pass the thong through the plaited work so that it will not be visible after the suède lining is applied (*see* FIG. 166E). As the lacing progresses the lining is cemented down on the outside piece of the braided part. A piece of suède is next folded over and cemented in place over the ends of the braided straps. To insure that it is securely held in place until the cement dries the suède piece should be held down with a clamp. The snap fastener is attached with a pair of pliers to complete the case, as at FIG. 166F.

Holes for the buckle are then punched in the ends of the shoulder strap. The strap is then cut into three strips of equal width, allowing three inches on the end for attaching the strap to the case. The thongs are then braided down a short distance and the end of the strap is passed through the braiding to remove the tangles incident to the braiding operation. This is continued until the strap is complete (*see* FIG. 166G.) The completed case is shown in FIG. 166H.

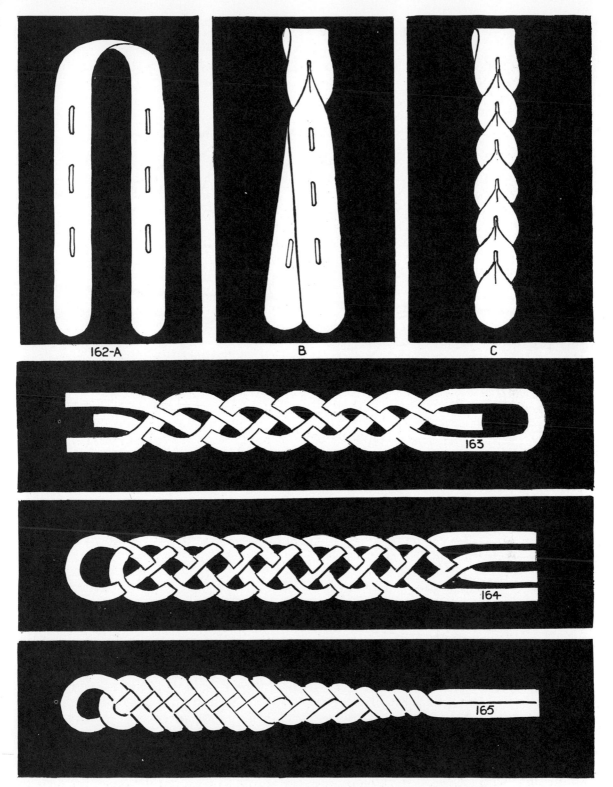

162-A B C

163

164

165

PLATE 211—LEATHER BELTS AND FALSE BRAIDS

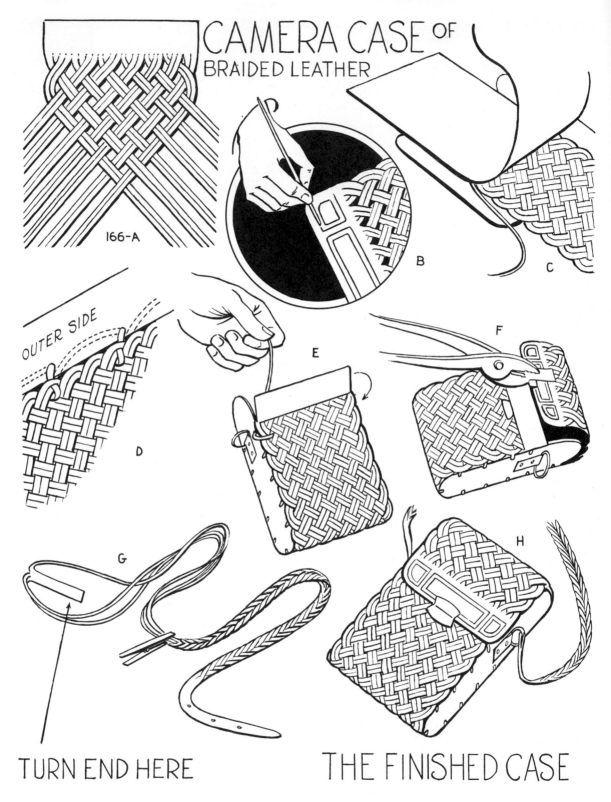

CAMERA CASE OF BRAIDED LEATHER

166-A

B

C

OUTER SIDE

D

E

F

G

H

TURN END HERE

THE FINISHED CASE

PLATE 212—A BRAIDED LEATHER CAMERA CASE

[*Plate 213*]   Macramé Tatting, Fringe, Needle-Work   399

Plate 213—A Square Knot Cord Camera Case

FIGS. 167A to H: *A Square Knot Case for a Vest Pocket Size Camera.* The materials required include one outline cord two feet long, of any color, and twenty-two working cords of the same color about twelve feet long. Two glass push pins and a hook to be fastened around the waist for holding the filler cords are also needed.

To start the work double two parts of cord and loop them to the middle of the outline cord, then make a Square Knot by using the two inside cords for the filler and the two outside cords to form the knot. Next, secure the work to a table with a push pin to hold it in a convenient working position. The outline cord will then hang down in an inverted V-shape, which will serve to form the shape of the flap. To add other working cords to each side simply loop each additional cord over the outline cord, as shown in FIG. 167A. Then for each additional row of Square Knots across the flap it is necessary to add another working cord to each side.

After all of the working cords have been added then proceed to make thirty-five rows of Square Knots, at the same time double looping the outside working cords over the outline cord in every other row. This will form an even edge along the strip. Next, add four double cords ten feet long and of any contrasting color to each side of the outline cord as shown at FIG. 167B. Proceed by knotting the enlarged strip, making thirty-five rows of Square Knots, after which the outline cord is returned to its original position in the strip.

Continue by forming eight rows of Square Knots in the middle or the breadth of the original strip. This forms the bottom of the case which should be measured over the camera to determine the correct size. The outline cord is then returned to the outside on either side of the strip and the knotting is continued with the additional contrasting cords. After nine rows of Square Knots have been made proceed by dropping a knot on each side in the center while making each row. This is done to form an inverted V. Next, knot the middle of a three foot cord of contrasting color to the two middle strands (*see* FIG. 167C). Bring these additional cords down the inverted V on either side by making Hitches around the working strands (*see* FIG. 167D). This forms the pattern for the front of the case. Square Knotting is then continued in the center and at the sides until a heart-shaped design is outlined with the cords of the contrasting color. The ends of these are knotted together at the back of the case and secured with cement (*see* FIG. 167E).

Square Knotting is again resumed until the body of the case is finished, which ordinarily is about thirteen and one-half inches, depending of course upon the size of the camera. To finish the strip bring the outline cords to the middle and make Hitches around them with the working cords on both sides. The knots are then cemented and the ends cut short. FIG. 167F shows the completed strip.

A length of cord is then threaded into a sail or darning needle and the sides of the case are sewed together in the manner illustrated in FIG. 167G. The snap fastener is then added to complete the case.

Two lengths of cord are used to make the shoulder-strap, if one is desired. One of these should be about thirty feet in length and the other nine feet long. Run both of these cords through one side of the case at the top. The shorter of the two cords is used as a filler and the longer cord is used to form the Square Knots. After forming several feet of knot work—the length of the strap to be made to suit the individual—the ends of the cords are then attached to the opposite side of the case, where they are tied securely and the ends cut short. The finished case is shown in FIG. 167H, without the shoulder-strap.

SQUARE KNOT CORD
CAMERA CASE

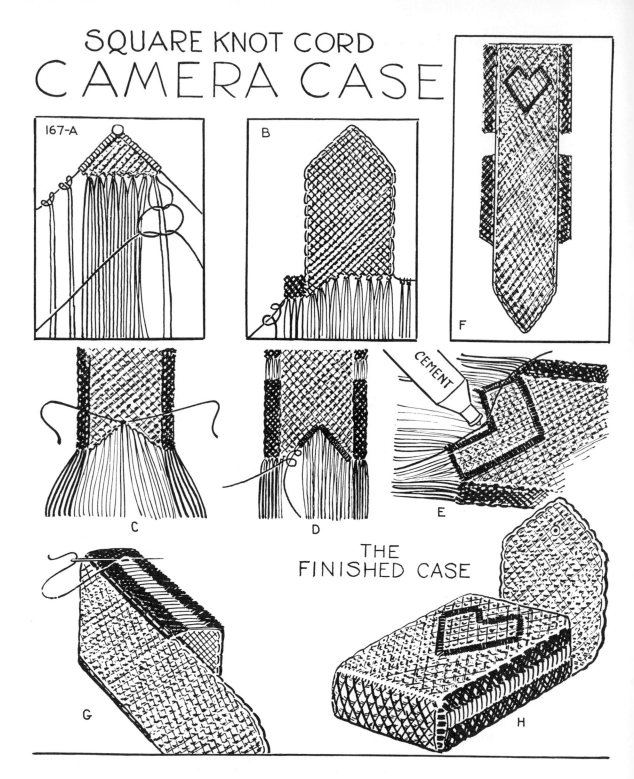

167-A

B

F

C

D

E

CEMENT

THE
FINISHED CASE

G

H

PLATE 213—A SQUARE KNOT CORD CAMERA CASE

Plate 214—A Knotted Cord Key Case

Figs. 168a to f: *A Key Case Made with Square Knots.* The materials required include one tan cord, three feet long, and twenty-three blue cords, five feet long or, any color combination may be used with the same number of cords. A snap **fastener** set and a swivel key plate with six hooks attached are also needed.

To start the case select one of the long blue cords and secure it to two screw-eyes in the manner shown in Fig. 168a. These screw-eyes are set seven inches apart and the blue cord is so attached that its center is three and one-half inches from the eyes. Next, take the twenty-two blue cords and form two rows of Square Knots with them on the blue cord attached to the eyes. After completing the first two rows of knots make another row of Square Knots in the third row, which is followed by pulling the top half of the second Square Knot up taut. Then pass the tan cord through as shown at Fig. 168b before pulling the bottom half of the Square Knot up taut. This method is continued with all of the blue cords, across the entire row, except that the last knot remains the same as the first (*see* Fig. 168c). The tan cord is then worked into each knot in each successive row, under the second and twenty-first Knots of the first row. This will form a border around the edge of the case.

Secure the work to the edge of a table with push pins and thus allow the filler cord to hang down on either side. It is then included in the work by forming a Double Half Hitch around it on each side with the outside cord on every other row (*see* Fig. 168d). Continue knotting until the work is three inches long and then bring the ends of the cords back to the middle. They should then be crossed inside an Open Knot with a drop of cement added before the knot is pulled taut. The ends are then cut short from the back.

Next, add several additional rows of Square Knots and bring the filler cords around from the sides and form Half Hitches over them with the other cords. Pull these Hitches up tight and add a little cement after which cut the ends off short.

The snap fastener is secured in place by setting a piece of wood over the spring and tapping the wood with a hammer until the post of the fastener and the spring are joined. A larger hole is then used to secure the top part. The rivets for the key plate and posts are inserted between the open diamond spaces of the Square Knots by placing them over the end of a nail set and tapping them into place with a hammer. Fig. 168e shows the completed case while Fig. 168f shows the case with the key plate attached.

Plate 215—Miscellaneous Fringe Knots

Fig. 169:   *This Diamond Fringe Design* is made up of a series of interlocked Overhand Knots. The cords are pulled through the material, and starting from the left of the illustration, are spaced as follows: Between the first two cords, ¼-inch, between the second and third cords, ¾-inch, between the next six cords, ¼-inch, which is followed by a space of ¾-inch, after which the same spacing may be continued for the remainder of the design. The manner in which the knots are tied is shown clearly in the pattern.

Fig. 170:   *This Flat Knot Diamond Fringe Design* is made by using Flat Knots as shown on Plate 168, Fig. 1, in groups of two. The cords are spaced as follows: Between the first two cords from the left, ¼-inch, between the second and third cords, ⅜-inch, then allow ¼-inch between the next two cords, to be followed by seven spaces of ¼-inch and then ¾-inch once,

A KEY CASE of KNOTTED CORD

168-A

B

C

D

E

F

KEY PLATE AND
HOOKS INSERTED

PLATE 214—A KNOTTED CORD KEY CASE

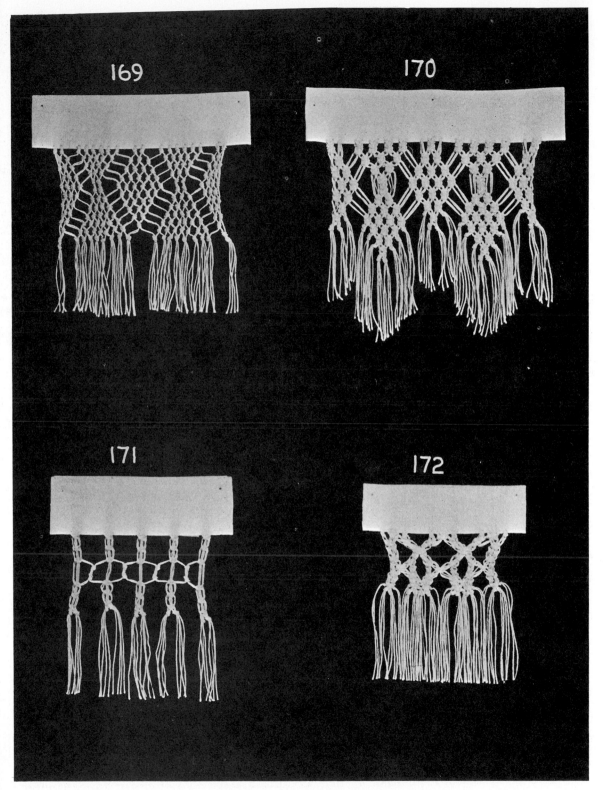

PLATE 215—MISCELLANEOUS FRINGE KNOTS

⅜-inch once and ¼-inch, after which the manner of spacing is reversed. These groups may be continued alternately to make a fringe of any desired length.

FIG. 171: *This Square Fringe Design* is made by using Flat Knots such as those shown on PLATE 168, FIG. 1. The cords are drawn through the material as previously and are spaced at intervals of once ⅜-inch, once one inch, once ⅜-inch, etc.

FIG. 172: *A Fringe Design* made up of a combination of different knots. The cords are spaced at intervals of once ¼-inch, three times ⅛-inch, once ¼-inch and once one inch. A Flat Knot (PLATE 168, FIG. 1) is made on the cords spaced ⅛-inch apart and a Single Lark's Head Knot is made as in PLATE 169, FIG. 17, on each side of the Flat Knot. A Collecting Knot, PLATE 168, FIG. 16, is made where the groups of cords meet.

Plate 216—Fringe Designs

FIG. 173: *An Overhand Knot Fringe Design.* The cords are drawn through the material at regular intervals of ⅜-inch. The design can be followed easily by reference to the illustration.

FIG. 174: *Another Overhand Knot Fringe Design,* made with ordinary Overhand Knots. These cords are also spaced at intervals of ⅜-inch.

FIG. 175: *An Ordinary Overhand Knot*

Fringe Design in which the cords are spaced at regular intervals of ½-inch. In making the fourth row of knots two groups of two cords each are brought together and the Overhand Knots are tied with them.

FIG. 176: *A Design Made with Ordinary Overhand Knots and Collecting Knots.* The latter are shown on PLATE 168, FIG. 16. The cords are pulled through the material at intervals of ¼-inch four times, once ⅞-inch and ¼-inch four times.

Plate 217—Miscellaneous Fringe Designs

FIG. 177: *The Attractive Fringe Design* shown in this illustration is made by starting the pattern with Half Hitches after the cords have been pulled through the material. A Flat Knot is made next and the two groups of cords are joined with a Collecting Knot. The Lark's Head design shown on PLATE 169, FIG. 17 is then made. The remainder of the design is but a repetition of the first part, while the fringe of tassels may be made any length. The cords are spaced in the material at intervals of ¼-inch once, one inch once, ¼-inch twice and one inch once, etc.

FIG. 178: *This Looped Square Knot Fringe* is made with Flat Knots and Looped Square Knots, PLATE 168, FIG. 10. The cords are spaced at intervals of ¼-inch once, one inch once, ¼-inch once, etc., repeating for any desired length.

FIG. 179: *The Open Spiral Mesh Fringe* is made by twisting the cords in groups of two before tying the Flat Knots. To start the work the cords are spaced as follows: ¼-inch five times, ⅞-inch once and ¼-inch five times, repeating as before.

FIG. 180: *This is a Sennit Fringe.* It is made by braiding a Sennit by going over one and under one, in the center of the fringe. The groups of cords are finished off with Collecting Knots as shown in PLATE 168, FIG. 16. The cords are spaced at regular intervals of ¼-inch.

FIG. 181: *The Double Chain Fringe* is made by using a combination of Collecting Knots and Double Chain Knots. The latter are shown on PLATE 168, FIG. 9. The Cords are spaced as follows: ¼-inch once, one inch once, ⅛-inch five times and once at one inch.

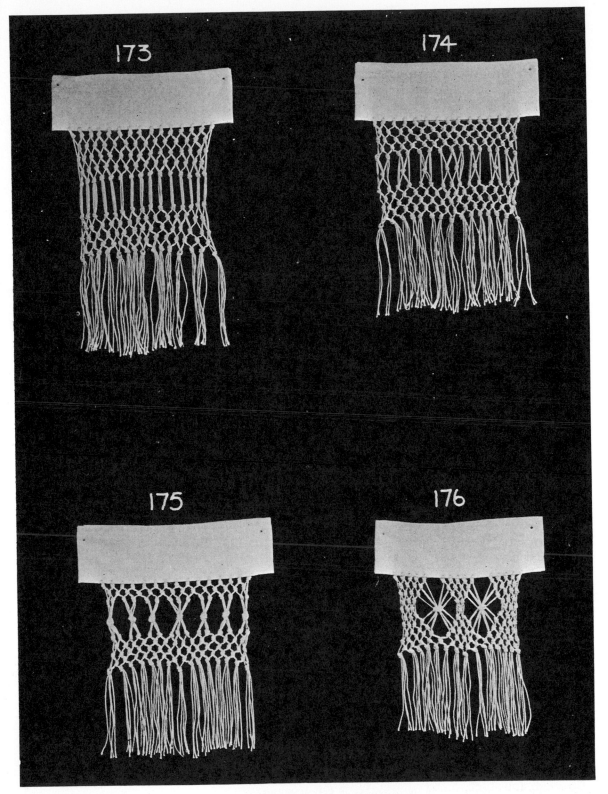

PLATE 216—FRINGE DESIGNS

FIG. 182: *The Open Mesh Fringe* shown in this illustration is made with Flat Knots in an open mesh form. When four rows of Flat Knots have been made, then tie two bars of Continuous Flat Knots with six knots in each. Between these two groups a Double Chain Knot with six Hitches is made. These are then joined by a Collecting Knot. Proceed by making two more bars of six Flat Knots and add the six Hitch Double Chain Knots as before. Continue with four more rows of Flat Knots. The cords are spaced at intervals of ⅜-inch.

Plate 218—Suggested Fringe Designs

FIG. 183: *The Inside Olive Fringe* is made by following the details of the design shown on PLATE 169, FIG. 18. The cords in this pattern are spaced at ¼-inch intervals.

FIG. 184: *The Outside Olive Fringe* is made much like that described above, except that close observation of the illustration will show that at the tops of the Olive Knot the cords enter at the back of the knot whereas in FIG. 183 the cords enter at the front of the Olive Knot. It will be noticed too that there is no row of Flat Knots separating the Olive Knots. The cords in this pattern are drawn through the material at ⅜-inch intervals (*see* PLATE 169, FIG. 18).

FIG. 185: *The Open Mesh and Chain Knot Fringe* is made with Open Mesh Flat Knots, PLATE 169, FIG. 23, the Double Chain Knot, PLATE 168, FIG. 9, and the Collecting Knot, PLATE 168, FIG. 16. The cords are spaced at intervals of ¼-inch.

FIG. 186: *The Chain Knot and Looped Square Knot Fringe* is made with the Double Chain Knot, the Looped Square Knot, and the Collecting Knot. The cords are drawn through the material at intervals of ⅜-inch.

FIG. 187: *The Open Mesh and Spiral Knot Fringe* is made by first tying four rows of Open Mesh Flat Knots followed by a Spiral Knot containing twelve Hitches, after which these are followed by three more rows of Open Mesh Flat Knots and another group of Spirals to finish. The cords are spaced at intervals of ¼-inch, ⅜-inch and ¼-inch, etc.

FIG. 188: *A Macramé Hook* with the cords which are used to secure it to the weaver's waist. Such hooks as this are used in making Flat Knots but are not necessary in forming Half Hitches. The two strands or cords on which the Knots are tied are hitched to the barb shown near the end of the piece of wood.

Plate 219—Stitches Used in Needle-Work

FIG. 189: *A Running Stitch.* It is made by going over two threads and then under two threads of a cross-stitch fabric. It is used mostly with other stitches in complicated work.

FIG. 190: *Back-Stitching.* Carry the needle backwards two threads to the right of the place where the thread was drawn through and then bring it out in front, four threads to the left of the place where the thread was drawn through. This is a more practical stitch than the Running Stitch.

FIG. 191: *Another Method of Back-Stitching.* It is similar to FIG. 190, except that the needle is brought out only two threads to the left of the place where the thread was drawn through. This stitch is used for ornamental purposes.

FIG. 192: *A Hemming Stitch.* Pass the needle in two threads on the left of the

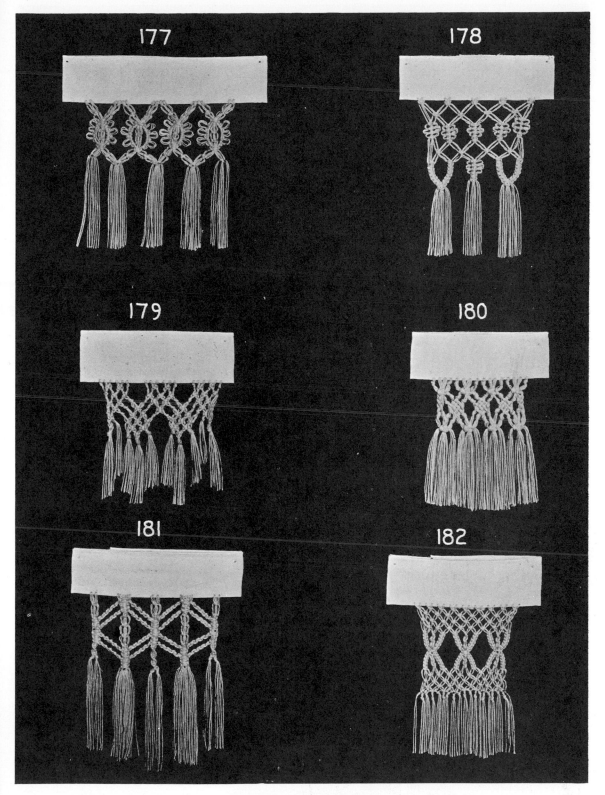

PLATE 217—MISCELLANEOUS FRINGE DESIGNS

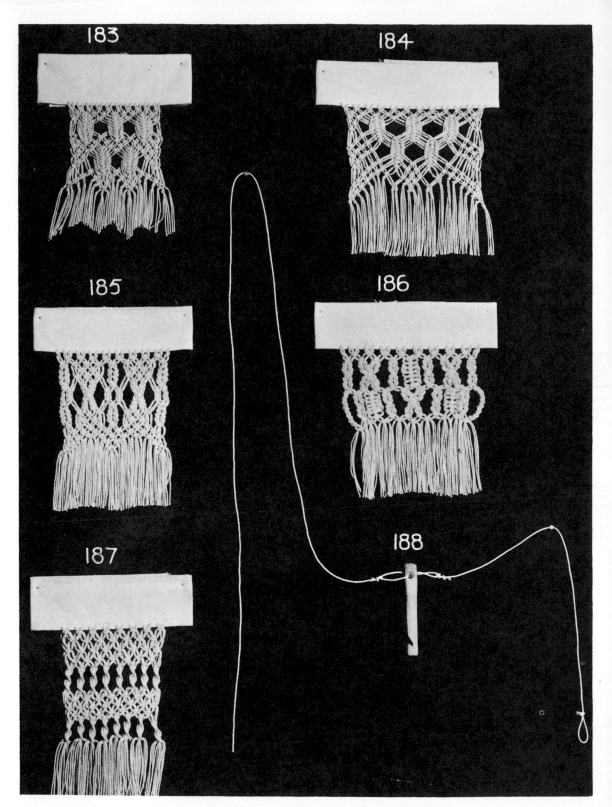

PLATE 218—SUGGESTED FRINGE DESIGNS

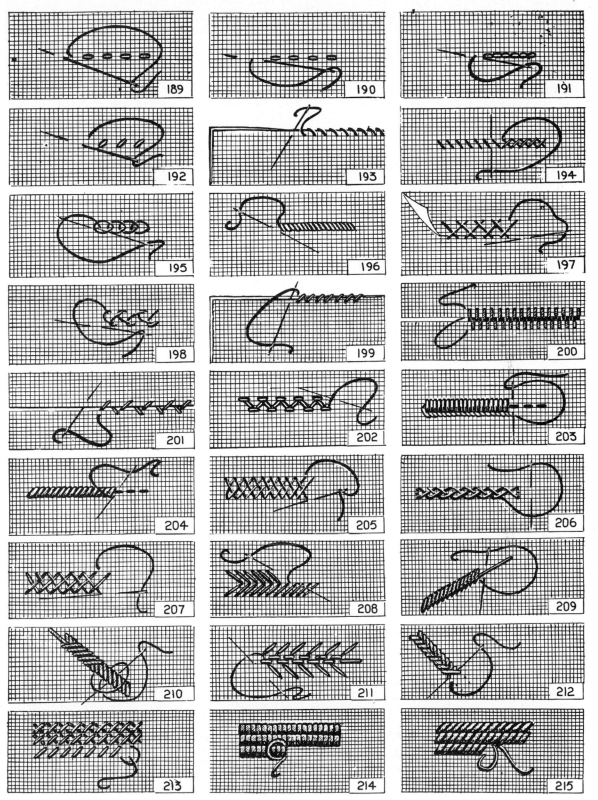

PLATE 219—STITCHES USED IN NEEDLE-WORK

place where the thread was drawn through but one thread lower down, and then bring it out again two threads further to the left and one thread higher up. It is used for making plain hems and on the fold-over of flat hems.

FIG. 193: *An Over-Sewing Stitch*. It is worked from right to left in the manner shown and is used for joining the edges of two pieces of material together.

FIG. 194: *A Plain Cross Stitch*. It is made with two rows of slanting stitches which cross each other, by working the first row from left to right with the slanting stitches made over two threads of the material in both length and height. The needle then comes out two threads higher up in a vertical position, ready to start over again. Work the second row back again in the same manner but from right to left, taking care to cross the stitches in a uniform manner. This stitch is used for tapestry, linen, and embroidery work.

FIG. 195: *A Chain Stitch*. It is begun by making a loop on the right side of the material by passing the needle through again at the same place it came out of and continued by passing it back through the loop and inserting it three threads lower down, repeating these moves over again. Adjust the thread to form a loop in a uniform manner each time. It is used in following the outline of different designs.

FIG. 196: *A Stem Stitch*. It is worked in a vertical manner from the bottom up and is used to embroider the straight lines of simple designs.

FIG. 197: *A Herringbone Stitch*. It is worked from left to right but the needle is passed through the material from right to left just above and below the seam. In this manner the stitches will cross each other. It is used for joining two pieces of material which are not folded, such as flannel. It also makes a neat ornamental stitch.

FIG. 198: *A Single Coral or Feather Stitch*. It consists of a series of passes worked from one side to the other. Start by laying a loop of thread obliquely which is then secured with a vertical thread by passing the needle in one thread lower and three threads to the right or left of the place where the thread came out. It is then passed through again two threads lower in the middle of the loop. Continue with the same method to repeat the stitches.

FIG. 199: *A Dressmaking Seam*. The stitches are worked from right to left. These are used for patching and dress seams.

FIG. 200: *An Antique Seam*. Start by inserting the needle under two threads of the material on the left side, then cross over and pass the needle again under two threads on the right side. In this manner the threads cross each other between the two pieces of material in similar fashion to a baseball stitch.

FIG. 201: *Another Antique Seam* with the stitches lying at an angle.

FIG. 202: *A Chevron Stitch*. Begin on the left by using a horizontal stitch which is passed over four threads, then back two threads to the left which will bring the needle out in the middle of the last stitch. Proceed with a stitch slanting to the right over four threads, then pass the needle under two threads to the left. This completes the lower horizontal stitch. Bring the needle back to the middle for the second slanting stitch up and repeat the same method as already described for the next top horizontal stitch.

FIG. 203: *A Blanket or Button-Hole Stitch*. It is worked from left to right with a running stitch serving as a base. The stitches are set side by side in a very close snug fit.

FIG. 204: *A Slanting Overcast Stitch*. It is also worked from left to right but at an angle over a running stitch which serves as a base.

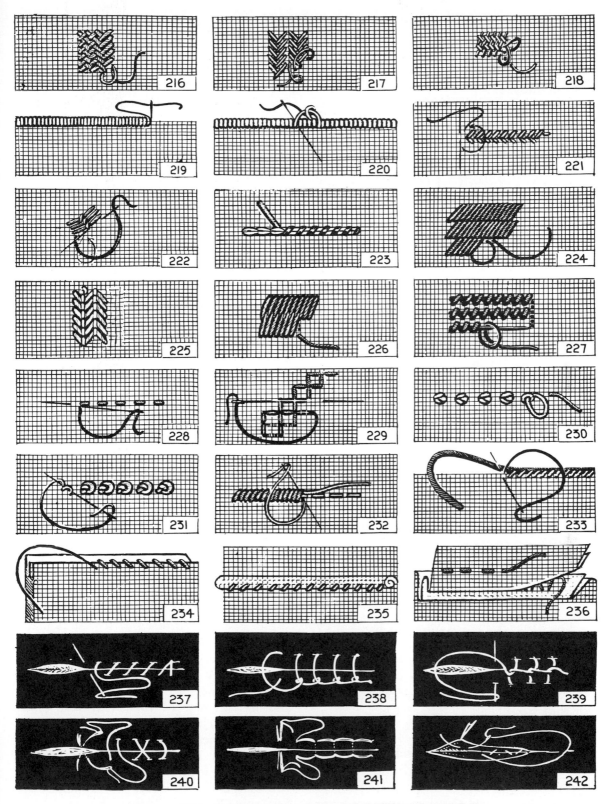

PLATE 220—STITCHES USED IN NEEDLE-WORK

FIG. 205: *A Crossed Back Stitch with Interlacing Threads*. It is used on transparent fabrics.

FIG. 206: *A Plaited Slav Stitch*. It is worked over three and six threads respectively and is easy to duplicate from the illustration.

FIG. 207: *A Plaited Algerian Stitch*. The stitch advances only one or two threads at a time and it is advisable to begin over an uneven number of canvas or cross-stitch threads. Continue by using the same method as illustrated throughout.

FIG. 208: *A Plaited Spanish Stitch*. It consists of a series of slanting stitches which go over five and then three threads, three threads apart respectively. It is a very fast and easy stitch to make and can be used for ornamental designing.

FIG. 209: *A Raised Stem Stitch*. It is worked with a thick thread, such as No. 1 D. M. C., with an additional thread running along the line of the pattern to serve as a base for the work which consists of a Slanting Stem Stitch.

FIG. 210: *An Overcast Raised Stem Stitch*. It is made similar to FIG. 209, except that an additional Overcast Stitch is brought back over the body of the work.

FIG. 211: *A Fish Bone Stitch*. It consists of two long Button-hole Stitches, one to the right and the other to the left with the inside threads forming a vertical vein. Used as a filling for leaves on linen embroidery.

FIG. 212: *The Basket Stitch*. It is made by passing the needle downward, from left to right and under from three to six threads of the foundation, then return the needle to the right with a second slanting stitch upwards which is followed by a third stitch, starting from the same hole as the first stitch and so on. This stitch can be worked on any kind of material.

FIG. 213: *A Plain Cross Stitch*. It is worked in a double journey to and fro. To start the thread is carried diagonally from left to right across two vertical and two horizontal threads, then down underneath the horizontal threads. The stitch is made from right to left in the return journey. This is the foundation of tapestry stitches.

FIG. 214: *A Straight Goblin Stitch*. It is worked in horizontal rows. The thread is carried over two threads of canvas in a vertical position, leaving one thread of material between the stitches each time.

FIG. 215: *An Oblique Goblin Stitch*. It is worked on canvas and the thread is carried over one vertical and two horizontal threads in an oblique direction.

Plate 220—Stitches Used in Needle-Work

FIG. 216: *A Plaited Stitch*. It is made by taking the thread back each time to the starting point, then from left to right downward over four vertical and two horizontal threads, then on the back side under two threads from right to left, and so on.

FIG. 217: *A Fern Stitch*. The thread is passed over two double threads of the canvas each way, running horizontally from right to left under the center pair of threads and then slanting upwards over two double threads to the right.

FIG. 218: *A Knotted Stitch*. It is made by carrying the thread over two horizontal and six vertical threads. The needle is then brought back vertically four threads lower down and inserted two threads higher up and to the rear of the stitch just made which will bring it over the middle threads. It is then taken down to the line of stitches and in the following rows extend the stitches over four threads downward which will then encroach upon two threads of the first row. This will bring the stitches of one row between those of the previous row.

[Plate 220]   Macramé Tatting, Fringe, Needle-Work   413

FIG. 219: *A Hem Stitch Ornamented with Picots.*

FIG. 220: *A Hem Stitch with Looped Picots.* The thread is carried from left to right, forming a loop which is held with a pin, after which the thread is carried back to the middle of the loop and twisted around it to form the picot.

FIG. 221: *A Beaded Stitch.* It is worked upwards in the direction of the arrow. Used on ancient church embroideries.

FIG. 222: *A Roman Stitch.* It can be followed easily by observing the illustration.

FIG. 223: *An Overcast Chain Stitch.* First make an ordinary Chain Stitch and then overcast it with a colored thread which is carried around each loop of the chain as illustrated.

FIG. 224: *A Wide Goblin Stitch.* This stitch is made by covering two vertical and three horizontal threads on canvas and advancing one thread of canvas at a time.

FIG. 225: *A Stem Stitch.* A Slanting Stitch is made over four vertical and horizontal threads and then the needle is brought back over two threads above where the first stitch was started. Proceed by setting the stitches in the opposite way for the second row, then include Back Stitching between them of a contrasting color to finish off.

FIG. 226: *An Encroaching Goblin Stitch.* This stitch consists of a series of oblique stitches which are carried over five vertical threads and one horizontal thread, at the same time leaving one thread of canvas between each stitch.

FIG. 227: *A Half Cross Stitch.* It can be followed easily from the illustration.

FIG. 228: *A Simple Knot Stitch.* Two Back Stitches are placed side by side, covering the same threads.

FIG. 229: *A Two Sided Line Stitch.* This stitch can be followed from the pattern which shows how the threads run.

FIG. 230: *A Knotted Stitch* which consists of a Compound Chain and Back Stitch worked together.

FIG. 231: *A Twisted Knot Stitch.* The thread is twisted twice around the needle and the needle is then pointed from left to right and passed back through the fabric after which it is drawn out at the place where the next stitch is intended to be.

FIG. 232: *A Straight Overcast Stitch.* This stitch is worked from left to right over a foundation thread in the manner illustrated. It is used for embroidering monograms and letters.

FIG. 233: *A Stitch for Sewing on Round Cord.* A very strong thread should be used for this kind of work.

FIG. 234: *A Hemming Stitch for Double Seams.* The two edges are turned in and layed one upon the other after which the sewing is done in the manner illustrated. It is used for fastening down linings in dressmaking.

FIG. 235: *An Open Hem Double Seam Stitch.* Two edges are laid together, then turned in twice and hemmed in the regular way.

FIG. 236: *A French Seam Stitch.* Two pieces of material are placed together back to back with the edges even. They are then turned over close to the seam in order to bring the right sides next to each other. This will enclose the two raw edges in between. This stitch is used for joining light fabrics in dressmaking.

FIG. 237: *A Continuous Stitch.* This and the following stitches are different kinds of stitches used by surgeons for sewing and closing flesh wounds.

FIG. 238: *A Blanket Stitch.*

FIG. 239: *A Ford Stitch.*

FIG. 240: *A Boot Lace Stitch.*

FIG. 241: *A Cobbler's Stitch.*

FIG. 242: *A Sub-Cuticular Stitch.*

Plate 221—Suggestions for Macramé Designing

FIGS. 243 to 258: *Elementary Types of Macramé Patterns.*

FIGS. 259 to 270: *Various Designs in Macramé* work are shown in these illustrations.

FIGS. 271 to 280: *Macramé Designs* applicable for a wide variety of uses.

FIGS. 281 to 285: *Elaborate Patterns in Macramé* of exceptionally broad designs in contrasting colors.

Plate 222—Patterns in Macramé Work

FIGS. 286 to 294: *Additional Suggestions for Macramé Color Designs* with various forms of hitching worked into the elaborate and attractive color blending of contrasting colors. These are offered as outstanding examples to select from for duplication.

FIGS. 295 to 302: *Other Examples of Macramé Work* are shown in these illustrations.

FIGS. 303 to 307: *Larger Designs of Blended Macramé Work* represent artistic patterns that may be used for belts and other similar articles.

Plate 223—Macramé Designs Using Half Hitches

FIGS. 308 to 313: *Macramé Work* lends itself to an almost unlimited selection of patterns and color schemes, several of which are shown in these illustrations. Designs and schemes of color blending of many kinds may be worked out by the student of this work with but little effort.

FIGS. 314 to 317: *Other Designs in Macramé* are shown here which may be made up in many contrasting colors.

FIGS. 318 to 322: *More Macramé Patterns* are illustrated as suggestions for the students of this art.

Plate 224—Macramé Designs for Belts

FIGS. 323 to 345: *Macramé Designs for Belts.* These are Macramé patterns showing advanced work in flower and French-style designing, in which are included a variety of methods of half hitch weaving in different color combinations.

Plate 225—Variated Macramé Belt Designs

FIGS. 346 to 357: *Additional Macramé Patterns* which represent an extension of many different designs. Duplication of such work as this will help to improve the skill of the amateur in mastering the art of Macramé work.

Plate 226—Macramé Designs in Colors

FIGS. 358 to 372: *Additional designs and patterns in Macramé work* in which are included a great variety of color combinations and weaves, worked into an interesting assortment of designs to serve as illustrations of Macramé work.

Plate 227—Variated Macramé Designs

FIGS. 373 to 383: *Macramé Designs in colors* such as these may be used in making belts and other useful articles. The student of this work can easily devise and create any number of beautiful arrangements of colors and different weaves.

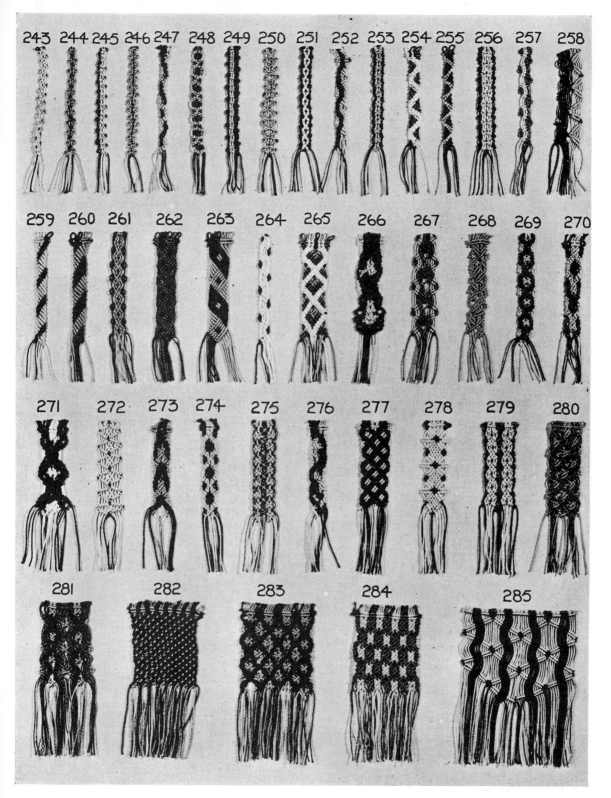

PLATE 221—SUGGESTIONS FOR MACRAMÉ DESIGNING

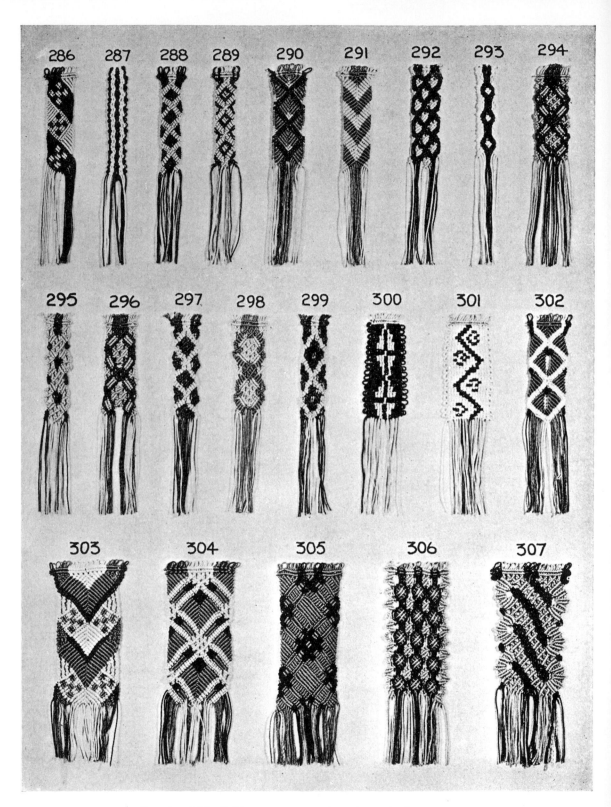

PLATE 222—PATTERNS IN MACRAME WORK

PLATE 223—MACRAMÉ DESIGNS USING HALF HITCHES

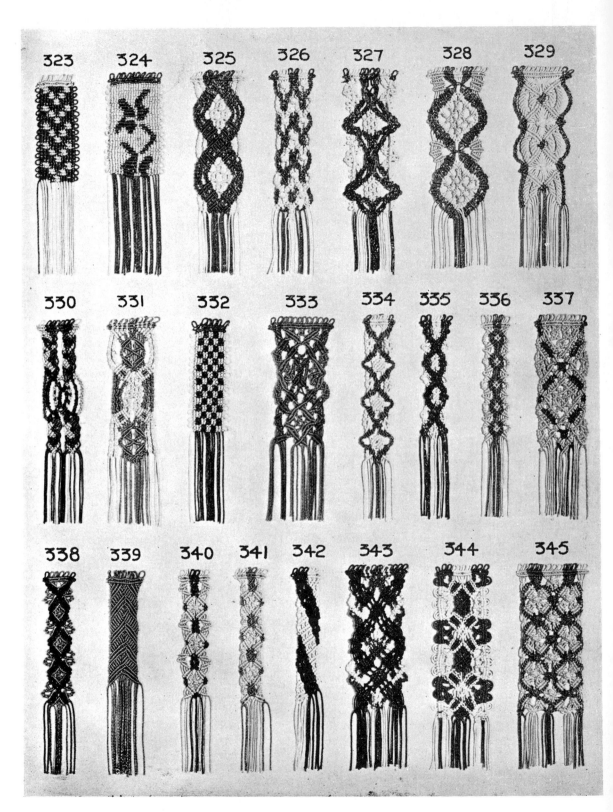

PLATE 224—MACRAME DESIGNS FOR BELTS

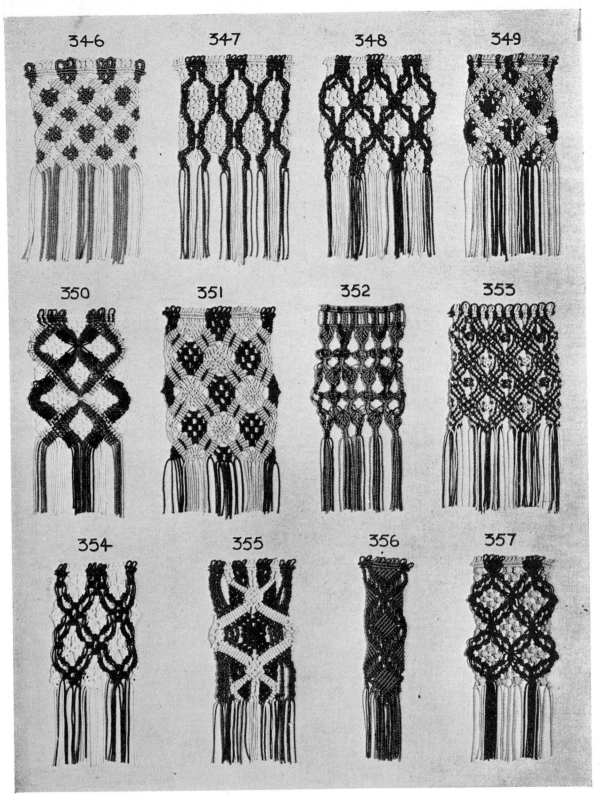

PLATE 225—VARIATED MACRAME BELT DESIGNS

PLATE 226—MACRAMÉ DESIGNS IN COLORS

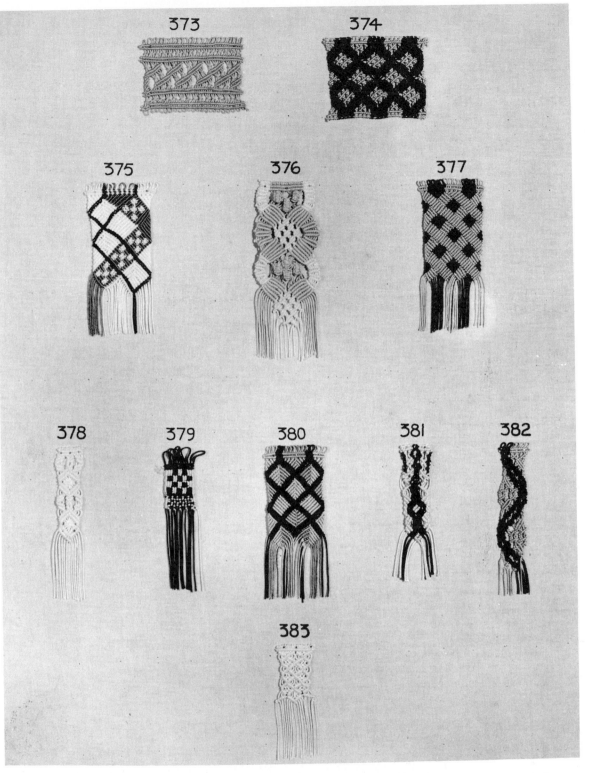

PLATE 227—VARIATED MACRAMÉ DESIGNS

Chapter X

Useful Rope Designs

I N THIS CHAPTER a number of rope designs are presented which may be used to make many beautiful articles of practical value, such as for instance, Knife Lanyards, Watch Fobs, Picture Frames, Comb Hangers, and Wall Bags. Unfortunately, the fine art of making such useful things as these is almost forgotten today. At one time, however, this type of fancy rope work was in high favor among the seamen of sailing-ships, who adapted many practical designs and ideas to their own individual needs.

This phase of knotting has never before been covered comprehensively in book form and it is hoped that by offering it here for the first time that interest in this valuable and fascinating art may be revived.

Before undertaking to make any of the articles described here, however, the student of this work should have first mastered the art of simple knotting as well as the procedure in combining the simple knots into more intricate designs, many of which he can devise himself.

Plate 228—Comb Hanger Designs

FIG. 1: *The Comb Hanger Design (No. 1)* is made as follows: form an eye in the desired amount of rope, then place a seizing around it, and unlay the strands from both ends down to the seizing. Next, tie a Lanyard Knot, and follow with a Double Lanyard, a Walled Crown, and another Lanyard Knot to finish off. Each knot should be pulled up snug before proceeding with the next one. After completing the last knot, fray the yarns out with a comb.

FIG. 2: *The Comb Hanger Design (No. 2)* begins with a Sailor's Breastplate. Seize both parts of the rope together, and make a Lanyard Knot, following this with a Turk's Head Weave. Then pull taut and fray out the yarns.

FIG. 3: *The Comb Hanger Design (No. 3)* is formed by first tying a Diamond Knot to form the eye. Follow this with a Lanyard Knot, finishing off with a Walled Crown and fraying out the yarns to complete the design.

Plate 229—Other Examples of Comb Hanger Designs

FIG. 4: *The Comb Hanger Design (No. 4)* is made in the following way: begin by tying a Hackamore Knot in the bight of a rope, then seize the two rope parts together, and tie a Diamond Knot of six strands (after unlaying the rope). Pull this knot up taut, and fray the yarns in the usual manner. All knots in comb hanger designs are tied with six strands, unless working with four-strand rope, which requires an eight-strand knot.

FIG. 5: *The Comb Hanger Design (No. 5)* is made by first unlaying and seizing the rope in the usual way to form the eye. Then tie a Lanyard Knot, followed by a Double Lanyard on top of the first one. A Star Knot is tied next and pulled up snug before finishing off with a Turk's Head Weave. Before fraying them out, make a Five-Strand Turk's Head with five passes around the rope yarns, using a needle and small white line.

PLATE 228—COMB HANGER DESIGNS

FIG. 6: *The Comb Hanger Design (No. 6)* begins with a Spanish Bowline. Seize the two parts of rope together, and unlay the strands. Then form a Six-strand Matthew Walker Knot, pull taut, and fray out the yarns.

Plate 230—Interesting Comb Hanger Designs

FIG. 7: *The Comb Hanger Design (No. 7)* is made as follows: take a length of rope and make a Three-Strand Coxcomb with small white line. Continue coxcombing until the desired amount has been completed for the eye. Then bend in the eye and clap on a seizing. Unlay the strands, tie a Double Diamond Knot, and pull up snug. Next, tie an ordinary Single Diamond Knot, and fray out the yarn. A Five-Strand Turks' Head with two passes or any other type of Turk's Head can be placed around the base of the eye, as illustrated.

FIG. 8: *The Comb Hanger Design (No. 8)* is tied by first coxcombing the rope as explained in FIG. 7. Next, form an eye, put on a seizing, and make a Lanyard Knot for a base. Tie a Star Knot and pull up taut. Then finish off with a Matthew Walker Knot, and fray out the yarns. A Five-Strand Turk's Head with two passes is placed around the base of the eye.

FIG. 9: *The Comb Hanger Design (No. 9)* begins with a Lanyard Knot for a base. after coxcombing and bending in the eye in the usual manner. Then make a Sennit Knot, pull it up taut, and place a Matthew Walker Knot on top of the Sennit Knot. Fray out the yarns to finish.

Plate 231—A Wall Bag and Turk's Head Designs

FIG. 10: *The Four-Strand Inverted Turk's Head with Nine Crosses* can be flattened out as illustrated and used as a table pad on which to set hot dishes. It is tied as described in Chapter VI. (*See* PLATE 150, FIG. 177.)

FIG. 11: *The Watch Fob Design* is tied as follows: attach two strands to the watch handle, and add two more strands at *a*. Begin to crown the four strands, first one way and then the other, forming a Single Nelson Braid. Continue this until the desired length for the fob is reached. Then finish with a Double Stopper Knot, and cut the strands off short.

FIG. 12: *The Six-Strand Inverted Turk's Head with Five Crosses* is another type of Flat Turk's Head, with very neat basket-like shape, but no practical value.

FIG. 13: *The Sailor's Bunk or Wall Bag Design* is formed in the following fashion: First, strip a piece of canvas the desired length, according to the number of designs required. Then count the threads or ravels, in order to equalize each separate bunch. Taking each bunch in turn, form a Clove Hitch or two Half Hitches with one of the outside strands, and draw the knot up snug. Do this with each bunch across the front, until the first row is completed. Then split each bunch, and form diamond designs by working in the same manner. Three rows of diamonds have been made in this illustration. The design is next worked into a series of Square Knot plaits, with a Carrick Bend on each side. Continue by working the diamond designs down into a point, and finish off with large tassels. A military ribbon is then passed through the Square Knot plait, and the canvas is folded up and overlapped to form pockets, which are basted in at different intervals with a needle and sail twine. The sides are sewed up to complete the bag, and three Japanese Knots are added as shown, by sewing them to the canvas. The top is turned back and secured to the back of the canvas.

PLATE 229—OTHER EXAMPLES OF COMB HANGER DESIGNS

PLATE 230—INTERESTING COMB HANGER DESIGNS

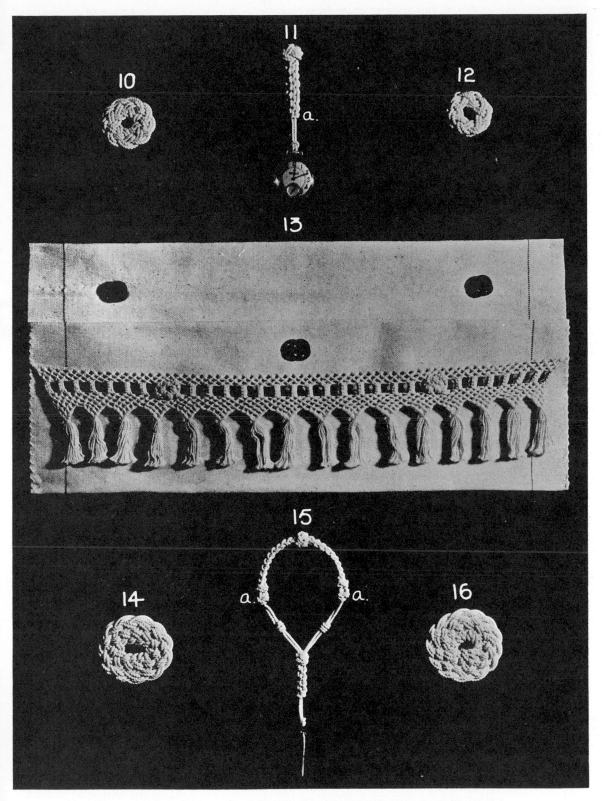

PLATE 231—A WALL BAG AND TURK'S HEAD DESIGNS

Fig. 14: *The Six-Strand Inverted Turk's Head with Seven Crosses.*

Fig. 15: *The Knife Lanyard Design* is begun by attaching two strands of white line, or any other suitable material, to the ring in the end of a knife. Next, add two more strands, an inch or so from the beginning, and form Four-Strand Crown Knots, reversing them each time as in a Single Nelson Braid. Braid up a short way, and tie a Four-Strand Diamond Knot with two passes on top of the Crown Braid. Then split the strands into separate pairs, and form Blood Knots with four passes on each pair. Lead the strands out in the shape of a fork after separating them, in order to judge the distance required for each set of designs. At the points marked *a*, two more strands are added on each side, and a Double Stopper Knot is tied with both sets of four strands each. Next, make Turk's Head Weaves, or any other suitable knots, and tie a Four-Strand Round Braid with each set, until the proper length is reached, in order to bring them together in the center of the design. Place a whipping on each braid. Then marry them, tie a Clipper-Ship Shroud Knot with two passes, pull the knot up snug, and cut the ends off short.

Fig. 16: *The Seven-Strand Inverted Turk's Head* is extended from a Five-Strand Irregular Turk's Head.

Plate 232—Knotting in Picture Frame Work

The Sennit Picture-Frame Design (No. 1), one of the finest examples of the art in existence, represents the last word in what was once a great pastime among the old-time sailormen. Such frames make unique decorations for a club-room or home, and are easy to construct, once the many different designs illustrated and explained in different parts of this book have been mastered. The average beginner will find it more satisfactory to have the frame constructed by a carpenter or wood-worker, instead of trying to make it himself. A frame can be made any size or shape desired and the work proportioned to it in regard to the length of braids, the size, shape, and number of designs, the general method of laying out the various types of knot work as the covering of the frame proceeds.

Before starting, the frame can be covered with drill if desired. The outside of the frame is then covered with a Paunch Mat Weave all the way around, and sewed together with a bag needle and sail twine. White line in the 84-thread size can be used for the larger work, and any other size can be employed for the smaller designs, such as 48, 60, or 72-thread. Next, make a Cable-Laid Sennit to go around the inside edge, after completing the outside Paunch Matting. Then use a Three-Strand Sennit around the outside edge of the frame, taking care to sew each piece of work on securely. Cover the top corners with an additional piece of Paunch Matting, after first using Portuguese Square Knot Sennits next to the large Cable-laid Sennit all the way around.

A cardboard heart is used for the Portuguese Sennit. Make another small Cable-Laid Sennit, and sew it all the way around. In the meantime, leave off the bottom part of the corner Paunch Mat covers until all other work that goes underneath is attached. It can be observed by following the design that Sword Matting is next placed around the interior of the frame. This should be made in four separate pieces; then join and sew the ends together diagonally in each corner. A Six-Strand Tripple-Passed Flat Sennit is next laid on and secured in the same way. A Five-Strand Running Sennit is used for a border between the Sword Matting and Flat Sennit. Pull the bottom of the Paunch Mat corner covers down and attach them.

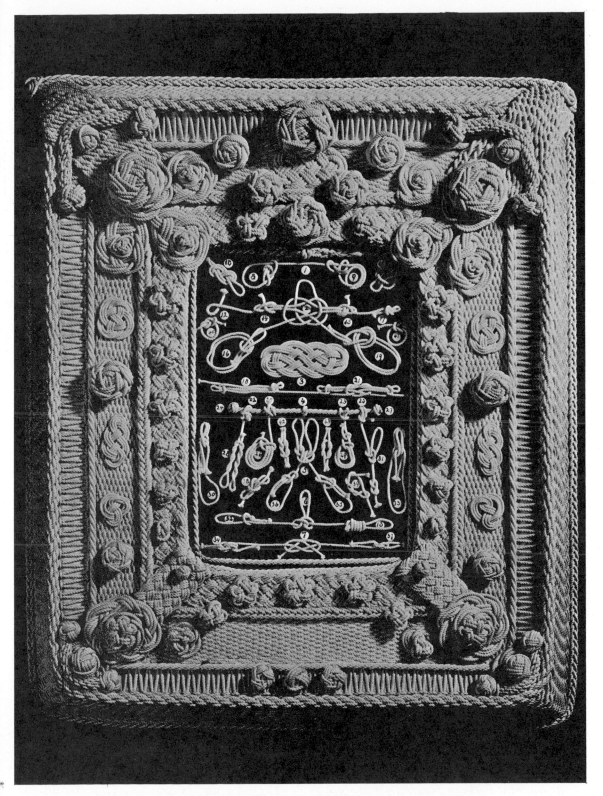

PLATE 232—KNOTTING IN PICTURE FRAME WORK

Crowned Spiral Braids with Triple-Passed Stopper Knots on the ends are used in each corner. A small Rose Knot is set in the middle of the Spiral Sennit, where it curves at each corner, and is secured with a screw. It is better to screw the large or protruding knots to the frame, but the flat weaves can be sewed on. Gunner's Knots are used in clusters of three each for both upper corners, and a Triple-Passed Three-Strand Turk's Head is placed over the base of these knots. A large Rose Knot, well sewed together, is then set on top of each Turk's Head and screwed on. Trinity Bends are used on the upper outside corners of the frame. In the lower corners, Triple-Passed Three-Strand Turk's Heads are used, with a Six-Strand Star Knot set in the middle of each in rose-bud form, after first placing a Seven-Strand Triple-passed Flat Sennit over each corner to serve as a foundation and cover the spot where the rope ends from the previous work meet. Covering the Sword Matting on both sides are Japanese Knots, then medium-sized Rose Knots, two different ornamental weaves, and another pair of Rose Knots. On the inside of the bottom Star Knot Cluster in each corner will be found another Three-Strand Star Knot set on an ornamental weave. And just above these knots, on top of the Five-Strand Running Sennit, are Four-Strand Star Knots. In the upper center of the picture is a large Rose Knot attached to the Portuguese Sennit, and flanked by two smaller Rose Knots on either side. Directly underneath is a Napoleon Bend with three passes which is also flanked at both lower corners by Rose Knots. Three-strand Star Knots are set in each cluster of Gunner's Knots on both upper sides. Small Terminal Knots, or

Monkey Fists, are placed near the top of the Seven-Strand Flat Sennits in both lower corners.

On the inside Seven-Strand Flat Sennit, underneath the Napoleon Bend, a Rose Knot is placed, flanked by two Five-Strand Star Knots. Two Five-Strand Star Knots are also on the bottom part of this same Sennit, with a Six-Strand Star Knot between them. On each side of the same Sennit will be found a Two, Three, Four, Five, Six and Seven-Strand Star Knot in the order named, starting from the bottom. The frame is finished with another Cable-Laid Sennit on the inside of the Seven-Strand Flat Sennit and underneath its edge.

The names of the knots on the inside panel (which is covered with black velvet and can be removed) are as follows: 1. Shroud. 2. Jury Mast Head. 3. Square Mat. 4. Wall. 5. Spanish Bowline. 6. Lineman's Bowline. 7. Flemish Carrick Bend. 8. Running Bowline. 9. Round Turn and two Half Hitches. 10. Flemish Eye. 11. Hackamore or Theodore. 12. Black Wall Hitch. 13. Hangman's Noose. 14. Single Sheet Bend. 15. Double Sheet Bend. 16. Double Bowline. 17. Heaving Knot. 18. Sheepshank. 19. Bowline on Bight. 20. Rolling Hitch. 21. Man O'War Sheepshank. 22. Buntline Hitch. 23. Clove Hitch. 24. Double Matthew Walker. 25. Bucket Hitch. 26. Topsail Halyard Bend. 27. Single Matthew Walker. 28. Cats Paw. 29. Fisherman's Bend. 30. Longshoreman's Knot. 31. Stopper or Ring Bowline. 32. Horse or Cow Hitch Knot. 33. Dutchman's Knot. 34. Double Carrick Bend. 35. French Bowline. 36. Bowline. 37. Single Carrick Bend. 38. Tomfool's Knot. 39. Timber Hitch. 40. Thief's Knot. 41. Reef or Square Knot.

Plate 233—A Combination of Knots and Braids

The Sennit Picture Frame Design (No. 2) is another artistic example of frame decorating. Although it is somewhat less complicated than design No. 1, it should furnish many new ideas of the different ways of constructing and covering frames with

PLATE 233—A COMBINATION OF KNOTS AND BRAIDS

Sennits and fancy rope work. The wooden frame is measured according to requirements, or the amount of designing contemplated. Then it is joined at the corners, and the work of covering is ready to start.

First, a Spiral Sennit is made and measured off in four pieces to match the length of the sides, top, and bottom. It is then placed all the way around the outer edge of the frame, and secured. Next comes a Four-Strand Round Sennit, a Portuguese Square Sennit, another Round Sennit, a Square Sennit, and Round Sennit, in the order named, working toward the inside of the frame. Follow this with still another Round Sennit and then a Three-Strand Running Sennit with two passes. Attach these braids as previously explained, and sew them all together with a bag or tufting needle and sail twine.

A Portuguese Square Sennit is placed around the inside edge; and the Square Knots (or Flats, as they are commonly called) are begun by attaching smaller line of about 12- or 15-thread to the bottom part of this Sennit all the way around, or to the framework if desired. The Square Knot diamond designs are then worked in toward the center of the frame and attached to the oval framework used as a basis for the inside designs. Four rows of knots are used to decorate the outside of the oval, and either Diamond, Stopper, or Manrope Knots can be employed for this purpose. An interlaced Hitch Weave is used to go around the inside of the oval. It has three passes with a row of large knots all the way around in the center of the weave. Diamond, Stopper, or Manrope Knots can also be used here. These knots are all attached with screws, as explained

in the description of Frame Design No. 1.

White line of any size can be utilized. But it is better to use 72- or 84-thread for the larger work, and smaller line for the small work. Two Nine-Strand Turk's Heads with three passes are used to go around the frame on the top and bottom. Two Ten-Strand Turk's Heads are used on each side. Seven-Strand French Sennits are used to cover the four corners, with two rows of five Diamond Knots on each side of all four Sennits. A Spiral Sennit is then placed around the outside edge of the two sides and bottom, with a Flat Sennit used for the same purpose on top. Four Five-Strand Turk's Heads with five passes are made, and then pulled up into a knob-like form by stuffing them with spun yarn or any other suitable material. These Turk's Heads are next attached on the inside of all four corners as the picture illustrates.

The design that decorates the top of the frame is made by Coach-Whipping a piece of rope, or small hose, with a Four- or Six-Strand Round Sennit, using three strands together in sets of four or six each, depending upon which type of braid is chosen. A Five-Strand Turk's Head of the type previously described is then placed on each end of the Coach-Whipping, and pulled taut. Three-Strand Turk's Heads are placed around the Coach-Whipping near the Turk's Head Knobs on the end, and another Turk's Head of five strands is attached to the center of the design. Two more Turk's Heads of three strands each are used to secure the bights on both sides of the design. This completes the description of the frame. The picture in the center shows the Seamen's Church Institute in New York City.

Plate 234—A Typical Frame Design

The Sennit Picture Frame Design (No. 3) is constructed in the same general way as Design No. 2, except for several slight differences in laying out the work and arranging the various patterns. It is better to cover these Sennit frames with light drill

PLATE 234—A TYPICAL FRAME DESIGN

PLATE 235—COLOR COMBINATIONS IN PICTURE FRAMES

[Plate 235]   Useful Rope Designs   435

or canvas before beginning work, sewing or tacking the material to the frame. But there are a number of other ways to handle the work, limited only by the skill and initiative of the individual. The frame is covered with a Spiral Sennit on the outside edge all the way around, followed with a row of Diamond Knots, a Four-Strand Round Sennit and two more rows of Diamond Knots around all four sides. Next, place another row of Diamond Knots on the inside edge of the frame, and carry it all the way around. The Square Knot work is similar to that explained in Design No. 2, but in addition to being smaller, it has a row of Spiral Sennits encircling the oval, which in this case is horizontal instead of vertical.

To complete the interior, use an Interlaced Hitch Weave with Diamond Knot designs, as explained in Frame Design No. 2. Close observation will disclose that there are six Five-Strand Star Knots attached to the Four-Strand Round Sennit on both sides of the frame. Four more Five-Strand Star Knots are placed on the top part, and nine on the bottom part. Seven-Strand French Sennits are used to cover all four corners, which are flanked by Star Knots

on each side. Around the bottom part of the frame are two Nine-Strand Turk's Heads with four passes. A Seven-Strand Turk's Head with four passes is formed around the center of the top side of the frame, with a cluster of twelve Five-Strand Star Knots encircling it on top and at the sides. Five-Strand Turk's Heads with four passes, made as already noted, are hung on the ends of the Four-Strand Round Sennit used to form the Carrick Bend design in the upper center part of the frame, just under the Five-Strand Turk's Head.

A small Five-Strand Turk's Head is utilized to seize the Carrick Bend design on both sides to the Four-Strand Round Sennit, of which the Sennit forms a part. It will be noted that the Sennit is attached to the upper underneath corner on each side, after leaving enough slack to hang down properly. An Ornamental Weave is placed in both lower corners, with a Diamond Knot on top. All Sennits are measured in the same way, and all knots are attached and sewed on in this frame as in the other frames already described.

The picture in the center shows the old Seamen's Church Institute also in New York City.

Plate 235—Color Combinations in Picture Frames

The Sennit Picture Frame Design (No. 4) is an ornamental knotted picture frame. To make it, first construct a wood base, consisting of flat pieces of wood, one and one-quarter inches wide. The frame's actual size is nine inches wide and seven inches high. Begin by making a Thirteen-Strand Double French Sennit, braided long enough to cover all four sides. Next, carefully measure off enough for one of the sides, sewing diagonally on both ends before cutting off. This will be the covering for one side of the frame. Then measure off the bottom piece, sew the ends diagonally, and cut off. Repeat this procedure for the other side and the top. When all four

pieces have been sewed and cut, they are fitted together, and their ends joined and sewed. This provides a base on which to work. The Sennit Braid, now in the form of a square, is tacked to the frame in each corner. This part of the work was made with small white cotton line.

The Sennits in each corner are Seventeen-Strand Single French Sennits. They are put diagonally over the corners, and their ends are joined and sewed together on the reverse side of the frame. These were made from blue dreadnaught cord. Next, make six Five-Strand Turk's Heads around the frame, two on the top, two on the bottom, and one on each side. These were

PLATE 236—A SUGGESTED DESIGN FOR A PICTURE FRAME

[*Plate 236*] Useful Rope Designs 437

made with red cord. Continuing, tie two Three-Strand Inverted Turk's Heads and tack one of them to the middle of the frame on the bottom and one on top. An Ornamental Knot was placed inside at the bottom of the frame. Figure-of-Eight Knots were sewed to the basic Sennit Braid all around the inside of the frame. When this has been done, braid four Three-Strand Sennits and sew them on the outside edge of the frame, leaving six ends in each cor-ner. With each set of six strands, form an English Rose Knot in the four corners, draw them up taut, and cut the ends off short. At the top of the frame, make two Sennits by using the Macramé Square Knot in a continuous chain. These are tied then to form a Double Carrick Bend and are sewed to the frame to finish the design.

The picture in the center of the frame is the five-masted Danish Barque "Copenhagen."

Plate 236—A Suggested Design for a Picture Frame

This Sennit Picture Frame Design (No. 5) is a good example of another elaborate style of fancy decorative rope work. The same general methods were employed in making this frame as have been explained previously in connection with the construction of similar frames.

A Sixteen-Strand Triple-Passed Coach-Whipping is placed around a length of rubber hose to form the top piece. It has two Three-Strand Turk's Heads on its ends and two Four-Strand Turk's Heads with three passes near the center. Twenty-six-Strand Paunch Matting is used to cover all four sides of the frame, after which the top piece is attached with screws.

A large piece of Cable-Laid Sennit is then made of the proper length and secured to the outer edge on all four sides of the frame. A Portuguese Sennit is formed around a piece of two-inch cardboard which has been covered with muslin. It will be noticed that this Sennit is placed at an angle on each of the four sides of the frame. Another Cable-Laid Sennit is attached to the frame on the inside of the Portuguese Sennit. Seven-Strand Triple-Passed Flat Sennits are placed diagonally across each upper corner. These are secured underneath the Cable-Laid Sennit with a large Rose Knot placed on top on either side just inside of the second Cable-Laid Sennit.

Twenty-one Rose Knots are attached in the form of an arc from one side of the top part to the other and these are followed with fourteen Triple-Passed Star Knots with three to seven strands each. Seventeen Star Knots, consisting of from three to seven strands are next attached in a straight line across the front as illustrated. These three rows of knots are all sewed to a Paunch Mat base which is secured to the frame first and carried all the way around the four sides of the frame to serve as a base for the remainder of the knot work.

Eleven Rose Knots are placed in a row on top of the Paunch Matting on either side of the frame between the inside Cable-Laid Sennit and the Eight-Strand Square Sennit which is attached next. Fourteen Rose Knots are then placed in a row between these two Sennits on the bottom part of the frame. A Strip of Sword Matting is next made the proper length and is attached all the way around the frame. This is flanked with an Eight-Strand Square Sennit and a Six-Strand Half Round Sennit with seven Flat Ornamental Knots on both the top and bottom parts and with five Flat Ornamental Knots on each side piece.

A Three-Strand Triple-Passed Inverted Turk's Head with a Star Knot set in the center is attached on the inside part of each of the Flat Sennits leading diagonally across the upper part of the frame on both sides. On the inside of these Inverted Turk's

Heads is a cluster of three Gunner's Knots which are placed over the Seven-Strand Triple-Passed Flat Sennit on each inside corner. A strip of Sword Matting is now placed diagonally across each lower corner and is carried to the inside of the frame and secured. Square Mats are placed on each lower outside corner over the Sword Matting and these are followed by three Flat Ornamental Weaves and one Rose Knot attached to the Sword Matting on both sides of the frame at intervals.

The back of the frame is covered with canvas and each piece of the work is sewed on in a manner as previously explained.

The painting in the center of the frame is that of the five-masted twin-screw auxiliary French Barque "France," built at Rouen, France, in 1912. This vessel was of 7,500 gross tons and 430 feet long over all.

Useful Rope Designs

Frontispiece. The detail of the weaving can be followed by carefully studying the flukes of the anchor, its stock, and its ring. The weaving of the Elongated Diamond Knot appearing just below and above the ring is explained in the chapter on ornamental rope-work. The Four-Strand Triple Pass Sennit used to make the shank, and the Four-Strand Single Pass Sennit in the chain, are both explained in the chapter dealing with Sennit braiding. The Sennit Rose Knot made at the end of the anchor-chain is illustrated in its different forms of construction in the chapter on end-rope work. The material used is 84-thread seine twine; 180 feet of twine were used in its construction; and the anchor measures 14 x 22 inches actual size. The small knots at each side are Sailor's Breastplates. *See* chapter on simple knotting.

To make the anchor, first take six pieces of line, each thirty feet in length. Select three of these and middle them, with fifteen feet of line on each side, and put a seizing on them. Then, take the other three pieces and do the same. Lay them on a large surface, with one set of ends going to the right and the other to the left. Begin by making a loop in the center with one piece, and weaving the other piece through, so that they lock. This is the beginning loop as it is shown in the illustration at the bottom of the anchor between the flukes.

The ends are then woven out and back, as in the illustration. When all the ends are back in the center again, begin to braid the Sennit, which will make the shank. The shank from the flukes to the stock should measure twice the distance between the flukes, after they have been bent up into the proper curve and all the slack has been drawn out after the weaving. The Elongated Diamond Knot is made with two strands of three each. The other two are drawn up through the center of it before it is drawn tight. After it has been drawn tight, six single strands are cut off close to the top of the knot. The ring is then woven with the remaining six strands. After the ring has all the slack drawn out of it, another Elongated Diamond Knot is made with two single strands. The remaining four are then brought up through the center, the knot is drawn up taut, and two strands are cut off. The chain is then braided with the four remaining strands, and made as long as desired. At the end, after the Sennit Rose Knot has been made, the ends are cut off close to finish the job.

PLATE 270, (page 497). Remarkable type of Sennit frame construction. The knotting and designing used are quite obviously very intricate; but if the pattern is studied closely, it will be of invaluable aid in serving as a criterion, since all of the basic knots and braids have been described in Chapter X.

Chapter XI

Miscellaneous Knotting

THE CONTENTS OF this chapter include Lashings, Netting, Rope-Pointings, Slings, Rope Ladders, and various types of Mats with many other miscellaneous kinds of rope work, such as Boat Fenders, Trick Knots, novel Sennit Braids and unusual ornamental weaving.

All kinds of knots and ties which can be used for any practical or unusual purpose are included. Numbered among the many kinds of work that will be found of interest are the different methods of jug covering and a great variety of angler's and fish-hook ties, with numerous kinds of sack knots and package ties, which are all illustrated and described according to their various forms of construction and uses.

Plate 237—Miscellaneous Hanger and Ring Designs

FIG. 1: *The Oriental Door-Hanger Design No. 1* shows a variety of knots made up in the form of a design that can be used for hanging on the interior of a door as a decoration. This type of knot-work is used extensively in the Orient, where it is usually found on doors in business establishments, etc. Any form of ornamental knotting can be used.

FIG. 2: *The Shroud Knot Ring with Two-Strand Coxcomb.*

FIG. 3: *The Oriental Door-Hanger Design No. 2.*

FIG. 4: *The Closed Bugler's Braid* in this illustration has Sailor's Breastplates on each side which are tied as the braid is being made.

FIG. 5: *The Oriental Door-Hanger Design No. 3.*

FIG. 6: *The Double Chinese Knot* shown here has braided ends which are finished off with Four-Strand Star Knots and capped with Lanyards on both ends.

FIG. 7: *The Bell-Ringer Design* is formed by using a Four-Strand Flat Braid for the eye. Then continue with a Double Nelson Braid or Double Reverse Crowning until the body is long enough. Finish off with a Diamond Knot, Turk's Head Weave, or any other suitable knot. Designs like this, or similar ones, are still found aboard ships, where they are attached to the ringers on bells.

FIG. 8: *The Horse or Hitching Knot* was once used for the purpose its name indicates. It can be duplicated easily by observing the illustration.

FIG. 9: *The Lineman's Bowline* is similar to the Lineman's Knot, except that the Hitches lay flat and the ends run in opposite directions.

FIG. 10: *The Four-Strand Coach-Whipping Around a Core* is pictured here. Each strand has a set of five strands, or in other words, four five-strand sets, making twenty strands in all, which are braided in the same way as a four-strand single type. Four-Strand Turk's Heads with five passes each are used to cover the ends.

FIG. 11: *The Extended Antique Sennit Turk's Head.*

FIG. 12: *The Three-Strand Coxcomb with Four-Strand Turk's Heads.* The Turk's Heads have four passes on each end.

FIG. 13: *The Danish Shroud Knot Ring with a Single-Strand Cackling.*

FIG. 14: *The Triple-Passed Manrope Rosette.*

FIG. 15: *The Cotton Line, Comb-Hanger Design* is first tied with a Walled Crown, then a series of Reverse Crowns, a Lanyard Knot, and finally a Round Braid and a Diamond Knot. The strands are frayed out and combed.

FIG. 16: *Serving on a Rope* showing both ends whipped with black line.

Plate 238—Stopper Knots, Trick Knots, and Hitches

FIGS. 17A and B: *The Figure-of-Eight Trick Knot* is an interesting design. FIG. 17A shows how the end of the line is passed through the open Figure-of-Eights, and FIG. 17B indicates how they appear when the line is pulled taut.

FIG. 18: *The Triple-Passed Three-Strand Stopper Knot* is tied in the same way as the other Stopper Knots in the chapter on End Ropes, except that it has an additional pass.

FIG. 19: *The Triple-Passed Four-Strand Stopper Knot.*

FIG. 20: *The Triple-Passed Three-Strand Manrope Knot* follows the regular method.

FIG. 21: *The Triple-Passed Four-Strand Manrope Knot.*

FIG. 22: *The Triple-Passed Three-Strand Diamond Knot* is tied in the same way as the ordinary method, with the exception of an additional pass.

FIG. 23: *The Triple-Passed Four-Strand Diamond Knot.*

FIG. 24: *The Single Blackwall Hitch* consists of a Half Hitch crossed through a hook. This is a quick and easy way to temporarily secure a rope to a hook.

FIG. 25: *The Government Eye Splice in Three-Strand Rope* was used on ridge ropes in former years, in order to give them a neat taper so that they could be passed through the small chocks that were used in those days. It is made by taking two tucks with the first strand, three tucks with the second strand, and four tucks with the third, after making the first tuck in the usual manner. This brings all the strands out on the same side, as illustrated.

FIG. 26: *The Double Blackwall Hitch* is made by placing the bight of the rope across the strop on the block. Cross it behind the hook, and then cross it again in front of the hook as illustrated. It holds much better than the Single Hitch.

Plate 239—A Fender, Comb Hanger and Other Designs

FIG. 27: *The Comb-Hanger Design* shown here is tied in white cotton line. It consists of a Diamond Knot, Lanyard Knot, Star Knot, and Turk's Head Weave.

FIG. 28: *The Rope Fender* is begun by unlaying a sufficient amount of rope from each end, after first forming the eye with a Flat Seizing. Then proceed by reversing each set of Crowns until the body is long enough. To finish off, stick the ends down through the middle and out through the body. Pull taut and cut off short.

FIG. 29: *The Antique Rose Knot* is a slight variation of the English Rose. The strands are crossed on top to form a Crown Weave. Then each strand is tied with an Overhand Knot, to finish off after making the last tuck. Knots like this are largely a matter of individual origin, as anyone can produce new ideas of his own by combining various weaves.

FIG. 30: *The Combination Basket Weave.*

FIG. 31: *The Double Figure-of-Eight Loop* is tied by forming two bights and passing each working end of the line under

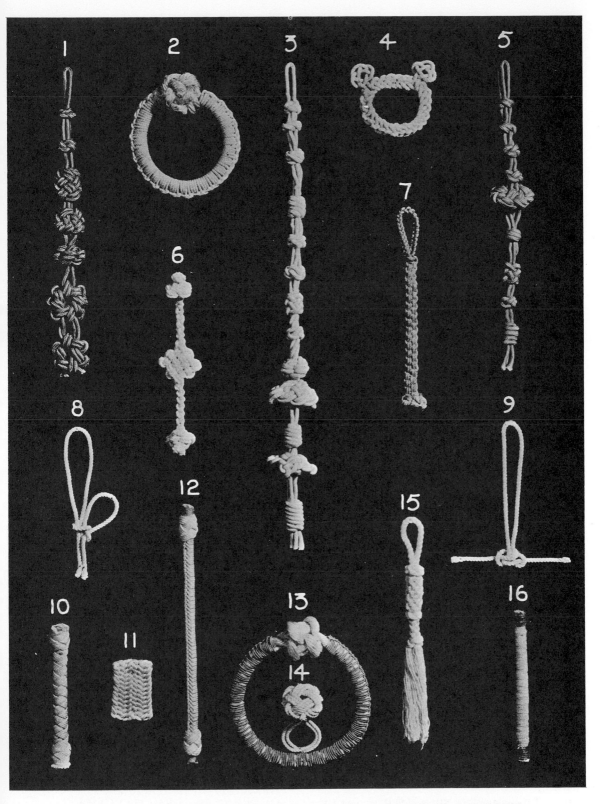

PLATE 237—MISCELLANEOUS HANGER AND RING DESIGNS

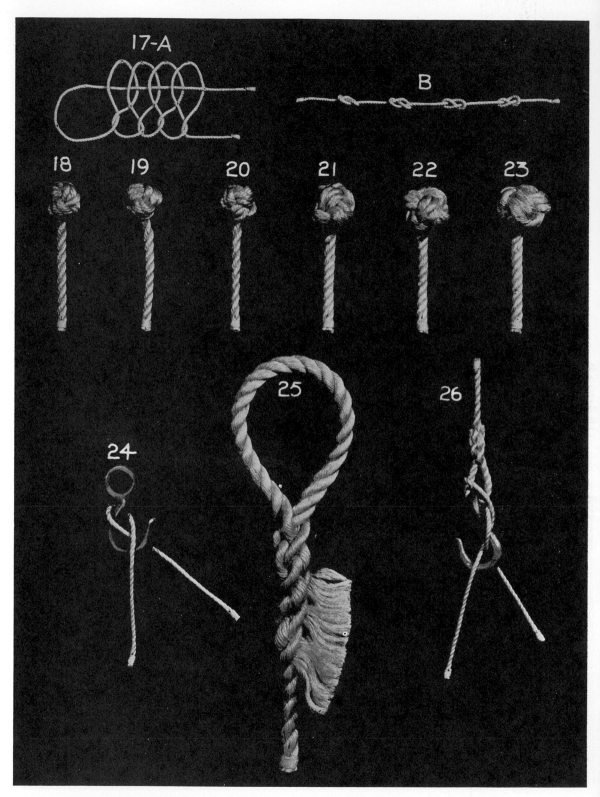

PLATE 238—STOPPER KNOTS, TRICK KNOTS, AND HITCHES

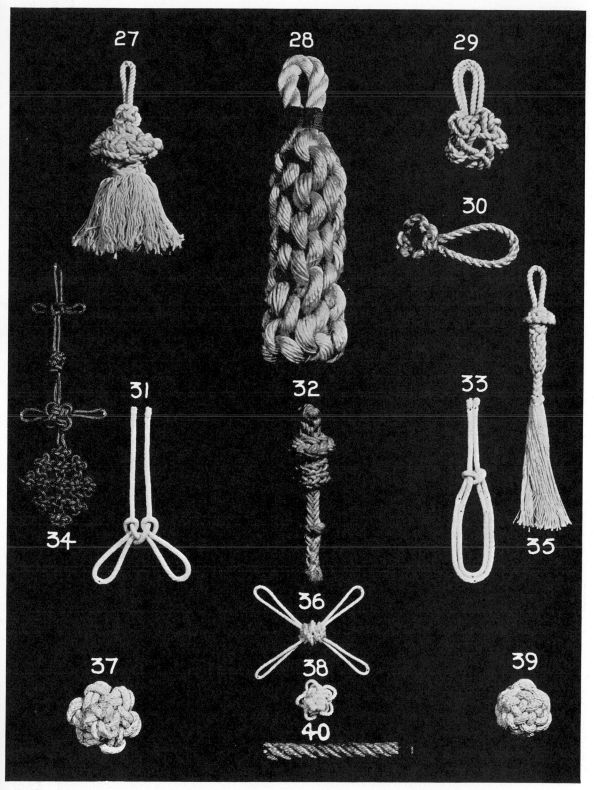

PLATE 239—A FENDER, COMB HANGER, AND OTHER DESIGNS

its own bight. Then cross them in the center by passing each strand out through the opposite eye formed by the other strand.

FIG. 32: *The Bell Rope Cord Design* shown here is begun at the base. It starts with six double strands, which are used for the Double Nelson Braid. Next, a Double Wall Knot is formed, which is followed by a Twelve-Strand Star Knot after splitting the strands. When the Star Knot has been completed, pull it taut. A Turk's Head Weave is now tied with all twelve strands, and then a Combination Walled Crown and Turk's Head Weave. After finishing this knot, braid the strands into a Twelve-Strand Square Sennit, and seize the end of this braid with a Double Wall Knot of six strands. Continue with a Double Six-Strand Round Sennit, and finish off with a Spritsail Sheet Top Knot.

FIG. 33: *The Double Running Knot* variation in this figure is made by tying an Overhand Knot, and passing the ends through the body of the knot as illustrated.

FIG. 34: *The Oriental Door-Hanger Design No. 4* shows a variety of oriental knots.

FIG. 35: *The Comb-Hanger Design*

shown here is made of white cotton line. It is tied in a slightly different way from the others by using a Combination Knot, a Diamond Knot, Single Nelson Braid, and Lanyard Knot.

FIG. 36: *The Spider or Windmill Knot* is tied by building a Spritsail Sheet body up in the middle of four bights.

FIG. 37: *The Combination Star and Lanyard Knot Rosette.*

FIG. 38: *The Five-Pointed Star Knot* with the ends pulled out.

FIG. 39: *The Combination Diamond Weave Crowned Down through the Center.*

FIG. 40: *The Hitched Rope Pointing* is made by first opening the rope up and scraping the heart or the underneath yarns down to a taper. Next, marl them, and proceed by sewing small strands of Marline or tarred line under two or three yarns of rope all the way around. Fender Hitch these strands together, and drop each alternate strand as the work tapers down to a point. Finish off by tying a Square Knot with the last two strands on the end.

Plate 240—Various Types of Mat Weaves

FIGS. 41A, B, and C: *The Square Mat Weave* is shown in FIG. 41A with the rope laid out to begin the weave. FIG. 41B illustrates the second stage of the work after one end has been closed up and FIG. 41C pictures it when completed, with the drawn lines showing how it is closed.

FIGS. 42A, B, and C: *The Sailor's True Lover Mat Weave* has the ends coming out on the bottom. FIG. 42A shows the first stage of the work. FIG. 42B presents it as it appears when the right bight is crossed and laid over the left bight, which has also been crossed. The drawn lines indicate how to

close it up. FIG. 42C shows how it looks when finished.

FIG. 43: *The Crowned Double Bight.*

FIG. 44: *The Crowned Double Bight Sheepshank.*

FIGS. 45A and B: *The True Shamrock Knot* is tied by forming two Interlacing Overhand Knots, as illustrated. Then pull the bight of each one through the opposite side as shown by the drawn lines. The knot will finally appear as in FIG. 45B, after it is pulled taut.

FIG. 46: *The True Shamrock Knot Doubled.*

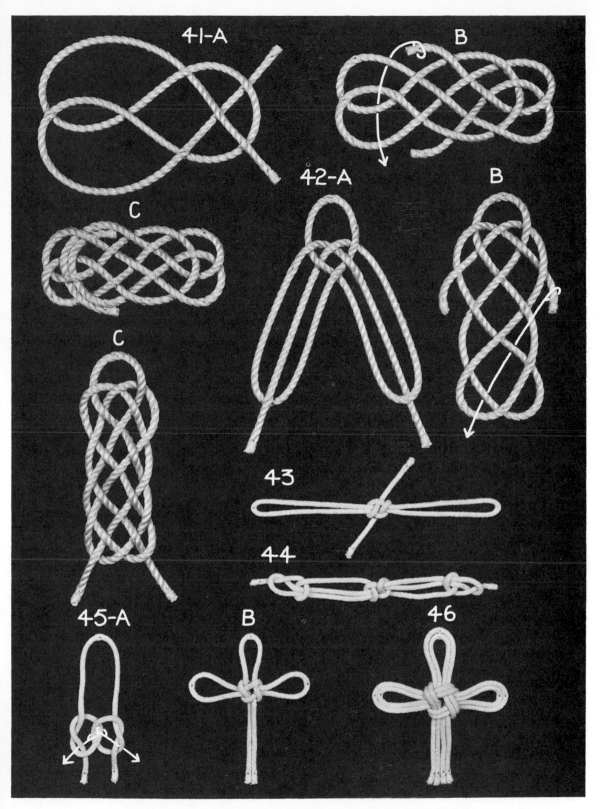

PLATE 240—VARIOUS TYPES OF MAT WEAVES

Plate 241—Lashes, Splices, and Weaves

FIGS. 47A, B, and C: *The Napoleon Bend Mat Weave* is shown here with the ends closed. In FIG. 47A, the rope is laid out to begin. The drawn lines indicate how to proceed with the working end of the line. FIG. 47B is the second stage of the work, after the first passes are completed. The mat is closed up as shown by the drawn lines. It will then appear as in FIG. 47C.

FIG. 48: *The Four-Strand Flemish Eye Cringle* is laid up on the same principle as an ordinary Flemish Eye, and can be used as a Cringle.

FIG. 49: *The Eight-Strand Irregular Turk's Head* extended from a Four-Strand Irregular Turk's Head with five crosses, and flattened out. The method of making these Turk's Heads is described in Chapter VI.

FIG. 50: *The Loop Lashing* pictured here has the ends of the line seized on opposite sides.

FIG. 51: *The Lashed Cut Splice.*

FIG. 52: *The Loop Lashing* in this illustration has the ends of the line seized in the middle of the body of the eyes.

FIG. 53: *The Ornamental Design* shown here can be used for decorative purposes. It represents a Double Nelson Braid, Star Knot, Outside Matthew Walker Knot, a Single and then a Double Nelson Braid, finished off on the left side with two Turk's Head Weaves, one on top of the other.

Plate 242—Masthead Knots, Rose Knots, and Weaves

FIG. 54: *The Sailor's True Lover Mat Weave* is shown here with both ends closed. It can be doubled or tripled, if desired, to form a more compact body. This knot makes a very handsome rope mat.

FIG. 55: *The Napoleon Bend Mat Weave* in this illustration has the bottom end left open. It is tied in a slightly different way from FIG. 47, but can be duplicated without difficulty.

FIG. 56: *The Five-Part Variated Masthead Knot* here has the body pulled together.

FIG. 57: *The Five-Part Masthead Knot* is tied in the same manner as a three- or four-part knot, except that it has additional parts.

FIGS. 58A to E: *The Rose Diamond Knot* is shown here formed with two strands. To make it, first form a bight and seize the strands together. Wall both strands as in FIG. 58A, and crown both strands on top of the Wall as shown in FIG. 58B. Next, each strand is passed under the other's part, between the Crown and Wall, and then passed out through the middle of the knot, as in FIG. 58D. This will bring each strand out under two parts. Pass each strand under the other strand's part again, as the drawn line indicates. Then tuck them under the strands that lead out from the seizing and up through the top. Pull taut, and the knot will appear as in FIG. 58E.

FIG. 59: *The Davenport Brothers' Trick Knot* is so called because it was used by these celebrated performers in doing a rope trick on the stage. It is tied by joining two lines together with an Overhand Knot. Then two running knots are made just below the Overhand Knot.

FIG. 60: *The Overhand Knot* shown here is tied in the middle of four bights.

FIGS. 61A and B: *The Trick Chain of Overhand Knots* in this illustration has the Hitches laid out in the fashion shown in FIG. 61A. Then the end of the line is passed through and pulled taut, bringing the knots out as they appear in FIG. 61B.

FIG. 62: *The Four-Strand Double Nelson or Cackling Braid* is tied around a core, which is made by Reverse Crowning with four double strands.

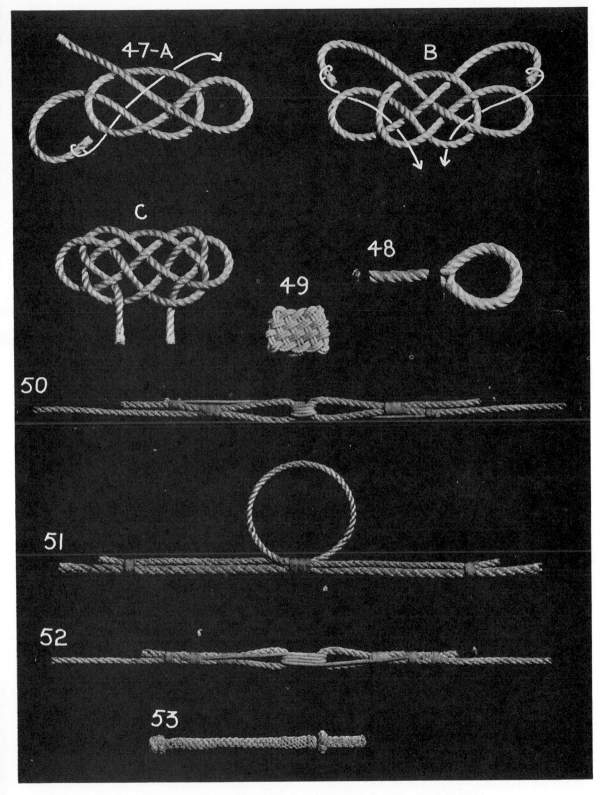

PLATE 241—LASHINGS, SPLICES, AND WEAVES

Plate 243—The Peruvian Quipu

FIG. 63: *The Unit "One" in the Ancient Inca Method of Counting*, which is said to be still used by Peruvian shepherds. Each additional turn in the cord, in lengthening the knot, increases the numeral. The cords are hung vertically or attached to a basal cord, and units of tens, hundreds, and thousands are placed in the order named from bottom to top, spaced at proper intervals.

FIG. 64: *Unit "Two"* (2).

FIG. 65: *Unit "Three"* (3).

FIG. 66: *Unit "Four"* (4).

FIG. 67: *Unit "Five"* (5).

FIG. 68: *Unit "Six"* (6).

FIG. 69: *Unit "Seven"* (7).

FIG. 70: *Unit "Eight"* (8).

FIG. 71: *Unit "Nine"* (9).

FIG. 72: *Number "Three Thousand"* (3000).

FIG. 73: *Number "Three Thousand, Four Hundred"* (3400).

FIG. 74: *Number "Two Thousand, One Hundred, Twenty"* (2120).

FIG. 75: *Number "One Thousand, One Hundred, Eleven"* (1111).

FIG. 76: *Number "Four Thousand, Thirty"* (4030).

FIG. 77: *Number "Five"* (5).

Plate 244—A Cask Sling, Gaskets, and a Sennit Weave

FIG. 78: *The Snaking on Backstays* was used when preparing for action on sailing-ship men-o'-war. A small rope was seized alternately from one stay to another, to keep either one from falling if shot away.

FIG. 79: *The Cask Sling* shown here was used in former years aboard sailing ships. It was made with a Bowline Knot in the yard-whip. Then the end was stuck back, in order to form a short bight to which the stay-whip was bent. The bight of the Bowline was next turned over its own part, and the two bights thus formed were slipped over the cask.

FIG. 80: *The Reefing Becket Sennit* can be made in a variety of designs. The eye of this design is formed with a Three-Strand Sennit, then closed together and continued with a Six-Strand Running Sennit. After it is plaited down for a certain distance, the strands are separated again with two Three-Strand Braids to form another eye. It is then closed up and continued as before, until the next eye has to be formed in the same way as the previous one. Next, the eye is closed up again, and the Braid tapered down from six strands to a Four-

and then a Three-Strand Sennit to finish off. On sailing-ships, the eye was constructed around a toggle, which remained in. When fitted to go around a jack-stay, the plaiting was carried down six inches from the toggle, and the foxes or strands were separated and an eye eight inches long formed. It was finally plaited down another nine inches, and the end whipped to finish off.

FIG. 81: *The Gasket* pictured here was made in former years by taking three or four foxes and middling them over a pin or pump-bolt. The three or four parts were then plaited together for the length of the eye. The plaiting was formed by bringing the outside fox on each side alternately over the middle, as in making a Running Sennit. It was tapered toward the end by removing a fox at intervals. When completed, one end was laid up—the others were plaited—and then the one end was hauled through. Foxes are made by taking a number of rope-yarns and twisting them on the knee by rubbing them back and forth with a piece of canvas. Spanish foxes are made by twisting single rope-yarns back-handed in the same way.

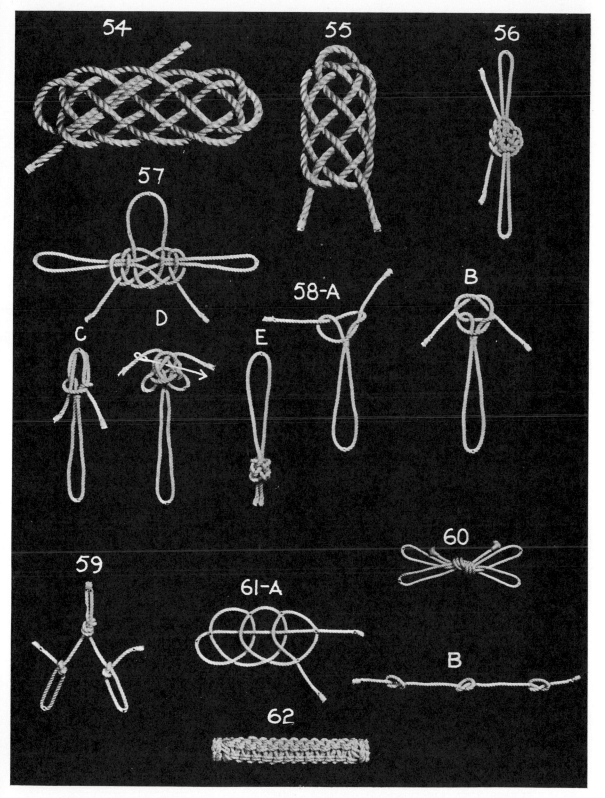

PLATE 242—MASTHEAD KNOTS, ROSE KNOTS, AND WEAVES

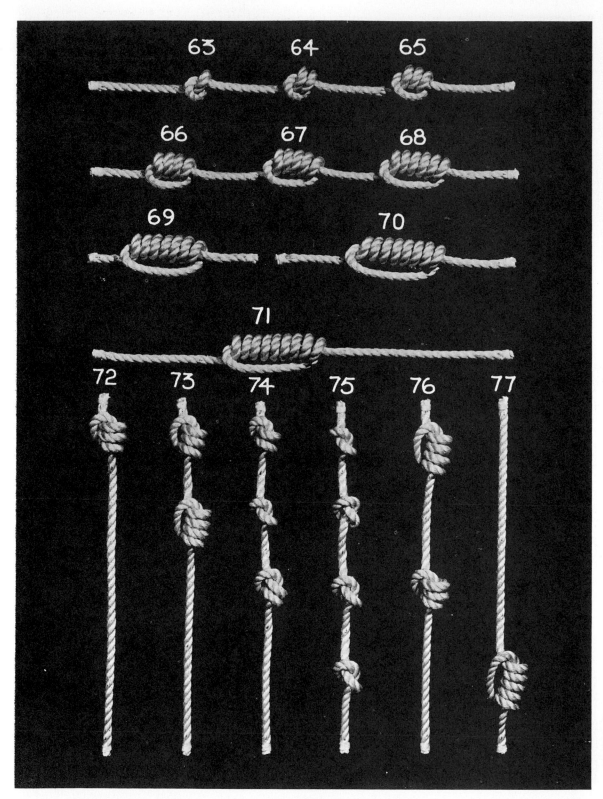

PLATE 243—THE PERUVIAN QUIPU

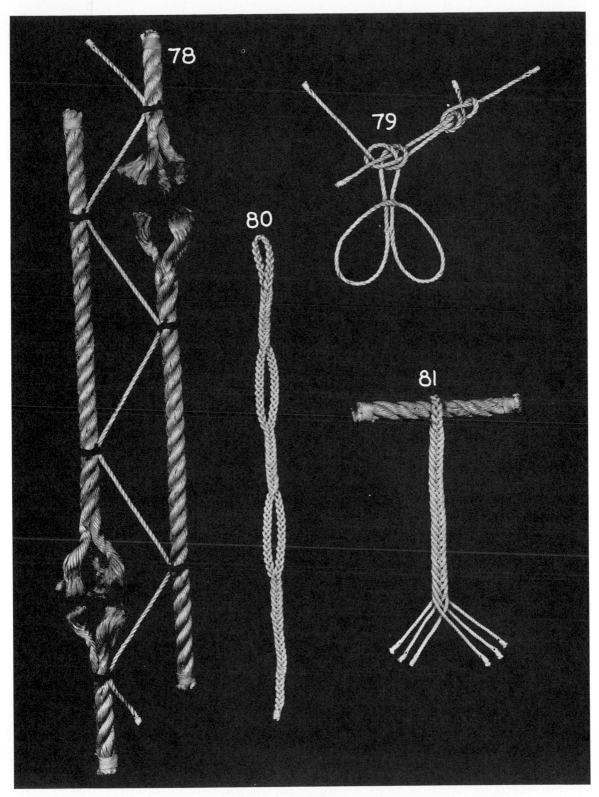

PLATE 244—A CASK SLING, GASKETS, AND A SENNIT WEAVE

Plate 245—French, Russian, Spanish, and Sword Mats

FIG. 82: *The French Mat* is made by middling any number of strands over a lashing—the number depending on the width of the mat required. Proceed by crossing each set of strands with the bottom strand, going over the top strand in each set. Then continue with a Flat or English Sennit type of braid, going under one and over one, etc., until the desired length is reached. Sew the ends together to finish.

FIG. 83: *The Spanish Mat* can be made with any number of strands suited to the width desired. Middle the strands over a lashing. Then crown them downward from left to right. On the upper left side, at the top of the weave, note that the underneath strand is taken over the top strand, of which it forms a part. It is then crowned down through the bight of the next strand. The other strands are also crowned down through the bight of the following strand in the same way, until the opposite side of the weave is reached. The next row is reversed, and crowned back from right to left, as shown in the bottom part of the weave. The outside strand on the left side and the outside strand on the right side are used as filler strands. Around them are passed the other strands used for Crowning, in order to close the weave on both sides, as the alternate Crowning continues. To finish off, take the outside strands across the bottom, hitch the other strands around them, and pull the ends out at the back. Tuck each end up through the back of the mat, pull taut, and cut them off.

FIGS. 84A and B: *The Russian Mat* is tied by first taking a piece of cordage and securing it to any convenient fastening. Any suitable number of strands are then middled over the lashing. Next, cross the underneath strand on the left side over the top strand, of which it forms a part, just as in the preceding method. Continue by walling each strand through the bight of the following strand, until the opposite side of the weave is reached. After making the last wall tuck—and using the underneath strand on the right side—pass this strand under, around, and over the outside strand. Then wall the strands back toward the left side again in the same way. Filler strands on both sides form a part of the weave, as in FIG. 83. The ends are hitched to finish off, as previously described. FIG. 84A shows the weave as it appears when opened up. FIG. 84B pictures it as completed.

FIGS. 85A and B: *The Wrought or Paunch Mat* is begun by taking any desired number of strands and middling them over a lashing. Next, bring the underneath strand over the top strand of each set from right to left, all the way across. Pass each strand under two strands toward the right side, and back over the same two strands toward the left side. Follow this procedure with each strand in turn, until the weave reaches the required length. The outside strand on each side serves as a filler for attaching the other strands. FIG. 85A shows the strands worked down into a point in the middle, which is the best way to keep the weave pulled up in place as the work continues. However, the method commonly used in this kind of work is illustrated in FIG. 85B. In this method, it will be noted that the strands are worked down into a point on the left side, by tapering the weave from the right side down. This is one of the old-type mats once used for heavy rigging on sailing-ships. It also makes an attractive design for covering Sennit Frames.

FIG. 86: *The Sword Mat* is formed by first middling the strands over a lashing, as in the preceding designs. Then middle a length of sail twine by passing it between the top and bottom parts of the strand next to the lashing. Proceed by taking every other strand up across the weave, with the

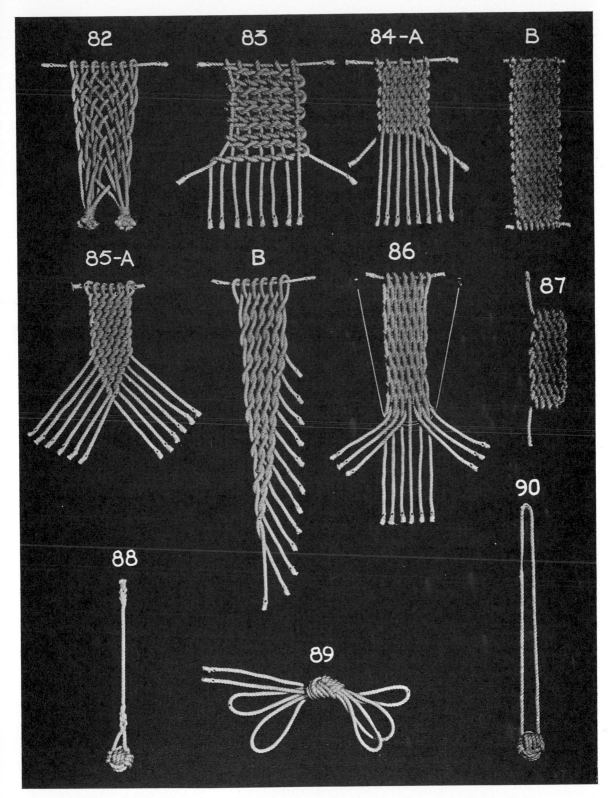

PLATE 245—FRENCH, RUSSIAN, SPANISH, AND SWORD MATS

alternate strands laying down, and pass the sail twine, or warp, from each side. Next, bring the bottom strands up, with the top strands laying down, and again pass the warp between the strands as illustrated. Continue this method until the mat is of the desired length, and then sew the ends together to finish off. There are various ways to make these mats, differing only in certain details. The old method of using a primitive loom is still frequently followed. But the method described here will be found much quicker and easier. The Sword Mat is a suitable design for covering Sennit Frames, etc. Any size line can be used for the work.

FIG. 87: *The Sword Mat* in this illustration is made from one piece of line. It

can be used as a deck mat on any type of boat. To make it, follow the directions given in FIG. 86, but use only one line.

FIG. 88: *The Three-Strand Monkey Fist* is tied in white line, with the working end spliced back into the standing part. Finish it off with a Back Splice on the end of the standing part.

FIG. 89: *The Bow Knot Shortening* is a slight variation of the ordinary Overhand Knot Shortening. It is made with the ends coming out in the form of a bow, and can be cast off easily if necessary.

FIG. 90: *The Four-Strand Monkey Fist on a Loop* is made with the standing part of the line knotted and tucked on the inside before the knot is pulled up taut.

Plate 246—Rose Knots, Star Knots, and Bag Knots

FIG. 91: *The Small Combination Rose Knot* is tied by first forming a Triple-Pass Monkey Fist or Terminal Knot, and then a Six-Strand Rose Weave, followed by a Turk's Head Weave triple-passed around the outside. The knot is sewed securely with sail twine to finish off. (See Chapter IV for the various keys of End Rope Knots.)

FIG. 92: *The Large Combination Rose Knot* is tied with a Triple-Passed Monkey Fist or Terminal Knot, a Turk's Head Weave, a Seven-Strand Rose Weave, and another Turk's Head Weave triple-passed around the outside body. Sew each part of the knot together, as previously mentioned.

FIG. 93: *The Medium Combination Rose Knot* is formed with a Triple-Passed Monkey Fist or Terminal Knot, a Six-Strand Rose Knot, a Triple-Passed Turk's Head Weave around the body, with another Triple-Passed Turk's Head Weave around the base. The ends are then tucked into the knot, which is sewed in the usual manner.

FIG. 94: *The Seven-Strand Star Knot* is

shown here, with the top part triple-passed.

FIG. 95: *The Topsail Halyard Bend* in this illustration is tied in the orthodox manner. This method is never used on merchant marine ships, but is sometimes employed on yachts. It is formed by first taking three round turns around a spar. Next, bring the working end back around the standing part, and pass it back under all three turns, then back over the last two, and under the first turn again.

FIG. 96: *The Fisherman's Bend* shown here follows the orthodox method of construction. First, take two round turns around the object to which it is to be attached. Then pass the working end around and under the standing part and make a round turn, forming a Half Hitch. Form another Half Hitch to make it secure. This knot is used for bending a rope to beckets.

FIG. 97: *The Magnus Hitch* pictured here illustrates the orthodox method of tying this knot. To begin, take two round turns over a spar, with the working end of the rope. Then bring the line back in front of the standing part, and make another

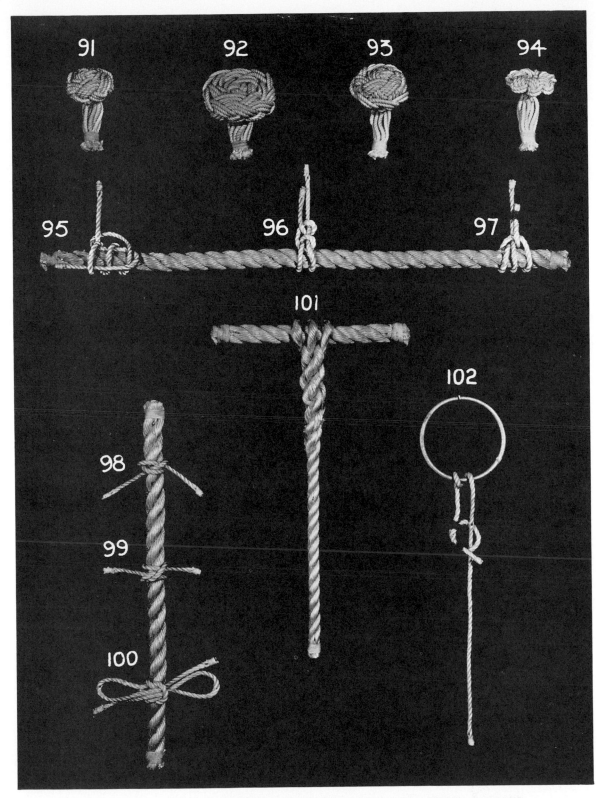

PLATE 246—ROSE KNOTS, STAR KNOTS, AND BAG KNOTS

turn, bringing the line back under its own part. Finally, seize it to the standing part.

FIG. 98: *The Miller's Sack or Bag Knot* is made by first taking a round turn. Then cross the body of the turn with the working end, going over the opposite end, and out under its own part. This knot was once used by millers to tie sacks.

FIG. 99: *The Double Builder's Knot* can be tied easily from the illustration.

FIG. 100: *The Double Bow or Rosette Knot.*

FIG. 101: *The Lashing Splice* is begun by unlaying the strands a sufficient distance. Next, pass each strand around the object the rope is to be lashed to, and tuck each one back into the standing part. Then splice and taper the strands as usual.

FIG. 102: *The Round Turn and Slip Clinch* is a very secure form of Slip Knot.

Plate 247—Mat Weaves, a Braided Eye, and Other Knots

FIG. 103: *The Three-Pass Sailor's True Lover Mat Weave* is closed at both ends.

FIG. 104: *The Three-Pass Japanese Knot.* (Same as PLATE 152, FIG. 226.)

FIG. 105: *The Three-Pass Napoleon Bend Mat Weave* is closed at both ends. This weave has only eight points, whereas FIG. 103 has ten points. (Same as PLATE 241, FIG. 47.)

FIG. 106: *The Three-Pass Square Mat Weave.* (Same as PLATE 141, FIG. 66.)

FIG. 107: *The Bow Hitch or Running Knot* is tied through the eye of a rope. This is one of the simplest methods that can be utilized for fastening the end of a rope to a ring, loop, or eye, etc.

FIG. 108: *The Four-Strand Braided Eye* is joined together with a Lanyard Knot. Then a Turk's Head Weave is placed on top. After the knot is pulled taut, a whipping is put around the strands and the strands themselves are opened up and frayed out to form a tassel.

FIG. 109: *The Five-Cross Four-Strand Turk's Head* is pulled tight to form a Knob

or Stopper Knot. The ends are led out on each side, or at top and bottom as illustrated here. (See Chapter VI for a description of Turk's Heads.)

FIG. 110: *The Strop Knot* is tied with each strand formed into a loop, or double strand. It is started from the bottom end with a Double Nelson Braid, which is braided up a short way. Then the strands are split, and a Turk's Head Weave is tied with single strands. A whipping is placed around the strands to finish off. The Strops on the bottom are finally walled around the end of the braid, and pulled taut.

FIG. 111: *The Cargo Net* in this illustration is made with brown-line. It will be shown in a different design in PLATE 255, FIG. 146.

FIG. 112: *The Turk's Head Bow* is formed by first making a Four-Strand Turk's Head with five crosses. Next, pull the bights of the ends through the knot in the form of a bow. Then pull the body of the Turk's Head up tight, and cut and whip the ends.

Plate 248—The Bell Ringer's Knot, and French Shroud Knots

FIG. 113: *The Chain of Artilleryman's Knots* shown here illustrates the formation used in tying these knots on the line attached to a heavy gun, when the gun is to be moved by man-power. The bights are placed around the shoulders of the men.

FIG. 114: *The Carrick Bend Design* in this illustration is tied in a Three-Strand Turk's Head, and inverted or flattened out.

FIG. 115: *The Eye Splice* pictured here has the body fender hitched in four-strand

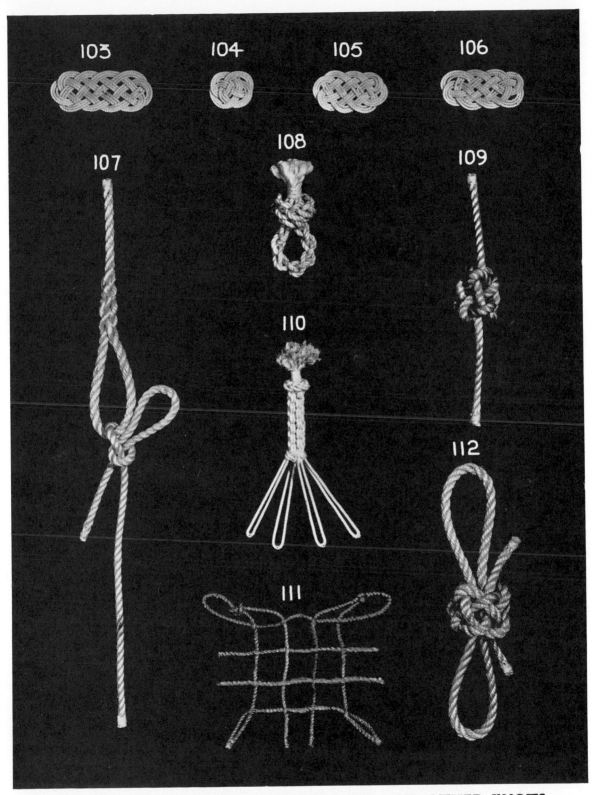

PLATE 247—MAT WEAVES, A BRAIDED EYE, AND OTHER KNOTS

rope. After the first tuck of the Eye Splice is made, the strands are hitched together for a short distance, then tucked back into the rope and cut off.

FIG. 116: *The Bell Ringer's Knot* is designed for a particular purpose. Church bells have a wheel on the axle to which they are hung. The bell rope passes around this wheel, to obtain leverage enough to raise the mouth of the bell upwards when it is rung. This operation requires a long rope, most of which lies on the belfry floor when the bell is down. After ringing the bell, this slack is tied up out of the way, with the knot illustrated here. It is nothing more than a Hitch on the end of the standing part. The working end of the line is passed back through the Hitch to form a Slip Eye, which will hold securely if the Hitch is kept pulled up close to the standing part. A slight pull with the end of the line will release the whole knot instantly. Tufting is usually found on the standing part above the Hitch, for use in grasping

the line. It is made by opening the strands and placing short pieces of worsted through them. Then trim off these pieces until they are all the same length.

FIG. 117: *The Three-Strand French Shroud Knot* shown here has been joined together in the usual way. Next, the strands of one rope are formed into a Crown Knot, and the strands of the other are made into a Wall Knot. This brings all the strands out the same way. The whole knot is then doubled, and a Lanyard Knot is tied on top for security.

FIG. 118: *The Racking Hitch* is practically the same as a Cat's Paw. Two bights are made in a rope, and turned over two times. Then the eyes of both bights are attached to the hook of a block, or whatever object they are going to be used in connection with.

FIG. 119: *The Four-Strand French Shroud Knot* is made in the same way as FIG. 117.

Plate 249—Eight Types of Barrel Slings

FIG. 120: *The Vertical Barrel Sling* may be used when a barrel is to be slung in an upright position. It is formed by first placing the barrel upright on the rope. Then join the end and standing part of the rope with an Overhand Knot above the barrel. Open up the knot, and slip the middle down over the barrel. This will bring half of the knot on each side. Pull both parts of the line up securely, and join the end to the standing part with a Bowline.

FIG. 121: *The Horizontal Barrel Sling* is also used, at times, for heavy sacks, and is therefore often called a Sack Sling.

FIG. 122: *The Butt Sling* is made with an Eye Splice on one end and two Half Hitches on the other, after allowing enough slack for a long loop which has a rope passed around and then secured with a Bowline.

FIG. 123: *The Parbuckle Sling* is used as a purchase for raising or lowering heavy casks, guns, etc. When hauling, equal force should be applied to both ends of the rope. A plank is used to form an incline in order to make the leverage more effective.

FIG. 124: *The Vertical Barrel Sling* shown here is made with two Overhand Knots instead of one, as in FIG. 120. This gives both a top and bottom seizing around the barrel, and is a very good method to use where extra care and safety are necessary.

FIG. 125: *The Cask Sling* is employed for slinging casks or barrels that have the heads knocked in. It is made by slipping the bight of the rope under the cask, and taking a hitch with each part over the head. Then the end is joined to the standing part with a Bowline.

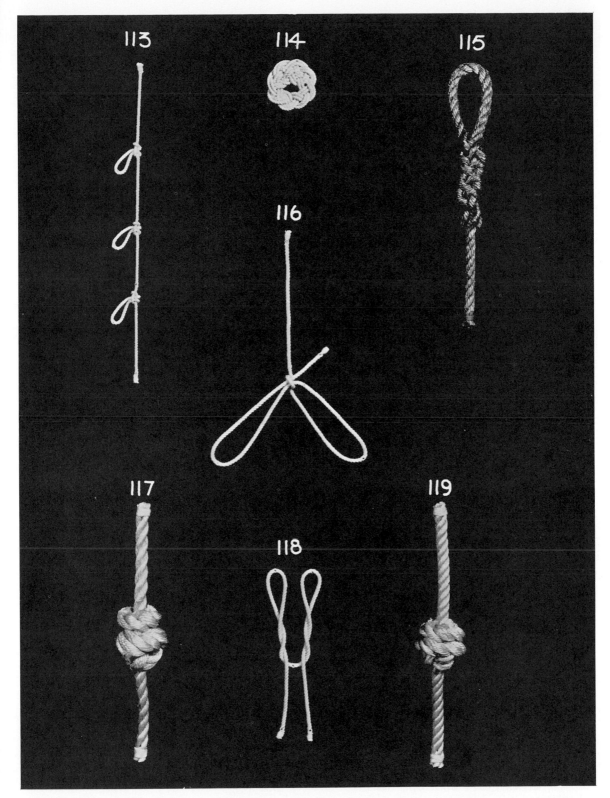

PLATE 248—THE BELL RINGER'S KNOT, AND FRENCH SHROUD KNOTS

FIG. 126: *The Bale Sling on a Barrel* is made with a piece of line spliced together and passed around the barrel. It is then passed under its own bight, pulled taut, and attached with a Bowline fastening.

FIG. 127: *The Hogshead Sling* is used to sling large heavy casks. It is more secure than can hooks or most other slings. Splice an eye in one end of the line. Then take the other end around the cask and through the eye, as in FIG. 122. Next, take the line around the other end of the cask and make it fast with two Half Hitches, after pulling the connecting part of the line down taut to the cask. It is then seized with a Bowline or hook, to make fast for lifting.

Plate 250—A Package Tie, and a Stationer's Knot

FIG. 128: *The Package Tie* shown here is the regular tie used in department stores and elsewhere for tying packages. It is made by first forming a Slip Eye in the end of a line, and bringing it to the center of the package. Pass the line around it in a horizontal direction, then through the eye, and pull tight. Next, pass the line around the parcel again in a vertical direction, bring it under the first pass, and over its own part, as illustrated. Pull this up tight, and it will hold securely. But for added safety, it is best to finish off with a Half Hitch.

FIG. 129: *The Stationer's Knot* is also handy for tying up parcels, as it can be made rapidly and can be untied instantly by pulling on the end of the line. First, form a Slip Eye. Next, pass the line around the parcel in a vertical direction, back through the eye, and pull tight. When this has been done, the line is passed around in a horizontal direction, and passed around the vertical and then the horizontal part. A Slip Eye is then formed, as shown in the illustration.

FIG. 130: *The Rope Ladder* shown here has its rope rungs made as in FIG. 131. For every other rung, the knot is reversed.

FIG. 131: *The Ladder Rung Knot* is tied with two parts of rope. One part is laid out with a bight at each end. The other part is passed through the top bight on the right as shown. Any number of round turns can be taken, suitable to the length of the rung. The rope is then passed through the lower bight on the left, and the knot is pulled taut.

FIG. 132: *The Column Sling* is made by taking two ordinary slings and joining them together with a Basket Hitch. They are then placed around the column as illustrated.

Plate 251—Rope Ladder Making

FIG. 133: *The Single Rope Ladder with Chocks* is begun by splicing an eye with a Thimble at one end. Next, run one of the chocks down the rope with the large side up, to about 28 or 30 inches from the end of the eye. A Footrope Knot is then tied underneath with any suitable line, and double-passed. Continue in the same way with the other chocks, leaving about 15 inches between each Footrope Knot, which is tied underneath. Chocks are usually made of oak, and turned from 4 to 5 inches in diameter, then tapered down in proportion. They are 4 to 5 inches long. The diameter of the hole through the center depends on the size of the rope to be used.

FIG. 134: *The Rope Ladder with Wooden Rungs* always has the ladder rungs spaced about 12 inches apart. If the ladder is to be from 24 to 25 feet long, it will require about two dozen rungs, each one a foot long, with the ends scored according to the size of the rope being used. After stretching and laying out the proper

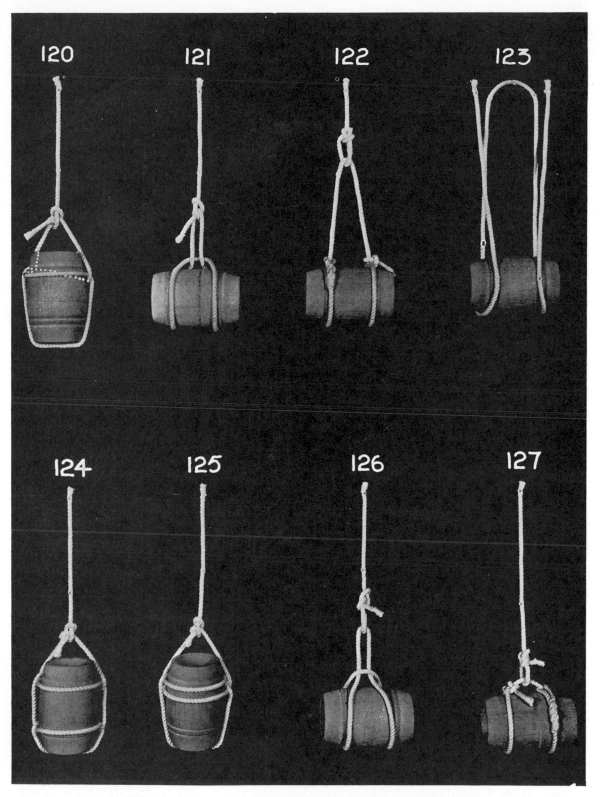

PLATE 249—EIGHT TYPES OF BARREL SLINGS

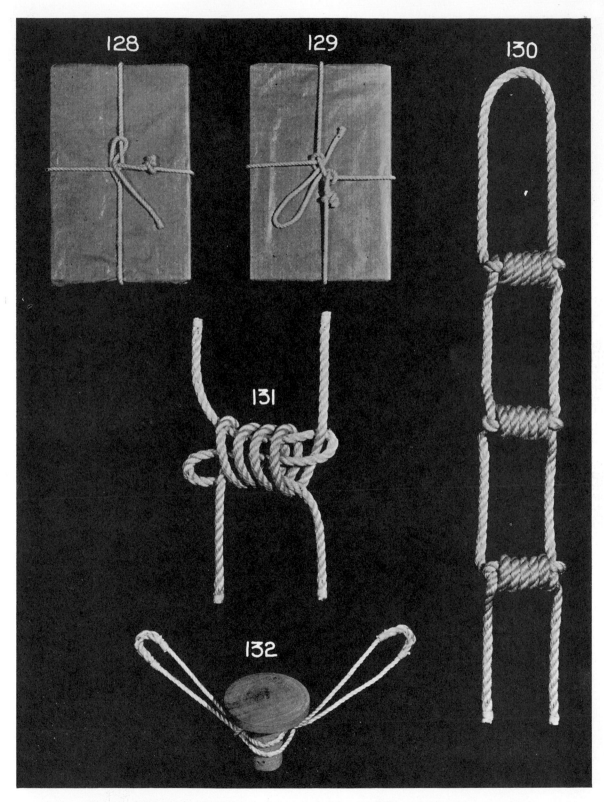

Plate 250—A PACKAGE TIE, AND A STATIONER'S KNOT

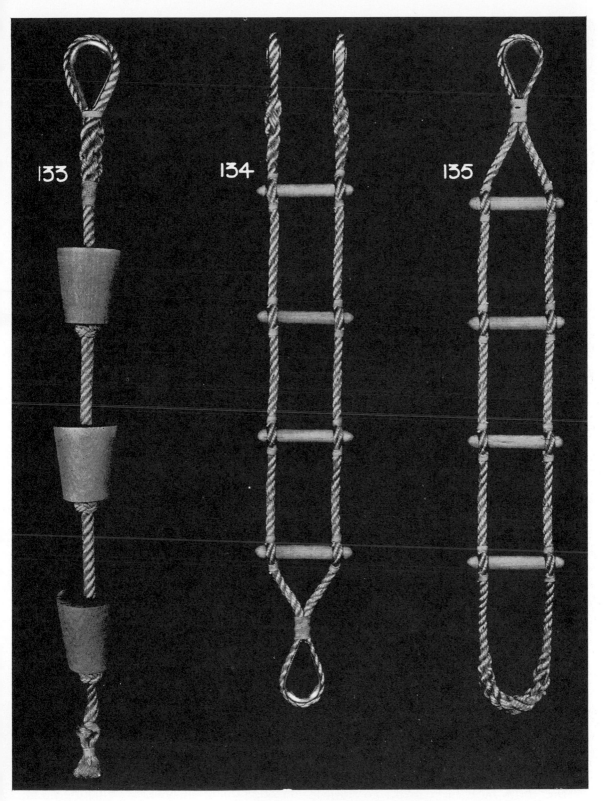

PLATE 251—ROPE LADDER MAKING

amount of rope, middle it and seize it around a thimble. Then mark off on both parts of the rope the place intended for each rung, spacing them about a foot apart. Beginning at the end nearest the thimble, open the rope up with a fid and push a rung in. Repeat on the opposite side, and continue until all the rungs are placed. Then, using a 7- or 8-turn whipping, seize the rope on both sides just above and below each rung. Splice both the ends around the thimbles, to form an eye on the end of each part.

FIG. 135: *The Stern Rope Ladder with Wooden Rungs* is made in the same way as FIG. 134, except that the two parts of rope on the bottom are spliced together at the finish.

Plate 252—A Boatswain's Chair, Fenders, and a Ladder

FIG. 136: *The Long Round Fender* is a duplication of the Round Fender in PLATE 253, FIG. 142, except that the bag should be made in the shape of the fender in FIG. 138.

FIG. 137: *The Pilot Ladder* is the most popular type of ladder, due to its sturdy and simple construction and the ease with which it may be handled. Each rung has four holes drilled in it, two on each side. To make it, take two lengths of rope, each one about twelve feet longer than twice the desired length of the finished ladder. Middle these, leaving one end on each rope six feet longer than the other. A thimble or a plain rope eye is seized in each bight (although this is optional). Then these eyes are lashed to a convenient horizontal object, the eyes being the same distance apart as the holes across the rungs. All the rungs are put on the ropes, each rope going through one of the four holes. The four ropes are stretched out, so as to suspend the entire ladder in mid-air. Next, the first rung is pushed up flush against the eye seizings in the bights, and a strong cross-seizing is put on just below the rung on each side, binding the two ropes together. Make two more cross-seizings the desired distance from the first rung, and bring the next rung up flush against these. Then another seizing is put on just below this rung. The same procedure is continued, until all the rungs have been used. To finish, splice the shorter of the two ends into the longer end on each side. The long ends are then utilized as Lanyards to lash the ladder when in use. If preferred, the ends may be finished off as in the illustration, with a round thimble. In this case, Lanyards are spliced into the thimbles.

FIG. 138: *The Long Round Fender* (Canvas Covered Rubber) has a rubber filling, and is much more durable than the cork-filled canvas fender. This type of fender must be purchased, because of the special construction of the rubber filling.

FIG. 139: *The Bos'ns or Rigger's Chair* is used by sailors or riggers when painting or making repairs aloft. The chair consists of a flat piece of board, at least eight inches wide, the length depending on the dimensions of the person it is to accommodate. Ordinarily it will be about twenty-two inches long. Four holes, two on each end of the seat, are drilled. It may be reinforced on the bottom, as in the illustration, although this is not necessary. To rig it, take a piece of rope the desired length (usually about fourteen feet). Put one end through one of the holes on one side, inserting it from the bottom, pulling it through almost to the end, and then passing it down through the hole directly opposite on the other side of the chair. The rope is now brought back to the beginning, crossing over on the bottom of the chair (never on top). Then pass it up again through the other hole. After taking up all the slack, the rope is passed down through the remaining hole, and both ends are

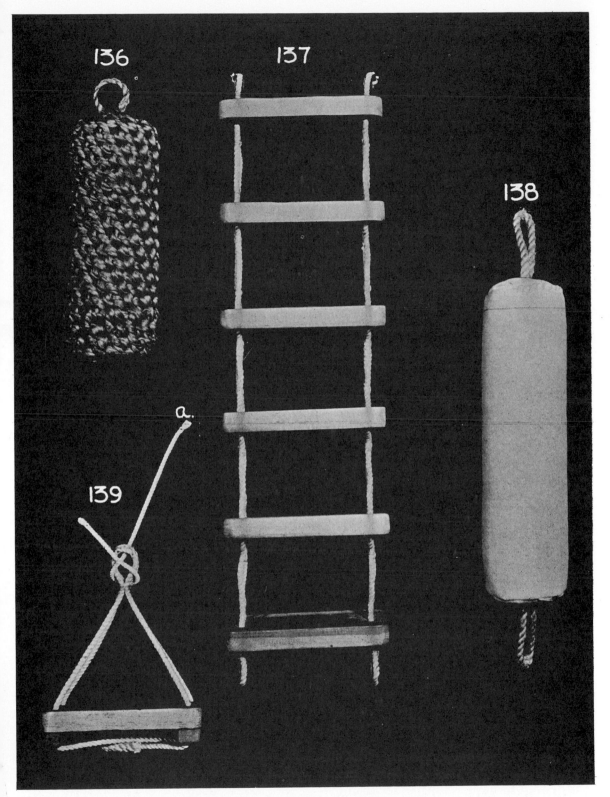

PLATE 252—A BOATSWAIN'S CHAIR, FENDERS, AND A LADDER

short-spliced together. The bights on top of the chair are adjusted so as to be of equal length, and seized together, leaving an eye. A Gantline is now made fast in this eye. The proper knot to use for this pur-

pose is a Double Sheet Bend. A Single Sheet Bend was used in the illustration for the sake of clarity. End *a* is rove through a block, and made fast to the chair as shown in PLATE 257, FIG. 163.

Plate 253—A Sling, and Two Types of Fenders

FIG. 140: *The Canvas Cargo Sling,* First Method, is used for cargo in bags, such as sugar, beans, etc. To make it, first take two lengths of rope and Long-Splice each one into its own ends, so as to form two Strops. Then take a piece of No. 00 canvas and sew the Strops to it in the manner shown. Another length of rope is next taken, and one end passed through one of the bights of the Strop and eye-spliced. The other end is passed through the bight of the other Strop, and another Eye Splice made. This same procedure is followed on the other side to complete the job.

FIG. 141: *The Oblong Flat Fender* is used over the side of boats and ships, to prevent the vessel's side from coming in contact with the dock, which might scrape off the paint and perhaps damage the boat. To begin, make a large Grommet, forming the handle as at the top. Then sew a piece of canvas or burlap into the shape of the finished fender. Make it in the form of a bag, and fill it with ground cork or rope-yarns cut in short lengths. When about one-quarter full, the Grommet is placed inside the bag, and the remainder of the bag filled with the cork or rope-yarn. After filling, the top is sewed, with a suffi-

cient amount of the Grommet remaining out for the handle. Next, take a long piece of rope, and unlay the strands for its entire length. Taking one strand, place a turn around the middle of the fender at point *a*. Then begin half-hitching the strand on this turn, and continue half-hitching until one side is completely covered. (Note that in the upper half of the fender the Half-Hitching is placed in a position exactly the reverse of that of the lower half.) When the upper half has been finished, take another strand, and beginning at the strand in the center (*a*), half-hitch the other half with Fender Hitching, illustrated in PLATE 105, FIG. 16.

FIG. 142: *The Round Fender* is made in the same way as the preceding fender. But instead of being oblong, it is round. A round thimble is spliced into the end of a piece of rope, and the other end is passed through a hole in the lower end of the canvas bag. After the bag has been filled and sewed, the rope coming out of the bottom is unlaid, and the three strands of each rope are sewed to the outside of the bag. Now proceed to half-hitch as in the previous fender.

Plate 254—A Canvas Cargo Sling, and Fenders

FIG. 143: *The Canvas Cargo or Oil Drum Sling,* Second Method, is used for the same purpose as the Sling, PLATE 253, FIG. 140. First, take a heavy piece of canvas (heavy sheet-rubber is sometimes used). If it is desired to have a Sling wider than the single piece of canvas, another section is sewed to the first. Sew both ends, using a

flat stitch. Cut eight holes through the canvas as shown. Then put Grommets into these as indicated in PLATE 296, FIG. 498. A piece of rope of adequate length is next passed through these eyelets. After this has been done, the ends are short-spliced together on the bottom of the Sling. The illustration shows a top view of the Sling.

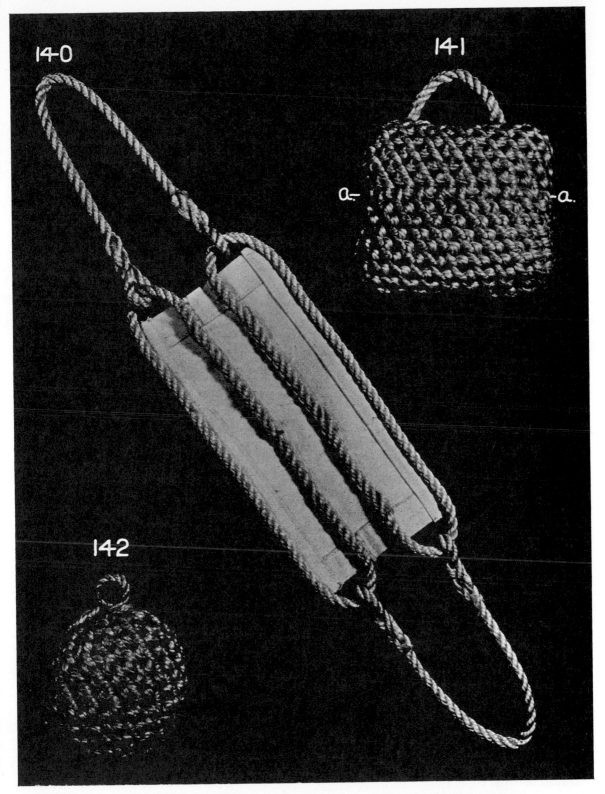

PLATE 253—A SLING, AND TWO TYPES OF FENDERS

FIG. 144: *The Vertical Fender* is made for small boats. It is hung over the side in a vertical position, suspended by the Lanyard spliced into the eyelet. To make it, take a piece of No. 1 canvas (heavier can be used if necessary), and cut it to the proper size. Double it over lengthwise, and sew up one side with a double seam, using a flat stitch. Next, take a small piece of canvas and measure out the bottom. This is then sewed on with either a single or double seam. The bag is now turned inside out and filled with rope-yarns, cork, or waste cotton. Fold in the top and sew in the form of a half-circle, using a round stitch. Then punch a hole in the canvas at this point, and insert a metal eyelet (*see* PLATE 296, FIG. 498). Splice a Lanyard into the eyelet to finish.

FIG. 145: *The Horizontal Fender* is made much in the same manner as the preceding fender, except that eyelets are made in both top and bottom. For the handles (which are put in before the bag is filled), a Grommet may be made, or two small Stopper Knots can be tied with their bights passed through the eyelets. This type of fender is suspended horizontally over the side of a boat, and made fast with a Lanyard spliced into each loop.

Plate 255—A Rope Cargo Net, and Footrope Knots

FIG. 146: *The Rope Cargo Net* is usually made of three-strand rope although four-strand is occasionally used. The size of the rope varies according to the type and weight of material to be handled. It is customary to make the frame (the rope running around the outer edge of the net into which the mesh ropes are spliced) of heavier rope than the mesh.

To begin, take a length of rope and long-splice the ends together in such a manner as to make a frame the proper size when the splice is completed. Next, cut the mesh ropes, leaving about one and one-half feet over the frame on each side. First splice in all the vertical mesh ropes. The ends are spliced into the frame after having tucked the mesh rope under two strands. The common Eye Splice is used. Take another mesh rope and splice it into the frame. Then unlay one strand from this rope until it has been unlaid down to the first vertical mesh rope nearest the eye. This strand is then tucked under one strand of the vertical mesh rope. Next lay the strand up again until it reaches the next mesh rope. The single strand is then tucked under one strand of this rope again. Proceed to lay the rope up again until the next mesh rope is reached. This process is repeated until the opposite frame rope is reached. The mesh rope is then laid up completely, tucked under two strands in the frame rope and spliced.

This procedure is carried out until all the horizontal mesh ropes have been spliced in place. The rope forming the "V" at the top of the net is called a Becket, which is spliced into the frame rope in each corner (this rope is not tucked under two strands but passed completely around the frame rope instead). Another such Becket is spliced into the lower end of the net. These are placed over a cargo hook and serve as a means of lifting the net.

FIG. 147: *The Double Half Hitch Stopper* is used when stopping off a wire topping lift on a boom. In such cases small steel chains are used instead of ropes. The chain is made fast to the swivel eye just below the shell of the block.

FIG. 148: *A Splice in the Standing Part of a Rope.* When making a Footrope Knot of three strands it is necessary to splice a short piece of Marline into the middle of another piece of rope. This splice is placed in the center of the footrope and therefore is not visible.

FIG. 149A: *Three-Strand Diamond Foot-*

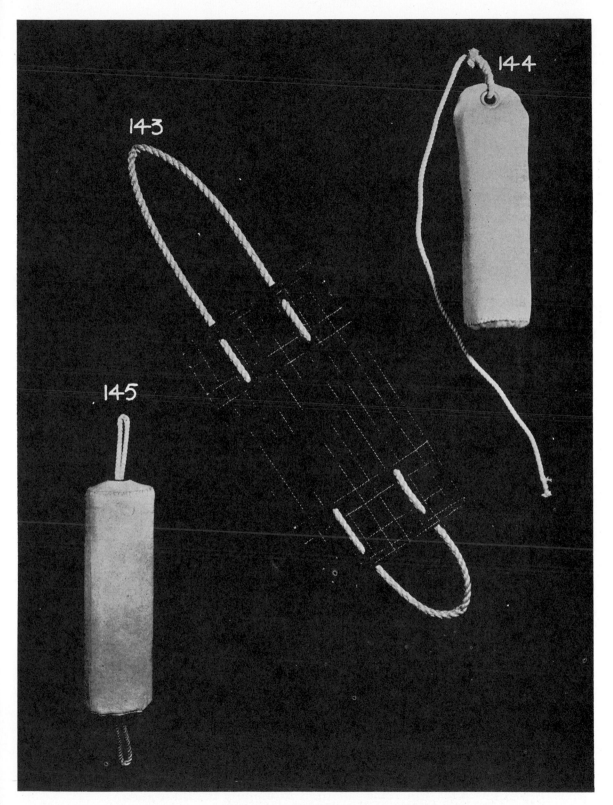

PLATE 254—A CANVAS CARGO SLING, AND FENDERS

rope Knot is begun by first tying the Diamond Knot (PLATE 60, FIG. 140). It is followed around twice, making three passes in all. Draw the entire knot up tight and cut the ends off short to finish. Footrope Knots are used on the footropes on the yards of sailing ships to prevent the sailor's feet from slipping. The finished knot is shown at *b*.

FIG. 150A: *A Three-Strand Crown Wall Footrope Knot* is made by first forming a Crown Knot, PLATE 53, FIG. 1, and then a Wall Knot, PLATE 53, FIG. 2, below it. Two

additional passes are made and the entire knot is drawn taut to complete. The finished knot is shown at *b*.

FIG. 151A: *The Three-Strand Long Footrope Knot* is tied as follows: First make a Diamond Knot, PLATE 60, FIG. 140, then turn the rope over (end for end) and tie another Diamond Knot. The ends will now come out in the middle of the knot as illustrated.

Two more passes are made, the slack is drawn up, and the ends cut off close to finish.

Plate 256—Various Footrope Knots, and a Railway Sennit

FIG. 152A: *The Crown and Wall Footrope Knot,* Four Strands, is made in four-strand rope. Take two pieces of Marline or white line of any suitable length. Pass one under one strand of the rope, and the other under another strand of the rope, but directly opposite the strand under which the first piece was tucked.

B: Then form a Crown Knot (PLATE 53, FIG. 1), followed by a Wall Knot (PLATE 53, FIG. 2), using all four strands of Marline. The Crown and Wall are followed around, to make three passes in all. Finally, the cords are drawn taut, and cut off short.

C: This shows the completed knot.

FIG. 153A: *The Diamond Footrope Knot,* Four Strands, is made in precisely the same manner as the preceding knot, but instead of tying a Crown and a Wall, form a Diamond Knot, PLATE 60, FIG. 140.

B: The finished knot, with three passes, is illustrated in this picture.

FIG. 154A: *The Diamond Long Footrope Knot,* Four Strands, is made as follows. The cords are passed through the rope as in FIG. 152. Then tie a Diamond Knot, (PLATE 60, FIG. 140), turn the rope over (end for end); and form another Diamond Knot. The ends will come out in the middle of the knot as illustrated. Follow the knot around twice, making three

passes in all. Draw up all the slack, and cut the ends off close to finish.

B: This shows the completed knot.

FIG. 155: *The Harpoon Lashing,* First Method, is used on the end of a harpoon, when there is no metal ring in which a line may be secured. First, take a suitable length of rope, middle it, and put on a seizing, forming an eye. Unlay the strands and the yarns, and lay up the yarns again to form two yarn nettles. The seizing of the eye is next placed on the end of the harpoon, and the nettles laid down along the shaft. With a good strong piece of Marline, cross-point the harpoon shaft for a distance of six inches (or more, depending on the length of the harpoon). The nettles are finally scrape-tapered and marled down on the shaft.

FIG. 156: *The Cat's Paw on a Hook* shows how a Cat's Paw is placed on a hook in practical use. Either of the two ends can be utilized as a hauling part.

FIG. 157A: *Knotting a Rope-Yarn* is done as follows: clutch the two strands of each rope-yarn together, and form a single Overhand Knot with the two strands *a* and *b*, as shown. (Heavy cord was used in order to simplify the illustration.)

B: This shows the Rope-Yarn Knot after it has been drawn up taut. (This specimen

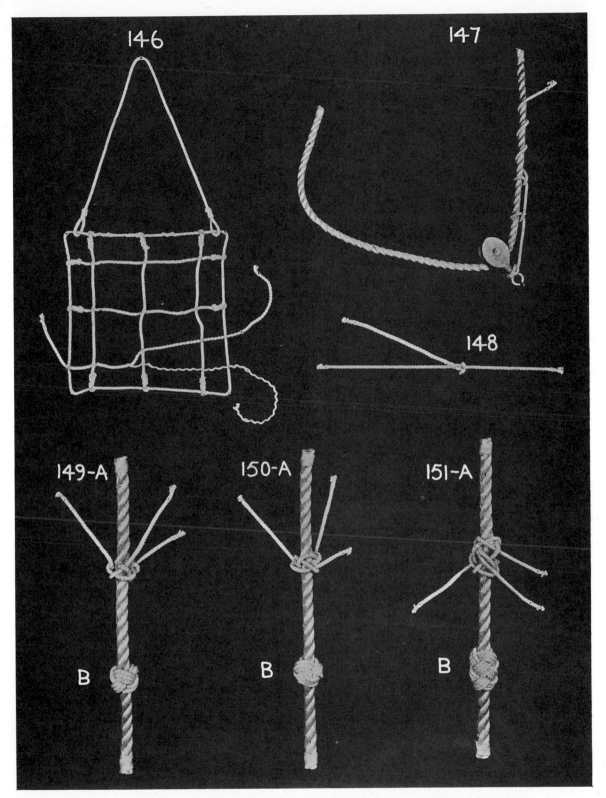

PLATE 255—A ROPE CARGO NET, AND FOOTROPE KNOTS

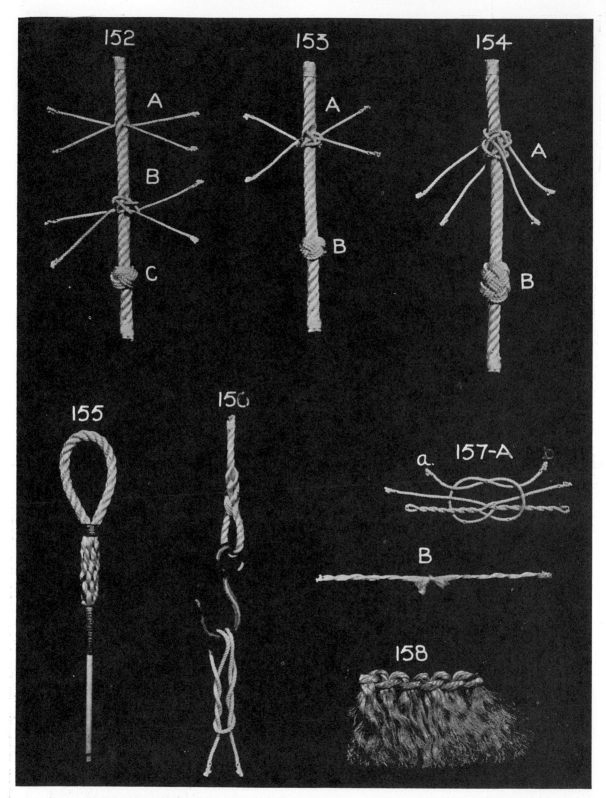

PLATE 256—VARIOUS FOOTROPE KNOTS, AND A RAILWAY SENNIT

was made with rope-yarn, instead of the cord used in the preceding illustration.) The ends are now trimmed off close to complete the knot. The Rope-Yarn Knot is employed when making Selvage Strops (*see* PLATE 262, FIG. 196).

FIG. 158: *The Railway Sennit,* First Method, is begun by unlaying two strands from a rope and twisting them together. The remaining strand is cut into three-inch lengths. Then each piece is middled

and passed through the rope between the two strands, one end on each side of the point where the strands cross. Continue until the desired length has been attained. This type of Sennit is used as chafing gear, being wrapped around stays and lifts and lazy jacks to protect sails in sailing-ships. It can also be used on the booms of steam-vessels, in order to prevent the wire cargo-runners from striking the underside of the boom and chipping off the paint.

Plate 257—Shell, Deadeye, and Regulating Lashings

FIG. 159: *The Shell Lashing* is another method of joining two ropes. A small lignum vitae ball having two grooves in its outer surface at right angles to each other forms the principal part of the lashing. The ropes are passed as shown and securely seized.

FIG. 160: *The Deadeye Lashing* was at one time used on the mast stays of sailing ships in place of turnbuckles. In this case, too, the principal part of the lashing is a lignum vitae oval disc. These discs have a groove cut in their outer surface, and at right angles to the groove three holes are drilled through the discs as shown in the illustration. The discs are then lashed much in the manner of the Shell Lashing. A smaller rope is rove through the holes in the discs, called the tackle, and one end of it is securely seized to the lower main rope as shown. A Handy Billy is attached to the other end of the tackle rope to apply the desired tension to the mast stay after which the upper end of the tackle is seized to the upper part of the stay as shown in the illustration.

FIG. 161: *The Regulating Lashing* is used when it is necessary to change the tension on a rope at frequent intervals. Guy ropes for tents and awnings are frequently secured in this manner, since they must be slacked off in wet weather and hauled taut when the weather is dry. When lashings

such as this are used the bight of the rope *a* is slipped over any fixed object and tension is applied by altering the position of the wooden block.

FIG. 162: *The Deadeye Block* is used when it is desired to alter the course or position of a rope. It is made up of a lignum vitae block having a groove in its outer surface and a hole through its center at right angles to the groove, a hauling line being seized around the block in the manner shown.

FIG. 163: *Rigging for a Boatswain's Chair* is shown in the accompanying illustration. After the Gantline has been rove through the block and secured to the chair bridle as shown and the workman has been hauled up he places the hauling part of the rope in front of him, grasps a bight and draws it through the bridle. The line is then passed over the workman's head and body, down under the chair and up in front of him again as shown by the arrow. All of the slack is hauled out of the line and it is then secured. To lower the chair all that is necessary is to slack off on the knot and allow the line to run out.

FIG. 164: *The French Multiple Cox-comb* is made with a single strand of cord in the manner illustrated on PLATE 107, FIG. 33. But, instead of hitching only once a hitch is taken around each preceding loop as the work continues around the object being covered.

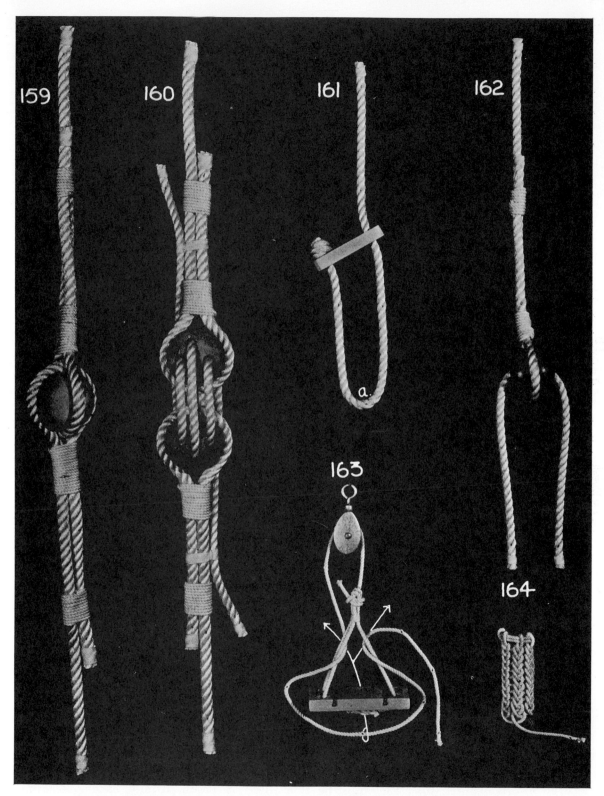

PLATE 257—SHELL, DEADEYE, AND REGULATING LASHINGS

Plate 258—Various Types of Pole Lashings

Fig. 165: *Poles Lashed and Wedged* in the manner shown in this illustration are held securely, with but little liability of their slipping or working loose. After the lashings have been applied small wooden wedges are driven between them and the poles as shown. This tends to take up any slack in the lashings.

Fig. 166: *The Telegraph Hitch* is used on long poles and piles when it is required to hoist them vertically. To make the hitch take a piece of line of sufficient length, middle it and make cross turns around the pole as shown. A short bar is then placed under the final cross turn and a turn is taken about it, after which the ends of the rope are secured with a Reef Knot forming a bight for the hoisting hook.

Fig. 167: *The Putlog Lashing* is employed when it is required to lash two square timbers together. The manner in which it is formed is clearly shown in the illustration.

Fig. 168: *The Packing Knot* is frequently used to hold large pieces of timber together. It is also used in stone quarries to secure large blocks of stone on the cars which haul them. The small block of wood used in the illustration is intended to represent a slab of stone. Two or three turns with a heavy line are taken around both the slab of stone and the dolly or car upon which the stone rests. A piece of timber or a metal bar is then inserted under

the lashing rope and it is twisted until all of the slack is taken out of the lashing. The piece of timber used as a lever is then in turn lashed to the body of the dolly as illustrated.

Fig. 169: *The Double Chain Lashing* shows the manner of making a line fast to a pair of crossed shears. The end is seized to the standing part of the rope after a sufficient number of turns have been taken about the shears.

Fig. 170: *A Loop Lashing* such as that shown serves to illustrate the manner in which the bight of a hawser is made fast to a pair of crossed shears. The bight of the hawser is passed over, under, and around the legs of the shears in the manner shown, after which the loop of the bight is placed over the top of one of the legs, leaving the standing part of the hawser as shown.

Fig. 171: *The Crossed Lashing* is another method used to make a line fast on the head of a pair of crossed shears. Any number of turns may be taken as shown, being crossed in back, after which the end of the lashing is made fast to its standing part with a seizing.

Fig. 172: *The Square Lashing* shown in this illustration is used for much the same purpose as that shown above. It is made in the same manner except that the turns are parallel and not crossed.

Plate 259—Tripod, Shear Leg, and Other Pole Lashings

Fig. 173: *The Shear Head Lashing* is used to lash the heads of a pair of shears together. The shears are laid parallel to each other on the ground; a number of turns are taken around them, after which several cross turns are taken. The ends are then finished off with a Reef Knot.

Fig. 174: *The Shear Leg Lashing* is em-

ployed to attach a cross member to the lower ends of the legs of a pair of crossed shears. The methods employed are clearly evident in the illustration.

Fig. 175: *The Tripod Lashing* is an interesting method frequently employed for holding the three legs of a tripod together. The three members are first placed in the

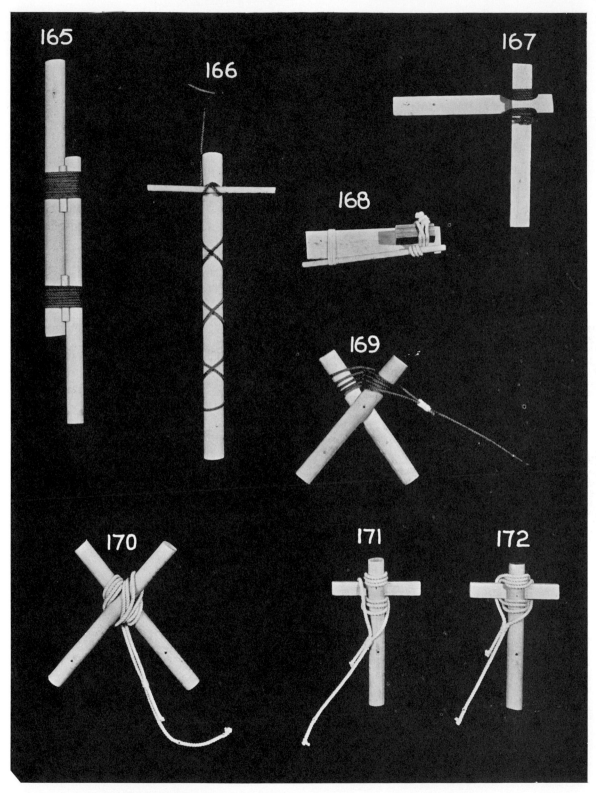

PLATE 258—VARIOUS TYPES OF POLE LASHINGS

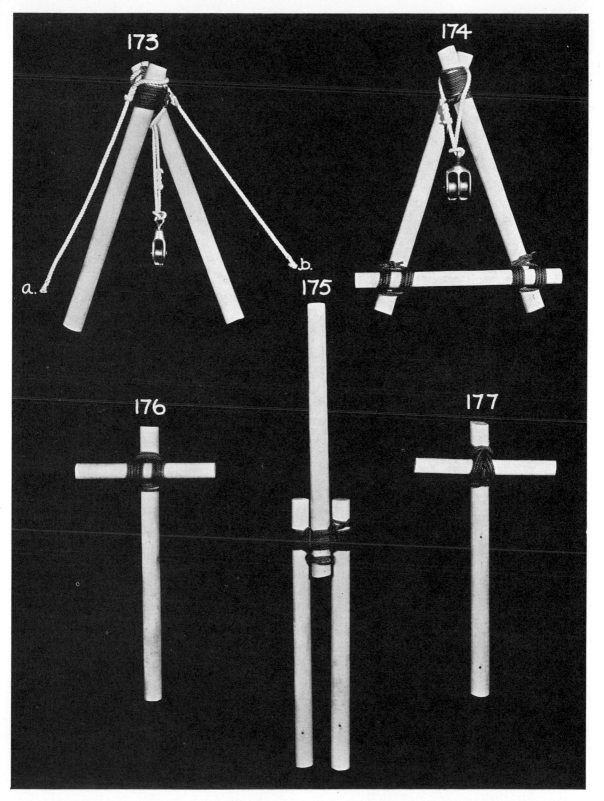

PLATE 259—TRIPOD, SHEAR LEG, AND OTHER POLE LASHINGS

position shown and a strong lashing is passed around all of them. Cross turns are then made between the shear heads, and the ends of this line are secured with Clove Hitches as shown.

Fig. 176: *The Square Cross Shear Lashing* is a very simple but secure method of passing a lashing which is commonly used.

Fig. 177: *The Herringbone Cross Shear Lashing* is made by taking a number of Figure-of-Eight Turns about the two members, after which cross turns are added above and below the cross shear. These tend to make the lashing more secure.

Plate 260—Various Methods for Securing Hawsers

Fig. 178: *Placing Hawsers Over a Bollard* on a dock should be done in such a manner that no matter how many hawsers are used each can be removed or cast off without in any manner interfering with the others. This is done in the following manner: assume that the bight of the hawser marked *a* was placed over the Bollard first, then when the second hawser *b* is passed its bight is brought up through the bight of hawser *a* as illustrated. If the bight of hawser *b* were not brought up through that of *a* it would not be possible to cast off hawser *a* without first releasing hawser *b*, which would not in all cases be desirable.

Fig. 179: *The Single Chain Fastening* is used over a single pile in the water. It consists of a series of Figure-of-Eight Turns taken around the pile and over the standing part of the line, after which the end is secured with two Half Hitches.

Fig. 180: *Securing a Hawser on a Bollard with a Round Turn.* It occasionally happens that when a hawser is passed over a Bollard it is given a round turn such as is indicated with the hawser *a* in the accompanying illustration. When this is the case such a hawser would not run free when cast off, as was the case with Fig. 178. To prevent such an occurrence the bight of the second hawser *b* is rove through the bight of hawser *a* as shown before being put over the pile. Either of the two hawsers can then be cast off without interfering with the other.

Fig. 181: *Three Hawsers on One Bollard.* When occasion demands it is often the practice to pass as many as three or more hawsers over the same Bollard. If this is done the bight of each line *a, b* and *c* must pass up through the eyes of all of the others, as shown in the illustration. By performing the operation in this manner any single line may be cast free.

Fig. 182: *The Lark's Head Mooring Hitch* is another simple method for securing a mooring line to a pile.

Fig. 183: *The Clove Hitch Mooring* is used for the same purpose as that in the example above.

Fig. 184: *The Round Turn Mooring Hitch* is made by passing several turns around a pile after which the end is made secure with two Half Hitches.

Fig. 185: *The Slippery Hitch* is a knot that should always be used on the sheets of small sailboats. One pull on the end of the line will release the sheet. This is often desirable when a sudden puff of wind hits the sail and there is danger that the boat might capsize.

Fig. 186: *Securing a Mooring Line,* First Method. This is a method of securing a mooring line with a series of Figure-of-Eight Turns about a pair of Bitts. The end of the line may be half hitched to one of the Bitts or it may be seized as shown in Fig. 187.

Fig. 187: *Securing a Mooring Line,* Second Method. This illustration is the same as Fig. 186, except that the end of the line is shown seized to prevent its running out. A seizing such as this is always applied when wire rope is used.

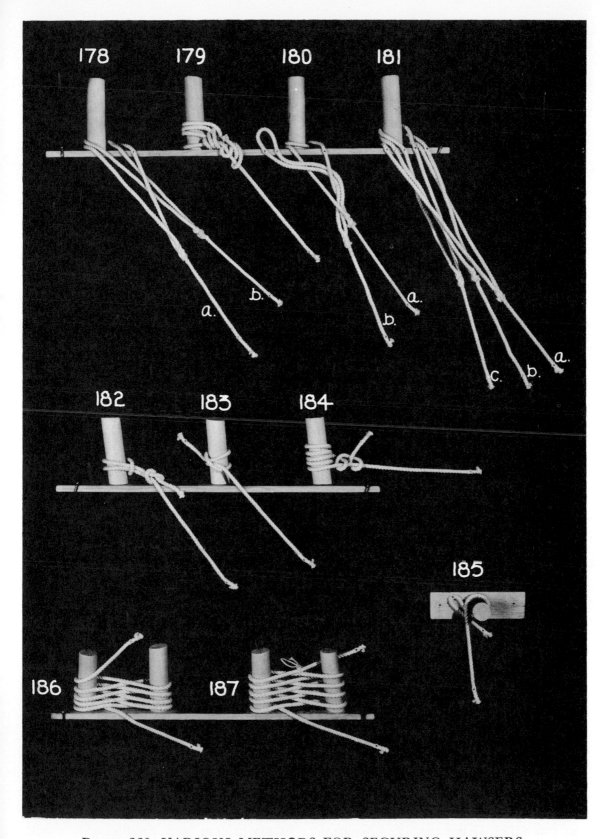

PLATE 260—VARIOUS METHODS FOR SECURING HAWSERS

Plate 261—A Stage Sling, and a West Coast Stage Sling

Fig. 188a: *The Stage Sling* is a rope design often found very useful by sailors. When working over the side of a ship or in a shipyard, it is frequently necessary to have a light yet sturdy scaffold capable of supporting one or two men. This need can be served by what is known as a stage, consisting of a long flat plank with two "horns," bolted at right angles to the plank. The purpose of these horns is to keep the plank away from the surface being worked on. In order to suspend the stage from— let us say—a ship's side, it must be rigged with ropes. This is done as follows: first, lay out the rope as shown, into a Marline-Spike Hitch. This is made a short distance from the end.

b: Next, place the knot under the horn, bringing part *a* over the top of the stage, Bights *b* and *c* are then brought over and on top of the horns on each side.

c: The end is now brought up and a Bowline formed, using the end and the standing part as indicated. But, before drawing the knot taut, be certain that both parts are even, so that the stage will not be canted when it hangs on the rope. One of these knots is made on each horn. The standing parts may be rove through the blocks on the deck above, with the ends brought down and made fast to the stage. This eliminates climbing back up on deck to lower the stage—which would be necessary if it were made fast to a railing.

Fig. 189: *The Overhand Wharf Tie* is an easy method of making a line fast to a pile on a dock when only the bight of the line is available. A simple Overhand Knot is first made in such a way that when the operation has been completed the bight will face upward. All that then remains is to cast the bight over the top of the pile.

Fig. 190a: *The West Coast Stage Sling* may be made in preference to the Sling described in Fig. 188. It will be noticed that this Hitch is not made on the stage

horns, but on the plank itself. To form it, take two full turns on the stage. (More may be made if desired, but two will be sufficient.) Next, bring the middle turn inside and under the standing part to the right, then to the left, over all the turns, and finally back to the right again—but underneath the plank, as indicated by the line.

b: The slack is now drawn up, and the end and the standing part finished off with a Bowline.

Fig. 191: *The Heaving Line Bowline* is another knot of great usefulness to seafaring men. When docking a ship and sending the hawsers ashore, the process must as a rule be carried out as quickly as possible. After the heaving line has been cast ashore, there is usually a good deal of unnecessary fumbling in making the end fast to the eye of the hawser. This can be eliminated by tying a Bowline, using the method illustrated here. The end of the line is first rove through the eye of the hawser. Then take the standing part of line *a* in the left hand, and place it in the position shown. End *b*, which is in the right hand, is next passed under the middle strand as noted by the arrow. Now cast end *b* away from you, and at the same time give standing part *a* a sharp jerk. The knot will automatically fall into a Bowline. Although this method appears to be a bit drawn out, a little practice will enable anyone to tie the knot in half the time required to tie a Bowline in the ordinary manner. This method can be used also when making fast to a pile (as in the illustration), or in any other situation where a Bowline is advisable.

Fig. 192: *The Stopper* may be applied as follows: when tying up a ship, or when a heavy load is to be suspended and it is desired to take the rope off the niggerhead or capstan. End *a* is the part leading to the capstan, and standing part *b* leads

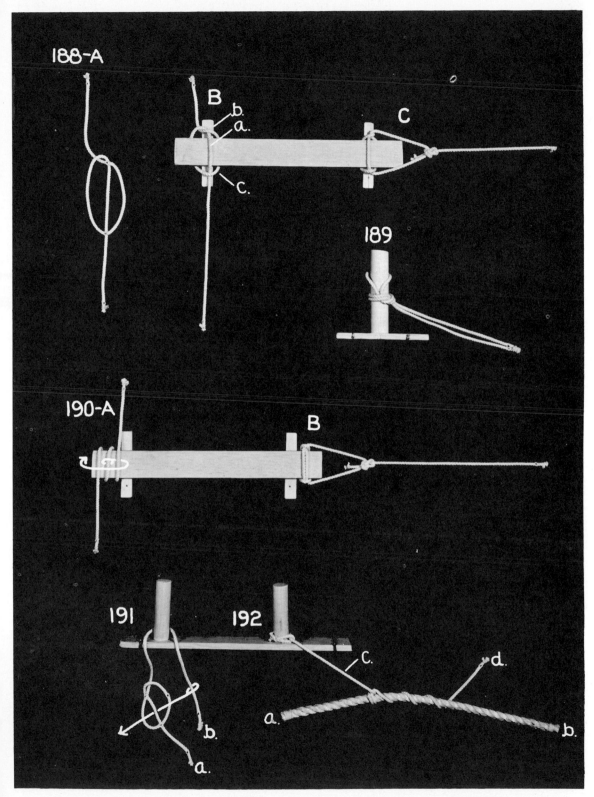

PLATE 261—A STAGE SLING, AND A WEST COAST STAGE SLING

to the load. The Stopper, *c*, is made fast to the Bitts and secured to the working line with a Stopper Hitch (*see* PLATE 4, FIG. 92), the end being "dogged" with the lay, and the bitter end *d* held in the hand. End *a* is

next slacked off the capstan until the Stopper is bearing all the strain. Then make end *a* fast to the Bitts or Chock, whichever is used, and remove the Stopper to complete the operation.

Plate 262—Mousing a Hook, and Securing a Grommet Strop

FIG. 193: *The Yoke Line* is used on the yoke of the rudder in small boats, dories, dinghies, etc. A Manrope Knot (PLATE 294, FIG. 485) is first made on one end. Then the other end is rove through the hole on one end of the yoke, and pulled through until the Manrope Knot lies flush against it. The other end is cross-pointed (*see* PLATE 287, FIG. 430). A Bunting Fringe is generally added to finish the job. This can easily be made by taking some blue or red linen yarns and laying them evenly around the beginning of the pointing, seizing them down tightly. Then stroke all the yarns downward, and put on a Snaked Whipping. It is customary to use white cotton line in making Yoke Lines.

FIG. 194: *The Edge Plank Sling* is often utilized to sling a plank on its side. First, take several turns around the plank. When near the ends on each side, make a Hitch as shown in the illustration.

FIG. 195: *The Method of Mousing a Hook* is a valuable thing to know when using a hook in which the rope is to be allowed to remain for some time. There is always a danger, when the lines slack, that

the hook will throw off its load. Hence, to safeguard against this, a hook should always be moused. This is done as follows: with a sufficient length of Marline, take several turns around the bill and the back of the hook. When enough turns have been taken, make a few frapping turns, which will draw it up tight. The ends are finished off by square-knotting them together.

FIGS. 196A and B: *The Selvage Strop* is stronger than a Spliced Strop of the same number of yarns. It is usually made of small line (Marline, rope-yarns, spun-yarn) or of rope, warped around two spikes spaced the desired distance apart. When enough turns have been made, the ends are square-knotted together, and temporary seizings placed on the strop. Its entire length is then lashed with Marline Hitching (PLATE 4, FIG. 112), to finish.

FIGS. 197, 198, 199: *Three Methods of Hitching a Grommet Strop to a Rope*. This type of Strop is usually made from a piece of rope short-spliced together. It can also be made from a single strand as a Grommet. But the former method is the more practical.

Plate 263—A Whistle Lanyard and Various Other Knots

FIG. 200: *The Mainstay*, a part of which is shown here, is begun by measuring a short distance from the end of the rope and then taking some spun-yarn and begin building up a mouse into the shape of a pear. Each turn of the spun-yarn must be hove taut and beaten down well. When the mouse is large enough, cover it with a piece of canvas. Next, cover the entire mouse with pointing (*see* PLATE 287, FIG.

430), adding or taking out nettles to conform to the taper. An eye is spliced into the short end and served up to the mouse with good heavy white line or Marline. The standing part of the rope is then served for a short distance, to complete the work.

FIG. 201: *The Whistle Lanyard* is made as follows: first, tie a Lark's Head Knot in the ring of the whistle. Make two Hack-

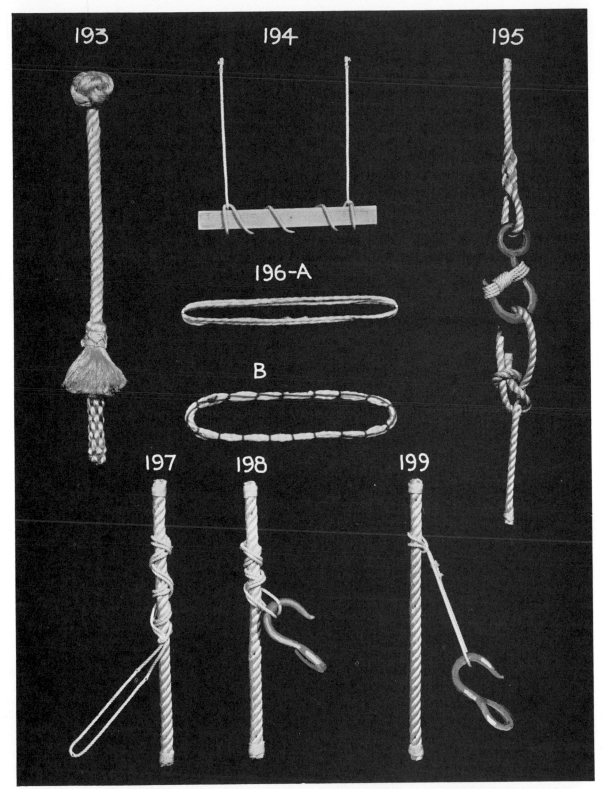

PLATE 262—MOUSING A HOOK, AND SECURING A GROMMET STROP

amore Knots (PLATE 21, FIG. 1), and just below these, a Fisherman's Knot. Next, form two Seven-Turn Blood Knots (PLATE 22, FIG. 16). Tie a Figure-of-Eight Knot in each cord, and add another long piece as illustrated in PLATE 35, FIG. 179. Continue to form Macramé Square Knots until the desired length has been reached. Then make a Double Elongated Diamond Knot (PLATE 165, FIG. 407). Bring the two remaining ends up through the center of the knot, draw it taut, and cut off four strands. With the two strands that are left, form a Brief Knot (PLATE 27, FIG. 83), and bring the ends up to make a double loop. On each side of this loop, make a Seven-Turn Blood Knot (PLATE 22, FIG. 16), and finish off the ends with Two-Strand Monkey Fist Knots (PLATE 49, FIG. 361). By tying the Blood Knots around the standing parts, the loop which goes around the neck can be made adjustable.

FIG. 202: *The Harpoon Lashing*, Second Method, is made in the same manner as the knot shown in PLATE 256, FIG. 155, except that when the strands return to the beginning they are spliced into the standing part, instead of being passed back through the body of the knot. An eye is spliced into the other end of the standing part into which the harpoon line is secured. By inserting the shaft of a harpoon into this knot, it automatically jams on itself, and the knot must then be pushed together in order to free the harpoon.

FIG. 203: *The Hammock Clew* is formed in the following way: take twelve pieces of Marline or white line, two and one-half times the desired length of the completed ends of the Clew. Middle these lines, and coxcomb all in the center (*see* PLATE 104, FIG. 6). Bring both sides together and pass an eye seizing, PLATE 18, FIG. 282, to form an eye. Next, bring one strand up and one strand down, as though for a Sword Mat, PLATE 245, FIG. 86. Bring the outside strand on each side across for

the filling, and leave them out. Continue this, leaving out two strands at each crossing. When the strands have been reduced to four, form a Macramé Square Knot to complete the work. Since there are usually twelve eyelets in a canvas hammock, two strands are spliced into each hole.

Heavy canvas is used for the construction of the hammock, which can be any length and breadth desired, with about two inches allowance for seams.

FIG. 204: *The Key Methods for Tying Various Knots*. All the keys illustrating how the following knots are tied will be found in Chapter III. This is a Five-Strand Wall Knot, PLATE 53, FIG. 2.

FIG. 205: *The Five-Strand Double Matthew Walker Knot*, PLATE 53, FIG. 5.

FIG. 206: *The Five-Strand Lanyard Knot*, PLATE 60, FIG. 131.

FIG. 207: *The Five-Strand Double Lanyard Knot* is made by merely following around the strands of the previous knot.

FIG. 208: *The Five-Strand Single Diamond Knot*, PLATE 60, FIG. 140.

FIG. 209: *The Five-Strand Double Diamond Knot*, PLATE 61, FIG. 141.

FIG. 210: *The Five-Strand Single Manrope Knot*, PLATE 53, FIG. 6.

FIG. 211: *The Five-Strand Double Manrope Knot*, PLATE 294, FIG. 485.

FIG. 212: *The Five-Strand Sennit Rose Knot*, PLATE 55, FIG. 33.

FIG. 213: *The Five-Strand Outside Matthew Walker Knot*, PLATE 54, FIG. 18.

FIG. 214: *The Five-Strand Single Crown and Wall Knot*, PLATE 54, FIG. 10.

FIG. 215: *The Five-Strand Double Crown and Wall Knot*, PLATE 54, FIG. 13.

. FIG. 216: *The Five-Strand Round Turn Knot*, PLATE 65, FIG. 207.

FIG. 217: *The Five-Strand Single Pineapple Knot*, key, PLATE 57, FIG. 72.

FIG. 218: *The Five-Strand Double Pineapple Knot*, key, PLATE 57, FIG. 72.

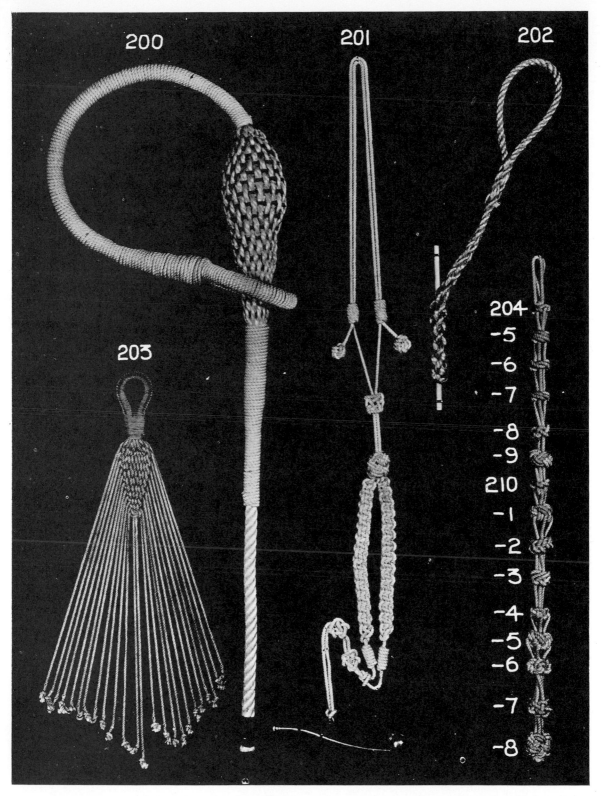

PLATE 263—A WHISTLE LANYARD, AND VARIOUS OTHER KNOTS

Plate 264—Lanyard, Manrope, Rose and Other Knots

FIG. 219: *Keys for Tying Various Knots* are illustrated on this plate. This is the Seven-Strand Wall Knot, PLATE 53, FIG. 2.

FIG. 220: *The Seven-Strand Double Matthew Walker Knot,* PLATE 53, FIG. 5.

FIG. 221: *The Seven-Strand Lanyard Knot,* PLATE 60, FIG. 131.

FIG. 222: *The Seven-Strand Double Lanyard Knot,* PLATE 263, FIG. 207.

FIG. 223: *The Seven-Strand Single Diamond Knot,* PLATE 60, FIG. 140.

FIG. 224: *The Seven-Strand Double Diamond Knot,* PLATE 61, FIG. 141.

FIG. 225. *The Seven-Strand Single Crown and Wall Knot,* PLATE 54, FIG. 10.

FIG. 226. *The Seven-Strand Double Crown and Wall Knot,* PLATE 54, FIG. 13.

FIG. 227: *The Seven-Strand Outside Matthew Walker Knot,* PLATE 54, FIG. 18.

FIG. 228: *The Seven-Strand Sennit Rose Knot,* PLATE 55, FIG. 33.

FIG. 229: *The Seven-Strand Single Manrope Knot,* PLATE 53, FIG. 6.

FIG. 230: *The Seven-Strand Double Manrope Knot,* PLATE 294, FIG. 485.

FIG. 231: *The Seven-Strand Round Turn Knot,* PLATE 65, FIG. 207.

FIG. 232: *The Seven-Strand Single Pineapple Knot,* PLATE 57, FIG. 72.

FIG. 233: *The Seven-Strand Double Pineapple Knot.* PLATE 57, FIG. 72.

FIG. 234: *The Eight-Strand Wall Knot,* PLATE 53, FIG. 2.

FIG. 235: *The Eight-Strand Double Matthew Walker Knot,* PLATE 53, FIG. 5.

FIG. 236: *The Eight-Strand Lanyard Knot,* PLATE 60, FIG. 131.

FIG. 237: *The Eight-Strand Double Lanyard Knot,* PLATE 263, FIG. 207.

FIG. 238: *The Eight-Strand Single Diamond Knot,* PLATE 60, FIG. 140.

FIG. 239: *The Eight-Strand Double Diamond Knot,* PLATE 61, FIG. 141.

FIG. 240: *The Eight-Strand Single Manrope Knot,* PLATE 53, FIG. 6.

FIG. 241: *The Eight-Strand Double Manrope Knot,* PLATE 294, FIG. 485.

FIG. 242: *The Eight-Strand Sennit Rose Knot,* PLATE 55, FIG. 33.

FIG. 243: *The Eight-Strand Outside Matthew Walker Knot,* PLATE 54, FIG. 18.

FIG. 244: *The Eight-Strand Single Crown and Wall Knot.* PLATE 54, FIG. 10.

FIG. 245: *The Eight-Strand Double Crown and Wall Knot,* PLATE 54, FIG. 13.

FIG. 246: *The Eight-Strand Round Turn Knot,* PLATE 65, FIG. 207.

FIG. 247: *The Eight-Strand Single Pineapple Knot,* PLATE 57, FIG. 72.

FIG. 248: *The Eight-Strand Double Pineapple Knot,* PLATE 57, FIG. 72.

FIG. 249: *The Nine-Strand Wall Knot,* PLATE 53, FIG. 2.

FIG. 250: *The Nine-Strand Double Matthew Walker Knot,* PLATE 53, FIG. 5.

FIG. 251: *The Nine-Strand Lanyard Knot,* PLATE 60, FIG. 131.

FIG. 252: *The Nine-Strand Double Lanyard Knot,* PLATE 263, FIG. 207.

FIG. 253: *The Nine-Strand Single Diamond Knot,* PLATE 60, FIG. 140.

FIG. 254: *The Nine-Strand Double Diamond Knot,* PLATE 61, FIG. 141.

FIG. 255: *The Nine-Strand Single Manrope Knot,* PLATE 53, FIG. 6.

FIG. 256: *The Nine-Strand Double Manrope Knot,* PLATE 294, FIG. 485.

FIG. 257: *The Nine-Strand Sennit Rose Knot,* PLATE 55, FIG. 33.

FIG. 258: *The Nine-Strand Outside Matthew Walker Knot,* PLATE 54, FIG. 18.

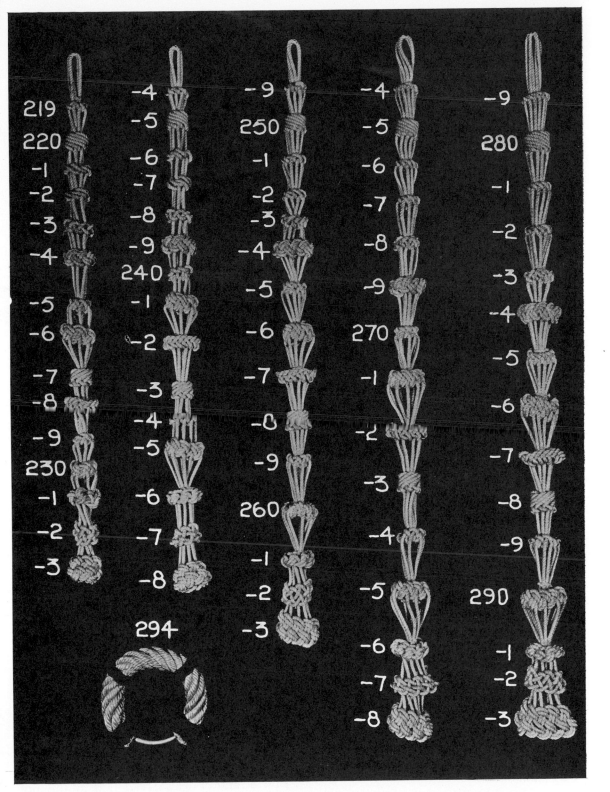

219
220
-1
-2
-3
-4
-5
-6
-7
-8
-9
230
-1
-2
-3

-4
-5
-6
-7
-8
-9
240
-1
-2
-3
-4
-5
-6
-7
-8

294

-9
250
-1
-2
-3
-4
-5
-6
-7
-8
-9
260
-1
-2
-3

-4
-5
-6
-7
-8
-9
270
-1
-2
-3
-4
-5
-6
-7
-8

-9
280
-1
-2
-3
-4
-5
-6
-7
-8
-9
290
-1
-2
-3

PLATE 264—LANYARD, MANROPE, ROSE AND OTHER KNOTS

FIG. 259: *The Nine-Strand Single Crown and Wall Knot,* PLATE 54, FIG. 10.

FIG. 260: *The Nine-Strand Double Crown and Wall Knot,* PLATE 54, FIG. 13.

FIG. 261: *The Nine-Strand Round Turn Knot,* PLATE 65, FIG. 207.

FIG. 262: *The Nine-Strand Single Pineapple Knot,* PLATE 57, FIG. 72.

FIG. 263: *The Nine-Strand Double Pineapple Knot,* PLATE 57, FIG. 72.

FIG. 264: *The Ten-Strand Wall Knot,* PLATE 53, FIG. 2.

FIG. 265: *The Ten-Strand Double Matthew Walker Knot,* PLATE 53, FIG. 5.

FIG. 266: *The Ten-Strand Lanyard Knot,* PLATE 60, FIG. 131.

FIG. 267: *The Ten-Strand Double Lanyard Knot,* PLATE 263, FIG. 207.

FIG. 268: *The Ten-Strand Single Diamond Knot,* PLATE 60, FIG. 140.

FIG. 269: *The Ten-Strand Double Diamond Knot,* PLATE 61, FIG. 141.

FIG. 270: *The Ten-Strand Single Manrope Knot,* PLATE 53, FIG. 6.

FIG. 271: *The Ten-Strand Double Manrope Knot,* PLATE 294, FIG. 485.

FIG. 272: *The Ten-Strand Sennit Rose Knot,* PLATE 55, FIG. 33.

FIG. 273: *The Ten-Strand Outside Matthew Walker Knot,* PLATE 54, FIG. 18.

FIG. 274: *The Ten-Strand Single Crown and Wall Knot,* PLATE 54, FIG. 10.

FIG. 275: *The Ten-Strand Double Crown and Wall Knot,* PLATE 54, FIG. 13.

FIG. 276: *The Ten-Strand Round Turn Knot,* PLATE 65, FIG. 207.

FIG. 277: *The Ten-Strand Single Pineapple Knot,* PLATE 57, FIG. 72.

FIG. 278: *The Ten-Strand Double Pineapple Knot,* PLATE 57, FIG. 72.

FIG. 279: *The Eleven-Strand Wall Knot,* PLATE 53, FIG. 2.

FIG. 280: *The Eleven-Strand Double Matthew Walker Knot,* PLATE 53, FIG. 5.

FIG. 281: *The Eleven-Strand Lanyard Knot,* PLATE 60, FIG. 131.

FIG. 282: *The Eleven-Strand Double Lanyard Knot,* PLATE 263, FIG. 207.

FIG. 283: *The Eleven-Strand Single Diamond Knot,* PLATE 60, FIG. 140.

FIG. 284: *The Eleven-Strand Double Diamond Knot,* PLATE 61, FIG. 141.

FIG. 285: *The Eleven-Strand Single Manrope Knot,* PLATE 53, FIG. 6.

FIG. 286: *The Eleven-Strand Double Manrope Knot,* PLATE 294, FIG. 485.

FIG. 287: *The Eleven-Strand Sennit Rose Knot,* PLATE 55, FIG. 33.

FIG. 288: *The Eleven-Strand Outside Matthew Walker Knot,* PLATE 54, FIG. 18.

FIG. 289: *The Eleven-Strand Single Crown and Wall Knot,* PLATE 54, FIG. 10.

FIG. 290: *The Eleven-Strand Double Crown and Wall Knot,* PLATE 54, FIG. 13.

FIG. 291: *The Eleven-Strand Round Turn Knot,* PLATE 65, FIG. 207.

FIG. 292: *The Eleven-Strand Single Pineapple Knot,* PLATE 57, FIG. 72.

FIG. 293: *The Eleven-Strand Double Pineapple Knot,* PLATE 57, FIG. 72.

FIG. 294: *The Method of Puddening an Anchor Ring* is as follows: First, cover the ring with well-tarred canvas. Next, take several strands of small line (from four to six strands. Six were used on the one illustrated). Each one should be about twice the circumference of the ring being used. Lay them on top of the ring. Put a temporary seizing on them and proceed to lay them in around one half of the ring. They are then hove taut. A Three-Strand Turk's Head is worked on near the top, and a Five-Strand Turk's Head tied at the bottom. Both are drawn up very tight. The same procedure is followed on the other

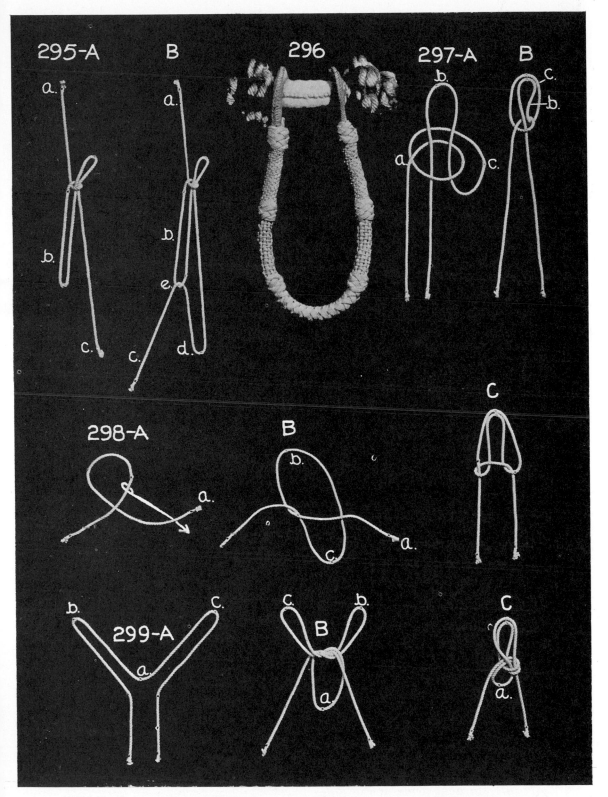

PLATE 265—SLING SHORTENINGS, AND A SEA CHEST SHACKLE

half of the ring. The temporary seizing is removed, and the remaining ends of the strands cut off. The short ends of the strands remaining near the Turk's Heads at the bottom of the ring are finally frayed out and tarred, to complete the job.

Plate 265—Sling Shortenings, and a Sea Chest Shackle

FIG. 295A: *The Dutchman* is a knot generally used in the circus and by truckmen. A very useful design, it forms a strong purchase and may be utilized where a block and tackle is not available. By using this knot, the amount of tension which can be applied to part *a* increases 75%. In use, part *a* leads from the object to be fastened down. Two bights, *b*, are next taken, and a Half Hitch passed over it, as shown in this illustration. End *c* is then passed through an eye or hook, or around some object.

B: After end *c* has been passed around the object indicated at *d*, it is passed through the lower end of bight *b*, at point *e* and made fast to complete the operation.

FIG. 296: *The Sea Chest Shackle or Handle* shown here was tied with four-strand rope. First, the rope is unlaid at each end, two strands are now taken and frayed out. The remaining two strands are temporarily not used. Next, the two frayed strands are served tightly and covered with Coxcombing. Then they are bent to form eyes, and the frayed portions laid up to make two strands, which are long-spliced into the original two strands of the rope. When this has been done, worm the rope, measure equal distances from both eyes, and cover the center portion with Coach Whipping (*see* PLATE 107, FIG. 34). With the ends of the cords used for the Coach Whipping, pointing is placed on each side of the handle (*see* PLATE 287, FIG. 430). These ends are then stopped down. The remaining portion is covered with Palm and Needle Hitching, and Fender Hitching (PLATE 108, FIG. 44). Five-Strand Turk's Heads are next made at the point where each design ends. The pin was made with a length of six-strand rope in this par-

ticular specimen, although six strands of any suitable size cordage may be used. A metal bar forms a core. The center portion is covered with canvas or thin leather. Work a Star Knot on one end, PLATE 57, FIG. 78, and crown with a Lanyard Knot, PLATE 60, FIG. 131. The other end is passed through the eyes of the handle, and the design is completed with another Star Knot, and Lanyard Knot.

FIG. 297A: *Another Longshoreman's Knot.* Can often be of real service when handling cargo aboard ship, or whenever a Sling or Strop must be used. At such times, it is sometimes necessary to shorten the Sling; but this must be done without tying knots in the rope, which might jam if this were attempted. The problem can be solved easily by using one of the various Sling-Shorteners. To make the knot shown here, first form a loop (*a*). Bight *b* is next drawn up through the loop as illustrated. Then parts *b* and *c* are brought together.

B: This pictures the finished knot. Bights *b* and *c* are now placed on the hook.

FIG. 298A: *The Regular Sling Shortener,* First Method, is begun by first laying out the rope as shown. Half of this loop is passed under part *a*, as indicated by the arrow.

B: The rope will then assume the position shown here. Bights *b* and *c* are next taken and brought together.

C: When this has been done, these two bights are placed over the hook. The Sling can be shortened as much as desired by simply pulling on bights *b* and *c* in FIG. 298B.

FIG. 299A: *The Regular Sling Shortener,* Second Method, is begun by divid-

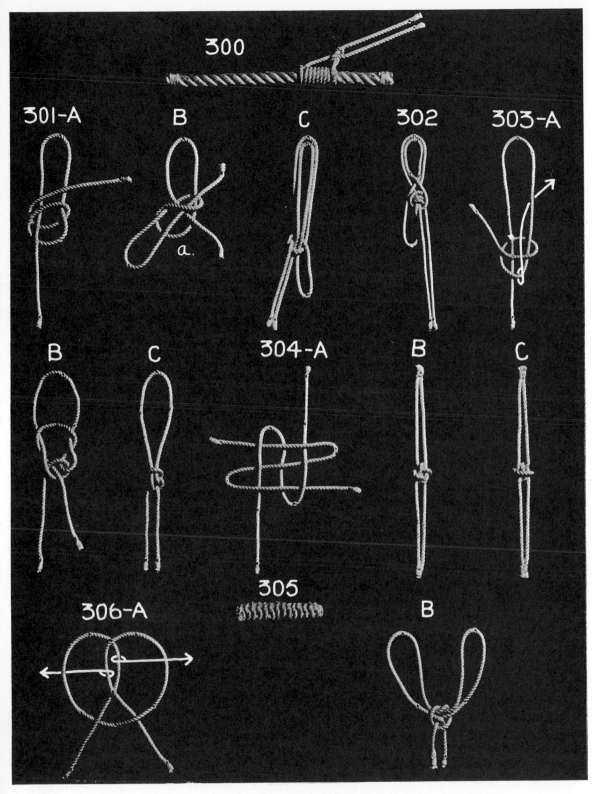

PLATE 266—FALSE HANDCUFF HITCHES, AND TYPES OF CARGO SLINGS

ing the rope into two bights *b* and *c,* as illustrated. Next, make an Overhand Knot, using both bights *b* and *c.*

B: This shows the rope after the first stage has been completed. Bights *b* and *c* are now brought together and placed on a hook.

c: The completed knot is pictured here. In actual use, loop *a* hangs free, because the knot itself jams and prevents this slack from being drawn up. This, in fact, is one of the functions of the knot. If the loop were drawn up tight, the knot would be hopelessly jammed.

Plate 266—False Handcuff Hitches, and Types of Cargo Slings

FIG. 300: *The Messenger or Cable Hitch* is used by linemen for hauling heavy cables. It is formed by taking eight or ten turns around the end of a cable, after a Half Hitch has been made. Place another Half Hitch on the cable after the turns have been made and pull the line taut. Then hitch the two parts of the line together on the hauling end to finish off. This is a very effective manner for attaching a hauling line to a cable, as it forms a very secure tie which holds without slipping.

FIGS. 301A, B, and c: *The San Francisco Longshoreman's Double Sling Shortener* is formed by taking a bight in the body of a line to start, then take a round turn around the bight and bring the working end of the line across the front as illustrated in FIG. 301A. Next, form another bight by passing the line down through the round turn as shown in FIG. 301B, after which take the bottom bight up alongside the top bight and pull the part marked *a* down. FIG. 301c shows how the Sling Shortener appears when completed.

FIG. 302: *The West Coast Sling Shortener.* This is somewhat similar to the double sling shortener shown in FIG. 301.

FIGS. 303A, B, and c: This Knot is a *Single Bowline on the Bight.* First form a bight and then take a round turn as shown at FIG. 303A. Pull the bottom part up through the bight on top, as the drawn line indicates, and at the same time pull the top bight down. The knot will then appear as in FIG. 303B. The finished Bowline, after being pulled taut, is shown in FIG. 303c.

FIGS. 304A, B, and c: This is a *Japanese Crown Knot* tied with four parts. FIG. 304A shows how the knot is formed while FIG. 304B shows the knot as it appears in the front after being pulled up. FIG. 304c shows a back view of the knot.

FIG. 305: *A Combination Wall and Crown Braid.* It is tied by forming alternate Wall and Crown knots, one after the other, with any number of strands.

FIGS. 306A and B: *False Handcuff Hitches.* They are tied by forming two Half Hitches in the opposite way, after which the inside part of one Hitch is laid on the inside part of the other Hitch, as shown at FIG. 306A. Pull each part through as the drawn line indicates and the knot will appear as at FIG. 306B.

Plate 267—A Jacob's Ladder, and a Round Rung Ladder

FIG. 307: *The Round Rung Ladder* is a light, sturdy ladder which can be used on ships when painting over the side or in any other place where it is constantly necessary to change the position of the

ladder. Begin with two lengths of rope, preferably four-strand, the length depending on the size of ladder wanted. Splice a round thimble into one end of each rope. Lash these eyes to a rail or any con-

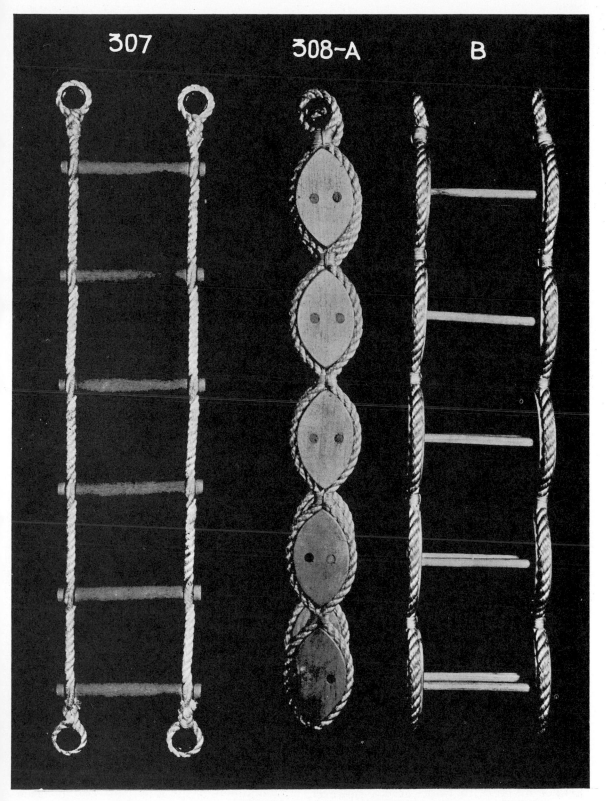

PLATE 267—A JACOB'S LADDER, AND A ROUND RUNG LADDER

venient object. Take the other ends, stretch them out full length, and make them fast to another object. Next, take a rung (usually one inch in diameter and fifteen inches long, with a groove cut in each end), and with the aid of a fid pass it through the center of one rope until the strands lie in the grooves. The other end of the rung is passed through the other rope. Be careful to keep it the same distance from the thimble as the first end. A seizing is put o i the rope on each side of the rung. (In order to show more clearly how the rungs are passed through the rope, seizings have not been put on the rope in the specimen illustrated.) Another rung is now taken, and the same procedure carried out, measuring carefully the distance between rungs, so as to have them all parallel. It will simplify the work if a stick is cut to the proper length and used as a spacer for the rungs.

FIG. 308A.: *The Jacob's Ladder* is shown here in a side view. This is a much more elaborate and expensive method of making a rope-ladder. Moreover, it is quite heavy, and when rolled up makes a bulky object that cannot be stowed easily. This ladder has two round rungs placed in two flat oval-shaped pieces of wood on each side. These pieces of wood, or "cheeks,"

have grooves cut in their edges, to accommodate the rope. To make the ladder, take two lengths of rope about two and one-quarter times the desired length of the completed ladder. Middle them, and seize a thimble into each bight. The ends are next stretched out as in the preceding ladder, and the first rung inserted. Another seizing is then placed on the two ropes just below the "cheeks." The rungs, if preferred, may be spaced farther apart in the following way: after putting on a seizing, a space is left of the desired distance, and another cross-seizing is placed on the ropes on each side. The next rung "cheek" is then placed against this seizing, and another cross-seizing put on just below the "cheeks." This procedure is repeated until the ladder has reached the intended length. Another thimble may be seized to the lower end of the ladder, or the ends can be long-spliced together. Short Lanyards are spliced into the thimbles on the upper end of the ladder, in order to secure it to an object when in use.

B: This shows a front view of the Jacob's Ladder. Note: Thimbles can be put into the lower ends of the ladder, so that should it at any time prove to be too short, another smaller ladder can be lashed to it.

Plates 268, 269 and 270—Sea Bag and Picture Frame

FIGS. 309A to I: *A Sea Bag* such as that which is shown in the various stages of its construction in the accompanying illustrations is more or less a relic of the bygone days of sailing ships. Some of them used by the sailors of years ago were of tremendous size and in them were stored all of the sailor's worldly possessions, such as clothing, bedding, dishes, tools of their trade, and many other articles which they carried about with them from ship to ship and from port to port. Today, however, the once well-known "Duffle Bag" is rarely seen along the waterfronts of the world.

In their stead sailors are using the more conventional types of luggage. However, a Sea Bag is a useful article for the storage aboard ship of many articles and those in use now are made in sizes suitable for the purpose for which they are intended. Most of them are made about one foot in diameter and three feet in length. No. 2 canvas is the material used, or for a lighter bag No. 7 or No. 8 canvas can be used. To make a bag of the size mentioned will require a piece of canvas of the weight desired, 36 inches wide by 42 inches long.

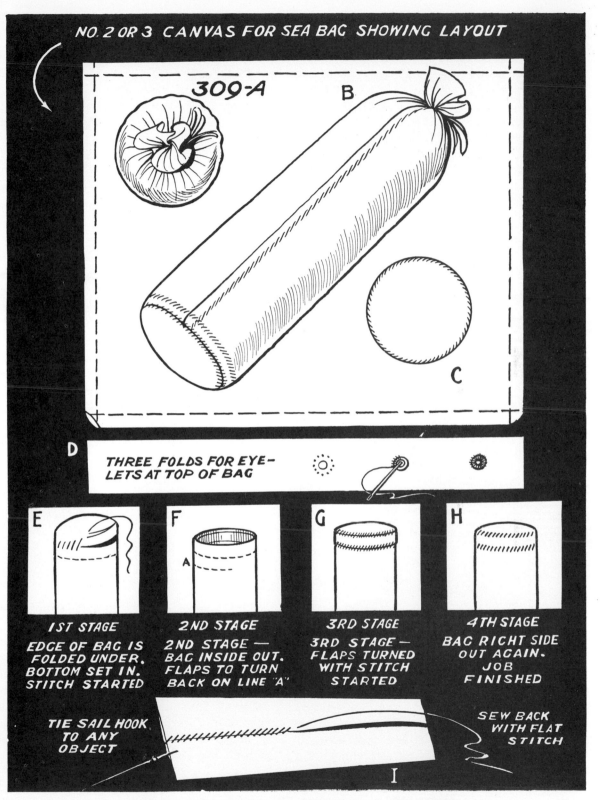

NO. 2 OR 3 CANVAS FOR SEA BAG SHOWING LAYOUT

309-A

B

C

D THREE FOLDS FOR EYE-LETS AT TOP OF BAG

E 1ST STAGE
EDGE OF BAG IS FOLDED UNDER. BOTTOM SET IN. STITCH STARTED

F 2ND STAGE
2ND STAGE — BAG INSIDE OUT. FLAPS TO TURN BACK ON LINE "A"

G 3RD STAGE
3RD STAGE — FLAPS TURNED WITH STITCH STARTED

H 4TH STAGE
BAG RIGHT SIDE OUT AGAIN. JOB FINISHED

TIE SAIL HOOK TO ANY OBJECT

SEW BACK WITH FLAT STITCH

I

PLATE 268—STEPS IN MAKING A SEA BAG

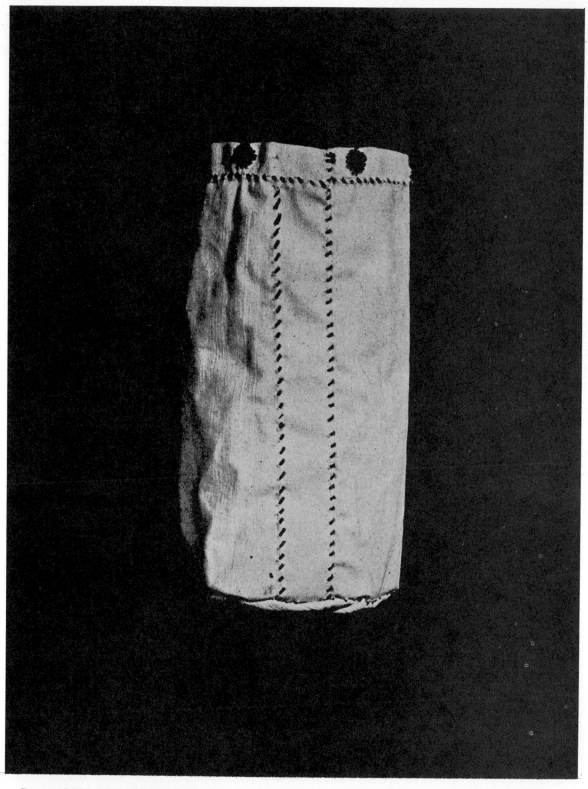

PLATE 269—ANOTHER TYPICAL SEA BAG, WITH SINGLE BOTTOM SEAM

PLATE 270—REMARKABLE TYPE OF SENNIT FRAME CONSTRUCTION
(*Description of this plate on page 438.*)

In the working of canvas, it will be noticed as it is unrolled from the bolt, that there are two colored threads woven into each strip about one inch from each selvage edge. These are intended as guide lines or markers in sewing the strips together. The strips are so overlapped that the edges of both coincide with these colored threads. Then, no matter whether the seam is made by hand or with a machine, the stitches are taken near the edge of each strip of canvas, using both the edge and the colored threads as guides. After a row of stitches has been made along one edge of the canvas the material is turned over and a second row of stitches is taken along the other edge of the material, thus making an overlapping flat seam. If the material is wide enough but one seam may be needed, but when narrow canvas is used it is frequently necessary to join two cloths, making two such seams, one on each side of the bag.

After the work of forming the sides of the bag has been completed the next step is to make the top of the bag. This is done by folding one edge of the tubular sack back over itself twice, thus making a seam of three thicknesses. This is sewed down by taking a row of stitches around the bag about one and one-half inches from the top edge. A flat stitch is used in the seam.

The next step is to form the eyelets for the draw cords. These are placed in the seam at the top of the bag and their number may be as many as required by the size of the bag. The first step in making the eyelets is to punch holes through the material, slightly smaller than the desired size of the finished eyelet. Place several turns of sail twine inside of each of the holes in the form of Grommets and proceed to sew these into place. Make two complete turns of stitches around each eyelet, overlapping the stitches the second time around to make a neat appearing job.

As the finishing touch the bottom is attached to the bag. There is a definite method for determining the size of the material needed for such a bag as that being described. The first step is to lay the tubular section of the bag out flat, then fold it in such a manner that there will be three equal folds. In other words, the width of the folded bag will be equal to one-third of the bag when it is folded out flat. In the case of the bag being made this will be about six inches, this amount is now doubled which makes twelve inches. Then, allowing about one half-inch for a seam all around the bottom, proceed to cut out a circular piece of canvas thirteen inches in diameter. Make a pencil mark around this circular piece about three-quarters of an inch in from its outer circumference. This line is intended as a marker or guide in sewing the bottom in the bag.

Next, turn the tubular section of the bag inside out and fold the bottom edge back upon itself, making a pencil mark around the edge of the fold as a guide or marker for placing the bottom in its correct position. Match the guide line on the bottom material with that on the tubular section and proceed to sew the bottom on the bag. It should be understood that the outside edge or perimeter of the bottom is placed inside the bag when the work is finished. If desired another seam may be made around the outer edge of the bottom of the bag after the bottom has been attached, but before the bag is turned right side out. This is not necessary but it adds to the strength of the bottom seam.

Finish off the work by running a drawstring of suitable size through the eyelets.

Plate 271—Temporary, Crown, and Other Lashings

FIG. 310: *A Temporary Lashing* is formed by passing a line a number of times through the two eyes formed in the ends of two ropes, after which the ends of the Lashing are brought down and under and are joined in a Square Knot. Mar-

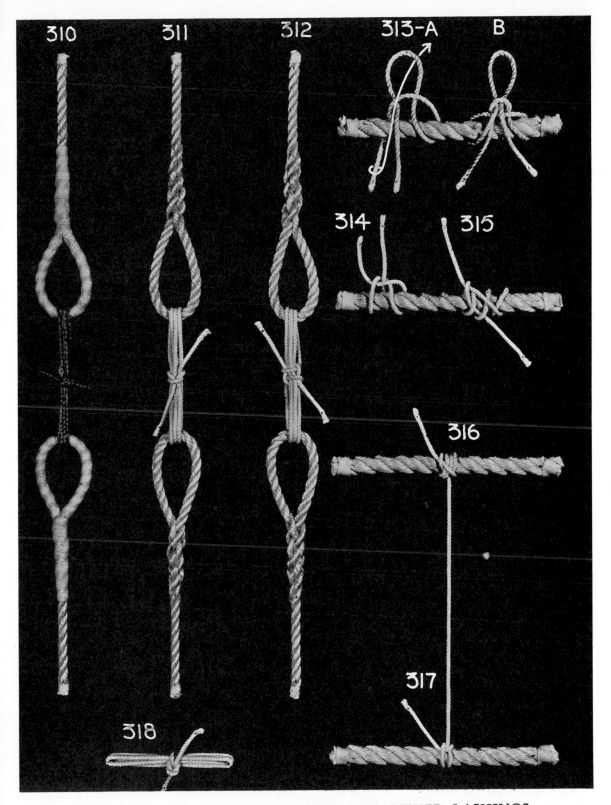

PLATE 271—TEMPORARY, CROWN, AND OTHER LASHINGS

line is used for making such a Lashing.

FIG. 311: *A Racking Lashing* is made by passing a line a number of times through two eyes in the same manner as shown in PLATE 17, FIG. 277. Finish off the Lashing by tying a Square Knot with both ends around the body of the Lashing.

FIG. 312: *A Crown Lashing* is formed by passing a line a number of times through two eyes in the manner explained, after which hitch each end around the body of the Lashing and form a Crown by tucking the ends under the opposite Hitch.

FIG. 313A and B: *A Draw Hitch* is tied by first forming a bight, after which bring one part of the line around the object to which it is being secured and then over the bight. Pass the line around the object again from the opposite side and up over its own part, then pass the line in the form of a bight through the eye of the first bight, which is then pulled down on the standing part with its own end. This will close the second bight in the form of an eye, which can be released instantly if

desired. A Draw Hitch is generally employed for securing a line to a ring or post. FIG. 313A shows the first stages of the knot and FIG. 313B shows it as it appears when finished.

FIG. 314: *An Ossel Hitch* is used for attaching the Ossels or short lengths of a net to the heavy rope or backing of the net. The manner in which the knot is formed is clearly shown in the illustration.

FIG. 315: *An Ossel Knot* is used on the Head Rope, or small rope along the top of a net, for the same purpose as the Ossel Hitch.

FIG. 316: *An Ossel Knot* is shown attached to the Head Rope with a connecting line to the Backing.

FIG. 317: *An Ossel Hitch* is shown as it is secured to the Backing, as explained in the other illustrations in this group.

FIG. 318: *A Rose Tie* is made by taking a number of turns over two hooks, or through two eyes, after which the ends are joined around the center of the Tie in a Square Knot.

Plate 272—A Tie Lashing, Fishhook Ties, and Blood Knot

FIG. 319: *A Tie Lashing* is formed by wrapping the cord tightly around the parts to be seized, with one end of the Lashing lying in the groove which is covered by the wrapping turns. The other end of the Lashing is pulled through, under the wrapping turns to the opposite side, by means of a needle and small thread secured to the wrapping line with a Sheet Bend. A Tie Lashing may be used for such purposes as binding together the fractured parts of a fishing rod.

FIG. 320: *A Muzzle Lashing*, such as that shown, was used in the by-gone days of sail for securing a housing over the end of a gun.

FIGS. 321A, B and C: *A Single Cat's Paw* is a knot used for attaching a line to a hook. It is made by forming two bights in

a line, as shown in FIG. 321A, after which one end of the line is passed around the middle part of the two bights, as indicated. Take two round turns, as shown in FIG. 321B, then bring the line down over the front. FIG. 321C shows the knot as it is attached to a hook.

FIG. 322 and FIG. 323: *Sack Knots* have several different forms, two of which are shown in the illustrations. The manner in which these are tied is so simple that no instructions should be necessary.

FIG. 324: *A Blood Knot* is another simple method used in tying sacks. Its form, like the others, is so simple that the method of tying it needs no explanation.

FIG. 325: *A Temporary Stopper Knot* is tied by laying a bight on the rope to be stopped off and then taking two or three

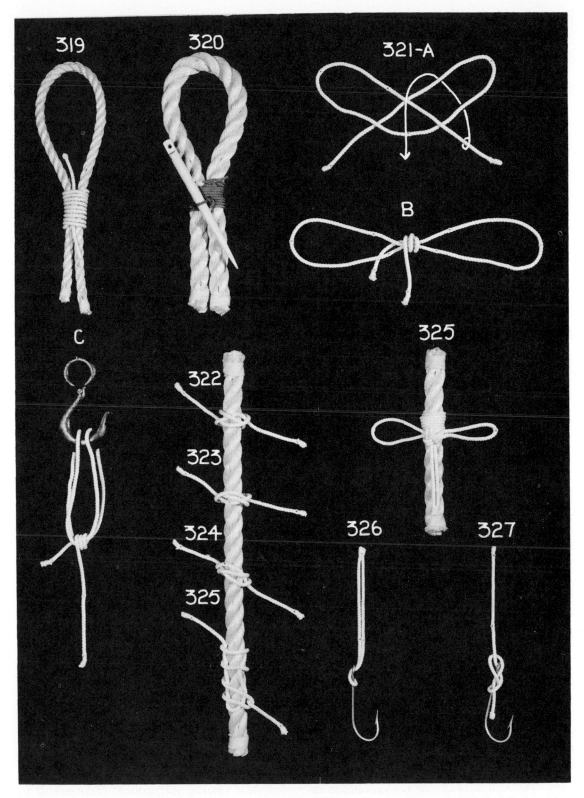

PLATE 272—A TIE LASHING, FISH HOOK TIES, AND BLOOD KNOTS

turns around the rope, against its lay, after which the Stopper is completed by hauling the end of the lashing taut by passing it through its own component part as shown.

FIG. 325A: *A Japanese Tie* is made by doubling, or middling, a line and running it under the last two turns of a whipping, after which the ends of the lashing are pulled through to form two bights as shown. These bights are used to form a Crown by laying one of them over both parts of the lashing line and then bringing the

other bight over the first bight and under the two parts of the line.

FIG. 326: *Fish Hook Ties* have many different forms, one of which is shown. This is a Jamming Reef Knot. With a leader having a loop in one end this is a simple method for securing it to the eye of a hook or fly.

FIG. 327: *A Single Cairnton Knot* is a form of attaching a line or a gut leader to a fishhook. The manner in which it is tied is evident from the illustration.

Plate 273—Various Knots for Attaching Fishhooks, etc.

FIG. 328: *A Fishhook Tie* of still another form is shown in the illustration. Like other knots used for the same purpose it is easily tied without a descriptive explanation.

FIG. 329: *A Fisherman's Knot Tie* is a simple method of securing a line to a hook, or for joining the ends of two leaders together.

FIG. 330: *A Jamming Reef Knot with a Blood Knot* added just above the eye of a fishhook is another typical form of securing a line or leader to a hook.

FIG. 331: *A Fisherman's Fly Knot* represents an effective method of attaching a line to a fly. Take a length of colored silk and a hackle from a cock's neck and secure the latter to the hook with a whipping immediately below the eye of the hook, after which run the line through the eye of the hook as shown. This colored line can be joined to another line by the use of a Reef Knot, as illustrated.

FIG. 332: *The Fisherman's Fly Knot* shown in this illustration is somewhat different from that shown in FIG. 331, in that the line above the hook is attached to another line by a Double Sheet Bend.

FIG. 333: *A Fisherman's Swivel Tie* is employed for attaching a swivel to a line or leader. It is shown as attached to a hook

instead of an eye for convenience. It is not intended for use on a hook.

FIG. 334: *A Diver's Life Line or Firemen's Rescue Knot* is an effective means for securing a line around a diver as a safety precaution when he is being lowered into a hatch or other dangerous parts of submerged ships.

Start by tying a Double Bowline on the Bight. Both loops of the Bowline are then pulled up over the diver's legs, after which a Hitch is taken around his waist with the long end of the line, thus pulling the loops of the Bowline up tight in the crotch. Tie a Slip Knot in the Hitch so that it will not pull up tight around the waist and then bring the short end of the line up and pass it under both parts of the eye that forms the Slip Knot. To finish off, run the end back under its own part and over both parts of the eye in the Slip Knot.

FIG. 335: *A Hawser Pointing* is formed in the same manner as an Artificial or Spindle Eye. The yarn is marled down on the standing part after which both the eye and the standing part are served and the eye is finished off with tape. This is followed by taking a single length of Marline and sewing it through each strand at the end of the serving until the Marline is middled. The body is then covered with

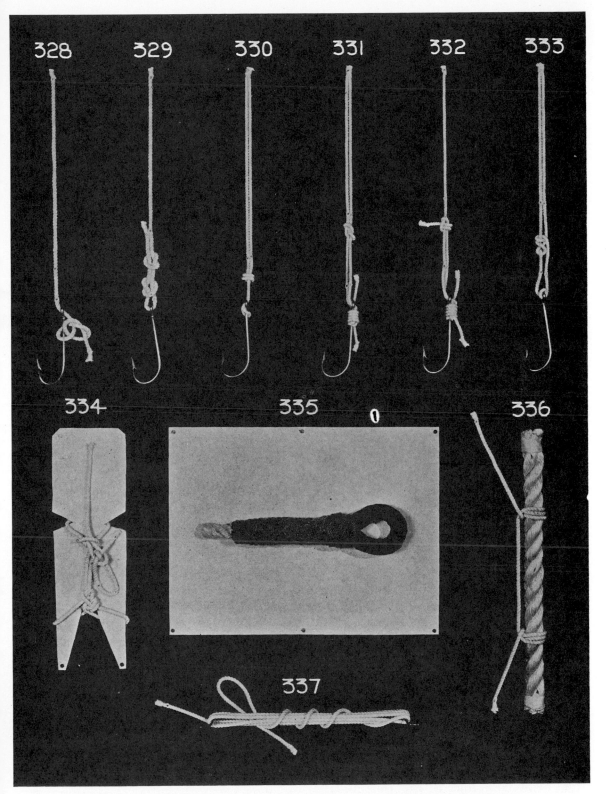

PLATE 273—VARIOUS KNOTS FOR ATTACHING FISHHOOKS

Fender Hitching and a Turk's Head Seizing is placed at the base of the eye.

Fig. 336: *A Twin Stopper,* which is easily tied, can be used to prevent a rope or any other object from turning by applying it as illustrated.

Fig. 337: *An Awning Tie,* as the name implies, is used for securing an awning to a stanchion, a rope, or some other object.

The most practical and the simplest form, such as that shown, is to take several turns around both hooks, leaving enough line at the end to permit of making a few turns crosswise around the first turns. At the last crosswise turn form a bight with the end of the line and tuck the end of the line through the first turns. This will hold fast and at the same time is easy to unfasten.

Plate 274—Ornamental Package Ties

Figs. 338A and B, and Fig. 339: *The Japanese Package Tie* is shown in two forms in these illustrations. Fig. 338A represents the beginning of one form and Fig. 338B shows the completed tie. Another and somewhat more complicated Tie is shown in Fig. 339.

Figs. 340A and B: *The Slip Package Tie* is made by forming a Bowline in one end of the cord after which the cord is passed around the package and its end is secured in the eye of the Bowline with a Slip Knot. Fig. 340A shows the Bowline and the Slip Knot loosely tied while Fig. 340B shows it as it appears when pulled up tight.

Figs 341A and B: *A Simple Package Tie* which is easily made is shown in these illustrations. Fig. 341A shows the front of the package and Fig. 341B the opposite side,

illustrating the manner of securing the cord to prevent it from slipping. Any form of loop may be used in one end of the cord, and the other end of the line, after having been wrapped about the package, is secured in the loop with a series of Half Hitches.

Fig. 342: *The Four-Strand Package Tie* shown in this illustration is so simple that no explanation as to how it is formed is required.

Figs. 343A and B: *A Diamond Package Tie* is started with an Overhand Knot tied in a loop which is placed on top of the package to form the diamond, after which the Tie is completed in the manner shown. Fig. 343B shows the opposite side before the Tie is completed.

Plate 275—Rope Coils and Pack Hitch

Fig. 344 and Fig. 345: *To Flemish Down a Coil* of rope is to lay down the coil in such a manner that each fake is outside of the other, beginning at the center of the coil and working outward, with each coil flat on the deck. Two methods of Flemishing Down rope are shown in the illustrations. One shows a flat concentric coil and the other two concentric coils. In coiling rope in this manner it is the practice to lay down right-handed rope in a right-hand coil, that is, the rope is laid down from left to right—clockwise, or with the sun. The opposite is the case with left-

handed rope. It is laid down from right to left—counter-clockwise, or against the sun. In all coils of this type it is important that the running part of the coil be in the center, while the end of the line is on the outside. This is done to insure free running.

Fig. 346: *To Fake Down a Coil* of rope it is laid down right-handed or left-handed. as the lay of the rope requires, with one fake directly over the fake below it. The coil is then capsized to insure free running.

Fig. 347: *Over-lapping Figure-of-Eight*

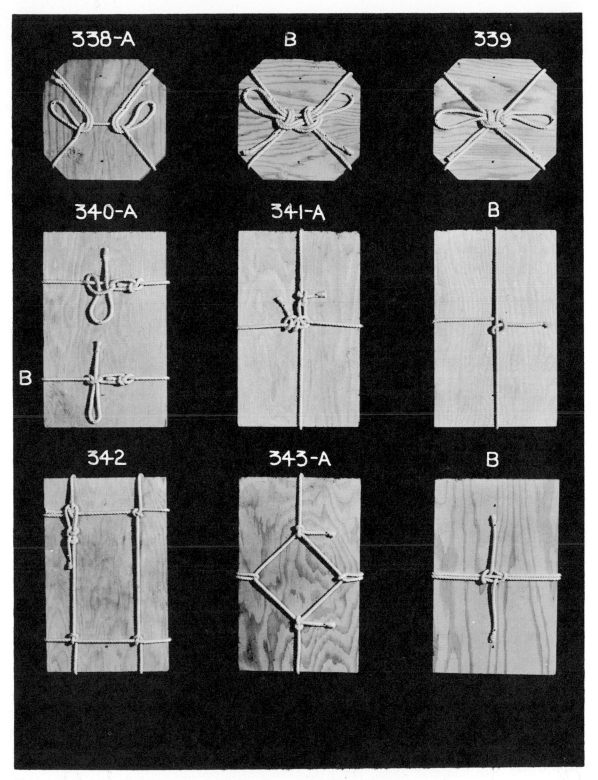

PLATE 274—ORNAMENTAL PACKAGE TIES

coiling is done in the manner illustrated. This is simply a Flemish Coil in which two of the opposite sides are overlapped after the coil has been laid down.

Fig. 348: *Faking Down Hawsers* is at times done in the manner illustrated. The first step is to lead the line out, removing all kinks and twists. Then begin by winding the rope, at its secured end, in a criss-cross manner, with each fake directly over the fake below it.

Figs. 349A and B: *A Diamond Pack-Mule Hitch* is one of the several methods

employed in securing packs to the backs of animals. It is tied much in the manner of the *Diamond Package Tie* shown in Fig. 343. Fig. 349B illustrates the manner of tying the ends of the Hitch on the underneath side. (See PLATE 327, Fig. 2.)

Fig. 350: *A Deck Stopper* is a short length of line with a round thimble spliced in one end and a Stopper Knot tied in the other. The rope is served with Marline, or tarred small stuff, and a Lanyard is spliced around its neck. In the illustration the hook, which is usually attached to the thimble, is omitted for convenience.

Plate 276—Initial Steps in Making Nets

Fig. 351: *Hammock Making* involves the use of a Netting Needle and a Mesh Stick, such as are used in weaving nets. The width of the Mesh Stick determines the size of the mesh in the netting or web of the hammock and at the same time it serves the purpose of making all of the meshes of the same size. That is, a Mesh Stick two inches wide will form a mesh one inch square. The Netting Needle carries the cord of which the hammock or net is made. It serves as a Shuttle for interweaving the cord and for tying the knots. It should be of such size that after being wound with cord it will pass easily through a mesh of the net. The illustration shows a common Sheet Bend as it is used in Hammock Making or in weaving nets.

Fig. 352: *Net Making* is started with a Slip Eye in an Overhand Knot as shown in the illustration. The first step is to pass the Netting Needle through the loop of the Slip Eye, then bring the Needle around that part marked *a* and at the same time hold the thumb over the part marked *c*. Throw the cord to the position marked *b* and then pass the Needle through the bight as shown and pull tight. Hold the cord securely with the thumb when pulling the knot up, as considerable care is necessary in order that all of the meshes

are uniform and that the knot is pulled tight. After the first mesh of the net has been made it serves as the loop in place of the Slip Eye and the same sequence of operations is followed as before. That is, the cord is led over the Mesh Stick, through the loop formed by the first mesh, as at *a*: hold the thumb at *c* as before and then cast the cord around as at *b* and reeve the Needle through the bight at *b* after which pull the knot tight. The mesh thus formed serves as the loop for the next successive step.

Fig. 353: *Netting Meshes* are shown in this illustration, but with all of the knots forming them tied loosely. A chain of about fifty such meshes are required for a Hammock. After the first chain has been completed the Slip Eye used to form the first mesh may be untied, making all of the meshes of uniform size and shape. The next step is to open the chain and then turn the mesh over, working another row of meshes back across and into the first row. This process of turning the net over and successively weaving additional rows of meshes is continued until the Hammock is of the desired width.

Fig. 354: *An Alternate Form of Meshing* which is slightly different from the method described previously. There are

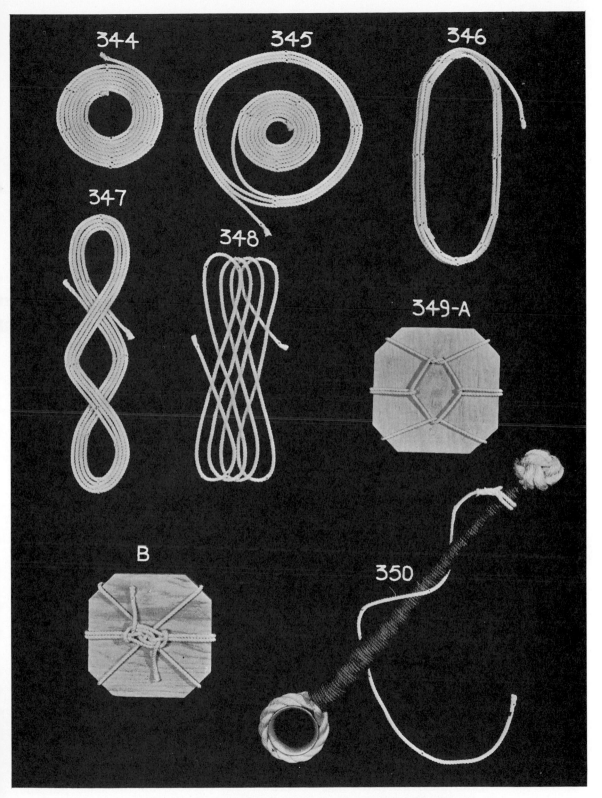

PLATE 275—ROPE COILS AND PACK HITCH

various other ways for forming meshes. Where the net is to be made round a metal ring or circular base, it is attached to the base with Clove Hitches and the meshes are then worked round from right to left.

Fig. 355: *An Eye and Seizing for Hammocks* is formed in the manner shown in the illustration. Pass a stout cord through the end meshes of a hammock and splice its ends together, making the loop of the splice long enough for a Thimble Seizing. A stick of sufficient length may be used at the ends of a hammock or the regular Hammock Clews may be used, such as are illustrated in PLATE 263, FIG. 203.

Plate 277—A Typical Rope Hammock

Fig. 356: *A Hammock* such as that shown is a very common type used in South America. It will be noticed that the end meshes are seized to round metal rings.

Plate 278—Splices, Sheepshanks, and a Monkey Fist

Fig. 357: *A Toggle Splice,* or a *Belaying Pin Splice,* is made up in the manner shown. A Belaying Pin is stopped on the end of a line with an Eye Splice, after which the Pin is passed through an Eye Splice in the end of another rope. In the lower end of the rope in which the Belaying Pin is spliced it will be noticed that another eye has been formed by using a Blood Knot. Another part of rope is passed through a Button and knotted securely with an Overhand Knot. Splices made by either of these two methods are easily and quickly unfastened or cast off.

Fig. 358: *A Cut Sheepshank* with a *Spanish Knot* is used to attach a line to a spar and is frequently used when a man desires to lower himself from aloft without leaving a line hanging. The Sheepshank is secured to the fixed object, as a spar, and the outside part is cut, as shown, just above the Spanish Knot. Such a tie as this is sufficiently strong to support a man and the lower part of the knot and line can be shaken out and hauled down.

Fig. 359: *A Hitched Monkey Fist* is made with four-strand rope. Unlay the strands back far enough to allow sufficient length for forming the knot. Next, separate each strand into two parts, making eight working ends. Proceed by fender hitching the strands together, as illus-

trated in CHAPTER V, PLATE 105, FIG. 16, after first placing an egg-shaped piece of wood or any other suitable object in the center of the knot to serve as a body over which the Hitches are formed. Finish the work by bringing the ends together on the end of the Monkey Fist with a Sprit Sail-sheet Knot, then pull all of the strands taut and cut them off short.

Fig. 360: *A Rigger's Hitch* is used primarily as a Sling such as those used for hoisting purposes. The manner in which the Hitch is made is so clearly illustrated that no explanation is necessary.

Fig. 361: *A Four-Strand Racking Nipper* is a very rare knot. It is a method of joining the bodies of four ropes together and was first found in China years ago by the authors among some ancient specimens of Chinese rope and knot work. The manner in which the Nipper is tied is so involved that even the authors were compelled to untie the specimen in order that they might understand how it was formed. For this reason an explanation of this difficult Nipper would hardly prove sufficient to give the proper understanding that is necessary to follow its construction.

Fig. 362: *A Cut Sheepshank* such as that shown may be used for the same purpose as the Cut Sheepshank with a Spanish Knot, shown in FIG. 358. In the Cut Sheepshank

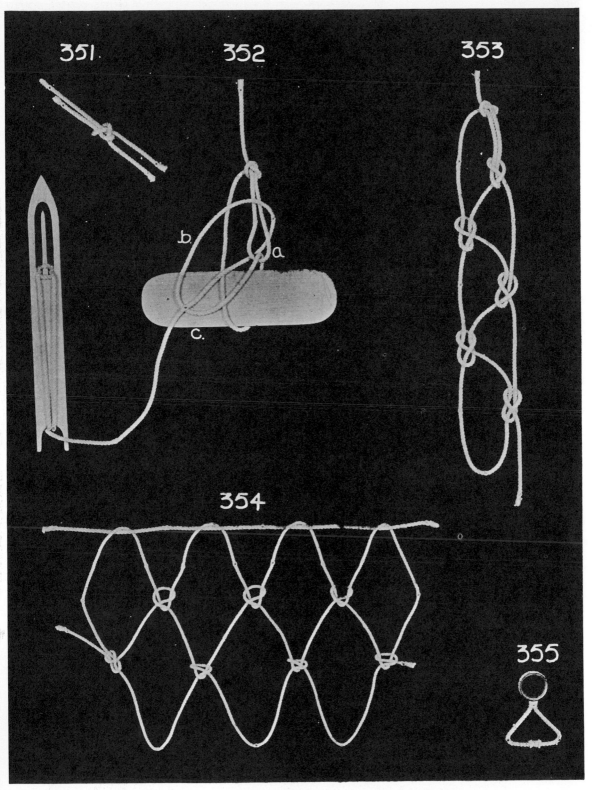

351   352   353

b

a

c

354

355

PLATE 276—INITIAL STEPS IN MAKING NETS

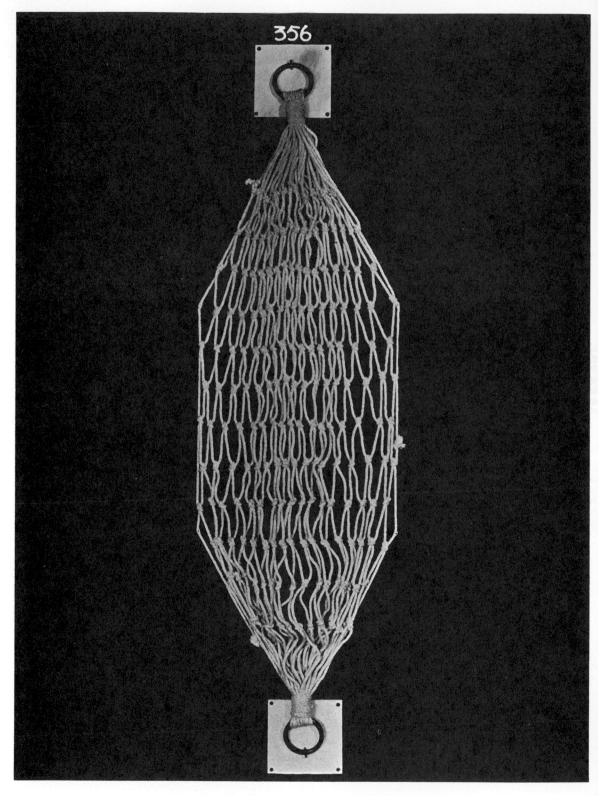

Plate 277—A TYPICAL ROPE HAMMOCK

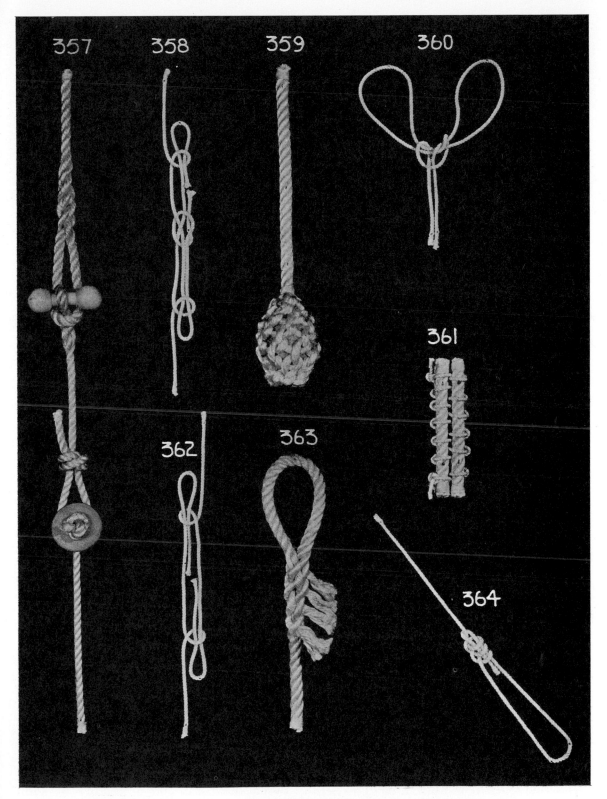

PLATE 278—SPLICES, SHEEPSHANKS, AND A MONKEY FIST

the middle part is cut, instead of the out-side part, as when a Spanish Knot is used. The lower end of this line can also be shaken out and hauled down.

FIG. 363: *A Four-Strand Government Eye Splice* is very similar to the three-strand method described in PLATE 238, FIG. 25. The first tucks are the same as for a regular Eye Splice in four-strand rope. The first strand is left under two strands, after its first tuck. The second strand is tucked twice and this is followed by three tucks

for the third strand and four tucks for the fourth. The result is that all of the strands of the Splice are brought out on the same side of the standing part of the rope, after which they are cut off.

FIG. 364: *A Triple Bowline* is a knot in which there are two additional Half Hitches or one more than is used in the Water Bowline which has two. Such a knot as this gives added security against jamming when the line is wet. However, it is somewhat odd and seldom used.

Plate 279—A Railway and a Thrum Sennit

FIG. 365: *The Railway Sennit,* Second Method, is very common, often used as chafing gear for sails. To start, take a line, double it and seize its two ends together. Next, middle strands of yarn and starting at the top of the doubled line lay on the yarns and pass their ends between the two strands of the rope.

FIGS. 366A, B, and C: This is a *Thrum Sennit* whose front side has the appearance of a Three-Strand Braid. It is started by middling a Thrum around a length of line or any other suitable lashing. This will give the Thrum two parts, as shown by the letters *b* and *c*, FIG. 366A. Next, lay another Thrum over the line and cross the top part over both parts of the previous Thrum, as shown at *a*. Then, bring the underneath part, shown at *d*, down parallel with part *c* of the previous Thrum. Add another Thrum by middling it around the body of the previous Thrums, then cross the left part over the right part, as shown at *c* and *b*. Continue by bringing part *f* down across the front and over part *c* and then keep on adding Thrums in the same manner until the Sennit is finished. The Lashing can then be pulled out at the beginning and the ends of the Thrum Sennit are seized together to finish it off. This Sennit as it would appear after being worked down to considerable length is shown at *c*.

Sennits such as this are used aboard sailing ships for Paunch Mats.

FIG. 367: *A Figure-of-Eight Weave, Knotted on Each End.*

FIGS. 368A and B: *A Single Bottle Knot* such as that shown can be used for slinging any object having a rim or a collar, but this method is not as dependable as other similar knots which are used for the same purpose. The knot is made by first splicing the ends of a piece of rope together, after which a loop is formed as shown in FIG. 368A. Pull the top part out underneath the left side and the bottom part over the right side. The knot will then appear as shown in FIG. 368B. The center of the knot is placed over the object to be slung and the bights on each side are used as handles, or they may be attached to a hook for hoisting.

FIG. 369: *An Inside Clinch With Double Seizing.*

FIG. 370: *A Wedding Lashing* is used to join the two eyes which have been previously made in the ends of two ropes. The Lashing line is passed successively through the eyes a number of times, after which the ends of the Lashing are passed down between the turns and a number of additional turns is taken over the body of the Lashing, each end of the Lashing line be-

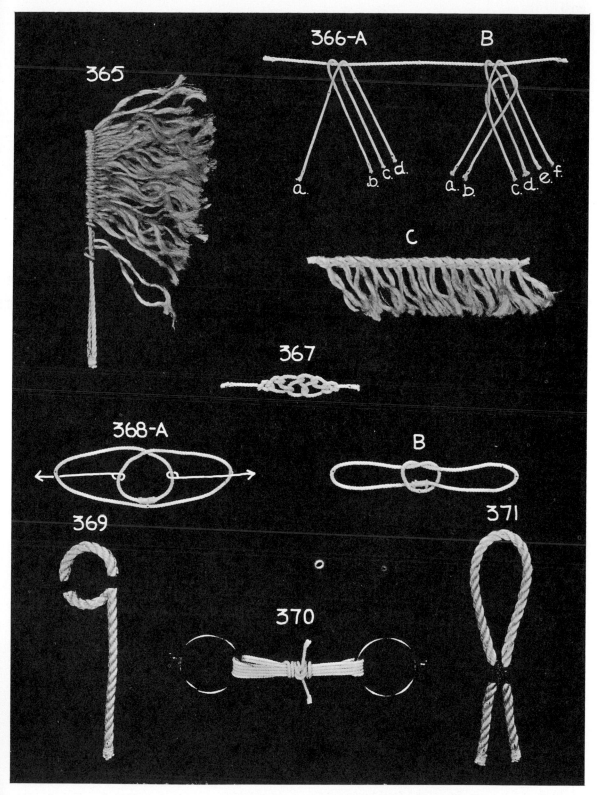

PLATE 279—A RAILWAY AND A THRUM SENNIT

ing passed in opposite directions. The ends are finally secured with a Square Knot in the center, as shown.

Fig. 371: This is a *Flat Seizing Finished Off With a Clove Hitch* after making the cross turns in the usual manner.

Plate 280—Dragonfly Knots, and a Center-Piece Design

Fig. 372A: *The Bocher Dragonfly Knot* is tied by tracing the cords as illustrated.

B: By pulling the loops on each side and the top and also the two ends the knot will then appear as in this illustration.

Fig. 373: *This Center-Piece* shows the knot illustrated in Plate 140, Fig. 42, opened and woven with a single strand rather than with three.

Fig. 374: *The False Sheet Bend Sheepshank* is made by forming two bights and tying a Sheet Bend on one bight, and a Hitch on the other bight as illustrated.

Fig. 375A: *The Persian Mat Weave* is begun as illustrated here.

B: The two ends are passed as shown in this illustration.

C: The final tucks are made to complete the knot.

Fig. 376: *The Double Round False Overhand Knot* is made by following the method shown in the illustration.

Fig. 377: *A Secure Sheet Bend* is tied by first forming a bight in the end of one rope and then making an Overhand Knot on the standing part with the moving part. The other rope is bent to the bight by using the Sheet Bend.

Fig. 378: *The Hitched False Carrick Bend* can be tied easily by observing the illustration.

Plate 281—A Persian Round Mat, and a Lamp Stand

Fig. 379: *The Seized Dragonfly Knot* is made by tying the Dragonfly Knot shown in Plate 137, Figs. 1A to 1E. The top bight is then seized together and brought down in back of the body of the knot and the two ends are passed through the loop to finish.

Fig. 380A: *A Persian Round Mat* is made by beginning as shown in the illustration.

B: The ends are now passed as shown in this illustration, which completes half the knot.

C: The ends are now passed as shown to complete the weave. Next draw the knot up evenly and cut off the ends.

Fig. 381: *This Lamp Stand* is a beautiful and useful piece of work which can be made in from nine to eleven hours. To make it a piece of ⅛-inch pipe 15 inches long and threaded on one end is used as a standard. Seven pieces of ¼-inch rope are then seized to the threaded end for a dis-

tance of three inches. Now begin to tie a Star Knot, Plate 57, Fig. 78, of seven strands. Next, two Single Diamond Knots are made, Plate 60, Fig. 140, one following the other. Each knot is drawn up taut just as soon as it has been completed. A Matthew Walker Knot, Plate 53, Fig. 5, is now made followed by another Single Diamond Knot. Two Lanyard Knots, Plate 60, Fig. 131, are then made, one following the other. Another Single Diamond Knot is made followed by a Triple Pass Diamond Knot. This is not drawn taut at this point.

A round disc of wood ½-inch thick and four inches in diameter is now cut. Drill a ½-inch hole through the center of the block and cut a small groove along the bottom for the wire. Place the block on the pipe at the bottom of the stand. The Triple-Pass Diamond Knot is now worked over the wooden disc, the knot worked taut and the ends cut off short. Pass the

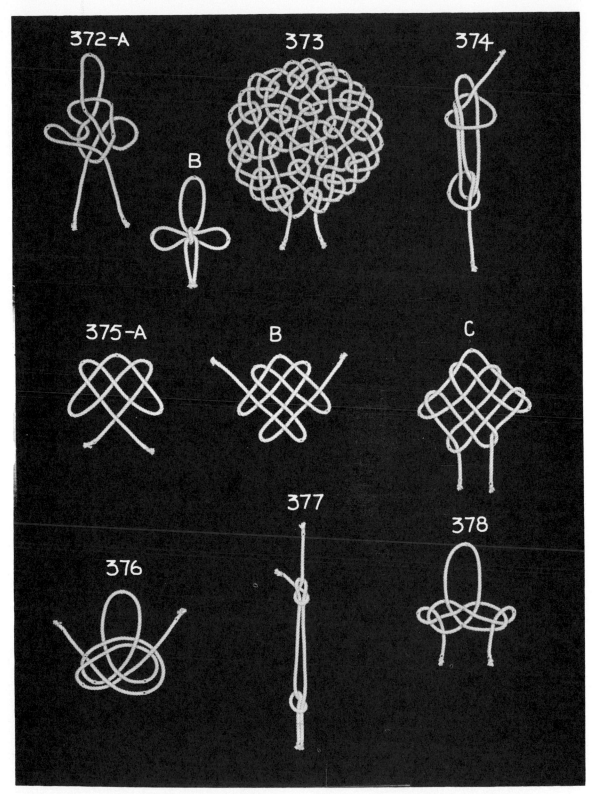

PLATE 280—DRAGONFLY KNOTS, AND A CENTER-PIECE DESIGN

wire through the pipe and join it to the socket screwed on the pipe. The set screw holding the socket is then tightened. Cut off any excess rope which overhangs the socket. Next, take a length of silk cord and starting at the Star Knot begin serving the neck of the lamp, until the serving reaches the socket. A Five-Strand Turk's Head, PLATE 109, FIG. 3, is then made on top of the serving. To finish the lamp three coats of varnish are applied to the rope, which not only preserves the rope but fills up the spaces between the yarns. It is therefore a simple matter to keep such a

stand as this clean with soap and water.

FIG. 382: *The Carrick Arrow Head Knot* shown in this illustration is made similar to the common Carrick Bend.

FIG. 383: *The Celtic Weave* is shown here. It can be duplicated easily by observing the illustration.

FIG. 384: *An Interlocking Bight Dragonfly Knot.* It is made by tying the Dragonfly Knot (*see* PLATE 137, FIG. 1).

FIGS. 385 and 386: *French Ornamental Knots* which can be made by tracing the designs.

Plate 282—Securing Ratlines to Shrouds

FIG. 387: *The Proper Way to Rattle Down,* i.e., secure a Ratline to a shroud is shown in the accompanying illustration. The eyes spliced into the ends of the Ratlines are made fast to the shrouds by lashings. These are passed through the eyes as illustrated and after a sufficient number of turns have been taken with the lashing, several cross turns are taken and the ends are secured with a Clove Hitch. It will be noticed in this connection that the eyes spliced in the Ratlines are always secured to the shrouds with the flat surface of the eye facing upward. This eliminates the possibility of rain water from lying in the cup on the bottom of the eye.

FIG. 388: *Rattling Down a Ratline* for its entire length is done in the following manner: make an Eye Splice in one end of a small line, or the line to be used as a Ratline, and lash it to the first shroud in the manner explained above. Pass the line to the next shroud and secure it with a Clove Hitch. Again pass the line from shroud to shroud and at each, secure it with a Clove Hitch. Starting from the left, or the first shroud on the port side, proceed to take up all of the slack in the line by readjusting and tightening the Clove Hitches from left to right. Then allow enough material and splice an eye in the

end of the Ratline at the last shroud and lash the eye in place as has been explained.

FIG. 389: *The French Rabbit Head Knot* can be tied easily by observing the accompanying illustration. The four bights *a* are drawn out to finish off the knot.

FIG. 390: *The French Dragonfly Knot* is the French variation of the Dragonfly Knot shown on PLATE 137, FIG. 1.

FIG. 391: *An Ornamental Knot* that can be tied easily from reference to the accompanying illustration. The bights *a* are pulled down slightly when the knot is pulled taut.

FIG. 392: *The Variated Pyramid Knot* is also an ornamental knot used for decorative purposes.

FIG. 393: *Tricing in Two Ropes* is done in the following manner: a short piece of line is made fast to one of the two ropes and then several turns are taken around both of them as illustrated. Pull all of the slack out of the two ropes by hauling on the free end of the lashing and then secure one end of the latter to either of the ropes with a Clove Hitch.

FIGS. 394A and B: *A Combination Ornamental Shamrock Knot.* Two Shamrock Knots (PLATE 240, FIG. 45) are made in

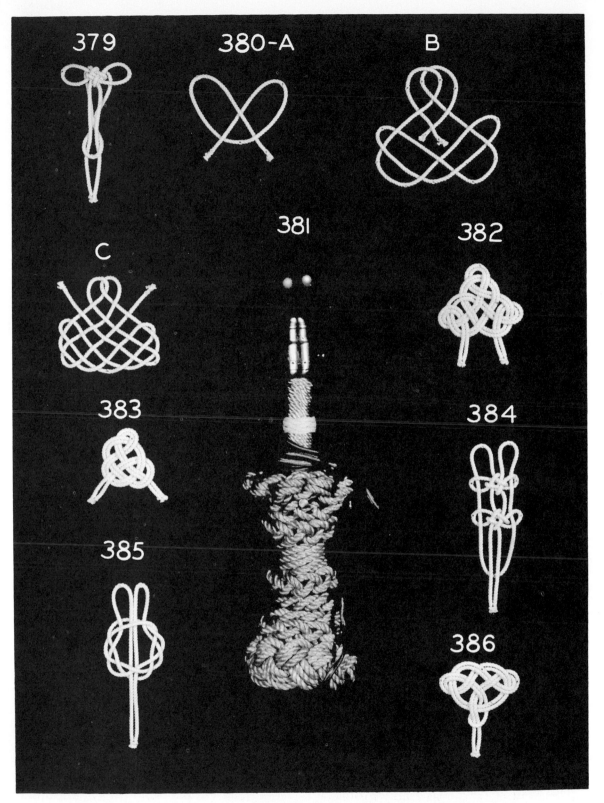

PLATE 281—A PERSIAN ROUND MAT, AND A LAMP STAND

series to start the pattern, after which a third Shamrock Knot is made below the two in series, but the two free ends of the cord are pulled out of the knot after it

has been formed and these free ends are used to interlace the wings of all three Shamrock Knots together as may be seen from the illustration.

Plate 283—Lashings, Knots, and a Spanish Windlass

FIG. 395: *The Rose Lashing*, First Method. It is used to secure a rope, having eyes spliced into each of its ends, around a mast or spar. A Lanyard is spliced through one eye and then passed in Figure-of-Eight fashion over and back under one eye, then over and back under the other. This process is continued until a sufficient number of turns have been made. The end is then taken round and round in coil fashion between the cross turns as shown.

FIG. 396: *The Rose Lashing*, Second Method. It was used on sailing ships to lash the footropes to the yards. It can also be used to lash an eye to a spar as illustrated. The method of tying the knot is self-explanatory.

FIG. 397: *The Log Packing Knot* is another method of applying the Packing Knot, illustrated in PLATE 258, FIG. 168.

FIG. 398: *Hitching a Tailblock*. A Tailblock is one of the most useful pieces of gear which can be used on a ship. It consists of a single sheave block with a Lanyard spliced into it. It is made fast in a number of ways depending on the circumstances. In this particular instance the illustration shows it made fast to a rope; the knot used is a Stopper Hitch (*see* PLATE 4, FIG. 92).

FIG. 399A: *Making Up a Gasket*. When sails are taken in on sailing vessels they are lashed to the yards with ropes which are called Gaskets. When under sail the Gaskets are of course not in use and therefore

must be coiled up in a fashion that will permit them to be released instantly when it is so desired. A Gasket is made in the following manner: Take the bight of the Gasket about four feet from the end which is made fast. Now begin coiling it up in the hand. When the entire line has been coiled it is flattened out but take care that none of the bights in the coil are dropped out of the hand. Next take several turns around the coil with the standing end. The bight of the standing end is now passed through the upper portion of the coil and then passed over the top of all the bights as shown by the arrow. The part *a* represents the bight which is passed through the bight.

B: The standing end is now drawn taut and the bight then comes to rest at the point *a*. (See PLATE 331, FIG. 2.)

FIG. 400: *Taking a Ropeyarn Out of a Strand*. It is surprising how few people know how to execute such a simple operation as taking a ropeyarn out of a strand. The method usually used is to extract it from the end. The proper method is to grasp the yarn *a* from the center of the strand and then withdraw it.

FIG. 401: *The Spanish Windlass* is an old device used to exert a drawing force by heaving two ends of a rope together. It is made as shown in the illustration with two Marline spikes, *a*, a steel or stout wooden bar, *b*, and a well-greased line, *c*. It is useful when clapping on a throat seizing.

Plate 284—Belaying Lines to Cleats

FIG. 402: *A Knot in a Lifeboat Line*. It happens occasionally, in lowering the lifeboats over the side of a ship, that an Over-

hand Knot will tie itself into a boat painter automatically as the painter is played out from aboard. This may be caused by the

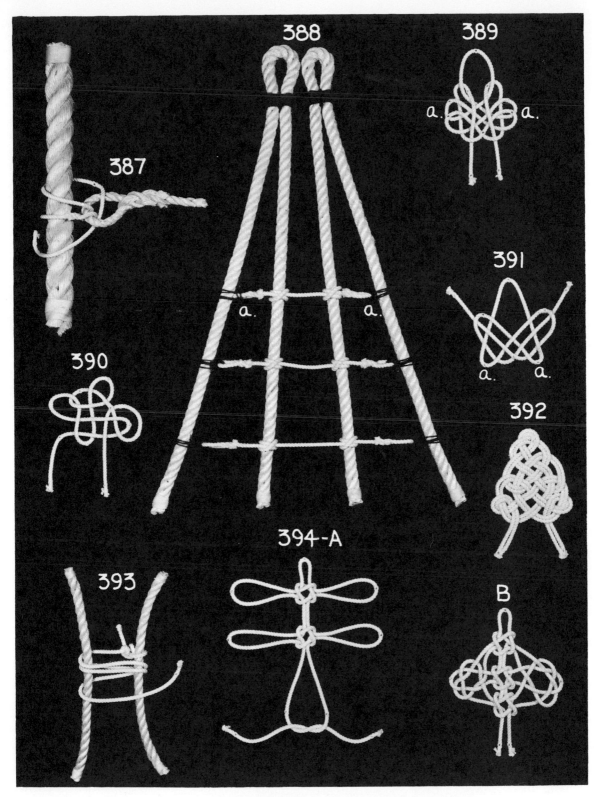

387 **388** **389**

a.   a.

390 **391**

a.   a.

392

394-A

393 **B**

PLATE 282—SECURING RATLINES TO SHROUDS

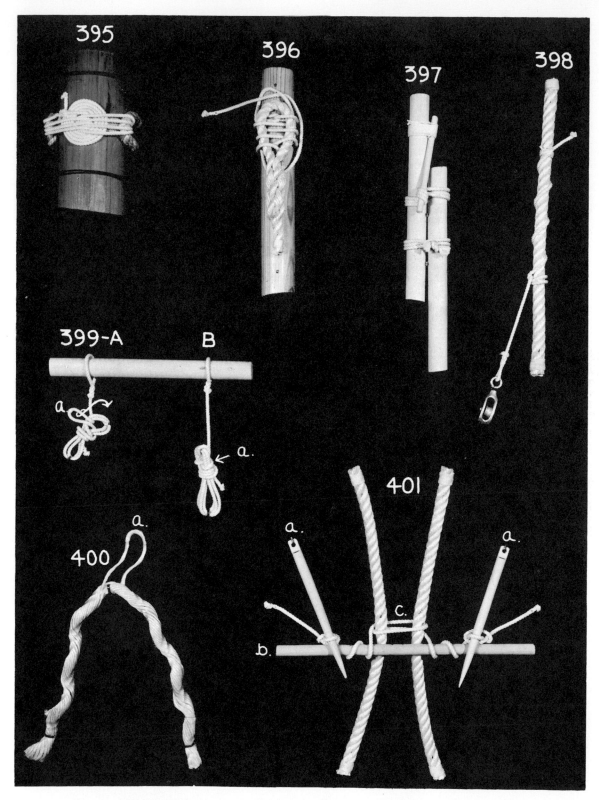

PLATE 283—LASHINGS, KNOTS, AND A SPANISH WINDLASS

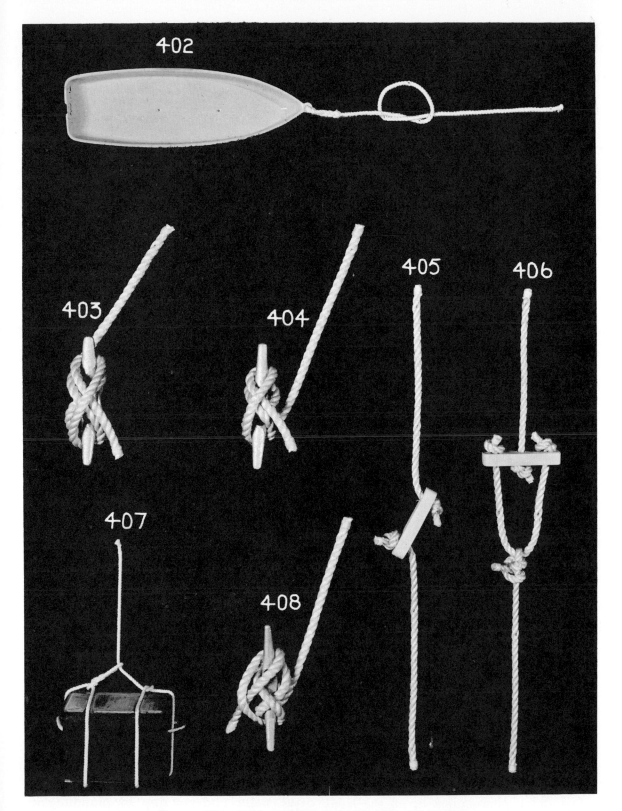

PLATE 284—BELAYING LINES TO CLEATS

boat drifting through a bight allowed to form in the line or it may be caused by the wind whipping the line back and over the lifeboat. To remove such a knot one method is to open the knot sufficiently to form a bight large enough to pass back over the lifeboat, or if the boat is in the water it may be allowed to float through the bight in the rope.

Fig. 403: *Belaying a Halyard to a Cleat* (incorrect method). This illustration depicts one of the many incorrect ways to belay a Halyard to a Cleat. Belaying running rigging, halyards and sheets is an important operation aboard ship and if not done correctly may result in damage to the rigging. It will be noticed in this illustration that the hauling part of the line is pulling against the Cleat, whereas it should pull away from it as shown in Fig. 404. Moreover, the hauling part of the line is also pulling against the turns taken around the Cleat and this would prevent them from being cast off quickly, which is often necessary in handling lines of this kind.

Fig. 404: *Belaying a Halyard to a Cleat* (correct method). This is the correct method of belaying a line to a Cleat. The end should not be secured in any manner other than that shown, that is, it should not be further secured by Hitches or other methods. Notice that the end of the line can be quickly slipped free and the turns on the Cleat cast off.

Figs. 405 and 406: *Swivels*. The devices shown in these illustrations are called Swivels, and the manner in which they are made is so clear as not to need explaining.

Fig. 407: *A Lashing* such as that shown in this illustration is used for handling sea chests. The Lashing is made with a length of line having an eye spliced into one of its ends and the manner in which the line is passed about the chest may be easily observed.

Fig. 408: *Belaying a Line to a Cleat* (landlubber's style). This is called the landlubber's method of belaying a line to a Cleat. The correct method is shown in Fig. 404.

Plate 285—Securing Lines to Belaying Pins and Jug Covers

Fig. 409: *Lashing a Cleat to a Stay* is done in the following manner: on small sailboats the flag halliards are usually made fast to a turnbuckle or hitched on any convenient object, which makes quite a sloppy method of securing the rigging. A much neater means to this end is to make a small cleat out of wood, which is grooved on the bottom and then lashed to the stay as illustrated. A rope can be kept from swinging in the air by using a fair-lead such as is shown just below the Cleat.

Fig. 410: *Coiling Rope on a Belaying Pin*. This is the correct method for coiling the end of a rope on a belaying pin. When a considerable amount of rope remains left over after a rope has been belayed, the remainder is then coiled up in the hand and when near the end, the coil is placed against the pinrail and several more turns

taken on the belaying pin. This uses up the remaining end and also secures the coil as illustrated. *a* is the standing part.

Fig. 411: *The Correct Method of Belaying an Eye-Spliced Line*. When the standing part of the rope leads from above, the end is brought around in back of the belaying pin, beneath the pinrail, and then the eye is placed over the top of the belaying pin.

Fig. 412: *This Is a Belaying Pin*. They are made of hard wood or metal, depending of course upon the strain they are required to bear.

Fig. 413: *The Leadline* is used to take soundings, that is to determine the depth of the water under a ship by plumbing its depth. The weight of the lead varies from two pounds to fourteen pounds, depending

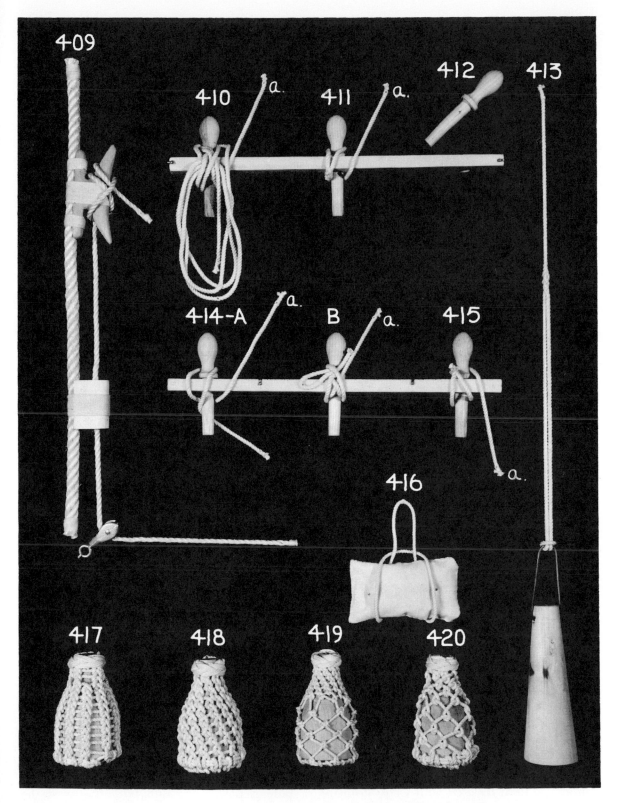

PLATE 285—SECURING LINES TO BELAYING PINS

on the depth of the water, or whether it is rough or calm, etc. Markings are made in the line at various intervals so that the depth may be known as soon as the lead touches bottom. To secure the line to the lead a long eye must be spliced into it. This line is then passed through the wire handle. The eye is then opened up and the lead dropped through it. The line is now drawn taut to finish.

FIGS. 414A and B: *Belaying a Line to a Belaying Pin* is done as shown. The rope is first brought around the pin, up and around the top of it, after which a number of Figure-of-Eight turns are taken around the line and the pin. *a* represents the standing part. When enough turns have been taken the end is finished off with a Slippery Hitch as illustrated in FIG. 414B.

FIG. 415: *Another Method of Making an Eye Fast to a Belaying Pin*. When the standing part *a* leads from below, the end is first brought around the top of the belaying pin, and the eye is passed over the bottom of the pin to finish.

FIG. 416: *Passing a Strop on a Sack* is done as shown in the illustration.

FIG. 417: *A French Hitched Jug*. The sides and necks of the jugs pictured here are covered first. The bottoms are then covered with Half Hitching (PLATE 108, FIG. 44, and PLATE 107, FIG. 33). The top of the neck is finished off with a Three-Strand Turk's Head (PLATE 109, FIG. 1).

FIG. 418: *A Jug Covered with Half Hitching*.

FIG. 419: *A Jug Covered with Netting*, as shown on PLATE 295, FIG. 487, and the neck is covered with Half Hitching.

FIG. 420: *A Jug Covered with Open Net Half Hitching* as shown on PLATE 105, FIG. 16.

Plate 286—Joining Ropes with Toggles, and Other Knots

FIGS. 421 and 422: *Joining the Ends of Ropes with Toggles*. In FIG. 421 an eye has been formed in the end of one of the ropes while a wooden disc has been knotted into the end of the other. In FIG. 422 a long eye has been spliced in the end of the rope to the left of the illustration while a Toggle is spliced directly into the end of the other rope.

FIG. 423: *A Toggle Lashing* is made by splicing eyes into the ends of the ropes as shown. A short piece of line then has its ends secured to two small round wooden pins and these are applied as shown.

FIG. 424: *Puddening a Fender* is done by taking a short piece of line and forming eyes in each of its ends, after which a mouse is built up out of spun yarn in the middle of the rope, with its ends tapered off as shown (*see* PLATE 68, FIG. 241). The entire mouse is then covered with Cross-Pointing (*see* PLATE 287, FIG. 430). Each end is then finished off with a Footrope Knot (*see* PLATE 255, FIG. 149), which is made from three strands of nettles taken from the Cross-Pointing.

FIG. 425: *The Topsail Halyard Toggle* was formerly used in the days of sailing ships. An eye is spliced into one end and a Manrope Knot (*see* PLATE 294, FIG. 485) is made on the other. As the Toggle was used the Manrope Knot was slipped through the eye, thereby forming a Ring or Grommet. It could be slipped easily by merely pushing the knot back through the eye.

FIG. 426: *The Curtain Ring* is completely covered with a series of Lark's Head Hitches.

FIG. 427: *The Tourniquet Lashing* is made as follows: First make a Grommet from a short piece of line which will just fit around the objects to be lashed, then a pole is passed through both bights of the Grommet and twisted until the desired tension is applied.

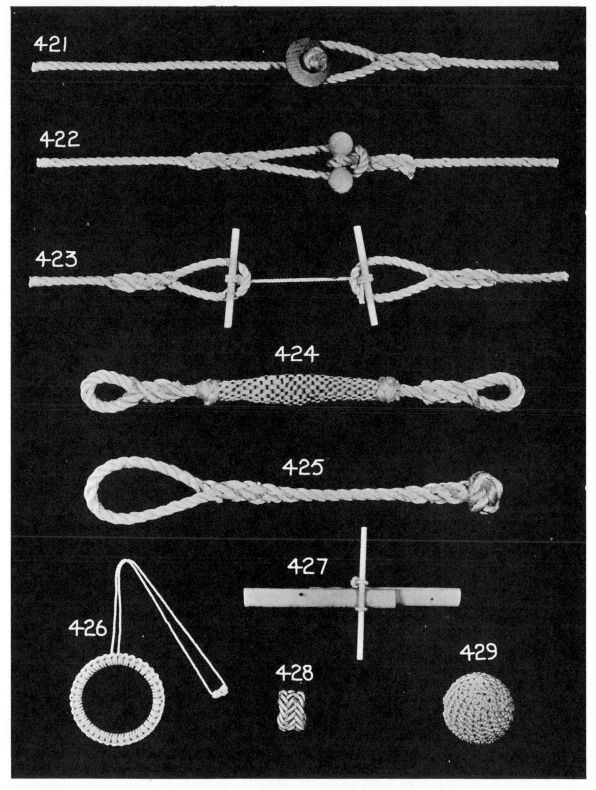

PLATE 286—JOINING ROPES WITH TOGGLES, AND OTHER KNOTS

Fig. 428: *The Headhunter's Ring.* The knot shown in this illustration is in reality a variation of Turk's Heading and was shown to the authors by one of the descendants of an ancient tribe of head hunters. The manner in which the knot is made was explained only after our promise never to show anyone how the weave is formed. For this reason we are prevented from explaining how the knot is made.

The original rings of this kind were made from bamboo reeds and were supposed to bring good fortune to those who wore them. It differs from any other type of Turk's Head Knot in that each strand passes over three strands and under three strands, instead of as in the Common Turk's Head which has one strand passing over one strand and under one.

Fig. 429: *A Rubber Ball Covered With Half Hitches.* Pass two turns of cord around the center of the ball and proceed to make Half Hitches with the cords until one-half of the ball has been covered. Turn the ball over and continue in the same manner, dropping a Half Hitch at intervals as the ball tapers. To finish off the work the cords are tucked under the Half Hitches half way around the ball and are cut off short (*see* PLATE 108, FIG. 44).

Plate 287—Various Forms of Rope Pointing

Fig. 430A: *The Common Rope Pointing* is one of the best methods for finishing off the end of a rope to prevent the strands from fraying. It also stiffens the end of the rope so that it can be passed easily through a block. To start the work clap a stout seizing on the rope about ten inches back from its end. Unlay the strands and make enough nettles to completely cover the rope. These nettles are shown in the illustration at *a*. The number of nettles should always be an even number, in this case twelve. The remaining yarns are then tapered by scraping, after which they are marled securely together as shown at *b*. Next, pass each alternate nettle down and the remainder up, laying the latter along the conical center. At the point where the two groups of nettles separate take two turns around the upright nettles and the cone with a piece of Marline, securing the second turn with a Blood Knot. Next, bring the vertical nettles down on the standing part of the rope and the other nettles up along the center. The Marline is again brought up and two turns taken about the now vertical nettles and the cone, after which the last turn of the Marline is again secured with a Blood Knot . Repeat this sequence of operations until the desired length has been reached.

B: To finish off the work do not stop all of the nettles to the work but instead take three loose turns around the one set of nettles and the core. Next, take each nettle from the second group and bring them up over the turns of Marline and then back down underneath them as shown at *d*. The nettles shown at *c* have not been tucked. When all of the nettles of the second group have been tucked as explained the turns of the Marline are brought up taut. All of the ends of the nettles and the core as well are cut off and the work will look as shown in FIG. 430c.

Fig. 431: *The Spiral Pointing,* First Method, is done much in the manner previously explained, except that two nettles are taken down and the third is kept up, thus making four groups out of the twelve nettles in this instance. The Marline in this case is passed around four nettles each time instead of six as was done before. The pointing shown in the illustration is finished off with a Footrope Knot, PLATE 255, FIG. 149.

Fig. 432: *The Spiral Pointing,* Second Method, is made in the same manner as that just explained, except that three nettles are kept down and only one is brought

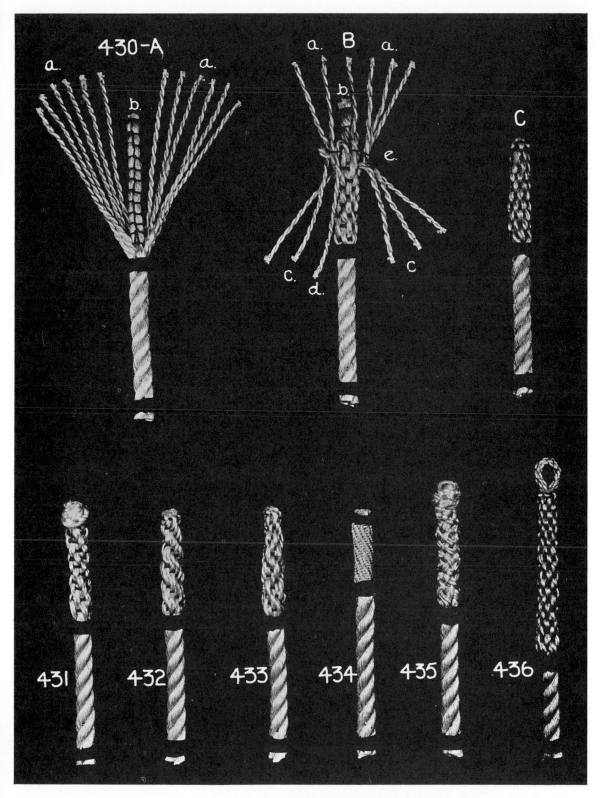

PLATE 287—VARIOUS FORMS OF ROPE POINTING

up. This divides the nettles into three groups. This form of pointing shows the spiral effect better than the other method.

FIG. 433: *Zig-Zag Pointing* such as that shown is made much like the other methods previously explained. Four Hitches are made to the left, three to the right, three to the left, and so on.

FIG. 434: *The Half Hitch Pointing* is done with Half Hitches (*see* PLATE 108, FIG. 44). A Five-Strand Turk's Head (PLATE 109, FIG. 3) was made on the standing part of the rope in this case with a Three-Strand Turk's Head (PLATE 109,

FIG. 1) formed on the end to finish off the work.

FIG. 435: *The Coach-Whipped Pointing* is made by covering the core of the rope with Coach-Whipping (PLATE 107, FIG. 34), after which the work is finished off with a Footrope Knot (PLATE 255, FIG. 149).

FIG. 436: *The Hawser Pointing* is made as follows: After the nettles have been separated, as was done previously, those remaining are laid up to form a three-strand rope. An eye is spliced in the end of this rope, after which the work of pointing is carried on as was explained under FIG. 430.

Plate 288—Rope Pointing, and Rope Ending

FIG. 437: *The Hitched Rope Pointing* is made by first unlaying the strands of the rope into yarns, after which the heart of the rope is scraped down to form a taper which is marled in the usual manner. A Whipping is placed around the rope at the point where the unlayed strands stop. Next lay the strands or yarns up into two-yarn nettles and fender hitch them together, working the Hitches down to a point at the end. Another Whipping is added at the pointed end using sail twine or small stuff.

FIG. 438: *The Spiral Hitched Rope Pointing* is started by unlaying the strands of the rope for a sufficient distance, after which a piece of Marline that will serve for a warp is whipped around the rope, at the same time seizing the end of the Marline underneath. Then, unlay the strands into yarns and separate them from the heart. Next, scrape the heart down to a taper and marl it. Proceed by hitching each of the strands around the Marline which is used as a warp passed around the heart of the rope in a spiral fashion. Continue with the Hitching until near the end, then place a Whipping over the Marline where the Hitching is left off. Another Whipping can then be placed on the end of the heart, as

illustrated, which will give a neat and attractive appearance to the point.

FIG. 439: *A Four-Strand Braid with Manila Rope* is started by middling one part around the other as illustrated. The weave can be followed from reference to the illustration. It can be made any desired length and the ends are seized to finish off the work.

FIG. 440: This is a *Spiral-Hitched Eye Pointing* which is made in the same manner as FIG. 438, after the eye has been formed and seized.

FIG. 441: *A Hard Boat Fender Design.* This is made by first forming an eye in the end of the rope by placing a seizing around the two parts with a piece of Marline underneath to serve as a warp. Next, unlay the strands into yarns and lay the outside yarns up into two-strand nettles. Proceed by hitching these nettles around the warp as it is passed around the heart of the rope in spiral fashion, after which finish off with a Whipping. The heart can then be worked down to the end as illustrated by trimming the yarns.

FIG. 442: *A Rope Ending.* The strands are unlayed and a Diamond Knot is tied

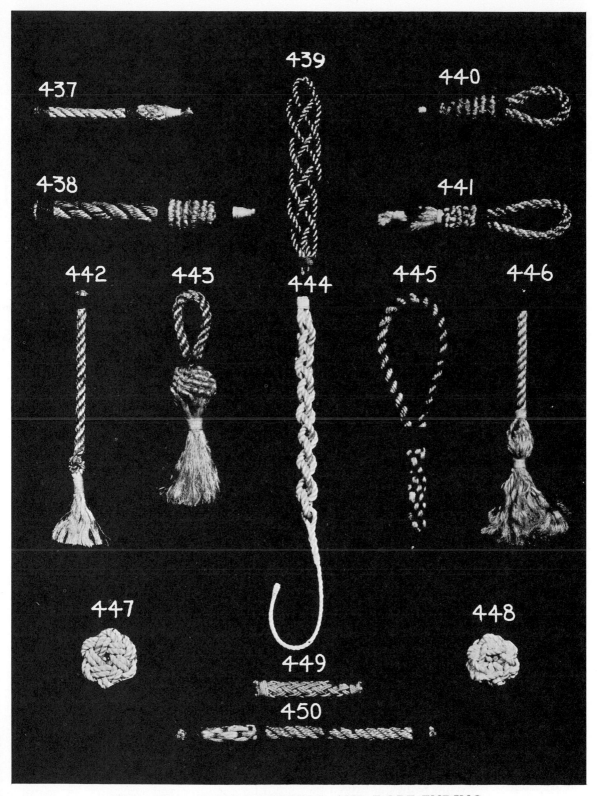

PLATE 288—ROPE POINTING, AND ROPE ENDING

with a Whipping placed just below the knot. The strands are then opened up and frayed out.

FIG. 443: This is called a *Coiffure Eye Pointing*. An eye is formed with a seizing in the usual manner and the Spiral Hitching is done as in FIGS. 438 and 440, except that the heart of the rope is not tapered down. The Hitching is done with the outside yarns and a Whipping is placed around the yarns to finish off the work.

FIG. 444: *A Braided Rope Fender*. To make it lay up the four ends of two pieces of rope into a Four-Strand Round Sennit, then place a seizing of lobster twine, tarred line, or Marline around the ends. To complete the Fender splice a small line through the first bight for a Lanyard.

FIG. 445: Represents *An Ordinary Eye Pointing*. Form the eye and place a seizing around the two parts of rope, then unlay the strands and select the outside yarns which are laid back and tied to the body of the rope. Taper the strands forming the heart and marl them down in the usual

manner. Make two Round Turns with Marline to start the Pointing, after laying each alternate pair of yarns back and the others down. Continue with another pair of Round Turns, bringing each alternate pair of yarns down and the others back with each additional pass. Make a secure Whipping on the end to finish the job.

FIG. 446: *A Rope Ending With the Strands Unlaid and Opened* which is started and finished with Whippings as illustrated.

FIG. 447: This is *A Combination Rosette Knot Tied with Cotton Line*.

FIG. 448: An example of still *Other Variations in Rope Knotting* with cotton line.

FIG. 449: *An Eight-Strand Coach-Whipping Around a Rope Core*. It is the same as an ordinary Round Sennit of eight double strands.

FIG. 450: *An Ordinary Rope Pointing* done in the same manner as the work illustrated in FIG. 445.

Plate 289—A Spindle Eye, and Sennits

FIGS. 451A and B: *An Artificial or Spindle Eye in Braided Hemp*. First, unlay the rope back far enough to allow sufficient material to form the eye and then open and separate each strand. Then take a spar of a diameter slightly larger than that of the size of the eye and raise a mousing on each side with Marline or spun yarn, placing the mousings so that the space between them is equal to the diameter of the rope in which the eye is to be formed. This is necessary to keep the unlaid strands of the rope in place during the making of the eye. The next step is to take the strands and divide them into sets of four strands each, after which they are joined together around the spar with Overhand Knots, as shown in FIG. 451A. Care should be exercised in making the Overhand Knots to insure that they

are spaced equally around the spar, in order that the eye will be circular and regular in shape.

The next procedure is to lay the ends of the strands down on the standing part of the rope. Continue by fraying out and scraping the ends down to a taper after which apply a Marline Hitch Seizing with sail twine to keep the open yarns secured to the standing part of the rope. Proceed by marling and coxcombing the eye and then serve the rope to finish off. This is a very practical method for forming an eye in braided hemp.

FIG. 452: *A Four-Strand Alternating Overhand Sennit*. To start, seize four parts of line together and continue by joining each alternate pair with Overhand Knots, one on top of the other. Strands *c* and *d*

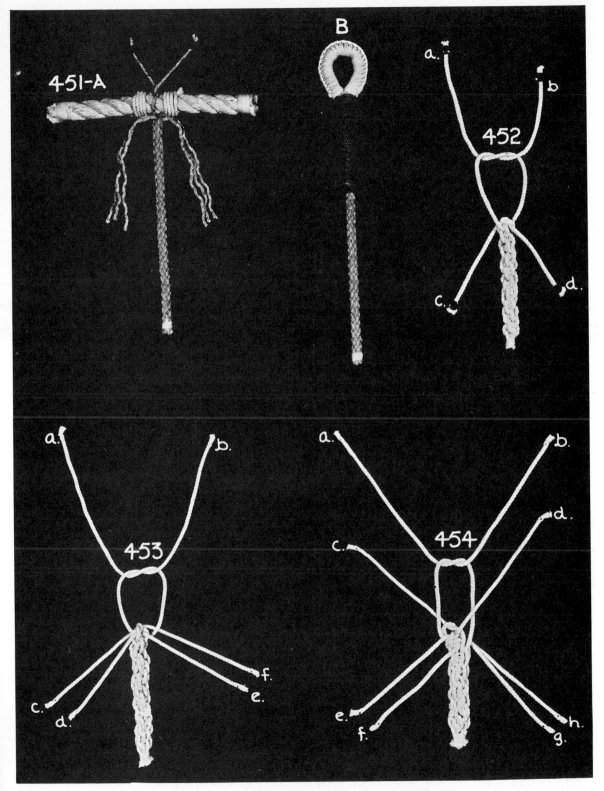

PLATE 289—A SPINDLE EYE, AND SENNITS

are joined and pulled taut, and then strands *a* and *b* are brought together in the same manner, on top of the previous Overhand Knot. Repeat this procedure until the braid is made to the length desired.

FIG. 453: *A Six-Strand Alternating Overhand Sennit.* It is made by forming Overhand Knots with each alternating pair of strands in the same manner as in the previous example. Strands *c* and *e* are joined, then *d* and *f* and finally strands *a* and *b* are brought together. This procedure is continued until the Sennit is of the desired length.

FIG. 454: *An Eight-Strand Alternating Overhand Sennit.* It is made in the same way as the other types, in that strands *f* and *h* are joined in the usual manner and then in successive order strands *e* and *g*, *c* and *d* and finally *a* and *b*.

Repeat this sequence until the Sennit is of the desired length.

Plate 290—Sennits, and an Artificial Spindle Eye

FIG. 455: *A Six-Strand True Overhand Sennit.* It is made slightly different from the alternating types previously described. Two pairs of strands are joined by the side of each other with Overhand Knots and then the odd pair is brought up over the other two pairs and joined in the opposite direction. This procedure is followed until the braid is completed. Strands *c* and *f* are joined first and then strands *d* and *e* are brought together, after which strands *a* and *b* are brought over the top from the opposite side and are knotted together.

FIG. 456: *An Eight-Strand True Overhand Sennit.* It is made in the same way as the six-strand type, except that two pairs of strands are joined one way and then two pair in the opposite way, over the top of the first two. Strands *d* and *f* are joined first and they are followed by strands *e* and *g*, which are brought together in the same way. Next, bring strands *c* and *h* up over the top of the two pairs of strands that were knotted first and join them with an Overhand Knot. Follow with strands *a* and *b* which are joined by the side of *c* and *h*. This method is followed until the braid is completed.

FIGS. 457A, B, and C: *An Artificial or Spindle Eye in Four-Strand Manila Rope.* Place a Whipping on the end of the rope at a distance from its end of about three times its circumference. Unlay the strands back as far as the Whipping and separate them into yarns, which are to be divided into two equal groups. There are two ways in which this eye can be formed. The yarns can be either knotted together or they can be laid up into nettles and then knotted together around a spar having a diameter equal to twice the circumference of the rope. Take care not to make all of the Overhand Knots at one place around the spar, but rather, space them equally distant from each other. After all of the yarns have been knotted together lay them down around the eye and on the standing part of the rope. Next, take a length of Marline and bind the knotted yarns with Marline Hitches all around the eye. Scrape and taper the ends of the yarns down on the standing part of the rope and marl them in the same manner as the eye. The eye and the standing part are then served, or the eye can be parceled before serving, to make a neat job. FIG. 457A shows the first stage of the work and FIG. 457B as it looks when marled. FIG. 457C shows the completed eye.

This type of eye is used for the collars of stays and was used also for the lower end of manropes when the Lanyard was spliced in back.

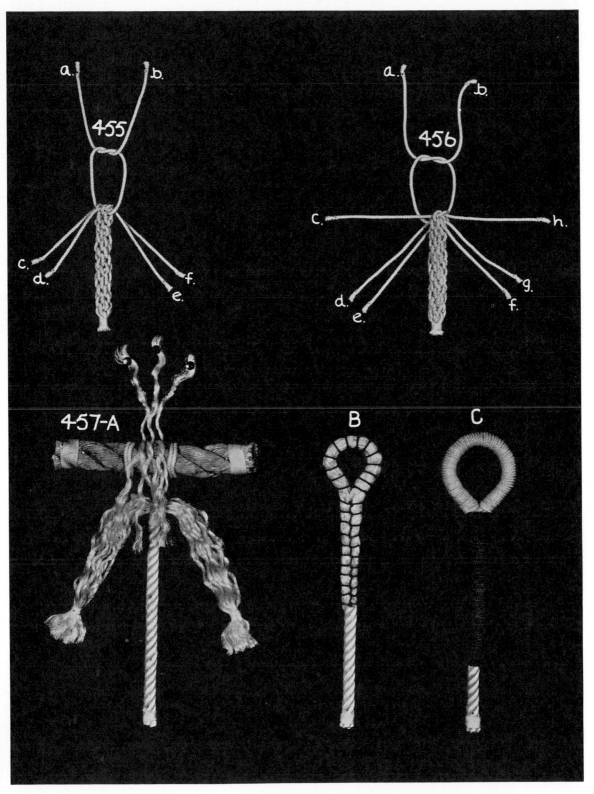

PLATE 290—SENNITS, AND AN ARTIFICIAL SPINDLE EYE

Plate 291—Tourniquets, and a Soft Boat Fender

FIG. 458: *One Form of a Tourniquet.* Such a device as this is very useful to stop the flow of blood from a wound. A piece of cord, rope, rubber tubing, a handkerchief, or any suitable piece of cloth may be used. To apply a Tourniquet wrap it around the injured member above the wound, draw it fairly tight and tie a Square Knot with the ends. Insert a short stick between the two parts and under the knot and twist the material until the Tourniquet presses the artery sufficiently to stop the flow of blood. Care should be exercised in twisting the Tourniquet so as not to bruise or injure the flesh. A Tourniquet should never be twisted up tight for more than a few minutes at a time as it is necessary to slack it off at intervals, to permit blood to circulate below the wound.

FIG. 459: *A Form of Soft Boat Fender.* It is made by forming a Grommet with a piece of Manila rope and then laying long lengths of rope yarns, spun yarn, or any other suitable material over the Grommet by middling the lengths around the bottom part, after which a series of Marline Hitches is formed for the entire length of the Fender.

FIG. 460: *Another Form of Tourniquet* which is made with an additional Square Knot. This form is effective when no stick is available, as it can be twisted by means of the second Square Knot, after which the knot is tucked in under the bandage to hold it tight.

FIG. 461: *A Bill Hitch.* It is formed in the same manner as a Becket Hitch, which is the same as a Sheet Bend, except that it is used to hitch a line to a Becket instead of bending two ropes together.

FIG. 462: *A Four-Strand Monkey Fist Tied Around a Small Ball,* with a Hangman's Noose formed in the end of the line.

FIG. 463: *A Double Three-Leaf Chinese Temple Knot.* It is tied in the same way as the regular method, except that each bight is doubled while forming the knot.

FIG. 464: *A Double Blackwall or Stunner Hitch.* It is more secure than the Single Blackwall Hitch.

FIG. 465: *A Form of Figure-of-Eight Handcuff Hitches.* It is an ingenious way of forming two bights into Handcuff Hitches through a Figure-of-Eight Knot.

FIG. 466: *Two Interlocking Carrick Bends in a Loop.* This knot is a replica of the Sword-Knot design used on the golden sword presented to George Washington by Louis XVI, King of France, at the time of the American Revolution. It is also a duplicate of the Sword-Knot design on the sword presented to La Fayette by the Colonial Army in the same period. These two swords were exhibited in New York during the World's Fair of 1939.

FIG. 467: *An Odd Type of Railway Sennit* that is seldom seen. It is made by bringing a lashing back against its own part, then middle each yarn and starting from the end lay the eye of the middle part across the two parts of the lashing, after which bring both parts of the yarn around the lashing and tuck the ends down through their own eye and between the lashing. Pull each one taut and continue the same method.

Plate 292—A French and a Thrum Sennit, and an Eye Splice

FIG. 468: *Ten-Strand Variated French Sennit.* The key, or the method by which it is made, is as follows: Place one strand over two and then under two from one side and follow with one strand over two and under three from the opposite side.

FIG. 469: Shown in this illustration is *Eleven-Strand Variated French Sennit.* The

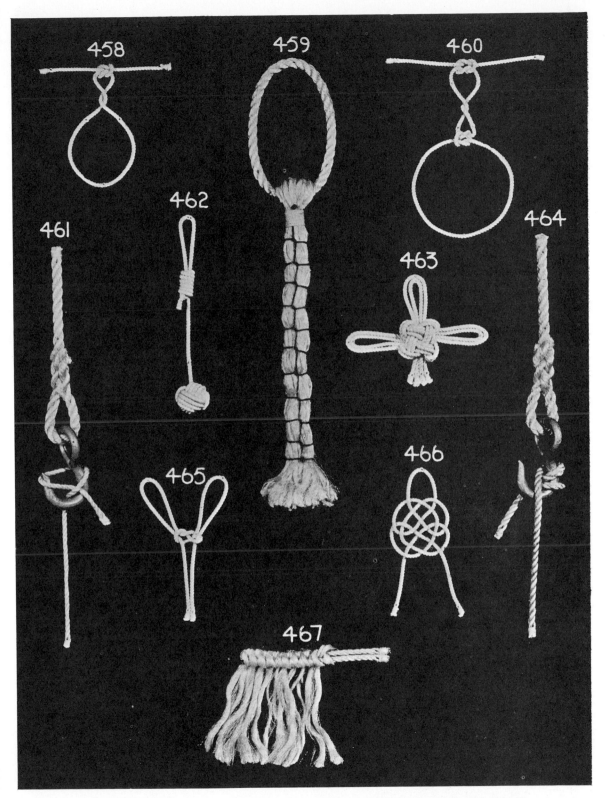

PLATE 291—TOURNIQUETS, AND A SOFT BOAT FENDER

key for making it is: one strand under two and over one from one side followed by one over two and under two from the opposite side.

FIG. 470: *A Yacht Eye Splice* such as that shown here may be made by any of several methods. One of the methods is as follows: Unlay the strands for a sufficient distance, after the customary seizing has been clapped on, then divide the strands into halves and proceed to splice one-half of each strand into the body of the rope, at the same time tapering down the Splice by dropping one yarn from each half-strand. Next, take the remaining half of each strand and form a series of Spiral Crowns around the outside body of the Splice. Finish off with a Walled Crown Knot, tuck the ends into the rope and cut them off short. Such a Splice as this is used more or less for ornamental purposes.

FIG. 471: *Criss-Cross Sennit of Four Strands* such as this can be made easily by careful attention to the illustration.

FIG. 472: *Nineteen-Strand Variated French Sennit* such as this is simply made by following the key, which is: one strand is brought down over three, under two, over two and then under one, from one side. From the opposite side bring one strand down over three, under two, over two and then under two and over one. Continue by repeating these several different moves from each side until the braid is of the desired length.

FIG. 473A: *Thrum Sennit* such as this is used as chafing gear aboard ships but they may be used for other purposes such as fenders and mats. In this illustration white line was used instead of the common rope yarn, merely for the purpose of photographic clearness. When rope yarns are used they should be about six inches long, the number required being determined by the length of the work. To start the Sennit take one strand and form a bight and then insert another strand in the bight, as shown

at FIG. 473A. The manner in which the strands are twisted is indicated by the arrows in both FIGS. 473A and B. FIG. 473C shows the two strands or yarns after the twist has been made, while the arrow indicates the position of the next additional yarn. This method of twisting the yarns and adding each additional yarn may be continued indefinitely until the Thrum has been made long enough for the purpose for which it was intended. FIG. D shows the completed Thrum.

FIG. 474: *A Spiral Fender* is made in the following manner: to make a Fender sixteen inches in length and two and one-half inches in diameter requires three fathoms of three-quarter-inch rope. The first step is to middle the rope and then clap on a stout seizing to form a small eye. Next, unlay all the strands and whip the end of each. Take the strands and form a continuous series of Crowns in one direction. Continue these Crowns until the Fender is about eighteen inches in length. Do not pull the Crowns up taut but, as they are made, merely take out the slack. Next, pass a stout piece of twine up through the center of the Fender. All of the six strands of the rope are then attached to this piece of twine and are pulled up inside the Crowns after which each one of the strands is pulled out separately through the six openings just below the seizing. Then, with the use of a fid, proceed to draw the slack out of the Crowns until the entire Fender has been drawn up as tight as possible. Pull the ends of the strands out until they are drawn up tightly and cut them off short below the seizing.

FIG. 475A: *A French Brief Knot.* It is a variation of the Brief Knot shown on PLATE 27, FIG. 83. The first step is to make a Square Knot, leaving a bight in the line as shown. The ends are then brought up and an inverted Square Knot is made on the loop as shown at FIG. 475B. To complete the knot the ends of the line are then

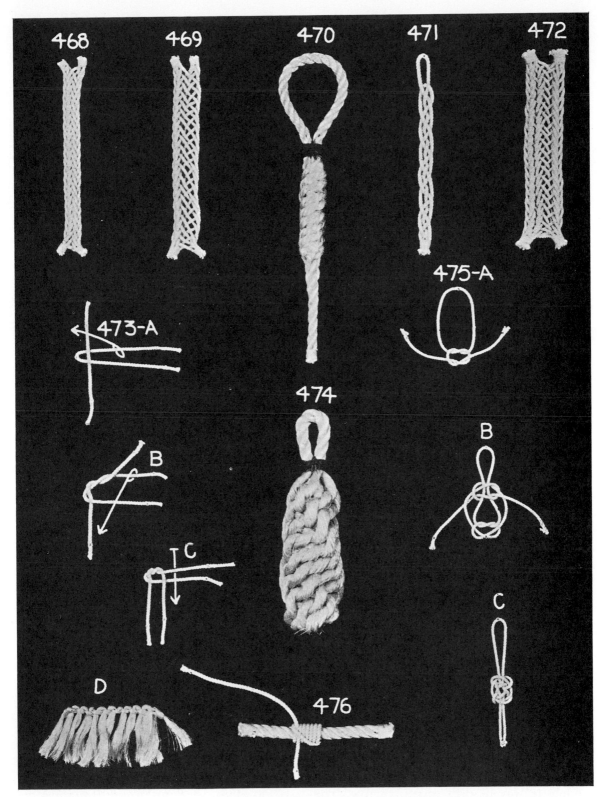

PLATE 292—A FRENCH AND A THRUM SENNIT, AND AN EYE SPLICE

brought down through the body of the lower Square Knot as shown in FIG. 475c.

FIG. 476: *The Fire Hose Hitch* is used extensively for hauling water hose to the upper floors or to the roof of a building. The knot is usually placed just below one of the couplings connecting the lengths of hose together. The Hitch is made as follows: Take several turns about the hose, bring the end back over the turns and form a Half Hitch. The end on top in the illustration is the hauling end while the lower end may be used to secure the hose in any position on the building or to a ladder.

Plate 293—A Circular Net, and an Extended Antique Sennit

FIGS. 477A and B: *A Circular Net.* A ring is made to form the center and a line is clove hitched around the ring in circular fashion as shown at FIG. 477A, taking care to space each of the six parts equally distant from each other. Next, take another length of line and attach it to both sides of the six open parts with Sheet Bends, working around the net in circular fashion. As this is done the six parts should again be spaced equally. After this additional work has been done the net will appear as in FIG. 477B. The net can be made any size by adding to the same parts that were added to previously.

FIG. 478: *A French Hitching* with the end of one part passing through the body of the following part.

FIG. 479: *An Ornamental Carrick Bend Net Design.*

FIG. 480: This illustration shows *A Hemp-Laid Long-Spliced Grommet.* A single strand of tarred hemp is laid up into three strands. When the strand is laid up two turns, cross the strand from the left under or inside the strand from the right, then continue around until the strands meet again and tie an Overhand Knot. Next, unlay the strands at the Overhand Knot by a half turn, to make them flat, then continue by tucking the ends with a Tapered Sailmaker's Splice.

FIG. 481: *A Cape Horn Knot.* Form four Half Hitches, one on top of the other, and then pull the left part of the two top Hitches through the body of the bottom Hitches, and at the same time pull the right part of the two bottom Hitches through the body of the two top Hitches. The knot will then appear as illustrated.

FIG. 482: *An Extended Antique Sennit.* It is made in a manner similar to that employed in making the design shown in PLATE 136, FIG. 412, except that the body of the weave is doubled or extended to form two weaves into one piece.

Plate 294—Making Tennis and Fishnets

FIG. 483: *The Making of Tennis Netting.* It is formed in the usual way with Sheet Bends, but with double lines and without using a Mesh Stick or a Shuttle.

FIG. 484: *Another Fish Net Design* formed with Lock-Knot Sheet Bends. The design is simple and may be followed easily. The knots are reversed from row to row or, in other words, they are tied in the opposite way in each successive row. The open knot on the lower right shows the opposite method of construction. This is a very effective method of making nets.

FIG. 485: *A Three-Strand Double Manrope Knot.* Tied in the same manner as the knot shown on PLATE 53, FIG. 6, except that the strands are doubled. It is used on the ends of gangway lines and for various other purposes.

FIG. 486: *A Four-Strand Double Manrope Knot.*

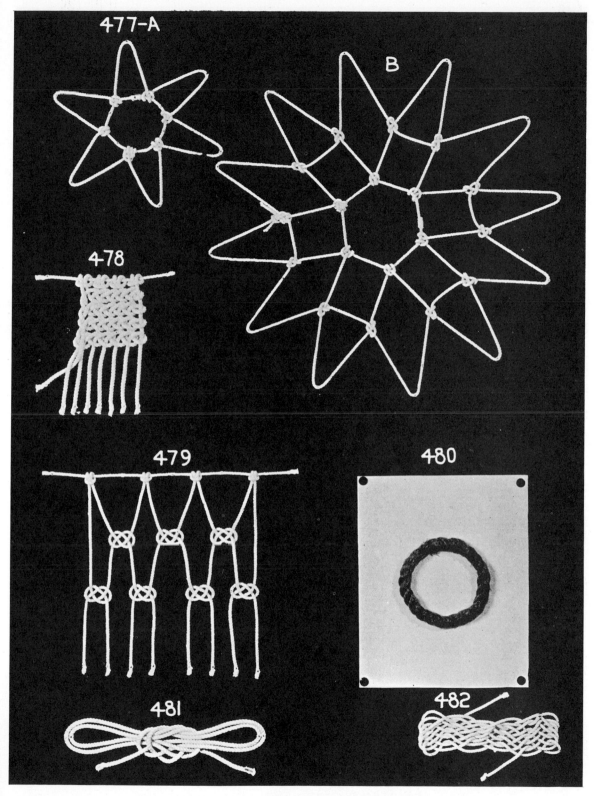

PLATE 293—A CIRCULAR NET, AND AN EXTENDED ANTIQUE SENNIT

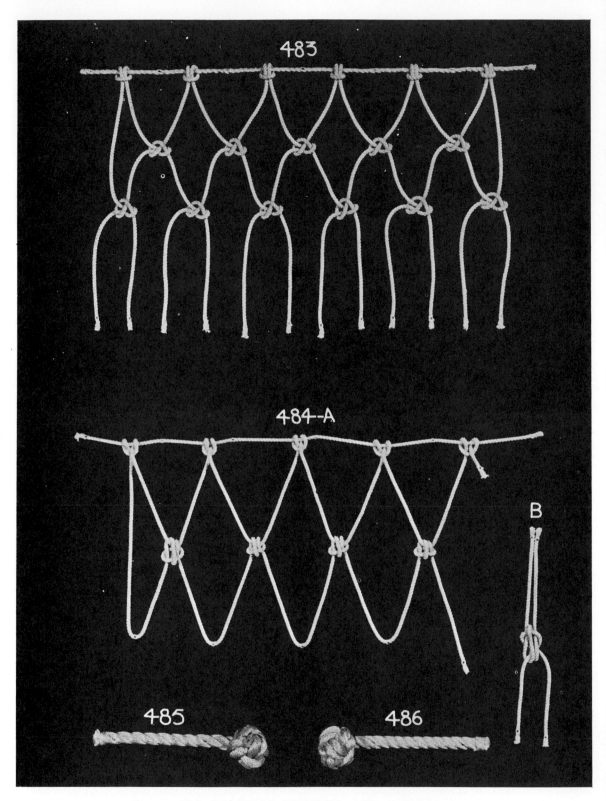

PLATE 294—MAKING TENNIS AND FISHNETS

Plate 295—Types of Nets, Worming, Parceling, and Serving

FIG. 487: *Meshes Used in Making Various Kinds of Nets* are shown in this illustration. The work is easy to follow and needs no explanation.

FIG. 488: *A Type of Netting Made by Seizing the Bights of Small Stuff Together*, such as Ratline stuff, leaving uniformly spaced meshes between. To make such a net first mark off a rope in equal spaces and seize the parts together with small seizing twine.

FIG. 489: *Worming, Parceling, and Serving*. These are the three essential types of work necessary to protect a rope from chafing or from rotting, due to dampness.

Worming consists of laying strands of Marline, spun yarn, or other suitable material along the spiral grooves of the rope, in the direction of the lay of the rope. This is done to fill in the hollow grooves in the rope and to give it a smooth, round appearance.

Parceling consists of small strips of canvas, usually tarred, which is wrapped around the rope, with the lay, by overlapping one turn over the other. This is done to give the overlapping turns a tendency to shed water.

Serving consists of a tight binding of Marline or spun yarn around and against the lay of the rope which has previously been wormed and parceled. This work is done with a Serving Mallet and two men are necessary to do the work. The Marline is wrapped around the handle of the Serving Mallet as illustrated. It is then passed around the rope, two or three turns being made, depending upon how tight the Service is to be. The Mallet is passed around the rope with each revolution adding an additional turn to the service.

Remember the old adage:

"Worm and parcel with the lay;
Turn and serve the other way."

FIG. 490: *A Rope Wormed with Spun Yarn.*

Plate 296—A Circular Net, and a Shrimp Net

FIG. 491: *A Fisherman's Method of Attaching a Line to a Leader with a Slip Knot.* It is often called a *Tiller Bend.*

FIG. 492: *A Circular Net* which is often called a Shot or Treasure Net. To begin, fill the Meshing Needle with line of the required size. Stretch the Head Rope in circular fashion and start on the left side by securing the line with a Clove Hitch to the Head Rope. The meshes are formed in the usual way, and the circumference of the net is reduced as the work continues down toward the end, by bringing two meshes into one at regular intervals. At first one mesh in a row is brought in, then in the next row two meshes. Next, take up every fourth mesh, and then every third in a row and so on. Work a small Grommet through the meshes at the bottom to hold them together. Reeve two straps through the head to be used as Beckets, for hauling apart in order to draw the mouth of the net up.

FIG. 493: *An Angler's Method of Attaching a Line to a Leader with a Figure-of-Eight Tie.*

FIG. 494: *An Angler's Method of Attaching a Line to a Leader with a Sheet Bend.*

FIG. 495: *A Shrimp Net.* It is made in a manner similar to the Circular Net, except that the bottom forms one piece with the rest of the net.

FIG. 496: *An Angler's Method of Attaching a Line to a Leader with a Double Sheet Bend.*

FIG. 497A and B: *A Sheet Brass Grommet* before it is put in the canvas. FIG. A

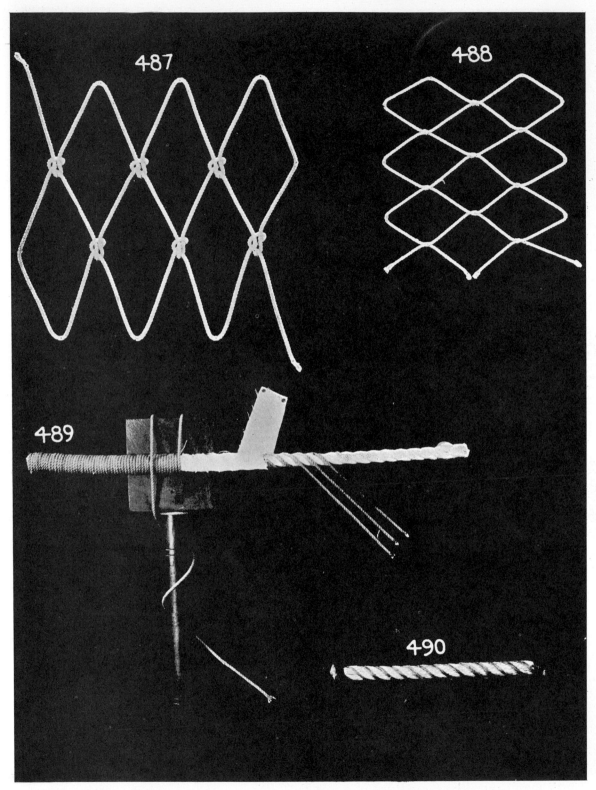

PLATE 295—TYPES OF NETS, WORMING, PARCELING, AND SERVING

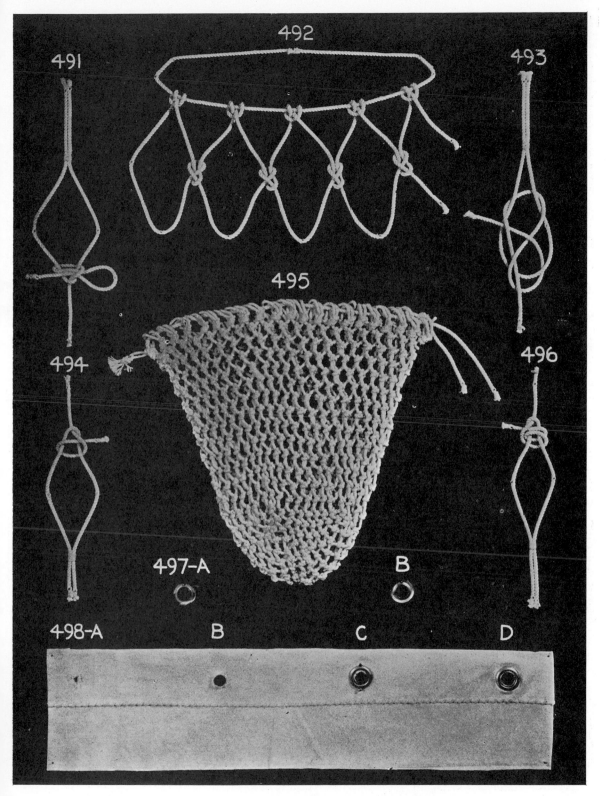

PLATE 296—A CIRCULAR NET, AND A SHRIMP NET

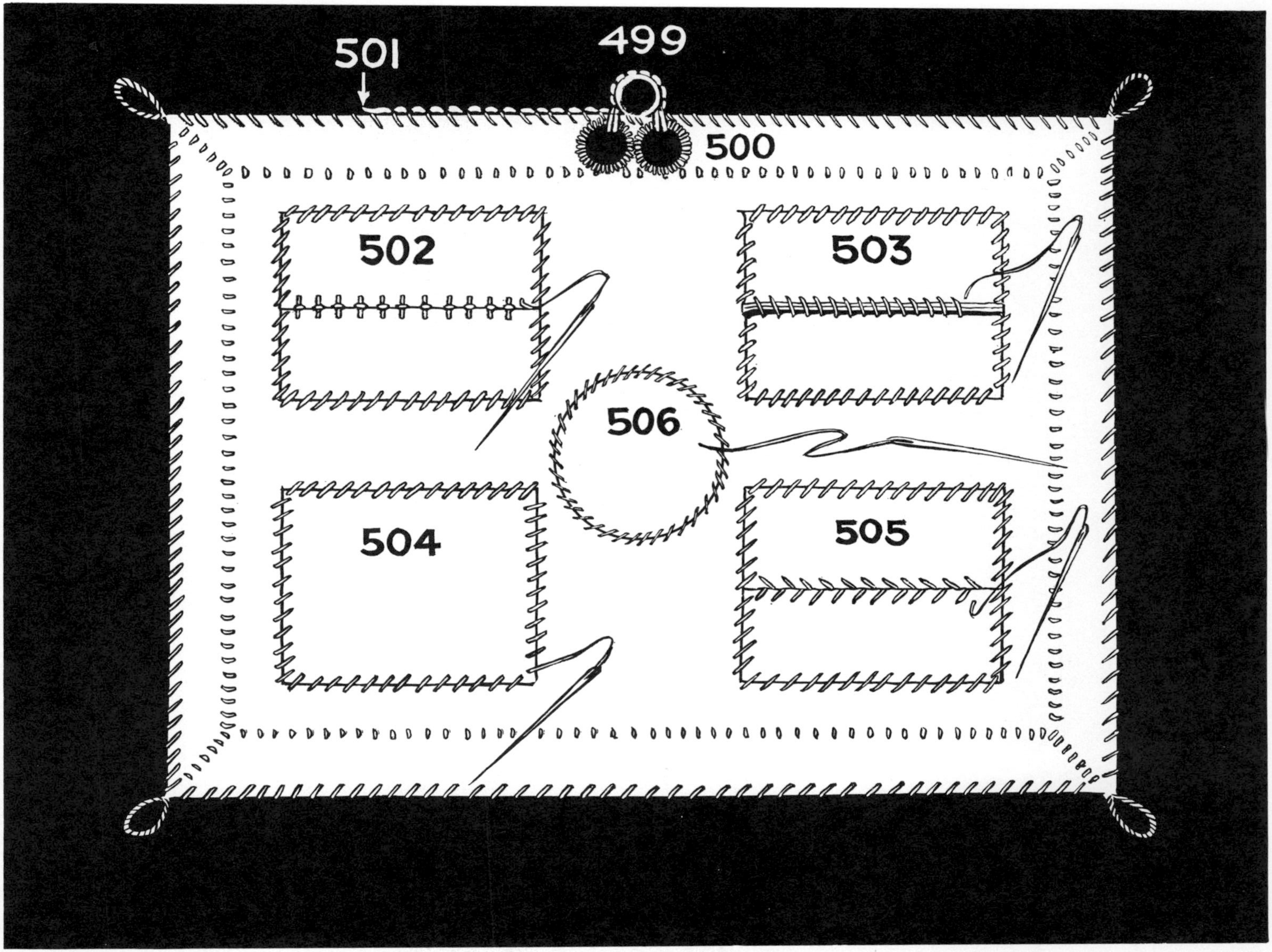

PLATE 297—STITCHES USED IN SEWING CANVAS

shows the male part which has a lip rising from the hole around the center. FIG. B shows the female part which has no lip.

FIG. 498A: *Inserting a Grommet in Canvas* is done as follows: A hole is first punched in the canvas with a pricker, the hole being slightly smaller than the lip in the male part of the Grommet.

B: The male part is pushed through the hole.

C: The female part is placed over the male part.

D: A Grommet Die (PLATE 309, FIG. 31) is placed on a table or other convenient place and the Grommet is placed in the die, making certain that the male part of the die comes in direct contact with the die and not the punch. The punch is now tapped gently with a hammer until the lip is rolled down firmly against the female part as shown in this illustration.

Plate 297—Stitches Used in Sewing Canvas

FIG. 499: *A Cringle Made Round a Thimble.* Reeve the end of an unlaid strand through the eyelet holes in the sail, then lay the strand up on itself and around the Thimble and through the eyelet holes again, after which continue by laying both ends up a second time until they meet on top of the Thimble. Work the strands taut with a Marline Spike, taper the ends and tuck them over one and under one as in splicing, making the last tuck on the inside and under the Thimble. Cut the ends off short to finish.

Another method, slightly different, is to unlay a rope the required size of the Cringle, as before, then whip the ends, and reeve the end of the strand through the eyelet hole on the left side, leaving one end of the strand about a third longer than the other; at the same time be sure that the roping of the sail is toward you. If a Thimble is desired in the Cringle, lay up the three parts of the strand together. This is done by starting with the short end of the strand towards you, then reeve the long end of the strand from you through the eyelet hole on the right side, taking it through the Cringle which will bring it into the proper place for laying up in the space that is still vacant. When this is completed, one end will be inside the right side eyelet hole and the other end will be outside the left side eyelet hole. The ends are next rove through their respective eyelet holes, then over the Leech Rope and under their own parts, in the form of a Hitch. This will bring one Hitch out toward you and the other Hitch out away from you. Next, bring the ends down under one strand on the right and two strands on the left of the Cringle nearest to it, and proceed by tucking the ends under the two strands nearest to the Hitch. Fid the Cringle out and put the Thimble in on the fore-part of the sail. Tuck the ends of the strand back in alternating fashion, heaving them taut. They are then whipped and cut short.

A Cringle is finished off on the Crown. However, instead of forming a Hitch with the ends, they are rove through their respective eyelet holes and then tucked back under two strands of the Cringle, and laid up again to the Crown, forming a Four-Stranded Cringle. Finish off by tucking the ends under two strands, then cross them under the Crown of the Cringle and trim the ends.

FIG. 500: *Hand-Worked Eyelets.* The modern eyelet is made of brass which is set in the canvas with a steel punch. The old-fashioned hand-worked eyelets were much stronger for use as Reef Cringles, as they would not chafe or pull out under a heavy strain. Mark the location for the eyelets and then punch circular holes through the canvas near the roping. These holes should be a trifle smaller than the desired size of eyelet. Next, make a Two-or-Three-Strand Grommet with a yarn of Marline and stretch the Grommet over a fid to make it hard and round. Proceed to sew the eyelet with a needle threaded with two parts of heavy sail twine, twisted and waxed. Sew all around the Grommet and through the canvas in circular fashion, keeping each stitch well back from the edge of the hole in the canvas. To finish off, stick the end of a fid through the hole and stretch the eyelet round.

FIG. 501: *Sewing Bolt Ropes to a Sail or Awning.* Place the rope along the edge of the canvas and pick up one strand with each successive stitch, the length of each stitch being governed by the size of the strands in the rope. Bolt Ropes are often sewn to the selvage edge of canvas, but when sewn to a raw edge, the edges must first be folded under and the rope sewn on so that it covers the raw edge.

FIG. 502: *A Herring-Bone Stitch* that is used on painted or very stiff canvas. Bring the needle across the opening each time and then through from the opposite side and out toward the middle. Next cross over the

stitch and then stick the needle in from the inside and out through the side the stitch was started from.

FIG. 503: *A Round Stitch,* which is used to join two edges together or for quick repair work on heavy canvas. It is made by holding the two edges together and passing the needle through both pieces at right angles to the canvas.

FIG. 504: *A Flat Stitch on a Square Patch.* It is the commonest method of sewing two pieces of canvas together. The stitch is made by lapping two pieces of canvas and pushing the needle through the lower piece and up through the edge of the canvas to be joined. When sewing on a patch be sure to smooth the edge of the parts that are folded under, to make a neat-looking job. To finish off a stitch take about two turns around the needle and pull up taut, then cut short.

FIG. 505: *A Baseball Stitch.* It is used for sewing up rips in canvas where a snug fit is required.

FIG. 506: *A Flat Stitch on a Round Patch.*

Plate 298—Bell Rope Lanyard and Tassel Designs

FIG. 507: *Bell Rope Lanyard Design No. 1,* shows a Four-Strand Cable-Laid Sennit formed into a bight and then used as a filler for the body of the Lanyard. It is then finished off on the opposite end with Triple-Passed Crowning. An Eight-Strand Star Knot is next added on the end of the Crowning with an Eight-Strand Triple-Passed Manrope Knot tied around the base. The eight strands are then led out from the bottom of the Manrope Knot and formed into a Double Spiral Crown Weave around the filler which extends to the middle of the Lanyard. The strands are then changed into a Triple-Passed Manrope Knot and the Weaving is then continued with an Eight-Strand Single Spiral Crown

Weave to the end, which is finished off with a Manrope Knot the same as before.

FIG. 508: *Bell Rope Lanyard Design No. 2.* Three strands are used for the Cable-Laid Filler which is doubled and brought to the opposite end, the same as before, then Triple-Crowned. A Triple-Passed Manrope Knot is next formed with twelve strands which are then led out from the bottom and continued around the filler with á Triple-Nelson or Reverse Crown Braid down to the next Manrope Knot, where four strands are dropped and the work is then continued with a Four-Strand Double Spiral or Crown Weave to the next Manrope Knot. Now proceed by changing the weave into an Eight-Strand Round Sen-

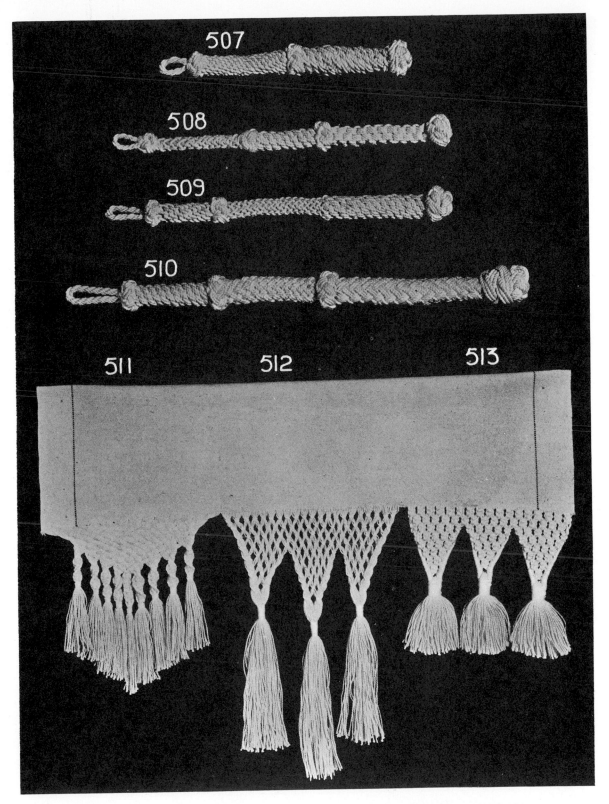

507

508

509

510

511   512   513

PLATE 298—BELL ROPE LANYARDS, AND OTHER DESIGNS

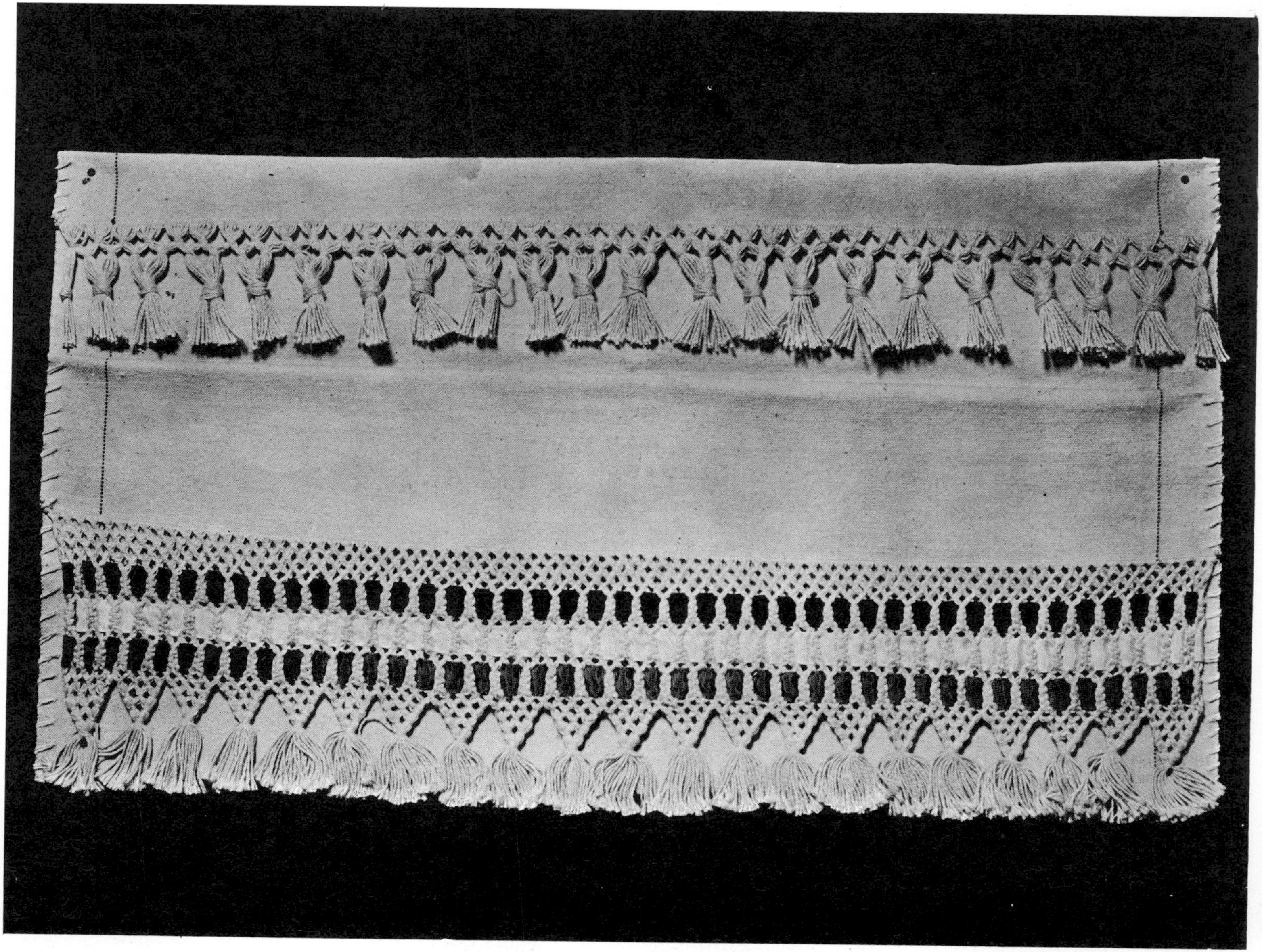

PLATE 299—A WALL BAG DESIGN

nit or Coach-Whipping down to the eye near the end and finish off with another Manrope Knot.

FIG. 509: *Bell Rope Lanyard Design No. 3* is made similar to the second design except that the weave starts with a Double Six-Strand Spiral Crown below the Manrope Knot and is then changed into a Twelve-Strand Single Coach-Whipping or Round Sennit. It is then continued with a Twelve-Strand Single Spiral Crown Weave after the next Manrope Knot and is finished off the same as before.

FIG. 510: *Bell Rope Lanyard Design No. 4* is a beautiful example of the old-time bell ropes. It is made with a Three-Strand Cable-Laid Filler which is doubled back to form the core after leaving an eye to secure it to the bell ringer. A Rose Knot is formed on the end with the six filler strands and then Coach-Whipping with ten triple-strands is started and braided down to the first Manrope Knot, where two strands are dropped.

A Four-Strand Turk's Head with three passes is then placed around the base of the Rose Knot on the end. After forming the Triple-Passed Manrope Knot the weave is then changed into a Fourteen-Strand Double Coach-Whipping and is carried down to the next Manrope Knot, where twelve more strands are dropped. The weave is then continued with an Eight-Strand Double Spiral Crown Braid and is finished off with another Manrope Knot.

FIG. 511: *A Braided Drawn Thread and Tassel Design*. When the filling threads have been drawn out of the canvas as described in PLATE 299, bunches of fiber yarn are taken and divided into groups. Proceed to braid a Common Sennit, passing one strand over one and under one. When the desired length has been reached, then form Spiral Knots with two groups of fine yarns for each Spiral. The end of the Spiral is then whipped and the ends of the yarns combed out to form tassels.

FIG. 512: *A Diamond Drawn Thread and Tassel Design* is made by taking the warp threads in groups of ten when beginning. They are hitched as illustrated in PLATE 169, FIG. 21. As the design tapers each preceding group is brought down and hitched together with the next group of fives. When the end of the design is reached all the yarns are seized together, then combed out and cut off evenly.

FIG. 513: *The Double Flat Knot Drawn Thread and Tassel Design* is made as follows: The Flat Knots are tied with groups of eight yarns, which is two yarns in each strand. Then two Flat Knots are made and separating the cords make two more Flat Knots. This is continued, gradually tapering the design to a number of points. Two yarns are then taken from the apex of each group and begin serving the yarns, continuing round and picking up each group and serving around them also, until the end is reached. The yarns from both sides of the point are then served together and the ends trimmed off evenly to finish.

Plate 299—A Wall Bag Design

PLATE 299: *An Elaborate Type of Design for a Wall Bag* which exemplifies one of the old-time sailor's arts. To start the bag, trim the outer edge of the canvas on both sides up as far as desired. Draw the horizontal threads out alternately from each side, starting from the end of the piece and working up to as far as the edge has been removed on both sides. This will be found to be a very effective method for stripping canvas as it simplifies an otherwise very difficult task. After the desired amount of canvas has been stripped, begin to form the diamond designs as described in PLATE 231, FIG. 13. Continue with the procedure until four rows have been completed, then form alternate Flats and Spirals all the way across.

Three Square Knots are used in each Flat and six Half Hitches in each Spiral. Join each of them together at the bottom and repeat the same method by forming the next row of alternate Flats and Spirals just below and between the row previously formed. Repeat this method for the third time and then join each design at the bottom as before. Continue with the diamond designs which are worked down to a point and then formed into tassels in the same manner as illustrated. Next, reeve three tri-colored military ribbons between the Flats and the Spirals which were formed previously and tuck the ends through the back. This completes the bottom piece.

The top piece is next stripped in the same manner and one row of Clove or Half-Hitched Diamonds is formed, which is followed by a row of Overhand Knot Diamond designs to finish off. Turn the bottom piece up to form the pockets for the bag and leave the end with the design hanging down. Sew the sides with a sail needle and twine and baste the pockets in at different intervals. Fold the top piece over with the design hanging down in front, as before, and sew the sides up to finish the bag.

When it is necessary to rip canvas for any required work, first spread the canvas out and pick up one thread at the measured mark, then with a sharp knife which is held at an angle, press lightly while moving the blade forward and at the same time keep a strain on the thread. In this way the thread is removed while leaving a straight thin line for the blade to follow as the actual cutting is done.

Decorative designs in drawn thread and tassel work are also used as trimmings and for curtains on power boats.

Chapter XII

Splicing Wire Rope

WIRE ROPE, WHICH has nowadays almost entirely replaced chains and fiber ropes for haulage and hoisting purposes, is made with a varying number of wires to the strand and a varying number of strands to the rope, according to the service for which the different ropes are intended and the degree of flexibility required.

There are five principal grades of wire rope manufactured, as regards the material from which the wires are drawn, viz.: Crucible steel, plow steel, extra strong crucible steel, iron, and a so-called blue-center steel. Occasionally copper and bronze wires are used in wire rope designed for light service and as a means of preventing corrosion. In so far as the flexibility of the rope is concerned there are but three commonly used classifications, viz.: Ordinary flexible, extra flexible, and special extra flexible.

Regular Lay of Wire Rope comprises the wires in the strands laid up from right to left with the various strands making up the rope laid up from left to right. This is also known as right lay rope; wires laid up to the left with the strands laid up to the right. Standard rope is made right lay.

In lang lay rope the wires in the strands and the strands in the rope are laid up in the same direction, either from left to right or the reverse. Lang lay rope is somewhat more flexible than standard rope, and as the wires are laid up more axially in the rope longer surfaces are exposed to wear, thereby increasing the endurance of the rope. Regular lay rope is the most commonly used since it hangs without twisting.

Classes of Wire Rope. Such wire rope as is used for haulage in mines, and around docks, usually consists of six strands of seven wires each laid up around a hemp core or center. Hoisting rope for elevators, derricks, mine lifts, and other similar purposes consists of six strands of 19 wires each wound around a hemp core. A more flexible rope for crane service and the like is made up of six strands of 37 wires each, wound around a hemp core.

In general the flexibility of the rope is increased by increasing the number of wires in each strand. Probably the most flexible rope made consists of six strands of 61 wires each. Other types comprise flattened strands for haulage, hoisting and transmission, non-spinning rope for the suspension of loads at the end of a single line, steel clad rope for severe conditions of service, guy and rigging rope and hawsers for towing and mooring.

Standard Types of Wire Rope are made up of 7, 12, 19, 24, and 37 wires each. Such a rope consisting of six strands of 12 wires each is commercially known as 6 by 12 rope, which is obtainable in varying degrees of flexibility, as previously explained, as are the other sizes.

When rope is used for ship's rigging, derrick guys, or under similar conditions involving continued exposure to the elements, the wires should be galvanized. Rope subjected to constant bending around drums and sheaves is not usually so treated.

Strength of Wire Rope. In determining the working strength of wire rope it was formerly the practice for each manufacturer to test the strength of each wire in the rope and then base the ultimate strength of the entire rope upon the number of wires and strands. However, the strengths arrived at in this manner were usually in excess of the actual breaking strength of the rope. Today there are fixed standards for the strength of wire ropes of different sizes. In general a factor of safety of five is allowed in giving the working loads. These are given in the accompanying tables for four of the most commonly used sizes.

Although wire rope possesses great strength it must be used with considerable care if a full measure of service is to be obtained. In the manufacture of wire rope particular care is exercised to see that each wire in each strand and each strand in the rope is laid up with an equal amount of tension, so that when stresses are applied to the finished rope an equal amount of the strain will be carried by each component part of the rope.

Handling Wire Rope. Wire rope should not be coiled or uncoiled like fiber rope. If it is received in a coil it should be rolled upon the ground like a hoop and straightened out before being placed on a drum. If the coil is on a reel the latter should be placed on spindles or flat on a turntable and properly unwound. In any event every effort should be made to prevent the rope from kinking or untwisting.

Sizes of Drums. In like manner considerable care should be exercised in the choice of the size of the drums and sheaves. Whenever possible the diameter of the drum or sheave should be at least 700 times that of the smallest wire in the rope, and under no circumstances is it recommended to use a drum or sheave which is less than 300 times the diameter of the smallest wire. Care should be exercised too in the size and shape of the grooves in the drums and sheaves. These grooves should have a radius at the bottom slightly larger than that of the rope, their sides must be free from scratches or grooves and they should be so located upon the drum to permit of free running of the rope without its scraping on the sides or outer edges of the grooves.

Another consideration in the care of wire rope is the manner of reeving it around the drums and sheaves. In so far as is possible these should be so placed that there will be no reverse bending of the rope. This practice will wear out a rope quicker than any other abuse. A little care will usually eliminate circumstances which contribute to reverse bending.

Lubricating Wire Rope. Wire rope should be protected by a suitable lubricant, both internally and externally, to prevent rust and to keep it pliable. The lubricant used should not only cover the outer surface of the rope but it should also penetrate into the hemp center, to prevent it from absorbing moisture, and at the same time lubricate the inner surfaces of the wires and strands. Best results cannot be obtained from thick, heavy grease and oils and the sticky compounds frequently used for this purpose.

Seizings. Before cutting wire rope it is essential to place several sets of seizings around the rope on each side of the intended cut, to prevent disturbing the lay of the rope after the cut has been made.

It is important to use the proper grade and size of wire in making seizings such as annealed iron wire in the following sizes:

Size of Wire Rope (Diameter)	Size of Seizing Wire (Diameter)
⅜″ to ½″	.047″
⅝″	.054″
¾″	.063″
⅞″ to 1⅛″	.080″
1¼″ to 1⅞″	.105″
2″ and larger	.135″

Applying Seizings. The following instructions should be followed carefully in applying seizings to wire rope. The wire should be wound uniformly and firmly.

Unless a serving mallet is used there is no advantage in making more than ten wraps of the wire for each seizing.

After the seizing has been applied and the wire pulled up taut, cross the ends of the wire over the seizing and twist the wires counterclockwise. Grasp the ends of the seizing wire with wire cutters and twist up the slack. Do not attempt to tighten up on the seizing by twisting its ends. Cut off the ends and hammer the twisted end of the seizing back against the standing part of the rope.

Number of Seizings Required. Two seizings are necessary on iron rope, three on steel rope, and four should be used on independent wire rope center ropes, while for larger ropes even more should be used.

Splicing Wire Rope. The splicing of wire rope is usually entrusted to workmen who possess some degree of mechanical skill and ability in handling tools. It follows that the greater the degree of the skill of the workman and the care employed the more satisfactory will be the result.

It would, therefore, be well for those who are entirely lacking in experience to make several practice splices before attempting to splice a wire rope subject to severe conditions in actual use.

Plate 300—A Liverpool or Spiral Eye Splice

Fig. 1a: *The Liverpool or Spiral Splice,* First Method. To make this splice involves the use of worming, parceling, and serving, and the application of a metal thimble in the eye of the splice. The first step is to determine the amount of rope required to completely encircle the thimble. Mark this length off on the rope allowing enough rope, about 18 inches, in addition, to form the splice. That part of the rope which will be enclosed by the thimble is next coated with a good preservative, after which it is wormed, parceled and served as shown on Plate 303, Figs. 9b and c.

Next bend the rope to form a bight in which to place the thimble and clamp both the rope and the thimble in a vise in the manner shown in the illustration. Proceed to unlay the strands of the short end and seize the end of each strand. Cut out the core of the rope close to the serving around the eye.

To prepare the standing part of the rope for splicing insert a marline spike under two strands of the rope, making certain that the spike is inserted with the lay of the rope and not against it. The spike is inserted under the strands close to the thimble and then rolled out to the position shown. This is done to open up the strands because a strand of wire cannot be tucked with a short bend in the strand as is done with fiber rope, which is the reason for the longer opening between the strands.

With the marline spike in place the strand *a* is then inserted under the two strands, working the strand *a* from the point of the spike toward the handle. With strand *a* in place it is pulled up taut and then rolled back toward the thimble until it occupies the position shown in Fig. 1b. The method employed in rolling the different strands back into place is shown in the views at Figs. 1b and c.

b: As the next step one strand of the standing part of the rope is raised with the marline spike in the manner previously explained. Strand *b*, the strand next to *a*, is placed in this opening and is in a like manner rolled back toward the thimble. This procedure is followed with the remaining strands in succession, tucking each strand of the end under one strand of the standing part.

c and d: Other operations in completing the Liverpool Splice are shown in the accompanying illustrations, in their various stages as the work progresses.

PLATE 300—A LIVERPOOL OR SPIRAL EYE SPLICE.

[*Plate 301*]　　　Splicing Wire Rope　　　555

Plate 301—A Rigger's Bench and Tools

Fig. 1e: *The Liverpool Splice,* First Method continued. In this illustration strand *e* has been tucked into place and the strand *b* is shown rolled into its final position. The work is continued by tucking all of the strands again, in the same order, taking care to tuck them over and around the strands they were first tucked under. In this manner three more rounds of tucks are made with all of the strands, making four rounds of tucks in all. Strands *a*, *b*, and *c* are given one more tuck each, making four and one-half tucks, which is sufficient for ordinary use.

If it is desired to taper the splice this is done in the following manner: After having made four and one-half tucks separate each strand into halves. Tuck one half of each of the half-strands twice more and then halve the strands again and proceed to again tuck one-half of each of the half-strands once more.

The splice is then beaten well, beginning at the thimble, to lay the various strands more correctly in position. The manner in which the strands are tucked in making eye splices is shown more clearly on Plate 304, Figs. 10a to g.

Fig. 2: *A Wire Net Cargo Sling.* Nets or slings such as these are employed in such work as is too severe for the ordinary rope sling. The frame ropes *b* may be in one piece with the ends short-spliced together, or they may be made up of four separate pieces of rope with eye splices made in all four corners of the net. The frame ropes are usually larger in diameter than those used for forming the mesh of the net.

The mesh ropes *a* are put in by unlaying two strands from a length of rope. Then begin by laying up these two strands again and each time one of these ropes intersects one of the other mesh ropes running at right angles to it the two unlayed strands are tucked under two of the strands of the cross-rope. This method is continued until the frame on the opposite side of the net is reached. Both ends of the cross-rope are then spliced into the frame-rope. The Beckets *c* may be made of either wire or fiber rope, and as may be seen from the illustration they are joined to the corners of the frame-rope with eye splices in one end while a metal ring for the hoist is spliced in the other end.

Fig. 3: *A Rigger's Vise.* This is one of the tools that is very essential in splicing wire rope. It acts both as a press for forming the splices in the ends of a rope and at the same time it acts as a vise for securing and holding the rope while the splice is being made. After the bight for the eye has been formed in the end of the rope, it and the thimble are placed between the jaws of the vise. The jaws, operated by screw threads on a bar passing through them, clamp the rope and thimble and hold them firmly. This threaded bar is shown at *e*. In putting the rope into the vise the end should be on the right with the standing part on the left next to the workman. Sufficient material should always protrude from the vise jaws to allow for forming the splice.

After the rope and thimble have been clamped in the vise a strop is placed around the rope and a block and tackle is attached to this, as at *a*. A pair of sister hooks, *b*, which are suspended from the ceiling, are then placed on the rope, between the vise and the block and tackle, *a*. The next step is to take up on the block and tackle until the wire rope is pulled taut. When this is done another strop *d* is placed on the rope, between the sister hooks and the vise. A bar *c* is then placed through the bight of the strop *d* and several turns are taken with the bar about the rope, to take out some of the turns in the lay of the rope. It will be found that the use of this bar aids materially in untwisting the lay of the

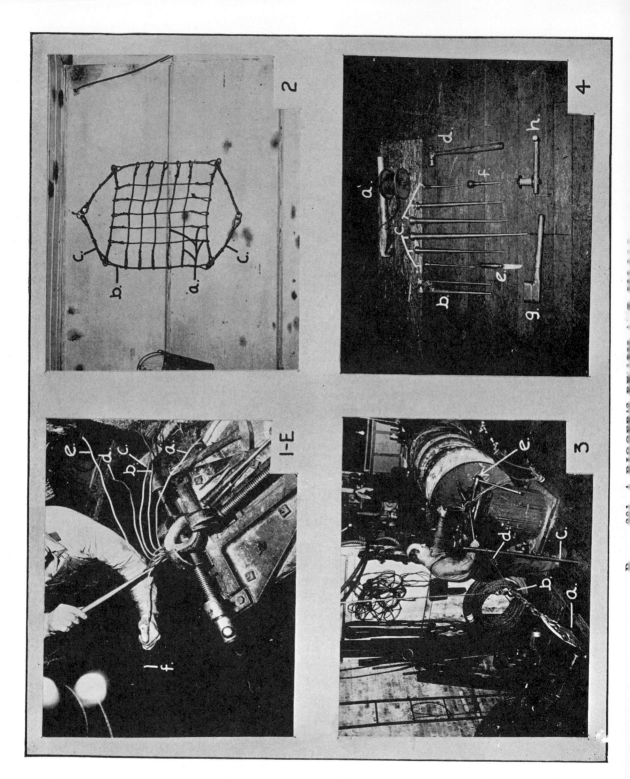

2

4

3-1

3

Pl. 231. A RIGGERS DEVICES AT A BULL

[*Plate 302*] Splicing Wire Rope 557

rope in order that the marline spike may be more easily inserted between its strands. Also, when a splice is made in a wire rope held under tension as explained, the work is easier to perform and at the same time the splice presents a much neater appearance.

FIG. 4: *Tools Used in Splicing Wire Rope.* Three serving mallets are shown at *a, g,* and *h.* PLATE 303, FIG. 9c, shows how serving mallets are used on wire rope. The tool shown at *b* is a pair of nippers or wire cutters such as are used for cutting the wires of the various strands of the rope and the wires of any seizings that may have been used. The slender pointed implements shown at *c* are various forms of marline spikes. These are used for separating the strands in the process of making splices. A ball-peen hammer is shown at *d.* These are typical mechanic's hammers common to the mechanical trades. A knife such as that shown at *e* is used for the various operations of cutting the core of the rope or for trimming Marline and serving materials. The pricker shown at *f* is used as a marline spike in splicing the smaller sizes of ropes.

Plate 302—A French Eye, and a Logger's Eye Splice

FIG. 5: *The Liverpool Splice,* Completed. The Liverpool Splice illustrated on PLATE 300, FIG. 1A to D, and on PLATE 301, FIG. 1E, is shown here as it appears after having been wormed, parceled and served.

FIGS. 6A to C: *The French Lock Eye Splice with a Thimble.* The method employed in making this splice is essentially the same as that followed in making the Liverpool Splice. The first set of tucks is made in precisely the same manner as illustrated on PLATE 304, FIGS. 10A to 10F, after which the strands *a, b,* and *c* are given one additional spiral tuck each, as shown on PLATE 304, FIG. 10G.

The next step, shown on PLATE 302, FIG. 6B, is to tuck each strand over one and under two, against the lay of the rope until three more tucks have been made. There will then be four and one-half tucks. The core of the rope, which was pushed down beside the eye, is then cut off short and the strands are each cut off, after the splice has been beaten into shape with a hammer or mallet. The splice will then appear as shown in FIG. 6c.

This type of splice is used in ropes on which the load hangs free and might have a tendency to untwist the lay of the rope, thereby allowing the strands forming the splice to slip or pull out, such as might be the case with a Spiral or Liverpool Splice.

FIG. 7: *The French Lock Eye Splice Without a Thimble.* It is made in precisely the same manner as that previously explained. It should be understood in this connection that an eye splice with a thimble is considerably stronger than one without and that all of the wear is placed directly upon the rope instead of being absorbed by the thimble.

FIGS. 8A to D: *The West Coast or Logger's Splice.* This splice is practically the only type used by logger's and stevedores on the Pacific coast. Although it may appear to be weaker than other types the authors have never heard of a case in which the eye in such a splice pulled out or slipped. It is one of the simplest forms of wire rope splicing.

As the first step cut out the core close to the seizing on the end. The strand *a* is then tucked under two strands of the rope. Next, the strand *b* is passed under the following two strands in the rope. This process is repeated until all six strands of the splice have been passed successively under two strands each of the rope.

After the first round of tucks has been

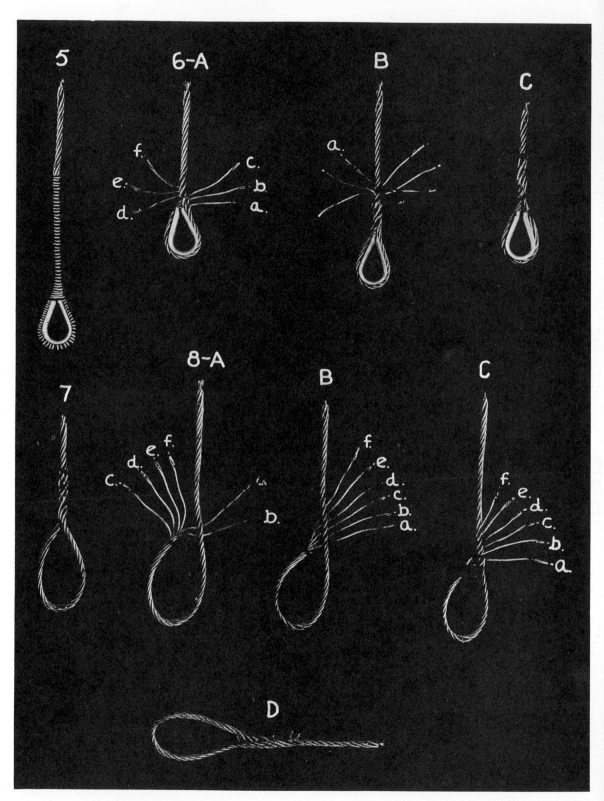

PLATE 302—A FRENCH EYE, AND A LOGGER'S EYE SPLICE

made, that is, after all six strands have been tucked, the work will appear as shown in FIG. 8B. The next step, taking the strands in their respective order from *a* to *f*, is to pass each strand back to the left over one strand and under two of the rope, with each strand tucking over one to the left and under two to the right, as shown in FIG. 8C in the accompanying illustration.

This completes the splice, except that it is beaten with a hammer or mallet and the strands are cut off. They should not be cut off too short, however, as it is better to allow them to extend through the rope about one-half to three-quarters of an inch. The finished splice is shown in FIG. 8D.

Plate 303—Worming, Parceling, and Serving

FIGS. 9A to D: *Worming, Parceling, and Serving a Splice.* Some riggers when starting to make a splice take the first tucks in the manner shown in FIG. 9A, that is, one strand under two strands, against the lay of the rope. This method does make a neater job. The other tucks are then made in the same manner as was explained in making the Liverpool Splice.

The next step, after all the tucks have been made and the splice has been beaten out, is to worm the grooves between the strands of the rope with a strand of spun yarn. This is represented by *a* in FIG. 9B. The splice is then parceled with a strip of burlap or tarred canvas, shown in FIG. 9B at *b*.

After the worming and parceling have been completed the entire splice is then served over the parceling with spun yarn. This is applied with a serving mallet as shown at *c* in FIG. 9C. Notice that the parceling is applied by starting it at the thimble and working it out along the rope to the end of the splice, while the serving is applied by starting it at the end of the splice and working it toward the thimble. This is more aptly explained in the following adage:

> Worm and parcel with the lay,
> Turn and serve the other way.

The completed splice is shown in FIG. 9D. It should be remembered that in making a splice that the lay of the strands of the rope has been disturbed and that in order to protect the rope from the effects of moisture the splice should be wormed, parceled and served carefully.

The rope is wormed in order to fill out the grooves between the strands of the rope. The parceling is applied in order to keep the moisture out of the Splice and also to make a smoother and even surface upon which the parceling is applied. The parceling is put on of course to secure the whole job, which is shown in FIG. 9D.

Plate 304—Diagrammatic Steps in Splicing and Seizing

FIGS. 10A to G: *The Liverpool Splice,* Second Method. The Liverpool or Spiral Splice is the method most commonly used in splicing wire rope. Not only can it be made rapidly but at the same time it makes a neat, strong and dependable splice.

As explained in the First Method, PLATE 300, FIG. 1, a rigger's vise was used for holding the work. When no such vise is available an ordinary mechanic's vise may be used, but in doing so the thimble must be held in the eye by seizings as shown at *b* in FIG. 10A. The rope itself should also be seized about one and one-half feet from its end. This end seizing is placed at *a*, FIG. 10A, when seizing the thimble in the bight forming the eye.

All of the strands of the end of the rope are then unlaid back to this seizing, a marline spike is inserted under three strands of the rope and the strand 1 is tucked as shown in FIG. 10A. As the next step the

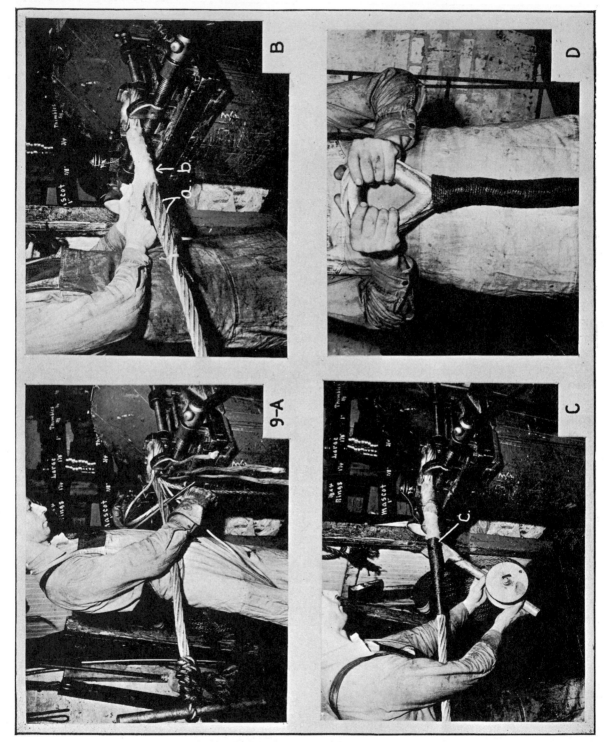

Plate 303—WORMING, PARCELING, AND SERVING

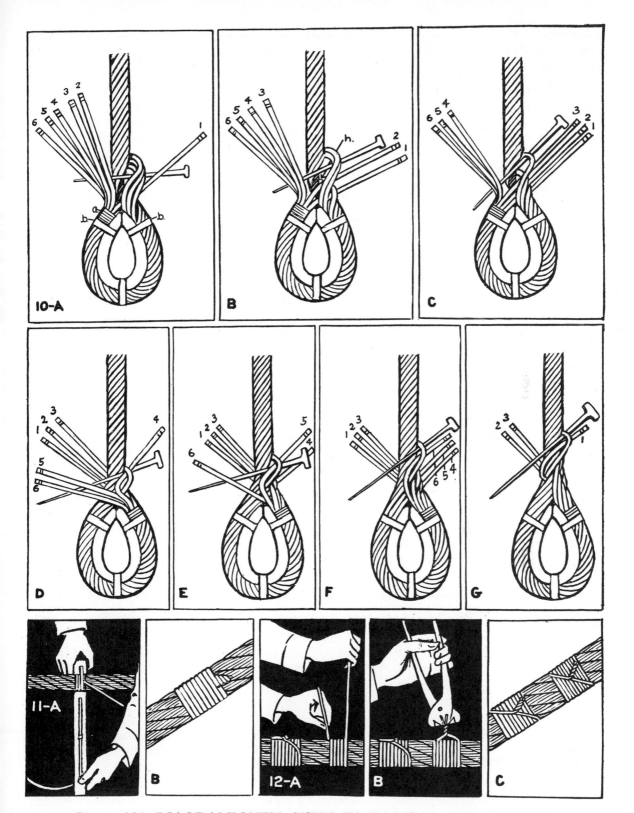

PLATE 304—DIAGRAMMATIC STEPS IN SPLICING AND SEIZING

spike is withdrawn from the rope and again inserted in the rope but this time under two strands, after which strand 2 is tucked as shown in FIG. 10B. After this operation has been completed the spike is again inserted in the rope, but under only one strand, and the strand 3 is tucked. This is shown in FIG. 10C.

As may be noticed in this view, FIG. 10D, the splice has been turned completely over from left to right, hence, strands 1, 2, and 3 now appear in back of the standing part of the rope. This was done in order to more clearly explain the following steps, but is not necessary in making a splice of this kind.

Continuing the work the spike is inserted under the next strand to the left of the strand under which strand 3 was tucked and strand 4 is tucked in alongside the spike. This is followed by lifting the next strand of the rope and tucking strand 5 in alongside the spike. The same procedure is followed in tucking strand 6. These operations are clearly shown in FIGS. 10E and 10F.

After all of the strands have been tucked in the manner explained the work is continued by again starting with strand 1 and tucking it under the next strand of the rope. Notice, however, that in the follow-ing successive steps the strands are tucked around and around the strands in the standing part which they were previously tucked under, that is, the tucks are made from left to right, as shown in FIG. 10G. This is commonly known as the Spiral Tuck.

FIGS. 11A and B: *Applying Wire Seizing*, First Method. Seizings are applied to wire rope in the same manner and for the same purpose they were used on fiber rope; to prevent the strands of the rope from becoming unlayed. It should be remembered also that before a wire rope is cut seizings should be clapped on the rope on both sides of the intended cut. The correct number to use for ropes of different kinds was given in the introductory paragraphs to this chapter.

The manner in which a serving mallet is used and the finished seizing are shown in FIGS. 11A and 11B, respectively.

FIGS. 12A, B, and C: *Applying Wire Seizing*, Second Method. These three illustrations show the progressive steps in applying wire seizing when no serving mallet is used. The wire is wound first as shown in FIG. 12A: the ends are twisted as in FIG. 12B, after which they are cut off. The finished seizing is shown in FIG. 12C.

Plate 305—The Lock Tuck in a Liverpool Eye Splice

FIGS. 13A and B: *The Liverpool or Spiral Splice* as it appears after having completed the first steps previously explained (*see* PLATE 304, FIG. 10). When the work has advanced to the stage shown in the accompanying illustration three more rounds of tucks are made. The splice may or may not be tapered as desired. That shown here is not. The finished splice is shown in FIG. 13B.

FIG. 14: *A Finished Liverpool or Spiral Splice* in which four and one-half rounds of tucks were made.

FIGS. 15A, B, and C: *The Liverpool Eye Splice with a Lock Tuck*. The strand *a* is tucked under two strands against the lay or from right to left. Next proceed as in other splices to tuck the first strand *b* under two and each following strand under one as in PLATE 300, FIG. 1. When strands *c*, *d*, *e*, and *f* have been tucked turn the splice around. Strand *a* will then appear in front. It is then tucked under the next strand in the standing part of the rope to the left of strand *f*.

The view at FIG. 15B illustrates the manner in which strand *a* is tucked. The other strands are tucked in the same manner as

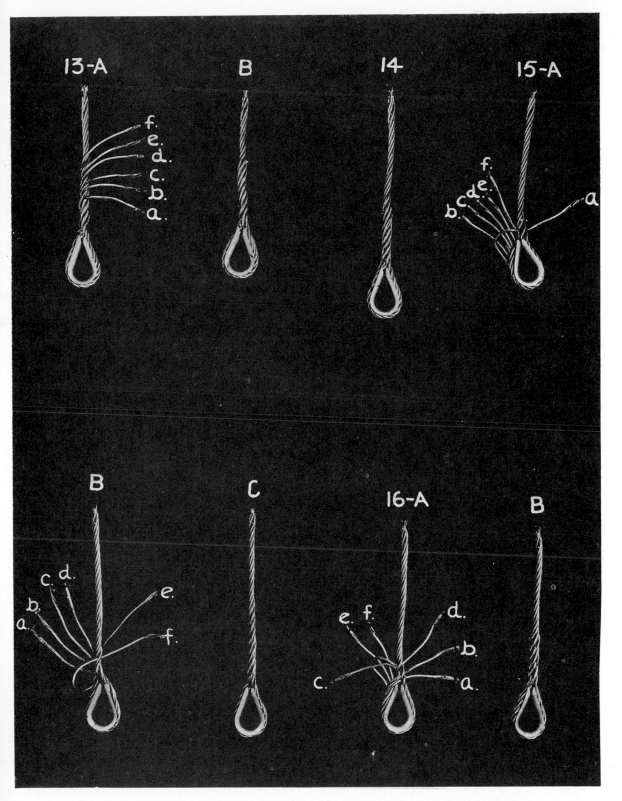

PLATE 305—THE LOCK TUCK IN A LIVERPOOL EYE SPLICE

was used in making the Liverpool Splice shown on PLATE 304, FIG. 10.

Three and one-half additional tucks are taken and the strands are cut off to finish the splice. This form of splicing is employed when it is desired to make a closer and neater job, especially in that part adjacent to the thimble. The finished splice is shown in FIG. 15c.

FIGS. 16A and B: *The French Eye Splice*

with a Lock Tuck. The strands *a* and *b* are tucked under two and one strands respectively. The strands *c* and *d* have their positions reversed as may be seen in the illustration. Strands *e* and *f* are to be tucked with the lay of the rope. Strands *a, b,* and *c* are each tucked again, after which proceed to tuck over one and under two as shown in PLATE 302, FIG. 6B.

The finished splice is shown in FIG. 16B.

Plate 306—A Long Splice, and a Tiller Rope Splice

FIGS. 17A, B, and C: *The Long or Endless Splice.* It is extremely important, in the making of a long splice in wire rope, to use great care in laying the various rope strands firmly into position. If, during any of the various operations, some of the strands are not pulled tightly into their respective places in the finished splice, it is doubtful if satisfactory results will be obtained.

When such a splice is placed in service those strands which are relatively slack will not receive their full share of the load, thus causing the other strands to be stressed excessively. This unbalanced condition will result in a distorted relative position of some of the rope strands so that they will be projected above the normal diameter of the rope and consequently will be subjected to abnormal abrasion and abuse. In addition, the unequal stress distribution will decrease the possible ultimate strength of the splice.

It is strongly recommended, therefore, that during each of the steps explained in the following method, particular attention be paid to maintaining as nearly as possible the same degree of tightness in all of the strands in the splice.

When ropes are to be used in places in which their failure may result in material damage or might endanger human lives the splicing should be done only by men who are well experienced in this work. It is considered good practice with such splices

as these to test them under stresses equal to at least twice their maximum working load before the ropes are placed in service.

As an aid in making long splices the accompanying tables show the amount or length of rope to be unlaid on each of the two ends of the ropes for ropes of different diameters. It will be noticed that the data given in the table are for regular lay wire rope. If lang lay rope is to be spliced doubling the lengths of the splices is recommended.

The instructions included in the following explanation are for making a 30-foot splice in ¾-inch diameter rope. The first step is to determine the total or overall length desired in the rope after the splice has been made, bearing in mind in measuring this length that an additional length of 15 feet will be required in each piece of rope, to be used in making the splice.

After the rope has been cut and a seizing applied 15 feet from the end of each rope, unlay the strands of each section up to the seizing. Cut off the cores close to the seizing and then clutch or marry both ends in such a manner that the various strands of each section will interlace with the corresponding strands of the other section (*see* PLATE 87, FIG. 74 and PLATE 88, FIGS 78A and B).

After both ropes have been married they are pushed together as tightly as possible, until the cores butt against each other. Another seizing is placed on the ropes at

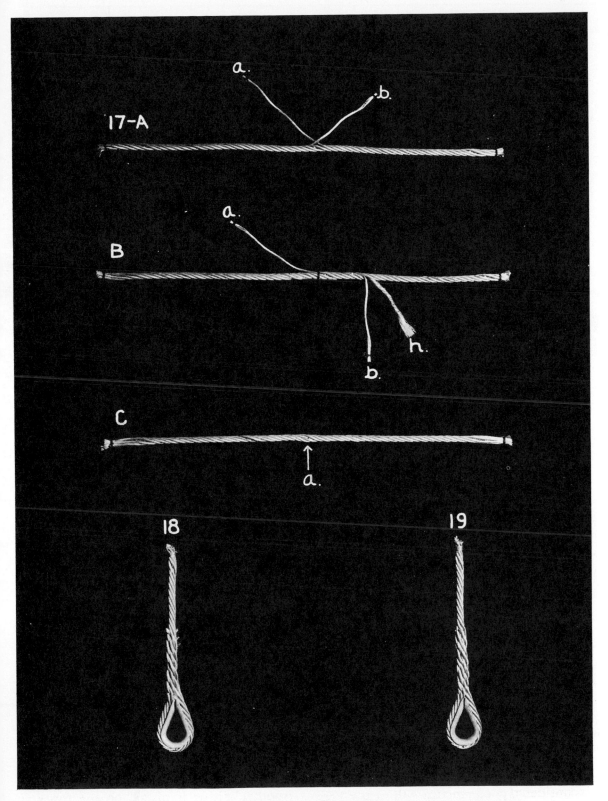

PLATE 306—A LONG SPLICE, AND A TILLER ROPE SPLICE

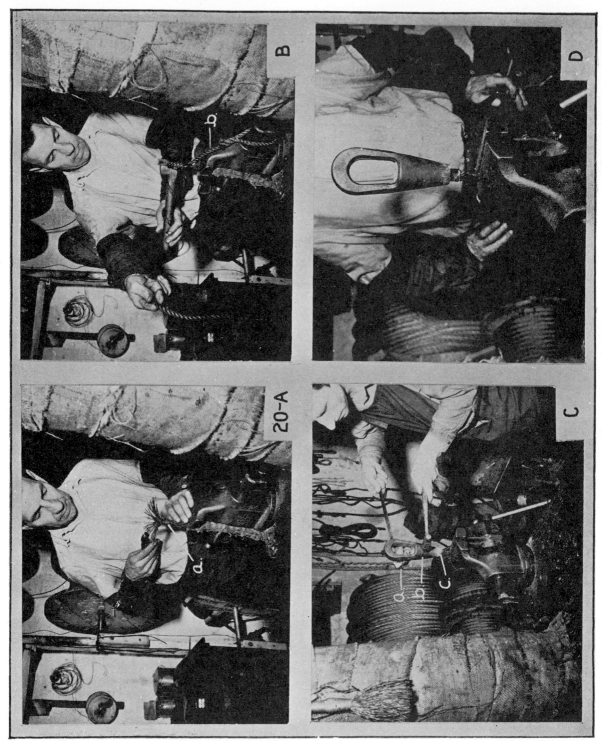

PLATE 307—A WIRE ROPE SOCKET AND ITS APPLICATION

[*Plate 307*]   Splicing Wire Rope   567

the point where they join; this will serve to hold both ropes firmly together. The two original seizings which were put directly on the ropes are now removed. Lift one of the unlaid strands of the rope on the left and put a stout seizing on the remaining five strands. Remove the last seizing put on both ropes at the point where they joined. Next unlay the strand just lifted to the left for a distance of thirteen feet. Now fill this groove with a strand from the rope on the right. When this has been done there will remain only two feet of this follow up strand as shown at *a* in Fig. 17A. The long strand *b* is then cut, leaving only two feet of the end remaining.

The strands remaining in the center are unlaid from one rope and are followed up with the strands from the other rope. Care should be exercised in laying up the strands from the two ropes in that alternate strands are brought into their proper positions. That is, one strand from the rope to the right is used to replace its corresponding strand in the rope from the left. In other words, three strands are laid up from the rope to the right with the three corresponding strands from the rope to the left, each spaced equally distant apart.

The ends of the strands must now be secured without increasing the diameter of the rope. The first step is to straighten out all of the ends and then wrap each strand with a length of friction tape, making the strand of the same diameter as that of the core of the rope.

When this has been done take a sharp knife and cut the fiber center of the rope at the point where both strands meet, and pull it out to the right for a short distance. Insert a marline spike under one strand and at the same time strand *b* is worked into the center of the rope in place of the heart *h* that has been pulled out. Continue to work the strand *b* into the rope as the core is pulled out until all of the wire strand has been worked into the rope in place of the core. Cut the core off at the end of strand *b* and work the remaining part of the core back into the rope center.

This same procedure is again carried out in order to dispose of strand *a* but working to the left this time rather than to the right as for strand *b*. There now remain five more sets of strands to be tucked. These are disposed of in exactly the same manner as has just been outlined. The rope is hammered well at the points where the strands enter the rope in order to give a smooth and neat appearance to the finished splice.

The finished splice is shown in Fig. 17C, the symbol *a* being the point at which the two strands cross. (*Also see* Figs. 32A to F, Plate 310.)

Fig. 18: *The Liverpool Splice in Tiller Rope.* This kind of rope is usually made of copper or bronze wire and at times of galvanized wire laid up left handed. The splice is made exactly as with right hand rope except that the various steps are reversed.

Fig. 19: *The French Eye or Lock Splice in Tiller Rope.* It is made in the same manner as the splice shown on Plate 302, Fig. 6, except that it is worked to the right rather than toward the left.

Plate 307—A Wire Rope Socket and Its Application

Figs. 20A to D: *Attaching a Socket to Wire Rope.* Sockets of the proper construction, if carefully and properly attached to a wire rope with melted spelter form a very effective method for attaching the ends of such ropes to other objects.

The first step in attaching a socket is to seize the end of the rope as at *a*. The material used for this purpose is soft iron wire such as that used for ordinary seizings. After the end has been seized the strands are opened up and the core is cut off short.

Next, separate the wires of each strand and thoroughly clean each of them in preparation for applying the spelter.

To clean the wires they should be washed thoroughly in either gasoline or kerosene and wiped dry. Next, dip the frayed wires only into a solution of one-half commercial muriatic acid and one-half water, from thirty seconds to one minute, or until the acid has thoroughly cleaned each of the wires. (Use extreme precautions to prevent the acid from coming into contact with the rope strands). Remove the wires from the acid bath and dip them into a solution containing soda, to neutralize the effect of the acid, after which dry the wires thoroughly. In making the acid bath the solution should under no circumstances be stronger than one-half acid and one-half water, otherwise serious damage might be done to the wires.

Continue the work by compressing the wires together until they are of such diameter that the socket can be slipped down over them. This may be done by the aid of a length of fiber rope and a serving mallet, as shown in FIG. 20B. The rope has an eye in one end which is passed over the horn of the vise, after which the free end is served about the frayed wires with sufficient tension applied to them to force them back into a small cylindrical mass. As the socket is slipped down over the compressed wires the rope serving is slowly unwound until the socket can be forced down to the seizing previously placed upon the rope.

As the next step in the work a small wad of fire-clay or asbestos cement is placed around the bottom of the socket to retain the molten spelter, as shown at *c* in FIG. 20c. The entire end of the rope as well as the socket is then heated with an oil or gas flame to a temperature equal to or slightly above that of the molten spelter. Care should be exercised in the heating to prevent the heat from becoming great enough to effect the temper of the wires in the rope.

The individual wires of the rope should not be allowed to extend above the top of the basket or pocket-like opening in the socket and in pouring the spelter a ladle of sufficient capacity should be used to permit of completely filling the socket in one operation. Care should be exercised too in aligning the socket with the rope and as the spelter is poured the socket should be tapped lightly with a hammer to insure that the spelter fills all of the small spaces in and around the wires.

The finished job is shown in FIG. 20D after any excess spelter and the fire clay around the bottom of the socket have been removed.

Plate 308—Splicing Multiple Strand Wire Rope

FIGS. 21A and B: *Splices in Ropes of More than Six Strands.* In some types of rope used principally for special services the ropes are composed of more than six strands and these are laid up differently than is the practice with regular right or left laid rope. In one of the types of special wire rope there are 18 strands. These are divided into inner and outer groups which are both laid up one over the other around a fiber rope core. The arrangement of the strands is that six of them are laid directly around the core while the other 12 strands form an outer layer around the six strands and the core. In other words the inner six strands are laid up as in regular rope while the remaining 12 strands form an outer layer around it.

In making an eye splice in rope of this kind it is seized and placed around a thimble in the usual manner. After this has been done the strands are divided as follows: The 12 strands in the outer layer are separated into six groups of two strands

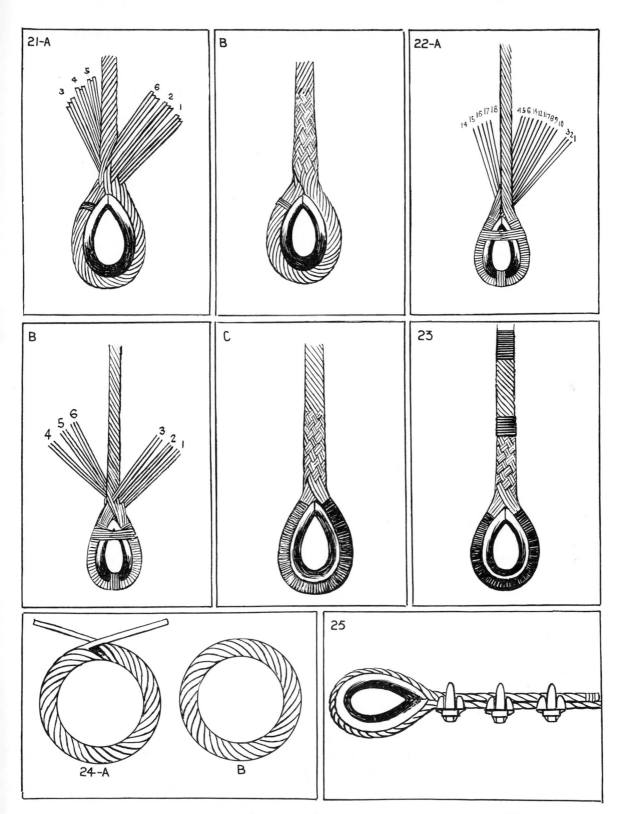

PLATE 308—SPLICING MULTIPLE STRAND WIRE ROPE

each, in the standing part of the rope only, the core and its six surrounding strands being left intact. In the working or splicing end of the rope all of the 18 strands are used. These are divided into groups of three strands each. Then, as the work of splicing progresses, three strands in the splicing or working end of the rope are tucked under two strands in the standing part of the rope. This is clearly shown in Fig. 21A.

Before starting to make the splice the core of the rope is cut off short near the thimble and all of the working strands are laid out, care being taken that none of them cross over each other. The work of tucking the strands is done exactly as in making a Liverpool Splice, until all six of the outer strands of three strands each have been tucked under the six groups of two strands each in the standing part of the rope.

The next step is to tuck each group of three strands each in the outer layer over one group of two strands in the inner layer of the standing part and then under one group of two strands, working toward the left or against the lay of the rope. This completes the second round of tucks. The third and fourth rounds are made in the same manner as just explained.

Before starting to make the fifth round of tucks turn back one strand each in all of the six groups of three strands each in the outer layer, leaving two working strands in each of the six groups. Proceed then to tuck these groups of two strands each over one group of two strands in the standing part and under one group of two. This is repeated to complete the sixth and last round of tucks.

After all of the tucks have been made beat the splice well with a mallet and cut off the ends of the six strands, taking care to secure the ends well. The completed splice is shown in Fig. 21B.

Fig. 22A: *Splicing Single Strand Cable.* This kind of wire rope is not generally used in commercial work, although some of it is used in airplane construction. It is usually constructed with the outer wires laid up left handed and varies from 7 to 37 wires per rope. It is twisted 18 strands around 12 strands, around 6 strands, around one strand, the latter forming the core. In a rope of 19 wires these would be laid up or twisted 12 strands of wire around 6 and the 6 around one.

In the accompanying illustration the rope is shown with the thimble turned in ready for splicing. In this case the single wire core is cut off at the thimble and is not used in making the splice, thereby leaving 18 wires to be worked into the splice.

These are divided into groups and the work of splicing is carried out exactly as explained in Fig. 21A. Remember, however, that this is left laid rope and not right lay, making it necessary to make all of the tucks in the reverse manner to that used for right laid rope.

In Fig. 21B the first round of tucks is shown completed and the finished splice is shown at Fig. 21C.

Fig. 23: *Splicing Single Strand Rope of Thirty-Seven Wires.* Such rope as this is laid up 18 wires around 12 wires, around 6 wires, around one wire. The six inner wires and the single core wire are not used in making this splice but are cut off short at the thimble, leaving 30 working wires, which are divided into six groups of five wires each.

The splice is made as has been explained, except that the wires in the standing part of the rope are divided into groups of three wires each and that each of the five-wire groups is inserted or tucked under nine wires in the standing part, or three groups of three wires each. After the first row of tucks has been made the groups of five wires are tucked under two groups of three wires and in the next pass under one group of three wires.

After four full rounds of tucks have been made in this manner bend back two of the

[*Plate 309*] Splicing Wire Rope 571

wires in each five-wire group and tuck three wires under three wires. In the next round bend back one wire and tuck two wires under three, taking two more turns with the remaining two wires in each group, going over three and under three in the standing part. The splice is then beaten out in the usual manner, after which it is good practice to put a small wire serving at the end of the splice to cover the ends of the wires.

FIGS. 24A and B: *A Wire Rope Grommet.* These are made from a single strand of wire rope, which is laid up around a fiber rope core. The ends are finished off in the same manner as was used in making the Long Splice, shown on PLATE 306, FIG. 17.

FIG. 25: *Wire Rope Clips.* These are used as shown to form an eye in the end of a wire rope. This is not the most satisfactory method of forming an eye and is frequently used in an emergency or when it is not possible to make one of the standard types of eyes.

The number of clips to be used and the distance they should be spaced apart is determined by the size of the rope and the service for which it is intended. The number of clips may vary from 2 to 8 for different sizes of ropes, while the length of the short end of the rope extending back from the thimble may be as much as from 35 to 50 times the diameter of the rope.

The illustration shows $5/8$-inch diameter rope with three clips spaced $51/2$ inches apart. In the case of 1-inch rope the length of the end would be from 35 to 50 inches, which would require from six to eight clips.

To apply the clips place the thimble in the bight of the eye and seize the rope temporarily at the end of the thimble. Clap on the first clip farthest from the thimble and pull it up tight. Be certain that the base or saddle of the clip rests upon the standing part of the rope and that the U-shaped member is applied over the short end of the rope. This applies to all clips. The next step is to apply the clip nearest to the thimble, but it is not pulled up tight. If more than two clips are to be applied each of them should be clapped on equally distant from each other.

In applying clips in this manner it is advisable, whenever possible, to apply tension to both members in order to equalize the stresses in both, after which all of the clips may be pulled up tight. After the clips have been in service for short intervals the clips should again be tightened as the strains to which the rope may be subjected tend to work them loose.

Plate 309—A Tail Splice, and a Short Splice in Wire Rope

FIG. 26: *The Tail Splice.* Such a splice as this is used for splicing fiber rope tails to the ends of wire rope. Usually they are made on the flexible wires of the running rigging such as on sailing yachts and small sailboats.

In the accompanying illustration, for the purpose of illustrating the work, a piece of $1/4$-inch rope is shown spliced to a length of $1/2$-inch diameter manila rope. The manila rope is shown at *a* and the wire rope at *b*.

To start the splice the wire rope is unlaid back about 12 inches, after which three of its alternate strands are unlaid for another 12 inches, where a seizing is clapped on. The next step is to unlay the manila rope back 24 inches, after which the first three strands of the wire rope are married to the three corresponding strands of the manila rope. Lay up the strands of the two ropes again, covering the three strands of the wire rope. There will now be 12 inches of manila rope with three strands of the wire rope as a heart or core. There will also be three strands of the wire rope each protruding at two different points. The strands are now unlaid and with the aid of a sailmaker's palm and a sail needle each individual wire is stitched through the strands. Some workmen prefer to dispose of the strands intact without unlaying them. When this is done a special tubular needle is required. They are tucked around similar to a short splice in manila rope, but instead of going over and under they are stitched right through the manila strands. In either method the wires are completely covered.

In the illustration the strand *d* is being tucked, strand *e* has been tucked, while strand *c* is to be unlaid and stitched into the rope. The strands *f* still remain to be tucked into the rope. The ends of the manila rope at *g* are scrape-tapered, after which the entire splice is marled and served with sail twine.

FIG. 27: *A Bulb on a Wire Rope End.* This method is used in securing a socket to the end of a wire rope instead of attaching it with spelter. A seizing is clapped on the rope a short distance from its end, the strands are unlaid and straightened out, after which each strand is bent back individually over the seizing. If the rope has a wire core it too must be bent back with the other strands, but if the core is made of fiber rope it is cut off short at the seizing.

After the wires have all been bent back they are hammered down to form a solid wire bulb. The next step is to cut off each wire so as to form a taper similar to that in the socket. The taper is formed by cutting the ends of the wires at different intervals from their ends back to the end of the bulb.

After the bulb has been formed as explained the entire end is served with spun yarn, or, for a better job, with fine copper wire. The socket, which was slipped over the rope before the bulb is completed, is now slipped into place on the bulb to finish the work.

FIG. 28: *A Back Splice in Wire Rope.* A seizing is clapped on the rope at about 12 to 18 inches from the end, the strands are unlaid and the fiber rope core is cut off short at the seizing. When this has been done proceed to tuck the strands over one and under two, against the lay, making four rounds of tucks in all.

FIG. 29: *A Short Splice in Wire Rope.* Clap on a seizing on the ends of each of the two ropes about two or three feet back from the ends. The length of the splice or rather the distance back at which the seizings are clapped on is of course determined by the size of the rope, the larger the diameter the greater the length of the splice.

Unlay the ends of both ropes and open up the strands back to the seizings. Marry the two ropes and clap on a temporary seizing at the point where they join. At this point remove one of the temporary seizings clapped on before unlaying the strands. The splice must be clamped in a vise, otherwise it will be loose and might pull out.

Now select any strand on the side from which the seizing was removed and begin to tuck over one and under two strands against the lay of the rope. Make four rounds of tucks and then divide the strands into two parts. Bend one-half of each strand back and tuck each half-strand twice. This will make six rounds of tucks. The wire is then turned around and the seizing removed, after which the strands are spliced as was done with the other end of the rope. Pull up each strand as tightly as possible after each tuck. Remove the temporary seizings, beat out the splice well, working from the center to the ends, after which cut off the strands to finish the splice.

FIG. 30: *Turning in a Thimble.* When no vise is available a good method to use in clamping a thimble in the bight preparatory to forming an eye is to use ordinary wire clamps to hold the wire in place against the sides of the thimble. The clamps are removed after the splices have been made.

FIG. 31: *A Grommet Die* such as that

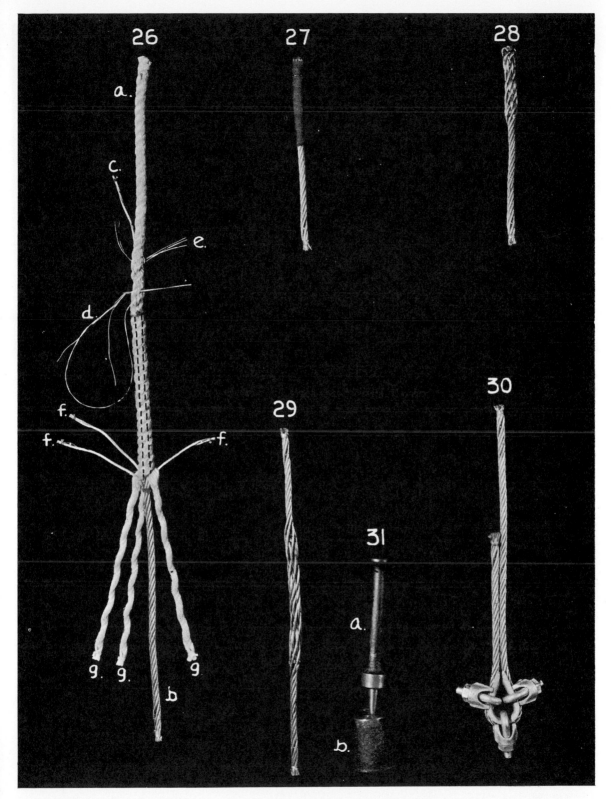

PLATE 309—A TAIL SPLICE, AND A SHORT SPLICE IN WIRE ROPE

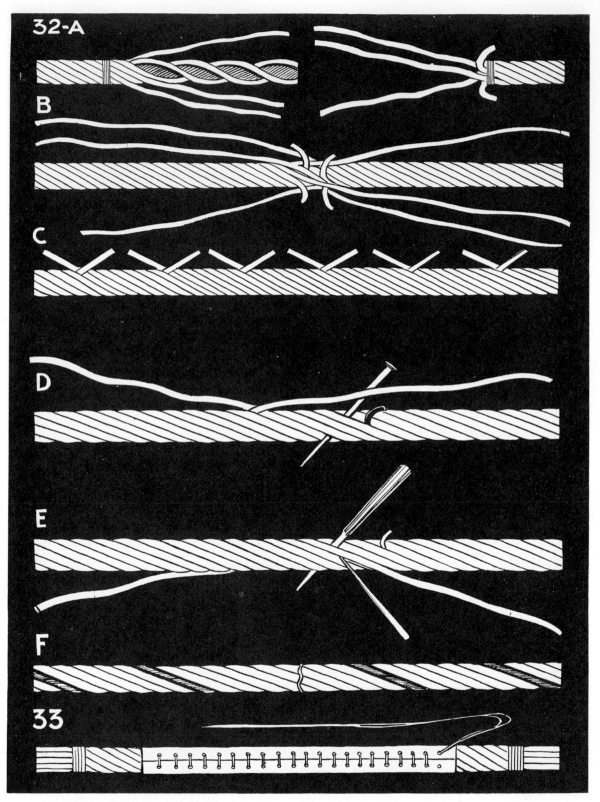

PLATE 310—A LONG SPLICE, AND STITCHING RAWHIDE ON WIRE ROPE

shown is used for setting circular metal Grommets in canvas. The male half of the Grommet is placed on the die *b* and the female part of the Grommet is placed over the male half. The point of the punch *a* is placed in the hole in the Grommet and the punch is struck with a hammer until the Grommet is set up firmly in place (*see* PLATE 296, FIG. 498), which illustrates the completed work.

Plate 310—A Long Splice, and Stitching Rawhide on Wire Rope

FIGS. 32A to F. Additional illustrations showing the different stages of a method employed to form a long splice in wire which is similar to the one described in FIGS 17A, B and C. These drawings are included to clarify the operation.

FIG. 33: The accompanying illustration shows the proper method employed for stitching rawhide on wire rope. However, elkhide is preferable, as rawhide has a tendency to absorb salt and moisture and consequently to rust the wire.

The total amount of rope to allow for making both Short and Long Splices in wire rope is shown in the following table.

Diameter of Rope		$\frac{1}{4}$-$\frac{3}{8}$	$\frac{1}{2}$-$\frac{5}{8}$	$\frac{3}{4}$-$\frac{7}{8}$	1-$1\frac{1}{8}$	$1\frac{1}{4}$-$1\frac{3}{8}$	$1\frac{1}{2}$
Total Length of Rope to Allow in Feet	Short Splice	15	20	24	28	32	36
	Long Splice	30	40	50	60	70	80

The total amount of wire rope to allow for various sizes of thimbles is shown in the following table.

Diameter of Rope	$\frac{1}{4}$-$\frac{3}{8}$	$\frac{1}{2}$	$\frac{5}{8}$-$\frac{3}{4}$	$\frac{7}{8}$-1	$1\frac{1}{8}$	$1\frac{1}{4}$	$1\frac{1}{2}$
Length to Allow in Feet	1	$1\frac{1}{2}$	2	$2\frac{1}{2}$	3	$3\frac{1}{2}$	4

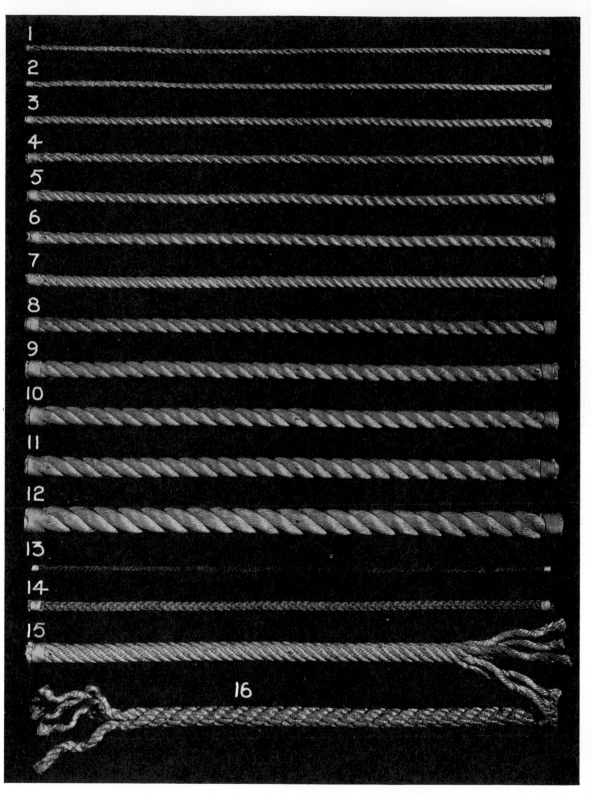

PLATE 311—THE RELATIVE SIZES OF VARIOUS ROPES

[*Plate 311*]   Fiber and Wire Rope Characteristics   577

Fiber and Wire Rope Characteristics

In the tables on pages 578-79 and on PLATE 311, are given the sizes and many of the characteristics of some of the different kinds of both fiber and wire rope most commonly used. Many sizes of Manila rope and wire cable, other than those described here, are manufactured, usually for special applications, or for some specific purpose requiring that the rope or cable have certain definite properties.

Plate 311—The Relative Sizes of Various Ropes

FIG. 1. 3/16-Inch Size Three-Strand Manila Rope.

FIG. 2. ¼-Inch Size Three-Strand Manila Rope.

FIG. 3. 5/16-Inch Size Three-Strand Manila Rope.

FIG. 4. ⅜-Inch Size Three-Strand Manila Rope.

FIG. 5. 7/16-Inch Size Three-Strand Manila Rope.

FIG. 6. ½-Inch Size Three-Strand Manila Rope.

FIG. 7. ½-Inch Size Four-Strand Manila Rope.

FIG. 8. 9/16-Inch Size Three-Strand Manila Rope.

FIG. 9. ⅝-Inch Size Three-Strand Manila Rope.

FIG. 10. ¾-Inch Size Three-Strand Manila Rope.

FIG. 11. 13/16-Inch Size Three-Strand Manila Rope.

FIG. 12. 1-Inch Size Three-Strand Manila Rope.

FIG. 13. The Spun Yarn shown here is drab brown in color, and does not photograph very clearly.

FIG. 14. Eight-Strand Braided Hemp.

FIG. 15. The Old-Fashioned Six-Strand Wheel Rope is seldom seen nowadays in any country outside of France, where it is called "Septin" and still used extensively. The end is unlaid to show the heart.

FIG. 16. The Cable-Laid Rope is composed of three right-handed hawser-laid ropes laid up together left-handed, giving it nine strands in all. The end is unlaid to illustrate its method of construction.

Fiber Rope Sizes and Characteristics

SIZES (Inches)		GROSS WEIGHTS (Lbs. and Decimals)		LENGTHS (Ft. and Decimals)		STRENGTHS (Pounds)	
Diameter	Circumference	Full Coils	Per 100 Ft.	Full Coils	Ft. in 1 Lb.	Breaking Strengths	Working Strains
3/16	5/8	25	1.43	1,750	70	450	90
1/4	3/4	30	1.72	1,750	58	550	110
5/16	1	45	2.63	1,700	38	950	190
3/8	1 1/8	60	3.71	1,625	27	1,300	260
7/16	1 1/4	75	5.26	1,425	19	1,750	350
1/2	1 1/2	90	7.5	1,200	13.3	2,650	530
9/16	1 3/4	125	10.4	1,200	9.6	3,450	690
5/8	2	160	13.3	1,200	7.5	4,400	880
3/4	2 1/4	200	16.7	1,200	6.0	5,400	1,080
13/16	2 1/2	234	19.5	1,200	5.13	6,500	1,300
7/8	2 3/4	270	22.5	1,200	4.45	7,700	1,540
1	3	324	27.0	1,200	3.71	9,000	1,800
1 1/16	3 1/4	375	31.3	1,200	3.20	10,500	2,100
1 1/8	3 1/2	432	36.0	1,200	2.78	12,000	2,400
1 1/4	3 3/4	502	41.8	1,200	2.40	13,500	2,700
1 5/16	4	576	48.0	1,200	2.09	15,000	3,000
1 1/2	4 1/2	720	60.0	1,200	1.67	18,500	3,700
1 5/8	5	893	74.4	1,200	1.34	22,500	4,500
1 3/4	5 1/2	1,073	89.5	1,200	1.12	26,500	5,300
2	6	1,290	108.0	1,200	.930	31,000	6,200
2 1/8	6 1/2	1,503	125.0	1,200	.800	36,000	7,200
2 1/4	7	1,752	146.0	1,200	.685	41,000	8,200
2 1/2	7 1/2	2,004	167.0	1,200	.600	46,500	9,300
2 5/8	8	2,290	191.0	1,200	.524	52,000	10,400
2 7/8	8 1/2	2,580	215.0	1,200	.465	58,000	11,600
3	9	2,900	242.0	1,200	.414	64,000	12,800
3 1/8	9 1/2	3,225	269.0	1,200	.372	71,000	14,200
3 1/4	10	3,590	299.0	1,200	.335	77,000	15,400
3 1/2	11	4,400	367.0	1,200	.273	91,000	18,200
3 3/4	12	5,225	436.0	1,200	.230	105,000	21,000

This table gives the sizes and characteristics of medium lay, three-strand Manila rope. The working strains are figured at about 20% of breaking strengths for efficiency in everyday service, but somewhat higher loads are not unsafe for temporary use.

Four-strand rope has approximately the same tensile strength as three-strand and runs 5 to 7% heavier.

Wire Rope Sizcs and Characteristics

GALVANIZED IRON RIGGING AND GUY ROPE

Composed of 6 Strands and a Hemp Center, 7 Wires to the Strand

Diameter in inches	Approx. circumference in inches	Approx. weight per foot	Breaking strength in tons of 2000 lbs.	Circum. of manila rope of nearest strength
1¾	5½	4.60	37.00	10
1⅝	5⅛	3.96	32.40	9
1½	4¾	3.38	27.70	8½
1⅜	4⅜	2.84	23.70	7½
1¼	3⅞	2.34	19.90	7
1⅛	3½	1.90	16.50	6
1 1/16	3⅜	1.70	14.80	5½
1	3⅛	1.50	13.20	5¼
⅞	2¾	1.15	10.20	4¾
¾	2⅜	.84	7.10	3¾
⅝	2	.59	5.30	3¼
9/16	1¾	.48	4.32	3
½	1⅝	.38	3.43	2½
7/16	1⅜	.29	2.64	2¼
⅜	1⅛	.21	1.95	2
5/16	1	.15	1.36	1½
9/32	⅞	.125	1.20	1⅜
¼	¾	.090	.99	1¼
7/32	11/16	.063	.79	1⅛
3/16	⅝	.040	.61	1

EXTRA PLIABLE HOISTING ROPE

Composed of 6 Strands and a Hemp Center, 37 Wires to the Strand

Diameter in inches	Approx. circumference in inches	Approx. weight per foot	Breaking strength in tons of 2000 lbs.
3½	11	19.00	451.0
3¼	10¼	16.37	392.0
3	9⅜	13.95	337.0
2¾	8⅝	11.72	285.0
2½	7⅞	9.69	237.0
2¼	7⅛	7.85	194.0
2	6¼	6.20	155.0
1¾	5½	4.75	119.5
1⅝	5⅛	4.09	103.3
1½	4¾	3.49	88.2
1⅜	4⅜	2.93	74.3
1¼	3⅞	2.42	61.5
1⅛	3½	1.96	49.9
1	3⅛	1.55	39.5
⅞	2¾	1.19	30.5
¾	2⅜	.87	22.8
⅝	2	.61	16.1
½	1⅝	.39	10.6
⅜	1⅛	.22	6.1
¼	¾	.10	2.8

GALVANIZED STEEL MOORING LINES AND HAWSERS

Composed of 6 Strands and a Hemp Center, each Strand composed of 24 Wires and a Hemp Core

Diameter in inches	Approximate circumference in inches	Approximate weight per foot	Breaking strength in tons of 2000 lbs.	
			Plow steel	Cast steel
2 1/16	6½	5.87	118.00	98.00
2	6¼	5.52	112.00	92.00
1 13/16	5¾	4.53	92.30	76.20
1¾	5½	4.23	86.20	71.20
1⅝	5⅛	3.64	74.50	61.60
1½	4¾	3.11	63.60	52.60
1⅜	4⅜	2.61	53.60	44.40
1¼	3⅞	2.16	44.40	36.70
1⅛	3½	1.75	36.00	29.90
1	3⅛	1.38	28.50	23.70
⅞	2¾	1.06	22.00	18.30
¾	2⅜	.78	16.40	13.60
⅝	2	.54	11.60	9.59
½	1⅝	.35	7.63	6.37
⅜	1⅛	.194	4.40	3.67

GALVANIZED STEEL HAWSERS

Composed of 6 Strands and a Hemp Center, 37 Wires to the Strand

Diameter in inches	Approximate circumference in inches	Approximate weight per foot	Breaking strength in tons of 2000 lbs.
2⅜	7½	8.74	173.3
2¼	7⅛	7.85	156.2
2⅛	6⅝	7.00	140.2
2	6¼	6.20	125.0
1¾	5½	4.75	96.5
1⅝	5⅛	4.09	83.4
1½	4¾	3.49	71.2
1⅜	4⅜	2.93	60.0
1¼	3⅞	2.42	49.7
1⅛	3½	1.96	40.3
1 1/16	3⅜	1.75	36.0
1	3⅛	1.55	31.9
⅞	2¾	1.19	24.6
13/16	2½	1.02	21.3
¾	2⅜	.87	18.3

Appendix

Plate 312—Sixteen-Strand Belt and Other Designs

Fig. 1: Shows an enlarged view of an opening for the belt tongue to go through, which has already been described in detail in Chapter IX.

Fig. 2: Shows an enlarged view of how to join the belt loop together, which is the most up-to-date method when a belt is started from the buckle. It has been described in the instructions on how to make a sixteen-strand belt.

Fig. 3: Is another illustration of how the loop is joined together, then finished off as previously described.

Fig. 4: Shows how a belt is half-hitched to finish off, after having been worked to a point, an operation likewise described thoroughly in the previous instructions in Chapter IX on belt making.

Fig. 5: Illustrates another one of the many examples of finished belts. This belt contains twenty strands, and can be duplicated easily if the pattern is followed closely. The following description of how to make a sixteen-strand belt can be applied to belts with any number of strands, with due allowance made for additional strands.

To make a sixteen-strand belt without a design, cut eight strands eight times the length of the desired belt, then take a piece of wood two by four by six and clamp it to the edge of a table. Hammer two four-penny nails into the piece of wood about three inches apart, then double one strand over these nails and make it fast at each nail with Clove Hitches. This strand now becomes two strands. The strand on the right being number one, and the strand on the left number two. Now double another strand and make a Lark's Head knot, Plate 1, Fig. 15, in the the center between the two nails. This will be Lark's Head number one, with strand number three on the right, and number four on the left. Continue by doubling a strand to the right of the first Lark's Head. This will be Lark's Head number three, and the strands will be numbers five and seven. Another strand is then doubled to the left of the first Lark's Head which will be known as Lark's Head number two, and the strands will be numbers eight and six.

The work is continued by using strands three and four as a filler; next tie a Square Knot with strands five and six. Now proceed by doubling a strand to the right of Lark's Head number three, and make Lark's Head number five, these strands to be called numbers nine and eleven; then double a strand to the left of Lark's Head number two and make Lark's Head number four, these strands to be known as numbers ten and twelve. Now use strands five and seven as a filler and tie a Square Knot with strands three and nine. Next use strands six and eight as a filler and tie a Square Knot with strands three and nine. Next use strands six and eight as a filler and tie a Square Knot with strands four and ten. The work is continued in the same way by using strands three and four for a filler, with a Square Knot tied by strands five and six. Now double a strand to right of Lark's Head number five, and make Lark's Head number seven, these strands to be known as numbers thirteen and fifteen. Strands nine and eleven are next used as fillers, with a Square Knot tied by strands seven and thirteen. Strands five and seven are used as fillers for the next Square Knot, which is tied with strands three and nine. Double a strand on the left of Lark's Head number four and make Lark's Head number six. These strands will then be known as strands fourteen and sixteen. Proceed by using strands ten and twelve for the next filler, and tie a Square Knot with strands eight and fourteen; then use strands six and eight as a filler, and tie a Square Knot with strands four and ten. Strands three and four are next used as a filler, and a Square Knot is tied with strands five and six.

Now untie strand two on the left and strand one on the right, and remove the nails. Take the point of the belt that has been completed and make it secure on top of the piece of wood by inserting a few small nails through openings in the work. Continue by using strands fourteen and sixteen as a filler, and tie a Square Knot with strands two and twelve. Strands ten and twelve are next used as a filler, and the Square Knot is made with strands eight and fourteen.

The work is now continued in the following order: Use as fillers strands six and eight, thirteen and fifteen, nine and eleven, five and seven, four and three, two and fourteen, ten and twelve, and then back to strands six and eight, which are again used in the same manner. The Square Knots are tied in the same order with strands four and ten, one and eleven, seven and thirteen, three and nine, five and six, twelve and sixteen, eight and fourteen, then back to four and ten, which are used for the second time.

Now proceed by using the following strands as fillers: One and thirteen, nine and eleven, five and seven, then three and four. The Square Knots are tied in their proper sequence by using the following order to go with the fillers: strands eleven and fifteen, seven and thirteen, three and nine, then five and six.

By switching the strands in this order, a crossed chain-like effect will be obtained which will give even edges to the belt. In the process of belt making always work to a point whenever possible, as by doing so lots of mistakes can be avoided.

To make the openings in the flap of the belt for the buckle tongue to go through, skip a Square Knot in the center every one and one-half inches until the desired amount of holes have been obtained.

Continue by working belt down to within six inches of the desired length, and leave three openings two inches apart for adjustment of buckle to proper length.

To finish off the belt and put a strap on it, work the square knots to a point. *See* PLATE 170, FIG. 28. Now take the belt and place it horizontally, with a small piece of wood or a ruler on top of belt near point, right side up. Strands three,

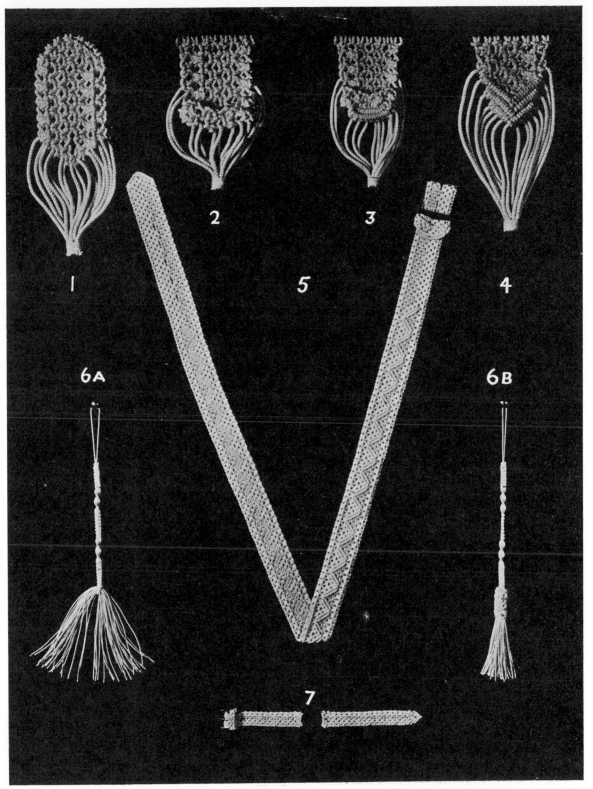

PLATE 312—SIXTEEN-STRAND BELT AND OTHER DESIGNS

five, seven, nine, eleven, thirteen, fifteen and one are facing the front, while strands four, six, eight, ten, twelve, fourteen, sixteen and two are lying on the table facing toward the back.

Now proceed by using as fillers strands three and seven, then nine and eleven, and make Square Knots with strands five and nine, then seven and thirteen in turn. Drop strands one and fifteen, and bury the ends underneath the belt by slightly opening a knot or two with a pricker. Continue by using as fillers strands three and seven, nine and eleven, and then strands three and seven, nine and eleven for the second time. Square Knots are tied in the same manner as previously described, with strands five and nine, seven and thirteen, then five and nine and seven and thirteen again.

Unclamp the work and it will now resemble PLATE 171, FIG. 33. Next take the belt and place the other side in front, with a small piece of wood or ruler on top of belt, near the point right side up. Strands four, six, eight, ten, twelve, fourteen, sixteen and two will now be in front. Use strands four and eight and ten and twelve as fillers, and proceed in the usual manner by making Square Knots with strands six and ten, then eight and fourteen. Drop strands two and sixteen and bury the ends in the usual way. Using as a filler strands four and eight, ten and twelve, then four and eight and ten and twelve once again, tie Square Knots with strands six and ten, then eight and fourteen, then repeat with the same strands as before.

Unclamp the work once again and place the belt with the wrong side up this time, then put a small piece of wood over it in front of what is to be the strap, and fasten it down. Take strand fourteen from the left side of strap and strand thirteen from the right side of strap and use them as a filler, then tie a Square Knot with strands twelve and eleven. This will be the first step in bringing the sides of the strap together to form a loop. Continue by using as fillers, strands ten and twelve, then strands nine and eleven, at the same time making Square Knots with strands eight and fourteen, seven and thirteen.

The strands will now number from left to right, fourteen, twelve, ten, eight, six, four, thirteen, eleven, nine, seven, five, and three. Cut strands eight and eleven off up close to knot, then use strand five as a filler and tie two Half Hitches with strands seven, nine, thirteen, four, six, ten and twelve in turn. Next take strand fourteen to be used as a filler, then tie two Half Hitches with strand five, then repeat the same performance with strand twelve and stick strand five through the loop of the second Half Hitch. Proceed by tying two Half Hitches with strands ten, six, four, thirteen, nine, seven and three in turn and stick through the loop of each second half hitch strands twelve, ten, six, four, thirteen, nine and seven in turn.

The work is now unclamped and strands five, twelve, ten, six, four, thirteen, nine and seven are pulled taut. These are the strands that are passed down through the loops of the second Half Hitches. Bury strand fourteen underneath in the usual way. Do not cut any strands off until the belt is washed and stretched while drying.

FIGS. 6A and 6B: Show a Light or Shade Pull Design slightly different and more intricate than PLATE 210, FIG. 158.

Cut two strands—one strand two feet long and the other eight feet long. Fasten a clamp vise on the top of the table, double the two foot strand over the top of the screw handle of the vise clamp, and fasten the two strands to the body hook that all square knotters use.

Double the eight foot strand and make a Square Knot about two inches down on the two-stranded filler, and continue to make eight Square Knots in all, one on top of the other. This type of work is known as a flat. Make sixteen Half Hitches or half a Square Knot going in the same direction; this makes what is known as a spiral; make eight more Square Knots, sixteen Half Hitches, and eight Square Knots, and the pull part of the shade pull is made. Proceed by cutting twenty-four strands eight feet long. Place the middle of these strands at the bottom of the pull just finished, and make a Square Knot with the two strands that you made the flats and spirals with. Let all strands hang down to form the tassel, remove from clamp.

Cut eight strands twenty inches long and lay these strands out straight on the table; place on top a ruler or a flat stick across the middle, and clamp it down on the edge of the table. Tie a Square Knot in the middle of these eight strands, using strands four and five as the filler and tying the knot with strands three and six; tie another Square Knot, using strands two and three as the filler, and tying your knot with strands one and four; tie another Square Knot, using strands six and seven as the filler, making knot with strands five and eight. You have now made three Square Knots with eight strands. Unclamp your eight strands with the three knots, then fasten the clamp vise on the top of the table, and place the eye part of the shade pull over the screw handle of the clamp vise. Put the eight strands round the top of tassel with one knot in the back, and one on each side. Use strands four and five as the filler and tie a Square Knot with strands three and six. This will make all strands fast to the pull on top of the tassel; tie another Square Knot, using strands six and seven as the filler, making knot with strands five and eight. You now have sixteen working strands. Continue to make four Square Knots all round till the desired length of crown is reached. By using sixteen strands you can make a round handle, and if you wish to make a square handle, reverse your Square Knots.

A Turk's Head may be placed below the Square Knots. The easiest way to start a Turk's Head is to make a sailor's breast-plate knot. PLATE 21, FIGS. 10A and 10B. Turk's Heads are on page 215. If you wish to put a binding round it, *see* PLATE 19, FIG. 296.

Trim off the bottom to the desired length, and you will have the nicest and most durable shade or light pull of its kind in square knotting. Any kind of cord can be used to make this article.

FIG. 7: Shows a Wrist Watch Strap. It is started from a four-penny nail, which is used as a filler. Cut eight strands thirty-six inches long, using braided silk fish line. Double each strand to form a Lark's Head, which gives sixteen working strands, then form a complete body of Square Knots approximately four inches long, and bring work to a point the same as for finishing off a belt that has been started from the buckle.

Now proceed by cutting eight additional strands thirty-six inches long, then double them to form Lark's Heads the same as before, and use another fourpenny nail as a filler. Continue the Square Knots to a length of three inches

for this end of the strap. The loop is then made on the end, the same as for finishing off a belt that has been started from the point.

In order to attach strap to wrist watch, remove pins from both ends of watch, then remove nails from where strap was started, and insert pins in the same openings. This is a very neat and attractive method of making a strap, which will be found suitable for any wrist watch.

Plate 313—Ladies' Handbags

FIG. 1A: Shows a partly completed ladies' evening handbag which has been made smaller than the average size in order to illustrate the method of construction in a more simplified form. FIG. 1B shows the same bag as it looks when completed.

For the average size handbag, as illustrated in FIGS. 2 and 3, eighty double strands, thirteen feet long are used. The bag is started from the point of the flap, on a nail, the same as for starting a belt from the point. Sixteen strands are used to form the tongue of the flap. Additional strands are then added on both sides, the same as in belt construction, and the manner in which they are used depends on the pattern of the desired flap. After the necessary amount of strands have been added, and the flap has been completed, four strands are dropped on both sides, then buried underneath (*see* upper portion of FIG. 1A). The work is then continued until the required length is obtained for both sides and the bottom. Twenty-six rows of Square Knots are used for the length of the back and twenty-five rows are used for the front, with five rows being used for the bottom.

Any kind of design can be used for decorative purposes depending, of course, upon individual initiative and the kind of pattern desired. After both sides have been completed, one strand is cut from each top row. As the work progresses, it will be found necessary to eliminate other strands accordingly. For the sides, ten double strands six feet long are used. Two double strands are inserted up through one square knot loop and down through the next square knot loop, until five rows of Square Knots have been used. This gives twenty strands for the sides. Continue by passing outside strands alternately up through then down through each following square knot loop until both sides have been completed, and filled in with Square Knots.

In order to make the first row of Half Hitches around the top, take the strands nearest to the inside on both sides, pass them through the square knot openings, and use them as fillers. The work is then continued by making two Half Hitches with each strand through the opposite side, from right to left of the bag; then take inside strands of the Square Knot

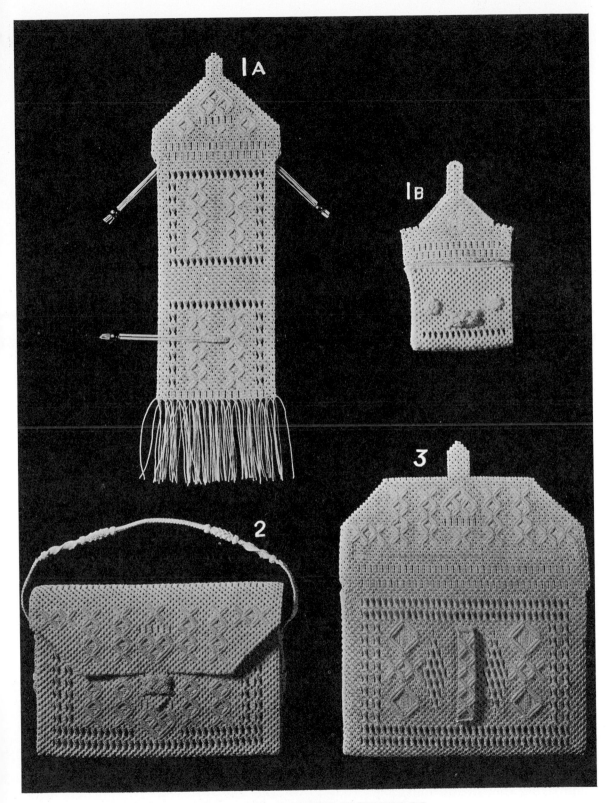

PLATE 313—LADIES' HANDBAGS

on the left side of bag and pass them through the square knot openings, the same as before, and make two Half Hitches with each strand toward the right side of the bag, burying them at the finish the same as for finishing off a belt.

Before the lining is attached, a block of wood is cut approximately the size of the bag, which is placed on the inside. The bag is then washed and allowed to dry on this pattern.

A piece of silk or satin can be used for lining. It must be cut to fit both front and back and come up just below the two top rows of half hitches. Sew both sides of the lining after ample room has been left to cover the interior. Next, lap the top over on the outside of the lining and sew the edge all the way around.

The zipper is next attached by sewing the side first. At each end the strands are alternately passed up through in front of zipper, then down through the top and in between every second Half Hitch.

A Carrick Bend design, or a row of flats are used to hold the point of the flap. See the partly completed design in FIG. 1A.

To make the handle, fourteen strands six feet long and two strands eleven feet long are worked down in the usual way and brought to a point, then secured to the bag by passing the strands down on the outside of the bag and tying them with Square Knots underneath or on the inside of the bag, which completes the work.

FIG. 2: Shows front view of a modern Ladies' Handbag with handle attached.

FIG. 3: Shows back view of a handbag that has a strap attached to the back for a handle. These two bags represent the last word in modern design.

Plate 314—Various Special Knots

FIG. 1: An *Open Bowline* with a bight. It can be tied easily from the illustration.

FIG. 2: A *Tugboat Bowline,* which is used extensively on tugboats.

FIG. 3: A variation of the regular *French Bowline.*

FIG. 4: A *Mexican Bowline* (end method), which is a rather uncommon style of forming a Bowline.

FIG. 5: A *Mexican Bowline* (left-handed loop method), which is very similar to the right-handed loop method, but its slightly different method of construction can be readily observed by comparing the illustrations.

FIG. 6: Represents an unusual method of forming a *Mat Design*.

FIG. 7: A *Mexican Bowline* (right-handed loop method).

FIG. 8: A *Ganging Knot*. It is often used by fishermen on the Grand Banks to snell their hooks.

FIG. 9: A *Climber's Rig Knot*. It is made with a French Bowline and Rolling Hitch.

FIG. 10: A *Mat Design* tied with two lines which can be double or triple passed, and then pulled up snug to form a compact body.

FIG. 11: A *Climber's* or *Pruner's Saddle.* It is used by the Park Department of the City of New York, where it is known as a Taut Knot. First make a chain braid, and then join the lines to-

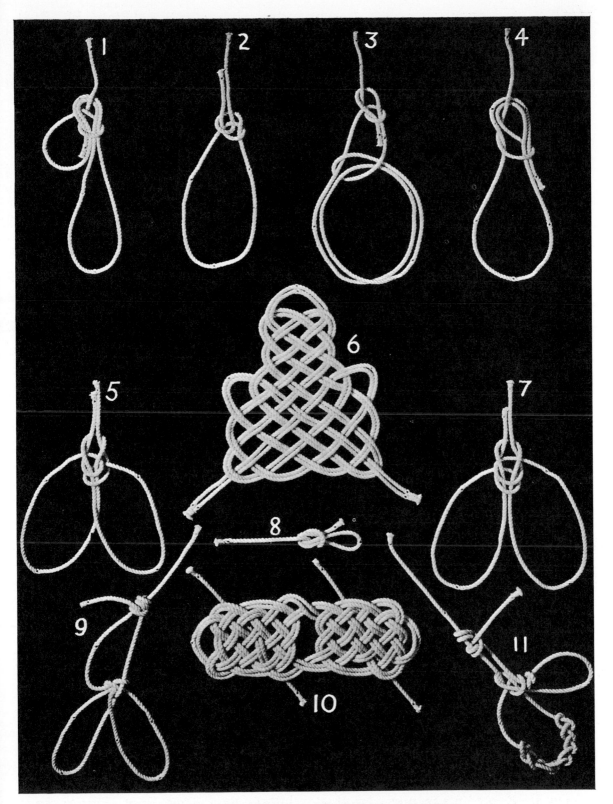

PLATE 314—VARIOUS SPECIAL KNOTS

gether with a Bowline. An Overhand Knot is then tied below the Bowline, and the line is passed up through this knot and joined to the other end of the line with a Round Turn and two Half Hitches.

Plate 315—Miscellaneous Knot Designs

FIG 1: A *Miniature Bell Rope Cord design* which includes a cable laid filler and body with a Matthew Walker Knot and Turk's Head Weave on one end, and a Turk's Head, Lanyard and Star Knot Weave on the other.

FIG. 2: An interesting design for a *Dog Leash,* tied with cotton line instead of the usual method of using dreadnaught cord for such purposes. An explanation of its construction isn't necessary, as the illustration shows its various weaves and knots, which should be plain and easy to follow by the experienced knot worker.

FIG. 3: A novel method for constructing a *Shirt Pocket Watch lanyard.* It has the same cable laid principle as Bell Rope Lanyards, and is finished off with a seven strand Turk's Head which is formed around a crowned filler. The other knots at different intervals are Turk's Heads, which can be formed with as many strands as desired.

FIG. 4: Another example of the old-time *Bell Rope* designs. Ornamental things such as these are the result of individual initiative; and by observing the various weaves and style of knotting, anyone should find it easy to create new and original ideas of their own.

FIG. 5: A *Sea Chest Shackle* done by a slightly different method than FIG. 296, PLATE 265. The eyes are coxcombed with one strand cackling, and the other designs can be easily followed.

FIG. 6: *Eight Strand Star Knot Rosette* with triple passed crowned heart.

FIG. 7: A very novel and attractive way of making a *Comb Hanger Design.* A rubber heart was used for the core, with a cork foundation for the two large Turk's Head designs, which are double passed and of thirteen and fifteen strands respectively. The thimble that is used to form the eye has a Running Sennit, which can be of any number of strands, depending on the size of the seizing around the base, and the work is continued with a Spiral Hitching that is finished with Running Sennits on each end, and small Turk's Head seizings, which are followed at different intervals with brass bands, as illustrated. To finish off, seize the rope yarns around the core before making the last series of Turk's Heads around the end.

FIG. 8: Another interesting suggestion for making a *Bell Rope Cord Design,* with an eye on the bottom for the lanyard attachment. To attempt a detailed explanation of its construction would be superfluous, as similar designs in Chapter XI have been explained thoroughly.

FIG. 9: A *Star Knot Rose Bud* of six triple passes.

FIG. 10: A *Twelve Strand Star Knot* with a *Matthew Walker* and *Double Nelson* base.

FIG. 11: An *Eight Strand Star Knot Rose Bud* with triple passes.

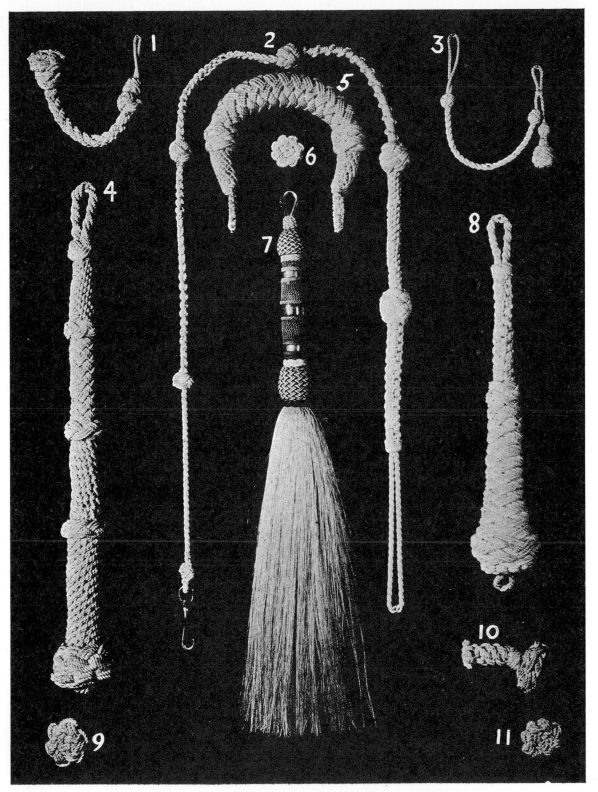

PLATE 315—MISCELLANEOUS KNOT DESIGNS

Plate 316—Miscellaneous Knots and Ties

FIG. 1: The *Combination Comb Hanger Design* shown here is started with a Lanyard, which is followed by a Sennit Weave, then a Star Knot and Turk's Head Weave is used to finish.

FIG. 2: The *Hangman's Noose Braid* represents a Hangman's Noose with the bight pulled out and cut in the center. The ends are then braided into the bottom part in the manner shown.

FIG. 3: The *Crowned Monkey Fist* has a series of Spiral Crowns worked around a core and then finished off with a Spritsail Sheet top.

FIG. 4: Is a *Manrope Knot* with the bottom or wall part double and the top or crown part single.

FIG. 5: This is another method of forming a *Comb Hanger Design,* which consists of a Lanyard covered by a Double Diamond that is followed with a Star Knot and finished off by using a Walled Crown Weave.

FIG. 6: The *Ornamental Lacing* shown here can be easily followed.

FIG. 7: The *Combination Carrick Weave Design*. Another of the many variations that can be obtained.

FIG. 8: Is a *Heaving Line Bend,* which is used for the purpose that its name implies. (*See* PLATE 24, FIG. 34.)

FIG. 9: Is a *Two-Strand Inverted Turk's Head* with three passes.

FIGS. 10A and B: Shows a *Saddle Girt Weave* that is used by Mexican Cowboys in the making of fancy saddle girts. Use any number of strands desired, and proceed by taking the outside strand from the left each time, then lead it across the full width of the body by hitching the other strands in turn as FIG. A indicates. FIG. B shows the underneath part of the weave that goes next to the horse's body.

FIG. 11: Is a *Racking Bend* which is used for towing purposes.

FIG. 12: A *Hickory Bend* as shown here is useful for slippery material.

FIG. 13: Is a *Slip Eye Bight* tied in the form of a Figure-of-Eight.

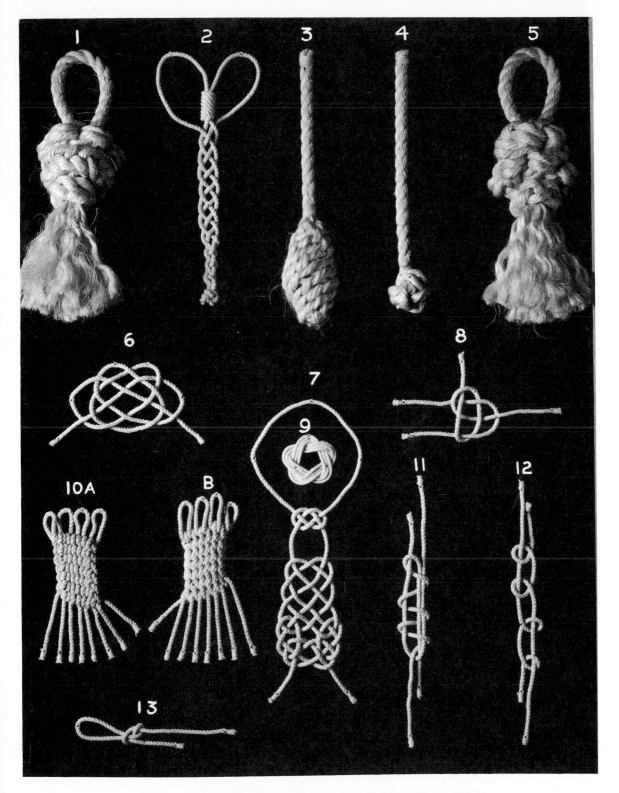

PLATE 316—MISCELLANEOUS KNOTS AND TIES

Plate 317—Miscellaneous Knots and Ties

FIG. 1: A *Single Riverman's Bend* as shown here is similar to a Sheet Bend, except that the first turn is taken around the outside. It is very secure for a line that is slippery.

FIG. 2: Is a *Strop and Becket Hitch* attached to a ring.

FIG. 3: Is a *Ring Hitch,* which can be easily followed from the illustration.

FIG. 4: Is a *Lark's Head* hitched to a ring.

FIG. 5: A *Double Riverman's Bend,* the same as the single method except for an additional round turn.

FIG. 6: A *Riverman's Bend with Bow.* It is easy to upset and cast off.

FIG. 7: An *Overhand Bend* as shown here is tied in a slightly different way from PLATE 7, FIG. 151.

FIG. 8: Is a *Lath Knot* which is used for tying bundles of laths with small tarred cordage.

FIG. 9: Is known as a *Harness Bend.*

FIG. 10: Shows a *Treble Lark's Head* with Half Hitches.

FIG. 11: Is a *Stoppered Ring Hitch.*

FIG. 12: Another method for tying a *Stoppered Ring Hitch.*

FIG. 13: Is a *Figure-of-Eight Bend.*

FIG. 14: A *Tack Bend* is formed with a Slip Eye in one end of the line with an Overhand Knot in the other line.

FIG. 15: Shows a *Double Square Knot Bend.*

FIG. 16: A *Thread Knot* is tied in the manner shown.

FIG. 17: Shows a *Double Granny Bend.*

FIG. 18: Is a *Cord Bend.*

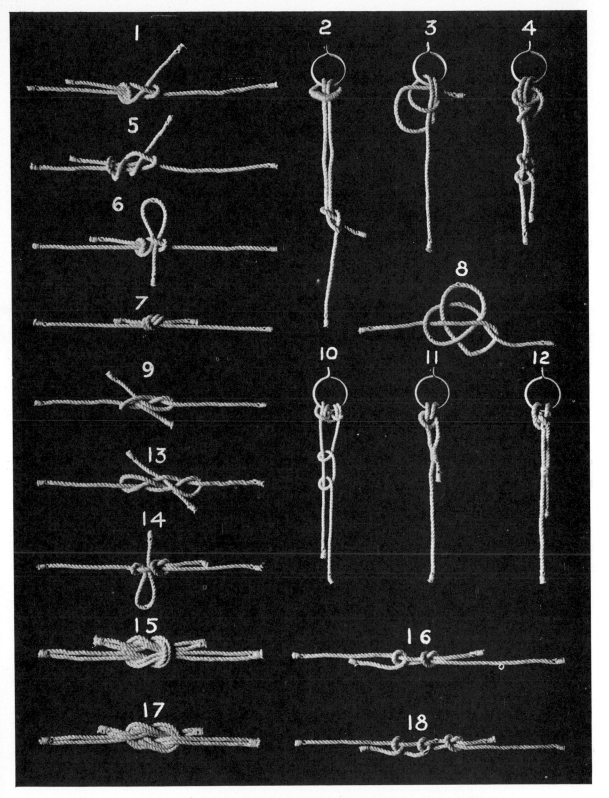

PLATE 317—MISCELLANEOUS KNOTS AND TIES

Plate 318—Miscellaneous Knots and Ties

FIG. 1: Is a *Safety Link Fishhook Tie.* This and the following ties are used by fishermen to attach flies and lines to fishhooks.

FIG. 2: Is a *Fly Hitch.*

FIG. 3: Is a *Turtle Knot.*

FIG. 4: Is another *Fishhook Tie.*

FIG. 5: Represents another of the many different methods that are used for attaching fishhooks.

FIG. 6: Is a *Stoppered Lark's Head Ring Hitch.*

FIG. 7: Is a *Simple Ring Hitch Stoppered.*

FIG. 8: Shows a method for making *Sheepshank Bights.*

FIG. 9: Is a *Japanese Bowline.*

FIGS. 10A and B: Shows a *Dropper Loop* or *Double Harness Hitch.* First form the knot illustrated in PLATE 27, FIG. 75. Next pull the bottom part underneath, then out through the bight as the drawn line indicates, and the completed knot will then appear as in FIG. B.

FIG. 11: Is a *Bedford Bend.* It is called by that name when tied with two bights, otherwise it is a common Sheet Bend.

FIG. 12: Is a *Swedish Bend* that is also a Sheet Bend tied with a bight and double line.

FIG. 13: Another of the many variations for tying *Gut Leader.*

FIG. 14: Is a *Gut Leader Tie* that is slightly different from the above.

FIG. 15: The method of forming this tie is called a *Canadian Bowline.*

FIG. 16: This is the opposite way to form a *Canadian Bowline.*

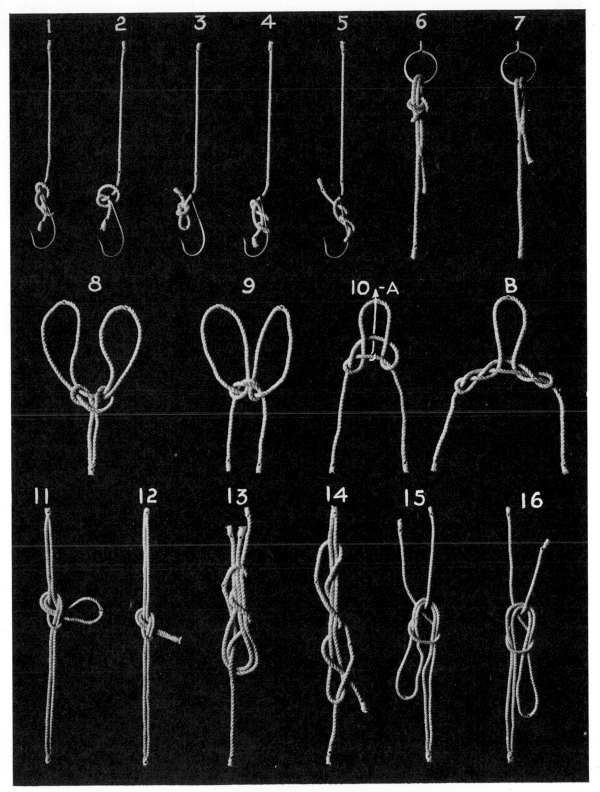

PLATE 318—MISCELLANEOUS KNOTS AND TIES

Plate 319—Miscellaneous Knots and Ties

FIG. 1: This and the following are *Latigo Ties,* that are used by horsemen for securing the strap or saddle girt to the cinch ring. The top rings represent the saddle rings and the bottom rings represent the cinch rings.

FIG. 2: *Latigo Tie,* Second Method.

FIG. 3: *Latigo Tie,* Third Method.

FIG. 4: *Latigo Tie,* Fourth Method.

FIG. 5: Is a good method for *Attaching a Line to a Ring.*

FIG. 6: The *Oyster Hitch* shown here will withstand severe usage.

FIG. 7: Is an *English Bowline* which is made much like other similar ties.

FIG. 8: The *Fisherman's Loop* shown here makes a good knot for a Leader.

FIG. 9: The *Cow Hitch* shown here is similar to PLATE 48, FIG. 349, except for the Figure-of-Eight.

FIG. 10: Is one of the many different methods of *Farmers' Loops.*

FIG. 11: Another *Farmer's Loop* method.

FIG. 12: Is a *Bowline with a Bight.*

FIG. 13: Is a *Tractor Hitch,* which can be easily followed.

FIG. 14: The *Granger Hitch* is of simple construction.

FIG. 15: The *Russian Hitch* is the same as the above, except for an additional Half Hitch.

FIG. 16: Is a *Single Spanish Bowline.*

FIG. 17: Is a *Rawhide Hitch* which has a Slip Eye.

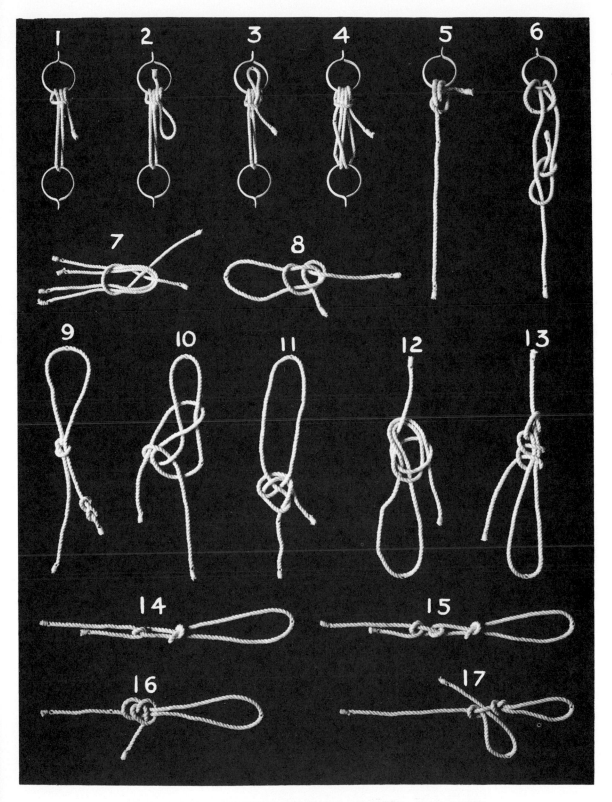

PLATE 319—MISCELLANEOUS KNOTS AND TIES

Plate 320—Miscellaneous Knots and Ties

FIG. 1: Shows a form of knot that is commonly called a *Doughnut Loop*.

FIG. 2: Is a *Mattress-maker's Knot* that is used to tie tufts together in the making of mattresses.

FIG. 3: Is a *Bosun's Hitch,* which is nothing more than a Figure-of-Eight Slip Eye.

FIG. 4: This form of *Sheet Bend* is often called a Cuban Bend. (*See* SWEDISH BEND.)

FIG. 5: The *Loop Knot* shown here includes a Manharness Knot with a Sheet Bend Eye.

FIG. 6: This *Ralph Hitch* is a handy way of making a line fast, and is easily made.

FIG. 7: Is a *Trapper's Hitch*. It is similar to a Bosun's Hitch.

FIG. 8: This shows a *Trapper's Hitch with a Bow.*

FIG. 9: Is a *Camper's Hitch*. It is handy for certain uses around camp.

FIG 10: Shows how to form a *Norwegian Bowline*.

FIG. 11: The *Waldo Hitch* shown here needs no explanation, as it can be followed easily.

FIG. 12: This is a *Wanagan Loop*.

FIG. 13: Is a *Flunkey's* or *Handyman's Hitch*. Practically the same tie as PLATE 24, FIG. 42.

FIG. 14: The form of tie shown here is known as a *Cayuse Hitch*.

FIG. 15: Is a *Bowline Hitch*.

FIG. 16: Is a *Bowline Hitch with Bow.*

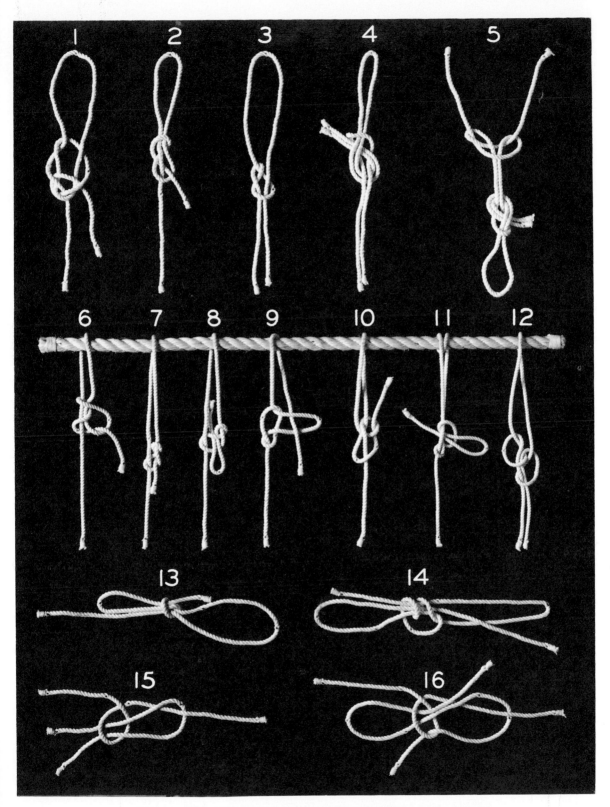

PLATE 320—MISCELLANEOUS KNOTS AND TIES

Plate 321—Miscellaneous Knots and Ties

FIG. 1: The *Mogul Bend* or *Sampan Hitch* shown here is used as a mooring for skiffs, and is handy for lowering certain objects so the line can be drawn up again.

FIG. 2: Is used as a *Buoy Hitch*.

FIG. 3: The *Anchor Knot* can be used for making fast to an Anchor Ring.

FIG. 4: Is a *Rolling Slip Hitch*.

FIG. 5: The *Packer's Hitch* is used by packers on packboards and in connection with Diamond Hitches.

FIG. 6: Shows the method of forming *Double Backhanded Sailors' Hitches*.

FIG. 7: Is a *Finland Knot*. It is used for tying horses.

FIG. 8: Is a *Slack Hitch and Round Turn*.

FIG. 9: Is one of the many methods of forming *Stoppered Hitches*.

FIG. 10: Another way of forming a *Stoppered Hitch with Round Turns*.

FIG. 11: Is a *Stoppered Hitch* that is similar to PLATE 42, FIG. 271.

FIG. 12: A *Reef Pennant Hitch* that is used to secure the reef cringle to the boom. A Reef Pennant is a rope that passes through a comb cleat on the end of the boom, through the reef cringle on the sail, then down through a comb cleat on the opposite side of the boom.

FIG. 13: Is a *Clifford's Loop*.

FIG. 14: Is a *Farmer's Noose*. (*See* COW HITCH.)

FIG. 15: Is a *Marten Knot* which is used as a temporary tie to prevent the unlaid strands on the end of a rope from fraying.

FIG. 16: Is a *Temporary Hitch*.

FIG. 17: The *Shank Hitch* shown here is used on a hook with small rope.

Fig. 18: Another form of *Shank Hitch* that is easily upset when strain is removed.

FIG. 19: Is a *Racking Hitch* on a hook.

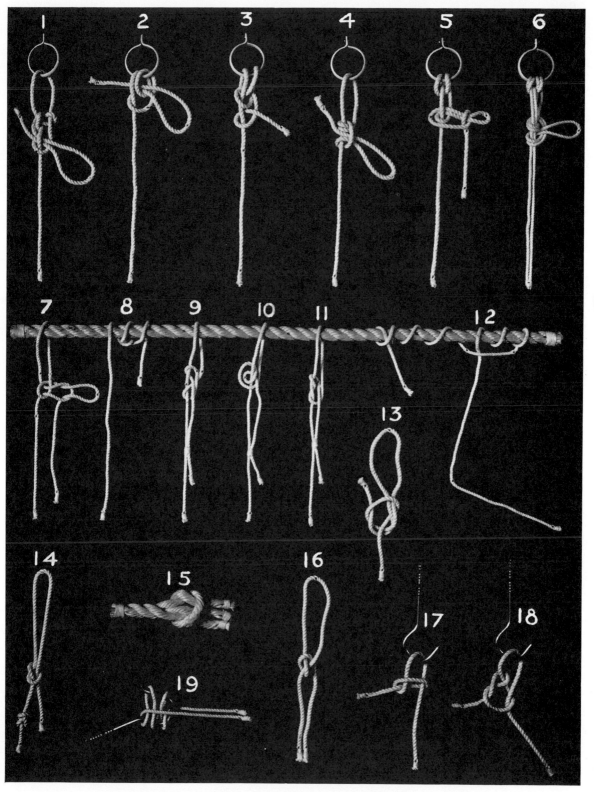

PLATE 321—MISCELLANEOUS KNOTS AND TIES

Plate 322—Miscellaneous Knots and Ties

FIG. 1: Is a *Twin Mooring Hitch*.

FIG. 2: Is another form of *Twin Mooring Hitch,* which shows a way to make a boat fast with one line between two docks.

FIG. 3: Shows a *Variated Midshipman's Hitch.*

FIG. 4: Is another variation of the *Midshipman's Hitch.*

FIG. 5: Is a *Midshipman's Hitch* variation that is similar to the above.

FIG. 6: Another one of the many different ways of forming *Midshipman's Hitch* variations. (*See* PLATE 3, FIG. 68 for the true Midshipman's Hitch.)

FIG. 7: Is a *Hoisting Hitch* which can be used for a variety of purposes that require rigging ties for certain lifts.

FIG. 8: The tie shown here is known as an *Alaska Bowline.* (*See* PLATE 10, FIG. 185 for a similar Bowline.)

FIG. 9: Is a *Variated Hitch* of very little practical utility.

FIG. 10: Is a *Circular Carrick Lacing.*

FIG. 11: The *Plumb Bob Hitch* is used for suspending a plumb bob beneath a transit.

FIG. 12: Is a *Drawing Bend.* It is a secure tie for dry ropes.

FIG. 13: The *Chain Bend* is used for joining chains. It is very secure, but jams hard under a severe strain.

FIG. 14: Shows a *Stag Hitch.* It can be formed with both ends of the line fast.

FIG. 15: The *Hog's Eye* is used to sew sail thread in the hole of a sail or other canvas of any kind to prevent the cloth from fraying.

FIG. 16: *Shows a way to break twine with the fingers.* Jerk the bottom end while holding the top part fast, and the twine will break at the cross on top of the finger.

FIG. 17: Is a *Clam Shortening.* It is similar to a Regular Sling Shortener (PLATE 265, FIG. 298) except tied on a hook.

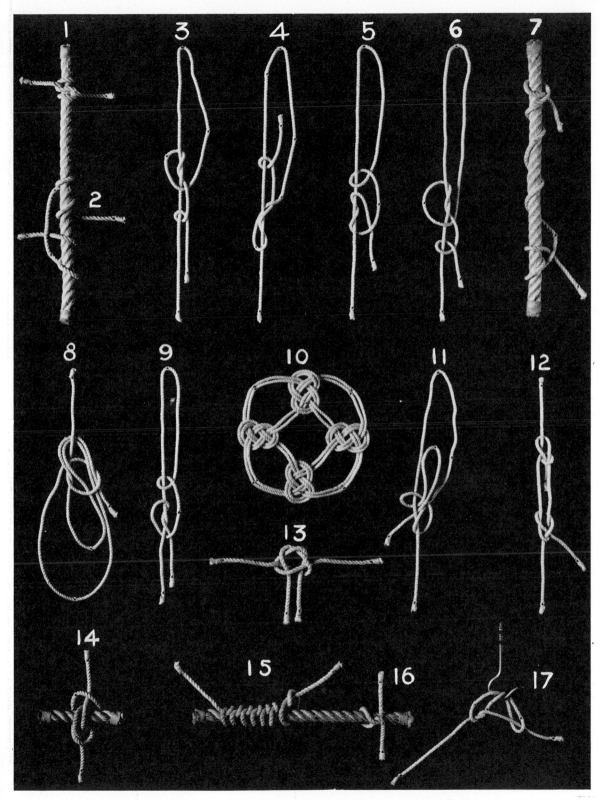

PLATE 322—MISCELLANEOUS KNOTS AND TIES

Plate 323—Miscellaneous Knots and Ties

Fig. 1: Is a *Game Carrier Tie,* which is a method that is used by hunters for carrying game.

Fig. 2: The *Cub Hitch* is used for mooring purposes.

Fig. 3: The *Roofing Hitch* is used by roofers and painters for lowering themselves down a roof. *a* is the standing part; *b* indicates where the knot is grasped by the hands; while *c* is the part that is made fast around the body.

Fig. 4: Is a *Ladder Sling.* Each bight is placed around the side pieces of the ladder.

Fig. 5: Is a *Painter's Hitch.* It shows how painters make the fall rope fast when they suspend the staging with tackles.

Fig. 6: Is a *Chator's Knot* that is used for Gut Leaders. (*Similar to* PLATE 7, FIG. 145.)

Fig. 7: The *Gill Net Knot* is used for repairing gill nets.

Fig. 8: The *Double Plumb Bob Hitch* shown here is slightly different from the Single Method. It is used for raising or lowering the Plumb Bob on transits.

Fig. 9: Is a *Rope Buckle Tie* which can be duplicated easily.

Figs. 10A and B: Is a *Converted Carrick Diamond Knot.* It has the Carrick Knot tied in the manner shown in FIG. A. The ends are then pulled out, and the knot will appear as in FIG. B. (*See* PLATE 36, FIG. 190 for an extended version of this knot.)

Fig. 11: Is a *Johnson Hitch.*

Fig. 12: The *Slack Bend* can be cast off under strain.

Fig. 13: The *Baldwin Bend* is used for towing.

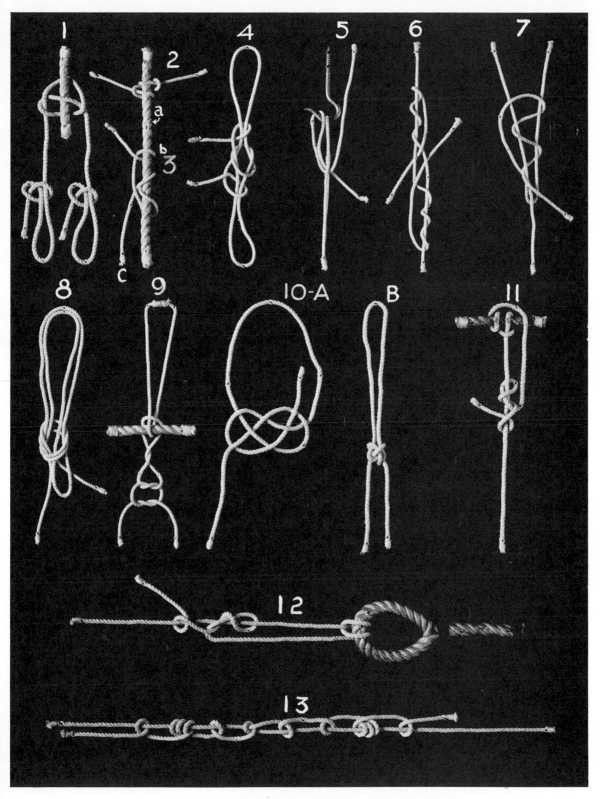

PLATE 323—MISCELLANEOUS KNOTS AND TIES

Plate 324—Miscellaneous Knots and Ties

FIG. 1: Is a *Hoisting Hitch* that can be used for a variety of purposes.

FIG. 2: Another one of a wide variety of *Hoisting Hitches,* that are included to show that almost any lifting obstacle can be overcome by employing the right hitch to suit the proper occasion.

FIG. 3: A *Cub Sling* that is rigged for hoisting purposes.

FIG. 4: *Hoisting Hitches* such as this and the following are adaptable to many different uses.

FIG. 5: Is another type of *Hoisting Hitch.*

FIGS. 6A and B: Is a *Dutch Sling.* The drawn line indicates how the end of the line is passed through the eye in FIG. A. FIG. B shows the Sling after proper adjustment on round object.

FIG. 7: Is a *Hoisting Hitch* that is similar to the others.

FIG. 8: Is a *Hoisting Hitch* also.

FIG. 9: Shows a *Packer's Ligature,* which is used for tying packages.

FIG. 10: Is a *Skidder's Hitch,* which represents a way of fastening a chain to small logs for skidding. Used by lumberjacks in logging camps.

FIG. 11: Is a *Bosun's Knot and Half Hitch Package Tie.*

FIG. 12: Is a *Claw Hitch with Bow.*

FIG. 13: Is a *Miller's Knot with Bow.*

FIG. 14: Shows a way of forming a *Sheet Bend* in the bight of a rope.

FIG. 15: The *Claw Hitch* shown here is used for making picket lines fast to stakes. (*Similar to* PLATE 272, FIGS. 322 and 323.)

FIG. 16: Is a *Crab Hitch.* It is the same as PLATE 272, FIG. 323, except that it is tied on a horizontal object instead of vertical.

FIG. 17: Is a *Strangle Knot.*

FIG. 18: The *Studding Sail Halyard Hitch* shown here is tied in the opposite or reverse way to PLATE 1, FIG. 20. It is used for fastening Studding Sail, Top Gallant, and Gaff Topsail Halyards.

FIG. 19: Is a *Carpenter's Hitch* that is used by carpenters to fasten chalk lines to nails or hooks.

FIG. 20: The *Picket Line Hitch* is used to make picket ropes fast to round objects, etc.

FIG. 21: Is a *Picket Line Hitch with Bow.*

FIG. 22: Shows a *Rolling Hitch with Bow.*

FIG. 23: Is a simple way of making a *Transfer Sling,* that is useful for transferring sea bags on difficult landings.

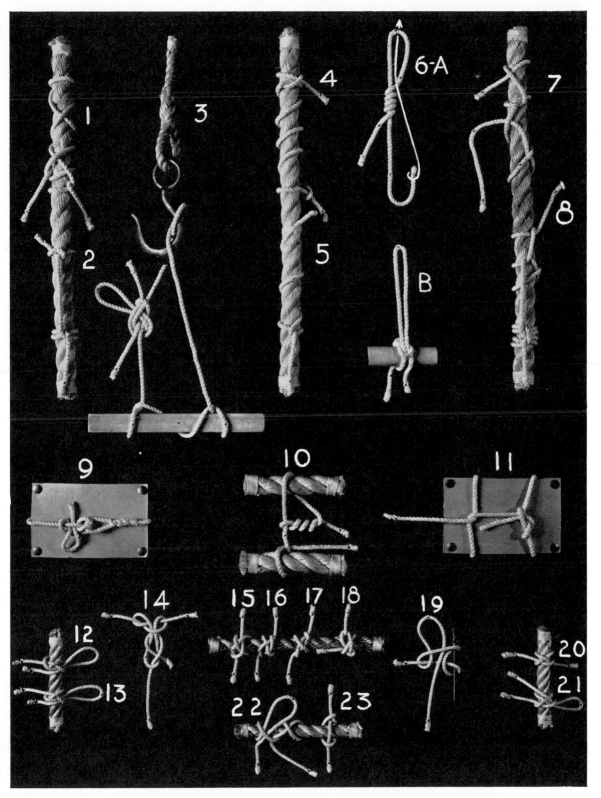

PLATE 324—MISCELLANEOUS KNOTS AND TIES

Plate 325—Miscellaneous Knots and Ties

Figs. 1A and B: Is an *Underwriter's* or *Electrician's Knot*. Used by electricians for securing wires in electrical fixtures. Fig. A shows the method by which the two strands are walled to the left, and Fig. B shows the knot as it appears when pulled up snug.

Fig. 2: Shows a *Round Turn and Buntline Hitch*.

Fig. 3: Is a *Buntline Hitch*. Used as a mooring for skiffs, etc. (*See* Plate 1, Fig. 21 for similar hitch.)

Fig. 4: Is a *Double Buntline Hitch*.

Fig. 5: The *Round Turn and Two Half Hitches* is tied with an eye as illustrated.

Fig. 6: The *Shank Hitch with a Bow* has a slip eye formed in the manner shown.

Fig. 7: Is a *Bulkhead Hitch*. Used for suspending rope coils over a peg or any other suitable object.

Fig. 8: Is another *Bulkhead Hitch*.

Fig. 9: Shows the proper method of forming a *Rope Coil Hitch*.

Fig. 10: Is a *Coil Hitch* that is used for tackles.

Fig. 11: Is another way of forming a *Rope Coil Hitch* which is slightly different from Fig. 9.

Fig. 12: The *Florist's Knot* is used by florists for securing twine.

Fig. 13: The *Grocer's Hitch* is used around the top of paper sacks, etc. The round turns at the bottom indicate how twine is passed around the neck of sacks in order to secure them.

Fig. 14: The *Round Turn and Bosun's Hitch* is the same as a Bosun's Hitch except for the round turn. Upsets easily when strain is removed.

Fig. 15: Shows a way of *making a Hammock fast to a Ring*.

Fig. 16: Shows how *to join Leather Strap Lines*.

Fig. 17: Is a good way *to make a Line Fast between two Rings*.

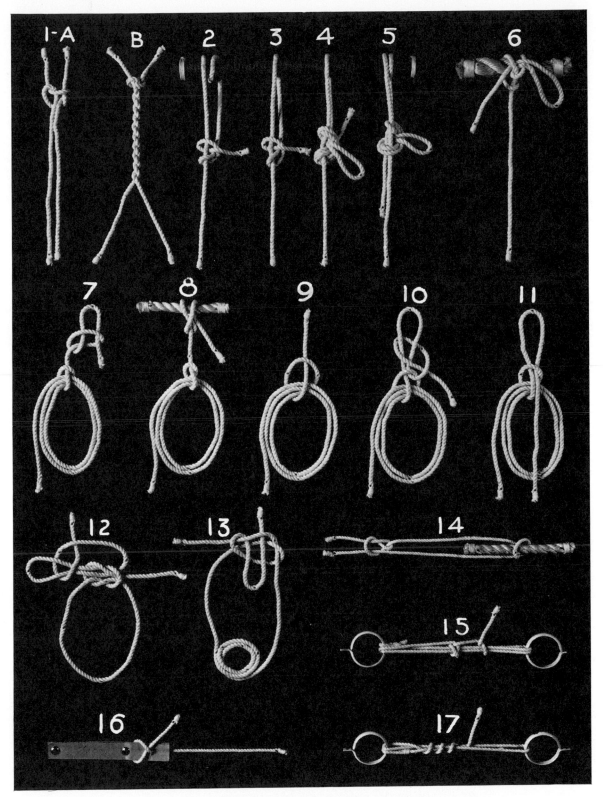

PLATE 325—MISCELLANEOUS KNOTS AND TIES

Plate 326—Miscellaneous Knots and Ties

FIG. 1: Shows a *Pin Hitch* that is used for belaying a sheet to a belaying pin.

FIG. 2: Is another *Pin Hitch* that is tied the reverse or opposite way to FIG. 1.

FIG. 3: Is a *Belaying Pin Hitch*. It can be slacked away gradually when there is a strain on the line. (*See* PLATE 284, FIG. 404.)

FIG. 4: Shows the ordinary way to form a *Rolling Hitch* (*See* PLATE 2, FIGS. 29 and 30.) A good knot for making lines fast on the side of awnings to the taffrail on the poop deck.

FIG 5: Is a *Rolling Hitch with Bow*, tied differently than PLATE 324, FIG. 22.

FIG. 6: The *Mechanic's Hitch* is used on angle irons, pipes, beams, etc.

FIG. 7: Is a *Haywire Bend*. A good way to join the ends of wire together with pliers.

FIG. 8: The *Barrel Knot* shown here is used on gut leaders.

FIG. 9: Is a *Packet Loop* that can be used for a variety of purposes.

FIG. 10: The *Bavin Hitch* is used on small cordage, and can be cast off easily.

FIG. 11: A *Tent Stake Hitch* such as that shown here can be used when rope and stakes are dry. Pressure is applied to tighten by heaving on line *a*.

FIG. 12: Is a *Tent, Stake* or *Storm Hitch*. Used by circus men to make ropes fast. To make the line tight push down at *b*. To slacken, push up at *c*. Two men work together as one heaves on line *a*.

FIG. 13: Is a *Lark's Head and Rolling Hitch*.

FIG. 14: Is a *Sack Hitch* that can be used for bags of potatoes, coal, or anything else in a sack that requires a secure tie.

FIG. 15: The *Eagle Hitch* is used where it is necessary to keep the line from sliding down.

FIG. 16: Shows a *Bag Hitch* opened up to clarify the method of tying.

FIG. 17: Is a *Double Rolling Hitch* formed with an eye in one end of the line.

FIG. 18: The *Round Turn and Shank Hitch*.

FIG. 19: Is a *Combination Square Knot Braid*, which embraces a chain of square knots tied in the manner indicated.

FIG. 20: Is a *Snubber's Hitch*. (*See* PLATE 2, FIG. 38 for a knot with a similar name. PLATE 4, FIG. 92 shows a method that is slightly different.)

FIG. 21: The *Flagpole Hitch* shows a way by which a flagpole can be raised or lowered.

FIG. 22: Is called a *Hanging Hitch*. Used to hold the line in place along the side of fish nets.

FIG. 23: Is a *Mechanic's and Rolling Hitch*.

FIG. 24: The *Deadhead Hitch* is tied in the manner indicated.

FIG. 25: A *Rolling Hitch with Bow* that is tied around an object in a different manner than FIG. 5.

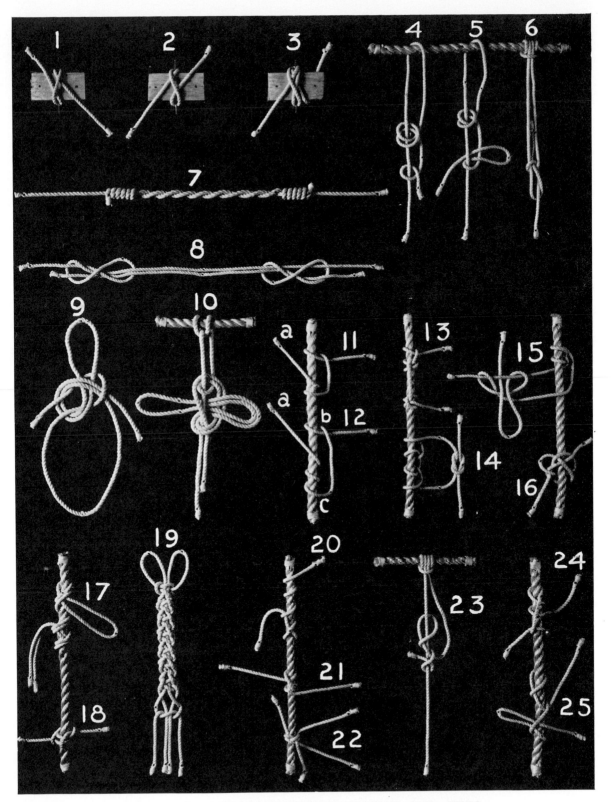

PLATE 326—MISCELLANEOUS KNOTS AND TIES

Plate 327—Miscellaneous Knots and Ties

FIG. 1: The *Ranger Hitch* as it is illustrated here is one of the several different methods that are used for packing on animals. It is hardly necessary to describe the tie, as the picture shows "plainer than words" how this tie is formed.

FIG. 2: Is a *True Diamond Hitch*. The old frontiersmen have passed into memory, and the early days of the West with their buffaloes, Indians, and intrepid horsemen have forever gone; but this Diamond Pack Mule Hitch which played such a prominent part in the winning of the West "from the Yukon to the Rio Grande" is here preserved for posterity and as a tribute to man's resourcefulness in his conquest of the wilderness, from the time of Custer's epic battle with the Sioux on the Little Big Horn to the present day. It can be made fast with an Overhand Slip Eye Knot, which also applies to the other pack ties.

FIG. 3: The *Lone Jack Diamond* of the western prairie can be thrown by one person, and is tied in the manner illustrated.

FIG. 4: Is a *Shipper's Knot*. Used for tying parcel post and other packages.

FIG. 5: Is a *Box Hitch*. A good way to tie a box.

FIG. 6: The *Lumber Hitch* shown here can be used for tying up stakes, flooring, bundles of lath, etc. The method of tying is clearly shown in the illustration.

FIG. 7: Is a *Bingo Hitch* which can be used for tying parcels, etc.

FIG. 8: Shows a way of forming what is commonly known as a *Paper Hitch*.

FIG. 9: The *Shanty Hitch* is pictured plainly, and can be duplicated easily.

FIG. 10: Shows how to form a *Bundle Hitch*.

FIG. 11: The *Crate Sling* can be used for hoisting crated machines, etc.

FIG. 12: The *Stopper Whipping* is nothing more than a series of Overhand Knots, tied on first one side, then the other, until the desired length of the object has been covered.

FIG. 13: Is a *Hangman's Noose with Nine Turns*, opened up in order to clarify the method of tying this form of knot. (*See* PLATE 29, FIGS. 102 to 104 for further details.)

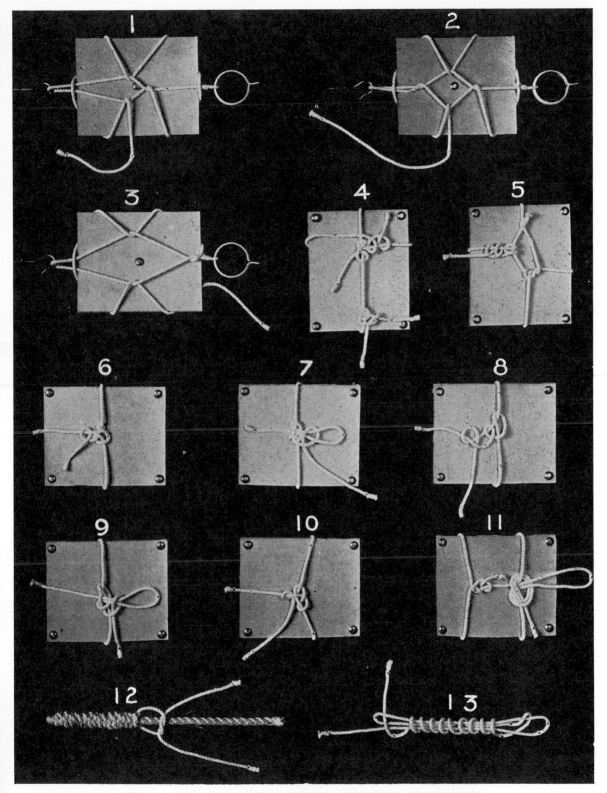

PLATE 327—MISCELLANEOUS KNOTS AND TIES

Plate 328—Miscellaneous Knots and Ties

FIGS. 1A and B: Shows a *Squaw Hitch* which was formerly used by the early Indians for packing their bedding together— hence the name. No packsaddle nor cinch rope is required with a hitch of this type. A shows the way to start the tie and B shows it as it appears when finished. It can be secured by using any kind of knot desired.

FIG. 2: Is a *Roband Hitch,* shown in a different form from that on PLATE 3, FIG. 73.

FIG. 3: Shows a *Magnus Hitch with Bow.* No instructions should be necessary with any hitch as simple as this, for the illustration shows quite clearly how the knot is tied.

FIG. 4: The *Slack Hitch* can be used for taking up slack in loose lines.

FIG. 5: Is a *Round Turn and Paper Hitch,* opened up so that the method of tying can be followed easily.

FIG. 6: Is another of the various types of *Transfer Slings* that can be used for suitcases and many other different objects.

FIG. 7: Shows a way to form a *Figure-of-Eight Horizontal Barrel Sling.*

FIG. 8: A *Hoisting Sling* such as this can be used by two men, to lift heavy trunks, etc.

FIG. 9: Is a *Badger Hitch,* which is a handy tie for small cordage. It can be secured with Half Hitches.

FIG. 10: The *Transfer Sling* shown here can be used for boxes, etc. It is also adaptable for all sorts of light material.

FIG. 11: A *Box Sling* which can be used for any number of purposes, such as lifting chests, boxes, trunks, etc.

FIG. 12: Is a *Transfer Sling* for lifting light objects.

FIG. 13: Is another *Transfer Sling* that is slightly different from the other types.

FIG. 14: Shows the *proper way to suspend a Quarter of Beef.* Used by butchers.

FIG. 15: Is an *Usher's Hat Strap* or *Surgeon's Knot* that is used as a band or strap on ushers' hats. (*See* PLATE 22, FIG. 15.)

FIG. 16: The *Flag Hitch* is a method commonly used to make a halyard fast to a flag. Its form of construction can be easily followed.

FIG. 17: Is a *Dressmaker's Decoration Knot.* Used by dressmakers for tying ribbons, etc., attached to the waists of dresses. It is nothing more than a simple Granny Knot with the ends of the top half of the knot reversed, or pointing in the opposite direction from the way they lead out.

FIG. 18: The *Lark's Head Transfer Sling* shown here can be used for surface landings that require ties on long objects.

FIGS. 19A and B: Shows the way to form a *Fireman's Hitch.* FIG. A illustrates the start and FIG. B is how it appears after it has been completed with a number of round turns.

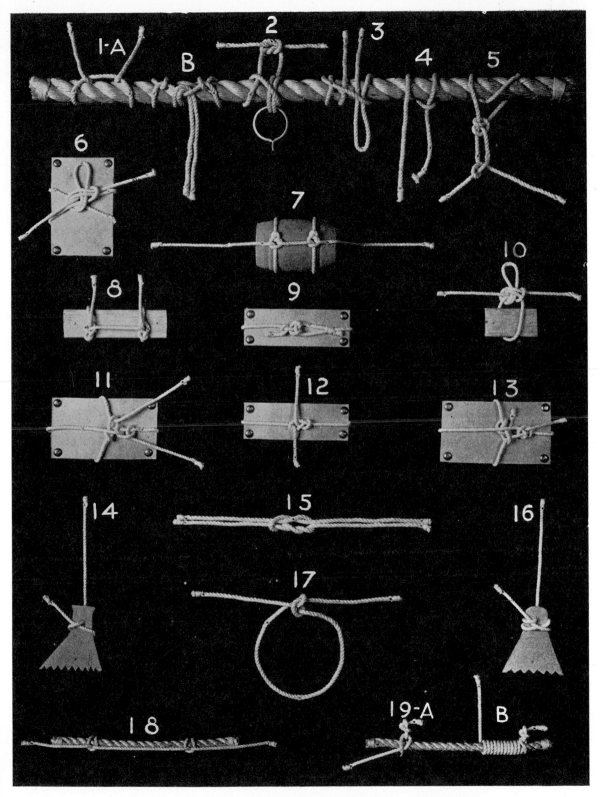

PLATE 328—MISCELLANEOUS KNOTS AND TIES

Plate 329—Miscellaneous Knots and Ties

FIG. 1: This *Packer's Hitch* is used by hunters and trappers to lash loads on pack boards carried on their backs. The load has to be kept up as high as possible on the shoulders in order to lessen the burden of traveling over long distances without tiring. The illustration will serve to clarify how the Hitch is formed in a much better manner than words could describe. It can be made fast with any knot that is satisfactory and easy to tie.

FIG. 2: Shows a *Ladder Hitch*, which is a very good way to make a line fast to a ladder.

FIG. 3: Is a *Lashing Tie*.

FIG. 4: Is a *Drayman's* or *Truckman's Hitch*. It is used for securing the tops of loads on drays, trucks, etc. *See* PLATE 265, FIG. 295 for a similar knot, that is used for practically the same purposes.

FIG. 5: The *Stakeman's Hitch* shown here is used by surveyors, or for any other purpose that requires bundles of stakes to be carried.

FIG. 6: Is a *Jug Sling*, which can be used to carry any kind of a jug or bottle.

FIG. 7: The *Hackamore Halter Tie* was used in the early days of the West for breaking wild and unruly horses. Loop *c* goes around horse's neck with the line *d* on top and *b* underneath. *a* goes over the muzzle to complete the adjustment.

FIG. 8: *Flagpole Strops.* This figure represents a method that can be used to climb a flagpole with the aid of a safety belt. One strop is placed above and one below the safety belt, thus permitting a person to walk up or down the pole easily.

FIG. 9: Is a *Telegraph Strop Hitch*. It can be used in the manner indicated on poles or long objects.

FIG. 10: Is a *Morrell's Seizing* which is used for temporary purposes. It is tied by pulling the end of the line through to form a slip eye, after first taking the necessary round turns. Can be released without difficulty.

FIG. 11: The *Purlin Hitch* is an excellent tie for hoisting horizontal timbers.

FIG. 12: Shows a *Vertical Strop Hitch*, that is passed around the object twice for added security.

FIG. 13: Shows a *Horizontal Strop Hitch*.

FIG. 14: Shows a *Vertical Strop Hitch*, which is the same as previous method except that it is tied for a vertical lift instead of a horizontal one.

FIG. 15: Is a *Binder Hitch*. Handy for securing bags.

FIG. 16: The *Waldo Hitch*, Second Method, is handy for securing the end of a rope to the limb of a tree in order to lower oneself over the edge of a cliff. The rope can be pulled down afterwards by swinging it over the knot.

FIG. 17: The *Bear's Claw Hitch* is another method that can be used for lowering a person down out of a tree or from a pole. By shaking the line free it can then be pulled down.

FIG. 18: Is a *Double Crate Sling*. A secure tie for heavy crates.

FIG. 19: The *Rider Hitch* shown here is the same as a Round Turn and Two Half Hitches, except that it has an additional turn.

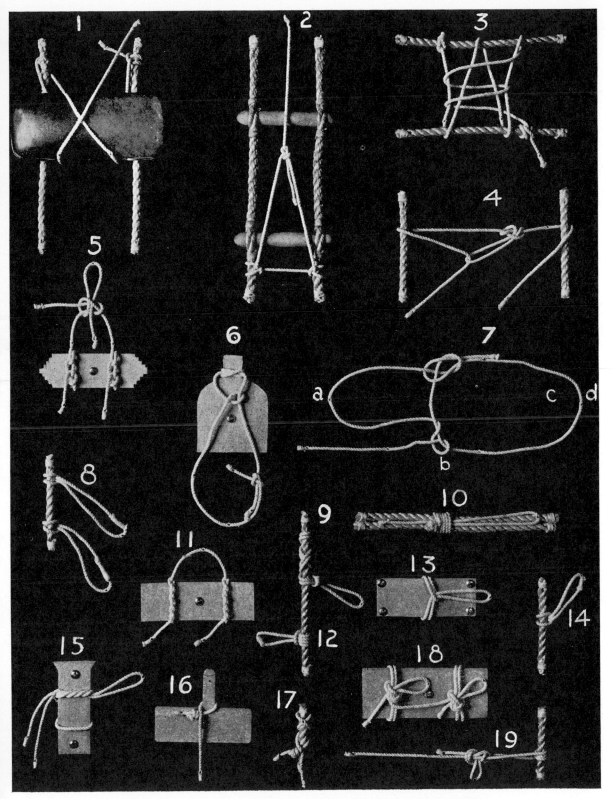

PLATE 329—MISCELLANEOUS KNOTS AND TIES

Plate 330—Miscellaneous Knots and Ties

FIG. 1: This form of tie is called an *Oyster Bend.* Used for any purpose where there will be a severe strain.

FIG. 2: The *Lineman's Hitch,* First Method, is a very good tie for hauling on the end of various objects.

FIGS. 3A and B: Is a *Grizzly Hitch,* which represents one of the numerous methods that can be used for lowering oneself down from the limb of a tree. FIG. A shows the back of the Hitch and FIG. B as it looks from the front side.

FIG. 4: The *Blarney* or *Slack Hitch* is used for holding slack that has been taken up temporarily.

FIG. 5: Shows a *Ball Hitch* that is used for making a line fast on a ball of twine in order to secure same after it has been done up properly.

FIG. 6: The *Boot Hitch* represents a good way to suspend rubber boots while they are drying in order to prevent cracking. The bottom part of the line goes around the toe in the manner indicated.

FIG. 7: The *Stalk Hitch* is a method that is used for binding cornstalks by hand. Its form of construction is easy to follow.

FIG. 8: Is an ordinary *Scaffold Sling* which represents the simplest way to form a tie of this kind.

FIG. 9: Is a *Commercial Fishing Tie.* A very good method for making a small line fast to a large line.

FIG. 10: The *Lineman's Hitch,* Second Method, is tied in a slightly different way from the first method. (*See* FIG. 2.) This type of hitch is very useful for securing pipes, hammers, etc., in order to send them to men working aloft.

FIG. 11: Is a *Can Top Hitch,* which can be used for tightening or loosening the tops of fruit jars after they have become stuck. The rope is intended to represent a stick of wood, which is twisted together with the line on the end, at the same time applying tension on the opposite end at the round turn where the top of the jar is placed. As many turns with the end of the line can be taken as found necessary for added leverage.

FIG. 12: Is a *Bag* or *Half-Moon Needle,* which is most adaptable for sewing on a flat surface, such as in knot work on picture frames, etc.

FIG. 13: Is a *Sail Twine Stopper Knot.* Used for stopping off the end of the twine by taking a number of turns in the manner indicated, after which the needle is drawn through to finish the work.

FIG. 14: A *Hardware Knot* is formed in the manner indicated. Used for various package ties.

FIG. 15: Is a *Line Lashing Tie.*

FIGS. 16A and B: Is an old-time *Bedding Hitch* which was usually thrown by two packers, one on each side. FIG. A shows the underneath side of the hitch, while FIG. B shows the top side after the tie has been completed.

FIG. 17: Is a *Trunk Hitch* which can be used on trunks, boxes, chests or similar objects.

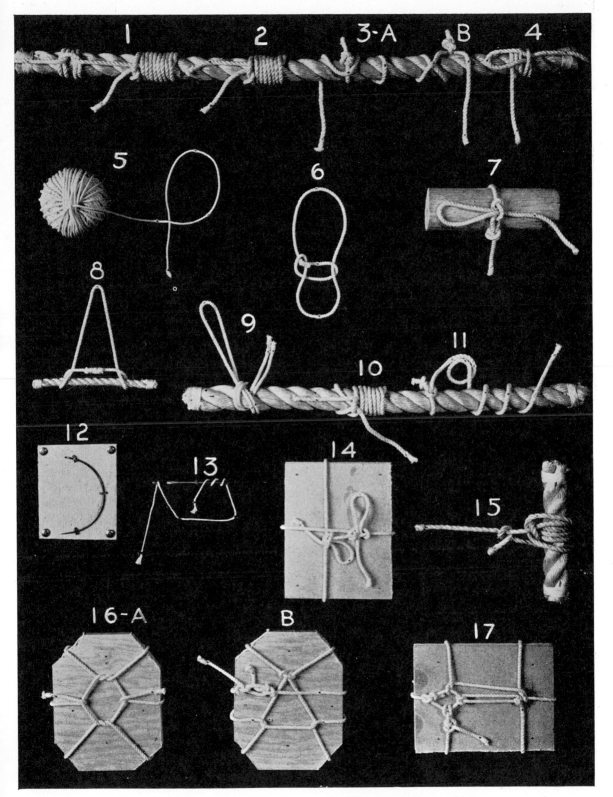

PLATE 330—MISCELLANEOUS KNOTS AND TIES

Plate 331—Miscellaneous Knots and Ties

FIG. 1: Is a *Fish Line Shortening*, which is used for fishing through the ice. When a fish jerks hard enough on the line it spills and runs out. The example shown is tied on rings for clearness.

FIGS. 2A, B and C: Is a *Gasket Shortening*. FIG. A shows how to start the operation of doing up a gasket, while FIGS. B and C show the second and third steps in securing a rope coil of this kind. The cross turns in FIG. C are purposely taken around above the point where the line leads out, for clearness. However, they are usually placed below, as shown in FIG. B. (For further details *see* PLATE 283, FIG. 399.)

FIGS. 3A and B: Is a *Halter Shortening*, that is used for doing up halter ropes. FIG. A shows how the operation is started, upside down, and FIG. B shows how it looks when finished.

FIG. 4: Is a *Heaving Line* or *Sash Cord Coil*. It is practically the same as a Gasket Shortening, except that the round turns are begun at the opposite or lower end.

FIG. 5: Shows a *Handy Way to Secure Small Cordage*.

FIG. 6: Is a *Round Turn and Rolling Hitch*.

FIG. 7: Is *Two Round Turns and a Rolling Hitch*.

FIG. 8: Shows the *proper way to lace Lumberjack's or Hunter's Boots*. The ends are tucked inside at the finish in the manner illustrated.

FIG. 9: Is a *Multiple* or *Six-Fold Figure-of-Eight Knot*. (See PLATE 22, FIG. 19 for an open illustration of this type of knot.)

FIG. 10: *Burlap Hitches* as they are illustrated here are formed so they can be untied from either end of a sack. Round turns around the sack's ears finish it off.

FIGS. 11A and B: Is a *Brickmason's* or *Cement Worker's Hitch*. Used by them to make their lines fast to rectangular stakes. FIG. A shows the back, while FIG. B shows it from the front side.

FIG. 12: Is an *Eleven-Strand Turkish Round Mat*, which is tied somewhat differently from the design on PLATE 158, FIG. 313. When the stage shown in FIG. 313A has been reached, instead of forming the bights parallel to their own parts, as illustrated, the bight leading toward the left is crossed over its own part and the bight leading toward the right is crossed under its own part. Next, close the outside up on both sides with the working end of the line, on each respective side; then pass each line through on the inside of the second pass, from the outside toward the opposite side of the knot. This will then form the third pass from the outside on each side. Each line is returned on the inside of the fourth line, thus forming the fifth line on each side as the weaving continues, with the customary over and under tucks until the knot is finished.

FIG. 13: Is another form of the many different types of *Rose Lashings*. It is tied by taking a number of cross turns, as illustrated. Next, pass the line on top down through between the opening and the crosses, while the underneath line is passed up through the same opening. Both lines are then passed around the crosses in opposite directions, forming two or three round turns, after which they are knotted together with a Square Knot. It is a handy way for seizing two eyes.

FIG. 14: Is a *Thirteen-Strand Turkish Round Mat.* The weaving is continued from PLATE 158, FIGS. 313A and B by following the same procedure as used in extending a seven-strand weave to a nine-strand weave. (See PLATE 158, FIGS. 310A and B.)

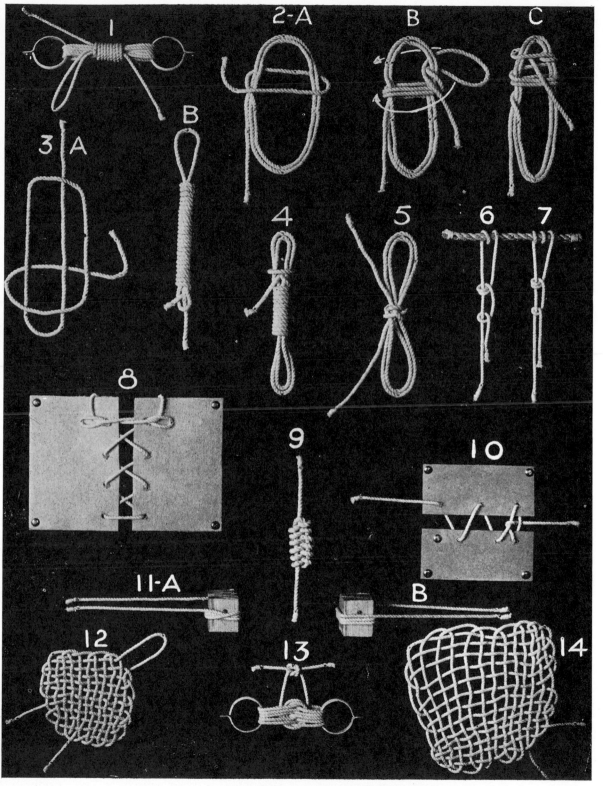

PLATE 331—MISCELLANEOUS KNOTS AND TIES

Plate 332—Boatswains Calls and Hammock Clews

Fig. 1: This is an *English Boatswain's Call with Lanyard.* It is one type of several different kinds that are used in the British Navy. The attached ·Lanyard can be made with *Double Flat* or *English Sennit,* using any number of strands that are suitable for the neck piece. Turk's Heads are applied as illustrated at intervals to serve as seizings and to give the work added distinction. Note the Half Hitch work on lower part of Lanyard.

A Boatswain's Call such as this is one of the oldest and most distinctive pieces of nautical equipment to be handed down from bygone centuries. A call pipe or flute was used in the days of antiquity by which the galley slaves of Greece and Rome kept stroke with their oars. According to history there is also a record that the call pipe was used by the English Crossbowmen in the Crusade of 1248, who were called on deck to attack by its signal. It is further related that when the French under the command of Chevalier Pregant de Bidoux defeated the British in the naval action off Brest on April 25, 1513, the English Commander Lord High Admiral Sir Edward Howard when certain the battle was lost, threw his gold Boatswain whistle into the sea rather than see this badge of honor humiliated in surrender.

Fig. 2: The *Hammock Clews* as shown here are formed in the following way. First measure off the desired length for the twelve bights that are attached to the canvas hammock by a Jackstay after being inserted through the Grommet Eyelets. In order to get the same uniform length in each bight, space twelve nails or screws an equal distance apart and the same length from the Hammock Ring. The other end of the line is now run back and forth between the ring and the screws until all twelve screws are covered with bights. After this operation is completed, the working end of the line is run through the ring in the opposite manner, or vice versa, to the side where the operation was

started. One end of the line will now be running through the ring from underneath, whereas the other end will be running through from the top. Continue by separating the strands with a rule which can be used for a spreader by passing it first over one strand and then under the next, thus bringing one strand up and the next strand down, as for a Sword Mat. After the spreader has been passed all the way through, the outside strands are used as a filler by running them through behind the spreader, and jamming them up snugly in place. This same operation is now continued until six passes of the filler strands have been made, taking care after each pass to drop a bight on each side until the end is reached. As the spreader is run through to separate the strands after each pass with the fillers has been made, caution should be used in picking up the proper strands; the strands that are up should be dropped down and the strands that are down should be picked up. A Square Knot is used to finish the operation. ·It is tied between the two center bights in the manner indicated, after the last pass has been made.

Fig. 3: An *American Navy Regulation Boatswain's Call with Lanyard and Sea Bean.* Note Pineapple Knot on lower part of Lanyard.

Fig. 4: Shows how the twelve bights are attached to the Jackstay after having been passed through the Grommet Eyelets on the edge of the canvas. Heavy canvas is used for the construction of the hammock, which can be any length and breadth desired, with about two inches allowed for seams.

Fig. 5: *Ripping Canvas* is performed by picking up one yarn on the outside. Then with the use of a sharp knife cut alongside of this yarn which is kept under a slight strain as the operation is continued. The canvas is hauled taut to simplify the work.

Fig. 6: Another Type of *British Boatswain's Call.*

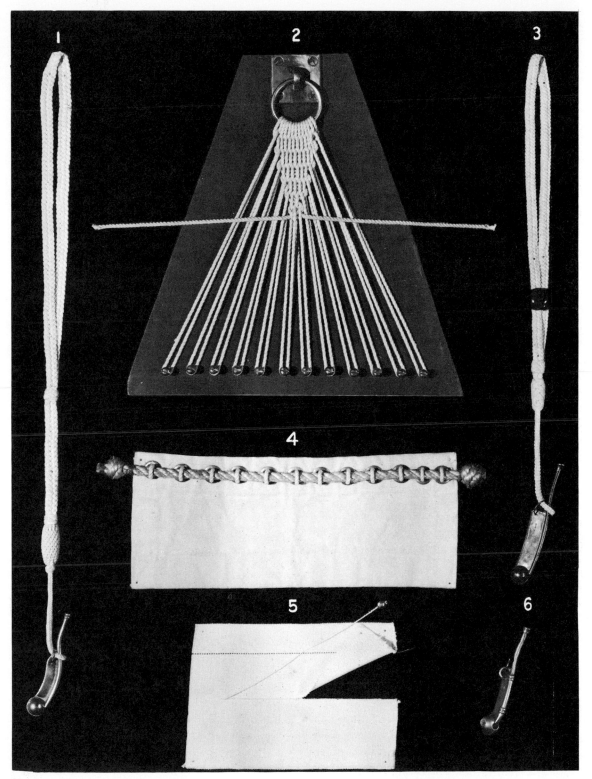

PLATE 332—BOATSWAINS CALLS AND HAMMOCK CLEWS

Plate 333—Mats

FIG. 1A: The *Single Diamond or Triangle Mat* is begun by forming two interlacing bights in the manner shown. The end of the line on the left is then crossed under the line on the right, in order to form additional bights to expand the weave.

B: With this line proceed in the formation of each succeeding bight by running the working end through the weave in the manner shown, after doubling it back to form another bight each time. The drawn-in line indicates how the weave is closed after the operation has been repeated often enough to expand the weave to the proper size.

C: This shows the completed design.

FIG. 2: The *Double Diamond or Triangle Mat* is worked in the same manner as the single method except that it has double strands to give the weave a larger, more compact body.

FIG. 3A: The *Single Queen Anne Mat* is begun with the line laid out in the position shown here.

B: Next form bights with both working ends, with one bight going over, and the other bight going under its own part in the manner indicated. The bights are now passed through each eye that was previously formed, in order to enlarge the weave. After this has been done, the operation will appear as illustrated, with the drawn lines indicating how the ends are passed through to complete the weave.

C: This shows the same weave as it looks when finished. By using the same key as previously described, this mat can be extended to any size desired merely by a repetition of additional bights, before

closing the mat with the last pass, after the desired size has been reached.

FIG. 4: The *Single Queen Anne Mat* is shown here after the weave has been filled in by extending the work with additional passes, as previously explained.

FIG. 5: The *Double Queen Anne Mat* is worked with double strands, otherwise it is the same as the single method.

FIG. 6A: The *Single Napolean Bend Mat Weave* is shown here with the line laid out in the form of an Overhand Knot with the bights pulled out and crossed over as indicated to start the weave. This method of construction is different from the example shown on PLATE 241, FIG. 47.

B: The bight on the right is now crossed over on top of the bight on the left, and the working parts of the line are next passed through the weave as indicated. This will close the pattern up and complete the operation.

C: This shows the finished mat. It can be double or triple passed if a larger mat is desired.

FIG. 7: The *Double Napolean Bend Mat Weave* is shown here with the strands doubled and pulled up in place to form a compact mat weave.

FIG. 8: The *Single Extended Napolean Bend Mat Weave* shows how the bights can be pulled out and crossed over to give additional length to the weave. They are then closed up as the drawn lines indicate.

B: This shows the completed mat design. Mats such as these were very popular among the old-time sailormen, who used them for floor mats and for the bottom of stairs on shipboard.

Plate 334—Miscellaneous Knots

FIGS. 1A and B: The *Prolonged Lanyard Knot* shown here is begun by tying a Granny Knot in a loop. The strands are then passed through the center of the knot as the drawn lines illustrate in FIG. A.

FIG. B shows the completed knot after the strands are pulled taut.

FIG. 2: A *Combination Half Hitch and Overhand Knot.*

FIGS. 3A and B: A *Japanese Brief Knot.*

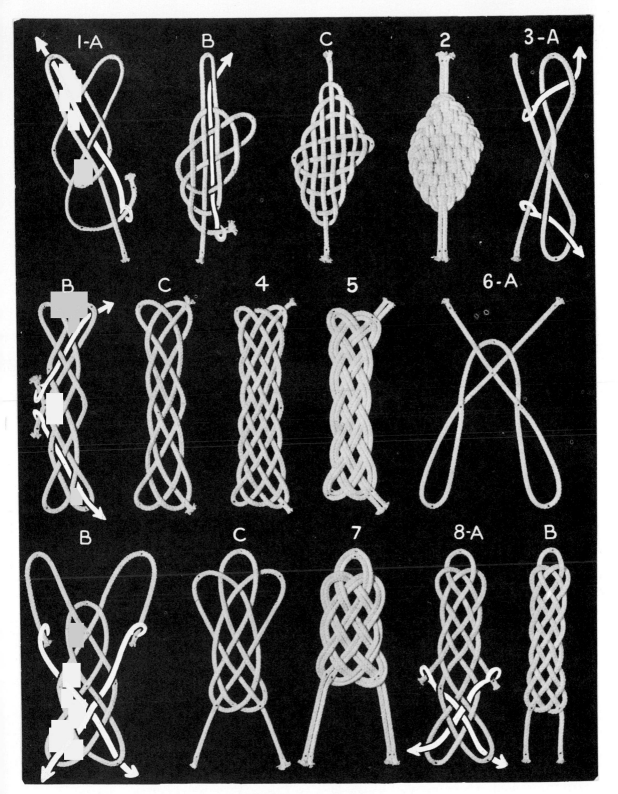

PLATE 333—MATS

FIG. A shows the knot opened up and FIG. B as it appears when closed.

FIGS. 4A and B: A *Japanese Hackamore Knot*. FIG. A is an open illustration while FIG. B pictures the knot closed.

FIG. 5: *Japanese Interlaced Hitches*.

FIG. 6: A *Japanese Combination Overhand Knot*.

FIGS. 7A, B and C: The *Japanese Dragon-fly Knot* as shown here is similar to PLATE 33, FIG. 157. FIG. A is an open illustration of the knot, while FIG. B shows the finished knot from the front and FIG. C as it appears from the back.

FIG. 8: A *Japanese Interlaced Overhand Half-Hitch Knot*.

FIG. 9: A *Japanese Double Overhand Knot* tied in a loop.

Plate 335—Carrick Bend Mat Weaves

FIG. 1A: Shows a *Double Carrick Bend Mat* that may be expanded by following the key illustrated here. It is begun by tying a Carrick Bend with two pieces of doubled line. Another piece of line is then run between each pair of doubled lines, as shown with the working part marked "a" on the right side of the design, which is left incomplete in this picture. The working ends of the extra parts are followed through between each pair of doubled lines to complete the job. It will be necessary to pick up the extra parts of line by tucking under them at times with the working end of a line that is being passed from the opposite direction, in order to make the proper over and under tucks. This brings the passes out in their correct sequence to complete the pattern.

B: After each doubled part has been filled in as previously explained the Mat will then assume the shape portrayed here. Ends may be cut off when the slack has been drawn out of the finished mat work. Such designs as these are novelties which can be used for decorative purposes or for such things as hot plate holders, etc.

FIG. 2: Shows a *Triple Carrick Bend Mat* which follows the same procedure as the double method, except that triple strands are used. Only one part of the design has been filled in here.

FIG. 3A: An *Enlarged Carrick Bend Mat* may be constructed by using additional bights to expand the weave in the manner shown, after first forming a Carrick Bend with single lines to begin the operation. The key to the work is easily understood by following the drawn-in lines that indicate the proper way to proceed.

B: After additional bights have been laid through the top part of the design, like the previous passes on the bottom, the nature of the work will then appear as shown at this stage.

C: The finished design presents the appearance of a slightly oblong shape, as may be observed from the accompanying illustration.

FIG. 4A: An *Extended Carrick Bend Mat* such as this may be developed from the previous example by the use of additional bights to expand the work. The extra bights are worked into the pattern by employing the lines in the manner shown. Follow the drawn-in lines of the previous example. The bights are used in the same manner at this point to expand the weave. They are used to help clarify the operation at this point. This type of mat may be enlarged to suit any requirements, simply by following the same "key" when adding more working parts. See bight marked "a".

B: This shows the shape the mat will assume after being filled in and worked up snug with the ends cut short.

FIG. 5: Portrays a *Carrick Bend Mat* which is worked in similar fashion to the preceeding designs. In this case it is developed into an oblong shape with the four ends on each corner formed into Diamond Knots with frayed out tassels.

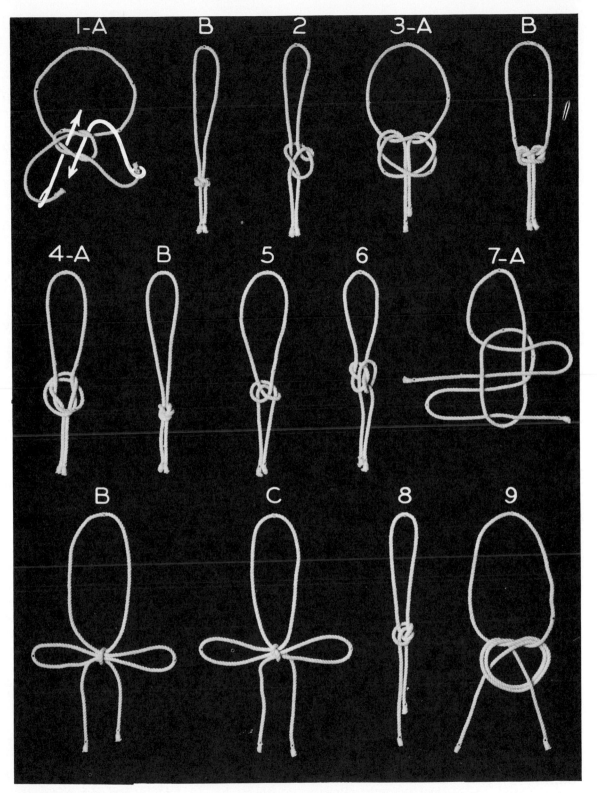

PLATE 334—MISCELLANEOUS KNOTS

Plate 336—Initial Steps in Making a Bath Mat

Fig. 1A: This shows the first step in the preparation of a *Canvas and Swab Twine Bath Mat*. For a 23 x 33 inch Mat, No. 4 or No. 6 canvas can be used, which is sewn down around the edge as shown in this illustration, to start the operation.

B: Using the contents of two deck swabs, lay half of the yarns lengthwise on the canvas, and the other half crosswise. Now lay a second piece of canvas over these yarns in the form of a sandwich, and sew the whole thing together in 2 inch squares, using a heavy-duty canvas sewing-machine, although it can be sewn by hand if no machine is available.

C: This illustrates the appearance of the proper way to sew the squares, as just described in the last paragraph.

D: The canvas is now cut with a sharp knife about 3/16 of an inch on the inside of the sewing, as indicated in the top panel on the left. After this has been completed, the yarns are now exposed as shown in the bottom panel on the left. Using a flat pointed wooden stick, under-run half the strands and cut same. Now underrun the other half of the strands and cut these also. This operation is illustrated with the use of a heavy line both lengthwise and crosswise in the top panel on the right. After the Swab Twine is cut, a ball will form at each corner of a 2 inch square as shown in the bottom panel on the right. The mat is now completed. To prevent the yarns from pulling out, soak the mat in very hot water for about two hours.

Plate 337—A Finished Bath Mat Design

The *Bath Mat* as previously described, will appear as it is pictured here after being completed. A mat of this kind should be a welcome addition to any home as it is made to last indefinitely and will be found a most useful article for the bath room.

Plate 338—Ornamental Knots

Fig. 1A: The *Four Leaf Flower Knot* resembles the Three Leaf Dragonfly (Plate 137, Fig. 1) in structural design, except that it has an additional bight which gives another leaf to this ornamental creation.

B: The same knot as it appears after being worked up neatly into shape.

Fig. 2: The *Crowned Four-Leaf Flower Knot* is formed in the same manner as Fig. 1, and then the bights are crowned, thereby transforming the knot into one of the most handsome and symmetrical designs in existence.

Fig. 3A: A *Two-Leaf Ornamental Knot* based on the Two Leaf Dragonfly (Plate 49, Fig. 363). Its method of construction is left open to illustrate the slightly different variation.

B: As the same knot appears when completed.

Fig. 4: The *Mathematical Design* shown here may be traced without much effort by simply observing the over and under tucks. If this knot is worked up closely into a compact body and crowned with the three bights, it then assumes another kind of pattern.

Fig. 5: After two crowns have been applied to the previous design it will appear as shown here. By using two or more crowns it is possible to build this knot up into a more compact body than can otherwise be obtained by using only one crown.

Fig. 6: The *Flower Knot with Closed Bights* has its five bights drawn together to form a closely knit compact body.

Fig. 7: Another *Four-Leaf Knot,* similar to Fig. 1, that resembles a flower. This knot is formed in a different manner to the previous method, as can be observed

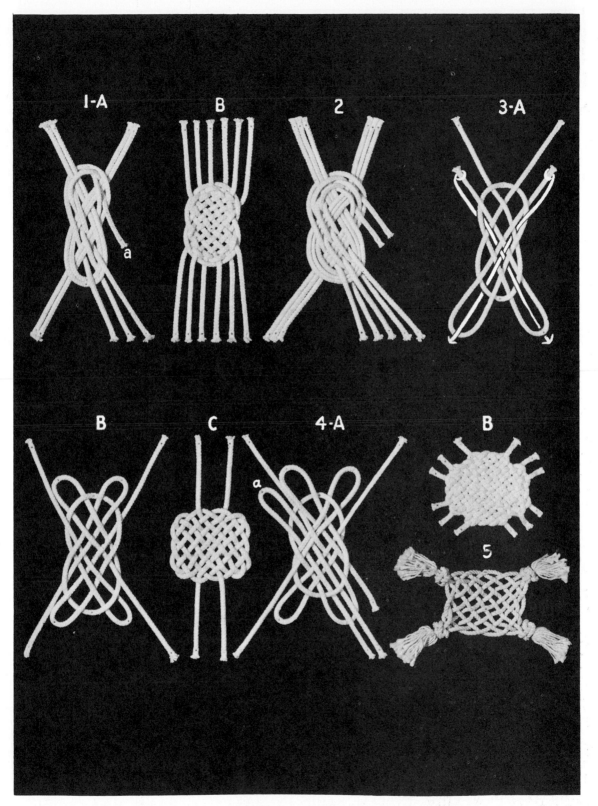

PLATE 335—CARRICK BEND MAT WEAVES

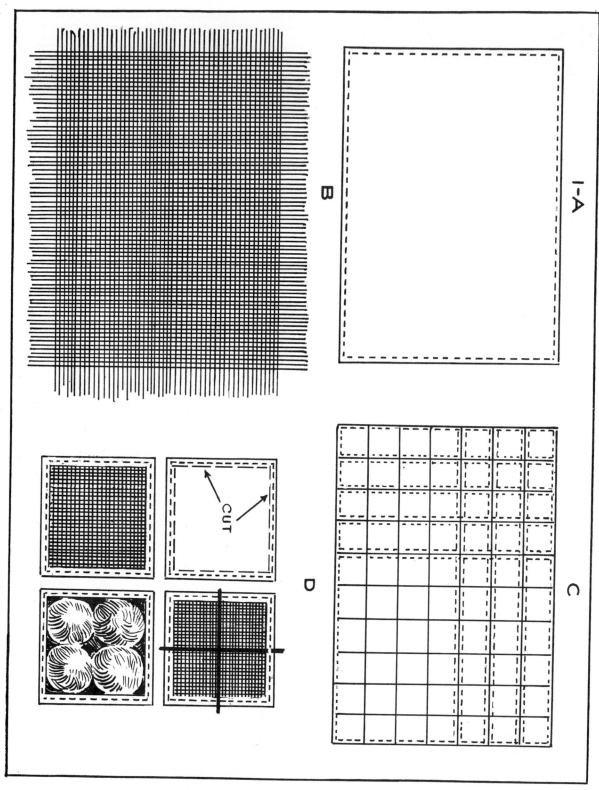

PLATE 336—INITIAL STEPS IN MAKING A BATH MAT

PLATE 337—A FINISHED BATH MAT DESIGN

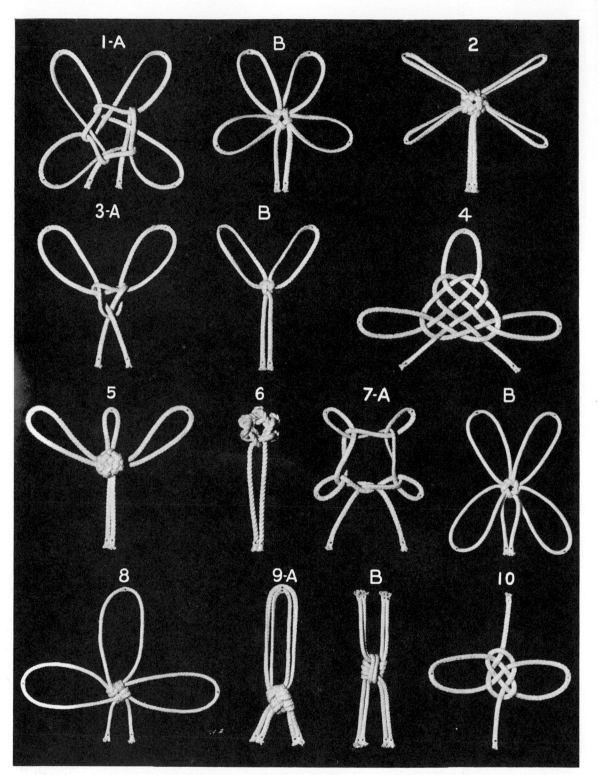

PLATE 338—ORNAMENTAL KNOTS

[*Plate 339–40*]   Appendix   635

from the open illustration, but after it is pulled up, it is transformed into an almost direct replica of its relationship with the other pattern.

B: This shows the structural appearance of the body. Its similarity of design can be seen at a glance, when compared with the previously mentioned method.

FIG. 8: *The Three-Leaf Dragonfly Knot with Doubled Body* has its interior tied with two passes instead of one, as for the regular method. This procedure gives it a different appearance and improves the structural design.

FIG. 9A: The *Double Extended Japanese Crown Knot* includes the same principle of construction as for the regular method (PLATE 22, FIG. 14) with the exception of an added extension of the weave.

B: This shows a back view of the same knot.

FIG. 10: The *Mathematical Design* shown here represents another of the many varieties of knot work that are used in certain kinds of calculations in scientific branches of mathematical reckoning.

Plate 339—Miscellaneous Knots

FIG. 1A: A *Japanese Three-Leaf Flower Knot*. Shows an open illustration of how the knot is woven in similar fashion to a Carrick Bend in a loop.

B: Pictures the knot as it appears when pulled up snug with each leaf adjusted to the proper size.

FIG. 2: A *Japanese Rope Shortening*. It can be followed easily from the photograph.

FIG. 3A: A *Japanese Interlocking Knot* that can be traced easily from the open illustration.

B: Shows how the knot appears when pulled up.

FIG. 4: A *Japanese Lock Knot* that can be followed without difficulty from the photograph.

FIG. 5: The *Japanese Masthead Knot*

shown here is made somewhat similar to PLATE 24, FIG. 44, except that the top part has another line on the inside that is woven through the knot in a manner that can be readily observed.

FIG. 6: A *Japanese Ornamental Knot* that can be traced by following the pattern.

FIG. 7: The *Japanese Sheet Bend* shown here is an open illustration of the *right-hand* method of tying this knot.

FIG. 8: The *Japanese Sheet Bend* shown here is an open illustration of the *left-hand* method of tying this knot.

FIG. 9A: A *Japanese Four-Fold Two-Leaf Blood Knot*. Illustration shows the open knot.

B: Pictures it as it appears when pulled up.

Plate 340—Miscellaneous Knots

FIG. 1A: A *Japanese Ceremonial Knot*. It is made in the manner illustrated, with the drawn line indicating how the ends of the cord are passed down around the bottom, then up underneath their own parts.

FIG. B: Shows the completed design.

FIG. 2A: A *Japanese Four-Loop Flower Tie* that is similar to the one shown in PLATE 147, FIG. 135 except that it is pre-

sented in a slightly different manner. This shows how the knot is laid out.

FIG. B: Shows how it appears after being tied with a Reef Knot in the center.

FIG. 3: A *Japanese Package Tie* that is formed in the opposite way to the regular manner of tying this knot.

FIG. 4: Another form of *Japanese Package Tie* that can be followed by closely observing the illustration.

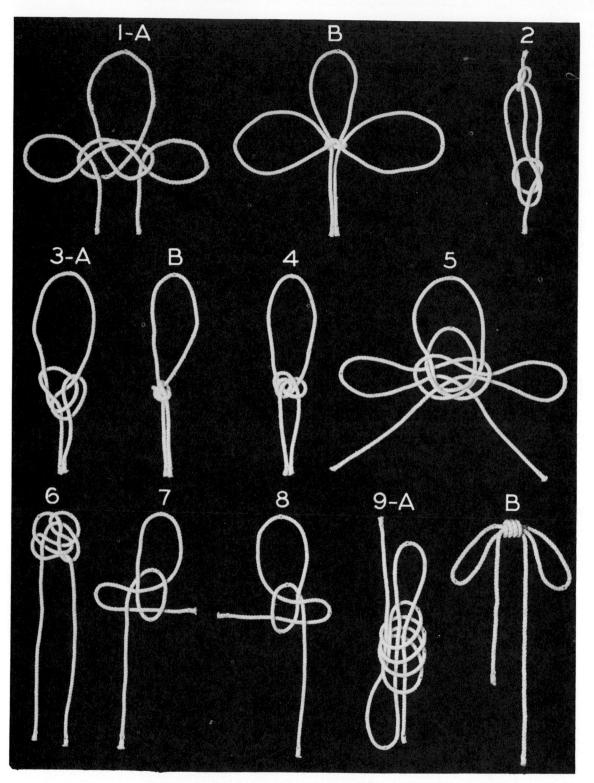

PLATE 339—MISCELLANEOUS KNOTS

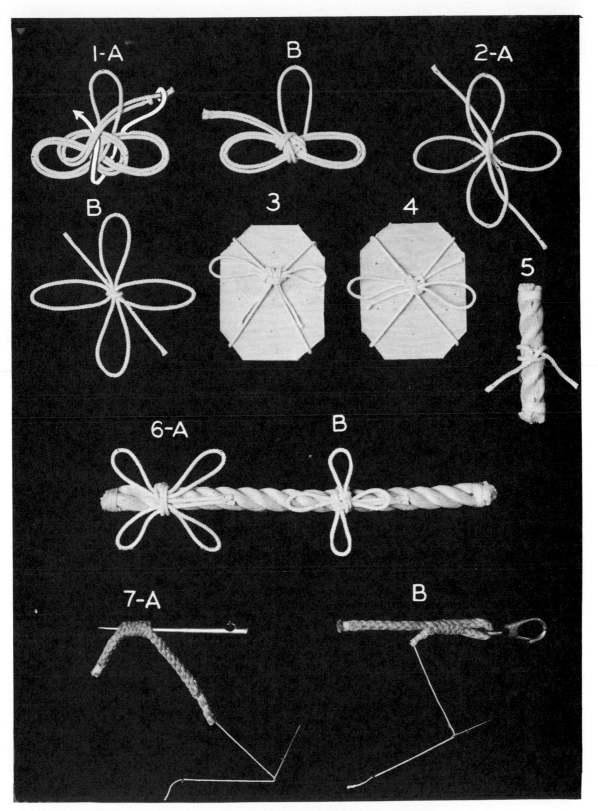

PLATE 340—MISCELLANEOUS KNOTS

FIG. 5: A *Combination Lock Hitch* made in the manner indicated.

FIG. 6: The *Four-Leaf Japanese Temple Knot* has the four leaves laid out as illustrated. They are then crowned and the knot will appear as in FIG. 6B.

FIG. 7A: A *Navy Signal-Halliard Splice.* It is an eye turned in the end of Signal Halliards for snap hooks and rings. About one and one-half inch from end of line, taper the halliard almost down to a point by cutting some of the strands out at different intervals. Insert sail needle and twine

about taper and make two or three marlin hitches to secure tapered end.

About six inches from end of halliard insert pricker or small marline spike as shown for about two inches down through the center. Haul sail needle twine and tapered end through ring or snap hook to be used, then withdraw pricker or marline spike and haul end of halliard through the opening that was made. (See FIG. 7B:) Cut off tapered part, leaving about one-half inch of end. Haul part way back and sew end through body of halliard to finish off.

Plate 341—Lacing Rawhide, etc.

FIG. 1: The *Cobbler's Stitch with Rawhide Lacing* is shown here. A leather punch is used to punch the required amount of holes.

FIG. 2: The *Marline-Hitched Rawhide* lacing is another way to perform work of this type.

FIG. 3: The *Crossed Rawhide Lacing* shows how the lacing is crossed back and forth for a stitch of this design.

FIG. 4: The *Running Rawhide Lacing* is one of the simplest ways to lace leather.

FIG. 5: The *Round Rawhide Lacing* is performed in the same manner as for a Round Stitch in canvas work.

FIG. 6: The *False Braid Eye Splice* in Leather shows how leather thongs are spliced into a strip of leather in similar form to a false braid.

FIG. 7: The *Double Eye Bend in Leather* is formed by running the end of each part through the eye of the opposite part. They are then pulled together until each eye fits snugly up against the other. The eyes are split the proper length with a knife. This operation is determined by the size of the piece of leather to be run through each eye.

FIG. 8: *Shoemaker's Hidden Stitch in Leather.* Using a Shoemaker's awl or any sharp-pointed instrument, cut the leather about half way through, then using a

sharp knife, cut the leather at a 45° angle. Punch out holes for sail twine with an awl along the groove where leather has been cut. As the work proceeds the sail twine should be left slack until sewing has been completed. Now pick up strands at the first stitch and haul them taut, bringing the edges of the leather together. After the operation has been completed a fid should be used to smooth the ridge down where the seams have brought the leather together. Leather should always be worked while wet, as it is softer, more pliable and thus easier to handle.

FIG. 9: *False Cross Pointing* joined with a Shoemaker's Hidden Stitch. The leather is laid out flat and scored diagonally to produce the cross-pointed effect.

FIG. 10: The *Eye Splice in Leather* is formed by cutting the eyes the required distance apart, then run the top standing part through the lower eye. Next bend the top part back and run the lower end through the eye of the top part. Pull the parts up and the operation is complete.

FIG. 11: *Square Crowning in Leather* is begun by first splitting the leather up a distance from both ends. The work is then started by crowning the four strands alternately, or first one way and then the opposite way until the work is as long as desired.

FIG. 12: The *Locked Herringbone*

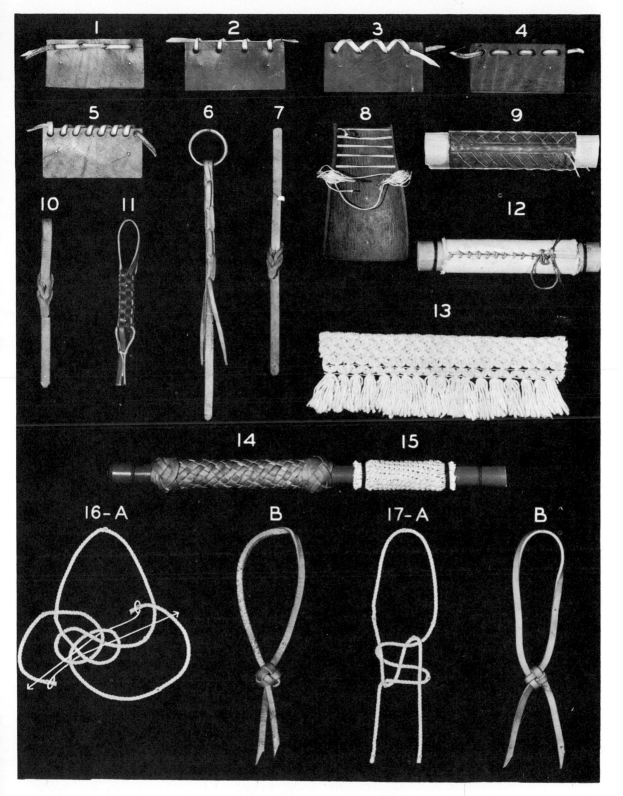

PLATE 341—LACING RAWHIDE, ETC.

Stitch is performed in the same manner as the regular method, except that a turn is taken around the top of each stitch with the needle in order to give the work a more secure finish. This type of stitch is more dependable than any other and is preferred by most sailmakers for mending sail.

FIG. 13: *McNamara Lace* such as this represents the usual way of forming design in stripped canvas, after the horizontal threads have been withdrawn from the canvas for the proper distance. The remaining vertical threads are then joined together with Clove Hitches to form diamond-shaped designs as shown. The work is finished off with tassels that are formed by taking half of each set of previous threads and joining them together in the usual manner.

FIG. 14: *Cross-Pointing with Leather.* Care should be taken when doing this type of work, as leather has a tendency to stretch and so should be worked very carefully. This kind of work is very attractive when neatly done. Three Strand Turk's Heads are used to finish off the ends in this case.

FIG. 15: *Square-Knot Pointing* represents a way of covering a cylindrical object with this type of work, which is nothing more than a series of Square Knots joined together.

FIG. 16A: The *Carrick Diamond Neckerchief Design* shows how the line is laid out and joined with a Carrick Bend. The ends are then pulled through the center of the knot as indicated.

B: This illustrates the same design in leather after being worked up snug.

FIG. 17A: The *Japanese Crown Neckerchief Design* is begun by laying the line out and lacing each part around and through the other part as pictured here.

B: This shows the completed design in leather after being snugly worked up.

Plate 342—Ornamental Knots

FIG. 1: The *Simple Ornamental Weave* shown here can be followed without difficulty by observing the over and under tucks that comprise the pattern of the knot.

FIG. 2A: The *Shamrock Brief Knot* embraces a combination of both these knots. Proceed as for the Brief Knot (PLATE 27, FIG. 3) but instead of closing the design up after the first two steps have been completed, Overhand Knots are added around the bight and then the knot is closed after the bights have been pulled out in same manner as PLATE 240, FIG. 45, to form the Shamrock part. The ends of the line are then run through both Square Knots from opposite sides, in the same way a Brief Knot is closed and which has only the first Square Knot to be tied included in this operation.

B: This shows the knot after the previously explained operations have been completed.

FIG. 3A: The *Shamrock Half-Brief Knot* includes the same principle of construction as the previous method, except there is only one Square Knot to run the ends through after bights have been pulled out to form the Shamrock part of knot.

B: This shows the completed design.

FIG. 4: The *Crowned Mathematical Design* is a reproduction of PLATE 338, FIG. 5 with the bights pulled out and crowned twice to form a compact body after the knot has been pulled up snug, with the weave drawn together, in order to apply the crowns more symmetrically.

FIG. 5A: The *Chinese Button Knot* has been used for centuries by Chinese tailors who employ it for a variety of purposes, such as the forming of soft buttons for pajamas and underwear. These are more comfortable for clothes of this sort, than the harder buttons of other varieties, and at the same time they are almost indestructible. The knot is shown here in a flat

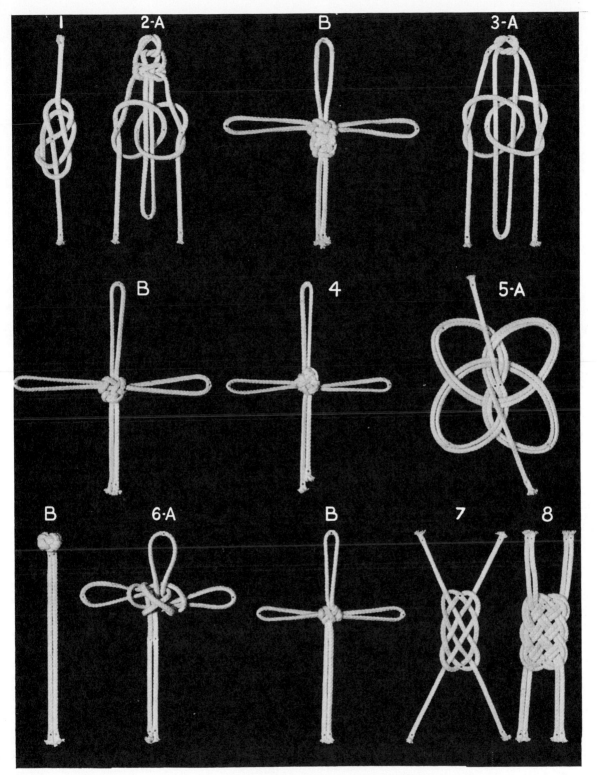

PLATE 342—ORNAMENTAL KNOTS

pattern exactly as it is tied by the Chinese. After this stage has been reached, the knot is next capsized or flipped over the two working ends of the line and worked taut.

B: After being adjusted and pulled up properly it will now appear as in this illustration.

Fig. 6a: A *Novelty Knot* that is based on the Three-Leaf Chinese Temple Design (Plate 137, Fig. 3). The weave is shown open here.

B: This pictures same design after being pulled up snug in a neat pattern of symmetry and beauty in its crossed-strand body effect.

Fig. 7: Shows the *Double Ornamental Mat Weave.*

Plate 343—General Knot Work

Fig. 1: The *Stevedore-Knot Becket Bend* shows a way of converting this knot into a Becket Bend in a Loop. The end of the line is passed through as indicated and the opposite end is then pulled taut to form an unusual type of this variety of knot. In this case the Stevedores Knot is tied in the reverse way.

Fig. 2: The *Snodder* forms a means of hoisting lumber in Navy yards on ships, etc. It is nothing more than a hook on a line with an eye splice at each end.

Fig. 3: The *Superior Hangman's Noose* is tied in the same manner as the usual way except that the bight is laid out with two passes instead of one, before taking the usual amount of turns to form the noose. The working end of the line is then put through the bottom part in the form of an eye which is then locked by passing the single end of the line through the eye. This type of Hangman's Noose is a novelty. However it has additional strength and is a fool-proof method of construction. Care should be taken in the adjustment of the two lines that form the noose, as the slack is worked back and forth until the two lines mate.

Fig. 4: The *Crowned Three-Leaf Dragonfly* is shown here with the three bights crowned on one side of the knot to form a novelty tie. This knot will be found illustrated on Plate 137, Fig. 1.

Fig. 5: The *Crowned Two-Leaf Dragonfly* is formed in the same manner as the previous method. This knot is illustrated on Plate 49, Fig. 363.

Fig. 6: The *Reverse Crabber's-Eye Knot* is formed into a False Bowline here.

Fig. 7: The *Life Ring* shown here has a jackstay seized to the Life Ring with five-strand Turk's Heads to form an ornamental design.

Fig. 8: The *Double-Passed Single Bowline on the Bight* is made the same as in Plate 266, Fig. 303, except that the line is double-passed on the bottom part as illustrated.

Fig. 9: The *Triple-Passed Single Bowline on the Bight.* This and the former method can be used on a heaving line or any other small line to drag a hawser with.

Fig. 10a: The *Triangle Knot* can be tied by taking a round turn in a line to form a loop. This will automatically bring the line together so that two bights can be separated at the upper end. Close these bights together by forming a Wall Knot which will then leave another bight on the bottom as the slack is worked out of the knot. This illustration shows one of the bights already walled.

B: As the knot will appear after both bights have been walled.

c: The same knot is shown here after the slack has been worked out and pulled taut.

Fig. 11: A *Baggy Wrinkle* such as that shown here is used in the form of a gasket to protect the paint on masts, or to keep new paint from running down on another color below. It is nothing more than a quantity of swab twine laid around an

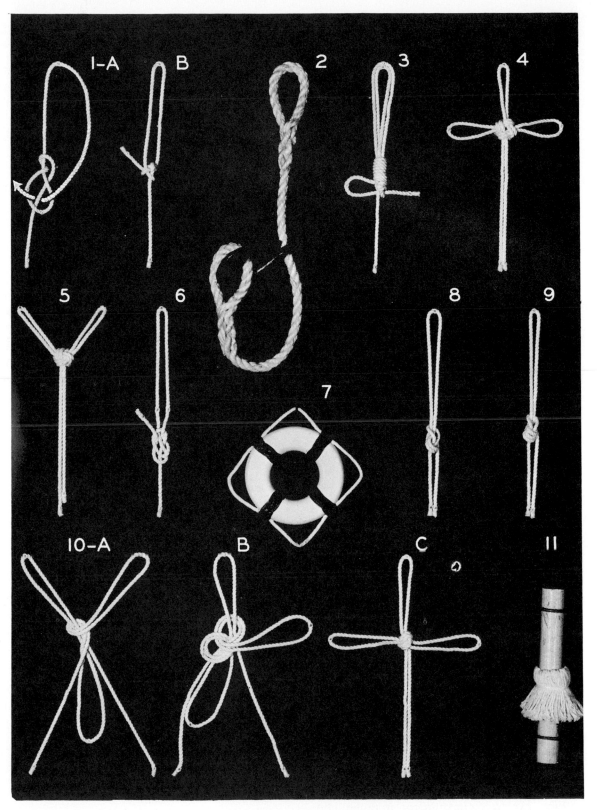

PLATE 343—GENERAL KNOT WORK

object, then seized in the middle. The twine is then folded down over the seizing

and another seizing is applied to secure the operation.

Plate 344—Diver's Hitches and other Ties

FIG. 1A: A Diver's Hitch as pictured here is often used in salvage diving operations. Divers become expert at making such ties and are capable of forming most any knot they need without being able to see the line they are working with. It is formed by simply taking a couple of twists in the line, then bring the bight of the working end back through the eye that was previously formed by the twists.

B: This shows the same tie after being pulled taut.

FIG. 2: The *Single Diver's Hitch "Rigged"* is shown here. It may be used to exert a strain between two objects, and if applied energetically enough the necessary leverage can be obtained to draw objects together, providing they are not too heavy.

FIG. 3: The *Double Diver's Hitch "Rigged"* increases the leverage where additional exertion is needed to heave two objects together or to keep them from drifting apart in an emergency.

FIG. 4: The *Double Diver's Hitch "Rigged"* may be secured as shown here and, if instant release is contemplated, a slipped bow can be used to finish off.

FIG. 5: A *Surgeon's Knot in the Bight* may be formed by laying the line out as for a Marline-spike Hitch; then pull the lower part up through the body of the knot as indicated with the drawn line and result will be the same as shown in FIG. B.

FIG. 6: A combination *Cask and Hackamore Knot* that defies description is shown here. It is a blending of these two knots and can be followed by tracing the weave much easier than it can be explained.

FIG. 7A: A *Square Knot* may be converted into a Lark's Head on the standing part over the top part, or by capsizing the knot, in other words. This operation can be accomplished in a matter of seconds

and the knot will then be transformed into a Lark's Head as shown in FIG. B.

FIG. 8: *Half Hitches* may be reinforced by running the line back around the object it is attached to, then back down through the Hitches.

FIG. 9: This shows the same tie pulled up snug, which makes a neat compact knot.

FIG. 10A: The *Overhand* or *Half-Knot Bowline* represents an ingenious way of forming a Bowline. After the Overhand Knot has been formed as shown, pull on the strand on the right hand side. This operation automatically transforms the knot into a Half Hitch and at the same time transfers the strand on the left side to the right side. The Bowline is then formed as indicated. See FIGS. B and C.

FIG. 11A: The *Tumble Bowline, Left-Handed Method* is formed in this manner. Next hold the working end designated as **a**, while at the same time turning the standing end **b** up and away from you. This maneuver will form the Bowline which is then hauled taut as the standing end is brought back down in place.

B: The completed Bowline is shown here. This and the previous method are often used by sailors and other people who prefer trick methods of forming this well known knot.

FIG. 12A: A line may be run through a ring with an independent eye formed in the bight afterwards and then passed back over the ring and onto the standing part where it assumes the position of a Lark's Head.

B: After the operation already described has transformed the line into a Lark's Head, it will appear as shown.

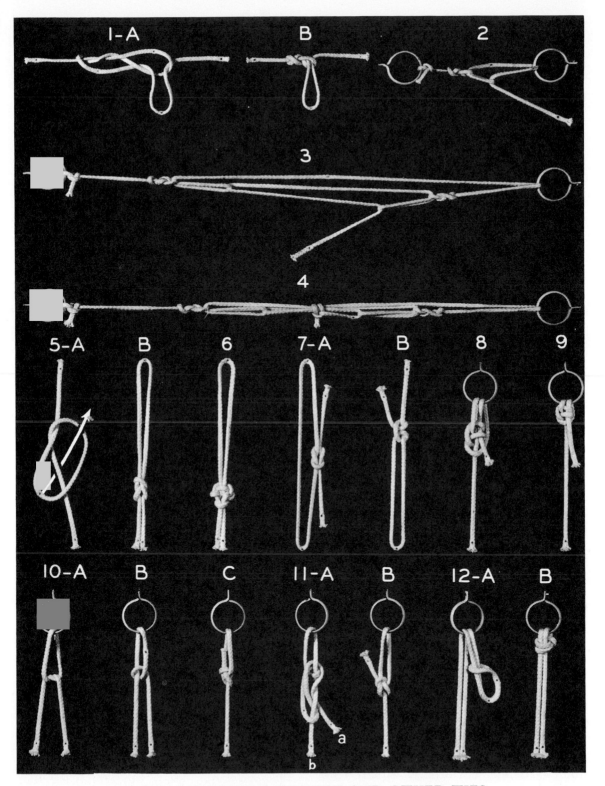

PLATE 344—DIVER'S HITCHES AND OTHER TIES

Plate 345—Sennit Braiding

Fig. 1: The *Interlocking Sennit*. It is of simple construction and may be formed with nothing more than a series of Interlocking Hitches, after first starting with an Overhand Knot for the base of the braid. Each succeeding pass is interlaced around and through the previous pass. This forms a Sennit of a slightly spiral nature.

Fig. 2: The *Spiral Sennit*. This design represents a serious of Half Knots that are formed one on top of the other, which produces a spiral pattern. Spirals such as these have invaluable use in numerous kinds of Square Knot work where they are used for creating different variations in the pattern of the design. Each Half Knot is tied the same way every time a new knot is formed, thus creating a true spiral effect.

Fig. 3: The *Square-Knot Sennit* shown here has the Square Knots pulled close together which produces a very neat uniform appearance. When tied around a core this work is known as "flats" in Square Knot vernacular.

Fig. 4: The *Square-Knot Loop Sennit*. It is tied by spacing each Square Knot an equal distance apart from the previous knot, thereby creating a loop effect in the general pattern.

Fig. 5: The *Four-Strand Square Half-Knot Sennit*. By working the strands in alternating pairs with a succession of left and right Half Knots, the design will acquire a handsome square effect with twin edges. Strands one and two are tied on top of strands three and four in the manner shown, and vice versa.

Fig. 6: The *Four-Strand Square-Knot Folding Sennit*. Form half a Square Knot with strands one and two, then fold strands three and four alternately over the top from their respective sides. Now form the other half of the Square Knot with strands one and two again and then repeat the same procedure as before. The result-

ing Sennit will have a handsome flat symmetrical appearance.

Fig. 7: The *Six-Strand Square-Knot Folding Sennit*. It is worked in similar manner to the four strand method except for the additional strands. In this case, strands one and two are used for tying each half of the Square Knot, while strands three, four, five and six are alternately folded over the top from their respective sides after each half of the Square Knot is formed. The resulting Sennit has a more compact body than the previous example.

Fig. 8: The *Four-Strand-Single Folding Sennit*. It is tied by first folding strands one and two over the top from each opposite side. Then repeat the same process with strands three and four from their respective sides. This Sennit builds very fast and has a most unusual and novel appearance.

Fig. 9: The *Four-Strand-Double Folding Sennit* (eight strands). It is worked the same way as the single method, except that the strands are doubled.

Fig. 10: The *Three-Strand-Double Triangle Crown Sennit* (six strands). By reversing the crowns each time, the resulting Sennit will assume a perfect triangular shape. It is a Sennit of unusual distinction and beauty.

Fig. 11: The *Three-Strand-Double Helixed Round Crown Sennit* (six-strand). By tying the crowns the same way each time, the Sennit will form a perfect helix with a handsome round surface. In this case the crowns revolve the same way each time.

Fig. 12: The *Eight-Strand Half-Knot Round Sennit*. Seize the strands together, then begin by tying a Right Half-Knot with each set of opposite strands. Next, tie two Left Half-Knots on top of the previous knots with the other two sets of opposite strands, in the same manner. Continue to alternate by tying first one

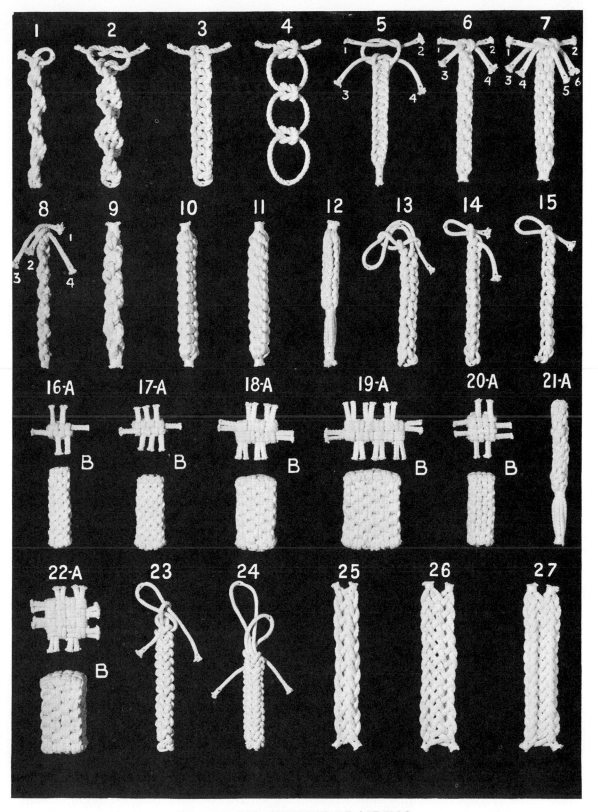

PLATE 345—SENNIT BRAIDING

pair of opposing strands and then the other with Right Half-Knots from one side, then with Left Half-Knots from the other side, etc., until the braid has reached a sufficient length. This operation will build into one of the oddest Sennits in existence. It forms a basically round braid, yet there are actually four individual weaves in its make up, each of which resemble an ordinary Three-Strand Sennit.

Fig. 13: The *Double Foundation Crocheting Stitch Sennit*. It comes from Caulfield and Saward's Dictionary of Needlework. Start by tying a Tom Fool's Knot, then form a bight through the left end with the right end of the Tom Fool's Knot. Continue forming eyes with each additional bight which in this case is worked from the right to left in the manner illustrated. Note, that after each bight is formed through the previous eye, the line is then run through the middle of its own two parts before being inserted through the eye of the last bight. It is then brought up to form another eye for each succeeding bight as the work proceeds. This Sennit can also be worked the opposite way, from left to right.

Fig. 14: The *Two-Strand Triangle Spool Sennit*. It comes from "Bocher's Cordes, Tresses et Noeuds." Each one of the three sides represents a different type braid. By forming a bight in a Slip Overhand Knot and then leading first one bight and then the other through the eye of the bight from the opposite end, the result will automatically assume a three-sided braid when each part is worked as pictured here.

Fig. 15: The *One-Strand Triangle Spool Sennit*. This braid was developed from the preceding example. Two of its sides are alike. Otherwise, as can be noted, it is worked in the same general way as its predecessor, except that only one strand is used in this case.

Fig. 16A: The *Single Six-Strand Oblong Sennit*. It is worked in Spritsail-Sheet fashion by leading the end strands parallel to each other across the body of the weave to the opposite side. These two strands are then crowned by alternately working from first one side and then the other with the side strands. This method can be readily grasped by observing the illustration at this point.

B: The body of the Sennit is shown here after it has been worked down a short way. This example makes an excellent handle for Handbags when worked with small material.

Fig. 17A: The *Single Eight-Strand Oblong Sennit* is formed the same way as the preceding example except that it has two additional strands which gives more bulk to the braid.

B: The same example when braided into a short length.

Fig. 18A: The *Double Six-Strand Oblong Sennit* (twelve-strands) makes an impressive design.

B: As it appears in final shape.

Fig. 19A: The *Double Eight-Strand Oblong Sennit*. It represents a pleasing type of Sennit with a handsome body. When working Sennits of this nature, take care to have the lengthwise strands about twice as long as the side strands when beginning the operation.

B: This shows the completed product.

Fig. 20A: The *Eight-Strand Cube Sennit*. It comes from "Alston's Seamanship," and was originally intended as a means of finishing off a fender. When worked in Spritsail-Sheet fashion by alternately crowning over and under with each strand from its respective side, the result will be a perfect cube as shown here.

B: The completed Cube Sennit. It forms a body of handsome appearance. All ends of strands may be trimmed and then tucked back into the body of Sennit like this and the preceding designs of a similar nature, when the work is finished.

Fig. 21: The *Six-Strand Round Crown Sennit*. It is made by arranging the cords into two equal sets of three strands each. First one set and then the other is alternately crowned to the right. To prevent confusion, it is best to extend the lower set each time another crown is formed and then bring the top set down alongside of the braid. As each lower set is brought up to form the next crown, it is necessary to pass the strands between two strands of the upper crown.

Fig. 22A: The *Eight-Strand Double Cube Sennit* (sixteen strands). This pictures the face of the braid after the correct starting formation of the strands has been arranged. They are laid out in the same manner as for the single method.

B: This illustrates the braid after being worked down a short ways. It builds into an extremely handsome and symmetrical pattern and may be carried to an enormous size by using large line to work with.

Fig. 23: The *Twin-Loop Higginbotham,* or *Double Idiot's Delight* as it is sometimes called, may be formed in similar manner to the Single Higginbotham, except that it is started by tying two Slip Overhand Knots instead of one and the braid is then worked by alternately employing the eye from the bight of each loop on its respective side, which is stuck through the eye of the previous bight from the opposite side, with the eye of the right bight going through the eye of the left bight in the manner shown at top of the braid. This Sennit does not require much patience to work, as it rapidly builds into a compact symmetrical braid.

Fig. 24: The *Twin Bugler's* Sennit. This extraordinary braid was developed by placing two Bugler's Sennits face to face at the start and then braiding them through each other by using the same principles as in preceding example, except that in this case the eye from the bight of each loop is run through the eye of the two previous bights from the opposite side, instead of one as in the former method. It may be readily observed that they are then interlaced in the same manner as the previous pattern, before continuing with the braid. This is one of the most handsome and pleasing Sennits that has been developed in the Authors' forty years of experiments along this line.

Fig. 25: The *Six-Strand Diagonal Reverse Weave Sennit.* It is braided across the front. The outside strand goes over one and under two from first one side and then the other. Each side has the opposite or reverse weave from the other side.

Fig. 26: The *Nine-Strand Twin-Row Channel Sennit.* Key: Under one, over two and under one, alternating from each side across the front with the outside strands. This illustration shows a back view of the Sennit. It forms a row on each side of the braid which resembles a Three-Strand Sennit, and has a Channel in the middle.

Fig. 27: The *Eleven-Strand Twin-Row Channel Sennit.* Key: Under one, over two and under two across the front from each side with the outside strands from their respective sides. This example presents a uniform braid with an upraised row on each side which forms a channel in the middle in similar fashion to the preceding braid.

Plate 346—Miscellaneous Knot Work

Fig. 1A: A *Crabber's-Eye Bowline.* This represents an odd way of converting a Crabber's-Eye Knot into a Bowline. In the illustration shown here the knot is opened up and turned upside down. This form of tie has definite possibilities, and will be found serviceable and dependable for a variety of uses, since it holds rigidly fast under a strain.

Fig. B: The same form of tie is shown here pulled taut, turned over and pointing the opposite way.

Fig. 2A: A *Crossed Running Bowline* illustrates how a Crossed Running Knot can be converted into a Bowline in the same manner as for the former method.

Fig. B: This shows how the knot appears when pulled taut, turned in the opposite way and illustrated from the other side.

Fig. 3: A *Secure Bight* can be formed as presented here.

Fig. 4A: The *Japanese Shamrock Knot*. It can be crowned with the three bights, which will transform it into an attractive design.

Fig. B: The same knot after being crowned and worked taut.

Fig. 5A: The *Crabber's-Eye Becket Bend* can be converted into a Becket Bend in a Loop by pulling on the working end of the line after the knot is formed as shown here.

Fig. B: Here is the same tie after being pulled up. It is formed similar to the way a Marline-Spike Hitch is converted into a Becket Seizing. It will be found a useful and quick way to seize a Loop.

Fig. 6: *Interlocking Hitches* on the Standing Part are formed as illustrated here. They have very little utility.

Fig. 7A: The *Figure-of-Eight Seizing in a Loop* is first formed in the manner shown. The working end is then pulled up gradually until the knot assumes the proper shape.

Fig. B: This pictures the tie completed.

Fig. 8: A *Toggled Bowline* is shown here after having Toggle secured with a

Lanyard to keep it from working out. This method will help cushion the strain on a knot when a line is subject to a continued heavy pull. It is also handy for use on shipboard when taking on fuel where it is occasionally necessary to cast off in a hurry.

Fig. 9: The *Turk's Head Needle* is useful for making complicated Turks Heads when they need additional passes. It can be made out of the handle of a tooth brush which is tapered down to a point with a hole made in the opposite end.

Fig. 10: The *Carrick Bend in Twin Loops* shows a method of forming a Carrick Bend in the manner illustrated.

Fig. 11: An *Upholsterer's Needle* will also be found useful in certain forms of rope work.

Fig. 12: The *Pommel Knot* is tied by unlaying the ends of a rope, which are then formed into an Overhand Knot. After the rope has been bent back on the standing part and the tie has been secured in the form of a slip eye with the Overhand Knot worked taut, the knot will appear as shown here. It is used by cowboys to make their lariat ropes fast to the pommel of their saddles.

Fig. 13: A *Roping Needle with Sail Twine* is used to apply Whippings on rope up to five inches in circumference. Over that Marline is used. Where a number of Whippings are applied, the distance between each one is usually about seven times the circumference of the line and as broad as the diameter.

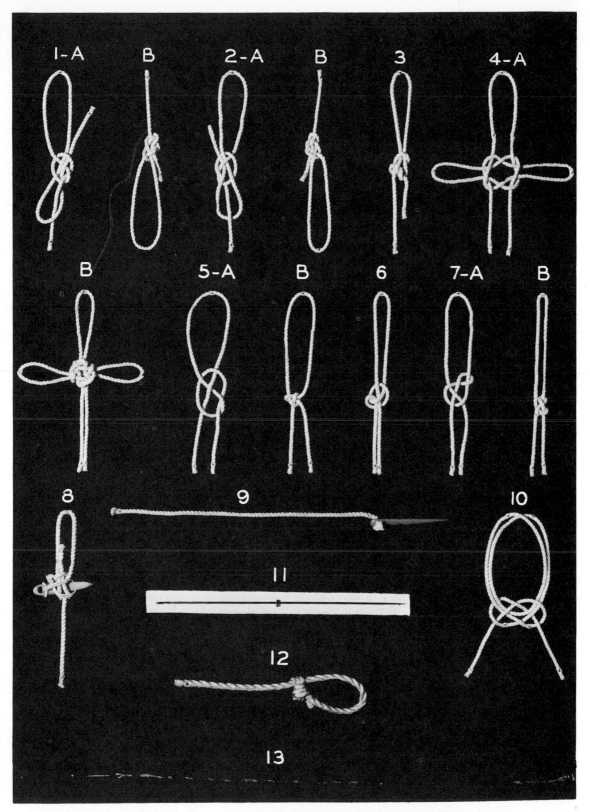

PLATE 346—MISCELLANEOUS KNOT WORK

Terminology

The following names, definitions, and terms apply to the various kinds and types of ropes and knots and their applications:

Rope Construction

Rope is made by twisting fibers into yarns or threads, then twisting the yarns into strands, and finally twisting the strands together to form the finished rope. As the rope is built up each part successively is twisted in an opposite direction; thus, when the yarns are twisted in a right-hand direction, the strands are twisted left-handed and the rope is twisted right-handed. This forms a right-handed plain laid rope. If three or more of these right-handed plain laid ropes are used as strands to form another rope, it will be a left-handed hawser, or **cable-laid** rope.

When a rope has four or more strands, it is customary to put a core or line in the center to retain the rounded form of its exterior, and this core or line is called the heart.

Rope is designated as right-laid or left-laid, according to the direction in which the strands are twisted. To determine which way the rope is laid, look along the rope, and if the strands advance to the right, or in a clockwise direction, the rope is right-laid; while on the other hand if the strands advance to the left or in a counter-clockwise direction the rope is left-laid.

Small Cordage

Small cordage: Commonly referred to as small stuff, may mean any small cord or line. However, halyards and other similar lines are not usually referred to as small stuff. Cords are generally designated by the number of threads of which they are made,

---

NAMES OF TOOLS SHOWN IN PLATE 347

1: Fid
2: Rope knife
3: Scissors
4: Thimble
5: Beeswax
6: Round thimble
7: Small bag needle
8: Palm
9: Sailmaker's needle
10: Meshing gage
11: Small sail needle
12: Small meshing gage
13: Meshing needle
14: Large bag needle
15: Sail twine
16: Sail hook
17: Meshing needle
18: Small meshing needle

Refer to the Glossary in the following pages for further definitions of these tools.

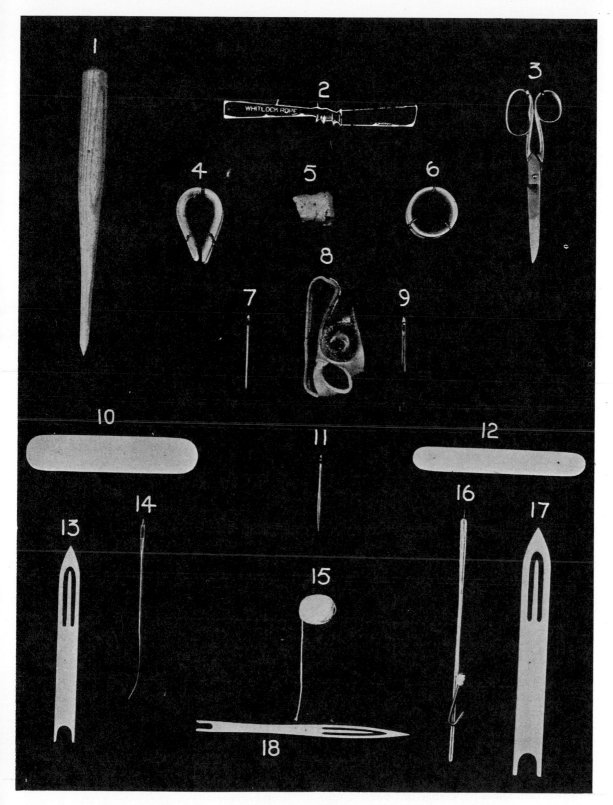

PLATE 347–TOOLS USED IN ROPE AND CANVAS WORK

twenty-four thread stuff being the largest. Aside from being known by the number of threads various kinds of small stuff have names of their own. As:

Spun yarn: This is the cheapest and most commonly used for seizing, serving, etc., where neatness is not important. It is laid up loosely, left-handed, in 2, 3 and 4 strands and is tarred.

Marline: Cord of this kind has the same applications as spun yarn but it makes a neater job. It is two-stranded and laid up left-handed. Untarred marline is used for sennit, a braided cord or fabric made from plaited yarns. Tarred yacht marline is used in rigging lofts.

Houseline and roundline: These lines are used for the same purpose as marline. They are three-strand cord; houseline being laid up left-handed and roundline right-handed.

Hambroline: This is right-handed, three-stranded small stuff made of fine back-handed untarred hemp yarns. Also called hamber line.

White line or Cod line: These lines are small stuff made of untarred American hemp or cotton.

Seizing stuff: This is a heavier line than any of the other small stuff and it is used when a strong neat job is required. It is a finished machine-made rope, commonly three-strand, of right-hand stuff. There may be 2, 3 or 4 threads to the strand, making 6, 9 or 12-thread seizing stuff. Tarred American hemp is the material used in its manufacture.

Ratline stuff: This is much the same as seizing stuff, except that it is larger. Its sizes usually run from .6 to 24 threads.

Foxes: This is comprised of two yarns hand-twisted, or one yarn twisted against its lay and rubbed smooth with the hands against the knee.

Rope Materials

Fiber rope: Under this heading are such materials as Manila, hemp, cotton and flax. It takes its name from the species of the plant from which the fiber is taken. Fiber rope is impregnated with oil when manufactured, which adds about ten per cent to its actual weight. The oil adds to the life of the rope by keeping out heat and moisture. As the oil leaves the rope the latter tends to deteriorate rapidly. The strength of fiber rope decreases with usage and a used rope is often deceptive, in that it may not be as serviceable as it looks. Unlike a wire rope the strands of fiber rope do not wear flat, thereby giving a visible sign of weakness. The fibers stretch and twist, but this does not always indicate decreased strength. It is not advisable to place a maximum strain on a rope that has been under a load for any considerable length of time, or one that has been strained to near its

breaking point. The safety of rope decreases rapidly with constant use, depending, of course, upon the circumstances and the amount of strain to which it is subjected.

Abaca, or Manila rope: This is the most important cordage fiber of the world today. It possesses a lightness and strength with which no other fiber can compare. Salt or sea water has but little effect upon it and therefore it is used almost exclusively for marine cordage. The material from which it is made is taken from the fibers of the abaca plant and its principal source is Manila, hence its name.

Hemp or sisal: The fibers of these plants are used extensively in rope making. The plants grow abundantly in Italy, Russia, the United States and Mexico. Most of the rope used in the United States Navy is made from the American hemp, which is equal in quality to that of any of the other countries from which the fibers are obtained. However, hemp rope is but little used, except for standing rigging, and seldom for that today, since most of the present-day standing rigging is made of wire rope. When used as rigging it is always tarred, the tar tending to protect it from moisture and increase its life, but decreasing its strength.

Coir: Coir is obtained from the fibrous husks of coconuts. Rope made from it is buoyant and does not become waterlogged easily. It has about one-half the strength of Manila rope and finds its chief usage in light lines.

Cotton and flax: These materials are both employed in rope making, although they find but little use aboard ship, except as small stuff. The taffrail log, signal halyards and lead lines are made of cotton, while braided flax is used for boat lead lines.

Notes on the Care and Handling of Rope

To open a coil of rope may seem very simple, yet many a seaman has found himself in "trouble" with a new line, because he did not stop to think before he grabbed an end blindly and started to measure off the amount he wanted. To prevent kinks; first inspect the coil and locate the *inside* end, which is within the eye. (By the expression eye is meant the opening in the center of the coil.) Turn the coil over so that the inside end is down; reach down inside of the eye and take hold of the end; pull it up through the eye and as it comes out it should uncoil counter-clockwise.

Rope manufacturers recommend that the lashings around a coil of rope should be cut from the inside of the eye, while the burlap coverings are left on the outside of the coil. Rope shrinks in length when it is wet. If it is held taut in dry weather it will be subjected to a great strain when it becomes wet, sometimes so great that it will part. Taut lines should be slacked off when they become wet. Even a heavy dew at night will penetrate an old line, therefore, running rigging should be eased off at night.

Both heat and moisture will cause rope to lose its strength and for this reason rope should always be stored in a cool but dry place. Wet rope should never be stored, nor should it be covered in a manner that will retain the moisture it contains. Rope should be covered to protect it from the weather and as protection against chafing it should be parceled.

Coiling Rope

Straight coil: Lay a bight of the secured end on deck and lay additional bights on top of it, using up the entire amount of line; keep out all kinks and coils. Turn the entire coil over and it will be clear for running.

To *Flemish* down a line, make a small circle of the free end and continue to lay small circles around it until the entire line is down and has the appearance of a coiled clock spring.

To *fake* down a line, lay the free end out in a straight line, then turn back a loop to form a close flat coil; continue to lay flat coils with the ends on top of the ends of the preceding coil. Always coil a line with the lay.

Right-handed rope should always be coiled "with the sun," that is, in a clockwise direction.

Left-handed rope should always be coiled "against the sun," that is, in a counter-clockwise direction.

Glossary

IN ITS TRUE SENSE the word "knot" is any fastening made by interweaving rope or cordage, yet in the common sense the term is generic in that it is considered as including many kinds and varieties of actual knots, as well as other rope fastenings, such as are known as bends, hitches, and splices.

The three principal classes of knots, in the commonly accepted meaning of the term are:

Bend, from the same root-word as "bind," is defined as a method of joining the ends of two ropes together, or in the language of the sea, the bending of two ropes together, as the Sheet Bend, Carrick Bend, etc.

Hitch, which is an Old English word, is defined as a method of securing a rope to some object such as a spar, as the Clove Hitch, or to another rope, as the Rolling Hitch.

Knot, from the Anglo-Saxon *cnotta,* refers to a method of forming a knob in a rope, by turning the rope on itself through a loop, as in the case of the Overhand Knot, the Bowline Knot, and the Running Knot.

The use of these three terms in connection with the word "knot" appears to be arbitrary, since there is but very little difference between the Fisherman's Bend and the Timber Hitch. In one sense the terms knot and seizing are considered as permanent fastenings, which must be unwoven or disentangled in order to be unfastened, while the bend or hitch can be unfastened by merely pulling the ropes in the opposite or reverse direction to that in which they are intended to hold.

There are many other terms used in connection with the tying of knots and with the uses of rope and cordage, most of which are given in the following glossary. This is quite general in its scope and contains many terms which do not apply to knots and rope, but which are closely related to their applications.

Knot and Rope Terms

Abaca: A plant which grows chiefly in the Philippine Islands from which the fibers are taken for making Manila rope. The Abaca is similar to a banana plant.

Abaca rope: Rope made from the fibers of the abaca plant; also called Manila rope, since most of the abaca fibers are obtained from that source.

Against the sun: A nautical term meaning rotation in a counter-clockwise, or left-handed direction, in contradistinction to clockwise, or right-handed, as in the direction of rotation of the sun.

Back-handed rope: In rope making the general practice is to spin the yarn over from left to right, or clockwise, making the rope yarn right-handed. The strand formed by a combination of such yarns becomes left-handed and three of these strands twisted together form a right-handed rope, or a plain-laid rope.

In making back-handed rope if instead of twisting the strand in a direction opposite to the direction of the twist of the yarn it is twisted in the same direction, that is, right-handed, then when brought together and laid up the rope is left-handed. This is called left-handed or back-handed rope. It is considered as being

656

more pliable than plain-laid rope and less liable to kinks.

Baseball stitch: A form of stitching or sewing used in sail making and repairing.

Becket: A rope eye for the hook of a block. Also; a rope grommet used as a row-lock or any small rope strop used as a handle.

Becket bend: An efficient bend used for uniting the two ends of a rope or the end of a rope to an eye. It jams tight with the strain, will not slip and is easily cast off.

Beeswax: This wax matter derived from the honey-comb found in bee-hives is used extensively in canvas work. It is applied to the sail twine to prevent the small threads from fraying as the twine is pulled through the canvas. Usually it is in the form of a wad as in FIG. 5.

Belay: To make a rope or line fast by winding it in figure-eight fashion around a cleat, a belaying pin, or a pair of bitts. Also; to stop or cease.

Belaying pin: A pin of either wood or metal set in such places as pin rails, etc., upon which to belay a rope or secure the running rigging.

Bend: As defined previously. Also; to secure, tie or make fast, as to bend two ropes together.

Bight: A loop in a rope, as that part of the rope between the end and the standing part, formed by bringing the end of the rope around, near to, or across its own part.

Bitt: One or more heavy pieces of wood or metal, usually set vertically in the deck of a vessel, for the purpose of securing mooring lines and tow lines.

Bitt a cable: To make a line fast by a turn under the thwartship piece and again around the bitt-head; or to double or weather-bitt a cable an extra turn is taken.

Bitt head: The upper part of a bitt, or its head or top.

Bitter-end: The last part of a cable that is doing useful work. In the case of an anchor chain its bitter-end is made fast in the bottom or side of the chain locker.

Block: A mechanical device consisting essentially of a frame or shell, within which is mounted a sheave or roller over which a rope is run. There are many varieties of blocks which are at times called pulleys, or when rigged, a block and tackle. The name pulley, as used in connection with a block, is a misnomer in that in this case the word pulley refers only to the sheave or roller.

Bollard: A heavy piece of wood or metal set in the deck of a vessel or on the dock to which the mooring lines are made fast. They are also called nigger heads.

Bolt rope: A piece of rope sewed into the edge of a piece of canvas or a sail to give added strength and to prevent the canvas from ripping. They are made of hemp or cotton cordage and the name Bolt rope is now applied to a good quality of long fiber, Manila or hemp.

Braid: To plat, plait or interweave strands, yarns, ropes or cords.

Breast line: A line leading from the breast of a ship to a cleat on the dock, without leading forward or aft, for the purpose of mooring the ship.

Bridle: Any span of rope with its ends secured.

Cable: A heavy rope used in attaching anchors or in towing. A cable is also a nautical measure of length. (See Cable-length.)

Cable-laid: Cable-laid rope is made up of three ropes laid up left-handed; the ropes comprising the strands being laid up right-handed. It is also called hawser-laid rope.

Cable-length: A nautical measure of length. Its name was derived originally from the length of a ship's cable which bears no relation today to the length of any cable. Many recognized authorities on the subject differ widely in their explanations of the definition of the term. Most of them, however, define a cable-length as being equal to 120 fathoms, although in some instances it is given as 100. fathoms. Admiral Luce, in his work on *Seamanship*, published in 1863, gives the most enlightening definition of a cable-length with a plausible reason for it. His explanation is that custom limited the length of cables to 120 fathoms for the reason that rope walks of earlier times were unable to lay up strands of greater length. This was due to the length of the early rope walks. To lay up a cable longer than 120 fathoms would require that the rope walks be one-third longer than the cable, as this extra length would be needed for drawing down the yarns and laying up the strands. Other difficulties in rope making also contributed in limiting the length of rope walks and hence cable lengths.

Canvas: A woven fabric of cotton or flax used for sails, awnings and many other shipboard purposes. It is made in varying degrees of weight or quality, numbered from 00, the coarsest, to 10, the finest weave. The term in nautical parlance is synonymous with sail.

Catch a turn: To take a turn, as around a capstan or bitt, usually for holding temporarily.

Caulking: To drive oakum or cotton into the seams of the deck or the ship's side, as a means for preventing leakage. Also; the pieces of oakum or cotton used for caulking purposes. Also called calking.

Cavil: A strong timber, bollard, or cleat used for making fast the heavier lines of a vessel. Also called kevel.

Chafe: To rub or abrade.

Chafing gear: A winding of small stuff, rope, canvas, or other materials around spars, rigging, ropes, etc., to prevent chafing.

Chafing mat: A mat made from woven ropes or cordage to prevent chafing.

Clap on: A nautical term with several meanings as: to seize or take hold of; clap on more sail, and clap on a Wall or Crown on the end of a rope.

Cleat: A heavy piece of wood or metal having two horns around which ropes may be made fast or belayed. Usually secured by bolts or lashings to some fixed object, as the deck of a vessel or the dock.

Clinch: A form of bend by which a bight or eye is made by seizing the end to its own part. Two kinds of clinches are used, an inside and an outside clinch. Also; an oval washer, at times called a clinch ring, which is used on spikes and bolts where they are employed in wooden construction.

Clockwise: Rotation in the direction of the hands of a clock, or right-handed, in contradistinction to counter-clockwise or left-handed.

Clothes stop: Small cotton line used for stopping clothes to a line or for securing clothes rolled up in bags or lockers.

Cod line: Small stuff made of eighteen thread untarred American hemp or cotton.

Coil: A series of rings, or a spiral, as of rope, cable and the like. Most rope is sold by the coil, which contains 200 fathoms. Also; to lay a rope or cable down in circular turns. If a rope is coiled right-handed, that is, in the direction of rotation of the hands of a clock, it is coiled from left to right, or with the sun. Hemp rope is always coiled in this manner.

Coir: The fibers of the outer husks of the coconut.

Coir rope: Rope made from coir fibers. It is extremely light in weight but is not as strong as rope or cable made from the other common rope materials.

Concluding line: A small rope or line rove through the middle of the steps of a Jacob's ladder.

Cord: Comprised of several yarns, usually cotton or hemp, with an extra twist, laid up the opposite way. Also a term employed as a distinction between small stuff and rope.

Core: A small rope run through the center of heavier rope. It is usually found in four-strand rope, lending to it a smooth, round outside appearance.

Cordage: A general term now commonly employed to include all ropes and cords, but, more specifically, it applies to the smaller cords and lines. Also used as a collective term in speaking of that part of a ship's rigging made up of ropes, etc.

Cotton: The fibers of the cotton plant, used in making ropes and small stuff.

Cotton canvas: Fabric made from cotton yarns.

Cotton rope: Rope made from cotton fibers or yarns.

Cow's tail: Frayed end of rope. Same as dead men and Irish pennant.

Counter-clockwise: Opposite in rotation to the hands of a clock, or left-handed, in contradistinction to right-handed or clockwise.

Creasing stick: A wood or metal tool slotted at one end used for creasing or flattening seams in canvas preparatory to stitching.

Cringle: A piece of rope spliced into an eye over a thimble in the bolt rope of a sail.

Cross turns: Turns taken around a rope at right angles to the turns of the lashings or seizing.

Crown: In knotting to so tuck the strands of a rope's end as to lock them in such a manner as to prevent unraveling by back-splicing the strands. A Crown over a

Wall Knot is the first step in tying a Man-rope Knot.

Dead men: The frayed ends of ropes. Same as cow's tail and Irish pennant.

Dead rope: A rope in a tackle not led through a block or sheave.

Earing: A short piece of rope secured to a cringle for the purpose of hauling out the cringle.

Elliott eye: A thimble spliced in the end of a cable or hawser.

End: In knotting that part of a rope extending from the bight to its extremity, in which the standing part of the rope is on one side of the knot and the end on the other.

End seizing: A round seizing on the ends of ropes.

Eye: A loop in the end of a rope, usually made permanent by splicing or seizing.

Eye seizing: A seizing used for shortening an eye, the turns of the seizing stuff being taken over and under each part and the ends crossed over the turns.

Fag end: An unraveled or untwisted end of rope, or as applied to flags and pennants, the ragged end.

Fair leader: Lines employed for the purpose of leading other lines in a desired direction. That is, they may be used to pull a line at an angle for the purpose of securing it to a belaying pin or cleat.

Fake: A circle or coil of rope in which the coils overlap and the rope is free for running. Also to fake down a rope is to coil down a rope.

Fall: A rope, which with the blocks makes up a tackle. A fall has both a hauling part and a standing part, the latter being the end secured to the tail of the block. In some cases only the hauling part is considered as the fall.

Fast: Attached or secured to. Also to make fast means to secure or attach.

Fibre: The smallest thread-like tissue of a rope, cord, or thread, as the fibers of flax, cotton, hemp, Manila, etc., which are twisted to make the yarn out of which the rope is made.

Fiber rope: Rope made from the fibers of abaca, hemp, coir, Manila, sisal, etc.

Fid: A tapered piece of hardwood or a pin similar in form to a marline spike and used for the same purpose, such as separating the strands of a rope in making splices (FIG. 1).

Flat seam: The most common method of sewing two pieces of canvas together. The seam is made by lapping the two pieces of canvas and then pushing the needle through the lower and up through the piece to be joined.

Flax: The fibers of the flax plant twisted into yarns for the purpose of making ropes, cords, and small stuff, as well as canvas fabric.

Flax canvas: Fabric made from yarns twisted from flax fibers.

Flax rope: Rope made from yarns twisted from flax fibers.

Flemish coil: There are several versions of the exact meaning of the term. One is that it is a coil in which each fake rides directly on top of the fake below it. Another version is that a Flemish coil, also called a Flemish fake or mat, is one in which each fake lies flat and concentrically, giving the appearance of a rope mat. Common practice, however, is to make a concentric rope mat when ordered to Flemish down a coil and when the order is to fake, or fake down, it is the practice to lay down a coil with one fake upon the other, for clear running.

Flemish eye: An eye in which the strands are not interwoven but are separated and bound down securely to the main part with seizing.

Foot rope: A stirrup or strap hanging in a bight beneath a yard in which the men stand when furling or reefing sail.

Foxes: As previously explained, two yarns hand-twisted, or one yarn twisted against its lay and rubbed smooth.

Frap: To bind or draw together and secure with ropes, as two slack lines.

Frapping turns: Same as cross turns.

Freshen the nip: To shift or secure a rope in another part to minimize wear.

Gantline: A whip or light line made fast aloft for the purpose of hoisting boatswain's chairs and for hoisting sails aloft for bending. Also called girtline.

Garland: A strop used primarily for the purpose of hoisting spars.

Garnet: An arrangement of tackle used for hoisting cargo.

Gasket: The term has several nautical meanings. In one sense a gasket is a rope or band of canvas by means of which sails are made fast to the booms or yards. Canvas and sennit bands used to secure a sail are called harbor gaskets, while a rope wound around a sail and a yard arm to the bunt is called a sea gasket. Gaskets are also defined as any kind of packing employed for making joints water- or gas-tight.

Geswarp: A hauling line laid out by a boat, a portion of which is coiled down in the boat. Also called guess warp, or a line for mooring a boat to a boom.

Girtline: Same as gantline.

Gooseneck: A bight made in the standing part of a rope in forming a bowline.

Grab rope: A rope used as a handrail, such as a line secured waist high above a boat-boom or gang-plank for steadying one's self.

Grafting: To cover a strap, ring-bolt or

any similar article with log-line, cord or small stuff.

Graft a rope: To taper the end of a rope and cover it completely with an ornamental arrangement of Half Hitches of small stuff.

Grommet: Eyelets made of rope, leather, metal, and other materials. Their chief uses are as eyelets secured to canvas and sails, through which stops or robands are passed.

Guess warp: Same as Geswarp.

Guest rope: A grab rope running alongside a vessel to assist boats coming alongside.

Guy: Any rope used for steadying purposes.

Gypsy: The drum of a windlass or winch around which a line is taken for hauling in.

Halyard: Any of the small ropes and tackles used for hoisting sails, flags and the like.

Hamber: Three-stranded seizing stuff tight-laid, right-handed. Also called Hambroline. It is usually made of untarred hemp and is similar to roundline.

Hambroline: Same as hamber.

Hand rope: Same as grab rope.

Hauling part: That part of the rope in a tackle which is hauled upon, or it might be described as the end of the falls or a rope to which power is applied.

Hauling line: Usually a line sent down from aloft for the purpose of hauling up gear. Also: any line used for hauling purposes.

Hawser: Any large rope, five or more inches in circumference, used principally for kedging, warping and towing.

Hawser-laid: Left-handed rope of nine strands laid up in the form of three, three-stranded, right-handed ropes.

Heart: Same as core.

Heave: To haul or pull on a line or to cast a heaving line.

Heaving line: A light flexible line having a monkey fist on its end. It is heaved ashore or to another vessel as a so-called messenger line, as when it is desired to pass a mooring line to a dock.

Heave taut: To pull tight or stretch.

Hemp: The fibers of the hemp plant used in making rope. The fibers of this plant are obtained from such sources as Italy, Russia, America and other countries. That obtained from New Zealand is called Phormium hemp, and that from the East Indies is known by the name of Sunn hemp. Rope made of hemp fibers is usually tarred, but if not it is called white rope. American hemp is distinguished by its dark gray color.

Hemp rope: Rope made from the fibers of the hemp plant.

Herringbone stitch: A form of stitching or sewing used in sail-making and in the sewing of canvas.

Hide rope: Rope made from strips of leather cut from green hides. It finds but little use today, except as wheel rope.

Hitch: As previously explained, or a combination of turns for securing a rope to a spar or stay.

Hook rope: A rope with a hook secured to its end used for clearing cable chains, etc.

House line: Three-stranded cord or small stuff laid up left-handed and used for seizings, etc. Sometimes called round line, although the latter is laid up right-handed.

Irish pennant: Same as cow's tail and dead men.

Jam: To wedge tight.

Junk: Salvaged rope which is made up into swabs, spun yarn, nettle-stuff, lacings, seizings, earings, etc., although little used today.

Jute: The fibers obtained from East Indian plants used in making sacking, burlap and twine.

Jute rope: Rope made from jute fibers.

Knife: Knives form an important part in the working of rope and canvas. One such as is used commonly by sailors is shown in Fig. 2.

Kedging: Moving a vessel by alternately laying out a small anchor or kedge and hauling the vessel up to it.

Keckling: Chafing gear applied to a cable, usually made up of old rope.

Kevel: Same as cavil. Also spelled kevil.

Kink: A twist in a rope.

Knittles: Rope yarns twisted and rubbed smooth for pointing and similar purposes. Two or more yarns may be twisted together or one yarn may be split and its halves twisted. Also called nettles.

Knot: As previously described, refers to a method of forming a knot in a rope, by turning the rope on itself through a loop.

Lacing: Small rope or cord used to secure canvas or sails by passing it through eyelets in the canvas.

Lang-lay rope: Wire rope in which the individual wires comprising the rope are twisted in the same direction as the strands which make up the rope.

Lanyard: Four-strand tarred hemp rope used for making anything fast. Also an ornamental braid or plait used by sailors in securing their knives and the like.

Lash: To secure by binding with rope or small stuff.

Lashing: A binding or wrapping of small stuff used to secure one object or line to another, as an eye to a spar.

Lashing eye: Loops in the ends of two ropes through which are passed the lashings which bind them together.

Lasket: Loops of small cord used to lace the bonnet to the jib. Sometimes called latchings or latch.

Latching: Same as lasket.

Lay: The direction in which the strands of a rope are twisted. This may be right-handed or clockwise, or left-handed, as counter-clockwise. It also refers to the degree of tightness with which the strands are twisted, as soft, medium, common, plain and hard lay. Also used in the expressions "against the lay" and "with the lay" as denoting a direction contrary to or with the lay of the strands of the rope.

Leading part: Same as hauling part.

Lead line: A line secured to the ship's lead which is used for sounding the depth of water under a vessel. A lead line is made of braided cotton twine for a boat; braided flax for a ship, and of hemp for deep sea purposes. Now being replaced with fine wire, wound on reels. (Pronounced led.)

Left-handed: Direction of rotation from right to left, counter-clockwise or against the sun, in contradistinction to right-handed, clockwise or with the sun.

Left-handed rope: Same as back-handed rope.

Line: Any rope or line, the word being more commonly used in marine practice than the term rope.

Log line: A line attached to a ship's log, an indicator for measuring speed and distance. The taffrail log line is made of braided cotton twine while the chip log line is made of hemp.

Loop: Same as bight.

Man rope: A rope hung over the ship's side for the purpose of ascending or descending.

Manila: A term used to describe rope made from the abaca fiber, which is obtained chiefly from Manila.

Manila rope: Rope made from the fibers

of the abaca; the chief source is Manila or the Philippine Islands.

Marl: To make secure or bind with a series of Marline Hitches.

Marline: See definition under Small Cordage.

Marline spike: A metal pin tapering to a point used chiefly for splicing wire rope, etc.

Marry: Binding two lines together temporarily, either side by side or end to end.

Match rope: An inflammable rope used as a fuse.

Meshing gage: These gages are used in making the meshes in nets. They may be of any length to suit the user's convenience, but their width determines the size of the mesh in the net. Thus, a meshing gage one inch wide will form a mesh one-half-inch square. (*See* Figs. 10 and 12.)

Meshing needle: Needles such as these are usually made of wood, but many have been made from light metal. They are used in the form of a shuttle for passing the cord and tying knots in the making of nets. In winding the cord on the needle it should be understood that both the needle and the cord it contains must be small enough to pass through the mesh of the net. They may be made of any desired length. Several forms are shown in Figs. 13, 17, and 18.

Messenger line: A light line such as a heaving line used for hauling over heavy lines, as from a ship to a dock.

Middle a rope: Doubling a rope in such a manner that the two parts are of equal length.

Mooring line: A line such as a cable or hawser used for mooring a vessel.

Mousing: A short piece of small stuff seized across the opening of the hook of a block as a measure of safety.

Nettles: Same as knittles.

Nip: A short turn in a rope or to pinch or close in upon.

Palm: A sailor's thimble, so to speak. It is comprised of a leather strap worn over the hand to which is attached a metal plate so placed as to fit into the palm of the sailor's hand. It is used primarily in sewing and mending sails and canvas (Fig. 8).

Painter: A short piece of rope secured to the bow of a small boat used for making the boat fast. Not to be confused with sea painter.

Parbuckle: A form of sling consisting of two ropes passing down a ship's side for the purpose of hauling a cask or similar object in the bight of the ropes, one end of each rope being secured and the other tended.

Parcel: To protect a rope from the weather by winding strips of canvas or other material around it with the lay preparatory to serving.

Part: To break.

Pass a lashing: Make the necessary turns to secure a line or an object.

Pass a line: Carry a line to or around something or reeve through and make fast.

Pass a stopper: To reeve and secure a stopper.

Payed: Painted, tarred or greased to exclude moisture, as payed rope.

Pay out: To slack off on a line or let it run out.

Plain laid: Rope in which three strands of left-handed yarn are twisted together to form a right-handed or plain laid rope.

Plat: Same as braid and plait.

Plait: Same as braid and plat.

Pendant: A length of rope with a block or thimble secured to its end.

Pointing: Any of numerous methods by which the end of a rope is worked into a stiff cone-shaped point.

Pricker: A light piece of metal, similar to a marline spike, but having a handle and used for the same purposes as a marline spike.

Quilting: Any covering of woven ropes or Sennit placed on the outside of a container used for water.

Rack: To seize two ropes together with cross turns of spun yarn or small stuff.

Rack seizing: Small stuff rove around two lines in an over and under figure-eight fashion.

Ratline: As previously described, three-strand, right-hand, tarred small stuff larger than seizing stuff. Also short lines of ratline stuff run horizontally across shrouds as steps.

Reef: To take in sail to reduce the effective area of a sail.

Reef cringle: A rope grommet worked into a thimble attached to a sail.

Reef earing: A short length of small stuff spliced into a reef cringle for the purpose of lashing the cringle to a boom or yard.

Reef points: Short pieces of small stuff set in the reef bands of sails for reefing purposes.

Reeve: To pass the end of a rope through an eye or an opening, as through a block, thimble, or bight.

Render: To pass through freely. Said of a rope when it runs easily through a fair-lead or a sheave.

Riders: A second layer of turns placed over the first layer of turns of a seizing.

Riding chock: Chocks over which the anchor chains pass.

Riding turns: Same as riders.

Right-handed: Direction of rotation from left to right, as clockwise and with the sun, in contradistinction to left-handed, counter-clockwise or against the sun.

Right-handed rope: Same as plain laid rope.

Robands: Short pieces of small stuff of Manila or spun yarn, used to secure the luff of a sail. Also called rope bands.

Rogue's yarn: Colored yarn worked into the strands of a rope as an identification mark and as protection against theft.

Rope: A general term used to describe any cord more than one inch in circumference. In this connection all rope was at one time measured by its circumference, except that used for power transmission, and it was measured by its diameter. Today, however, all rope is usually measured in terms of its diameter.

Rigging: A term applied to a ship's ropes generally.

Rope band: Same as roband.

Roping needle: A short spur needle used for sewing bolt ropes and other heavy work.

Roping twine: Nine- to eleven-ply small stuff.

Roping yarn: Untwisted strands of a rope used for rough seizings.

Rounding: Serving a rope to prevent chafing.

Round line: Three-stranded cord or small stuff laid up right-handed. Also called house line.

Round seizing: A method of securing two ropes together or the parts of the same rope to form an eye.

Round seam: A seam employed in sewing canvas and sails. It is used to join two edges together by holding them together and passing the needle through them at right-angles to the canvas.

Round turn: To pass a line completely around a spar, bitt or another rope.

Rouse: Heave heavily on a line.

Rubber: A flat steel tool used for rubbing or smoothing down seams in canvas. It is fitted with a wooden handle.

Rumbowline: Coarse soft rope made from outside fibers and yarns and used for temporary lashings, etc.

Running line: Any line such as a messenger line which may be used to run out for paying out a hawser or cable.

Running rigging: All the lines of a ship used to control the sails.

Sail: Generally, canvas used aboard ship in the form of sails.

Sail hook: A metal hook secured to a small line, used for holding sails and canvas while sewing seams, etc. (*See* FIG. 16.)

Sail needle: Long spur steel needles, triangular at the point and cylindrical in form at the eye. There are two types, known respectively as sewing and roping needles, and these are in turn called short and long spur needles. Sewing needles come in the sizes 6 to 14 and in half-sizes to 17½. Size 15, which is 2½ inches long, is the most used. (FIG. 7 is a small bag or tufting needle; FIG. 9, a sailmaker's needle; FIG. 11, one of the smaller needles, and FIG. 14 is a large bag or tufting needle.)

Sail twine: Small stuff in the form of thread made of either cotton or flax. It is available in several different sizes, usually wound into the form of a ball (FIG. 15).

Scissors: These are essential in canvas and fancy rope work. A pair is shown in FIG. 3.

Sea painter: A long rope, not less than 2¾ inches in circumference, for use in a ship's lifeboats.

Secure: To attach, fasten or make fast.

Secured end: That part of a line, or the end of a line which is attached or secured to an object.

Seize: To put on or clap on a seizing. That is, bind with small stuff, as one rope to another, a rope to a spar, etc. Seizings are named from their appearance or from the functions they serve, as throat seizing, flat, and round seizing, and others.

Seizing stuff: Small stuff.

Selvage: A woven border in fabric, or the edge of the fabric so closed by complicating the threads as to prevent raveling.

Selvagee: Rope yarn, spun yarn or small stuff marled together and used for stoppers, straps, etc.

Sennit: Braided cordage such as nettles or small stuff, usually of ornamental design, the different kinds being known by many different names, according to their design.

Serving: To wind a rope or wire, after worming and parceling with small stuff, the turns being kept very close together to make the end of the rope impervious to water after being tarred. The turns of the serving are made against the lay of the rope. Also called service.

Serving board: A small flat board having a handle, used with a serving mallet for serving rope. The mallet is a typical round, wooden maul with a groove cut lengthwise in its head. Their purpose is to keep the serving taut and the turns close together.

Shakings: Odds and ends of rope and scrap rope which are hand-picked into fibers for use as oakum.

Sheave: The roller of a tackle block.

Shoemaker's stitch: A sewing stitch used in making and mending sails and in sewing canvas and other fabrics.

Shroud-laid: Four-stranded rope laid up right-handed.

Shrouds: Ropes of hemp or wire used as side stays from the masthead to the rail.

Sisal: Fibers of the henequin plant which grows abundantly in Yucatan.

Sisal rope: Rope made from fibers of the sisal plant.

Slack: That part of a rope between

its secured ends which is hanging loose; the opposite of taut.

Sling: To sling a piece of cargo, as a barrel, by passing a line around it. Or, a sling is an arrangement of short pieces of rope or chain used for hoisting cargo and other similar purposes. Of these the rope sling or strap is the most common. A rope sling is made of short pieces of rope spliced together. It is passed around a cask, for instance, and one bight, the rove, is passed through the other, which is known as the bite. The cargo hook is attached in the rove. Other types of slings are known by such names as web, chain, platform, net, bale, butt, etc.

Spanish fox: Untwisted rope yarn retwisted in the opposite direction.

Splice: To join the ends of ropes together, or the end of a rope to its standing part, as in forming an eye, by interweaving the strands of the rope into themselves. Splices are known as long, short, chain, sailmaker's, etc.

Small Cordage: As previously described; small stuff which may be 1¾ inches in circumference or less.

Spar: A yard, mast, gaff, or boom.

Spun yarn: Two-, three- and four-stranded rough stuff twisted loosely together and laid up left-handed for use as small stuff, especially in applications where a smooth service is desired.

Standing part: In knotting, the standing part of a line is that part of the main rope as distinguished from the bight and the end.

Stay: A piece of rigging, usually a rope of hemp or wire used as a support for a mast.

Standing rigging: That part of a ship's rigging used to support its spars which is not altered with the ordinary working of the ship.

Stop: To seize or lash, usually temporarily.

Stopper: A short line, one end of which is secured to some fixed object, used to check or stop a running line.

Strand: Part of a rope, made up of yarns, the twist of the strand being opposite to that of the yarns.

Stranded: A rope is said to be stranded when a strand parts.

Strap: A form of sling, usually employed for handling cargo. Also called a strop. Permanent straps are spliced into the thimble with the hook of a tackle block. A sail strap is one in which the eye is made by a seizing and the bight is tucked through the eye instead of the strap itself.

Strop: Same as strap.

Take a turn: To pass a line around a cleat or a belaying pin.

Tackle: An arrangement of ropes and blocks, sometimes called block and tackle. Also pronounced tay-kle. Tackle is employed primarily for hoisting purposes.

Tackline: A short length of line, usually signal halyard, used for separating strings of signals.

Tapered rope: Rope used in places where most of the strain is taken by one end only. The part which bears the strain is full-sized while the remainder of the line tapers off to the hauling part, which is usually light and pliable.

Taut: Tight; the opposite of loose or slack.

Tarred fittings: Small stuff.

Tend: Man or attend.

Thimble: A grooved piece of metal, either circular or heart-shaped, to receive the eye of a rope (Figs. 4 and 6).

Thread: Yarn or small stuff made into strands. Small rope or cord is often designated by the number of threads or yarns it contains, as 6-thread seizing stuff.

Throat seizing: A seizing used to lash an eye in a rope; to hold it around a thimble, or to seize two parts of rope together at the point where they cross each other.

Thrums: Short pieces of small stuff secured by their bights to pieces of canvas for use as chafing gear. The verb thrum means to attach the small stuff.

Thrum mats: Small pieces of canvas with short pieces of rope sewed to them by a method called thrumming. They are used between the rowlocks and the oars to prevent noise.

Tie: That part of a halyard which hoists a yard. Also to make a knot.

Tiller rope: Wire rope made of copper, bronze and galvanized wire, laid up left-handed.

Timenoguy: A short piece of rope with a bull's-eye spliced in its end, employed as an intermediate support or guy for stays.

Toggle: A small wooden pin made of hardwood which is inserted into a knot to make it more secure or to make it more readily and quickly unfastened.

Tow line: A cable or hawser used for towing.

Trailing line: Small lines attached to the gunwales of small boats and around the loom of the oars to prevent them from falling overboard when the oars are trailed.

Trice: To haul up or pull taut.

Tricing line: Any small line used for suspending articles.

Turn: A single winding of rope, as around a bollard or cleat.

Twice-laid rope: Rope made from second-hand rope yarns or strands.

Unbend: Cast off or adrift, let loose or free; to untie.

Unlay: To separate the strands of a rope.

Unreeve: The opposite of reeve.

Veer: To permit a rope or chain to run out or slack off.

Veer and haul: To slack off and pull alternately.

Warp: Maneuver a ship as at a dock.

Wheel rope: Rope connecting the steering wheel with the drum of the steering gear. Composed of six strands and a heart, making seven strands in all.

Whip: To lash the end of a rope to prevent it from fraying. Also used to designate different kinds and arrangements of blocks and tackles.

Whipping: The lashings on the end of a rope or the small stuff used for whipping.

Whip upon whip: One lashing over the top of the other.

White line: Small stuff made of untarred hemp or cotton.

With the sun: Rotation in the direction of that of the sun, clockwise, or right-handed, in contradistinction to against the sun, counter-clockwise or left-handed.

Worming: Filling up the lays of a rope with spiral windings of small stuff preparatory to parceling in order to make a round, smooth surface.

Yarn: Any number of threads or fibers twisted together from the various fibers from which rope and cords are made.

Yoke lanyard: A small line rove through or secured to the ends of a yoke.

Index

Appendix Index